WEAKER SECTION IN INDIAN SOCIETY

CONCEPTS IN COMMUNICATION INFORMATICS & LIBRARIANSHIP (CICIL)

For a list of titles in this series,
see pp. 398-400 at the end of the book.

Concepts in Communication Informatics & Librarianship-33

General Editor: **S.P. Agrawal**

WEAKER SECTION IN INDIAN SOCIETY

Undiscovered Past, Uncertain Present and Unpredictable Future
Index to Writings in Indian Scholarly Journals and
10 National Newspapers Classified under 1500 Descriptors
1886-1990

S.P. AGRAWAL
Former Director
National Social Science Documentation Centre, ICSSR, New Delhi

RAJEEV KUMAR SHARMA
Librarian
Directorate of Education, Delhi

CONCEPT PUBLISHING COMPANY, NEW DELHI-110059

ISBN 81-7022-416-0

First Published 1992

Published and Printed by
Ashok Kumar Mittal
Concept Publishing Company
A/15-16, Commercial Block, Mohan Garden
NEW DELHI-110059 (India)

Lasertypeset by
Microtech Advance Printing Systems (Pvt.) Ltd.
H-13, Bali Nagar,
NEW DELHI-110015

GENERAL EDITOR'S INTRODUCTION

With the attainment of independence the depressed classes, which received some special concessions for improving their socio-economic condition during the British regime, were recognised by the Indian Constitution as backward classes and further categorised into four major groups – Scheduled Castes, Scheduled Tribes, Denotified Tribes and Other Backward Classes. In the caste hierarchical society of India the groups, who were at the bottom and in consequence suffered from economic and social disabilities as also treated as untouchables, were termed as Scheduled Castes. The communities, which were economically and socially backward and which lived in isolation having a distinct culture and language of their own, were considered as Scheduled Tribes. For proper educational, economic and social uplift of these backward classes, a number of provisions and safeguards were provided in the Constitution so as to integrate them with the other normal citizens of India. Numerous welfare programmes have been formulated for them under Five-Year Plans, both in the Central and State sectors. A number of measures have also been taken by the Government to protect these unfortunate segments of the society from social injustices which they are often subjected to, and to save them from being exploited by the so called privileged classes.

These welfare programmes have been constantly reviewed by various Commissions, Committees and the Study Teams set up for the purpose by the Government of India and State Governments from time to time, and in the light of the recommendations and suggestions made by these bodies, changes have been made in the strategies adopted by the Government for their advancement. Particularly, the Commissioner for Scheduled Castes and Scheduled Tribes has been made responsible for evaluation of the working of the safeguards provided for these communities in the Constitution. Moreover, there exists a Parliamentary Committee which overviews these welfare schemes and makes a critical assessment of the measures taken by the Government of India in this direction. These Governmental measures and development programmes have, in fact, made a dent in the economic and social life of these groups. There cannot be two opinions regarding the appreciable improvement in their status which followed. As a matter of fact a section of the Scheduled Castes is economically so well-off and socially so better placed that it can be bracketed with the upper echelon of the Indian society. There is, however, no denying the fact that still greater sizeable population of these communities is even at present below the poverty line, it continues to suffer from economic and social disabilities, and is still being subjected to social injustices and exploited by the members of the higher castes — this includes those of their own section which grabbed the opportunity to rise higher steps.

There have been numerous schemes for the development and welfare of the tribals as well. Nonetheless, though Governmental measures taken for their economic, educational and social uplift have improved their position to some extent rightly or wrongly, a lot remains yet to be done to achieve the desired goal in the right direction of bringing them on par with normal populace of the country. These tribals are not only being exploited by the unscrupulous dominant classes but are being misdirected by the well-intentioned too, in their zeal to do something, which may bring them (not tribals) some fame and name. In this connection it may be pointed out that while implementing the welfare schemes for the Scheduled Tribes, we have to be very cautious. It would not be in their interests if in our enthusiasm for doing good to them we disturb their life-style. We may perhaps take note of the observation made by Pandit Jawaharlal Nehru, the then Prime Minister of India, that people should develop along the lines of their own genius and we should avoid imposing anything on them. He further urged that we should try to encourage, in every way, their own traditional arts and culture.

As compared to Scheduled Castes and Scheduled Tribes, the groups, which come under the purview of Other Backward Classes, are a mixed lot of less socially disadvantages and still economically backward. Ironically, a large number of persons categorised under these classes are indistinguishable from the Scheduled Castes and the Scheduled Tribes. A segment of this group has also raised its status through its own efforts, and as such to provide any out-of-the-way assistance to them would not be fair to others. In the case of these backward classes it would be reasonable to apply economic criteria to determine the level of their backwardness. Recently, the decision of the National Front Government to implement recommendations of the Mandal Commission by giving 27 per cent job reservations to these OBCs, i.e., other socially and educationally backward classes in the Central Government and Public Sector Undertakings triggered a political convulsion throughout the country, perhaps unprecedented in the recent history. On no issue, such a large section of the student community reacted so violently and emotionally involved. On no problem in recent past so many innocent and precious lies were lost.

The present Index of articles which is based on the scholarly writings appearing in the Indian journals of standing during the last hundred five years or so (1886–1990) attempts to provide materials for the use of researchers and social scientists on various aspects of the problems, possibilities and the past status of these so termed backward classes. The articles included in this Index give a detailed picture of the economic and social conditions of these underprivileged groups. They not only indicate the Governmental measures taken so far for their uplift, but also provide critical assessment of such measures. In these articles we find the discussion on the reports of the Committees and Commissions submitted to the Government on the problems of the backward classes. The Index also includes such articles which highlight the important researches made on tribals for the benefit of those who are entrusted with the tribal administration. Reflections and notes on the life-style and modes of our tribal brethren, included in the writings, which are indexed in this volume may, one hopes so, open our eyes to the service and dis-service we are indulging ourselves in. Every effort has been made to make it as comprehensive as possible. The fact that it contains articles culled from as many journals as one hundred seventy one shows how wide is its coverage. Cautions note, however, that it is an Index, and not a Bibliography.

S.P. AGRAWAL

CONTENTS

ONE

DESCRIPTORS

ABOR HILLS : INDIA : ASSAM
ABORIGINAL CHILD
ABORIGINAL DEBT : INDIA : MADHYA PRADESH
ABORIGINALITY
ABORIGINALS
ABORIGINES
ABORS
ABUJHMADIAS
ABUJHMARAH/ABUJHMARH/ABUJMARH/ABUJMARIAS/
ABUJMARIYAS
ACADEMIC ACHIEVEMENT
ACCIDENTAL DEATHS: TRIBALS
ACCULTURATION
ACHIEVEMENT
ADIS
ADIVASI REVOLTS
ADIVASIS
ADJUSTMENT : PSYCHOLOGICAL ASPECT
ADMINISTRATION : TRIBAL DEVELOPMENT PROGRAMMES
ADMISSION TO PUBLIC PLACES
ADOLESCENTS : TRIBALS
ADOPTION BEHAVIOUR : TRIBAL FARMERS
ADOPTION STRATEGEM
ADULT EDUCATION : CONTRIBUTION TO TRIBAL DEVELOPMENT
ADULT LEARNERS : READING MATERIAL
ADULT TRIBALS : EDUCATION
AGARIA GONDS
AGARIYAS
AGGRESSIVENESS : SCHEDULED CASTE : CHILDREN
AGNA PANNA
AGRARIAN SITUATION : TRIBAL AREAS
AGRARIAN STRATIFICATION : WARLIS
AGRARIAN SYSTEM
AGRICULTURAL DEVELOPMENT : TRIBALS
AGRICULTURAL LABOURERS : TRIBAL AREAS
AGRICULTURAL PRACTICES : RIANGS
AGRICULTURE : TRIBALS
AHOMS : GIRLS
A J G A R
ALCOHOLIC BEVERAGES
ANCIENT INDIA
ANCIENT TRIBAL GROUPS : INDIA : ANDMAN AND NICOBAR ISLANDS
ANDAMAN AND NICOBAR ISLANDS : INDIA
ANDAMANEES
ANDHRA PRADESH : INDIA
ANDHRA PRADESH SCHEDULED TRIBES CO-OPERATIVE FINANCE DEVELOPMENT CORPORATION
ANIMAL HUSBANDRY : TRIBALS : INDIA : ARUNACHAL PRADESH
ANTHROPOLOGICAL APPROACH
ANTHROPOLOGY : SOCIO-CULTURAL APPROACH
ANTHROPOMETRIC CHARACTERS : MUNDAS : INDIA : ASSAM
ANTHROPOMETRY
ANTI BRAHMINISM
APA TANIS
APPLIED RESEARCH : BACKWARD CLASSES
ARAKU VALLEY : INDIA : KERALA : VISAKHAPATNAM
ARMFOLDING : TRIBALS
ARROW MARRIAGE
ARSON
ARTERIAL PRESSURE : ENDOGAMOUS COMMUNITIES : INDIA : WEST BENGAL
ARUNACHAL PRADESH : INDIA
ARYANS
ASHRAM SCHOOLS
ASIA : SOUTH EAST

DEVELOPMENT
IRULAS
ISLAM
ISLAMISATION
ISLANDS OF THE PACIFIC
ISOLATED FOOD GATHERING COMMUNITY : INDIA
ISOLATION

JAGDALPUR CONFERENCE : INDIA : MADHYA PRADESH
JAGJIVAN RAM : IMPACT ON HARIJANS
JAGJIVAN RAM : VIEWS ON CASTEISM AND UNTOUCHABILITY
JAINTIA HILLS : INDIA : MEGHALAYA
JALPAIGURI DISTRICT : INDIA : WEST BENGAL
JAMMU AND KASHMIR
JATI/CASTE : INDIA
JATS : INDIA
JATS : POWER POLITICS
JAUNSARIES
JEHANABAD MASSACRE : INDIA
JHABUA
JHARKHAND : INDIA : BIHAR
JHARKHAND STATE DEMAND : INDIA : BIHAR
JHARO
JHOOMING
JHUMIAS
JOBS : RESERVATIONS
JODHPUR CITY : INDIA : RAJASTHAN
JUANG DORMITORIES
JUANGS
JUGIS : INDIA : TRIPURA
JUSTICE FOR TRIBALS
JUTI MAKERS/SHOE MAKERS : WOMEN

KACHARIS
KAHARS : INDIA : KARNATAKA
KALADY : INDIA : TRAVANCORE
KALASHS
KAMAR TRIBE : INDIA : MADHYA PRADESH
KAMNAS : INDIA : ANDHRA PRADESH
KANAURAS/KINNARAS
KANDHAS
KANTHAPURAM : INDIA
KANWARS : INDIA : MADHYA PRADESH
KAPU SAVARAS
KAPUS : INDIA : ANDHRA PRADESH
KARBIS : INDIA : ASSAM
KARNATAKA : INDIA
KARPOORI FORMULA : RESERVATION
KASHMIR : INDIA
KATKARI LABOUR
KATKARIS
KAURS
KAWARS
KAYASTHS : INDIA
KEONJHAR DISTRICT : INDIA : ORISSA
KERALA : INDIA
KHAIRWARS : INDIA : MADHYA PRADESH
KHAMPTIS
KHANDESH
KHARIAS/KHERIAS
KHARKHARA PROJECT
KHASAS : WOMEN : INDIA : UTTAR PRADESH
KHASI HILLS : INDIA : MEGHALAYA
KHASI REVIVALIST MOVEMENT
KHASI SYNTENGS
KHASIS : INDIA : MEGHALAYA
KHASIS : WOMEN
KHATRIS : PHYSICAL CHARACTERISTICS
KHATRIS : SINDHIS
KHAWAS
KHERWAR MOVEMENT
KHOKRO
KHUTTO SAVARAS
KINNAUR : TRIBAL LANGUAGES : INDIA : HIMACHAL PRADESH
KINNAUR : WOMEN
KINNAUR POLYANDRY
KINSHIP AND MARRIAGE : IGBO OF NIGERIA
KINSHIP SYSTEMS : TRIBALS
KINSHIP TERMINOLOGY
KISAN CHILDREN : INDIA : ORISSA
KODAGU : INDIA : KARNATAKA
KODAL HILLS
KODAVA SOCIETY
KODHUS
KOKRO
KOLES
KOLES : GIRLS
KOLGHAS
KOLI HILLS
KOLIS
KOLS : EDUCATION : INDIA : UTTAR PRADESH
KOLS : INDIA : UTTAR PRADESH
KONDA KAMARAS

TRIBES AND TRIBALS : CENSUS : INDIA : WEST BENGAL
TRIBES AND TRIBALS : CHILDREN
TRIBES AND TRIBALS : CLUBS
TRIBES AND TRIBALS : DEFINITION
TRIBES AND TRIBALS : DIET
TRIBES AND TRIBALS : ECONOMIC CONDITIONS : INDIA : MADHYA PRADESH
TRIBES AND TRIBALS : ECONOMIC CONDITIONS : INDIA : ORISSA
TRIBES AND TRIBALS : ECONOMIC CONDITIONS : INDIA : WEST BENGAL
TRIBES AND TRIBALS : EDUCATION
TRIBES AND TRIBALS : FOOD : NUTRITION
TRIBES AND TRIBALS : HEALTH AND HYGIENE
TRIBES AND TRIBALS : HISTORY : INDIA
TRIBES AND TRIBALS : INDEBTEDNESS
TRIBES AND TRIBALS : INDIA
TRIBES AND TRIBALS : INDIA : ANCIENT
TRIBES AND TRIBALS : INDIA : ANDAMAN AND NICOBAR ISLANDS
TRIBES AND TRIBALS : INDIA : ANDHRA PRADESH
TRIBES AND TRIBALS : INDIA : ANDHRA PRADESH : HYDERABAD
TRIBES AND TRIBALS : INDIA : ARUNACHAL PRADESH
TRIBES AND TRIBALS : INDIA : ASSAM
TRIBES AND TRIBALS : INDIA : BIHAR
TRIBES AND TRIBALS : INDIA : BIHAR : BIBLIOGRAPHY
TRIBES AND TRIBALS : INDIA : BIHAR : CHOTANAGPUR
TRIBES AND TRIBALS : INDIA : BIHAR : JAMSHEDPUR
TRIBES AND TRIBALS : INDIA : CENTRAL PROVINCES
TRIBES AND TRIBALS : INDIA : DECCAN
TRIBES AND TRIBALS : INDIA : GUJARAT
TRIBES AND TRIBALS : INDIA : HIMACHAL PRADESH
TRIBES AND TRIBALS : INDIA : HIMALAYAN REGION
TRIBES AND TRIBALS : INDIA : JAMMU AND KASHMIR
TRIBES AND TRIBALS : INDIA : KARNATAKA
TRIBES AND TRIBALS : INDIA : KERALA
TRIBES AND TRIBALS : INDIA : MADHYA PRADESH
TRIBES AND TRIBALS : INDIA : MAHARASHTRA
TRIBES AND TRIBALS : INDIA : MAHARASHTRA : BOMBAY
TRIBES AND TRIBALS : INDIA : MANIPUR
TRIBES AND TRIBALS : INDIA : MEGHALAYA
TRIBES AND TRIBALS : INDIA : MID INDIA
TRIBES AND TRIBALS : INDIA : NORTH EASTERN
TRIBES AND TRIBALS : INDIA : NORTH EAST FRONTIER AGENCY
TRIBES AND TRIBALS : INDIA : ORISSA
TRIBES AND TRIBALS : INDIA : ORISSA : ECONOMIC CONDITION
TRIBES AND TRIBALS : INDIA : RAJASTHAN
TRIBES AND TRIBALS : INDIA : SIKKIM
TRIBES AND TRIBALS : INDIA : SINGHBHUM
TRIBES AND TRIBALS : INDIA : SUNDARBANS
TRIBES AND TRIBALS : INDIA : TAMIL NADU
TRIBES AND TRIBALS : INDIA : TAMIL NADU : MADRAS
TRIBES AND TRIBALS : INDIA : TRAVANCORE
TRIBES AND TRIBALS : INDIA : TRIPURA
TRIBES AND TRIBALS : INDIA : UTTAR PRADESH
TRIBES AND TRIBALS : INDIA : WEST BENGAL
TRIBES AND TRIBALS : ISLANDS OF THE PACIFIC
TRIBES AND TRIBALS : LAOS
TRIBES AND TRIBALS : LIBRARIES
TRIBES AND TRIBALS : MALASIYA
TRIBES AND TRIBALS : NIGERIA
TRIBES AND TRIBALS : NORTH EAST FRONTIER AGENCY
TRIBES AND TRIBALS : NUTRITION

TWO

JOURNALS/NEWSPAPERS SCANNED

JOURNALS

Adibasi (Q)
Tribal Research Bureau
Government of Orissa
Bhubaneswar
Orissa-751001

Administrator (Q)
National Academy of Administration
Charles Villa
Mussoorie
Uttar Pradesh-248179

Andhra Pradesh (M)
Department of Information and Public Relations
Government of Andhra Pradesh
Hyderabad
Andhra Pradesh-500001

Annals of the National Association of Geographers, India (HY)
C/o Indian Statistical Institute,
7, S.I.S., Sanswal Marg
New Delhi-110016

Anthropologist (HY)
Department of Anthropology
University of Delhi
Delhi-110007

Arthniti (HY)
Department of Economics
Calcutta University
Calcutta
West Bengal-700019

Asian Journal of Psychology & Education (Tri-A)
Agra Psychological Research Cell
Tiwari Kothi, Belanganj
Agra
Uttar Pradesh-282004

Asian Studies (Q)
Netaji Institute for Asian Studies
1, Woodburn Park
Calcutta
West Bengal-700020

Bengal Past and Present (HY)
Calcutta Historical Society
Bijay Manzil
10-A Diamond Harbour
Calcutta
West Bengal-700027

Bhartiya Shiksha Shodh Patrika (HY)
Indian Institute of Educational Research
Saraswati Kunj
Nirala Nagar
Lucknow
Uttar Pradesh-226001

Bihar Journal of Public Administration (HY)
Kadam Kuan
Patna
Bihar-800004

Bulletin of Anthropological Survey of India (HY)
(Continued from *Bulletin of the Department of Anthropology*)
Anthropological Survey of India
Indian Museum
27, Jawaharlal Nehru Marg
Calcutta
West Bengal-700016

Bulletin of Cultural Research Institute (Q)
P1/4 C.I.T. Scheme VII/M
V.I.P. Road
Calcutta
West Bengal-700054

Bulletin of the Deccan College Research Institute (Q)
Deccan College
Pune
Maharashtra-411006

Bulletin of the Department of Anthropology (HY)
(Continued from *Bulletin of Anthropological Survey of India*)
Anthropological Survey of India
Indian Museum
27, Jawaharlal Nehru Marg
Calcutta
West Bengal-700016

Bulletin of Institute of Traditional Cultures (HY)
University of Madras
Madras
Tamil Nadu-600005

Bulletin of the Madras Government Museum
Madras
Tamil Nadu-600005

Bulletin of Non-Formal Education (Q)
National Council of Educational Research and Training
NIE Campus
Sri Aurobindo Marg
New Delhi-110016

Bulletin of Tribal Research Institute (Chhindwara) (HY)
Chhindwara
Madhya Pradesh-480001

Bulletin of Tribal Research and Development Institute (Bhopal) (HY)
35, Simla Road
Bhopal
Madhya Pradesh-462002

Business India (F)
Wadia Building
17/19, Dalal Street
Bombay
Maharashtra-400001

Capital (W)
12, Old Cōurt House Corner
Calcutta
West Bengal-700001

Carvan (F)
Rani Jhansi Marg
Jhandewalan
New Delhi-110055

Children's World (M)
Children's Book Trust
Nehru House
New Delhi-110002

Cochin University Law Review (Q)
Department of Law
University of Cochin
Cochin
Kerala-682022

Commerce (W)
NKM International House
178, Bacbay Reclamation
Bombay
Maharashtra-400020

Contemporary Social Sciences (Irr)
Research Foundation
B4/245, Safdarjang Enclave
New Delhi-110029

Contributions to Indian Sociology (Old and New Series) (A)
Institute of Economic Growth
University of Delhi Campus
Delhi-110007

Co-operative Perspective (Q)
Vaikunth Mehta National Institute of Cooperative Management
University Road
Pune
Maharashtra-4110041

Co-operators Bulletin (M)
Jammu and Kashmir Co-operative Union
Vir Marg
Jammu
Jammu and Kashmlr-180001

Deccan Geographer (HY)
Deccan Geographical Society
Subhadra Bhawan
120-A, Nehru Nagar East
Hyderabad
Andhra Pradesh-500007

Development Policy and Administration Review (Q)
HCM State Institute of Public Administration
Jaipur
Rajasthan-302004

Eastern Anthropologist (Q)
Ethnographic & Folk Culture Society
Box 209
7-A, Ram Krishna Marg
Faizabad Road
Lucknow
Uttar Pradesh-226007

Economic Affairs (Q)
BC/144, Sector 1
Salt Lake City
Calcutta
West Bengal-700064

Economic and Political Weekly (W)
(Continued from Economic Weekly)
Skylark
284, Shahid Bhagat Singh Road
Bombay
Maharashtra-400038

Economic Trends (F)
Federation of Indian Chambers of Commerce and Industry
Federation House
Tansen Marg
New Delhi-110001

Economic Weekly (W)
(Continued from *Economic and Political Weekly*)
Sameksha Trust
Skylark
284, Shahid Bhagat Singh Road
Bombay
Maharashtra-400038

Education (M)
Teacher's Cooperative Education Journals and Publications Ltd
Kanyakubja College
10, Staff Colony
Lucknow
Uttar Pradesh-226001

Education Quarterly (Q)
Ministry of Human Resource Development
Department of Education
Government of India
Room No. 503
C. Wing Shastri Bhavan
New Delhi-110001

Educational India (M)
Hindu Press
Machilipatnam
Andhra Pradesh-521001

Educational Miscellany (Q)
Directorate of Higher Education Publications Unit
Government of Tripura
Old Flowers Corner Building
Melarmath
Agartala
Tripura-799001

Educational Review (M)
16, Sankuwar Street
Triplicane
Madras
Tamilnadu-600005

Experiments in Education (M)
S.I.T.U. Council of Educational Research
No. 3, Trust Link Street
Mandavelipakkam
Madras
Tamil Nadu-600028

Faculty of Social Work Magazine (A)
(Continued from *Social Work Review*)
Faculty of Social Work
Maharaja Sayajirao University of Baroda
Fatehganj
Vadodara
Gujarat-390002

Folklore (M)
(Continued from *Indian Folklore*)
Indian Folklore Society
Indian Publications
3, British Indian Street
Calcutta
West Bengal-700069

Gandhi Marg (M)
Gandhi Peace Foundation
221-223, Deen Dayal Upadhayay Marg
New Delhi-110002

Geographical Review of India (Q)
35, Ballygange Circular Road
Calcutta
West Bengal-700009

Goa Today (M)
Goa Publication
E/253, Dr. Gomes Pereira Road
P.B. No. 9
Panjim
Goa-403001

Guru Nanak Journal of Sociology (HY)
Guru Nanak Dev University
Amritsar
Punjab-143001

Haryana Review (M)
Public Relations Department
Government of Haryana
S.C.O. No. 189/191
Sector-17C
Chandigarh-160017

Health and Population : Perspective and Issues (HY)
National Institute of Health and Family Welfare
New Mehrauli Road
Munirka
New Delhi-110067

Illustrated Weekly of India (W)
Times of India Press
P.B. No. 207
Bombay
Maharashtra-400020

India Past and Present (HY)
Institute of Historical Research
9, New Marine Lines
Bombay
Maharashtra-400020

India International Centre Quarterly (Q)
India International Centre
40, Maxmuller Road
New Delhi-110003

India Quarterly (Q)
Indian Council of World Affairs
Sapru House
Barakhamba Road
New Delhi-110001

India Today (F)
Living Media India Ltd.
F-14/15, Connaught Place
New Delhi-110001

Indian and Foreign Review (F)
Ministry of Information and Broadcasting
Publication Division
Government of India
Patiala House
New Delhi-110001

Indian Anthropologist (HY)
Indian Anthropologist Association
Department of Anthropology
University of Delhi
Delhi-110007

Indian Archives (HY)
National Archives of India
Janpath
New Delhi-110001

Indian Behavioral Science Abstracts (Q)
Manasayan
Lalit Park
Laxmi Nagar
Delhi-110092

Indian Economic and Social History Review (Q)
Delhi School of Economics
University Enclave
Delhi-110007

Indian Economic Journal (Q)
Department of Economics
Bombay University Campus
Vidyanagri
Bombay
Maharashtra-400098

Indian Education (M)
All India Federation of Educational Associations
(V.P. Raghavachari)
2-1-408/3 University Road
Nallakunta
Hyderabad
Andhra Pradesh-500044

Indian Educational Review (HY)
National Council of Educational Research and Training
NIE Campus
Sri Aurobindo Marg
New Delhi-110016

Indian Folklore (M)
(Continued from *Folklore*)
Indian Folklore Society
Indian Publications
3, British Indian Street
Calcutta
West Bengal-700069

Indian Historical Review (HY)
Indian Council of Historical Research
35, Ferozshah Road
New Delhi-110001

Indian Journal of Adult Education (M)
Indian Adult Education Association
17-B Indraprastha Estate
New Delhi-110002

Indian Journal of Applied Psychology (HY)
Madras Psychology Society
Department of Psychology
University of Madras
Madras
Tamil Nadu-600005

Indian Journal of Community Guidance Service (Tri-A)
Annamalai University
Annamalainagar
Tamil Nadu-608002

Indian Journal of Extension Education (Q)
Indian Society of Extension Education
Division of Agricultural Extension
Indian Agricultural Research Institute
New Delhi-110012

Indian Journal of Physical Anthropology and Human Genetics (Tri-A)
Ethnographic and Folk Culture Society
P.B.-209
Lucknow
Uttar Pradesh-226007

Indian Journal of Political Science (Q)
University of Bhagalpur
Bhagalpur
Bihar-812007

Indian Journal of Political Studies (HY)
Department of Political Science
University of Jodhpur
Jodhpur
Rajasthan-342001

Indian Journal of Public Administration (Q)
Indian Institute of Public Administration
Indraprastha Estate
New Delhi-110002

Indian Journal of Social Research (Q)
B-47, Shastri Nagar
Tejgarhi
Meerut
Uttar Pradesh-250002

Indian Journal of Social Work (Q)
Tata Institute of Social Sciences
Deonar
Bombay
Maharashtra-400088

Indian Management (M)
All India Management Association
Management House
14, Institutional Area
Lodi Road
New Delhi-110003

Indian Museum Bulletin (HY)
Indian Museum
27, Jawaharlal Nehru Marg
Calcutta
West Bengal-700016

Indian Psychological Review (Q)
Agra Psychological Research Cell
Tiwari Kothi, Belanganj
Agra
Uttar Pradesh-282004

Indian Sociological Bulletin (Q)
Print Craft Publishers
Pili Kothi, Rakesh Marg, G.T. Road
Ghaziabad
Uttar Pradesh-201001

Interdiscipline (HY)
(Continued from *Social Science Abstracts*)
Gandhian Institute of Studies
Box 116, Rajghat
Varanasi
Uttar Pradesh-221001

International Journal of Dravidian Linguistics (HY)
Dravidian Linguistics Association
Kerala Panini Buildings
Kummumpuram
Trivandrum
Kerala-695001

Janata (W)
National House
6, Tulloch Road
Apollo Bundar
Bombay
Maharashtra-400039

Journal and Proceedings of Asiatic Society of Bengal (Irr)
1, Park Street
Calcutta
West Bengal-700019

Journal of Ancient Indian History (HY)
Calcutta University
51/2, Hazra Road
Calcutta
West Bengal-700019

Journal of Anthropological Society of Bombay
(*Old* and *New Series*) (HY)
Anthropological Society of Bombay
209, Dr Dadabhai Nauroji Road
Bombay
Maharashtra-400001

Journal of the Bihar Puravid Parishad (A)
Bihar Puravid Parishad
Patna
Bihar-800001

Journal of Dharma (Q)
Dharma Research Association Centre for the Study of World Religions
Dharmaram College
Bangalore
Karnataka-560029

Journal of Education and Psychology (Q)
M.B. Patel College of Education
Sardar Patel University
Vallabh Vidyanagar
Gujarat-388120

Journal of Educational Planning and Administration (Q)
National Institute of Educational Planning and Administration
17B, Aurobindo Marg
New Delhi-110016

Journal of Family Welfare (Q)
Family Planning Association of India
Bajaj Bhawan
Nariman Point
Bombay
Maharashtra-400021

Journal of Gujarat Research Society (Q)
Samshodban Sadan
Ramakrishna Mission Marg
Khar
Bombay
Maharashtra-400052

Journal of Haryana Studies (HY)
Kurukshetra University
Kurukshetra
Haryana

Journal of Higher Education (Tri-A)
University Grants Commission
35, Ferozshah Road
New Delhi-110001

Journal of Historical Studies (A)
Department of Post Graduate Studies and Research in History
University of Mysore
Manasagangotri
Mysore
Karnataka-570006

Journal of the Indian Anthropological Society (Tri-A)
Indian Anthropological Society
Indian Museum
27, Jawaharlal Nehru Marg
Calcutta
West Bengal-700016

Journal of Indian Education (M)
National Council of Educational Research and Training
NIE Campus
Sri Aurobindo Marg
New Delhi-110016

Journal of the Indian Law Institute (Q)
Indian Law Institute
Bhagwan Das Road
New Delhi-110001

Journal of Institute of Economic Research (HY)
J.S.S. Institute of Economic Research
Vidyagiri
Dharwar
Karnataka-580014

Journal of Institute of Educational Research (Tri-A)
59, Usman Road
Madras
Tamil Nadu-600017

Journal of Karnatak University (Social Science) (A)
Karnatak University
Dharwar
Karnataka-580003

Journal of Kerala Studies (Q)
Department of History
University of Kerala
Karyavattam
Kerala-695581

Journal of Maharaja Sayajirao University of Baroda (Irr)
M.S. University of Baroda
Vadodara
Gujarat-390002

Journal of North-East Indian Council for Social Science Research (HY)
B.T. Hostel
Laitumkhrah
Shillong
Meghalaya-793003

Journal of Psychological Research (Q)
Madras Psychological Society
University of Madras, Department of Psychology
Madras
Tamil Nadu-600005

Journal of Rural Development (BiH)
National Institute of Rural Development
Rajendranagar
Hyderabad
Andhra Pradesh-500030

Journal of Social and Economic Studies (HY)
A.N.S. Institute of Social Studies
Patna
Bihar-800001

Journal of Social Research (HY)
Council of Social and Cultural Research, Bihar and Department of Anthropology
Ranchi University
Ranchi
Bihar-834008

Journal of Social Sciences (HY)
Institute of Social Sciences
Agra University
Agra
Uttar Pradesh-282004

Journal of Sociological Studies (A)
Department of Sociology
University of Jodhpur
Jodhpur
Rajasthan-342002

Journal of the University of Bombay (5/yr)
University of Bombay
Fort
Bombay-400098

Khadi Gramodyog (M)
Erla Road
Ville Parle (West)
Bombay
Maharashtra-400056

Kurukshetra (M)
Ministry of Information and Broadcasting
Publication Division
Government of India
Patiala House
New Delhi-110001

Legal News and Views (M)
Social Action Trust
Indian Social Institute
Lodi Road Institutional Area
New Delhi-110003

Link (W)
Link House
Bahadur Shah Zafar Marg
New Delhi-110002

Mainstream (W)
F-24, Bhagat Singh Market
New Delhi-110001

Malayalam Literature Survey (Q)
Kerala Sahitya Academy
Town Hall Road
Trichur
Kerala-680001

Man and Development (Q)
Centre of Research in Rural and Industrial Development
1037, Sector 21B
Chandigarh-160002

Man and Life (Q)
Department of Anthropology
Calcutta University
35, Ballygunge Circular Road
Calcutta
West Bengal-700019

Man in India (Q)
Bharatiya Bhasha Mudranalaya
C-9/274 Chetaganj
Varanasi
Uttar Pradesh-221001

Management and Labour Studies (Q)
Xavier Institute
Jamshedpur
Bihar-831001

Marg (Q)
34-38, Bank Street
Bombay
Maharashtra-400001

Memoirs of the Asiatic Society of Bengal (Irr)
1, Park Street
Calcutta
West Bengal

Modern Review (M)
77/2/1 Dharamtalla Street
Calcutta
West Bengal-700013

Monthly Commentary on Indian Economic Conditions (M)
Indian Institute of Public Opinion (P)Ltd.
2A, National Insurance Building
P.B. No. 288
Parliament Street
New Delhi-110001

Mysore Economic Review (M)
Sáraswathi Building
N.R. Road
Bangalore
Karnataka-560002

N I E Journal (BiM)
National Council of Educational Research and Training
NIE Campus
Sri Aurobindo Marg
New Delhi-110016

National Geographer (HY)
Allahabad Geographical Society
University of Allahabad
Department of Geography
Allahabad
Uttar Pradesh-211002

National Geographical Journal of India (Q)
National Geographical Society of India
Banaras Hindu University
Department of Geography
Varanasi
Uttar Pradesh-221005

National Journal of Education (HY)
Faculty of Education
Banaras Hindu University
Kamachha
Varanasi
Uttar Pradesh-221010

New Age (W)
Ajoy Bhawan
Kotla Road
New Delhi-110002

New Frontiers in Education (Q)
C-6, Community Centre
Safdarjang Development Area
New Delhi-110016

Organiser (W)
Bharat Prakashan(Delhi) Ltd.
29, Rani Jhansi Marg
New Delhi-110055

Panjab University Research Bulletin (Arts) (Irr)
Panjab University
Arts Block No. 1 (Top Floor)
Chandigarh-160014

Parlance (M)
7B, Everest House
46C, Chowringhee Road
Calcutta
West Bengal-700071

People's Democracy (W)
Communist Party of India (Marxist)
4, Ashoka Road
New Delhi-110001

Political Science Review (Q)
Department of Political Science
University of Rajasthan
Jaipur
Rajasthan

Prabuddha Bharata (M)
Advatta Ashrama
5, Delhi Entally Road
Calcutta
West Bengal-700014

Prashasnika (Q)
H.C. Mathur State Institute of Public Administration
Jaipur
Rajasthan 302004

Primary Teacher (Q)
National Council of Educational Research and Training
NIE Campus
Sri Aurobindo Marg
New Delhi-110016

Probe India (M)
105, Rohit House
3, Tolstoy Marg
New Delhi-110001

Progress of Education (M)
Pune Vidyarthi Griha Prakashan
1786, Sadashiv Peth
Pune
Maharashtra-411030

Progressive Education Herald (Q)
3rd Floor, Palace Talkies Complex
Abid Centre
Hyderabad
Andhra Pradesh-800001

Purana (HY)
All India Kashiraj Trust
Fort, Ramnagar
Varanasi
Uttar Pradesh

Quarterly Journal of the Mythic Society (Q)
Mythic Society
Daly-Memorial Hall, Nrupatunga Road
Bangalore
Karnataka-560002

Quarterly Review of Historical Studies (Q)
Institute of Historical Studies
35, Theatre Road
Calcutta
West Bengal-700017

Quest in Education (Q)
Indian Council of Basic Education
Gandhi Shikshan Bhavan
Juhu
Bombay
Maharashtra-400045

Radical Humanist (M)
B-17, Maharani Bagh
New Delhi-110065

Rajasthan Economic Journal (HY)
Department of Economics
S.B.S.H.(New Campus)
Sukhadia University
Udaipur
Rajasthan-330001

Religion and Society (Q)
Christian Institute for the Study of Religion and Society
P.O. Box 4600, 17, Miller's Road
Bangalore
Karnataka-560046

Resarun (HY)
Directorate of Research
Government of Arunachal Pradesh
Shillong
Meghalaya-793001

Research Bulletin (Q)
Maharashtra State Council of Educational Research and Training
Pune
Maharashtra-411030

Research Journal of Ranchi University (Irr)
Ranchi
Bihar-834008

Rural India (M)
Adarsh Seva Sangha
Ishwaradas Mansions
Nana Chowk
Bombay
Maharashtra-400007

Sarvodaya (M)
Tamil Nadu Sarvodaya Sangh
Gandhi Nagar
Tirupur
Tamil Nadu-638603

Secular Democracy (M)
A 199, Pandara Road
New Delhi-110003

Seminar (M)
Malhotra Building
Janpath
New Delhi-110001

Sevartham (A)
St. Albert's College, P.B. No.5
Regional Major Seminary
Ranchi
Bihar-834001

Social Action (Q)
Indian Social Institute
Institutional Area
Lodi Road
New Delhi-110003

Social Change (Q)
Council for Social Development
53, Lodi Estate
New Delhi-110003

Social Science Abstracts (HY)
(Continued from *Interdiscipline*)
Gandhian Institute of Studies
P.B. No. 116, Rajghat
Varanasi
Uttar Pradesh-221001

Social Scientist (M)
B-1, 2nd Floor
LSC, J-Block
Saket
New Delhi-110017

Social Service Quarterly (Q)
Social Service League
Servants of India Society
Sardar Patel Road
Bombay
Maharashtra-400004

Social Welfare (M)
Central Social Welfare Board
Jeewan Deep
Parliament Street
New Delhi-110001

Social Work Review (A)
(Continued from *Faculty of Social Work Magazine*)
Faculty of Social Work
Maharaja Sayajirao University of Baroda
Fatehgunj
Vadodara
Gujarat-390002

Socialist Perspective (Q)
140/20E, South Sinthee Road
1st Floor
Calcutta
West Bengal-700050

Society and Change (Q)
Association for Studies in Society and Social Change
1/C, Madhu Gupta Lane
Calcutta
West Bengal-700012

Sociological Bulletin (HY)
Tata Institute of Social Sciences
Sion-Trombay Road
Deonar
Bombay
Maharashtra-400088

Southern Economist (F)
106-108, Saleh Ahmed Building
Infantry Road
Bangalore
Karnataka-560001

State and Society (Q)
Indian Institute for Regional Development Studies
Pullarkunnu
Kerala-686027

Survey (Irr)
Indian Institute of Social Welfare and Business Management
College Square West
Calcutta
West Bengal-700073

Teacher Today/Naya Shikshaks (Q)
Directorate of Primary and Secondary Education
Government of Rajasthan
Bikaner
Rajasthan-334001

Teaching Politics (HY)
Department of Political Science
University of Delhi
Delhi-110007

Theosophist (M)
Theosophical Publishing House
Adyar
Madras
Tamil Nadu-600020

Tribal Research Bulletin (HY)
Tribal Research and Training Institute
28, Queen's Garden
Pune
Maharashtra-411001

Tribe (Q)
Manikya Lal Verma Tribal Research Institute
Udaipur
Rajasthan-313001

Vanyajati (Q)
Bharatiya Adamjati Sewak Sangh
Thakkar Bapa Smarak Sadan
Dr. Ambedkar Marg
Jhandewalan
New Delhi-110055

Vedic Path (Q)
32, University Campus
Gurukula Kangri
Hardwar
Uttar Pradesh.249044

Vidura (Q)
Press Institute of India
Sapru House Annexe
Barakhamba Road
New Delhi-110001

Vishveshvaranand Indological Journal (HY)
Vishveshvaranand Vishva Bandhu Institute of Sanskrit and Indological Studies
Sadhu Ashram
Hoshiarpur
Punjab-146001

Vision (Q)
Journal of the Institute of Economic and Social Studies
Bhubaneswar
Orissa-751001

Vivekananda Kendra Patrika (HY)
Vivekananda Rock Memorial Committee
3, Singrachari Street
Triplicane
Madras
Tamil Nadu-600005

Voluntary Action (HY)
Association of Voluntary Agencies for Rural Development
5, Deen Dayal Upadhayay Marg
New Delhi-110002

Yojana (F)
Publication Division
Ministry of Information and Broadcasting
Government of India
Patiala House
New Delhi-110001

NEWSPAPERS

Economic Times (D)
7, Bahadur Shah Zafar Marg
New Delhi-110002

Financial Express (D)
Bahadur Shah Zafar Marg
New Delhi-110002

Hindu (D)
Kasturi and Sons Ltd.
Madras
Tamil Nadu-600002

Hindustan Times (D)
Hindustan Times Buildings
Kasturba Gandhi Marg
New Delhi-110001

Indian Express (D)
Bahadur Shah Zafar Marg
New Delhi-110002

National Herald (D)
Herald House
Bahadur Shah Zafar Marg
New Delhi-110002

Patriot (D)
Bahadur Shah Zafar Marg
New Delhi-110002

Statesman (D)
Statesman House
Connaught Circus
New Delhi-110001

Times of India (D)
Bahadur Shah Zafar Marg
New Delhi-110002

Tribune (D)
Chandigarh-160020

Legend

A	=	Annual
HY	=	Half Yearly
Irr	=	Irregular
M	=	Monthly
Q	=	Quarterly
Tri-A	=	Tri-Annual

THREE

BASIC INDEX

ABOR HILLS : INDIA : ASSAM

Sen Gupta, P.N., 1953, Population studies and living conditions of the tribes in Padam and Minyong areas of Abor Hills (Assam), *Bulletin of Department of Anthropology* 2(1) January, p 91-112, tables.

ABORIGINAL CHILD

Venkatraman, S.R., 1963, The life of the Aboriginal child, *Social Service Quarterly* 48(4) April, p 105-109.

ABORIGINAL DEBT : INDIA : MADHYA PRADESH

Dube, Krishna Chandra, 1960, Problem of Aboriginal debt in Bhindranawagarh subdivision of the Raipur district (M.P.), *Vanyajati* 8(2) April, p 73-80, tables.

ABORIGINALITY

Ehrenfels, U.R., 1962, Gifts of Aboriginality, *Journal of Social Research* 5(2) September, p 71-80.

ABORIGINALS

Anon, 1954, Aboriginal Education in Australia, *Educational Review* 60(4) April, p 57-76.

Baduri, Manindra Bhusan, 1941, The Aboriginal tribes of the Udaipur State (C.P.), *Man in India* 21(2-3), April-September, p 92-126, footnotes.

Basu, Minendra Nath, 1961, Suggestions for the educational plan of the Aboriginal peoples of India, *Vanyajati* 9(3) July, p 123-126.

Elwin, Verrier, 1942, The duration of marriage among the Aboriginals of the Maikat hills, *Man in India* 22(1) January-March, p 11-21, footnotes.

Grigson, W.V., 1946, The Aboriginal in the future India, *Man in India* 26(2) June, p 81-96, footnotes.

Kodanda Rao, P., 1954, Liquor and the Aboriginal, *Indian Journal of Social Work* 14(4) March, p 382-385.

Naik, T.B., 1950-51, Aboriginals of Gujarat, *Eastern Anthropologist* 4(1) September-November.

Parasnis, N.R., 1958, The problems of the education of the Aboriginal tribes (Adiwasis) in the Thana district, Bombay State, *Progress of Education* 32(8) March, p 254-259; 32(9) April, p 316-328.

Sahu, Laxminarayan, 1955-1956. The problem of the Aboriginals, *Adibasi* 1, p 16-18.

——, 1957, We and the Aboriginals, *Vanyajati*, 5(1) January, p 30-32.

——, 1961, The Aboriginal : From symbolic to individual life, *Vanyajati* 9(4) October, p 149-150.

Sarkar, Haribishnu, 1951, Disposal of the dead at the Indus valley and its survival among the Aboriginal peoples of India, *Man in India* 31(1) January-March, p 23-32, references, tables.

Satyarthi, Devendra, 1944, In Aboriginal India, *Rural India* 7(6) July, p 247-252.

Von Furer-Haimendorf, Christoph, 1945, Aboriginal rebellions in the Deccan, *Man in India* 25(4) December, p 208-217.

See also Aborigines; Tribes and Tribals.

ABORIGINES

Anon, 1965, Schools on wheels for Aborigines in Northern Territory, *Education* 44(10) October, p 26-28.

Bapat, N.V., 1962, Education of the Aborigines, *Educational Review* 68(7) July, p 161-165. [From the Presidential address to the Aborigines Education Section at the last All-India Education Conference].

Das, Nitayananda, 1958, Glimpses of Aborigines education, *Vanyajati* 6(3) July, p 122-129.

Mehta, B.H., 1949, The problem of Aborigines, *Indian Journal of Social Work* 10(2) September.

Minendra Nath, 1958, The role of anthropology in the education of the Aborigines in India, *Adibasi* 3(2) May-July, p 1-8.

Roy, Sarat Chandra, 1946, The Aborigines of Chotanagpur : Their proper status in the reformed constitution, *Man in India* 26(2) June, p 120-136.

Sahu, Laxminarayan, 1958, The problem of Aborigines, *Vanyajati* 6(4) October, p 170-173.

Sarkar, S.S., 1957, Finger prints of Orissan Aborigines, *Man in India* 37(3) July-September, p 182-191, tables.

Sharma, A.C., 1949, Illiteracy of Aborigines in India, *Educational Review*, 55(4) April, p 67-69.

_____, 1950, Report of the Aborigines Education Section, *Educational India* 16(10) April, p 286-287.

_____, 1951 Eradication of illiteracy among Aborigines, *Educational India* 17(7) January, p 216-218.

Social Service Quarterly (Perodical), 1940, Indian Aborigines Friends Society, *Social Service Quarterly* 26(2) October, p 79-81, editorial.

Venkatraman, S.R., 1950, Education of the Aborigines, *Educational Review*, 56(7) July, p 129-132; 56(8) August, p 150-152.

_____, 1962, Education of Aborigines, *Social Science Quarterly* 47(4) April, p 119-126.

See also Aboriginals; Tribes and Tribals.

ABORS

Gohain, B.C., 1974, Agricultural organisation among the Abor, *Bulletin of the Department of Anthropology* 3(2).

Ray, P.C., 1955, The tensional feeling among the Abor and Gallongs indicated by Rorschach Techniques, *Indian Journal of Psychology* 30(1-2), p 95-103.

See also Scheduled Tribes : India : Arunachal Pradesh.

ABUJHMADIAS

Kurup, A.M., 1963-1964, People of the unknown hills : The Abujhmadias, *Vanyajati* 11(1) January, p 38-41, 11(4) October, p 168-176; 12(1) January, p 46-55; 12(2) April, p 67-79; 12(4) October, p 180-189.

ABUJHMARAH/ABUJHMARH/ABUJMARH/ABUJMARIAS/ABUJMARIYAS

Anon, 1962, The culture studies (A socio-economic survey of Abujhmarh), *Bulletin*

Resarun 11(1) Spring-Summer, p 27-32.

———, 1985, Customs and laws of widow inheritance of the Adis, *Resarun* 11(2) Autumn-Winter, p 14-24.

———, 1986, Role of intergroup relations in communal harmony among the Adis, *Resarun* 12(1-2) Spring-Winter, p 9-13.

Roy, S., 1958, Hunting and fishing among the Adis, *Vanyajati* 6(2) p 140-152.

ADIVASI REVOLTS

Parulekar, Godavari, 1986, Glorious saga of the Warli Adivasis revolt, *People's Democracy* 10(8) February 23, p 6-7.

———, 1986, Saga of the Warli Adivasis revolt, *People's Democracy* 10(9) March 2, p 5 +

ADIVASIS

Anon, 1955, Problems of Adivasi and suggestions to solve them, *Vanyajati* 3(4) October, p 176-177.

———, 1957, Social reconstruction among Adivasis, *Vanyajati* 5(3) July, p 111-114.

———, 1985, Industry takes away Adivasi land, gives jobs to outsiders, *Link* 27(50).

———, 1987, (Book review), *Contributions to Indian Sociology* (NS) 22(1) January-June, p 116-118; *Social Scientist* 16(2) February, p 60-66.
Review of the book : **Hardiman, David**, 1988, *The coming of Devi* : Adivasi Assertion in Western India, Oxford University Press, New Delhi, 248 p.

Bhagat, Anupdev, 1956, Missionaries, anthropologists and Adivasi culture, *Social Action* 6(11) November, p 457-472, references.

Coelho, E.P., 1952, A new approach to Adivasi education, *Progress of Education* 27(12) July, p 340-344.

Das, G.N., 1957, The Adivasis of Orissa and their welfare, *Vanyajati* 5(2) April, p 74-82, references.

Ekka, P., 1962, The Adivasis of Chotanagpur : How will they adjust to the modern world? *Social Action* 12(4) April, p 188-189, tables.

Gaffoor, Khaja Abdul, 1954, The future of Hyderabad's Adivasis, *Vanyajati* 2(3) July, p 91-94.

Jena, Krishna Chandra, 1959, The Adivasis of Orissa, *Rural India* 22(1) January, p 39-40.

Kar, P., 1966, Educational survey of some Adivasi villages of Orissa, *Adibasi* 8(1) April, p 49-52.

Kaul, S.K., 1955, Adivasis and Indian army, *Vanyajati* 3(1) January, p 23-25.

Krishnan, Jalram, 1988, Adivasi upsurge at Dharol, *Economic Times*, January 17, p 3, col 1-6.

Kulkarni, Sharad, 1985, Adivasis, law and social justice, *Economic and Political Weekly* 20(28) July 13, p 1171-1174.

———, 1986, Adivasis, law and social justice, *Tribal Research Bulletin* 8(2) March, p 1-7, bibliography.

Mehatab, H.K., 1957-1958, Our Adibasi problem, *Adibasi* 2(1), p 1-2.

Mishra, Satish, 1986, A silver of hope for Adivasis, *Link* (Supplement) 28(30) March 2, p 4-19.

Nanal, V.M., 1961, Education of the Adivasis in Thana District, *Progress of Education* 35(12) July, p 382-386; 36(1) August, p 19-24.

Narain Prasad, 1961, Primary education among the Adivasis, *Vanyajati* 9(4) October, p 161-162.

Nehru, Jawaharlal, 1955, Place of Adivasis in our national life, *Vanyajati* 3(2) April,

Surgana taluka (Nasik district) in respect of paddy cultivation, *Tribal Research Bulletin* 9(2) March, p 15-17.

ADOPTION STRATEGEM

Parmanand Singh, 1987, Preventing exploitative acquisition of reservation benefits through adoption strategem, *Journal of Indian Law Institute* 29(1) January-March, p 100-109, footnote.

ADULT EDUCATION : CONTRIBUTION TO TRIBAL DEVELOPMENT

Jha, Raghunath, 1986, Adult Education and tribal development, *Mainstream* 24(50) August 16, p 35-36 +.

See also Adult Tribal: Education

ADULT LEARNERS : READING MATERIAL

Kundu, M., 1981, Preparing 'readers' for tribal adult learners: Some viable topics, *Indian Journal of Adult Education* 42(9) September, p 21-24, references.

ADULT TRIBALS : EDUCATION

Venkataih, N., 1980, Non-formal education for adult tribals, *Experiments in Education* 8(3) May, p 54-56.

See also Adult Education: Contribution to Tribal Development

AGARIA GONDS

See Gonds.

AGARIYAS

See also Gonds.

AGGRESSIVENESS : SCHEDULED CASTE : CHILDREN

Srivastava, Jai Prakash, 1954, Aggressiveness in Scheduled Caste children, *Education* 33(4) April, p 16-19; 33(5) May, p 10-13.

AGNA PANNA

Devi, Mahasveta, 1988, Story of Agna Panna, *Economic and Political Weekly* 23(42) October 15, p 2151-2152.

AGRARIAN SITUATION : TRIBAL AREAS

Pathy, Jaganath, 1987, The agrarian situation in tribal areas, *Journal of Social Economic Studies* 4(2) April-June, 143-162.

AGRARIAN STRATIFICATION : WARLIS

Mondal, S.K. and **Malhotra, R.**, 1984, Agrarian stratification among the Warlis of Gujarat : An observation, *Tribe* 16(3-4) September-December, p 36-43.

AGRARIAN SYSTEM

Chetan Singh, 1988, Conformity and conflict : Tribes and the agrarian system of Mughal India, *Indian Economic and Social History Review* 25(3) July-September, p 314-340.

AGRICULTURAL DEVELOPMENT : TRIBALS

Buch, M.N., 1969, Land improvement and agricultural development in tribal areas: Lack of motivation, *Bulletin of Tribal Research and Development Institute* (Bhopal) 7(1-2) June-December, p 1-4.

Jaiswal, N.K., et al, 1969, Attitude towards agricultural development among tribal and non-tribal people, *Man in India* 49 (3) July-September, p 267-280, tables.

Kulkarni, R.R. and **Borkar, S.T.**, 1986, Tribal leaders and their role in agricultural development, *Tribal Research Bulletin* 8(2) March, p 17-20.

Talesara, Rajendra, 1984, Agricultural development among tribals : Issues and aspects, *Prashnika* 13(1) January-March, p 27-33.

AGRICULTURAL LABOURERS : TRIBAL AREAS

Rajagopal, 1986, Agricultural labourers in tribal areas, *Kurukshetra* 34(4) January, p 17-18 +.

AGRICULTURAL PRACTICES : RIANGS

Thusu, Kidar Nath, 1962, The Riang agricultural practices, *Bulletin of Anthropological Survey of India* 11(3-4), p 157-174, appendix, references,

AGRICULTURE : TRIBALS

Gangwar, A. and **Ramakrishnan, P.S.**, 1987, Agriculture and animal husbandry among the Sulungs and Nishis of Arunachal Pradesh, *Social Action* 37(4) October-December, p 345-372, bibliography, figures tables.

See also Shifting Cultivation.

AHOMS : GIRLS

Sengupta, Sarthak, 1982, Study of sexual maturation in Ahoms girls, *Indian Journal of Physical Anthropology and Human Genetics* 8(1) April, p 63-66, bibliography, tables.

A J G A R

Mitra, Chandan, 1989, Moulded in caste : AJGAR versus the lesser OBCs, *Times of India*, August 23, p 6, col. 3-5.

ALCOHOLIC BEVERAGES

Sengupta, P.N., 1956, Studies on the nutritive values of tribal alcoholic beverages, *Bulletin of Department of Anthropology* 5(1) January, p 67-80.

See also Liquors.

ANCIENT INDIA

Das, Amal Kumar, 1963, Leadership : Its role in ancient India and among the tribals, *Bulletin of Cultural Research Institute* 1(3) p 1-7, references.

ANCIENT TRIBAL GROUPS : INDIA : ANDMAN AND NICOBAR ISLANDS

Bhupinder Singh, 1989, Between two worlds : Five ancient tribal groups of A & N Islands, *Vanyajati* 37(2) April, p 1-4.

ANDAMAN AND NICOBAR ISLANDS : INDIA

Agrawal, H.N., 1965, A B O blood groups in Andaman Islands, *Bulletin of Anthropological Survey of India* 14(1-2) January-June, p 59-60, tables.

Bose, Savadindu, 1964, Economy of the Onge of Andaman, *Man in India* 46(4), p 298-310.

See also Ancient Tribal Groups; Oraons; Geographical Area subdivision "Andaman Nicobar Islands" under main descriptor.

ANDAMANEES

See also Hill Tribes.

ANDHRA PRADESH : INDIA

Lakshmaiah, T. and **Yadappanavar, Arvind**, 1988, A survey of educational facilities for tribal students : Problems and impacts in Paderu Samithi in Andhra Pradesh, *Man in India* 68(4) December, p 380-400, bibliography.

Rayudu, C.S., 1985, New milestones in Andhra Pradesh, *Social Welfare* 32(3) June, p 17-19.

Shyama Nand Singh, 1986, Reservation controversy in Andhra Pradesh, *Mainstream* 25(2) September 20, p 2-5 +, tables.

See also South India; Geographical Area subdivision 'Andhra Pradesh' under main Descriptor.

ANDHRA PRADESH SCHEDULED TRIBES CO-OPERATIVE FINANCE DEVELOPMENT CORPORATION

Shrikant, L.M., 1967, Co-operative movement among tribals : Andhra Pradesh Scheduled Tribes Co-operative Finance Development Corporation, *Vanyajati* 15(2) April, p 94-97, tables.

ANIMAL HUSBANDRY : TRIBALS : INDIA : ARUNACHAL PRADESH

Gangwar, A. and **Ramakrishnan, P.S.**, 1987, Agriculture and animal husbandry among the Sulungs and Nishish of Arunachal Pradesh, *Social Action* 37(4) October-December, p 345-372, bibliography, figures, tables.

ANTHROPOLOGICAL APPROACH

Bage, S.K., 1965, Anthropologists and tribal administration, *Journal of Social Research* 8(1) March, p 11-16.

Basu, Minendra Nath, 1963, Anthropological approach to the tribal peoples of India, *Vanyajati* 11(1), January, p 4-8.

———, 1963 Anthropology in tribal education, *Bulletin of Cultural Research Institute* 2(1), p 22-27.

Bhagat, Anupdev, 1956, Missionaries, anthropologists and Adivasi culture, *Social Action* 6(11) November, p 457-472, references.

Biswas, P.C., 1955, Anthropology and tribal education, *Vanyajati* 3(2) April, p 81-83.

Bose, Nirmal Kumar, 1957, Anthropology and tribal welfare, *Man in India* 37(3) July-September, p 169-181.

Chattopadhyay, Gouranga, 1960, Application of anthropology to administration : Case studies in rural and tribal areas, *Journal of Social Research* 3(1) March, p 48-54, references.

Majumdar, D.N., 1951, Anthropology under glass, *Journal of the Anthropological Society of Bombay* (NS) 5(1) March, p 1-16.

ANTHROPOLOGY : SOCIO-CULTURAL APPROACH

Ahmed, Imtiaz, 1972, For a sociology of India, *Contributions to Indian Sociology*, New Series, 6, December, p 172-177.

Banerjee, Biswanath, 1965, An outline of background, theory and methods of socio-cultural anthropology, *Bulletin of Cultural Research Institute* 4, p 44-52, references.

Bhatt, G.S., 1964, Sociology and anthropology in India and the West, *Journal of Social Research* 7 (1-2) March-September, p 143-152, references.

Bulsara, Jal. F., 1969, Thoughts on approaches to the study of man and society, *Journal of Anthropological Society of Bombay* (NS) 14(2), p 109-124.

Das, Nityananda, 1968-1969, Methods of social anthropology and study of tribes in

India, *Adibasi* 10(3-4) October-January, p 40-50, references.

Dube, Leela, 1970, The craft of social anthropology, *Eastern Anthropologist* 23(3) September-December, p 285-297.

Ehrenfels, U.R., 1959, Anthropology and traditional cultures, *Indian Journal of Social Work* 19(4) March, p 323-324.

Father, P., and **Gisbert, S.J.**, 1951, Sociology's debt to anthropology, *Journal of Anthropological Society of Bombay* (NS) 6(1) March, p 1-13, references.

Ferreira, John V., 1964, Ethnology and history, *Sociological Bulletin* 13(1) March, p 1-11, references.

——, 1967, Towards integral man through integral anthropology, *Sociological Bulletin* 16(2) September, p 77-93.

Gisbert, P., 1961, Culture as the central interest of anthropology, *Journal of Anthropological Society of Bombay* (NS) 11(2), p 1-10.

Greenfield, Sydney M., 1984, Social anthropology and economic theory: Their place in study and policy formulation in the new nations, *Indian Sociological Bulletin* 1(4) July, p 24-31, references.

Hodson, K.C., 1962, Cultural anthropology, *Man in India* 6(2-3) June-September, p 84-89.

Knabe, Wolfang K., 1983, The role of sociology and anthropology in solving problems of Indian tribals, *Development Policy and Administration Review* 9(1-2) January-December, p 15-23.

Kochar, V.K., 1967, Objectification of research process in social anthropology, *Indian Journal of Social Work* 27(4) January, p 387-392, references.

Minendra Nath, 1958, The role of anthropology in the education of the Aborigines in India, *Adibasi* 3(2) May-July, p 1-8.

Minz, Nirmal, 1985, Anthropology and deprived, *Religion and Society* 32(4) December, p 3-19, bibliography.

Mitra, Sarat Chandra, 1921, Types of cultural theory, *Man in India*, 1(3) September, p 240-261, footnotes.

Mukerjee, Radhakamal, 1965, Unities and universals of culture, *Eastern Anthropologist* 18(1) January-April, p 1-11, references.

Mukherjee, Bhabananda, 1966, Social anthropology and its roles, *Vanyajati* 14(2) April, p 78-81.

——, 1990, Social anthropology and its roles, *Vanyajati* 37(1) January, p 17-21.

Paul, Gemini, 1957, Anthropology and tribal administration, *Vanyajati* 5(1) January, p 4-11.

Peter, Prince, 1939, The utility of psycho-analysis in social anthropology, *Indian Journal of Psychology* 14(1) January, p 23-25.

Pocock, David F., 1961, Psychological approaches and judgements of reality, *Contributions to Indian Sociology* 5 October, p 44-74.

Roy Burman, B.K., 1970, Family planning from the point of view of cultural anthropology, *Indian Journal of Social Work* 30(4) January, p 343-353, references.

Sarkar, S.S., 1960, Micro-revolution: A plea for coordination between physical and cultural anthropology, *Journal of Social Research* 3(1) March, p 1-6, illustrations, references.

Saxena, Davendra, 1965, Demography and social anthropology, *Indian Journal of Social Research* 6(3) December, p 246-250, references.

Srinivas, M.N., 1952, Social anthropology and sociology, *Sociological Bulletin* 1(1) March, p 28-37.

Vidyarthi, Lalit P., 1957, Anthropology, authority and tribal welfare, *Eastern*

Anthropologist 11(1) September-November, p 14-24, references.

——, 1959, Anthropology and administration in India, *Journal of Social Research* 2(1-2) March-September, p 59-71, references.

ANTHROPOMETRIC CHARACTERS : MUNDAS : INDIA : ASSAM

Buzarabarua, P.M., 1989, Effects of migration and environment on anthropometric characters of Munda population of Assam : A preliminary observation, *Man in India* 69(3) September, p 292-304.

ANTHROPOMETRY

Rao, V.V. Raman, 1984, Impact of supplementary feeding on tribal pre-school children of A.P. : An anthropometric assessment, *Man in India* 64(2) June, p 167-174.

ANTI BRAHMINISM

Anon, 1985, (Book review), *Hindustan Times* (Magazine) August 8, p 6-8.

Review of the book : **Rajagopal, Indhu**, 1985, *The tyranny of Caste: The non-brahmin movement and political development in South India*, Vikas, New Delhi, 195 p.

Jain, Meenakshi, 1985, Anti-Brahminism by another name, *Times of India* September 4, p 7-8; September 5, p 7-8.

See also Caste and Politics : India; Protest/Reform Movements.

APA TANIS

Von Furer Haimendorf, C., 1946, The agriculture and land tenure among the Apa Tanis, *Man in India* 26(1) March, p 20-49, footnotes, illustrations.

Von Furer Haimendorf, Elizabeth et al, 1946, Notes on tribal justice among the Apa Tanis, *Man in India* 26 (3-4) September-December, p 181-195.

APPLIED RESEARCH : BACKWARD CLASSES

Zutshi, G.L., 1959, Preliminaries regarding applied research among backward classes, *Vanyajati* 7(3) July, p 84-93.

ARAKU VALLEY : INDIA : KERALA : VISAKHAPATNAM

Prasad Rao, P.D., 1959, Tribal people of Araku Valley, Visakhapatnam, *Vanyajati* 7(3) July, p 103-105.

ARMFOLDING : TRIBALS

Datta, Upali and **Ghosh, G.C.**, 1988, A study of hand clasping and armfolding among the Jugi of Tripura, *Man in India* 68(23) June-September, p 211-215.

Datta Chaudhuri, S.S., 1984, A note on hand clasping armfolding and tongue rolling among the Mugi of Arunachal Pradesh (India), *Vanyajati* 32(2) April, p 12-13.

Mayanglambam, Manibabu and **Mayanglambam, Suniti Bala**, 1989, Patterns of hand clasping, armfolding and handedness among the Phayengs of Manipur, *Man in India* 69(1) March, p 87-93.

ARROW MARRIAGE

Dube, S.C., 1948, Arrow Marriage, *Eastern Anthropologist* 2(1) September, p 22-26.

ARSON

Balagopal, K., 1987, A tale of arson, *Economic and Political Weekly* 22(29) July 18,

p 1169-1171.

ARTERIAL PRESSURE : ENDOGAMOUS COMMUNITIES : INDIA : WEST BENGAL

Gangopadhyay, Prodyot and **Kundu, Shampa**, 1988, Familial trend in arterial pressure among few endogamous communities of West Bengal reared under diverse occupational environment, *Man in India* 68(2-3) June-September, p 235-242, bibliography.

ARUNACHAL PRADESH : INDIA

Das Gupta, K., 1979, A note on the Wancho language of Arunachal Pradesh, *Resarun* 5(1) Spring-Summer, p 25-37, bibliography.

Datta Chaudhuri, S.S., 1984, A note on hand clasping armfolding and tongue rolling among the Mugi of Arunachal Pradesh (India), *Vanyajati* 32(2) April, p 12-13.

Durrah, Dwijendra Kumar and **Das, Priya Bala**, 1984, A cross-sectional study of growth in four somatometric characters of the Khampti boys of Arunachal Pradesh, *Resarun* 10(1) Spring-Summer, p 15-24, bibliography, flags, tables.

Dutta, P.C., 1978, Social organisation of the Wanchos of Tirap district, Arunachal Pradesh, *Resarun* 4(1) January-March, p 14-35.

Sengupta, S. and **Dutta, M.N.**, 1985, A note on ridge count of finger patterns of the Wanchos of Arunachal Pradesh, *Resarun* 11(2) Autumn-Winter, p 23-26, bibliography, tables.

——, 1985, Palmar main line index and transversality in Wanchos of Arunachal Pradesh, *Resarun* 11(2) Autumn-Winter, p 39-41, bibliography, tables.

Sengupta, Sarthak, 1984, Finger prints of the Bangnis of Arunachal Pradesh, *Resarun* 10(1) Spring-Summer, p 25-30, bibliography, tables.

See also Geographical Area subdivision 'Arunachal Pradesh' under main Descriptor.

ARYANS

Anon, 1965, Brahmans in early Tamilaham, *Bulletin of Institute of Traditional Cultures* Part II, 1965, p 275-317.

Basham, A.L., 1963, Some reflections on Dravidians and Aryans, *Bulletin of Institute of Traditional Cultures* Part II, p 225-234.

See also Seminar on Brahmans in Early Tamilaham, 1965, Madras.

ASHRAM SCHOOLS

Shaw, Biswanath, 1958-1959, Vocational education in the Ashram Schools, *Adibasi* 3(3-4) August-January, p 31-34.

Vyas, Ambalal, 1957-1958, Why this emphasis on vocational bias in education in Ashrams? *Adibasi* 2(1), p 45-49.

ASIA : SOUTH EAST

See South East Asia; Geographical Area subdivision under main Descriptor.

ASOKAN PERSONS : SRI LANKA

Roberts, Michael, 1984, Caste feudalism in Sri Lanka : A critique through the Asokan persons and European contrasts, *Contributions to Indian Sociology* (New Series) 18(2) July-December, p 189-217.

ASSAM : INDIA

Anon, 1953, A plea for intensive non-official work in Assam, *Vanyajati* 1(3) July,

p 49-51.

——, 1953, Scheme of the Assam State Government for the welfare of Scheduled Tribes included in the Five Year Plans, *Vanyajati* 1(3) July, p 71-72.

Hutton, J.H., 1924, Assam and the Pacific, *Man in India*, 4(1-2) March-June, p 1-13, footnotes.

——, 1929, Cultural affinities of the Oraons with the Hill tribes of Assam, *Man in India* 9(1) January-March, p 1-6.

Paul, Gemini, 1956, Origin of certain tribal names pertaining to Assam, *Vanyajati* 4(4) October, p 147-154, references.

Sengupta, Gouranga Gopal, 1959, The Kacharis of Assam, *Indian Folklore* 2(3) July-September, p 226-227.

Vaid, Minnie, 1985, Gujarat is going the way of Assam, *Illustrated Weekly of India* 106(8) June 30, p 36-37.

See also Geographical Area subdivision "Assam" under main Descriptor.

ASSIMILATION

Kanekar, P.G., 1942, Isolation or assimilation? *Social Service Quarterly* 28(3) January, p 97-115.

Wilkinson, T.S., 1961, Isolation, assimilation and integration in their historical perspective, *Religion and Society* 8(3) September, p 13-25.

——, 1962, Isolation, assimilation and integration in their historical perspectives, *Bulletin of Tribal Research and Development Institute* (Chhindwara) 2(1) June, p 19-28.

ASSOCIATIONS : GIRLS

Gupta, Jaya Dutta, 1960, Ponung or girls association among the Padam Abor in the lower Abor hills, *Bulletin of Anthropological Survey of India* 9(2) July, p 71-73.

ASTHAPURAM : INDIA

Sivakumar, S.S. and **Sivakumar, Chitra**, 1979, Class and jati at Asthapuram and Kanthapuram : Some comments towards a structure of interests, *Economic and Political Weekly*, 19, Annual Number, February, p 263-286.

ATTAPPADY : INDIA : KERALA

Sankaranarayan, A.S. and **Lakshmanan, K.K.**, 1987, A tribal festival in Attappady, Kerala : An aspect of worship of nature as God, *Folklore* 28(10) October, p 235-36.

AUDUMBARA COIN

Mukherjee, D., 1984, A review of an Audumbara coin, *Indian Museum Bulletin* 19, p 66-68.

AUSTRALIA

Anon, 1954, Aboriginal education in Australia, *Indian Educational Review* 60(4) April, p 57-76.

AUSTRIC SPEAKING TRIBES : INDIA

Ishtiaque, M., 1989, Changing patterns of linguistic identity among the Austric speaking tribes in Mid-India, *National Geographical Journal of India* 35(2) June, p 140-152.

AUTONOMOUS STATE : INDIA : ASSAM

Hussain, Monirul, 1987, Tribal movement for autonomous state in Assam,

Economic and Political Weekly 22(32) August 8, p 1329-1332.

AVARNAS

See also Untouchability.

BACKWARD CLASSES

Adibasi (Periodical), 1965, Defence-cum-production orientation of the programme of backward classes welfare, *Adibasi*, October, p 1-4, editorial.

Anon, 1947, Government drive for uplift of backward classes, *Social Service Quarterly* 33(1) July, p 27-29.

——, 1966, Education Commission, Government of India : Questionnaire on the education of the backward classes, *Vanyajati* 14(3) July, p 139-144.

Aurora, G.S., 1968, Caste and backward classes, *Man in India* 48(4) October-December, p 297-306, footnotes.

Blair, Harry W., 1980, Rising Kulaks and backward classes in Bihar : Social change in the late 1970s, *Economic and Political Weekly* 15(2) January 12, p 64-74.

Dave, P.C., 1966, Voluntary organisations and welfare of backward classes, *Vanyajati* 14(4) October, p 156-164.

Dushkin, Lelah, 1979, Backward class benefits and social class in India, 1920-1970, *Economic and Political Weekly* 14(4), Annual Number, April, p 661-667.

Gopala Reddy, B., 1956, Welfare of tribals and other backward classes, *Indian Journal of Social Works* 16(4) March, p 294-296.

Gupta L.P., 1979, A study of personality syndromes and cognitive characteristics of Scheduled Castes, backward classes and non-Scheduled Caste students, *Journal of Higher Education* 4(3) Spring, p 381-387.

Hanumanta Rao, K., 1990, Job reservation for backward classes, *Mainstream* 28(46) September 8, p 6.

Husain, Syed Khaja Mahboob, 1949, The rural uplift of tribes and backward classes in Hyderabad, Deccan, *Man in India* 29(3-4) July-December, p 185-198.

Raju Cheluva, K.H., 1986, Backward classes in India : Issues and trends, *Indian Journal of Political Sciences* 47(4) October-December, 473-485.

Rangaya, D., 1955, Memorandum submitted to the Backward Classes Commission on behalf of the Bhartiya Adamjati Sevak Sangh, Delhi, *Vanyajati* 3(1) January, p 33-39.

Roy Burman, B.K., 1961. A list of research projects with operative significance for welfare of the backward classes (with special reference to West Bengal), *Vanyajati* 9(1) January, p 9-21.

Shrikant, L.M., 1966, Education Commission and backward classes, *Vanyajati* 14(3) July, p 95-98.

Zutshi, G.L., 1959, Preliminaries regarding applied research among backward classes, *Vanyajati* 7(3) July, p 84-93.

See also Backward Communities; Scheduled Castes and Scheduled Tribes; Tribes and Tribals, etc.; name of individual backward class, e.g., Harijans.

BACKWARD CLASSES COMMISSION, 1953-55, NEW DELHI

Vanyajati (Periodical), 1953, Backward Classes Commission, *Vanyajati* 1(2) April, p 25-26, editorial.

BACKWARD CLASSES COMMISSION, 1979-80, NEW DELHI : NEWS ANALYSIS AND CRITIQUE

Abraham, A.S., 1990, OBC forces in full cry: Bid for power in perpetuity, *Times of India*, September 4, p 8, col 2-4.

Amrik Singh, 1990, Mandal Commission: Educational impact, *Times of India*, August 18.

Badhwar, Inderjeet, 1990, Mandal Commission : Dividing to rule, *India Today*, September 15.

Bhatia, Prem, 1990, A mostly unread document, *Tribune*, September 7.

Business India (Periodical), 1990, Risking the Mandal Report, *Business India*, September 3-16, editorial

Chatterjee, Raj, 1990, First thing first, *Tribune*, September 7.

Dhawan, Harmohan, 1990, Text of Harmohan Dhawan's letter to P.M., *National Herald*, September 9.

Datta Ray, Sunanda K., 1990, Class into caste : V.P. Singh's political insurance, *Statesman*, September 9.

Dube, S.C., 1990, Against fraticidal caste war, *Mainstream* 28 (46) September 8, p 4-5.

——, 1990, A retrograde fetish, *Hindustan Times*, September 3, p 11, col. 2-5.

Gandhi, Rajiv, 1990, More politics than jobs, *Hindustan Times*, September 8, 1990.

Ganguli, Amulya, 1990, Divide and lose : Mandal in Shah Bano's wake, *Statesman*, September 5, p 6, col. 4-6.

Garg, R.K., 1990, For development sans divisions, *Patriot*, September 5.

Gill, M.S. and **Singh, A.M.**, 1989, Reactionary dissent by caste Hindu employees, *Social Change* 19(3) September, p 16-22.

Hindustan Times (Newspaper), 1990, The Mandal mess, *Hindustan Times*, September 19, editorial.

——, 1990, Time for second thoughts, *Hindustan Times*, September 13, editorial.

Hoshiar Singh and **Malik, Jagdish Kumar**, 1984, The Mandal Commission report: A plea for share in power, *Political Science Review* 23(3-4) July-December, p 250-268, bibliography, tables.

India Today (Periodical), 1990, Policy reservations, *India Today*, September, 15, editorial.

Jain, Meenakshi, 1990, The plight of Brahmins, *Indian Express*, September 18.

Karlekar, Hiranmay, 1990, Undermining India, *Indian Express*, August 25.

Khanna, H.R., 1990, Weakening the roots, *Hindustan Times*, September 13.

Khushwant Singh, 1990, Mandal mess, *Hindustan Times*, September 8.

Kothari, Rajni, 1990, Meaning of Mandal, *Hindustan Times*, September 24, p 13.

Mishra, Sudhanshu, 1990, Most party leaders keep aloof, *Link* 33(4) September 2, p 6-7.

Muthamma, C.B., 1990, Change the system, *Hindustan Times*, September 21.

Puri, Rajender, 1990, Mandal : A way out, *Hindustan Times*, September 11.

Rajappa, S., 1990, Tamil Nadu for it, rest of South quiet, *Statesman*, September 4.

Ramaiah, A., 1990, Mandal Commission's recommendations : A critical view, *Mainstream* 28(43) August 18, p 19-20 +.

Ramanathan, K.V., 1990, Lessons from experience, *Indian Express*, September 7.

Roy Burman, B.K., 1990, Burman questions 1931 Census, *Hindustan Times*, September 18.

Sangal, P.S., 1990, Re-examination of criteria necessary, *National Herald*, September 9.

Sardesai, Rajdeep, 1990, Mandal fails to agitate Maharashtra, *Times of India*, September 1.

Sharma, K.L., 1990, A backward step, *Indian Express*, September 19.

Shoure, Arun, 1990, Three sets of facts on Mandal : Rank 413? So sorry. Rank 14246? But of course. . . *Indian Express*, September 2.

Shukla Rajiv, 1990, Mandal Commission : Where does the Janata Dal stand? *Sunday*, September 9-15.

Srivastava, Manju, and **Srivastava, Saraswati**, 1983-84, The Mandal Commission Report : A critique, *Journal of State Politics and Administration* 6(2) July-December; 7(1) January-June, p 75-86, bibliography, footnotes.

Tharyan, P., 1990, Attack caste, not Mandal, *Hindustan Times*, September 8, p 11, col. 2-5.

Verghese, B.G., 1990, Quake remedies, *Indian Express*, September 12.

See also Mandal, B.P.: Report of Backward Classes Commission

BACKWARD CLASSES COMMISSION, 1979-1980, NEW DELHI : NEWS ITEMS

Anon, 1990, Advani assails V P on minorities quota, *Hindustan Times*, September 2.

——, 1990, Advani assails V P on Muslim quota, *Times of India*, September 2.

——, 1990, Agreement on four point says Upendra, *National Herald*, September 4.

——, 1990, Ahir and Gujjars 'left alone', *Statesman*, September 7.

——, 1990, All party meet not a failure : N F, *Hindustan Times*, September 5.

——, 1990, All party meet to discuss reservations, *Hindustan Times*, August 31.

——, 1990, Anger of the elite? *Statesman*, September 7.

——, 1990, Anti Mandal stir : No decision on Delhi rally, *Times of India*, September 9.

——, 1990, Anti quota stir hits grain trade, *Times of India*, September 8.

——, 1990, Anti-quota stir spreads, four killed in Patna violence, *Times of India*, September 5, p 1, col. 1-2.

——, 1990, Anti-quota stir toll rises to 7 in Orissa, *Statesman*, September 3, p 1, col. 3-5; p 7, col. 5.

——, 1990, Anti-reservation stir in Bihar : Situation needs mature handling, *Patriot*, September 1.

——, 1990, Anti-reservation stir unabated : 4 killed in Orissa police firing, *Times of India*, September 2.

——, 1990, Army alerted in Baroda: Curfew in three cities, *Hindustan Times*, September 6.

——, 1990, Army alerted in Simla, *Hindustan Times*, September 8, p 1, col. 5-7; *Tribune*, September 8.

——, 1990, Army called out in Kangra district : H P rejects Mandal report, *Times of India*, September 7.

——, 1990, B J P against quota for minorities, says Advani, *Hindustan Times*, September 3, p 1, col. 4.

——, 1990, BJP, CPM for talks with students, *Tribune*, September 7.

——, 1990, B J P flays Govt. on job quota issue, *Hindustan Times*, September 9

——, 1990, B J P for 50 per cent as quota limit, *Hindustan Times*, September 1

——, 1990, B J P-Left call for economic criterion, *Times of India*, August 18.

——, 1990, Backward quota a forward step, *Hindustan Times*, September 7.

——, 1990, Backwardness won't go by playing petty politics : Rajiv, V.P.S. Obstinacy will divide India' : Plea for uplift of poorest of poor in marathon L.S. speech, *National Herald*, September 7.

———, 1990, Bandh no way to do it, says traders, *Hindustan Times*, September 7.
———, 1990, Basu calls for modifications, *Indian Express*, September 1.
———, 1990, Be your own light, *Tribune*, August 19.
———, 1990, Beyond mere palliatives, *Hindu*, September 9.
———, 1990, Bill on job quota for SC, ST on anvil, *Hindustan Times*, September 3, p 18, col. 1-2.
———, 1990, Bommai warns of bloodshed, *Tribune*, September 9.
———, 1990, C.P.M. favours Karpoori formula, *Hindustan Times*, August 31.
———, 1990, C.P.M. view on quota against its policy, *Times of India*, September 2.
———, 1990, Cabinet not split over quota : V.P., *Times of India*, September 5.
———, 1990, Carrying the can, *Times of India*, September 5, p 8, col. 1.
———, 1990, Caste not basis, Says V.P. Singh, *Hindu*, September 7.
———, 1990, Cauldron of caste tensions, *Hindu*, September 4, p 8, col. 3-6.
———, 1990, Central order on job reservation, *Hindustan Times*, August 19, p 12, col. 5-8.
———, 1990, Centre accepts States plea, *Times of India*, September 3.
———, 1990, Chakha jam plan washed away, *Hindustan Times*, September 8, p 5, col. 2-5.
———, 1990, A challenge to political parties, *National Herald*, September 2.
———, 1990, .Congress-I flays Govt. move on quota, *Indian Express*, September 5, p 9, col. 1-5.
———, 1990, Congress to boycott all-party meet, *Hindustan Times*, September 3, p 1, col. 1-3, p 18, col. 1-2.
———, 1990, Consensus eludes all-party meet : Congress leaders attend, Govt. stand rigid, *Hindustan Times*, September 4, p 1, col. 1-4.
———, 1990, DUTA Chief's bid to scuttle discussion condemned, *Hindu*, September 2.
———, 1990, DUTA split over Mandal report, *Times of India*, September 2.
———, 1990, Dalit Christians allege bias, *Hindustan Times*, August 18, p 5, col. 5-8.
———, 1990, Dalit Christians demand SC status, *Times of India*, August 18.
———, 1990, Dalit Christians want S.C. Status, privileges, *Hindu* August 18.
———, 1990, Decision on Mandal report hasty : Dhawan, *Tribune*, September 9.
———, 1990, Decision on quota hasty : NF leader, *Times of India*, September 9.
———, 1990, Delhi incident-free, but stir continues, *Hindu*, September 2.
———, 1990, Divided they stand, *Tribune*, September 5, p 6, col. 1-2.
———, 1990, Do no destroy country : Dinesh, *Hindustan Times*, September 6.
———, 1990, Don't take a hasty decision on quota, Left tells V.P., *National Herald*, September 5, p 1, col. 1.
———, 1990, Double talk on castes, *Hindustan Times*, September 7.
———, 1990, End the drift, *Hindustan Times*, September 7.
———, 1990, Expert disagrees with Mandal report, *Hindustan Times*, September 1.
———, 1990, Extend reservation to education, MPs, *Patriot*, September 4.
———, 1990, Farmers blast quota policy, *Hindustan Times*, September 9.
———, 1990, Fire spreads, *National Herald*, September 8, p 6, col. 1-2.
———, 1990, Firing in Bihar, stir spreads to South, *Times of India*, August 19.
———, 1990, Five die in Bihar anti-quota stir, *Indian Express*, September 5.
———, 1990, Forum asks students to go back to classes, *Hindustan Times*, September 1.
———, 1990, Fresh violence in Bihar, Haryana, *Hindustan Times*, September 6.
———, 1990, From crisis to crisis : The unmaking of the Singh Government, *Probe*

India 11(7) September, p 8-12.
———, 1990, Full speed backwards by P.M., *Times of India*, September 4, p 8, col. 2-4.
———, 1990, Government has put students fate in jeopardy : Aiyer, *National Herald*, September 4, p 3-5.
———, 1990, Government pulled up for not tabling report, *Tribune*, September 7.
———, 1990, Govt. urged to seek apex courts advice, *Hindu*, September 8.
———, 1990, Gujarat coalition in fresh row, *Patriot*, September 8.
———, 1990, Gujarat 'no' to Mandal report, *Statesman*, September 3, p 1, col. 7-8.
———, 1990, Gujjar leader assails report, *Indian Express*, September 5, p 16, col. 1-3.
———, 1990, Haryana observes complete bandh, *Times of India*, September 1.
———, 1990, Haryana panel on backward classes, *Hindustan Times*, September 9.
———, 1990, High living, plain thinking : Mandalised metropolitan mind, *Times of India*, September 5, p 8, col. 2-4.
———, 1990, How a tragedy is enacted, *Indian Express*, September 5, p 8, col. 1
———, 1990, The impasse continues, *National Herald*, September 6.
———, 1990, In a bind of sports, *Hindu*, September 5, p 8, col. 1.
———, 1990, Injustice will be legalised, *Indian Express*, September 8, p 5, col. 6-7.
———, 1990, Irony of the Mandal: Meenakshi Jain, *Indian Express*, September 3, p 8, col. 3-6.
———, 1990, Is shoe-shining that shameful? *Times of India*, September 9.
———, 1990, JNU students join anti-quota stir, *Times of India*, August 19.
———, 1990, Janata party opposes, Mandal Report, *National Herald*, September 3, p 11, col. 5.
———, 1990, Job quota ends Manu's legacy, *Statesman*, September 8.
———, 1990, Job reservations for backward classes, *Patriot*, September 3.
———, 1990, Kanshi Ram assail V.P. on Mandal, *Hindustan Times*, September 6.
———, 1990, List of castes delayed, *Times of India*, September 9.
———, 1990, Lung power keeps pot boiling, *Hindustan Times*, September 7.
———, 1990, Mandal : Champion of backward classes? *Indian Express*, August 19, p 1, col. 1-5; p 9, col. 1.
———, 1990, Mandal : Myth of merit and equity, *Times of India*, September 4, p 8, col. 6-7.
———, 1990, Mandal Maria and social justice, *Indian Express*, September 5, 1990, p 8, col. 2-5.
———, 1990, Mandal not relevant to Orissa, says J.B. Patnaik, *National Herald*, September 3, p 12, col. 2.
———, 1990, Mandal panel report : Harvests of headcounts in caste politics, *Link* 33(4) September 2, p 4-5.
———, 1990, Mandal report not to be imposed on States : V.P., *Indian Express*, September 2.
———, 1990, Mandal report scientific : Gill, *Hindustan Times*, September 6.
———, 1990, The Mandal trap, *Hindustan Times*, September 1.
———, 1990, A messiah always in the news, *Times of India*, September 9.
———, 1990, Minority Govt. arrogance, *Tribune*, September 4, p 6, col. 2-4.
———, 1990, Mishra urges V.P. to accept Rajiv formula, *National Herald*, September 5, p 9, col. 5-8.
———, 1990, More politics than jobs, says Rajiv, *Hindustan Times*, September 8, p 1, col. 1-2; p 10.

_____, 1990, NF allies may seek changes in Mandal, *National Herald*, September 2.
_____, 1990, NF Parliamentary Party backs implementation, *Indian Express*, September 4, p col. 2-4; p 9, col. 5.
_____, 1990, National debate on reservation imperative, *Statesman*, September 1.
_____, 1990, Need for dialogue, *Indian Express*, September 6.
_____, 1990, Need, not caste, *Times of India*, September 8.
_____, 1990, Need to redefine backwardness, *National Herald*, September 1.
_____, 1990, Nehru or Lohia? *National Herald*, August 24.
_____, 1990, No compromises on Mandal : Mulayam, *National Herald*, September 3, p 11, col. 2-3.
_____, 1990, No confrontation with States : V.P., *Times of India*, September 2.
_____, 1990, No consensus on Mandal report; Cong attends All Party Meet, *Times of India*, September 4, p 1, col. 3-4; p 16, col. 2.
_____, 1990, No legal hurdles to job quota, *Hindustan Times*, August 19, p 1, col. 1.
_____, 1990, No plan to change quota formula : Nayanar, *Indian Express*, September 8, 1990, p 14, col. 1-4.
_____, 1990, No way to consensus, *Patriot*, September 5.
_____, 1990, Not by closure, *Patriot*, September 3.
_____, 1990, Not by violence, *Times of India*, August 18.
_____, 1990, Not without a consensus, *Hindustan Times*, September 5, p 14, col. 1.
_____, 1990, Now it is caste fanaticism. *Hindustan Times*, September 8, p 5, col. 1-3.
_____, 1990, Omens in Gujarat, *Times of India*, September 6.
_____, 1990, One killed in UP firing, *Times of India*, September 4, p 1, col. 5-7; p 16, col. 3.
_____, 1990, Orissa asks for Central forces, *Hindustan Times*, September 2.
_____, 1990, Orissa firing toll 6, agitation continues in many States, *Indian Express*, September 3, p 1, col. 6-8; p 12, col. 3-5.
_____, 1990, PM dividing nation on caste lines : Rajiv, *Times of India*, September 9.
_____, 1990, PM urged to defuse crisis, *Hindustan Times*, September 7.
_____, 1990, Patnaik orders probe into firing, *Patriot*, September 4.
_____, 1990, Pointless polemics, *Patriot*, September 8.
_____, 1990, Politicians view point, *Hindustan Times*, September 9.
_____, 1990, The politics of pell mell, *Hindustan Times*, September 2.
_____, 1990, Professors oppose job quota, *Hindustan Times*, August 18, p 1, col. 4; p 22, col. 1.
_____, 1990, Pro-quota men set for rally, *Hindustan Times*, September 6.
_____, 1990, Pro-quota rally a damp squid, *Indian Express*, September 8, p 1, col. 5-7; p 9, col. 1.
_____, 1990, Pro-quota youth rally today, *National Herald*, September 4, p 3, col. 5-6.
_____, 1990, Protest against Mandal report, *Tribune*, September 3, p 7, col. 2-5.
_____, 1990, Quota a hasty step, NF leader, *Hindustan Times*, September 9.
_____, 1990, Quota created caste divide in Muslims, says Mishra, *National Herald*, September 9.
_____, 1990, Quota for OBC *ad hoc* solution, *National Herald*, September 3, p 12, col. 3-4.
_____, 1990, Quota for OBCs in education also sought, *Hindustan Times*, September 4, p 1 col. 5 +.
_____, 1990, Quota should be availed of once only, *Indian Express*, September 8,

p 3, col. 4-6.
———, 1990, Quota stir spreads to many areas, *Hindustan Times*, September 7.
———, 1990, Rain God is anti Mandal : Paswan, *Hindustan Times*, September 8, p 1, col. 11 +.
———, 1990, Rajiv urges exhaustive paper, *Times of India*, September 4, p 16, col. 1.
———, 1990, Reservations are necessary, *Tribune*, September 3, p 6, col. 3-5.
———, 1990, Reservation doesn't mean mediocrity, *Times of India*, September 3.
———, 1990, Reservation partisan, *Tribune*, August 8.
———, 1990, Reservation won't lead to mediocrity : Paswan, *Patriot*, September 3.
———, 1990, Rift in Bihar Cong-I over quota issue, *Indian Express*, September 7.
———, 1990, Right to work demanded, *National Herald*, September 7, p 3, col. 2-4.
———, 1990, Road, rail traffic disrupted, *Times of India*, August 24.
———, 1990, Schools closed in three States, *Times of India*, September 9.
———, 1990, Sharad warning on stir, *Hindustan Times*, September 3, p 18, col. 2-4.
———, 1990, Sikkim also rejects report, *Times of India*, September 8.
———, 1990, Sikkim to benefit by Mandal report, *Times of India*, September 7.
———, 1990, Slamming the doors, *Indian Express*, September 8, p 8, col. 1-2.
———, 1990, Statement on extension of reservation policy, *Mainstream* 28(46) September 8, p 2.
———, 1990, States of unrest, *Statesman*, September 8.
———, 1990, Storm round the corner, *Link*, 33(4) September 2, p 7-8.
———, 1990, Students block roads in Haryana towns, *Hindustan Times*, September 1.
———, 1990, Students burn Mandal report, *Statesman*, August 18.
———, 1990, Students' clear warning, *Hindustan Times*, September 2.
———, 1990, Students get farmer's support, *Hindustan Times*, September 5, p 1, col. 4-7.
———, 1990, Students must join talks: Bommai, *Times of India*, September 4, p 4-6.
———, 1990, Talk to youth, Advani tells Government, *Indian Express*, September 5, p 9, col. 6
———, 1990, The talks fail, *National Herald*, September 5, p 6, col. 1.
———, 1990, Teachers' front back reservation, *National Herald*, September 4, p 3, col. 2-3.
———, 1990, This is not collectivism, *National Herald*, September 4, p 6, col. 1.
———, 1990, Tikait not to lead anti quota agitation, *Times of India*, August 18.
———, 1990, Toll figure inflated, says Bihar C.M., *Hindu*, September 6, 1990, p 4, col. 2-5.
———, 1990, Top Congress leaders held in Orissa, *Hindustan Times*, September 5, p 1, col. 1-2.
———, 1990, Troops patrol M.P. towns, *Times of India*, September 8.
———, 1990, U.P.C.C. Chief flays quota policy, *National Herald*, September 3, 1990, p 9, col. 4.
———, 1990, Uncharacteristic calm, political compulsions, *Hindu*, September 9.
———, 1990, Undertaking democracy right, *Hindu*, September 4.
———, 1990, The unmaking of the Indian Union, *Indian Express*, September 3, p 1, col. 1-4.
———, 1990, Upendra claim absurd, *National Herald*, September 5, p 1, col. 2,
———, 1990, V.P. : No going back on rights of minorities, *Tribune*, September 3, p 1, col. 7-8.

——, 1990, V.P. asks NF MPs to explain Mandal report to people, *Hindustan Times*, September 8, p 1, col. 2-3.
——, 1990, V.P. dares Cong. reverse decision, *Hindustan Times*, September 6.
——, 1990, V.P. gets backing of State J D Chiefs, *National Herald*, September 3, p 1, col. 4-5 +.
——, 1990, V.P. revised agenda, *Tribune*, September 4, p 1, col. 2-5.
——, 1990, V.P. Singh in a bind, *Patriot*, September 4.
——, 1990, V.P. working to divide nation on caste lines : Rajiv, *Hindustan Times*, September 7.
——, 1990, V.P. wrote to CMs before decision, *Hindustan Times*, September 2.
——, 1990, V.P.'s bid to score over Devi : Mishra, *National Herald*, August 19, p 4, col. 3-8.
——, 1990, V.P.'s challenge to Cong-I, *Indian Express*, September 6.
——, 1990, V.P.'s other storm-trooper, *Tribune*, September 7.
——, 1990, Vajpayee hails all party meet on quota, *National Herald*, September 3, p 12, col. 1.
——, 1990, Violence in more States : Cuttack curfew extended, *Hindustan Times*, September 1.
——, 1990, Violence mars bandh in Delhi, 214 rounded up, *Hindustan Times*, September 7.
——, 1990, Violence unabated in Orissa, *Link* 33(4) September 2, p 8-9.
——, 1990, Wages of silence, *Indian Express*, August 25.
——, 1990, Walkout by BJP, CPI, CPM, *Tribune*, September 4, p 1, col. 6-8.
——, 1990, A way out of caste war, *Tribune*, September 3, p 6, col. 1-2.
——, 1990, Who is to do it? *Hindustan Times*, September 7.
——, 1990, Woes of Mandal beneficiaries, *Tribune*, September 6.
——, 1990, Wrong move, *Indian Express*, September 6.

BACKWARD COMMUNITIES

Anon, 1986, (Book review), *Socialist Perspective* 13(4) March, p 275-278; *Journal of Sociological Studies*, January 6, p 187-190.
Review of the book: **Bag, D.C.**, 1985, *Impact of education on some backward communities of West Bengal*, OPS Publishing, Calcutta, 304.
——, 1987, (Book review), *Journal of Sociological Studies*, January 6, p 187-190.
Review of the book : **Bag, Dulal Chandra**, 1985, *Impact of education on some backward communities of the West Bengal*, OPS Publishing, Calcutta, 304 p.
Bhattacharya, Biswanath, 1965, A short note on clubs and libraries of the backward communities, *Bulletin of Cultural Research Institute*, 4, p 53-57, tables.
Deshmukh, B.D., 1957, Educational status of the backward communities, *Progress of Education* 32(3) October, p 97-98, letter to editor.
See also Backward Classes; Scheduled Castes and Scheduled Tribes

BACKWARD STUDENTS

Verma, B.P. and **Sharma, Keshav**, 1989, A comparative study of locus of control and self concept of higher, backward and Scheduled Caste students, *Progress of Education* 63(9) April, p 205-208.

BACKWARD TRIBALS

Das, Gananath, 1967, The programme of social education for backward tribals, *Adibasi* 8(4) January, p 56.

BACKWARDNESS

Educational India (Periodical), 1964, Backwardness, *Educational India* 30(9) March, p 308-09, editorial.

Parvathamma, C., 1986, Should caste be a basis for recognising backwardness, *Guru Nanak Journal of Sociology* 7(2) October, p 89-101, bibliography, tables.

See also Educational Backwardness: Tribal Students; Scholastic Backwardness: Tribal Children.

Vyas, Ambalal, 1970, How backward the tribal areas of Orissa State are? *Vanyajati* 18(3) July, p 131-133, tables.

BAIGAS : INDIA : MADHYA PRADESH

Shashi, S.S., 1971, The Baigas of Madhya Pradesh, *Children's World*, October 10, p 18.

BALVADIS : TRIBAL AREAS

Mehta, B.H., 1962, Social experiments in extension projects: The Balvadi in tribal areas, *Indian Journal of Social Work* 23(1) April, p 53-56.

BANDI SRIRAMULY

See Sriramuly, Bandi.

BANGLADESH

Bleie, Tone, 1987, Gender relations among Oraons in Bangladesh: Continuity and change, *Economic and Political Weekly* (Supplement) 22(17) April 25, p w527-w531.

See also Geographical subdivision 'Bangladesh'; under main Descriptor.

BANGNIS : INDIA : ARUNACHAL PRADESH

Sengupta, Sarthak, 1984, Finger prints of the Bangnis of Arunachal Pradesh, *Resarun* 10(1) Spring-Summer, p 25-30, bibliography, tables.

BANGNI SOLUNGS

See Solung Bangnis.

BANSWARA DISTRICT : INDIA : RAJASTHAN

Shyamlal, 1986, Socio-religious movements among the tribals of Banswara district, Rajasthan, *Man and Life* 12(3-4) July-December, p 159-172, bibliography.

BARTANG ISLAND

Sinha, A.K., 1986, Chotanagpur tribals of Baratang Island: A brief note, *Journal of Social Research* 29, September, p 73-79.

BASTAR : INDIA : MADHYA PRADESH

Athavale, M.C. and **Nahatakar, Sunil**, 1983, Evaluation study of tribal area development programme in Konta and Dontewara, Bastar district, M.P., *Cooperative Perspective* 18(3) October-December, p 93-100.

Brij Raj Singh and **Thapar, Rajiv**, 1985, Bastar: Impact of Change : A viewpoint, *Link* (Supplement) 27(26) February 3, p 34-37, tables.

Dubey, K.C., 1970, The Dorlas of Bhopalpatnam, Bastar district, *Bulletin of Tribal Research and Development Institute* (Bhopal) 8(1-2) June-December.

Elwin, Verrier, 1945, Funerary custom in Bastar state, *Man in India* 25(2) June, p 87-133.

Fuchs, Stephen, 1969, A royal "Saviour" of the Bastar tribals, *Journals of*

Anthropological Society of Bombay (NS) 14 (1), p 36-50, references.

Hazra, Durgades, 1959, The Dorla of Bastar, *Bulletin of Department of Anthropology* 8(2) July, p 75-84, references.

Naskar, Santosh K. and **Naskar, Indrani**, 1989, Pre-Independent tribal revolution in Bastar : A historical analysis, *Vanyajati* 37(2) April, p 30-34.

Negi, Raghunath Singh and **Ahmad, S. Hasim**, 1962, The Bhatra, Muria and Mahra of Bastar : A blood group genetic study, *Bulletin of Anthropological Survey of India* 11(3-4) p 201-209, references, tables.

——, et al, 1962, Distribution of middle phalangeal hair in some Bastar population, *Bulletin of Anthropological Survey of India* 11(3-4), p 175-191, appendix, references, tables.

——, et al, 1982, P T C taste variation in Bastar (Central India), *Indian Journal of Physical Anthropology and Human Genetics* 8(1) April, p 41-46, bibliography, tables.

Nigam, Raghuvir Sahay, 1961, Marias of Bastar, *Social Service Quarterly* 46(3) January, p 87-88.

Pawar, S.B., 1962-1963, An administrator looks at the culture (A report on Abujhmarah, Tahsil Narainpur, District Bastar), *Bulletin of Tribal Research Institute* 2(2) December; 3(1) June, p 22-65.

Porte, Swaroop Singh, 1970, Tribes of Bastar and forest rights, *Vanyajati*, 18(2) April, p 77-83.

Shamsuddin, 1988, Glimpses of Bastar, *Social Welfare* 34(11) February, p 2-3.

——, 1989, The tribal world of Bastar, *Social Welfare* 35(10) January, p 17-20.

Sharma, J.C., 1970, Convergence and divergence of dermatoglyphic traits in human populations based on a study of the four tribal groups of Bastar, *Eastern Anthropologist* 23(1) January-April, p 17-35.

Shukla, Ravi Shankar, 1955, Tribal welfare work in Bastar district (M.P.), *Vanyajati* 3(2) April, p 78-80.

Srivastava, R.N., 1988, Moving wheels of machine: The impact of mining-industrtialisation of the Bastar tribal region of Central India, *Man and Life* 14(3-4) July-December, p 119-137.

Tandon, J.S., 1959, The Bhatra of Bastar, *Bulletin of Department of Anthropology* 8(2) July, p 33-54.

Thusu, Kidar Nath, 1959, The Durwa of Marenga, Bastar district, *Bulletin of Department of Anthropology* 8(2) July, p 67-73, references.

——, 1963, The Dhurwa tribe of Bastar, *Vanyajati* 11(1) January, p 16-21.

See also Geographical Area subdivision under main Descriptor.

BAULS

Sarkar, R.M., 1984, Conflict, compromise and diversity unity oriented life philosophy of wandering community, *Indian Museum Bulletin*, 19, p 48-55.

BEDEES

Das, Manmatha Natha, 1956, Female infanticide among the Bedees and the Chouhans; Motives and modes, *Man in India* 36(4) October-December, p. 261-266.

BENGAL : INDIA

Roy Burman, B.K., 1954, A note on the taxonomy of the tribals with special reference to Bengal, *Vanyajati* 2(3) July, p 86-91.

See also West Bengal.

BHABHAR

Govila, J.P., 1959, The Tharus of Tarai and Bhabhar, *Indian Folklore* 2(3) July-September, p 228 +.

BHAGOLIAS

See Bhils.

BHAINAS

Sarkar, Jayanta, 1985, Antithetical activities of the Bhaina in local social hierarchy, *Journal of Indian Anthropological Society* 20(1) March, p 32-42, bibliography, tables.

BHANGIS

See also Sweepers.

BHANGIS : INDIA : MAHARASHTRA

Patel, Leela, 1954, A review of the report of the Scavenger's Living Conditions Enquiry Committee, State of Bombay, *Social Service Quarterly* 39 (4) April, p 102-106.

BHANGIS : INDIA : RAJASTHAN

Shyam Lal, 1970, Educational development among Bhangis in Jodhpur, *Tribe*, 7 (1) January, p 26-31, tables.

——, 1973, Sanskritisation and social change among Bhangis in Jodhpur city, *Indian Journal of Social Work* 34 (1).

BHANJDEO, PRAVIR CHANDRA

Fuchs, Stephen, 1969, A royal "Saviour" of the Bastar tribals, *Journal of Anthropological Society of Bombay* (NS) 14 (1), p 36-50, references.

BHANTUS : INDIA : ANDAMAN AND NICOBAR ISLANDS

Raha, Manish Kumar and **Coomar, Palash Chandra**, 1989, The kinship terms of the Bhantu of Andamans : Structural analysis, *Man in India* 69 (4) December, p 374-386.

BHARTIYA ADIMJATI SEVAK SANGH

Anon, 1965, Report of the Planning Committee of the B.A.J. Sevak Sangh on 4th Five Year Plan on tribal welfare, *Vanyajati* 13 (2) April, p 79-84.

BHATRAS : INDIA : MADHYA PRADESH

Negi, Raghunath Singh and **Ahmad, S. Hasim**, 1962, The Bhatra, Muria and Mahra of Bastar : A blood group genetic study, *Bulletin of Anthropological Survey of India* 11 (3-4), p 201-209, references, tables.

——, et al, 1982, P T C taste variation in Bastar (Central India), *Indian Journal of Physical Anthropology and Human Genetics* 8 (1) April, p 41-46, bibliography, tables.

Tandon, J.S., 1959, The Bhatra of Bastar, *Bulletin of Department of Anthropology* 8 (2) July, p 33-54.

BHIL DHOLIS

See Bhils.

BHILS DUNGWIS
See Bhils.

BHIL GARASIAS
See Bhils.

BHIL MEWASIS
See Bhils.

BHIL RAWALS
See Bhils.

BHIL SAINT

Thakkar, A.V., et al, 1939, Gul Maharaj : The Bhil saint, *Rural India* 1(5) March, p 250-259.

BHIL SEVA MANDAL

Maiji, Amba Shankar U., 1936, The Bhil Seva Mandal, Dohad, *Social Service Quarterly* 21 (3) January, p 92-94.

Social Service Quarterly (Periodical), 1928-31, Bhil Seva Mandal, *Social Service Quarterly* 13 (4) April, 1928, p 176-77; 15 (1) July, 1929, p 31-32; 17 (2) October, 1931, p 82, editorial.

BHIL TADVIS
See Bhils.

BHILALAS

Sinha, R.K., 1983, Self image and emerging identity of the Bhilala, *Vanyajati* 31 (3) July, p 9-16.

———, 1984, Birth rites and rituals among the Bhilala, *Vanyajati* 32 (3), July, p 5-8.

See also Bhils.

BHILS

Ahmad, S.H., 1987, The study of phalangeal hair among the Bhil and their allied groups of Malwa area, *Man in India* 67 (1) March, p 47-58.

Carstairs, Morris, 1954, The Bhils of Kotra Bhomat, *Eastern Anthropologist* 7 (3-4) March-August, p 169-181.

Haque, M., 1984, A note on earlobe attachment of the Bhil of Dungarpur, Rajasthan, *Vanyajati* 32 (4) October, p 20-22.

Khan, G. Ahmed, 1935, The Bhils of Khandesh, *Man in India* 15 (2-3) April-September, p 133-143.

Koppers, W., 1938-40, My Central Indian expedition, *Man in India*, 20 (3) July-September, p 178-181.

Mann, K., 1987, Status of Bhil and Khasi women: A comparative study, *Man and Life* 13 (1-2) January-June, p 57-66, bibliography.

Mehta, Manubhai N., 1938, The Bhils of the Gwalior State, *Man in India* 18 (4) October-December, p 264-284.

Navalakha, Surendra Kumar, 1959, The authority structure among the Bhumij and Bhils: A study of historical causalions, *Eastern Anthropologist* 13 (1) September-November, p 27-40.

Ray, P.C., 1951, Differences in concrete intelligence among the Bhils of Central India, *Indian Journal of Psychology* 36 (1-4), p 73-77.

———, 1953, Maze Test Performance of Bhils of Central India, *Bulletin of*

Department of Anthropology 2 (1), p 83-90.

Sebastian, M.K. and **Bhandari, M.M.**, 1987, Magico-religious beliefs about plants : Among the Bhils of Udaipur district, Rajasthan, *Folklore* 28 (10) October, p 244-247.

Shyam Lal, 1984, Planting a mission among the Bhils of South Rajasthan, *Man and Life* 10 (1-2) January-June, p 77-96, bibliography, tables.

Singh, C.S.K., 1985, Bhils participation in politics in Rajasthan in the 1920s, *Social Scientist* 13 (4) April, p 31-43, footnotes.

Singh, R.Y., 1972, Bhils of Malwa region: Their habitat economy and society, *National Geographical Journal of India* 15 (3-4), p 223-39.

Social Service Quarterly (Periodical), 1925, Bhils in South Gujarat, *Social Service Quarterly* 11 (1) July, p 28-29, editorial.

Thakkar, A.V., et al, 1939, Gul Maharaj: The Bhil saint, *Rural India*, 1 (5) March, p 258-259.

Varma, S.C., 1984, The Bhil kills, *Man in India* 64 (4) December, p 440-444.

BHILS : ECONOMIC CONDITION

Raval, Indubhai B., 1964, Sociology of tribal economic development, *Indian Journal of Social Work* 25 (1) April, p 43-51, tables.

BHINDRANAWAGARH : INDIA : MADHYA PRADESH

Dube, Krishna Chandra, 1960, Problem of Aboriginal debt in Bhindranawagarh sub-division of the Raipur district (M.P.), *Vanyajati* 8 (2) April, p 73-80, tables.

BHINE KOYAS

See Koyas.

BHOIS

See Khasis.

BHOTIAS

See Bhotiyas.

BHOTIYAS

Anon, 1987, Economy of a border region : The Bhotiyas of Kumaon, *Link* 29 (45) 14 June, p 17-20.

Chakraborty, Minakshi, et al, 1984, Post climb effects on hearing and oxygen consumption at moderate altitude among Bhutia boys, *Journal of Indian Anthropological Society* 19 (2) July, p 131-135.

Sah, B.L., 1985, Change and stagnation go together in Kumayun Himalaya, *Social Welfare* 32 (3) June, p 5-7 +.

Sah, Nirmal K., 1986, A tribe in transition : Bhotiyas of Uttarakhand, *Asian Studies* 4 (2) April, p 20-27.

Sidhu, L.S., et al, 1985, Sexual dimorphism, physique and body composition of adult Bhotia : A high altitude population, *Indian Anthropologist* 15 (2) December, p 115-126, bibliography.

Srivastava, R.P., 1953, Rang-Bang in the changing Bhotia life, *Eastern Anthropologist* 6 (3-4) March-August, p 190-203, footnotes.

BHOTS

See Bodhs.

BHUMIJ KSHATRIYAS : INDIA

Sinha, Surajit, 1959, Bhumij-Kshatriya social movement in South Manbhum, *Bulletin of Department of Anthropology* 8 (2) July 1959, p 9-32, references.

BHUMIJAN SEVA MANDAL

Anon, 1942, Appeal for help : Bhumijan Seva Mandal, *Rural India*, 5 (8) August, p 348-352.

Elwin, Varrier, 1945, Bhumijan Seva Mandal, *Rural India* 8 (3) March, p 72-73.

BHUMIJS

Navlakha, Surendra Kumar, 1959, The authority structure among the Bhumij and Bhils: A study of historical causations, *Eastern Anthropologist* 13 (1) September-November, p 27-40.

BHUTIAS

See Bhotiyas.

BIBLIOGRAPHIES

Anon, 1962, Bibliography, *Social Action* 12(4) April, p 199-201.

——, 1986, Annotated Bibliography, *Social Action* 36(2) April-June, p 220-225.

——, 1980, (Book Review), *Contemporary Social Sciences* Review of the book: **Mac, M.R.**, 1980, *Select Bibliography on Scheduled Castes*, Centre for Social Studies, Surat, 225 p.

——, 1988, (Book Review), *Man in India* 68 (2-3) June-September, p 305. Review of the book: **Gour, P.N.** ed., 1988, *Bihar tribal bibliography*, Patna Library Publishing, Patna, 135 p.

Barange, B.G., 1963, An annotated bibliography on tribal indebtedness, *Bulletin of Tribal Research and Development Institute* (Chhindwara) 3(1) June, p 60-66.

BIDISA EXPERIMENT

Bhowmick, P.K., 1987, Voluntary effort in tribal development : The Bidisa experiment, *Journal of Social and Economic Studies* 4 (2) April-June, p 175-186.

BIHAR : INDIA

Akhilesh Kumar, 1988, Genesis of caste riots in Bihar, *Mainstream* 26 (21) March 5, p 25-26.

Akhwari, N., 1958, Socio-cultural barriers to rural change in an East Bihar community, *Eastern Anthropologist* 11 (3-4), p 212-219.

Anirudh Prasad, 1985, People's perception of atrocities committed on Harijans in Bihar, *Journal of Social and Economic Studies* (New-Series) 2 (1) January-March, p 105-125.

Anon, 1953, Schemes of the Bihar State Government submitted to the Govt. of India under Act 275 of the constitution of India for the uplift of Scheduled Tribes during 1952-53, *Vanyajati* 1 (3) July p 72-74.

Jabbar Alam, M., 1986, Tribal unrest in Bihar: Demand for Jharkhand state revived, *New Age* 34 (5) February 2, p 8-9.

Sachchidananda, 1958, Study of culture change in tribal Bihar, *Adibasi* 3 (2) May-June, p 11-16.

——, 1959, Political consciousness in tribal Bihar, *Man in India* 39 (4) October-December, p 301-308.

See also Geographical Area subdivision 'Bihar' under main Descriptor.

BIRHORS

Lahiri, Kuntala, 1990, Will the Birhor survive modernization?, *Geographical Review of India* 52 (1) March, p 99-101.

BIRHORS : SOCIAL CONDITIONS

Sachchidananda, 1965, Directed change among the Birhor, *Eastern Anthropologist* 18 (3) September-December, p 172-176, references.

BIRHULS

See Birhors.

BIRSA

Sachchidananda, 1954, Birsa: An Adivasi fighter for freedom, *Vanyajati* 2 (4) October, p 120-124.

Sinha, Surendra Prasad, 1961, The native and religion of Birsa (1895-1900), *Journal of Social Research* 4 (1-2) March-September, p 316-322, references.

Zide, Norman H. and **Munda, Ram Dayal**, 1969, Revolutionary Birsa and the songs related to him, *Journal of Social Research* 12 (2) September, p 37-60, references.

BIRSA MOVEMENT

Dene, Steve, 1985, Religious movement as rite passage: Analysis of the Birsa movement, *Contributions to Indian Sociology* (New Series) 19 (2) July-December, p 251-268, bibliography.

BIRTH RITES AND RITUALS : BHILALAS

Sinha, R.K., 1984, Birth rites and rituals among the Bhilala, *Vanyajati* 32 (3) July, p 5-8.

BISON HORN MARIA

Dubey, K.C., 1968, Tikenpal: Some aspects of Bison Horn Maria village, *Bulletin of Cultural Research Institute* 7 (1-2), p 66-79, tables.

———, 1969, A note on the Bison-Horn Maria phratries clans and totems, *Eastern Anthropologist* 22 (3) September-December, p 371-376.

BLOOD GROUPS

Bose, Uma, 1952, Blood groups of the tribes of Travancore, *Bulletin of Department of Anthropology* 1 (1) January, p 19-24, references, tables.

Negi, Raghunath Singh and **Ahmad, S. Hasim**, 1962, The Bharta, Muria and Mahra of Bastar: A blood group genetic study, *Bulletin of Anthropological Survey of India* 11 (3-4), p 201-209, references, tables.

Piplai, Chumki, et al, 1985, A note on A B O, M N, Rh and in (a) blood groups of the Tamang and Oraon tea labourers of the Jalpaiguri district, West Bengal, *Journal of Indian Anthropological Society* 20 (1) March, p 66-70, bibliography, tables.

Rami Reddy, V. and **Subhashini, A.B.**, 1984, A B O blood groups among the Palli Reddies: A backward caste of Tirupati and other populations of Andhra Pradesh, *Man in India* 64 (2) June p 193-200, bibliography.

Roy, Sachin, 1955, Distribution of A B O, M N blood groups and the A B H secretor among the tribes of Central and Northern Travancore, *Man in India* 35 (1) January-March, p 57-65, illustration, references, tables.

BODHS

Chowdhury, A.K., 1988, P.T.C. taste sensitivity and colour blindness among the Bodh and Swangla of Lahaul, *Man in India* 68 (4) December, p 448-453, bibliography, tables.

BODOS

Chinal, Rupa, 1985, Fighting for a cultural identity, *Indian Education* (Magazine) 22 (3) September, p 1-8.

BOKARS

Krishan Kumar, 1984, The traditional economic life of the Bokars, *Resarun* 10 (1) Spring-Summer, p 5-15; 10 (2) Autumn-Winter, p 7-16.

BOKSAS

Verma, Ram Swaroop, 1985, Socio-psychological make up of Tharu and Boksa adolescents, *Bhartiya Shikhsa Shodh Patrika* 4 (2) July-December, p 27-33.

BOMBAY : MAHARASHTRA : INDIA

Anon, 1953, Scheme in Bombay Govt. sanctioned for 1952-53 for Scheduled Tribes under Act 275 of the Constitution, *Vanyajati* 1 (4) October, p 101-102.

——, 1981, (Book Review) *Education Quarterly* 33 (3) July, p 48-49.

Review of the book: **Aikara, Jacob**, 1981, *Scheduled Castes and Higher Education: A study of college students in Bombay*, Dastane Rama Chandra and Co., Pune, 112 p.

Kannan, C.T., 1961, Intercaste marriage in Bombay, *Sociological Bulletin* 10 (2) September, p 53-68, tables.

Shrikant, L.M., 1960, Evaluation of work of non-official associations in Bombay, Madras and Kerala, *Vanyajati* 8 (1) January, p 3-5.

Social Service Quarterly (Periodical), 1936, Harijan Sevak Sangh, Bombay, *Social Service Quarterly* 22 (1) July, p 24, editorial.

See also Geographical Area subdivision 'Bombay' under main Descriptor.

BOMBAY HARIJAN TEMPLE WORSHIP ACT

Anon, 1938, Admission of Harijans to Hindu temples, *Social Service Quarterly* 24 (1) July, p 39-41.

Social Service Quarterly (Periodical), 1938, Harijan Temple Worship Act, *Social Service Quarterly* 24 (1) July, p 28-30, editorial.

BONDAR : INDIA : MADHYA PRADESH

Bapat, N.V., 1953, Bondar: A unique tribal welfare centre in M.P., *Vanyajati* 1 (2) April, p 38-40.

BONDAS

Anon, 1986, Bondas opt for development, *Link* (Supplement) 28 (30) 2 March, p 22-23.

Misra, Kamal K., 1985, Life and development in Bonda hills of South Orissa, *Social Welfare* 32 (3) June, p 12-13.

BORDI CONFERENCE

Anon, 1959, The Tribal Welfare Conference at Bordi, *Social Service Quarterly* 44 (3) January, p 72-77.

BIRHORS

Lahiri, Kuntala, 1990, Will the Birhor survive modernization?, *Geographical Review of India* 52 (1) March, p 99-101.

BIRHORS : SOCIAL CONDITIONS

Sachchidananda, 1965, Directed change among the Birhor, *Eastern Anthropologist* 18 (3) September-December, p 172-176, references.

BIRHULS

See Birhors.

BIRSA

Sachchidananda, 1954, Birsa: An Adivasi fighter for freedom, *Vanyajati* 2 (4) October, p 120-124.

Sinha, Surendra Prasad, 1961, The native and religion of Birsa (1895-1900), *Journal of Social Research* 4 (1-2) March-September, p 316-322, references.

Zide, Norman H. and **Munda, Ram Dayal**, 1969, Revolutionary Birsa and the songs related to him, *Journal of Social Research* 12 (2) September, p 37-60, references.

BIRSA MOVEMENT

Dene, Steve, 1985, Religious movement as rite passage: Analysis of the Birsa movement, *Contributions to Indian Sociology* (New Series) 19 (2) July-December, p 251-268, bibliography.

BIRTH RITES AND RITUALS : BHILALAS

Sinha, R.K., 1984, Birth rites and rituals among the Bhilala, *Vanyajati* 32 (3) July, p 5-8.

BISON HORN MARIA

Dubey, K.C., 1968, Tikenpal: Some aspects of Bison Horn Maria village, *Bulletin of Cultural Research Institute* 7 (1-2), p 66-79, tables.

———, 1969, A note on the Bison-Horn Maria phratries clans and totems, *Eastern Anthropologist* 22 (3) September-December, p 371-376.

BLOOD GROUPS

Bose, Uma, 1952, Blood groups of the tribes of Travancore, *Bulletin of Department of Anthropology* 1 (1) January, p 19-24, references, tables.

Negi, Raghunath Singh and **Ahmad, S. Hasim**, 1962, The Bharta, Muria and Mahra of Bastar: A blood group genetic study, *Bulletin of Anthropological Survey of India* 11 (3-4), p 201-209, references, tables.

Piplai, Chumki, et al, 1985, A note on A B O, M N, Rh and in (a) blood groups of the Tamang and Oraon tea labourers of the Jalpaiguri district, West Bengal, *Journal of Indian Anthropological Society* 20 (1) March, p 66-70, bibliography, tables.

Rami Reddy, V. and **Subhashini, A.B.**, 1984, A B O blood groups among the Palli Reddies: A backward caste of Tirupati and other populations of Andhra Pradesh, *Man in India* 64 (2) June p 193-200, bibliography.

Roy, Sachin, 1955, Distribution of A B O, M N blood groups and the A B H secretor among the tribes of Central and Northern Travancore, *Man in India* 35 (1) January-March, p 57-65, illustration, references, tables.

BODHS

Chowdhury, A.K., 1988, P.T.C. taste sensitivity and colour blindness among the Bodh and Swangla of Lahaul, *Man in India* 68 (4) December, p 448-453, bibliography, tables.

BODOS

Chinal, Rupa, 1985, Fighting for a cultural identity, *Indian Education* (Magazine) 22 (3) September, p 1-8.

BOKARS

Krishan Kumar, 1984, The traditional economic life of the Bokars, *Resarun* 10 (1) Spring-Summer, p 5-15; 10 (2) Autumn-Winter, p 7-16.

BOKSAS

Verma, Ram Swaroop, 1985, Socio-psychological make up of Tharu and Boksa adolescents, *Bhartiya Shikhsa Shodh Patrika* 4 (2) July-December, p 27-33.

BOMBAY : MAHARASHTRA : INDIA

Anon, 1953, Scheme in Bombay Govt. sanctioned for 1952-53 for Scheduled Tribes under Act 275 of the Constitution, *Vanyajati* 1 (4) October, p 101-102.

——, 1981, (Book Review) *Education Quarterly* 33 (3) July, p 48-49.

Review of the book: **Aikara, Jacob**, 1981, *Scheduled Castes and Higher Education: A study of college students in Bombay*, Dastane Rama Chandra and Co., Pune, 112 p.

Kannan, C.T., 1961, Intercaste marriage in Bombay, *Sociological Bulletin* 10 (2) September, p 53-68, tables.

Shrikant, L.M., 1960, Evaluation of work of non-official associations in Bombay, Madras and Kerala, *Vanyajati* 8 (1) January, p 3-5.

Social Service Quarterly (Periodical), 1936, Harijan Sevak Sangh, Bombay, *Social Service Quarterly* 22 (1) July, p 24, editorial.

See also Geographical Area subdivision 'Bombay' under main Descriptor.

BOMBAY HARIJAN TEMPLE WORSHIP ACT

Anon, 1938, Admission of Harijans to Hindu temples, *Social Service Quarterly* 24 (1) July, p 39-41.

Social Service Quarterly (Periodical), 1938, Harijan Temple Worship Act, *Social Service Quarterly* 24 (1) July, p 28-30, editorial.

BONDAR : INDIA : MADHYA PRADESH

Bapat, N.V., 1953, Bondar: A unique tribal welfare centre in M.P., *Vanyajati* 1 (2) April, p 38-40.

BONDAS

Anon, 1986, Bondas opt for development, *Link* (Supplement) 28 (30) 2 March, p 22-23.

Misra, Kamal K., 1985, Life and development in Bonda hills of South Orissa, *Social Welfare* 32 (3) June, p 12-13.

BORDI CONFERENCE

Anon, 1959, The Tribal Welfare Conference at Bordi, *Social Service Quarterly* 44 (3) January, p 72-77.

BORIS

Borgohain, H., 1986, A tour to Payum: The Bori land, *Resarun* 12(1-2) Spring-Winter, p 14-19, bibliography.

BOUGLE, C : VIEWS ON CAST SYSTEM

Dumont, Louis and **Pocock, D.**, 1958, Hocart: On cast-religion relation and power; and Bougle: The essence and reality of the cast system, *Contributions to Indian Sociology*, 2, April, p 7-30.

BOWS AND ARROWS : TRIBALS

Mani, S.B., 1964, Bows and arrows in tribal India, *Vanyajati* 12 (1) January, p 40-45, references.

BRAHAMANS

Anon, 1965, Brahmans in early Tamilaham, *Bulletin of Institute of Traditional Cultures*, Part II, p 275-317.

See also Brahmins; Anti Brahminism.

BRAHAMPUTRA VALLEY

Rao, L.N., 1939, The Kacharis of Brahamputra Valley, *Rural India* 2 (3) September, p 136-139.

BRAHMINS

Jain, Girilal, 1988, Kshatriya-Brahmin equation: Historic shift under the Raj, *Times of India*, July 27, p 4, col. 3-5.

See also Brahamans; Anti Brahminism.

BRIDE CARRYING

Oberoi, R.C., 1989, They carry away the bride, *Man in India* 69 (4) December, p 403-405.

BUDDHIST TRIBES : INDIA : ARUNACHAL PRADESH

Das, A.K., 1984, Masks and masquerades among the Buddhist tribes of Arunachal Pradesh, *Indian and Foreign Review* 22 (10) March 15, p 18-19.

BUFFER COMMUNITIES : BORDER AREAS : INDIA

Roy Burman, B.K., 1966, Structure of bridge and buffer communities in the border areas, *Man in India* 46(2) April-June, p 103-107.

BULDBANA DISTRICT : INDIA

Surana, M.B., 1985, Socio-economic survey of tribals in the proposed M.A.D.A. pocket in Buldbana district, *Tribal Research Bulletin* 7 (2) March p 9-13.

BUNDELKHAND : INDIA : UTTAR PRADESH

Tripathi, R.S. and **Vishwakarma, J.P.**, 1990, Castes in rural areas of Bundelkhand (U.P.) : A study of major characteristics and process of change, *Geographical Review of India* 52 (1) March, p 84-88.

CAREER ORIENTATION

Indra Jeet Singh, 1967, Social rehabilitation and career orientation, *Journal of Social Research* 10 (1) March, p 18-21.

CAREER PATTERN : JATS : INDIA : HARYANA

Choudhary, Ram Krishna, 1987, Achievement, orientation and career pattern of

rural jat youths in a Haryana village, *Journal of Social Studies*, January 6, p 123-130, bibliography.

CARPET BAGGERS : INDIA : BIHAR

Anon, 1985, Industry, police, carpet-baggers run a muck in Chotanagpur, *Link* 27 (50) July 21, p 4-9.

CASTE

Anon, 1988, (Book review), *Hindustan Times* (Magazine), August 28, p 5. col 1-4. Review of the book: **Shah, A.M.** and **Desai, I.P.**, 1988, *Division and hierarchy: An overview of caste in Gujarat*, Hindustan Publication Corporation, Delhi, 150 p.

Banerjee, Hemendra Nath, 1989, Reconsideration of the principles of social stratification viewed through class-caste distinction: Social mobility in India: A sociological approach, *Man in India* 69 (4) December, p 393-402.

Bennur, C.S., 1967, Caste prejudice and children, *Progress of Education* 41 (10-11) May-June, p 292-293, letter to editor.

Bulsara, Jal F., 1958, Gnyati-Bandan or caste barriers: What are they? *Indian Journal of Adult Education* 19 (3) October, p 5-12 +.

Burling, Robbins, 1960, An incipient caste organisation in the Garo hills, *Man in India* 40 (4) October-December, p 283-299, references.

Das, Veena and **Uberoi, Jit Singh**, 1971, Elementary structure of caste, *Contributions to Indian Sociology*, New Series, 5, December, p 33-43.

Desai, Bharti S., 1982-1983, Channels of mobility used by a landowning peasant caste: An empirical study of the Woras of South Gujarat, *Journal of the Maharaja Sayajirao University of Baroda* 31-32 (2) p 125-143, bibliography, tables.

Goswami, B.B. and **Morab, S.G.**, 1988, Tribes and castes as functionaries in the temples of Karnataka, *Man in India* 68 (1) March, p 61-69.

Lindholm, Charles, 1986, Caste in Islam and the problem of deviant systems: A critique of recent theory, *Contributions to Indian Sociology*, New Series 20 (1) January-June, p 61-73, bibliography.

Mac Dougall, John, 1979, Dominant castes or rich peasant ? *Economic and Political Weekly* 14 (12-13) March 24, p 625-634.

Mc Gilvary, B. Dannis, ed., 1985, Caste ideology and interaction, *Man in India* 65 (2) June, p 192-195.

Madan, T.N., 1971, On the nature of caste in India: A review symposium on Louis Dumont's Homo Hierarchichus, *Contributions to Indian Sociology*, New Series, 5, December, p 1-13.

——, 1971, On understanding caste, *Economic and Political Weekly* 6 (3-4) August 21, p 1805-1808.

Mukherjee, Jayasree, 1987, The institution of caste in the eyes of Ramakrishna and Vivekananda, *Quarterly Review of Historical Studies* 27 (2), p 22-35, bibliography.

Rattord, B. Shyamak Devi, 1984, Class and caste differences among the Lambadas in Andhra Pradesh, *Social Scientist* 12 (7) July, p 47-56.

Roy, Sarat Chandra, 1934-1938, Caste, race and religion in India, *Man in India* 14 (1) January-March, p 39-63; 14 (2) April-June, p 75-220; 14 (3-4) July-December, p 271-311; 17 (3) June-September, p 147-76; 17 (4) October-December, p 212-254; 18 (2-3) April-September, p 85-105, footnotes.

Saran, Soubhagyalaxmi, 1986, Caste in modern setting, *Vision* 5 (3-4) January-June, p 56-61.

Sen, Sachin, 1964, Impact of modern forces on castes and tribes, *Journal of Social*

Research 7 (1-2) March-September, p 113-118.

Shah, A.M., 1982, Division and hierarchy: An overview of caste in Gujarat, *Contributions to Indian Sociology*, New Series, 16 (1) January-June, p 1-33.

Shah, Ghanshyam, 1985, Caste, class and reservation, *Economic and Political Weekly* 20 (3) January 19, p 132-136, footnote.

Shaileshwar Prasad, 1960, Where tribes and castes meet: Some preliminary observations, *Journal of Social Research* 3 (2) September, p 132-144, references, tables.

Sinha, Surajit, 1965, Tribe-caste and tribe-peasant continuum in Central India, *Man in India* 45 (1) January-March, p 57-83, footnote, bibliography.

Srivastava, S.L., 1967, The Jat: A caste stereotype, *Folklore* 8 (10) October, p 370-375.

Subba, Tanka Bahadur, 1984, Caste and agrarian structure: A study in hill Darjeeling and Sikkim, *Man in India* 64 (1) March, p 59-68, bibliography.

Volchock, B. Ya, 1964, The interaction of castes and tribal communities in Central India, *Journal of Social Research* 7 (1-2) March-September, p 104-112, references.

CASTE : ANTHROPOLOGICAL ASPECT : INDIA

Bose, Nirmal Kumar, 1957, Anthropology and tribal welfare, *Man in India* 37 (3) July-September, p 169-181.

Buchi, Ernst C., 1969, Caste and race in South India, *Anthropologist*, Special Volume, p 61-67, references.

Dube, S.C., 1955, Methods and problems of social anthropology in India, *Anthropologist* 2 (1) March, p 21-24.

Ehrenfels, U.R., 1958, Example and responsibility: Two acculuration problems, *Indian Journal of Social Work* 19 (2) June, p 143-149.

Ferreira, John V., 1969, Applied anthropology in India, *Journal of Anthropological Society of Bombay* (NS) 14 (1), p 15-25, references.

Gayre, G.R., 1956, The significance and usefulness of cultural anthropology to ethnological studies, *Vanyajati* 4 (1) January, p 18-28, illustrations.

Gopala Sarana, 1961, Professor Majumdar and anthropology of Indian religion, *Journal of Social Research* 4 (1-2) March-September, p 1-12, references.

——, 1970, Anthropology of Indian civilisation, *Journal of Indian Anthropological Society* 5 (1-2) April-October, p 31-39, references.

Gulati, R.K., 1970, Biological and cultural affinities: An interpretation, *Eastern Anthropologist* 23 (3) September-December, p 325-242.

Hiralal, 1922, Aborigines of Central India, *Man in India* 2 (1-2) March-June, p 12-32.

Majumdar, D.N., 1956-1957, What the sociologists can do, what they must do, how they can do and how they should do it, *Eastern Anthropologist* 10 (2) December-February, p 130-143.

Rakhshit, Hirendra K., 1970, Language, culture and race in South India, *Journal of Indian Anthropological Society of Bombay* 5 (1-2) April-October, p 205-232, appendix.

Sanghvi, L.D., 1969, Perspectives for study of racial origins in India, *Anthropologist*, Special Volume p 69-73.

Sen, D.K., 1967, Racial studies in India: Recent trends, *Journal of Indian Anthropological Society* 2(1) March, p 1-18.

Shah, P.G., 1952, Cultural synthesis in India, *Journal of Anthropological Society of Bombay* (NS) 6 (2) September, p 62-65.

Sills, David L., 1961, Social research and anthropology in India, *Journal of*

Anthropological Society of Bombay (NS) 11 (2), p 36-47.

Srivastava, S.K., 1960, Current trends in social anthropological research in India, *Journal of Social Sciences* 2 (2) July, p 107-115, references.

Von Furer-Haimendorf, Christoph, 1949, Problems and prospects of Indian anthropology, *Man in India* 29 (3-4) July-December, p 147-168.

CASTE : ASIA : SOUTHEAST

Laiq, Jawid, 1988, Ethnopolitical issues in South-East Asia, *Economic and Political Weekly* 23 (18) 30 April, p 909-917.

CASTE : BARRIERS

Bulsara, Jal F., 1958, Gnyati-Bandan or caste barriers: What are they? *Indian Journal of Adult Education* 19 (3) October, p 5-12 +.

CASTE : BRAHMANICAL VIEW

Berreman, Gerald D., 1971, Brahmanical view of caste, *Contributions to Indian Sociology*, New Series, December 5, p 16-23.

CASTE : CULTUROLOGICAL ASPECTS

Gupta, Dipankar, 1981, Caste, infrastructure and super structure: A critique, *Economic and Political Weekly* 16 (51) December, p 2093-2104.

CASTE : DETERMINANTS

See Determinants.

CASTE : DISCRIMINATION

Bhattacharya, S. and **D'Almeida, Fleur**, 1986, The caste system and discrimination in historical perspective, *New Frontiers in Education* 16 (2) April-June, p 25-32, tables.

CASTE : ETHNOPOLITICAL ISSUES : ASIA : SOUTHEAST

Laiq, Jawid, 1988, Ethnopolitical issues in South-East Asia, *Economic and Political Weekly* 23 (18) 30 April, p 909-917.

CASTE : ETHNOSOCIOLOGICAL ISSUES

Bhattacharya, Gayatri, 1983-1984, Bhudev Mukhopadhyay and ethnosociology of the caste system: A search for an identity? *Journal of Department of Sociology*, p 53-65, bibliography.

CASTE : HISTORY : INDIA

Bhattacharya, S. and **D'Almeida, Fleur**, 1986, The case system and discrimination in historical perspective, *New Frontiers in Education* 16 (2) April-June, p 25-32, bibliography.

Kalidas, Raju, 1984, Varna Samkara in ancient India, *Quarterly Journal of Mythic Society* 75 (4) October-December, p 374-387.

Maity, Sachindra Kumar, 1960, Note on caste in ancient India, *Man in India* 40 (1) January-March, p 65-67, references.

Sharma, Arvind, 1986, Manu on determinants of caste, *Man in India* 66 (3) September, p 255-258.

Sharma, R.S., 1984, Sudras in ancient India, *Journal of the Institute of Economic Research* 19 (2) July, p 32-33.

Sinha, B.C., 1985, Origin and evolution of caste system, *Vedic Path* 47 (4) March, p 31-34, bibliography.

Verma, O.P., 1979, Determinants of status in ancient India, *Journal of Bihar Puravid Parishad*, 3, p 87-90.

CASTE : HISTORY : INDIA : BIHAR

Jha, Jata Shankar, 1979, Some unpublished records relating to the caste movement in Bihar, *Journal of Bihar Puravid Parishad* 3, p 208-222.

CASTE : HISTORY : INDIA : KERALA

Malar, K.M., 1987, The Mappila riots of 1896, *Quarterly Review of Historical Studies* 26 (4) January-March, p 33-39, bibliography.

CASTE : HISTORY : INDIA : MAHARASHTRA

Tucker, Richard, 1980-1981, The early setting of the non-Brahmin movement in Maharashtra, *Indian History Review* 7 (1-2) July-January, p 134-159, footnotes.

CASTE : INDIA

Anon, 1958, Casteism as a social phenomenon, *Indian Journal of Adult Education* 19 (3) October, p 11.

——, 1958, Social education and casteism, *Indian Journal of Adult Education* 19 (3) October, p 1-11.

——, 1984, (Book Review), *India Quarterly* 40 (1) January-March, p 156-160; *Man in India* 64 (2) June, 219-221.

Review of the book : **Ostor, Akos**, et al, 1983, *Concepts of person, kinship, caste and marriage in India*, Oxford University Press, New Delhi, xiv, 271p.

——, 1984, (Book review), *Economic Times* 30 (6) December, p 1-4;

Review of the book: **Brass, Paul R.**, 1983, *Castc faction and parly in Indla politics*, Chanakya Publication, Delhi, 339 p.

——, 1984, (Book review), *Man and Life* 10 (1-2) January-June, p 107-109.

Review of the book: **Anantha Krishna Iyer, L.K.**, 1981, *The tribes and castes of Cochin*, Cosmo Publications, New Delhi, 3 vols.

——, 1985, (Book review) *Hindustan Times* (Magazine), August 8, p 6-8.

Review of the book: **Rajagopal, Indhu**, 1985, *The tyranny of caste: The non-brahmin movement and political development in South India*, Vikas Publication, New Delhi, 195 p.

——, 1985, (Book review), *Social Perspective* 13 (3) December, p 204-207.

Review of the book: **Alam, Javeed**, 1985, *Domination and dissent*: Peasant and politics, Mandira, Calcutta.

——, 1985-1986, Castes and tribes in economic transition: A regional study, *Arthaniti* 25, p 46-64

——, 1986, (Book review), *Indian Express*, August 31, p 4 col 1-5.

Review of the book: **Anon**, 1986, *Scenario of the 7 per cent*, Cenemart Foundation, New Delhi, 2 vols.

——, 1986, (Book review), *Indian Journal of Social Work* 47 (2) July, p 237-238.

Review of the book: **Sinha, Sachchidananda**, 1982, *Caste system: Myths reality challenge*, Intellectual Publication, New Delhi, 236 p.

——, 1986, (Book Review), *India Past and Present* 3 (2), p 315-323.

Review of the book: **O'Hanion, Rosalind**, 1986, *Caste, conflict and ideology: Mahatma Jatirao Phule and low caste protest in nineteenth century*, Western India, Cambridge University Press, Cambridge, 320 p.

——, 1986, (Book review), *Patriot*, February 4, p 4-7.

Review of the book: **Brass, Paul R.**, 1983, *Caste, faction and party in Indian politics*, Chanakya Publication, Delhi, 323 p.

——, 1986, Caste politics, *Economic Trends* 4 (5) June, p 1-2.

——, 1987, (Book Review), *Economic and Political Weekly* (Supplement) 22 (44) 31 October, p Ws75-Ws76; *Social Action* 37(2) April-June, p 199-201.
Review of the book: **Liddle, Joanna and Joshi, Roma**, 1986, *Daughters of Independence: Gender, caste and class in India*, Kali for Women, New Delhi, 264 p.

——, 1987, (Book review), *Economic and Political Weekly* 22 (26) 27 June, p 1030-1031.
Review of the book: **Srinivas, M.N.**, 1987, *The dominant caste and other essays*, Oxford University Press, New Delhi, ix, 195 p.

——, 1987, (Book review), *India Quarterly* 43 (3-4) July-December, p 345-348.
Review of the book: **Sinha, Sachidanand**, 1982, *Myths, reality, challenge*, Intellectual Book, New Delhi, ix, 236 p.

——, 1987, (Book review), *Journal of Social Economic Studies* 4 (4) October-December, p 387-389.
Review of the book: **Choudhary, Ram Krishna**, 1987, *Caste and power structure in village India*, Inter-India Publication, New Delhi.
Social Action 37 (2) April-June, p 199-201.

——, 1987, (Book review), *Times of India* (Sunday Review) March 15, p 1-5.
Review of Book: **Gould, Harold A.**, 1987, *The Hindu caste system: The Sacralization of a social order*, Chanakya Publication, Delhi.

Aurora, G.S., 1968, Caste and backward classes, *Man in India* 48 (4) October-December, p 297-306, footnotes.

Ayrookuzheie, A.M., 1985, Religion: A way of salvation or an ideology of oppression? *Religion on Society* 32 (1) March, p 3-23, footnote, tables.

Ayyangar, M.A., 1964, Impact of modern forces on the tribes and castes in India, *Journal of Social Research* 7 (1-2) March-September, p 1-6.

Banerjee, Hemendra Nath, 1989, Reconsideration of the principles of social stratification viewed through class-caste distinction: Social mobility in India: A Sociological approach, *Man in India* 69 (4) December, p 393-402.

Bennur, C.S., 1967, Caste prejudice and children, *Progress of Education* 41 (10-11) May-June, p 392-293, letter to editor.

Berreman, Gerald D., 1971, Brahmanical view of caste, *Contributions to Indian Sociology*, New Series, 5, December, p 16-23.

Bhattacharya, Gayatri, 1983-1984, Bhudev Mukhopadhyay and ethnosociology of the caste system: A search for an identity? *Journal of Department of Sociology*, p 53-65, bibliography.

Bhattacharya, S. and **D' Almeida, Fleur**, 1986, The caste system and discrimination in historical perspective, *New Frontiers in Education* 16 (2) April-June, p 25-32, bibliography.

Bishei, Ulrich, 1983, The dominant caste and its land scape expression in Indian villages, *Geographical Review of India* 45 (4) December, p 34-47, bibliography.

Bulsara, Jal F., 1958, Gnyati-Bandan or caste barriers: What are they? *Indian Journal of Adult Education* 19 (3) October, p 5-12 +.

——, 1959, Implications of a casteless and classless society, *Journal of Anthropological Society of Bombay* (NS) 11 (1), p 43-60.

Chaturvedi, K.N. and **Mishra, R.C.**, 1988, Children spontaneous recall in relation to their caste group affiliation, *Indian Journal of Community Guidance Service* 5 (2) May, p 23-30, bibliography, tables.

Choudhary, Kameshwar, 1988, Caste in politics: A rejoinder, *Times of India*,

August 12, p 78.

Das, Veena, 1968, A sociological approach to the caste puranas, *Sociological Bulletin* 17 (2) September, p 141-164, references.

Ganguly, Swati, 1983-1984, Buddhism, castes and outcastes: A sociological perspective, *Journal of Ancient Indian History* 14 (1-4), p 220-233.

Gupta, Dipankar, 1984, Continuous hierarchies and discreate castes, *Economic and Political Weekly* 19 (46) 17 November, p 1955-1958; 19 (47) 24 November, p 2003-2005; 19 (48) 1 December, p 2049-2053, bibliography.

Holmstrom, Mark, 1972, Caste and status in an Indian city, *Economic and Political Weekly* 7 (15) April 8, p 769-774.

Indra Deva and **Shrirama**, 1989, Varnashrama and the industrialization of violence, *Radical Humanist* 53 (1) April, p 21-23, bibliography.

Jagjivan Ram, 1958, Casteism and untouchability: An analysis, *Indian Journal of Adult Education* 19 (3) October, p 33-37.

Jain, Girilal, 1987, Intra-Hindu conflicts: Main sources of turbulence, *Times of India*, June 17, p 3-5.

——, 1988, Kshatriya - Brahmin equation: Historic shift under the raj, *Times of India*, July 27, p 3-5.

Jain, Meenakshi, 1985, Anti-Brahminism by another name, *Times of India*, September 4, p 7-8, September 5, p 7-8.

——, 1985, Coping with dominant castes: Ignored aspect of Mrs. Gandhi's politics, *Times of India*, June 17, p 3-5; June 18, p 7-8; June 19, p 7-8.

Kalelkar, Kaka, 1958, Casteism and untouchability: An analysis: Excerpts from the paper read at the Seminar on casteism and removal of untouchability, 1955, Delhi, *Indian Journal of Adult Education* 19 (3) October, 37-39.

Kamalakar, Jaya, 1988, Ethnic politics in Municipal Corporations, *Economic and Political Weekly* 23 (19) May 7, p 945-946.

Madge, Charles, 1958, Caste and community in India and Thailand: A contrast, *Indian Journal of Adult Education*, 19 (3) October p 13-15.

Maity, Sachindra Kumar, 1960, Note on caste in ancient India, *Man in Inida* 40 (1) January-March, p 65-67, references.

Malhotra, Inder, 1989, Political commentary: The Yadav and other factors, *Times of India*, August 10, p 3-5.

Mavalankar, Damodar K., 1987, Castes in India, *Theosophist* 108 (8) May, p 327-330.

Mehta, B.H., 1958, Towards a casteless rural community, *Indian Journal of Adult Education* 19 (3) October, p 40-46.

Mitra, Chandan, 1989, Moulded in caste: AJGAR versus the lesser OBCS, *Times of India*, August 23, p 3-5.

Nanavatty, Meher C., 1955, Seminar on casteism and removal of untouchability: A review, *Indian Journal of Adult Education* 16 (4) December, p 41-50.

——, 1958, Casteism and social education: Role of the social education, *Indian Journal of Adult Education* 19 (3) October, p 47-51.

Oommen, T.K., 1970, The concept of dominant caste: Some quarries, *Contributions to Indian Sociology*, New Series, 4, December, p 105-125.

Pal, Roma and **Dixit, Ashok K.**, 1984, Social class and marital status and correlates of modernization, *Asian Journal of Psychology and Education* 14 (1-4), p 25-33, bibliography.

Parvathamma, C., 1986, Should caste be a basis for recognizing backwardness, *Guru Nanak Journal of Sociology* 7 (2) October, p 89-101, bibliography, table.

Pathy, Suguna, 1987, Caste, class and violence: An appraisal, *Teaching Politics* 13 (2), p 61-75, bibliography.

Rajpal Singh, 1989, Rise of the Jat power, *Tribune* (Magazine) April 9, p 3-6.

Ram Sagar Singh, 1986, Caste consciousness, identity and protest: A sociological analysis of neo-Buddhist movement in India, *Journal of Social Studies*, 5, January, p 161-180, bibliography.

Ranadive, B.T., 1979, Caste, class and property relations, *Economic and Political Weekly*, 14, Annual Number, February, p 337-348.

Sanyal, B.S., 1987, Can they live outside in conflict with the mother society?, *Organiser* 39 (11) August 9, p 8-9.

Sayanna, V.V., 1950, The social class structure and its influence on rural economy with special reference to the prestige classes in rural society, *Rural India* 13 (5) June, p 198-200.

Shah, P.G., 1958, Caste and social education: Sublimation of caste impulse, *Indian Journal of Adult Education*, 19 (3) October, p 47-51.

Sharma, K.L., 1984, Caste and class in India: Some conceptual problems, *Sociological Bulletin* 33 (1-2) March-September, p 1-28, bibliography.

Shashi, S.S., 1988, Gujjars: The Nomads of the Himalayas, *Kurukshetra* 36 (4) January, p 13-14.

Sinha, Surajit, 1965, Tribe-caste and tribe-peasant continuum in Central India, *Man in India* 45 (1) January-March, p 57-83, references, tables.

Social Service Quarterly (Periodical), 1952, The abolition of caste distinctions, *Social Service Quarterly* 37 (1) July, p 10-12, editorial.

Srinivas, M.N., 1979, Future of Indian caste, *Economic and Political Weekly*, 14. Annual Number, February, p 237-242.

——, 1984, Some reflection on the nature of caste hierarchy, *Contributions to Indian Sociology*, New Series, 18 (2) July-September, p 161-167.

Subba, Tanka Bahadur, 1985, Caste relations in Nepal and India, *Social Change* 15 (4) December, p 23-26, bibliography.

Vazeruddin, Mohammad, 1985, Scientific analysis of caste system, *Tribune*, May 12, p 1-8.

Wadia, A.R., 1958, Casteism and untouchability: An analysis: Excerpts from the paper read at the Seminar on casteism and removal of untouchability, 1955, Delhi, *Indian Journal of Adult Education* 19 (3) October, p 28-33.

See also Aryans, Bhatras; Bhils; Bhumij-Kshatriyas; Caste and Tribes; Chamars; Chouhans; Coorgs; Dharampandit; Dhurwas; Dorlas; Dravidians, Gadabas; Garos; Gonds; Gujjars; Jats; Katkaris; Kayasthas; Kharias; Khatis; Kolis; Kui; Lambadis; Marwadis; Meos, Monpas, Mundas, Muslims, Konkani, Navayats, Nimadi; Oraons; Pahiras; Paundra-Kshatriyas; Rajputs; Riangs; Sansies; Santals; Satnam Pantha; Scheduled Castes and Scheduled Tribes; Social Classes; Shudras; Sikligars; Tharus; Todas; Tomars; Tribes and Tribals; Weavers.

CASTE : INDIA : ANCIENT

Kalidas, Raju, 1984, Varna Samkar in ancient India, *Quarterly Journal of Mythic Society* 75 (4) October-December, p 374-387.

Maity, Sachindra Kumar, 1960, Note on caste in ancient India, *Man in India* 40 (1) January-March, p 65-67, references.

Sharma, Arvind, 1986, Manu on determinants of caste, *Man in India* 66 (3) September, p 255-258.

Sharma, R.S., 1984, Sudras in ancient India, *Journal of the Institute of Economic Research* 19 (2) July, p 32-33.

Verma, O.P., 1979, Determinants of status in ancient India, *Journal of Bihar Puravid Parishad*, 3, p 87-90.

CASTE : INDIA : ANDHRA PRADESH

Abraham, A.S., 1986, Good-bye to modernism: Warring over reservations, *Times of India*, August 1, p 3-5.

Anon, 1989, (Book Review), *Economic Times*, February 5, p 6 col 1-4.
Review of the Book: **Nancharaiah, Gummadi**, 1989, *Land and caste*, Himalayan Publishing House, Bombsy, 112 p.

——, 1989, Ranga's murder raises many questions, *Times of India* (Section II) February 20, p 2-6 +.

Deep Kumar, V.S., 1985, A genetic study of Kamna and Kapu caste groups of Andhra Pradesh, *Journal of Indian Anthropological Society* 20 (1) March, p 59-65, bibliography.

Govinda Reddy, P., 1987, Effects of consanguineous marriages on fertility and infant mortality among the Mala of Southern Andhra Pradesh, *Indian Journal of Physical Anthropology and Human Genetics* 13 (1) January-April, p 43-49, bibliography, tables.

Ramachandran, R., et al, 1986, Caste and consciousness: An invested pyramid, *Indian Journal of Social Work* 47 (3) October, p 243-253, tables.

Rammi Reddy, V. and **Subhashini, A.B.**, 1984, A B O blood group among the Palli Reddies: A backward caste of Tirupati and other populations of Andhra Pradesh, *Man in India* 64 (2) June, p 193-200, bibliography.

Rattord, B. Shyamak Devi, 1984, Class and caste differences among the Lambadas in Andhra Pradesh, *Social Scientist* 12 (7) July, p 47-56, bibliography, tables.

Reddy, N.S., 1973, Caste in a tribal society: The formative process, *Contributions to Indian Sociology*, New Series, 7, p 159-167.

CASTE : INDIA : ASSAM

Anon, 1985 (Book review), *Hindustan Times* (Magazine) January 6, p viii, col 1-6.
1984, Review of the book: **Dev, Bimal J.**, and **Lehri, Dilip K.**, *Consmogony of caste and social mobility in Assam*, Mittal Publications, Delhi, 183 p.

Das, R., 1985, A study on variation of palmar fexion crease among three Assamese castes, *Indian Journal of Physical Anthropology and Human Genetics* 11 (3) August-December, p 175-177, bibliography, tables.

CASTE : INDIA : BENGAL

See Caste : India : West Bengal.

CASTE : INDIA : BIHAR

Akhilesh Kumar, 1988, Genesis of caste riots in Bihar, *Mainstream* 26 (21) 5 March, p 25-26.

Anon, 1987, A clash of rights, *Hindustan Times* (Magazine) June 21, p 1-6 +.

——, 1987, Class war in Bihar, *Hindustan Times* (Magazine) June 21, p 1-6.

——, 1987, Is there a cure for Bihar? *Hindustan Times* (Magazine) June 7, p 1-3.

——, 1987, Rural violence in Bihar, *Link* 29 (49) July 12, p 17-20.

——, 1988, Caste in Bihar's political mould, *Times of India* February 9, p 2-5 +.

——, 1989, (Book review) *Patriot*, April 9, p 3-6.
Review of the book: **Jain, S.K.**, 1989, *Castes and Politics in Bihar*, Common Health Publication, New Delhi, 134 p.

Arti Kumari, 1988, A study on the palmar dermatolyphics of the Kayasth of Ranchi,

Man in India 68 (2-3) June-September, p 216-227, bibliography.

Das, Arvind N., 1984, Class in itself, caste for itself: Social articulation in Bihar, *Economic and Political Weekly* 19 (37) 15 September, p 1616-1619.

——, 1985, Bihar society in perspective: Roots of regional imbalance, *Times of India* October 24, p 8, col 3-5; October 25, p 8, col 7-8.

——, 1985, Growing violence in Bihar: Social roots of the cult of the gun, *Times of India* November 21, p 8, col. 3-5.

——, 1987, Bihar disinformation: Caste killings and naxalite alibi, *Main Stream* 25 (40) 20 June, p 7-10.

Jha, Amar Kumar, 1987, Caste-politics interactions: Process and consequences: A case study of Sitamarhi parliamentary constituency, *Journal of Social Economic Studies* 4 (3) July-September, p 211-288.

Jha, Jata Shankar, 1979, Some unpublished records relating to the caste movement in Bihar, *Journal of Bihar Puravid Parishad*, 3, p 208-222.

Mishra, Girish, 1987, Agrarian violence in Bihar, *Mainstream* 25 (39) 13 June, p 6-8.

Pradhan, H. Prasad, 1979, Caste and class in Bihar, *Economic and Political Weekly* 14, Annual Number, February, p 481-484.

Ranjan, Sudhanshu, 1988, Bihar killings in retrospect, *Mainstream* 26 (21) 5 March, p 27-29.

Shyama Nand Singh, 1988, Roots of caste war in Bihar, *Mainstream* 26 (14) 16 January, p 28-29.

Sinha, Arun, 1986, Caste and faction in Bihar politics, *Times of India* July 9, p 7-8.

CASTE : INDIA : BUNDELKHAND

See Caste : India : Uttar Pradesh.

CASTE : INDIA : CENTRAL

Sinha, Surajit, 1965, Tribe-caste and tribe-peasant continuum in Central india, *Man in India* 45 (1) January-March, p 57-83, references, tables.

Volchock, B. Ya, 1964, The interaction of castes and tribal communities in Central India, *Journal of Social Research* 7 (1-2) March-September, p 104-112, references.

CASTE : INDIA : DELHI

Anon, 1987, (Book review), *Indian Journal of Social Work* 47 (4) January, p 464-466.

Review of the book: **Gangrade, K.D.**, 1986, *Social work and development: Role of religion and caste in three Delhi villages*, Northerrr Book Centre, Delhi, 130 p.

Channa, V.C., 1984, From childhood to youth: The learning process amongst the Aggarwals of the city of Old Delhi, *Indian Anthropologist* 14 (1) June, p 23-39, bibliography.

CASTE : INDIA : EASTERN

Goswami, Omkar, 1985, Then came the Marwaris: Some aspects of the changes in the pattern of industrial control in Eastern India, *Indian Economic and Social History Review* 22 (3) July-September, p 225-249, bibliography, footnote.

CASTE : INDIA : GOA

Mascarenhas, Lambart, 1985, Castes and integration, *Goa Today* 19(7) February p 12-13.

CASTE : INDIA : GUJARAT

Anon, 1988, (Book review), *Hindustan Times* (Magazine) August 28, p 1-4.
Review of the book: **Shah, A.M.** and **Desai, I.P.**, 1988, *Division and hierarchy: An overview of caste in Gujarat*, Hindustan Publication Corporation, Delhi, 150 p.

Majumdar, D.N. and **Kishen, K.**, 1948, Serological status of caste and tribes of central Gujarat, *Eastern Anthropologist* 2 (2) December, p 92-97.

Jain, Meenakshi, 1985, The Patels of Gujarat: Story of remarkable rise, *Times of India*, August 3, p 3-5.

——, 1985, Rise of a political caste in Gujarat, *Times of India*, July 8, p 7-8.

Shah, A.M., 1982, Division and hierarchy: An overview of caste in Gujarat, *Contribution to Indian Sociology*, New Series, 16 (1) January-June, p 1-33.

CASTE : INDIA : HARYANA

Choudhary, Ram Krishna, 1987, Achievement, orientation and career pattern of rural Jat youth in a Haryana village, *Journal of Social Studies* January 6, p 123-130, bibliography.

Phogat, Silak Ram, 1984, The original home of Toumraras: A new interpretation, *Journal of Haryana Studies* 16 (1-2) p 16-20, bibliography.

CASTE : INDIA : HISTORY

See Caste : History : India.

CASTE : INDIA : JAMMU AND KASHMIR

Khayal, Ghulam Nabi, 1985, The Gujjars of Kashmir: A forgotten community, *Indian Express* (Magazine) 13 (6) October 13, p 6 col 1-4.

CASTE : INDIA : KARNATAKA

Kusumakar, H., 1985, The name tag tells all in the South, *Time of India* (Sunday review) September 1, p 1, col 1-8.

Mahadevappa, N.G., 1984-1985, Implications of the Lingayata (Virasaiva) conception of liberation, *Journal of Karnataka University (Social Science)* 20-21, p 67-80, bibliography.

Narayana Reddy, G., 1984, Dominant caste and social interaction in a Karnataka village, *Social Change* 14 (4) December, p 25-30, bibliography, tables.

Shashi, S.S., 1988, Kurbas: Shepherds of Karnataka, *Mainstream* 26(14) January 16, p 27-28.

Srinivas, M.N., 1985, The Poleyas in the Kodava society, *Journal of Historical Studies* 19, p 75-79, bibliography.

CASTE : INDIA : KERALA

Achuthan, K.R., 1984, The social spectrum of Kerala, *Journal of Kerala Studies* 9 (1-4) March-December, p 103-162.

Alexander, K.C., 1988, Changing status of Pulaya Harijans of Kerala, *Economic and Political Weekly*, Special Number, July.

Gladstone, J.W., 1985, Caste, religion and people's movements in Kerala with particular reference to south Kerala, *Religion and Society* 32 (1) March, p 24-35, footnotes.

Joseph, M.J., 1988, Class, caste, church and the Left, *Economic and Political Weekly* 23 (49) 3 December, p 2573-2574.

Malar, K.N., 1987, The Mappila riots of 1896, *Quarterly Review of Historical Studies* 26 (4) January-March, p 33-39, bibliography.

Sivananda, P., 1979, Caste, class and economic opportunity in Kerala: An

emphirical analysis, *Economic and Political Weekly* 14, Annual Number, February, p 475-480.

Subhashini, A.V., 1987, Tharavads: Kerala's Nair homes, *Indian Management* 7 (8) July, p 52-63.

Sukumaran, Tatapuram, 1984, The Ezhavas in Kerala, *Malayalam Literature Survey* 8 (3-4) July-December, p 111-117, bibliography, footnotes.

CASTE : INDIA : MADHYA PRADESH

Keswani, Raaj Kumar, 1987, The survivors, *Illustrated Weekly of India* 107 (46) November 23, p 20-23.

CASTE : INDIA : MAHARASHTRA

Malhotra, K.C. and **Sen Gupta, B.**, 1985, Absolute and fluctuating asymmetry of digital ridge counts among Hatkars of Maharashtra, *Man in India* 65 (2) June, p 139-153, bibliography, tables.

Sonalkar, Wandana and **Shakir, Moin**, 1987, Caste, politics and development in Maharashtra, *Mainstream* 25 (30) 11 April, p 25-31, bibliography.

Tucker, Richard, 1980-1981, The early setting of the non-Brahmin movement in Maharashtra, *Indian History Review* 7 (1-2) July-January, p 134-159, footnotes.

CASTE : INDIA : NORTHERN

Jain, S.P., 1971, Religion and caste ranking in a North Indian town, *Sociological Bulletin* 20 (2), p 134-144.

CASTE : INDIA : NORTHWEST PROVINCE AND OUDH

Pant, Rashmi, 1987, The cognitive status of caste in colonial ethnography: A review of some literature of the North West Province and Oudh, *Indian Economic Social History Review* 24 (2) April-June, p 145-162.

See also Caste : India : Uttar Pradesh.

CASTE : INDIA : ORISSA

Patnaik, Binay Kumar, 1987, Tribe and caste: A case study in an Oriya village, *Man in India* 67 (4) December, p 335-351.

CASTE : INDIA : OUDH

See Caste : India : North West Province and Oudh.

CASTE : INDIA : RAJASTHAN : JODHPUR CITY

Shyam Lal, 1973, Sanskritisation and social change among Bhangis in Jodhpur city, *Indian Journal of Social Work* 344 (1).

CASTE : INDIA : SOUTHERN

Anon, 1987, (Book review), *Indian Economic Social History Review* 24 (3) July-September, p 341-342; *Tribune* (Magazine) September 14, p 5-8.

Review of the book: **Dumont, Louis**, 1986, *A South Indian subcaste: Social organisation and religion of the Pramalai Kallar*, Oxford University Press, New Delhi, 634 p.

Appadurai, A., 1974, Right and left-hand castes in South India, *Indian Economic and Social History Review* 11 (2-3), p 216-260.

Bhargava, G.S., 1986-1987, Caste war in South India, *Janata*, 41 (25) November 30, p 5-7; 41 (26) December 21, p 7-8; 41 (27) January 4, p 5-6.

Driver, Edwin D., 1982, Class, caste and status summation in urban South India, *Contributions to Indian Sociology*, New Series, 16 (2) July-December, p 226-253.

Dumont, Louis, 1987, A South Indian sub-caste: Social organization and religion of the Pramalai Kallar, *Economic Trends* 8(6) February, p 1-4.

Guru, Gopal, 1985, Casteism in the South, *Mainstream* 23 (47) 20 July, p 20-22, bibliography.

Kusumakar, H., 1985, The name tag tells all in the South, *Times of India* (Sunday review), September 1, p 1, col 1-8.

Menon, Venu, 1986, Requiem for an era, *Illustrated Weekly of India* 107 (29) July 20, p 28-29.

See also Caste: India, Tamil Nadu.

CASTE : INDIA : TAMIL NADU

Anon, 1987, (Book review), *Social History Review* 24 (3) July-September, p 341-342; *Tribune* (Magazine) September 14, p 5-8.

Review of the book: **Dumont, Louis**, 1987, *A South Indian subcaste: Social organisation and religion of the Pramalai Kallar*, Oxford University Press, New Delhi, xxiii, 502 p.

Dumont, Louis, 1987, A South Indian sub-caste: Social organization and religion of the Pramalai Kallar, *Economic Trends* 8 (6) February, p 1-4.

Sivakumar, S.S. and **Sivakumar, Chitra**, 1979, Class and Jati at Asthapuram and Kanthapuram: Some comment towards a structure of interest, *Economic and Political Weekly* 19, Annual Number, February, p 263-286.

See also Caste: India: Southern

CASTE : INDIA : UTTAR KHAND

See Caste : India : Uttar Pradesh.

CASTE : INDIA : UTTAR PRADESH

Chakraborty, Minakshi, et al, 1984, Post climb effects on hearing and oxygen consumption at moderate altitude among Bhutia boys, *Journal of Indian Anthropological Society* 19 (2) July, p 131--135.

Sah, Nirmal K., 1986, A tribe in transition: Bhotiyas of Uttar Khand, *Asian Studies* 4 (2) April, p 20-27.

Saxena, N.C., 1985, Caste and Zamindari abolition in U.P., *Mainstream* 23 (42) June 44, p 15-19, tables.

Sidhu, L.S., et al, 1985, Sexual dimorphism, physique and body composition of adult Bhotia: A high altitude population, *Indian Anthropologist* 15 (2) December, p 115-126, bibliography.

Tripathi, R.S. and **Vishwakarma, J.P.**, 1990, Castes in rural areas of Bundelkhand (U.P.): A study of major characteristics and process of change, *Geographical Review of India* 52 (1) March, p 84-88.

See also Caste : India : North West Province and Oudh.

CASTE : INDIA : WEST BENGAL

Anon, 1987, (Book review), *Contributions to Indian Sociology*, New Series, 21 (1) January-June, p 248-249.

Review of the book: **Das Gupta, Satadal**, 1986, *Caste, kinship and community: Social System of a Bengal Caste*, Madras University Press, Madras, xii, 291 p.

——, 1988, Castes and tribes in economic transition: A regional study, *Arthaniti* 25, p 46-63.

Bandhyopadhyay, Sekhar, 1985, Caste in the perception of the Raj: A note on the evolution of colonial sociology of Bengal, *Bengal Past and Present* 104 (1-2) January-December, p 56-80, bibliography, footnote.

——, 1985, The Raj, Risley and the tribes and the castes of Bengal, *India Past and Present* 2 (1) p 41-52, footnotes.

Banerjee, A.R. and **Chowdhuri, Lipi**, 1988, Caste exogamy and clan-gotra enologamy in the contemporary Bangalee society, *Man in India* 68 (2-3) June-September, p 200-210, bibliography, tables.

Basu, Swaraj, 1986, A case study of the Rajbansi caste movement in Northern Bengal, 1901-1921, *Quarterly Review of Historical Studies* 26 (3)October-December, p 59-61.

Bose, Sukla, 1985, Caste, tribe and female labour participation, *Social Change* 15 (2) June, p 15-20, bibliography, tables.

Gangopadhyay, Prodyot and **Kundu, Shampa**, 1988, Familial trend in arterial pressure among few endogamous communities of West Bengal reared under diverse occupational environment, *Man in India* 68(2-3) June-September, p 235-242, bibliography.

CASTE : ISLAM

See Caste: Muslim.

CASTE : MUSLIM

Lindholm, Charles, 1986, Caste in Islam and the problem of deviant systems : A critique of recent theory, *Contributions to Indian Sociology*, New Series, 20 (1) January-June, p 61-73, bibliography.

CASTE : NEPAL

Subba, Thanka Bahadur, 1985, Caste relations in Nepal and India, *Social Change* 15 (4) December, p 23-26, bibliography.

CASTE : OPPRESSION

Ayrookuzheil, A.M. Abrahi, 1985, Religion: A way of salvation or an ideology of oppression? *Religion and Society* 32 (1) March, p 3-23, footnote, tables.

CASTE : PREJUDICE

See Caste Prejudice.

CASTE : PROTEST/REFORM MOVEMENTS

See also Protest/reform Movements

CASTE : PROTEST/REFORM MOVEMENTS : INDIA

Anon, 1985, (Book review), *Hindustan Times* (Magazine) August 8, p 6-8.

Review of the book: **Rajagopal, Indhu,** 1985, *The tyranny of caste: The non-brahmin movement and political development in South India*, Vikas Publication, New Delhi, 195 p.

Basu, Swaraj, 1986, A case study of the Rajabansi caste movement in Northern Bengal, 1901-1921, *Quarterly Review of Historical Studies* 26 (3) October-December, p 59-61.

Gladstone, J.W., 1985, Caste, religion and people's movements in Kerala with particular reference to South Kerala, *Religion and Society* 32 (1) March p 24-35, footnote.

Jain, Meenakshi, 1985, Anti-Brahminism by another name, *Times of India*, September 4, p 7-8, September 5, p 7-8.

Jha, Jata Shankar, 1979, Some unpublished records relating to the caste movement in Bihar, *Journal of Bihar Puravid Parishad* 3, p 208-222.

Malar, K.M., 1987, The Mappila riots of 1986, *Quarterly Review of Historical Studies*

26 (4) January-March, p 33-39, bibliography.

Parvathamma, C., 1986, Role of protest movements in social transformation, *Guru Nanak Journal of Sociology* 7 (1) April, p 1-22.

Ram Sagar Singh, 1986, Caste consciousness identity and protest: A sociological analysis of neo-Buddhist movement in India, *Journal of Social Studies*, 5, January, p 161-180, bibliography.

Tucker, Richard, 1980-1981, The early setting of the non-Brahmin movement in Maharashtra, *Indian Historical Review* 7 (1-2) July-January, p 134-159, footnotes.

CASTE : RESERVATIONS

See Reservation Issues.

CASTE : RIOTS

See Caste Violence.

CASTE : SACRALIZATION OF SOCIAL ORDER

Anon, 1987 (Book review), *Times of India* (Sunday review) March 15, p 1-5.

Review of the book: **Gould, Harold A.**, 1987, *The Hindu caste system: The Sacralization of a social order*, Chanakya Publication, Delhi.

CASTE : SRI LANKA

Roberts, Michael, 1984, Caste feudalism in Sri Lanka: A critique through the Asokan persons and European contrasts, *Contributions to Indian Sociology* (New Series), 18 (2) July-December, p 189-217.

CASTE : THAILAND

Medge, Charles, 1958, Caste and community in India and Thailand: A contrast, *Indian Journal of Adult Education* 19(3) October, p 13-15.

CASTE : VIOLENCE

See Caste Violence.

CASTE : WAR

See Caste Violence.

CASTE AND POLITICS : INDIA

Anon, 1984, (Book review), *Economic Times* 30 (6) December, p 1-4.

Review of the book: **Brass, Paul R.**, 1983, *Caste faction and party in Indian politics*, Chanakya Publication, Delhi, 339 p.

——, 1985, (Book review), *Social Perspective* 13 (3) December, p 204-207.

Review of the book: **Alam, Javeed**, 1985, *Domination and dissent: Peasant and politics*, Mandira, Calcutta.

——, 1986, (Book review), *Patriot*, February 4, p 4-7.

Review of the book: **Brass, Paul R.**, 1983, *Caste faction and party in Indian politics*, Chanakya Publication, Delhi, 339 p.

——, 1986, Caste politics, *Economic Trends* 4 (5) June, p 1-2.

——, 1987, (Book review), *Journal of Social Economic Studies* 4 (4) October-December, p 387-389.

Review of the book: **Choudhary, Ram Krishna**, 1987, *Caste and power structure in village India*, Inter-India Publication, New Delhi, 178 p.

Blair, Harry W., 1980, Rising kulaks and backward classes in Bihar: Social change in the late 1970s, *Economic and Political Weekly* 15 (2) January 12, p 64-74.

Choudhary, Kameshwar, 1988, Caste in politics : A rejoinder, *Times of India*,

August 12, p 7-8.

Dorairaj, S., 1985, AIADMK's balancing tactic, *Link* 27 (37) April 28, p 12-13.

Jain, Girilal, 1987, Intra-Hindu conflicts : Main sources of turbulence, *Times of India*, June 17, 3-5.

——, 1988, Kshatriya-Brahmin equation: Historic shift under the Raj, *Times of India*, July 27, p 3-5.

Jain, Meenakshi, 1985, Coping with dominant castes: Ignored aspects of Mrs. Gandhi's politics, *Times of India*, June 17, p 3-5; June 18, p 7-8; June 19, p 7-8.

——, 1985, Failure of Indira strategy: Backward castes support not enough, *Times of India* 13 (8) July, p 3-5.

Kamalakar, Jaya, 1988, Ethnic politics in municipal corporations, *Economic and Political Weekly* 23 (19) May 7, p 945-946.

Malhotra, Inder, 1989, Political commentary: The Yadav and other factors, *Times of India*, August 10, p 3-5.

Mitra, Chandan, 1989, Moulded in caste: AJGAR versus the lessor OBCs, *Times of India*, August 23, p 6, col 3-5.

Rajpal Singh, 1989, Rise of the Jat power, *Tribune* (Magazine) April 9, p 3-6.

Sheth, D.L., 1979, Politics in caste conflict, *Seminar*, 233, January.

See also Anti Brahminism.

CASTE AND POLITICS : INDIA : ANDHRA PRADESH

Abraham, A.S., 1986, Good-bye to modernism: Warring over reservations, *Times of India*, August 1, p 8, col 3-5.

Anon, 1989, Ranga's murder raises many questions, *Times of India* (Section II) February 20, p 2-6 +.

CASTE AND POLITICS : INDIA : BIHAR

Anon, 1988, Caste in Bihar's political mould, *Times of India* February 9, p 2-5 +.

——, 1989, (Book review), *Patriot* April 9, p 3-6.
Review of the book: **Jain, S.K.** 1989, *Caste and politics in Bihar*, Common Health Publication, New Delhi, 134 p.

Jha, Amar Kumar, 1987, Caste-politics interactions : Process and consequences: A case study of Sitamarhi parliamentary constituency, *Journal of Social Economic Studies* 4 (3) July-September, p 211-228.

Sinha, Arun, 1986, Caste and faction in Bihar politics, *Times of India*, July 9, p 7-8.

CASTE AND POLITICS : INDIA : MAHARASHTRA

Sonalkar, Wandana and **Shakir, Moin**, 1987, Caste, politics and development in Maharashtra, *Mainstream* 25 (30) 11 April, p 25-31, bibliography.

CASTE AND POLITICS : INDIA : SOUTHERN

Anon, 1985, (Book review), *Hindustan Times* (Magazine), August 18, p 8, col 6-8.
Review of the book: **Rajagopal, Indhu**, 1985, *The tyranny of caste: The non-Brahmin movement and political development in South India*, Vikas, New Delhi, 195 p.

CASTE CONFLICT

Anon, 1985, (Book review), *Patriot*, May 12, p 4, col 1-4.
Review of the book: **Desai, I.P.**, et al, 1985, *Caste, caste-conflict and reservations*, Janata Publication Delhi, viii, 218 p.

Sunil, K.P., 1989, Crucible of conflict, *Illustrated Weekly of India* 110(41) October 8, p 22-25.

CASTE DETERMINANTS : INDIA : ANCIENT

Sharma, Arvind, 1986, Manu on determinants of castes, *Man in India* 66 (3) September, p 255-258.

Verma, O.P., 1979, Determinants of status in ancient India, *Journal of Bihar Puravid Parishad* 3, p 87-90.

CASTE DISCRIMINATION

See Caste : Discrimination.

CASTE DISTINCTION : INDIA

Banerjee, Hemendra Nath, 1989, Reconsideration of the principles of social stratification viewed through class-caste distinction: Social mobility in India: A Sociological approach, *Man in India*, 69(4) December, p 393-402.

Social Service Quarterly (Periodical), 1952, The abolition of caste distinctions, *Social Service Quarterly* 37 (1) July, p 10-12, editorial.

CASTE EXOGAMY : INDIA : WEST BENGAL

Banerjee, A.R. and **Chowdhuri, Lipi**, 1988, *Caste exogamy and clan/gotra endogamy in the contemporary Bengali Society, Man in India* 68 (2-3) June-September, p 200-210, bibliography, tables.

CASTE HIERARCHY

Anon, 1988, (Book review), *Hindustan Times* (Magazine) August 28, p 1-4. Review of the book: **Shah, A.M. and Desai, L.P.**, 1988, *Division and hierarchy: An overview of caste in Gujarat*, Hindustan Publication Corporation, Delhi, 150 p.

Gupta, Dipankar, 1984, Continuous hierarchies and discreat castes, *Economic and Political Weekly* 19 (46) November 17, p 1955-1958; 19(47) November 24, p 2003-2005; 19(48) December 1, p 2049-2053, bibliography.

Radetotad, N.K., 1966, Caste hierarchy among the untouchables of Dharwar, *Eastern Anthropologist* 19 (3) September-December, p 205-214, references, tables.

Shah, A.M., 1982, Division and hierarchies: An overview of caste in Gujarat, *Contributions to Indian Sociology*, New Series, 16 (1) January-June, p 1-33.

Srinivas, M.N., 1984, Some reflections on the nature of caste hierarchy, *Contributions to Indian Sociology* (New Series) 18 (2) July-September, p 161-167.

CASTE MOVEMENT : INDIA

Basu, Swaraj, 1986, A case study of the Rajbansi caste movement in Northern Bengal, 1901-1921, *Quarterly Review of Historical Studies* 26 (3) October-December, p 59-61.

CASTE PREJUDICE : CHILDREN

Bennur, C.S., 1967, Caste prejudice and children, *Progress of Education* 41 (10-11) May-June, p 392-93, letter to editor.

CASTE RANKING : INDIA

Jain, S.P., 1971, Religion and caste ranking in a North Indian town; *Sociological Bulletin* 20 (2) p 134-44.

CASTE RESERVATIONS

Mathew, P.M., 1988, Caste reservations: A critique, *Social Change* 18 (2) June, p 93-99, bibliography.

See also Reservation Issues; Reservation Policy.

CASTE RIOTS : INDIA : BIHAR

Akhilesh Kumar, 1988, Genesis of caste riots in Bihar, *Mainstream* 26 (21) March 5, p 25-26.

CASTE STRUCTURE

Bhadra, Ranjit K., 1979, Rural class structure in post-independence Assam, *Economic and Political Weekly* 14 (4) January 27, p 165-167.

Das, Veena and **Uberoi, Jit Singh**, 1971, Elementary structure of caste, *Contributions to Indian Sociology*, New Series 5, December, p 33-43.

CASTE VIOLENCE : INDIA

Indra Deva and **Srirama**, 1989, Varnashrama and the industrialization of violence, *Radical Humanist* 53 (1) April, p 21-23, bibliography.

Pathy, Suguna, 1987, Caste, class and violence: An appraisal, *Teacher Politics* 13 (2), 61-75, bibliography.

CASTE VIOLENCE : INDIA : BIHAR

Anon, 1987, A class of rights, *Hindustan Times* (Magazine) June 21, p 1-6 +.

——, 1987, Class war in Bihar *Hindustan Times* (Magazine) June 21, p 1-6.

——, 1987, It there a cure for Bihar? *Hindustan Times* (Magazine) June 7, p 1-3.

——, 1987, Rural violence in Bihar, *Link* 29 (49) July 12, p 17-20.

Akhilesh Kumar, 1988, Genesis of caste riots in Bihar, *Mainstream* 26 (21) 5 March, p 25-26.

Das, Arvind N., 1985, Growing violence in Bihar : Social roots of the cult of the gun, *Times of India* November 21, p 8 col 3-5.

——, 1987, Bihar disinformation: Caste killings and naxalite alibi, *Mainstream* 25 (40) June 20, p 7-10.

Mishra, Girish, 1987, Agrarian violence in Bihar, *Mainstream* 25 (39) June 13, p 6-8.

Ranjan, Sudhanshu, 1988, Bihar killings in retrospect, *Mainstream* 26 (21) 5 March, p 27-29.

Shyama Nand Singh, 1988, Roots of caste war in Bihar, *Mainstream* 26 (14) 16 January, p 28-29.

CASTE : VIOLENCE : INDIA : GUJARAT

Abraham, A.S., 1985, Caste war in Gujarat: Wider objectives of agitation, *Times of India*, June 14, p 6.

Anon, 1985, Gujarat caste war, *Times of India*, April 17, p 8, col 1-2.

CASTE VIOLENCE : INDIA : SOUTHERN

Bhargava, G.S., 1986-1987, Caste war in South India, *Janata* 41 (25) November 30, p 5-7; 41 (26) December 21, p 7-8; 341(27) January 4, p 5-6.

CASTEISM

Nanavatty, Meher C., 1955, Seminar on casteism and untouchability: A review, *Indian Journal of Adult Education* 16 (4) December, p 41-50.

See also Caste.

CASTES : INDIA

See Caste: India

CATTLE HUSBANDRY : TRIBALS

Srivastava, R.M. and **Kharde, R.L.**, 1983, Traditional beliefs of tribal Mundas

p 65-69.

CHARCOAL MAKING : INDIA

Sathe, Madhusudan Dattatraya, 1988, Katkari labour in charcoal making, *Economic and Political Weekly* 23 (34) July 30, p 1565-1567.

CHARMAKARS : INDIA

Misra, P.K., 1963, A note on an organized effort to bring a change in the caste status by the charmakars, *Bulletin of Anthropological Survey of India* 12 (1-2) January-June, p 127-128.

See also Chamars.

CHATTRIS

See Kanwars.

CHENCHUS

Bhowmick, P.K., 1985, Social organization of the Chenchus: A gathering hunting tribe of Andhra Pradesh, *Journal of Asiatic Society* (Bengal) 27 (3), p 35-78, bibliography, tables.

Mukhopadhyay, Rajatsubhra, 1984, Dilemma of tribal transformation: The case of Chenchus, *Vanyajati* 32 (2) April , p 19-24.

Sirajuddin, S.M., 1984, Reproduction and consanguinity among Chenchus of Andhra Pradesh, *Man in India* 64(2) June, p 181-192, bibliography.

CHERWAS

See Kanwars.

CHHOTA UDEPUR : INDIA

Krishnan, Jalram, 1986, The Chhota Udepur experiment, *Economic Trends* (Supplement) 16(11) March, p 1-4.

CHILDREN : INDIA

Bennur, C.S., 1967, Caste prejudice and children, *Progress of Education* 41 (10-11) May-June, p 392-393, letter to editor.

Chaturvedi, K.N. and **Mishra R.C.**, 1988, Children spontaneous recall in relation to their caste group affiliation, *Indian Journal of Community Guidance Service* 5 (2) May, p 23-30, bibliography, tables.

Om Prakash, 1980, Educational attainment of children in the sweeper community at AIIMPS campus: An exploratory study, *Indian Educational Review* 15 (4) October, p 97-103.

Sunil, K.P., 1989, Children of a lesser God, *Illustrated Weekly of India* 110 (26) June 25, p 36-39.

See also Caste Prejudice: Children; Kisan Children; Tribal Children.

CHINALS

Sharma, D.D., 1988, Language loyalty and maintenance: A case of Chinals of Lahaul, *Panjab University Research Bulletin (Arts)* 19 (2) October, p 111-119, footnotes.

CHINGLEPUT DISTRICT : INDIA : TAMILNADU

Venktraman, S.R., 1984, Villis of Chingleput district, *Vanyajati* 32 (2) April, p 5-11.

CHIPKO MOVEMENT : INDIA : BIHAR CHOTANAGPUR

Bahuguna, Sunderlal, 1990, INTACH Seminar on problems facing tribals and launching of Chipko movement in Chotanagpur, held at the Grove, Hazaribagh on October 22 and 23 1989, *Man in India* 70(1) March, p 96-97.

CHITTOR DISTRICT : INDIA : ANDHRA PRADESH

Ramachandra Reddy, M. and **Chengal Reddy, P.**, 1986, Fertility behaviour in the Sugalis of Chittor district, Andhra Pradesh, *Health and Population* 9 (4) October-December, p 205-217.

CHOLANAICKANS : INDIA : KERALA

D'Monte, Darryl, 1986, Cholanaickans: Homeless in Kerala, *Hindustan Times* (Mag) August 17, p 5 col 1-6.

CHOTANAGPUR : INDIA : BIHAR

Anon, 1985, Industry, police, carpet-baggers runamuck in Chotanagpur, *Link* 27 (50) July 21, p 4-9.

Sinha, S.C., Sen, Jyoti and **Panchbhai, Sudhir**, 1969, The Concept of Diku among the tribes of Chotanagpur, *Man in India* 49 (2) April-June, p 121-138, references.

See also Geographical Area subdivision 'Chotanagpur' under main Descriptor.

CHOUHANS

Das, M. N., 1966, Female infanticide among the Bedees and the Chouhans: Motives and modes, *Man in India* 36(4) October-December, p 261-266.

CHOWDWAR HARIJAN CONFERENCE (ORISSA)

Anon, 1945-46, Chowdwar Harijan Conference, *Social Service Quarterly* 32(2) October, p 61-64; 33(1) July, 1946, p 12-21.

CHRISTIAN APPROACH TO TRIBALS

Anon, 1961, A Christian approach to tribal communities in India today, *Religion and Society* 8(3) September, p 60-83.

CHRISTIAN GROUPS : UCHAIS : INDIA : TRIPURA

Das, Biplas, 1986, The Uchais of Tripura : Some religious functions of the Christian groups, *Folklore* 27(8) August, p 171-176, bibliography.

CHRISTIANITY : IMPACT ON TRIBALS

Das, Anirudha, 1968, Impact of Christianity on the tribals in Orissa : The historical background, *Adibasi* 10(1) April, p 87-99.

Pugh, B.M., 1961, Christianity and the tribal communities of Assam, *Religion and Society* 8(3) September, p 46-52, appendix.

CHURCH

Joseph. M.J., 1988, Class, caste, church and the Left, *Economic and Political Weekly* 23(49) December 3, p 2573-2574.

Marrison, G. E., 1962, Language in the tribal churches of North India, *Religion and Society* 9(4) December, p 72-79.

Moasosang, P., 1962, Social and cultural changes in the tribal communities today and the responsibility of the churches, *Religion and Society* 9(4) December, p 40-45.

CITY LIFE: IMPACT ON TRIBALS

Das, Amal Kumar, 1962, Influence of city life on educated tribals, *Bulletin of Cultural Research Institute* 1(2), p 69-78, tables.

CIVILISATION CRISIS : IMPACT ON TRIBALS

Mukherjee, Charulal, 1943, The Santal in a changing civilization, *Indian Journal of Social Work* 4(2) September, p 171-181.

CLAN BASED SOCIETIES : INDIA

Mehta, B. H., 1966, The heterogeneous character of clan based societies with special references to Gonds of the Central Indian high lands, *Journal of Anthropological Society of Bombay* (NS) 12(1), p 50-70.

CLAN/GOTRA ENDOGAMY : INDIA : WEST BENGAL

Banerjee, A. R. and **Chouwdhury Lipi**, 1988, Caste exogamy and clan/gotra endogamy in the contemporary Bengali Society, *Man in India* 68(2-3) June-September, p 200-210.

CLAN ORGANIZATION : GONDS : INDIA

Buradkar, M. P., 1947, The clan organization of the Gonds, *Man in India* 27(2) June, p 127-136, footnotes.

CLANS

Dubey, K. C., 1969, A note on the Bison-Horn Maria Phratries clans and totems, *Eastern Anthropologist* 22(3) September-December, p 371-376.

See also Tribes and Tribals.

CLANS AND CLAN SYSTEM

Anon, 1964, A note on locality in relation to descent, *Contributions to Indian Sociology* 7, March, p 71-76.

Buradkar, M. P., 1947, The clan organization of the Gonds, *Man in India*, 27(2) June, p 127-136, footnotes.

CLASSES : BACKWARD

See Backward Classes; Other Backward Classes.

CLASSICAL ECONOMICS : SOCIAL CLASSES

Hodges, Donald C., 1961, Classical economics and Marx's theory of social class, *Indian Journal of Social Research* 2(2) July, p 91-95, references.

CLASSWAR

Makwana, Yogendra, 1985, Reservation : Does it promote class war, *Link* 27(36) April 21, p 9-11.

CLUBS : BACKWARD COMMUNITIES

Bhattacharya, Biswanath, 1965, A short note on clubs and libraries of the backward communities, *Bulletin of Cultural Research Institute* 4, p 53-57, tables.

COCKS : IMPORTANCE IN KHASI AND JAINTA HILLS

Paul, Gemini, 1957, Importance of egg and cock in Khasi and Jaintia hills, *Vanyajati* 5(2) April, p 66-69, references.

COINS : AUDUMBARA

Mukherjee, D., 1984, A review of Audumbara coin, *Indian Museum Bulletin* 19,

p 66-68.

COLONIAL SOCIOLOGY : INDIA : WEST BENGAL

Bandhyopadhyay, Sekhar, 1985, Caste in the perception of the Raj : A note on the evolution of colonial sociology of Bengal, *Bengal Past and Present* 104 (1-2) January-December, p 58-80, bibliography, footnotes.

COLOUR VISION : TRIBALS : INDIA : ASSAM

Mukherjee, Deba Prasad, 1963 Variation in defective colour vision among some tribes of Assam, *Bulletin of Anthropological Survey of India* 12 (1-2) January-June, p 39-42, references, tables.

COMMERCIAL COMMUNITY

Agarwal, B.R., 1962 Nature and extent of social change in a mobile commercial community, *Sociological Bulletin* 11 (1-2) March-September, p 141-145.

COMMISSIONS/COMMITTEES: CENTRAL AND STATES (INCLUDING PRE-INDEPENDENCE RELEVANT REFERENCES)

See Appendix.

COMMUNAL LAND SYSTEM : TRIBALS

Roy Burman, B.K., 1987, Historical process in aspect of communal land system and poverty alienation among tribals, *Social Action* 37(4) October-December, p 391-420, bibliography, tables.

COMMUNALISM : TRIBAL AREAS

Jabbar Alam, M., 1986, Injecting communalism into tribal areas, *New Age* 34 (39) September 28, p 11.

COMMUNITIES : RESEARCH AND SURVEYS

Khan, A.H., 1956, The study of community in social studies, *Educational Forum* 1(1) January, 1956, p 9-11.

Lele, T.P., 1967, A comparative study of the students from different communities, *Education and Psychology Review*, 7 (3) July, p 117-124, tables.

COMMUNITY DEVELOPMENT BLOCKS : TRIBALS

Shrikant, L. M., 1968, Tribal Development Blocks: Community Development Blocks, *Vanyajati* 16 (4) October, p 119-122 +.

CONCEPT OF SOUL : TRIBALS : INDIA

Basu, Minendra Nath, 1965, The concept of soul among the tribal folk of India, *Bulletin of Cultural Research Institute* 4(1) p 5-8.

CONFERENCE FOR TRIBAL WELFARE, DELHI

Chattopadhyay, K. P., 1952, Conference for tribal welfare at Delhi, *Man in India* 32 (3) July-September, p 167-169.

CONFLICTS

See INTRA CONFLICTS

CONSANGUINEOUS MARRIAGES : INDIA : ANDHRA PRADESH

Govinda Reddy, P., 1987, Effects of consanguineous marriages on fertility and infant mortality among the Mala of Southern Andhra Pradesh, *Indian Journal of Physical Anthropology and Human Genetics* 13 (1) January-April, p 43-49, bibliography, tables.

CONSTITUTION AND WELFARE : INDIA

Anon, 1953, Scheme in Bombay Government sanctioned for 1952-53 for Scheduled Tribes under Act 275 of the Constitution, *Vanyajati* 1(4) October, p 101-102.

——, 1953, Schemes of the Bihar State Government submitted to the Government of India under article 275 of Constitution of India for the uplift of Scheduled Tribes during 1952-1953, *Vanyajati* 1(3) July, p 72-74.

Krishnan, P.G., 1985, Constitution and tribal welfare, *Cochin University Law Review* 9(1-2) March-June, p 49-66.

Leuva, K.K., 1964, Impact of constitutional safeguards on the Scheduled Tribes, *Journal of Social Research* 7 (1-2) March-September, p 62-69.

Parmanand Singh, 1987, Reservations, reality and the Constitution : Current crisis in India, *Cochin University Law Review* 11(3-4) September-December, p 284-318.

Rastogi, S.P., 1980, The impact of Constitutional provision upon the uplift of Harijans, *Indian Educational Review*, 15(4) October, p 76-80.

Ursekar, H.S., 1970, Constitutional concern for Harijans and Adivasis, *Social Service Quarterly* 55(4) April, p 97-105.

CONSTITUTIONAL LAW : RESERVATION

Sundaresh, Aruna, 1986, Constitution, law and reservations, *New Frontiers in Education* 16(2), p 33-40.

CONSTITUTIONAL PROVISIONS : HARIJANS

Rastogi, S.P., 1980, The impact of constitutional provision upon the uplift of Harijans, *Indian Educational Review* 15 (4) October, p 76-80.

CONSTRUCTIVE WORKERS : SCHEDULED AREAS

Shrikant, L.M., 1956, Some suggestions for constructive workers in scheduled areas, *Vanyajati* 4(2) April, p 58-59, references.

CONSUMPTION PATTERN : INDIA

Mohapatra, P.C., 1985, Consumption pattern of Scheduled Tribes : A case study of Koraput district, Orissa, *Vision* 5(2) October-December, p 15-22, bibliography, tables.

Sharma, H.R., et al, 1987, Pattern of income, consumption and employment, *Economic Affairs* 32(2) June, p 81-88, appendix, tables.

CONVERSION : MAHARAS

Patwardhan, Sunanda, 1968, Social mobility and conversion of Maharas, *Sociological Bulletin* 17 (2) September, p 187-202, references.

CONVERT COMMUNITY

Sharma, S.L. and **Srivastava, R.N.**, 1967, Institutional resistance to induced Islamization in a convert community : An empirical study in sociology of religion, *Sociological Bulletin* 16(1) March, p 69-80.

COOPERATIVE MOVEMENTS : TRIBALS

Anon, 1966, A short note on the working of the cooperative movement for benefit of tribal district of Raigarh (Madhya Pradesh), *Vanyajati* 14(1) January, p 40-43.

Apte, J.S., 1960, Cooperative movement among the tribals of district Thana, Bombay State, *Vanyajati* 8(3) July, p 102-104.

Shrikant, L.M., 1967, Co-operatives movement among tribals : Andhra Pradesh

Scheduled Tribes Cooperative Finance Development Corporation, *Vanyajati* 15(2) April, p 53-55 +, maps, tables.

——, 1967, Cooperative movement among tribals III : The Madhya Pradesh State Tribal Co-operative Development Corporation Limited, Bhopal, *Vanyajati* 15(3) July, p 101-108, Tables.

——, 1967, Cooperative movement among the tribes, *Vanyajati* 15(1) January, p 1-4; 15(3) October, p 101-108.

See also Cooperatives : Tribals; Tribal Cooperative Societies.

COOPERATIVES : TRIBALS

Naresh Kumar, 1985, Cooperatives for tribals, *Social Welfare* 32(3) June p 30-32.

Shah, U.M., 1984, Cooperatives and tribals, *Tribe* 16(3-4) September-December, p 7-19.

——, 1986, Cooperatives and tribals, *Khadi Gramodyog* 31(7) April, p 314-322.

——, 1986, Tribals and cooperatives, *Kurukshetra* 34 (4) January, p 4-8.

See also Cooperative Movement: Tribals; Tribal Cooperative Societies.

COORGS : RELIGION AND MYTHOLOGY

Anon, 1954, On the different aspects or levels in Hinduism, *Contributions to Indian Sociology*, 3 April, p 40-54.

COSMOGONY OF CASTE

Anon, 1984, (Book review), *Hindustan Times* (Magazine), January 6, p 8, col-6.
Review of the book : **Dev, Bimal J.** and **Lahri Dilip K.**, 1985, *Cosmogony of caste and social mobility in Assam*, Mittal Publication, Delhi, 183 p.

CREATIVE ABILITIES : TRIBAL CHILDREN

Krishna Kumari, P. et al, 1986, Study of creative abilities of tribal children in relation to their sex and socio-economic status, *Journal of Institute of Educational Research* 10(1) January, p 1-4, references.

CREATIVITY : TRIBALS : INDIA : MEGHALAYA

Dutta, Gitika, 1982, Sex differences in creativity among the tribe of Meghalaya, *Journal of Institute of Educational Research* 6(2) May, p 23-26, references, tables.

CRIMES : TRIBAL AREA

Banerjee, S.P., 1961, Crimes in tribal areas, *Bulletin of Tribal Research Institute and Development* (Chhindwara) 1(2) December, p 4-8.

Batria, P., 1963, Crime and witchcraft among the tribes of Madhya Pradesh, *Bulletin of Tribal Research and Development Institute* (Chhindwara) 3(1), p 21-29, references, tables.

See also Tribal Crime.

CRIMINAL TRIBES

See also Backward Classe; Ex Criminal Tribes; Tribes and Tribals.

CRIMINAL TRIBES : INDIA : NORTHERN

Sher, Sher Singh, 1960, Ex-criminal tribes of Northern India need reclassification on more authentic and scientific grounds, *Journal of Social Research* 3(2) September, p 35-42, tables.

CRIMINAL TRIBES : INDIA : TAMIL NADU : MADRAS PRESIDENCY

Radhakrishna, Meena, 1989, The Criminal Tribes Act in Madras Presidency:

Implications for itinerant trading communities, *Indian Economic and Social History Review* 26(3) July-September, p 269-295.

CRIMINAL TRIBES ACT, 1911

Radhakrishna, Meena, 1989, The Criminal Tribes Act in Madras Presidency : Implications for itinerant trading communities, *Indian Economic and Social History Review* 26(3) July-September, p 269-295.

CRITERIA FOR RECOGNITION

See Determinants.

CULTIVATION : WILD PLANTS : INDIA : RAJASTHAN

Sebastian, M.K. and **Bhandari, M.M.**, 1984, Cultivation of wild plants for the uplift of tribals in the forest areas of Rajasthan, *Tribe* 16 (3-4) September, p 30-35, bibliography.

CULTIVATORS : TRIBALS

Gaikwad, John S., 1987, Transformation of economy of the tribal cultivators through the electric motor pumps, *Tribal Research Bulletin* 9(2) March p 18-20.

CULTURAL ADAPTATION : YANADIS

Agrawal, Binod C. et al, 1984, Determinants of cultural adaptation in the process of change : A case of Yanadi, *Man in India* 64(2) June, p 133-142.

CULTURAL AFFINITIES : TRIBALS

Hutton, J.H., 1929, Cultural affinities of the Oraons with the Hill tribes of Assam, *Man in India* 9(1) January, March, p 1-6.

CULTURAL CONTACTS : TRIBALS

Anon, 1983, Book Review, *Sociological Bulletin* 32(2) September, p 224-227. Review of the book : **Vyas, N.N.** and **Manu, R.S.**, 1983, *Disease, culture contact and tribals*, MLV Tribal Research and Training Institute, Udaipur, p 14-86.

_____, 1983, Cultural contacts, *Sociological Bulletin* 32(2) September, p 224-227.

CULTURAL FACTORS IN DEVELOPMENT : TRIBALS

Roy Burman, B.K., 1965, Cultural factors in economic development and technological change in tribal area, *Journal of Social Research* 8(1) March, p 21-32.

CULTURAL INTEGRATION : TRIBALS

Ravindranathan, M.N., 1983, The problem of cultural integration of the tribals: Education as the chief instrument of change, *Education Quarterly* 35(4) October, p 20-24.

CULTURAL THEORY

Mitra, Sarat Chandra, 1921, Types of cultural theory, *Man in India* 1(3) September, p 240-261, footnotes.

CULTURE : TRIBALS

See Tribal Culture.

CUSTOMS AND TRADITIONS : TRIBAL WOMEN

Sarkar, R.M., 1968, Women in tribal India through custom and traditions, *Folklore* 9(1-2) December, p 458-467, references.

CUTTACK DISTRICT : INDIA : ORISSA

Mohapatra, Kulamani, 1958, The changing status of Harijans in a village of Cuttack district, *Adibasi* 3(2) May-July, p 26-30.

DAHAITS

See Kols.

DALITS

Anon, 1986, Shiv Sena enters rural politics : Campaign against Dalits in Marathwara village, *Economic and Political Weekly* 21 (50) December 13, p 2166-2167.

Bhuskute, R.V., 1989, Tribals, Dalits and government lands, *Economic and Political Weekly* 24(23) June 10, p 1265-1266 tables.

Gani, H.A., 1990, Dalit unity, *Janata*, 45, Annual Number, p 41 +.

Mishra, K.K., 1985, The Dalits reply back, *Link* 27(36) April 21, p 13.

Times of India (Newspaper), 1988, An effective reposite, *Times of India* February 9, p 6, col 1-2, editorial.

DALITS : INDIA : MAHARASHTRA

Anon, 1986, Shiv Sena enters rural politics : Campaign against Dalits in Marathwara villages, *Economic and Political Weekly* 21(50) December 13, p 2166-2167.

Times of India (Newspaper), 1988, An effective reposite, *Times of India* February 9, p 6, col 1-2, editorial.

DANCES : TRIBALS

Dutta, Dipak K., 1984, Dances of the Hrussos, *Resarun* 10(1) Spring-Summer, p 38-40.

Shashi, S.S., 1971, Songs and dances of the Gaddis, *Caravan*, p 14.

DANDAKARANYA PROJECT : INDIA

Anon, 1960, Dandakaranya and the tribals, *Vanyajati* 8(2) April, p 41-43.

——, 1961, A essay in migration, *Social Action* 11(12) December, p 575-576 +

DANTEWARA : INDIA : MADHYA PRADESH

Athavale, M.C. and **Nahatkar, Sunil**, 1983, Evaluation study of tribal area development programme in Konta and Dantewara, Bastar district, Madhya Pradesh, *Co-operative Perspective* 18(3) October-December, p 93-100.

DARJEELING (HILL) : INDIA

Subba, Tanka Bahadur, 1984, Caste and agrarian structure : A study in Hill Darjeeling and Sikkim, *Man in India* 64(1) March, p 59-68, bibliography.

DAROIS

See Gonds.

DASAS : INDIA : ANCIENT

Chanana, Dev Raj, 1959, The Sudra, the Dasa and Manu, *Indian Journal of Social Work* 20(3) December, p 201-208.

DAUGHTERS

Anon, 1987, (Book review), *Economic and Political Weekly* (Supplement) 22(44) October 31, WS75-WS76; *Social Action* 37(2) April-June, p 199-201.

Review of the book : **Liddle, Joanna** and **Joshi, Rama**, 1986, *Daughters of independence : Gender: A caste and class in India*, Kali for Women, New Delhi, 264 p.

See also Girls; Women.

DBULE DISTRICT : INDIA

Surana, M.B., 1986, Supply of milch animals to Adivasis in Dbule district, *Tribal Research Bulletin* 9(1) September, p 11-15.

DEAD PERSONS : DISPOSAL OF CORPSE : INDIA

Sarkar, Haribishnu, 1951, Disposal of the dead at the Indus Valley and its survival among the Aboriginal peoples of India, *Man in India* 31(1) January-March, p 23-32, references, tables.

See also Funerary Customs: India: Mortuary Practices: Nigeria: North Eastern.

DEATHS : ACCIDENTAL : TRIBALS

Batria, Puran, 1962, Accidental deaths among tribes, *Bulletin of Tribal Research and Development Institute* (Chhindwara) 2(1), p 43-48.

DECCAN : INDIA

Von Furer-Haimendorf, Christoph, 1945, Aboriginal rebellions in the Deccan, *Man in India* 25(4) December, p 208-217.

Prakash Rao, R., 1954, Village organization and authority among the Lambadas of the Deccan, *Eastern Anthropologist* 8(1) September-November, p 3-12.

DEDICATION TO PROSTITUTION : HARIJAN GIRLS

Anon, 1941, Problem of dedication of Harijan girls to prostitution in Karnataka, *Rural India* 4(6) June, p 303-308.

DEFENCE ORIENTATION : WELFARE : BACKWARD CLASSES

Adibasi (Periodical), 1965, Defence-cum-production orientation of the programme of backward classes welfare, *Adibasi*, October, p 1-4, editorial.

DELHI : INDIA

Chattopadhyay, Prasanta Kumar, 1950, Some physical studies among the Gujjars of Delhi, *Man in India* 50 (2) April-June, p 185-88.

See also Geographical Area subdivision under main Descriptor.

DEMOGENETIC STUDIES : TRIBALS : INDIA

Bhageshwar Singh and **Reddy, N.K.**, 1982, A plea for demogenetic studies of numerically small and large tribes, *Indian Journal of Physical Anthropology and Human Genetics* 8(1) April, p 67-70, bibliography.

DEMOGRAPHIC CHARACTERISTICS : TRIBALS : INDIA

Gaikwad, John S., 1986, A demographic profile of tribals in Maharashtra State, *Tribal Research Bulletin* 9(1) September, p 16-27.

Kuthiala, S.K., 1969, Demographic characteristics of tribal population in India, *Indian Sociological Bulletin* 7(1) October, p 57-58, references.

DEMOGRAPHIC FACTORS : TRIBALS : INDIA

Nag, Narendra Gopal, 1970, Implication of cultural and demographic factors on the socio-political trends among Scheduled Tribes, *Vanyajati* 18(2) April, p 51-58, references, tables.

DEMOGRAPHIC STUDIES : INDIA

Pandit, T.N., 1960, Demographic study of a Gujar village, *Anthropologist* 7(1-2) March-August, p 1-6, references, tables.

Sher, Sher Singh, 1962, A demographic study of Sansis, *Vanyajati* 10(4) October, p 145-160, references, tables.

DEMOGRAPHIC TRENDS : TRIBAL WOMEN : INDIA : ANDHRA PRADESH

Rohini, A., 1987, Some demographic trends among the tribal women of Andhra Pradesh, *Man and Life* 13(1-2) January-June, p 91-96, bibliography, tables.

DEMOGRAPHIC VARIABLES : WELFARE : SCHEDULED CASTES

Juyal, P.D., 1986, Some demographic variables influencing the attitude of Scheduled Caste towards the measures adopted for their welfare : An empirical study, *Progress of Education* 61(4-5) November-December, p 85-88, references.

Panda, S., 1969, Demography of Kondh village, *Adibasi* 11(3) October, p 27-35, tables.

Saxena, Devendra, 1965, Demography and social anthropology, *Indian Journal of Social Research* 6(3) December, p 246-250, references.

Sher, Sher Singh, 1963, Demography of Sikligars, *Vanyajati* 11(2) April, p 79-81, tables.

See also Tribal Demography.

DENOTIFIED TRIBES

Anon, 1982, Effect of parental deprivation on personality adjustment ; With special reference to the denotified tribes of U.P., *Indian Educational Review* 17(1) January, p 99-109.

Khan, M.A., 1979, Parental deprivation in relations to academic achievement of denotified tribes, *Indian Educational Review* 14(4) October, p 95-98.

Kundu, C.L., 1968, Education of denotified tribes, *Progress of Education* 42(10-12) May-June, p 351-354.

Sinha, V., et al, 1976, Parental deprivation in relation to intelligence of denotified tribes, *Asian Journal of Psychology and Education*, 1(2) July, p 38-39.

See also Scheduled Tribes

DEPOPULATION : PRIMITIVE COMMUNITIES

Hutton, J.H., 1922, Depopulation of primitive committees, *Man in India* 2(4) December, p 220-227, footnotes.

See also Detribalisation

DEPRESSED CLASSES

Social Service Quarterly (Periodical), 1923, Depressed Classes Mission Society, *Social Service Quarterly* 9(1) July, p 47-48, editorial.

Social Service Quarterly (Periodical), 1934, Disabilities of depressed classes, *Social Service Quarterly* 20(1) July, p 25-26, editorial.

See also Deprived Classes; Downtrodden Classes; Scheduled Castes and Scheduled Tribes; Tribes and Tribals, etc.; name of individual depressed class, e.g., Harijans.

DEPRESSED CLASSES (PROTECTION OF RIGHTS) BILL

Social Service Quarterly (Periodical), 1934, Mr. Bakhale's Depressed Classes (Protection of Rights) Bill, *Social Service Quarterly* 20(2) October, p 75-77, editorial.

DEPRESSED CLASSES INSTITUTE, BOMBAY

Social Service Quarterly (Periodical), 1927, Depressed Classes Institute, *Social Service Quarterly* 12(3) January, p 144-145, editorial.

DEPRESSED CLASSES MISSION SOCIETY

Social Service Quarterly (Periodical), 1923, Depressed Classes Mission Society, *Social Service Quarterly* 9(1) July, p 47-48, editorial.

DEPRIVATIONS : TRIBAL CHILDREN

Kulshrestha, Shivendra Kumar, 1979, Self situational deprivations in the school adjustment of tribal children, *Journal of Indian Education* 5(2) July, p 41-47.

See also Disadvantaged Classes: Education: Tribal Children.

DEPRIVED CLASSES

Minz, Nirmal, 1985, Anthropology and the deprived, *Religion and Society* 32(4) December, p 3-19, bibliography.

Sharma, R.S., 1985, Developing educational technology for deprived sections of the Indian society, *Bulletin of Non-formal Education* 3(3) December, p 1-17.

See also Depressed Classes; Downtrodden Classes.

DERMATOGLYPHIC STUDY : CASTES AND TRIBES : INDIA

Chakravarti, Manish Ranjan and **Mukherjee, Deba Prasad**, 1962, Dermatoglyphic study on the tribes and castes of Nagaland and Manipur, *Bulletin of Anthropological Survey of India* 11(3-4), p 233-234, tables.

DERMATOGLYPHIC TRAITS : TRIBALS : INDIA

Sharma, J.C., 1970, Convergence and divergence of dermatoglyphic traits in human populations based on a study of the four tribal groups of Bastar, *Eastern Anthropologist* 23(1) January-April, p 17-35.

DESAYA KONDHS

See Kondhs.

DESCENT GROUPS : MANNEDORAS

Suguna, A.V. et al, 1988, The role of descent groups among the Mannedoras, *Man in India* 68 (4) December, p 454-458, tables.

DETERMINANTS

Parvathamma, C., 1986, Should caste be a basis for recognizing backwardness?, *Guru Nanak Journal of Sociology* 7(2) October, p 89-101, bibliography, tables.

Rama, Badri, 1990, Connotation of merit, *Hindustan Times*, September 4, p 11, col. 6-7.

Sharma, Arvind, 1986, Manu on determinants of castes, *Man in India* 66(3) September, p 255-258.

Verma, O.P., 1979, Determinants of status in ancient India, *Journal of Bihar Puravid Parishad* 3, p 87-90.

DETRIBALISATION

See also Tribalisation.

DETRIBALISATION : INDIA

Bose, Nirmal Kumar, 1962, Some observations on industrialization and its effects of tribal life, *Man in India* 42 (1) January-March, p 5-9.

Das, Amal Kumar, 1966, Special problems in tribal transformation: Industrialization as a means of such transformation, *Bulletin of Cultural Research Institute* 5(1-2), p 5-10, references.

Das, G.N., 1964, Culture contact and social engineering, *Adibasi* November, p 19-22.

Das, T.C., 1960, Assimilation, integration, acculturation, *Journal of Social Research* 3(2) September, p 6-10.

Ebnother, Robert, 1967, Traditionalism or modernity in development, *Adibasi* 9(1) April, p 59-61.

Gisbert, P., 1962, Cultural change among the tribals, *Social Action* 12(4) April, p 179-187.

Kurup, A.M., 1963, Impact of industrialization on tribal life, *Vanyajati* 11(2) April, p 71-75.

Mathur, V.K., 1966, Modernity: The nexus of tribal development, *Adibasi* 8(3) October, p 17-22.

——, 1967, The traditional-modern continuum: An assumption in tribal development, *Journal of Social Research*, 10(2) September, p 11-25.

Oraon, Kartik, 1964, Tribes and tribalism of India, *Journal of Social Research* 7(1-2), March-September, p 36-52, references.

Rao, V.K.R.V., 1966, Social change and the tribal culture, *Journal of Social Research* 9(2) September, p 1-9.

Roy Burman, B.K., 1968, Some dimension of transformation of tribal societies in India, *Journal of Social Research* 11(1) March, p 88-94; *Vanyajati*, 17(1) January, 1969, p 1-4 +.

Sen Gupta, A.K., 1967, Hinduisation and tribalisation: Two case studies, *Folklore* 8(12) December, p 433-438, references.

See also Depopulation: Primitive Communities; Development; Tribal Development.

DETRIBALISATION : INDIA : BIHAR

Sachchidananda, 1958, Study of culture change in tribal Bihar, *Adibasi* 3(2) May-July, p 11-16.

Vidyarthi, L.P., 1964, The changing face of tribal Bihar : Some preliminary observations on the concept of deteribalization, *Journal of Social Research* 7 (1-2) March-September, p 53-61, references.

DETRIBALISATION : INDIA : NORTH EASTERN

Srivastava, L.R.N., 1969, The problem of modernization of the tribes of North-East India, *Bulletin of Cultural Research Institute* 8(1-2), p 21-25.

DETRIBALISATION : INDIA : WEST BENGAL

Das Gupta, Pranab Kumar, 1964, Impact of industrialization of tribal life, *Bulletin of Anthropological Survey of India* 13(1-2) January-June, p 85-106, tables.

DEVADASIS

Nadkarni, V.C., 1975, Devadasis: Married to God and Mammon, *Illustrated Weekly of India*, December 14.

DEVELOPMENT

Desai, Anjana P., 1985, On perceiving problems of rural development, *Deccan Geographer* 23(1) January-June, p 95-102, bibliography, tables.

Dinbandhu, Mahal, 1985, The role of Tribal Development Cooperative Corporation of Orissa Ltd for the development of tribals, *Tribal Research Bulletin* 7(2) March,

p 20-23.

——, 1985, The Tribal Development Cooperative Corporation of Orissa, *Cooperative Perspective* 20(3) October-December, p 42-46.

Ebnother, Robert, 1967, Traditionalism or modernity in development, *Adibasi* 9(1) April, p 59-61.

Gangwar, A.K., 1990, Tribals and forests of North-Eastern India: Strategies for sustainable development, *Vanyajati* 38(2) April p 14-21.

Gupta, Ram Pratap and **Sunil**, 1986, Madhya Pradesh : Development of tribals, *Economic Trends* 8(3), p 1-5 +.

Narayana, K.V., 1985, Tribals in rural development, *Kurukshetra* 34(2) November, p 7-8 +.

Patnaik, K.M., 1987, Industrialization for accelerating development in a tribal setting, *Vision* 6 (3-4) January, p 52-56.

Paul, S.P. and **Baghel, A.S.**, 1987, Sociological constraints and attitude to development of tribal farmers in the tribal areas of M.P., *Journal of Rural Development* 6(2) March, p 197-210.

Prasad, R.R., 1985, Tribal culture development, *Administrator* October-December, p 347-355, bibliography.

Raval, Indubhai B., 1964, Sociology of tribal economic development, *Indian Journal of Social Work* 25(1) April, p 43-51, tables.

Roy Burman, J.J., 1990, Tribal tradition and modern development in North-East India, *Vanyajati* 38(2) April, p 9-13.

Samuel, C.J., 1985, Development of tribal economy : Legislative and executive measures, *Cochin University Law Review* 9(1-2) March-June, p 87-104, footnotes.

Sanyal, Shubhendu, 1988, Primitive tribes of Bihar : Strategy for development, *Man in India* 68 (4) December, p 356-368.

Satish Kumar, 1985, Development in tribal areas : An overview, *Link* (Supplement) 27 (26) February 3, p 13-18, table.

Sharma, Suryanarayan, 1985, Accent on tribal area development, *Commerce* 151 (3873) August 17, p 325-326.

Srisalkar, P.R., 1985, Primitive tribes : Challenge for development, *Tribal Research Bulletin* 7(2) March, p 7-8.

Vyas, N.N., 1984, Some spatial aspects of tribal culture and development, *Tribe* 16(3-4) September-December, p 1-6.

See also Tribal Development

DEVELOPMENT PLAN : TRIBALS : INDIA : MADHYA PRADESH

Athavale, M.C. and **Nahatkar, Sunil**, 1983, Evaluation study of tribal area development programme in Konta and Dantewara, Bastar district, M.P., *Cooperative Perspective* 18(3) October-December, p 93-100.

Paul, S.P. and **Baghel, A.S.**, 1989, Elements of a development plan for tribal area farmers of Madhya Pradesh, *Journal of Rural Development* 8(1) January, p 71-78.

See also Development Planning: Tribals: India: Madhya Pradesh.

DEVELOPMENT PLANNING : TRIBALS: INDIA: MADHYA PRADESH

Sharma, K.N., 1969, Development planning for M.P. tribes, *Bulletin of Tribal Research and Development Institute* (Bhopal) 7(12) June-December, p 19-25.

See also Development Plan.

DEVELOPMENT STRATEGY : IMPACT ON TRIBAL DEMOGRAPHY

Ghosh, A., 1985, The political economy of development strategy and tribal

of the Malapantaram, Muthuvan and Ullatan tribes of Travancore, *Bulletin of Department of Anthropology* 5(2), p 9-19, tables.

See also Tribes and Tribals: Food: Nutrition.

DIGITAL RIDGE COUNTS : HATKARS : INDIA

Malhotra, K.C. and **Sen Gupta, B.**, 1985, Absolute and fluctuating asymmetry of digital ridge counts among Hatkars of Maharashtra, *Man in India* 65(2) June, p 139-153, bibliography, tables.

DIKU CONCEPT

Sinha, S.C., Sen, Jyoti and **Panchbhai, Sudhir**, 1969, The concept of Diku among the tribes of Chotanagpur, *Man in India*, 49(2) April-June, p 121-139, references.

DISADVANTAGED CLASSES : EDUCATION

Varma, R.P., 1984, Educating the disadvantaged : A few suggestions, *National Journal of Education* 6(2) May, p 1-6, references.

DISADVANTAGED CLASSES : EDUCATION : TRIBAL CHILDREN

Rath, R., 1986, Educational problems of the disadvantaged tribal children, *Vivekananda Kendra Patrika* 15(2) August, p 75-82.

See also Deprivations: Tribal Children.

DISEASES : TRIBALS

Vyas, N.N. and **Chaudhary, N.D.**, 1983, The socio-economic implications of Guinea worm : A disease in tribal setting, *Tribe* 15 (1-2) March-June, p 15-26.

DISPLACED FAMILIES : KHARKHARA PROJECT

Bahadur, F. ed., 1966, Kharkhara project: Survey of displaced families, *Bulletin of Tribal Research and Training Institute* (Bhopal) June, p 1-13, tables.

See also Displacement of Tribals.

DISPLACEMENT OF TRIBALS

Anon, 1987, Displacement of tribals due to location of Centre-State projects : Problems and related issues, *Tribals Research Bulletin* 9(2) March, p 21-26, bibliography.

See also Displaced Families: Kharkhara Project.

DIWALI CELEBRATIONS : TRIBALS : INDIA : TAMIL NADU

Dubey, S.N., 1964, Celebration of Diwali among the Gonds of Tamil, *Bulletin of Tribal Research and Training Institute* (Chhindwara) 4(1) June, p 37-43.

DOMINANT CASTE : INDIA

Bishei, Ulrich, 1983, The dominant caste and its land scape expression in Indian villages, *Geographical Review of India* 45(4) December, p 34-47, bibliography.

Jain, Meenakshi, 1985, Coping with dominant castes : Ignored aspect of Mrs. Gandhi's politics, *Times of India*, June 17, p 8, col 3-5; June 18, p 8, col 7-8.; June 19, p 6, col 7-8.

Narayana Reddy, G., 1984, Dominant caste and social interaction in a Karnataka village, *Social Change* 14(4) December, p 25-30, bibliography, tables.

Oommen, T.K., 1970, The concept of dominant caste : Some queries, *Contributions to Indian Sociology*, New Series 4, December, p 105-125.

DOMINANT EYES : TRIBALS : INDIA
Mayanglambam, Mani Babu and **Mayanglambam, Suniti Bala**, 1989, Earlobe attachment and dominant eye among the Phaynegs of Manipur, *Man in India* 69(3) September, p 285-291.

DONGRIA KONDHS
See Kondhs.

DORLAS : INDIA : MADHYA PRADESH : BASTAR
Dubey, K.C., 1970, The Dorlas of Bhopalpatnam, Bastar district, *Bulletin of Tribal Research and Development Institute* (Bhopal) 8(1-2) June-December.
Hazra, Durgadas, 1959, The Dorla of Bastar, *Bulletin of Department of Anthropology* 8(2) July, p 75-84, references.

DORMITORIES : TRIBALS
See Tribal Dormitories

DOWNTRODDEN CLASSES
Barve, V.N., 1942, A call from the downtrodden, *Social Service Quarterly* 28(4) April, p 145-147.
See also Depressed Classes; Deprived Classes.

DRAVIDIANS
Basham, A.L., 1963, Some reflections on Dravidians and Aryans, *Bulletin of Institute of Traditional Culture*, part II, p 225-234.
Sircar, D.C., 1955, The Dravidian problem, *Man in India* 35(1) January-March, p 31-38, references.

DRAVIDO-MUNDA CULTURE AREA
Bhattacharya, S., 1975, Linguistic convergence in the Dravido-Munda Culture Area, *International Journal of Dravidian Linguistics* 4(2), p 199-214.

DRESSES : TRIBALS
Srivastava, Shakuntala, 1961, A note in the question of dress for the tribals (with an apology to Dr. Verrier Elwin), *Sociological Bulletin* 10(2) September, p 42-45.

DROPOUTS : SCHEDULED CASTES AND SCHEDULE TRIBES : INDIA : ANDHRA PRADESH
Subrahmanyam, S., 1986, Problems of school dropouts: A study with a special reference to Scheduled Castes and Scheduled Tribes in Andhra Pradesh, *Education Quarterly* 38(3) Autumn, p 28-32.

DUDHI TRIBES
Mathur, K.S., 1951-1952, Sorcery and witchcraft among the tribes of Dudhi, *Eastern Anthropologist* 5(2-3) December-May, p 79-86.

DUNGRI BHILS
See Bhils.

DUNGRI GARASIAS
See Bhils.

DUSHADS
Singh, Ashok K., 1989, Socio-cultural characteristics of Dushads, *Vanyajati* 37(4)

October, p 56-61.

EACHATOLOGY : TRIBALS

Exem, A. Van, 1988, Tribal forever : The eachatology of the Sarna, *Sevartham* 13, p 27-42, footnotes.

EARLOBE ATTACHMENTS : TRIBALS : INDIA

Mayanglambam, Mani Babu and **Mayanglambam, Suniti Bala**, 1989, Earlobe attachment and dominant eye among the Phayengs of Manipur, *Man in India* 69(3) September, p 285-291.

EASTERN INDIA

Das. T.C., 1962, Nature and extent of social change in tribal society of Eastern India, *Sociological Bulletin* 11(1-2) March-September, p 221-228, tables.

Goswami, Omkar, 1985, Then came the Marwaris : Some aspects of changes in the pattern of industrial control in Eastern India, *Indian Economic and Social History Review* 22(3) July-September, p 225-249, bibliography, footnotes.

Maitra, Sunilranjan, 1970, Bachelor's dormitories of the tribes of Eastern India, *Bulletin of Anthropological Survey of India* 19(2) April, p 61-65, references.

See also Geographical Area subdivision under main Descriptor.

ECOLOGICAL ANALYSIS : TRIBALS : INDIA : SIKKIM

Anon, 1990, (Book review), *Man in India* 70(2) June, p 199-201.

Review of the book: **Bhasin, Veena**, 1989, *Ecology, culture and change : Tribals of Sikkim Himalayas*, Inter-India Publications, Delhi, p 407+22, photoplates.

Roy Burman, B.K., 1989, Society, ecology and land reform in tribal India, *Indian Journal of Public Administration* 35(1) January-March, p 41.

ECOLOGICAL DEVELOPMENTS : TRIBAL AREAS

Deogaonkar Warora, S.G., 1989, Role of voluntary agencies and tribal institutions in social and ecological developments in tribal areas, *Vanyajati* 37 (4) October, p 32-38.

Sachchidananda, 1989, Role of voluntary agencies in social and ecological development in tribal areas, *Vanyajati* 37(4) October, p 26-31.

ECONOMIC ANALYSIS : TRIBAL FARMERS

Chakravarty, M.I., 1989, Economic analysis of employment, income and consumption pattern of tribal farmers, *Journal of Rural Development* 8(1) January, p 97-108, tables.

ECONOMIC BACKWARDNESS

Hegde, Ramakrishna, 1990, Hedge for economic criterion, *Indian Express*, September 19, p 9.

Sheth, D.L., 1986 The problem of reservations : Economic backwardness and social injustice, *Indian Journal of Adult Education* 47(5) May, p 9-15; 47(6) June, p 4-7 +; 47(7) July, p 14-21.

ECONOMIC CONDITIONS : TRIBALS

Vyas, N.N., 1968, Economic aspect of tribal life, *Rural India* 31(6) July-August, p 216-218, tables.

ECONOMIC CO-OPERATION : TRIBALS

Sachchidananda, 1954, Economic co-operation in tribal India, *Man in India* 34(3)

July-September, p 220-224.

ECONOMIC DETERMINANTS : WAGHERS : INDIA : GUJARAT

Bajpai, Geeta, 1983, Economic determinants of social behaviour : A case study of the Waghers of Gujarat in the second half of the nineteenth century, *Journal of the Gujarat Research Society* 45(3) July, p 32-41, bibliography, footnotes.

ECONOMIC DEVELOPMENT : INDIA

Anon, 1985, (Book Review), *Rajasthan Economic Journal* 9(1) January, p 67-68. Review of the book: **Trivedi, Hari Vallash**, 1985, *Economic development of tribes in India*, Himanshu Publication, Udaipur, 195 p.

Kulkarni, M.G., 1985, Economic development of tribal people, *Tribal Research Bulletin* 7(2) March.

Sachchidananda, 1988, Economic development, education and social change in Arunachal Pradesh, *Man in India* 65(1) March, p 33-57.

ECONOMIC DIFFERENTIATIONS : TRIBALS

Anon, 1985, (Book review), *Tribune*, June 15, p 4, col 3-4. Review of the book: **Shah Ghanshyam**, 1985, *Economic differentiations and tribal economy*, Ajanta Publication, Delhi, 152 p.

ECONOMIC EXCHANGES : TRIBALS

Baboo, Balgovind, 1986, Economic exchange in a tribal village, *Man in India* 66(2) June, p 151-165.

ECONOMIC OPPORTUNITIES : SCHEDULED CASTES AND SCHEDULED TRIBES : INDIA

Premi, Kusum K., 1984, Educational equality and economic opportunities: A comparative study of Scheduled Castes and non-Scheduled Castes, *Journal of Higher Education* 9(3) Spring, p 363-72, references, tables.

Sivananda, P., 1979, Caste, class and economic opportunity in Kerala: An empirical analysis, *Economic and Political Weekly*, 14, Annual Number, February, p 475-480.

ECONOMIC ORGANISATION : TRIBALS : INDIA : MADHYA PRADESH

Anon, 1964, Economic organization of the tribes of Madhya Pradesh, *Bulletin of Tribal Research and Development institute* (Chhindwara) 4(2) December, 1-32, tables.

ECONOMIC PROJECTS : GONDS : INDIA : ORISSA

Mohapatra, K., 1964, Action programme on economic projects among the Gonds of Orissa, *Adibasi*, November, p 23-28.

ECONOMIC STATUS : SCHEDULED CASTES : INDIA : RAJASTHAN

Goel, N.P., et al, 1986, Changes in socio-economic status of the Scheduled Caste population in rural Rajasthan : 1961-1981, *Rajasthan Economic Journal* 10(1) January, p 65-73, bibliography, tables.

ECONOMIC TRANSFORMATION : TRIBALS : INDIA

Anon, 1988, (Book review), *Contributions to Indian Sociology* (New Series) 20(1) January-June, p 155-158. Review of the book : **Mishra, S.N.**, 1985, *Tribal economic transformation: The North East Indian pattern*, Institute of Development Economics, Tokyo, 88 p.

ECONOMIC TRANSITION : CASTES AND TRIBES

Anon, 1988, Castes and tribes in economic transition : A regional study, *Arthaniti*, 25, p 46-64.

ECONOMICS : PRIMITIVE

Halpern, Joel Martin, 1958-1959, Trade patterns in Northern Laos, *Eastern Anthropologists* 12(2) December-February, p 119-124.

Sachchidananda, 1954, Economic co-operation in tribal India, *Man in India* 34(3) July-September, p 220-224.

ECONOMY : TRIBALS

See Tribal Economy

ECOSYSTEM : TRIBALS

Maheshwari, J.K., 1987, Tribal ecosystem : An overview, *Tribal Research Bulletin* 9(2) march, p 1-4 +.

EDUCATED TRIBALS : INDIA

Patel, M.L., 1970, Spatial mobility of unemployed educated tribals of Mandala district, *Vanyajati* 18(2) April, p 70-76, references, tables.

EDUCATION

Anon, 1986, (Book review), *Socialist Perspective* 13(4) March, p 275-278; *Journal of Sociological Studies*, January 6, p 187-190.

Review of the Book : **Bag, Dulal Chandra** 1984, *Impact of education on some backward communities of West Bengal*, OPS Publishing, Calcutta.

Bennur, C.S., 1967, Education and prejudice. *Progress of Education* 41(8) March, p 294-98 +.

Bapat, N.V., 1962, Education of the Aborigines: *Educational Review* 68(7) July, p 161-165

[From the Presidential address to the Aborigines Education Section at the last All India Education Conference.]

Bernard, Thomas L., 1969, Implications of social class factors in contemporary English secondary education, *Indian Sociological Bulletin* 6(2) January, p 104-106, references.

Das, Amal Kumar, 1962, Influence of city life on educated tribals, *Bulletin of Cultural Research Institute* 1(2), p 69-78, tables.

Hasan, Amir, 1968, A note on education among the Kols of Uttar Pradesh, *Eastern Anthropologist* 21(1) January-April, p 83-86.

Minz, Nirmal, 1987, Religion, culture and education in the context of tribal aspirations in India, *Journal of Dharma* 12(2) April-June, p 150-164, bibliography, footnote.

Prasad, S., 1975, Implications of the 10+2+3 patterns for the education of tribal children, *Journal of Indian Education* 1(1) May p 75-79.

Rajaiah, B., 1982, Reservations in higher education and jobs, *Educational Review* 88(3), p 55-58.

Sachchidananda, 1988, Economic development, education and social change in Arunachal Pradesh, *Man in India* 65(1) March, p 33 57.

Seerval, H.M., 1985, Reservation in education and public service, *Monthly Commentary on Indian Economic Conditions* 27(1) August, p 79-86.

Shrivastava, L.R.N., 1968, Plans and programmes of social education for the tribal people, *Bulletin of Cultural Research Institute* 7(1-2) p 39-50.

See also Employment Bias: Education: Tribals; Pedagogy.

EDUCATION COMMISSION, 1964, DELHI

Anon, 1966, Education Commission, Government of India : Questionnaire on the education of the backward classes, *Vanyajati* 14(3) July, p 139-144.

Shrikant, L.M., 1966, Education Commission and backward classes, *Vanyajati* 14(3) July, p 95-98.

Srivastava, B.N., 1966, Education Commission and tribal education, *N I E Journal* 1(2) November, p 78-82.

EDUCATIONAL BACKWARDNESS : TRIBAL STUDENTS

Sharma, K.R., 1983, A study of educational backwardness of tribal students, *Education Quarterly* 35(2) April, p 33-38.

See also Backwardness; Scholastic Backwardness: Tribal Children.

EDUCATIONAL FACILITIES : TRIBAL STUDENTS

Lakshmaiah, T. and **Yadappanavar, Arvind**, 1988, A survey of educational facilities for tribal students : Problems and impact in Paderu Samithi in Andhra Pradesh, *Man in India* 68(4) December, p 380-400.

EDUCATIONAL IMPACT : BACKWARD CLASSES COMMISSION

Amrik Singh, 1990, Mandal Commission : Educational Impact, *Times of India*, August 18.

EDUCATIONAL OPPORTUNITIES : SCHEDULED CASTES

Sivadasan Pillai, K., 1988, Equality of educational opportunities and the Scheduled Castes, *Progressive Education Herald* (3)(1) October, p 40-42.

EDUCATIONAL RESERVATIONS

Patwardhan, Vidya and **Palshikar, Vasant**, 1990, Are educational reservations a waste? : The results of a survey, *Janata*, 45, Annual Number, p 35-39.

See also Reservation Issues.

EDUCATIONAL STAGNATION : TRIBAL CHILDREN

Ahuja, G.C., 1980, Educational wastage and stagnation among tribal children, *Journal of Indian Education* 6(1) May, p 58-70, references, tables.

EDUCATIONAL TECHNOLOGY FOR DEPRIVED SECTION

Sharma, R.S., 1985, Developing educational technology for deprived sections of the Indian society, *Bulletin of Non-formal Education* 3(3) December, p 1-17.

EDUCATIONAL WASTAGE : TRIBAL CHILDREN

Ahuja, G.C., 1980, Educational wastage and stagnation among tribal children, *Journal of Indian Education* 6(1) May, p 58-70, references, tables.

EGGS : IMPORTANCE IN KHASI AND JAINTIA HILLS

Paul, Gemini, 1957, Importance of egg and cock in Khasi and Jaintia hills, *Vanyajati* 5(2) April, p 66-69, references.

ELECTRIC MOTOR PUMPS : IMPACT ON TRIBALS

Gaikwad, John S., 1987, Transformation of economy of the tribal cultivators through the electric motor pumps, *Tribal Research Bulletin* 9(2) March, p 18-20.

EMPLOYMENT : TRIBALS

Chakravarty, M.I., 1989, Economic analysis of employment, income and consumption pattern of tribal farmers, *Journal of Rural Development*, 8(1) January, p 97-108, tables.

EMPLOYMENT BIAS : EDUCATION : TRIBALS

Shyam Manohar, 1964, Education in tribal areas with employment bias, *Indian Education* 3(10), p 18-24.

EMPLOYMENT PATTERN

Sharma, H.R., et al, 1987, Pattern of income, consumption and employment, *Economic Affairs* 32(2) June, p 81-88, appendix, tables.

EMPOWERMENT

Jetley, Surinder, 1968, Transfer of power to a low caste, *Interdiscipline* 5(3) Autumn, p 199-206.

ENDOGAMOUS COMMUNITIES : INDIA : WEST BENGAL

Gangopadhyay, Prodyot and **Kundu, Shampa**, 1988, Familial trend in arterial pressure among few endogamous communities of West Bengal reared under occupational environment, *Man in India* 68(2-3) June-September, p 225-242, bibliography.

ENTREPRENEURIAL SUCCESS : TRIBALS

Jarial, Gurpal Singh, 1984, Creativity as a prediction of entrepreneurial success among tribals, *Experiments in Education* 11(12) February, p 110-114, references.

ENVIRONMENTAL EFFECTS : TRIBALS : INDIA

Banerjee, Biswanath, 1968, Relation between environment and culture among some Indian primitive communities living in the hills, *Bulletin of Cultural Research Institute* 7(1-2), p 55-61, references.

Buzarburua, P.M., 1989, Effects of migration and environment on anthropometric characters of Munda population of Assam: A preliminary observation, *Man in India* 69(3) September, p 292-304.

Roy Burman, J.J., 1990, Environmental management in tribal areas through social forestry, *Vanyajati* 38(1) January, p 26-32.

Singh, K.S., 1990, Environment, technology and management in tribal areas, *Man in India* 70(2) June, p 123-130.

ENVIRONMENTAL HAZARDS : TRIBALS : INDIA

Chakravarti, M.R., et al, 1988, Environmental hazards in reproduction performance among Chotanagpur tribals, South Bihar, India, *Journal of Indian Anthropological Society* 20(2) July, p 137-140, bibliography, tables.

EQUALITY

Anon, 1984, (Book review), *Journal of Management* 14(1) September, p 104-107.

Review of the book: **Galanter, Marc**, 1984, *Competing equalities : Law and backward classes in India*, Oxford University Press, New Delhi, 650 p.

_____, 1986, (Book review), *Economic and Political Weekly* 21(33) August 16, p 1451-1454.

Review of the book: **Galanter, Marc**, 1984, *Competing equalities: Law and backward classes in India*, Oxford University Press, New Delhi, 650 p.

Chitnis, Suma, 1972, Education and equality, *Economic and Political Weekly* 7(31,

32, 33), p 1975-1981.

Man Mohan, 1987, In search of equality, *Hindustan Times* (Magazine) September 27, p 1, col 1-6.

Premi, Kusum K., 1984, Educational equalily and economic opportunities: A comparative study of Scheduled Castes and non-Scheduled Castes, *Journal of Higher Education* 9(3) Spring, p 363-372, references, tables.

Sharma, K.R., 1983, Scheduled Tribes and equality of educational opportunity, *Indian Education* 12(10) January, p 10-13.

Sundaresan, V. and **Subba Reddy, B.V.**, 1982, Equality for tribals : The role of education, *Experiments in Education* 9(12) February, p 213-215.

Uplaonkar, A.T., 1989, Protective discrimination and the equality of opportunity, *Social Change* 19(3) September, p 3-15.

EQUALISATION : EDUCATIONAL OPPORTUNITIES

Anon, 1980, (Book review), *Journal of Indian Education* 6(1) May, p 78-79.
Review of the book : **Nautiyal, K.C.** and **Sharma, Y.D.**, 1980, *Equalisation of educational opportunities for Scheduled Castes and Scheduled Tribes*, National Council of Educational Research and Training, New Delhi.

ETHNIC POLITICS

Kamalakar, Jaya, 1988, Ethnic politics in municipal corporations, *Economic and Political Weekly* 23(19) May 7, p 945-946.

ETHNOGRAPHY : INDIA

Anon, 1964, Tribal ethnography of Orissa, *Adibasi*, January, p 41 + illustrations.

Campbell, J., 1956, Ethnography of India, *Journal of Asiatic Society of Bengal*, 35.

Pant, Rashmi, 1987, The cognitive status of caste in colonial ethnography : A review of some literature on the North West Province and Oudh, *Indian Economic Social History Review* 24(2) April-June, p 145-162.

ETHNOLOGY

Ferreira, John V., 1964, Ethnology and history, *Sociological Bulletin* 13(1) March, p 1-11, references.

ETHNOPOLITICAL ISSUES : ASIA : SOUTH EAST

Laiq, Jawid, 1988 , Ethnopolitical issues in South East Asia, *Economic and Political Weekly* 23(18) April 30, p 909-917.

ETHNOZOOLOGY : TRIBAL AREAS : INDIA : MADHYA PRADESH

Joseph, A.N.T., 1989, Ethnozoology of reptiles in relation to health care among tribals in Madhya Pradesh, *Social Action* 39(4) October-December, p 405-422.

EXCLUSION : TRIBALS : CONSTITUTIONAL PROVISION : INDIA

Roy Burman, B.K., 1966, Questions relating to inclusion in and exclusion from the list of Scheduled Tribes, *Journal of Indian Anthropological Society* 1(1) March, p 7-14, references, illustration.

EXCRIMINAL TRIBES : INDIA

Kurian, K.V., 1985, The ex-criminal tribes of North Karnataka : A study, *Quarterly Journal of Mythic Society* 76(3-4) July-December, p 366-377.

Lala, Arjun, 1956, Welfare of tribes including ex-criminal tribes, *Indian Journal of Social Work* 16(4) March, p 300-305.

Sher, Sher Singh, 1960, Ex-criminal tribes of Northern India need reclassification

on more authentic and scientific grounds, *Journal of Social Research* 3(2) September, p 35-42, tables.

See also Criminal Tribes

EXECUTIVE MEASURES : TRIBAL WELFARE : INDIA : KERALA

Karunakaran, C.K., 1985, Legislative and executive measures for tribal welfare in Kerala, *Cochin University Law Review* 9(1-2) March-June, p 208-212.

EXPLOITATION OF TRIBALS : INDIA

Anon, 1958, The exploitation of Kerala tribals, *Link* 28(4) September 1, p 16-18.

Jena, A.C., 1986, Form of exploitation in tribals areas and their consequences : Some observation in Keonjhar district of Orissa, *Man and Life* 12(3-4) July-December, p 173-180, bibliography.

Mitra, Ashok T., 1968, Tribal exploitation: An overview, *Mainstream* 26(33) May 28, p 32-34.

EXTENSION PROJECTS : TRIBAL AREAS : INDIA

Mehta, B.H., 1962, Social experiments in extension projects : The Balvadi in tribal areas, *Indian Journal of Social Work* 23(1) April, p 53-56.

EXTERIOR CASTES

See Backward Classes; Scheduled Castes and Scheduled Tribes; Untouchability.

EXTINCTION : TRIBALS

Jabbar Alam, M., 1985, Tribals starving to extinction, *New Age* 35(25) June 23, p 5.

Pardesi, Ghanshyam, 1986, The Taraos: Threatened with extintion, *Indian Express* (Magazine), August 17, p 4, col 1-8.

EZHAVAS : INDIA : KERALA

Sukumaran, Tatapuram, 1984, The Ezhavas in Kerala, *Malayalam Literature Survey* 8(3-4) July-December, p 11-17, bibliography, footnotes.

FAMILIAL TREND : ENDOGAMOUS COMMUNITIES : INDIA : WEST BENGAL

Gangopadhyay, Prodyot and **Kundu, Shampa**, 1988, Familial trend in arterial pressure among few endogamous communities of West Bengal reared under diverse occupational environment, *Man in India* 68(2-3) June-September, p 235-242, bibliography.

FAMILY COMPOSITION : TRIBALS : INDIA : WEST BENGAL

Das, Amal Kumar and **Banerjee, Swapan Kumar**, 1963, The 'family' of tribals of West Bengal : Static and dynamic aspects of composition, *Bulletin of Cultural Research Institute* 2(1), p 12-21.

FAMILY PLANNING

Chatterjee, B.B., 1970, Functional literacy for family planning in tribal areas, *Indian Journal of Adult Education* 31(1) January, p 12-13+.

Naik, Shukadeb and **Sharma, A.K.**, 1985, Social structure and family planning : A case study of two tribal villages, *Journal of Family Welfare* 32(1) September, p 50-58, bibliography.

Ramachandra Reddy, M. and **Chengal Reddy, P.**, 1989, Family planning behaviour in the Sugalis of Andhra Pradesh, *Vanyajati* 37(1) January, p 3-8.

Roy Burman, B.K., 1958, Problem of family planning among the Scheduled Tribes of West Bengal, *Vanyajati* 6(4) October, p 160-164.

——, 1970, Family planning from the point of view of cultural anthropology, *Indian Journal of Social Work* 30(4) January, p 343-353, references.

FAMILY SYSTEM : TRIBALS : INDIA : ARUNACHA PRADESH

Bachi, R.N., Family system and inheritance of property among the tribes of Arunachal Pradesh, *Resarun* 5(1) Spring-Summer, p 38-41, bibliography.

FARMERS

See also Land owning peasants; Peastans: India: Goa.

FARMERS : TRIBALS

See Tribal Farmers.

FEMALE INFANTICIDE : TRIBALS

Das, M.N., 1966, Female infanticide among the Bedees and the Chouhans : Motives and Modes, *Man in India* 36 (4) October.

FEMALE LABOUR PARTICIPATION

Bose, Sukla, 1985, Caste, tribe and female labour participation, *Social Change* 15(2) June, p 15-20, bibliography, tables.

FEMALE WORKERS

Bose, Sukla, 1985, Caste, tribe and female labour participation, *Social Change* 15(2) June, p 15-20, bibliography, tables.

FERTILITY : TRIBALS : INDIA

Nagdo, B.L., 1988, Socio-cultural mores and high fertility among tribes in Banswara, *Social Welfare* 34(11) February, p 14-15 +.

FERTILITY BEHAVIOUR : TRIBALS : INDIA : ANDHRA PRADESH

Ramachandra Reddy, M. and **Chengal Reddy, P.**, 1986, Fertility behaviour in the Sugalis of Chittoor district, Andhra Pradesh, *Health and Population* 9(4) October-December, p 205-217.

FESTIVALS : TRIBALS : INDIA

Basu, Sunil Kumar, 1969, A note on important festivals among the major tribals of West Bengal, *Bulletin of Cultural Research Institute* 8(3-4), p 17-33, tables.

Behura, N.K. and **Misra, K.K.**, 1985, Religious rites and festivals among the tribes of Orissa, *Vision* 4(4), April-September, p 66-86, bibliography.

Dubey, S.N., 1964, Celebration os Diwali among the gonds of Tamia, *Bulletin of Tribal Research and Development Institute* (Bhopal) 4(1) June, p 37-43.

Durah, D.K., 1985, Festival of the Nishis of Arunachal Pradesh, *Resarun* 11(2) Autumn-Winter, p 29-31.

Sankaranarayan, A.S. and **Lakshmanan, K.K.**, 1987, A tribal festival in Attapady, Kerala: An aspect of worship of nature as God, *Folklore* 28(10) October, p 235-236.

FINGER PATTERNS : TRIBALS : INDIA : ARUNACHAL PRADESH

Sengupta, S. and **Dutta, M.N.**, 1985, A note on ridge count of finger patterns of the Wanchos of Arunachal Pradesh, *Resarun* 11(2) Autumn-Winter, p 23-26, bibliography, tables.

FINGER PRINTS : TRIBALS : INDIA

Sarkar, S.S., 1957, Finger prints of Orissan Aborigines, *Man in India* 37(3) July-September, p 182-191, references, tables.

Sengupta, Sarthak, 1984, Finger prints of the Bangnis of Arunachal Pradesh, *Resarun* 19(1) Spring-Summer, p 25-30, bibliography, tables.

FISH CULTURE : TRIBAL AREAS

Das, A.K., 1965, Prospects of fish culture in tribal area, *Man in India* 45(4) October-December, p 316-321, references.

FISHING METHODS : INDIA : ORISSA

Das, Harish Chandra, 1963-1964, The seafisherman of North Balasore and their way of fishing, *Adibasi* 5(2), p 25-28.

FIVE YEAR PLANS : TRIBAL WELFARE : INDIA

Anon, 1953, Scheme of the Assam State Government for the welfare of Scheduled Tribes, included in the Five Year Plan, *Vanyajati* 1(3) July, p 71-72.

——, 1956, Scheduled Tribes under the Five Year Plans, *Vanyajati* 4(4) October, p 97-99 +.

——, 1965, Report of the planning committee of the B.A.J. Sevak Sangh on 4th Five Year Plan on tribal welfare, *Vanyajati* 13(2) April, p 79-84.

Bhupinder Singh, 1984, Tribal development in retrospect and prospect : Sixth Plan mid-term appraisal, *Indian Journal of Public Administration* 30(4) October-December, p 1064-1081, tables.

FOLK CULTURE INSTITUTE

Chanderverker, Pushker, 1961, A scheme for Folk Culture Institute in Gujarat, *Folklore* 2(5) September-October, p 318-322.

FOLK SONGS

Upadhyaya, Ram Narain, 1959, The Nimadi folk songs, *Indian Folklore* 2(4) October-December, p 298-299.

See also Songs: Tribals.

FOOD AND DIETARY PRACTICES : TRIBALS : INDIA : ANDHRA PRADESH

Rajyalakshmi, P. and **Geervani, P.**, 1988, Tribal people: Traditions customs and attitudes related to food and dietary practices : A case study Vizianagram district, Andhra Pradesh, *Indian Journal of Social Work* 49(1) January, p 45-50.

FOOD GRAINS FOR TRIBALS

Satyanarayanana, T.V., 1986, Cheaper foodgrains for tribals, *Indian and Foreign Review* 23(16) June 16, p 8-9.

——, 1986, Subsidised foodgrains for tribals, *Yojna* 30(7) April 16, p 19-20.

FOREIGN MISSIONS AMONG TRIBALS

Mac Naughton, A., 1953, Foreign missions and their work among tribal peoples, *Indian Journal of Social Work* 14(3) December, p 276-81.

FOREST AREAS : INDIA : RAJASTHAN

Sebastian, M.K. and **Bhandari, M.M**, 1984, Cultivation of wild plants for the uplift of tribals in the forest areas of Rajasthan, *Tribe* 16(3-4) September, p 30-35, bibliography.

FOREST BILL OF 1980

Srivastava, Ratish, 1984, Tribals of Madhya Pradesh and Forest Bill of 1980, *Man in India* 64(3) September, p 320-327.

See also Forest Legislation: Tribals.

FOREST CO-OPERATIVE SOCIETIES : INDIA

Shrikant, L.M., 1970, Seminar on tribal forest labour co-operatives, *Vanyajati* 18(2) April, p 49-50.

Wandrekar, D.N., 1966, The progress of the movement of the forest labourer's co-operatives, *Vanyajati* 14(4) October, p 165-170.

——, 1967, Forest labour co-operatives or corporations, *Vanyajati* 15(4) October, p 184-187.

——, 1968, Co-operatives and the forest workers, *Vanyajati* 16(1) January, p 5-10, illustrations.

See also Cooperative Societies.

FOREST CO-OPERATIVE SOCIETIES : INDIA : MAHARASHTRA : BOMBAY

Shrikant, L.M., 1954, Forest co-operative societies in Bombay, *Vanyajati* 2(3) July, p 94-99.

FOREST DWELLERS : INDIA

Anon, 1986, (Book Review), *Indian and Foreign Review* 24(8) February 15, p 26.

Review of the book: **Chatrapati Singh**, 1986, *Common prosperity and common poverty : India's forests, forest dwellers and the law*, Oxford University Press, Delhi, 76 p.

Tripathy, Sangam, 1989, A silent revolution of forest dwellers and tribals, *Janata* 44(7) April 9, p 15-16.

FOREST ECONOMY

Anon, 1987, (Book Review), *Indian Express* (Magazine) January 10, p 5, col 6-8.

Review of the book: **Fernandes, Walter** and **Menon, Geeta**, 1987, *Tribal women and forest economy*, Indian Social Institute, New Delhi.

Mehta, B.H., 1959, Tribal welfare and forest economy, *Journal of Social Research* 2(1-2) March-September, p 72-81.

FOREST LEGISLATION : TRIBALS

Kulkarni, Sharad, 1987, Forest legislation and tribals : Comments on Forest Policy Resolution, *Economic and Political Weekly* 22(50) December 12, p 2143-2148.

See also Forest Bill of 1980.

FOREST POLICY RESOLUTION : TRIBALS

Kulkarni, Sharad, 1987, Forest legislation and tribals : Comments on Forest Policy Resolution, *Economic and Political Weekly* 22(50) December 12, p 2143-2148.

FOREST PRODUCE : TRIBAL ECONOMY

Gaikwad, John S., 1986, Role of minory forest produce in tribal economy, *Tribal Research Bulletin* 8(2) March, p 12-16.

FORESTRY : TRIBALS

Mehta, B.H., 1966, Forestry and tensions in tribal area, *Journal of Social Research* 9(2) September, p 10-25.

Brij Raj Singh and **Thapar, Rajiv**, 1985, Forestry and tribal development, *Link* (Supplement) 27(26) February 3, p 24-28.

FORESTS AND TRIBALS

Anon, 1985, (Book review), *Economic and Political Weekly* 23(4) January 23, p 148; *Patriot*, January 31, p 4, col 3.7.

Review of the book : **Basu, N.G.**, 1987, *Forests and tribals*, Manish Granthalya, Calcutta, vi, 196 p.

Bhaskara Rao, Digumastha, 1984, Educational problems of tribal children of forest and hill areas, *Experiments in Education* 12(1) March, p 15-18.

Gangwar, A.K., 1990, Tribals and forests of North-Eastern India : Strategies for sustainable development, *Vanyajati* 38(2) April, p 14-21.

Leelakrishnan, P., et al, 1985, Forests and tribal people : Law and practice, *Cochin University Law Review* 9(1-2) March-June, p 259-270 +.

Raha, Manis Kumar, 1963, Forest in tribal life, *Bulletin of Cultural Research Institute* 2(1), p 56-61, footnotes.

Zutshi, G.L., 1961, Place of forests in tribal economy, *Vanyajati* 9(1) January, p 32-36.

FUNCTIONAL LITERACY : TRIBALS

Chatterjee, B.B., 1970, Functional literacy for family planning in tribal areas, *Indian Journal of Adult Education* 31(1) January, p 12-13 +.

See also Informal Education; Non Formal Education.

FUNDAMENTAL RIGHTS

Chatterjee, Ramananda, 1933, A fundamental right, *Social Service Quarterly* 18(4) April, p 125.

FUNERARY CUSTOMS : INDIA

Elwin, Verrier, 1945, Funerary custom in Bastar state, *Man in India* 25(2) June, p 87-133.

See also Dead Persons: Desposal of Corpse: India: Mortuary Practices; Nigeria: North Eastern.

GADABAS

Khan, M.Y., 1990, Kinship in the Gadabas of Bastar, *Man in India* 70(2) June, p 192-194.

Paddiash, G. and **Reddy, G.G.**, 1982, Finger dermatoglyphics of the Gadaba, *Indian Journal of Physical Anthropology and Human Genetics* 8(1) April, p 57-62, bibliography, tables.

Ramadas, G., 1931, The Gadabas, *Man in India* 11(2) April-June, p 160-173.

Sahu, L.N., 1954, The Gadabas, *Vanyajati* 2(2) April, p 61-63.

——, 1957-58, The Gadabas, *Adibasi* 2(1), p 27-30.

Satpathy, Gopinath, 1964, Gadabas, *Adibasi*, January, p 151-156.

Somasundram, A.M., 1949, A note on the Gadabas of Koraput district, *Man in India* 29(1) January-March, p 35-45.

GADDIS

Shashi, S.S., 1969, A sociological study of the Gaddi tribe in Himachal Pradesh, *Tribe*, 4, June, 32.

——, 1970, Folk dances and dances of the Gaddis, *Folklore*, 11, March, p 91.

——, 1970, A sociological study of the Gaddi tribe in Himachal Pradesh, *Indian Behavioural Science Abstract* 1(3) July, p 259.

——, 1971, The Gaddis of the Himalayas, *Children's World*, August 29, p 11.

——, 1971, Songs and dances of the Gaddis, *Caravan* p 14.

——, 1973, Gaddi women of Himachal, *Hindustan Times* (Sunday Magazine) March 25, p 8, col. 1-4.

GADIA LOHARS

Jayaram, K.V., 1986, They carry on the tradition, *Economic Trends* 27(4) April, p 1-5.

GALLONG ADIS

See Adi Gallongs.

GALLONGS

Kumar, K., 1955, Traditional beverage of the Gallongs of Arunachal Pradesh, *Resarun* 11(2) Autumn-Winter, p 4-7.

Ray, P.C., 1955, The tensional feeling among the Abors and Gallongs indicated by Rorschach Techniques, *Indian Journal of Psychology* 30(1-2), p 95-103.

GAM LYNGNS

See Khasis.

GANDHI, INDIRA : VIEWS ON CASTE

Jain, Meenakshi, 1985, Coping with dominant castes : Ignored aspect of Mrs. Gandhi's politics, *Times of India*, June 17, p 8, col 3-5; June 18, p 8, col 7-8; June 19, p 6, col 7-8.

GANDHI, MOHANDAS KARAMCHAND : VIEWS ON UNTOUCHABILITY

Anon, 1932, The curse of untouchability, *Social Service Quarterly* 18(2) October, p 64-65.

Lele, P.R., 1933, Worthy of the forgiveness untouchability : Changed angle of vision, *Social Service Quarterly* 18(3) January, p 83-86.

Sachchidananda, 1970, Untouchability and Gandhi, *Interdiscipline* 7(4) Winter, p 37-47, references.

GARASIA BHILS

See Bhils; Garasias.

GARASIA DUNGRIS

See Bhils; Garasias

GARASIAS : INDIA : RAJASTHAN

Kundu, N.N., 1985, Tribal fair : A source of acquiring a mate : A study of Garasia, a Scheduled Tribe of Rajasthan, *Folklore* 26(5) May, p 91-94.

See also Bhils.

GARO HILLS : INDIA : MEGHALAYA

Burling, Robbins, 1960, An incipient caste organisation in the Garo hills, *Man in India* 40(4) October-December, p 238-299, references.

GAROS

Bose, J.K., 1938, Ordeals among the Garos, *Man in India* 18(2-3) April-September, p 174-176.

Mukherjee, Bhabananda, 1957, Garo family, *Eastern Anthropologist* 11(1) September-November, p 25-30, references.

Raha, Manis Kumar, 1966, The Garos, *Bulletin of Cultural Research Institute* 5(1-2), p 26-35, references, tables.

GHOLENG SCHOOL

Shamsuddin, 1966, Gholeng school : Adivasis' heaven, *Educational India* 33(4) October, p 123-126, illustrations.

GIPSIES

See Gypsies.

GIRLS

Gupta, Jaya Dutta, 1960, Ponung or girls' association among the Padam Abor in the lower Abor hills, *Bulletin of Anthropological Survey of Indian* 9(2) July, p 71-73.

Mukherjee, D.P. and **Das, N.K.**, 1985, Age at menarche in tribal girls: The Kanwar and Oraon of Surguja district, M.P., *Journal of Indian Anthropological Society* 20(2) July, p 153-158, bibliography, tables.

Patel, Harbans, 1985, Why tribal girls stay away : A case study in Gujarat, *Mainstream* 24(3) October 26, p 26-28, tables.

See also Daughters; Koles: Girls; Tribal Girls.

GNYATI-BANDAN

Bulsara, Jal F., 1958, Gnyati-Bandan or caste barriers : What are they?, *Indian Journal of Adult Education* 19(3) October, p 5-12 +.

See also Caste : Barriers.

GOA : INDIA

Anon, 1968, Goa peasants on hunger-strike, *People's Democracy* 4(11) March 17, p 5.

Mascarenhas, Antonio, 1984, Conversion : Coercion or conviction?, *Goa Today* 19(1) August, p 31-35.

Nair, P.K, 1970-1978, Welfare scheme for Goa miners, *Social Welfare* 24(9-10) December-January, p 71-73 +.

See also Geographical Area subdivision 'Goa' under main Descriptor.

GOND ARAKHS / GOND ARRAKHS

See Gonds.

GOND ASURS

See Gonds.

GOND BADAS

See Gonds; Marias.

GOND BHARS

See Gonds.

GOND BHATOLAS

See Gonds.

GOND BHIMMAS

See Gonds.

GOND BHUTAS

See Gonds.

GOND BISON HORN MARIAS
See Bison Horn Maria

GOND CHOTU MARIAS
See Gonds

GOND DANDAMI MARIAS
See Gonds.

GOND DHOBAS
See Gonds.

GOND DHULIAS
See Gonds.

GOND DORLAS
See Dorlas; Gonds.

GOND GAIKES
See Gonds.

GOND GAITAS
See Gonds.

GOND GOWARIS
See Gonds.

GONDOS
See Gonds.

GONDS

Acharya, P., 1938, Note on the Dharuas or the Gonds of Mayurbhanj State, *Man in India* 18(2-3) April-September, p 163-167.

Buradkar, M.P., 1940, Totemism among the Gonds, *Man in India* 20(3) July. September, p 114-143; 20(4) October-December, p 268-269, footnotes, tables.

——, 1947, The clan organisation of the Gonds, *Man in India* 27(2) June, p 127-36, footnotes.

Dubey, S.N., 1964, Celebration of Diwali among the Gonds of Tamil, *Bulletin of Tribal Research and Training Institute* (Chhindwara) 4(1) June, p 37-43.

Mehta, B.H., 1966, The heterogeneous character of clan based societies with special references to Gonds of the Central Indian high lands, *Journal of Anthropological Society of Bombay* (NS) 12(1), p 50-70.

Mehta, Behram H., 1985, Gonds of the Central Indian highlands, *Indian Journal of Social Work* 46(2) July, p 299-301.

Mohapatra, K., 1964, Action Programme on economic projects among the Gonds of Orissa, *Adibasi*, November, p 22-28.

Naik, T.B., 1965, Gond leadership, *Adibasi*, July, p 19-28.

Srivastava, P.K., 1963, The Gonds of Sagar district (M.P.): Culture contact and consequences, *Vanyajati* 11(1) January, p 12-14.

See also Hadias.

GOVERNMENT LANDS : INDIA

Bhuskute, R.V., 1989, Tribals, Dalits and government lands, *Economic and Political*

Weekly 24(23) June, p 1265-1268, tables.

GOVERNMENT ORGANISATIONS : ROLE IN TRIBAL WELFARE : INDIA : MADHYA PRADESH

Mehta, Shalini, 1988, Role of voluntary and government organisations in tribal welfare : A case study of Mandala district of M.P., *Eastern Anthropologist* 41(1) January-March, p 49-64, tables.

GOVERNMENT STAFF : INDIA

Anon, 1985, Government Staff in Gandhi Nagar strike work, *Times of India*, May 1, p 1, col 7-8.

GRAM PANCHAYATS : TRIBALS REPRESENTATION

Sahay, B.N. and **Singh, B.K.**, 1969, Representation of tribals in gram panchayats, *Journal of Social Research* 12(2) September, p 130-136, references, tables.

——, 1970, Political consciousness among the tribals and their representation in gram panchayats, *Vanyajati* 18(1) January, p 12-16, tables.

GRAMDAN

Vinoba Bhave, 1958, Tribal welfare workers and their role in gramdan work, *Vanyajati* 6(4) October, p 143-145 +.

GREEN REVOLUTION : IMPACT ON TRIBALS : INDIA : BIHAR

Thakur, Devendra, 1985, Bihar tribals share benefits of green revolution, *Link* 28(19) December 14, p 26-27; *Monthly Commentary on Indian Economic Conditions* 27(4) November, p 7-9.

GUDUVELLA AREA : INDIA

Anon, 1968, A study on the socio-religious life of tribals in Guduvella area, Bolongir district, *Adibasi* 9(4) January, p 3-30.

GUINEA WORM DISEASE : TRIBALS

Vyas, N.N., and **Chaudhary, N.D.**, 1983, The socio-economic implications of Guinea worm: A disease in tribal setting, *Tribe* 15(1-2) March-June, p 15-26.

GUJARAT : INDIA

Abraham, A.S., 1985, Caste war in Gujarat : Wider objectives of agitation, *Times of India*, June 14, p 6 col 3-5.

Anon, 1985, Gujarat Accord, *Times of India*, July 22, p 8, col 1-2.

——, 1985, Gujarat : Threat of fresh agitation, *New Age*, November, 24, p 2.

——, 1985 Gujarat caste war, *Times of India*, April, 17, p 8, col 1-2.

Bajpai, Geeta, 1983, Economic determinants of social behaviour : A case study of the Waghers of Gujarat in the second half of the nineteenth century, *Journal of the Gujarat Research Society* 45(3) July, p 32-41, bibliography, footnotes.

Baxi, Upendra, 1985, Reflections on reservation crisis in Gujarat, *Mainstream* 23(41) June 8, p 15-22; 23(42) June 15, p 20-25; 23(43) June 22, p 20-24.

Mandal, S.K. and **Malhotra, R.**, 1984, Agrarian stratification among the Warlis of Gujarat : An observation, *Tribe* 16(3-4) September-December, p 36-43.

Mehta, Dhawal, 1985, Anti-reservation agitation in Gujarat, *Radical Humanist* 49(4) July, p 25-31.

Shah, Ghanshyam, 1987, Middle class politics : Case of anti-reservation agitation in Gujarat, *Economic and Political Weekly* (AN) 22(19-21) May, p AN155-AN72.

Vaid, Minnie, 1985, Gujarat is going the way of Assam, *Illustrated Weekly of India*

106(8) June 30, p 36-37.

See also South Gujarat; Geographical Area subdivision under main Descriptor.

GUJARS

Khayal, Gulam Nabi, 1985, The Gujjars of Kashmir : A forgotten community, *Indian Education* 13(6) October, p 1-4.

Shashi, S.S., 1973, Gujjar women, *Hindustan Times*, (Sunday Magazine), May 27, p 4., col. 1-3.

——, 1988, Gujjars : The Nomads of the Himalayas, *Kurukshetra* 36(4) January, p 13-14.

GUJARS : PHYSICAL CHARACTERISTICS

Chattopadhyay, Prashant Kumar, 1950, Some physical studies among the Gujars of Delhi, *Man in India* 50(2) April-June, p 185-88.

Uma Singh, et al, 1969, Genetic investigation of the Gujars-I: Blood groups and ABH secretion; *Anthropologist* 16(1-2), March-September, p 57-61, references, tables.

GUJARS : SOCIAL CONDITIONS

Bhardwaj, A.N., 1956, The problem of Gujar tribe, *Vanyajati* 4(4) October, p 124-126, illustrations.

GUJARS : SOCIAL LIFE AND CUSTOMS : INDIA : JAMMU AND KASHMIR

Pandit, Trilokinath, 1959, The Gujar of Kashmir Valley : Some observations on their ecology and social organisation, *Vanyajati* 7(2) April, p 64-71.

GUJARS : STATISTICS : VITAL

Pandit, T.N., 1960, Demographic study of a Gujar village *Anthropologist* 7(1-2) March-August, p 1-6, references, tables.

GUL MAHARAJ

Thakkar, A.V., et al, 1939, Gul Maharaj : The Bhil saint, *Rural India* 1(5) March, p 258-59.

GWALIOR STATE : INDIA

Mehta, Manubhai N., 1938, The Bhils of the Gwalior State, *Man in India* 18(4) October-December, p 264-284.

GYPSIES

Khan, Masood Ali, 1987, Indologist on Gypsies affinity to India, *New Age* 25 (40) 4 October, p 14.

Shashi, S.S., 1982, Origin of Gypsies, *Link*, February 28, p 17.

——, 1986, Roma : The Indian gypsies, *Indian and Foreign Review* 24(1) 31 October, p 14-15.

See also Wandering Communities.

HABITATS : TRIBALS

Shrivastava, Aruna, 1986, Tribal habitats under the impact of urbanisation and industrialisation, *Man and Life* 12(1-2) January-June, p 69-76, bibliography.

HAJANGS

See Hajongs.

HAJONGS : INDIA : MEGHALAYA

Barua, Saumitra, 1985, Red green colour blindness and earlobe attachment among the Hajongs of Meghalaya (India), *Indian Journal of Physical Anthropology and Human Genetics* 11(3) August-December, p 151-154, bibliography, tables.

HAKKIPIKKIS

Mann, R.S., 1985, Hakkipikki : Trapper and seller, *Man and Life* 11(3-4) July-December, p 221-224.

HAND CLASPING PATTERN : TRIBALS

Datta Chaudhuri, S.S., 1984, A note on hand clasping, armfolding and tongue rolling among the Muji of Arunachal Pradesh (India), *Vanyajati* 32(2) April, p 12-13.

Datta, Upali and **Ghosh, G.C.**, 1988, A study of handclasping and armfolding among the Jugi of Tripura, *Man in India* 68 (2-3) June-September, p 211-215, bibliography.

Mayanglambam, Mani Babu and **Mayanglambam, Suniti Bala**, 1989, Patterns of hand clasping, armfolding and handedness among the Phayengs of Manipur, *Man in India* 69(1) March, p 87-93.

HANDEDNESS PATTERN : TRIBALS : INDIA : MANIPUR

Mayanglambam, Mani Babu and **Mayanglambam, Suniti Bala**, 1989, Patterns of hand clasping, armfolding and handedness among the Phayengs of Manipur, *Man in India* 69(1) March, p 87-93.

HANDICRAFTS : ROLE IN TRIBAL ECONOMY

Banerjee, Swapan Kumar, 1963, Role of handicrafts in tribal economy, *Bulletin of Cultural Research Institute* 1(3), p 15-19, references.

HARIJAN SEVAK SANGH

Lele, P.R., 1934, Harijan Sevak Sangh, *Social Service Quarterly* 20(2) October, p 60-63.

Social Service Quarterly (Periodical), 1936, Harijan Sevak Sangh, Bombay, *Social Service Quarterly* 22(1) July, p 24, editorial.

HARIJANS : INDIA

Abraham, A.S., 1985, Violence against Harijans : Integral part of rural change, *Times of India*, August 16, p 6, col 3-5.

Anon, 1941, problem of dedication of Harijan girls to prostitution in Karnataka, *Rural India* 4(6) June, p 303-308.

——, 1945-1946, Chowdwar Harijan Conference, *Social Service Quarterly* 32(2) October, p 61-64; 33(1) July, p 12-21.

——, 1967, On minimising social distance existing between the upper castes and Harijans, *Interdiscipline* 4(4) Winter, p 316-321, references.

——, 1969, The outsider: The dilemma of the Harijan, *Social Action* 19(3) July-September, p 249-253.

——, 1981, (Book review), *Education Quarterly* 39(4) Winter, p 49-50.

Review of the book : **Goyal, B.R.**, 1981 *Educating Harijans*, Academic Press, Gurgaon, xvii, 129 p.

——, 1982, (Book review), *Progress of Education* 56(8) March, p 200-01; *Quest in Education* 19(1) January, p 90-94.

Review of the book : **Goyal, Bhagat Ram**, 1981, *Educating Harijans,* Academic

Press (India), Gurgaon, xvii 129 p.
——, 1987, (Book review), *Social Change* 17(3) September, p 97-99.
Review of the book : **Roy, Ramashray** and **Singh, V.B.**, 1987, *Between two worlds : A study of Harijan elites*, Discovery Publishing House, Delhi, 176 p.

Desai, Haribhai G. and **Uchat, D.A.**, 1981, Self-concept of Harijan students and attitudes of other students towards them, *Indian Educational Review* 16(3) July, p 44-50.

Jhaveri, Krishnalal H., 1933, The uplift of the Harijans, *Social Service Quarterly* 18(4) April, p 126-127.

Kamila, Bana Behari, 1983, Occupational status of parents of Harijan and Tribal Welfare Department high school students of Orissa, *National Journal of Education* 6(1) September, p 56-64, references, tables.

——, 1985-1986, A study of attitude of students towards school of Harijans and Tribal Welfare Department high schools of Orissa, *Journal of Education and Psychology* 43(3-4) October-January, p 187-192, references.

Kaujalgi, H.S., 1941, Thakkar Bappa meets the Harijans, *Rural India* 4(3) March, p 147-148.

Madhara Rau, M.S., 1940, A Harijan conference and its lessons, *Social Service Quarterly* 26(1) July, p 14-19.

Malik, Neena, 1979, Helping Harijans in Haryana, *Haryana Review* 13(2) February, p 6 +.

Mehta, Vaikunth L., 1941, Harijans and municipalities, *Social Service Quarterly* 28(2) October, p 41-48.

Panchbhai, S.C., 1967, The levels of regional and national indentification and intergroup relations among Harijans and Adivasis, *Journal of Indian Anthropological Society* 2(1) March, p 75-83, references, tables.

Rastogi, S.P., 1978, Attitudes and beliefs of Harijan students, *Journal of Higher Education* 4(2) Autumn, p 251-258.

——, 1980, The impact of Constitutional provision upon the uplift of Harijans, *Indian Educational Review* 15(4) October, p 76-80.

Raymond, L., 1952, Harijan at school, *Social Action* 1(2) March, p 398-412.

Rice, Marion J., 1980, Harijan Wasti, *Progress of Education* 55(2) September, p 51-57.

Shanker, Prem, 1968, Education and Rorschach affective factors of the Harijans, *Indian Psychological Review* 4(2) July, p 95-100, references, tables.

Social Service Quarterly (Periodical) 1923, Depressed Classes Mission Society, *Social Service Quarterly* 9(1) July, p 47-48, editorial.

—— (Periodical), 1934, Admission of Harijans to public restaurants, *Social Service Quarterly* 19(4) April, p 159-160, editorial.

——, 1934, Disabilities of depressed classes, *Social Service Quarterly* 20(1) July, 25-26, editorial.

——, 1934, Harijan uplift, *Social Service Quarterly* 19(4) April, p 160-161, editorial.

——, 1934, Mr. Bakhale's Depressed Classes (Protection of Rights) Bill, *Social Service Quarterly* 20(2) October, p 75-77.

——, 1935, An appeal to all friends of Harijans, *Social Service Quarterly* 20(3) January, p 114-115, editorial.

——, 1938, Harijans in Savantvati, *Social Service Quarterly* 24(3) January, p 129-130, editorial.

Thakkar, A.V., 1935, The Harijan problem, *Social Service Quarterly* 21(1) July, p 6-8.

Ursekar, H.S., 1970, Constitutional concern for Harijans and Adivasis, *Social Service Quarterly* 55(4) April, p 97-105.

See also Bhangis; Bombay Harijan Temple Worship Act; Chowdwar Harijan Conference; Harijan Sevak Sangh; Pulayas; Untouchability.

HARIJANS : INDIA : HARYANA

Malik, Neena, 1979, Helping Harijans in Haryana, *Haryana Review* 13(2) February, p 6 +.

Mehra, Savita et al, 1984, Status improvement of Scheduled Castes in Haryana. *Haryana Review* 18(7) July, p 16 +.

See also Scheduled Castes and Scheduled Tribes: India: Haryana.

HARIJANS : INDIA : KARNATAKA

Anon, 1941, Problems of dedication of Harijan girls to prostitution in Karnataka, *Rural India* 4(6) June, p 303-308.

HARIJANS : INDIA : MADHYA PRADESH : INDORE

Social Service Quarterly (Periodical), 1938, Harijans in Indore, *Social Service Quarterly* 23(4) April, 1938, p 173, editorial.

HARIJANS : INDIA : MAHARASHTRA : BOMBAY

Anon, 1934, Admission of Harijans to public restaurants, *Social Service Quarterly* 19(4) April, p 159-160, editorial.

HARIJANS : INDIA : ORISSA

Mohapatra, Kulamani, 1958, The changing status of Harijans in a village of Cuttack district, *Adibasi* 3(2) May-July, p 26-30.

See also Chowdwar Harijan Conference (Orissa).

HARYANA : INDIA

See also Geographical Area subdivision 'Haryana' under main Descriptor.

HATKARS : INDIA : MAHARASHTRA

Malhotra, K.C. and **Sen Gupta, B.** 1985, Absolute and fluctuating asymmetry of digital ridge counts among Hatkars of Maharashtra, *Man in India* 65(2) June, p 139-153, bibliography, tables.

HEALTH AND HYGIENE

Anon, 1938, (Book review), *Sociological Bulletin* 32(2) September, p 224-227.
Review of the book : **Vyas, N.N.** and **Mann, R.S.**, 1983, *Diseases, culture contact and tribals*, MLV Tribal Research and Training Institute, Udaipur, p 14-86.

——, 1983, Health and hygiene, *Sociological Bulletin* 32(2) September, p 224-227.

See also Tribes and Tribals: Health and Hygiene.

HEALTH CARE : TRIBALS : INDIA : MADHYA PRADESH

Joseph, A.N.T., 1989, Ethnozoology of reptiles in relation to health care among tribals in Madhya Pradesh, *Social Action* 31(4) October-December, p 405-422.

HEALTH CENTRES : TRIBALS

Chakrabarti, A.K., et al, 1984, Socio-psychological correlates in the adoption of health innovations among tribals within intensive service of primary health centre, *Health and Population* 7(1) January-March, p 72-83, bibliography.

HEALTH PROBLEMS : TRIBAL WOMEN

Ramalingaswami, Prabha, 1986, Impact of social change on health problems of tribal women, *Society and Change* 16(2-3) June-September, p 100-103, bibliography, tables.

HEGDE, RAMAKRISHNA : ROLE

Anon, 1986, Mr Hegde surrenders, *Times of India*, October 9, p 8, col 1-2.

HEREDITARY PROLETARIAT

Malkani, N.R., 1970, A hereditary proletariat, *Interdiscipline* 7(4) Winter, p 32-36.

HIERARCHY : INDIA : GUJARAT

Anon, 1988, (Book review), *Hindustan Times* (Magazine) August 28, p 5, col 1-4. Review of the book : **Shah, A.M.** and **Desai, I.P.**, 1988, *Division and hierarchy : An overview of caste in Gujarat*, Hindustan Publication Corporation, Delhi, 150 p.

Shah, A.M., 1982, Division and hierarchy : An overview of caste in Gujarat, *Contributions to Indian Sociology*, New Series, 16(1), January-June, p 1-33.

HIGHER EDUCATION : SCHEDULED CASTES AND SCHEDULED TRIBES

Adiseshiah, M.S., 1975, Scheduled Castes and Tribes in higher education in Tamil Nadu, *Journal of Higher Education* 1(2), p 240-244.

Amba Rao, U., 1976, Higher education and occupational mobility among the Scheduled Caste youth, *Journal of Higher Education* 1(3) Spring, p 305-314, references, tables.

HILL AREAS

Banerjee, Biswanath, 1968, Relation between environment and culture among some Indian primitive communities living in the hills, *Bulletin of Cultural Research Institute* 7(1-2), p 55-61, references.

HILL DWELLERS

See Hill Areas; Hill Tribes; Ulladans.

HILL MARIAS

Jay, Edward J., 1959, The anthropologist and tribal welfare : Hill Maria: A case study, *Journal of Social Research* 2(2), p 82-89.

HILL MIRIS : INDIA : ARUNACHAL PRADESH

Kani, M. and **Bourai, R.A.**, 1985, Aryan tradition among Nishis and Hill Miris of lower Subawsiri district, Arunachal Pradesh, *Resarun* 11(2) Autumn-Winter, p 35-38.

HILL TRIBES

Hutton, J.H., 1929, Cultural affinities of the Oraons with the Hill Tribes of Assam, *Man in India* 9(1) January-March, p 1-6.

Krishna Iyer, L.A., 1945, The Hill-Tribes of Travancore, *Man in India* 25(3) September, p 194-198.

Meerawarth, A.M., 1989, The Andamanese, Nicobarese and Hill Tribes of Assam, *Marg* 40(4) p 90-91.

Sahu, L.N., 1959, My experiences of work among the Hill Tribes of India, *Vanyajati* 7(2) April, 49-52.

HIMACHAL PRADESH : INDIA

Amar Dev and **Banerjee Guha, Swapna**, 1986, Tribes in Himachal Pradesh: Socio-economic characteristics, *National Geographical Journal of India* 32(4) December, p 281-286.

See also Geographical Area subdivision 'Himachal Pradesh' under main Descriptor.

HINDU RELIGION

Nilkanth, Vidhya Ramanbhai, 1933, Untouchability : The supposed mainstay of Hindu religion, *Social Service Quarterly* 18(4) April, p 127-129.

HINDU TEMPLES

Anon, 1938, Admission of Harijans to Hindu temples, *Social Service Quarterly* 24(1) July, p 39-41.

HINDUISATION

Sen Gupta, A.K., 1967, Hinduisation and tribalisation : Two case studies, *Folklore* 8(12) December, p 433-438, references.

HINDUISM

Anon, 1954, On the different aspects or levels in Hinduism, *Contributions to Indian Sociology*, April 3, p 40-54.

HINDUS : COMPARISON WITH TRIBALS

Lal Bahadur Singh, et al, 1986, Modes of parental discipline among Santals and Hindus : Assessment across communities, *Indian Journal of Social Work* 47(3) October, p 315-322, bibliography, tables.

HINDUS : INTERACTION WITH TRIBALS

Chaudhuri, Buddhadeb, 1968, The nature and extent of Munda Hindu interactions, *Bulletin of Cultural Research Institute* 7(1-2), p 154-165, maps, references, tables.

HISTORICAL BACKGROUND : TRIBAL POPULATION

Mehta, B.H., 1953, Historical background of tribal population, *Indian Journal of Social Work* 14(3) December, p 236-244.

HISTORICAL PERSPECTIVE : CASTE SYSTEM

Bhattacharya, S. and **D'Almeida Fluer**, 1986, The caste system and discrimination in historical perspective, *New Frontiers in Education* 16(2) April-June, p 25-32, bibliography.

Gangmumei Kabui, 1989, Tribes in North-East India in historical perspective : The emerging pattern and the perspective for the future, *Vanyajati* 37(4) October, p 12-19.

HO TRIBES : INDIA : BIHAR : CHOTANAGPUR

Krishna Nandan Prasad, 1990, Incidence of bilingualism among the Ho-Tribes of Chotanagpur, *Man in India* 70(2) June, p 155-168.

HO WOMEN : INDIA : WEST BENGAL

Kishwar, Madhu, 1987, Toiling without rights : Ho women of Singhbhum, *Economic and Political Weekly* 28(3) 17 January, p 95-101; 22(4) 24 January, p 149-155; 22(5) 31 January, p 194-200.

HOCART, A.M. : VIEWS ON CASTE

Dumont, Louis and **Pocock, D.**, 1958, Hocart : On caste religion and power; and Bougle : The essence and reality of the cast system, *Contributions to Indian Sociology*, 2, April, p 7-30, p 45-63.

HOUSING PATTERNS : SCHEDULED CASTES

Singh, Y.P., 1986, Housing programme for Scheduled Castes in U.P., *Kurukshetra* 34(8) May, p 4-7.

Venkataramana, M., et al, 1989, Housing patterns in Scheduled Castes of Andhra Pradesh: A micro-empirical study, *Vanyajati* 37(4) October, p 62-75.

HOUSING PROBLEMS : TRIBALS

Bhattacharyya, Debasish and **Chattopadyay, R.N.**, 1987, Housing problems of dislocated tribals in industrial areas and a step towards solutions, *Man and Life* 13(1-2) January-June, p 49-55, bibliography.

Nair, S.P., 1960, Problems in tribal housing, *Vanyajati* 8(2) April, p 48-50.

HRUSSOS

Dutta, Dipak K., 1984, Dances of the Hrussos, *Resarun* 10(1) Spring-Summer, p 38-40.

HUMAN RIGHTS : SCHEDULED CASTES AND SCHEDULED TRIBES

Baxi, Upendra, 1989, Historic new law : Protecting SC/ST human rights, *Times of India,* September 1, p 3-5.

Venkataraman, S.R., 1967, Social welfare and exercise of human rights regarding tribes, *Social Service Quarterly* 53(2) October, p 54-58.

HYDERABAD : INDIA

Anon, 1954, Welfare of Hyderabad Tribes, *Indian Journal of Social Work* 15(1) June, p 59-60.

See also Geographical Area subdivision 'Hyderabad' under main Descriptor.

HYPERGAMY : INDIA : NORTHERN

Khare, R.S., 1970, On hypergamy and progeny rank determination in Northern India, *Man in India* 50(4) October-December, p 350-378 references, tables.

I R S PADDY : TRIBAL FARMERS

Bajaj, S.S., et al, 1985, Role of information sources in the adoption of IRS paddy by tribal farmers, *Tribal Research Bulletin* 7(2) March p 17-19.

IGBO OF NIGERIA

Onwurah, Emeka, 1989, Kinship and marriage among the Igbo of Nigeria, *Sevartham* 14, p 3-12, footnote.

ILLITERACY : ABORIGINES

Sharma, A.C., 1949, Illiteracy of Aborigines in India, *Educational Review* 55(4) April, p 67-69.

———, 1951, Eradication of illiteracy among Aborigines, *Educational India* 17(7) January, p 216-218.

See also Literacy : Tribals.

INCLUSION : TRIBES : CONSTITUTIONAL PROVISION : INDIA

Roy Burman, B.K., 1966, Questions relating to inclusion in and exclusion from list

of Scheduled Tribes, *Journal of Indian Anthropological Society* 1(1) March, p 7-14, references, illustrations.

INCOME PATTERN

Sharma, H.R., et al, 1987, Pattern of income, consumption and employment, *Economic Affairs* 32(2) June, p 81-88, appendix, tables.

INDEBTEDNESS

Anon, 1965, Indebtedness among the tribal people of the scheduled areas of Madhya Pradesh, *Bulletin of Tribal Research and Development Institute* (Bhopal) 5(1-2) June-December, p 1-18, tables.

Barange, B.G., 1963, An annotated bibliography on tribal indebtedness, *Bulletin of Tribal Research and Development Institute* (Chhindwara) 3(1) June, p 60-66.

Mitra, Mrinal K., et al, 1985, Some observations on rural indebtedness, *Rajasthan Economic Journal* 9(2) July, p 62-74, bibliography.

INDIA

Bhatt, G.S., 1964, Sociology and anthropology in India and the West, *Journal of Social Research* 7(1-2) March-September, p 143-152, references.

Subba, Tanka Bahadur, 1985, Caste relations in Nepal and India, *Social Change* 15(4) December, p 23-26, bibliography.

See also Geographical Area subdivision 'India', under main Descriptor, e.g. Caste: History: India.

INDIA : MEMBERS OF PARLIAMENT

See Members of Parliament: India: views on Reservation

INDIA : PRIME MINISTER

See Prime Minister: India

INDIAN ABORIGINES FRIENDS SOCIETY

Social Service Quarterly (Periodical), 1940, Indian Aborigines Friends Society, *Social Service Quarterly* 26(2) October, p 79-81, editorial.

INDIAN ARMY AND ADIVASIS

Kaul, S.K., 1955, Adivasis and Indian Army, *Vanyajati* 3(1) January, p 23-25.

INDIGENOUS POPULATION

See Natives.

INDUS VALLEY

Sarkar, Haribishnu, 1951, Disposal of the dead at the Indus valley and its survival among the Aboriginal peoples of India, *Man in India* 31(1) January-March, p 23-32, references, tables.

INDUSTRIAL AREAS : TRIBAL HOUSING PROBLEMS

Bhattacharya, Debasish and **Chattopadhyay, R.N.**, 1987, Housing problems of dislocated tribals in industrial areas and a step towards solutions, *Man and Life* 13(1-2) January-June, p 49-55, bibliography.

INDUSTRIAL CONTROL : INDIA : EASTERN

Goswami, Omkar, 1985, Then came the Marwaris : Some aspects of the changes in the pattern of industrial control in Eastern India, *Indian Economic and Social*

History Review 22(3) July-September, p 225-249, bibliography, footnotes.

INDUSTRIAL TRAINING : SCHEDULED CASTES AND SCHEDULED TRIBES

Anon, 1989, (Book review), *Tribune*, January 29, p 2, col 1-2.
Review of the book : **Premi, Kusum K.**, 1989, *Scheduled Castes and Scheduled Tribes in industrial training institutes*, Vikas Publishing, New Delhi, 134 p.

INDUSTRIALISATION

Anon, 1967, A summary of the study on impact of industrialisation on the tribals of Sundargarh district, *Adibasi* 8(4) January, p 46-51.

——, 1985, (Book review), *Contributions to Indian Sociology* (NS) 20(1) January-June, p 155-158; *Sociological Bulletin* 33(1-2) March-September, p 152-154.
Review of the book : **Sachchidananda** and **Mandal, B.B.**, 1985, *Industrialisation and the social disorganisation : A study of tribals in Bihar*, Concept Publishing Company, New Delhi, 164 p.

——, 1985, Industry, police, carpet-baggers run amuck in Chotanagpur, *Link* 27(50) July 21, p 4-9.

——, 1985, Industry takes away Adivasi land, gives jobs to outsiders, *Link* 27(50) July 21, p 10-15.

Bose, Nirmal Kumar, 1962, Some observations on industrialisation and its effects on tribals life, *Man in India* 42(1) January-March, p 5-9.

Das, Amal Kumar, 1966, Special problems in tribal transformation : Industrialisation as a means of such transformation, *Bulletin of Cultural Research Institute* 5(1-2), p 5-10, references.

Das Gupta, Pranab Kumar, 1964, Impact of industrialisation of tribal life, *Bulletin of Anthropological Survey of India* 13(1-2) January-June, p 85-96, tables.

Dayal, L., 1984, Industrialisation in tribal areas, *Bihar Journal of Public Administration* 1(1) Spring, p 62-64.

Hassan, M.K., 1986, Impact of industrialisation on mental health of tribals, *Social Change* 16(4) December, p 30-33, bibliography, tables.

Kurup, A.M., 1963, Impact of industrialisation on tribal life, *Vanyajati* 11(2) April, p 71-75.

Patnaik, K.M., 1987, Industrialisation for accelerating development in a tribal setting, *Vision* 6(3-4) January, p 52-56.

Rao, G.R.S., 1966, Process of industrialisation and direction of social changes in tribal society, *Journal of Social Research* 21(2) September, p 65-69.

Shrivastava, Aruna, 1986, Tribals habitats under the impact of urbanisation and industrialisation, *Man and Life* 12(1-2) January-June, p 69-76, bibliography.

Srivastava, R.N., 1988, Moving wheels of machine : The impact of mining industrialisation of the Bastar tribal region of Central India, *Man and Life* 14(3-4) July-December, p 119-137.

Uday Bhaskar Reddy, I., and **Chattopadhyay, R.N.**, 1986, Industrializing tribal areas: Boon or bann, *Yojana* 30(5) March 16, p 18-20.

INDUSTRIES : IMPACT ON TRIBALS : INDIA : BIHAR : CHOTANAGPUR

Anon, 1985, (Book review), *Management and Labour Studies* 10(1) January p 46-47.
Review of the book : **Biswas, R.K.**, et al, 1985, *Industries face to face with tribal people : The case of Chotanagpur in Bihar*, NIPM, Ranchi, 66 p.

INEQUALITY

Ramaswamy, Uma, 1986, Protection and inequality among backward groups, *Economic and Political Weekly* 21(9) May 1, p 399-403.

Sujatha, K., 1987, Inequality of educational development of Tribes : A case study of Andhra Pradesh, *Journal of Educational Planning and Administration* 1(2) April, p 108-125, bibliography, footnotes, tables.

INFANT MORTALITY : TRIBALS : INDIA : ANDHRA PRADESH

Govinda Reddy, P., 1987, Effects of consanguineous marriages on fertility and infant mortality among the Mala of Southern Andhra Pradesh, *Indian Journal of Physical Anthropology and Human Genetics* 13(1) January-April, p 43-49, bibliography, tables.

See also Female Infanticide: Tribals.

INFORMAL EDUCATION : TRIBALS

Ramchandra Naidu, A., 1966, Informal education among tribals, *Vanyajati* 14(4) October, p 183-191.

See also Non Formal Education; Functional Literary.

INFORMATION SOURCES : TRIBALS

Bajaj, S.S., et al, 1985, Role of information sources in the adoption of IRS paddy by tribal farmers, *Tribal Research Bulletin* 7(2) March, p 17-19.

INHERITANCE : TRIBALS

Hussain, Syed Khaja Mahmood, 1951, Tribal inheritance, *Man in India*, 3(2) April-June, p 84-87.

INHERITANCE : TRIBALS : INDIA : ARUNACHAL PRADESH

Bachi, R.N., 1979, Family system and inheritance of property among the Tribes of Arunachal Pradesh, *Resarun* 5(1) Spring-Summer, p 38-41, bibliography.

INNOVATIONS : IMPACT ON TRIBALS : INDIA : LITTLE ANDMAN

Venkatashan, D., 1988, Innovations and their impact on the Onge of Little Andaman, *Man in India* 68(4) December, p 413-423, bibliography.

INSTITUTIONAL FINANCE : TRIBALS

Roy Burman, B.K., 1986, Institutional finance and tribal development, *Mainstream* 24(20) January 18, p 16-22.

INTACH SEMINAR ON PROBLEMS FACING TRIBALS, OCTOBER 22-23, 1989, HAZARIBAGH

Bahuguna, Sunderlal, 1990, INTACH Seminar on problems facing Tribals and launching of Chipko movement of Chotanagpur, held at the Grove, Hazaribagh on October 22 and 23, 1989, *Man in India* 70(1) March, p 96-97.

INTEGRATED TRIBAL DEVELOPMENT

Moulik, T.K., 1987, Palamar tribals : Towards integrated development, *Economic Times*, May 21, p 5, col 3-6.

INTEGRATED TRIBAL DEVELOPMENT PROJECTS

Synghal, S., 1984, Integrated tribal development projects, *Kurukshetra* 32(12) September, p 6-8 +.

INTEGRATION

Mascarenhas, Lambart, 1985, Castes and integration, *Goa Today* 19(7) February, p 12-13.

Wilkinson, T.S., 1961, Isolation, assimilation and integration in their historical perspective, *Religion and Society* 8(3) September, p 13-25.

——, 1962, Isolation, assimilation and integration in their historical perspectives, *Bulletin of Tribal Research and Development Institute* (Chhindwara) 2(1) June, p 19-28.

See also Tribal Integration.

INTELLIGENCE : TRIBALS

Kundu, C.L., 1969, Intelligence and tribal delinquency, *Indian Journal of Applied Psychology* 6(1) January, p 29-30, references, tables.

INTERACTIONS : CASTES AND TRIBES : INDIA

Chaudhuri, Buddhadeb, 1968, The nature and extent of Munda Hindu interaction, *Bulletin of Cultural Research Institute* 7(1-2), p 154-165, maps, references, tables.

Volchok, B. Ya, 1964, The interaction of castes and tribal communities in Central India, *Journal of Social Research* 7(1-2) March-September, p 104-112, references.

INTER ETHNIC RELATIONS : INDIA

Anon, 1959, Inter-ethnic relation and social mobility movements among some Tribes and castes of Eastern and Central India C 1900-1959, *Bulletin of Department of Anthropology* 8(2) July, p 9-130.

INTER GENERATIONAL MOBILITY : SCHEDULED CASTES

Anon, 1979, Intergenerations mobility among the Scheduled Castes, *Journal of Indian Education* 5(4) November, p 61.

INTERGROUP RELATIONS AMONG ADIVASIS AND HARIJANS

Panchbhai, S.C., 1967, The levels of regional and national identification and intergroup relations among Harijans and Adivasis, *Journal of Indian Anthropological Society* 2(1) March, p 75-83, references, tables.

INTER TRIBAL RELATIONS

Dube, S.C., 1950, Inter-tribal relations: A study, *Man in India* 30(2-3), April-Septembner, p 73-80.

INTRA CONFLICTS : HINDUS

Jain, Girilal, 1987, Intra-Hindu conflicts : Main sources of turbulence, *Times of India*, June 17, p 3-5.

IRRIGATION : IMPACT ON TRIBAL DEVELOPMENT

Rao, N.V.N. and **Ram Reddy, R.**, 1986, Minor irrigation and tribal development : An empirical study, *Kurukshetra* 34(2) November, p 31-33.

IRULAS

Guruswamy, P.A., 1988, Irula tribes of Nellithorai, *Social Welfare* 34(11) February, p 20-22 +.

ISLAM

See Muslims.

ISLAMISATION

Sharma, S.L. and **Srivastava, R.N.**, 1967, Institutional resistance to induced Islamisation in a convert community : An empirical study in sociology of religion, *Sociological Bulletin* 16(1) March, p 69-80. references

See also Muslims.

ISLANDS OF THE PACIFIC

See Geographical Area subdivision under main Descriptor.

ISOLATED FOOD GATHERING COMMUNITY : INDIA

Das, Nityananda, 1967, The Hill Kharia of Simplipal Hills : A study of an isolated food gathering community, *Adibasi* 9(2) July, p 44-49.

ISOLATION

Kanekar, P.G., 1942, Isolation or assimilation ? *Social Service Quarterly* 28(3) January, p 97-115.

JAGDALPUR CONFERENCE ; INDIA : MADHYA PRADESH

Anon, 1955, Resolutions passed at the Third Tribal Welfare Conference held at Jagdalpur (M.P.) on 13th, 14th and 15th March, 1955. *Vanyajati* 3(2) April, p 84-85.

JAGJIVAN RAM : IMPACT ON HARIJANS

Jain, Meenakshi, 1986, The polities of consensus: Jagjivan Ram and the Harijans, *Times of India*, July 29, p 8, col 3-5.

JAGJIVAN RAM : VIEWS ON CASTEISM AND UNTOUCHABILITY

Jagjivan Ram, 1958, Casteism and untouchability: A analysis, *Indian Journal of Adult Education* 19(3) October, p 33-37.

JAINTIA HILLS : INDIA

Paul, Gemini, 1957, Importance of egg and cock in Khasi and Jaintia hills, *Vanyajati* 5(2) April, p 66-69, references.

JALPAIGURI DISTRICT : INDIA : WEST BENGAL

Piplai, Chumki, et al, 1985, A note on A B O, M N Rh and in (a) blood groups of the Tamang and Oraon tea labourers of the Jalpaiguri district, West Bengal, *Journal of Indian Anthropological Society* 20(1) March, p 66-70, bibliography, tables.

JAMMU AND KASHMIR

See also Kashmir; Geographical Area subdivision under main Descriptor.

JATI/CASTE : INDIA

Sivakumar, S.S. and **Sivakumar, Chitra**, 1979, Class and Jati at Asthapuram and Kanthapuram : Some comment towards structure of interests, *Economic and Political Weekly*, 19, Annual Number, February, p 263-266.

JATS : INDIA

Choudhary, Ram Krishna, 1987, Achievement orientation and career pattern of rural Jat youth in a Haryana village, *Journal of Social Studies* January 6, p 123-130, bibliography.

Kudryavtsev, M.K., 1964, On the role of the Jats in Northern India's ethnic history, *Journal of Social Research* 7(1-2) March-September, p 126-135.

Srivastava, S.L., 1967, The Jat : A caste stereotype, *Folklore* 8(10) October, p 370-375.

JATS : POWER POLITICS

Rajpal Singh, 1989, Rise of the Jat power, *Tribune* (Magazine) April 9, p 3-6.

JAUNSARIES

Ray, P.C., 1951, Difference in concrete intelligence among Jaunsaries, *Journal of Asiatic Society* 17, p 45-52.

JEHANABAD MASSACRE : INDIA

Abraham, A.S., 1988, Massacre in Jehanabad : Looking for a scapegoat, *Times of India*, August 19, p 4, col 3-5.

Tavleen Singh, 1988, Murder and mayhem in Jehanabad, *Indian Express*, September 4, p 1, col 1-8.

JHABUA

Deshpande, W.R., et al, 1988, Travails of the tribals of Jhabua, *Indian Farming* 38(8) November, p 33-35.

JHARKHAND : INDIA : BIHAR

Das, Victor, 1989, Tribals of Jharkhand and the question of their survival, *Social Action* 39(4) October-December, p 438-443.

JHARKHAND STATE DEMAND : INDIA : BIHAR

Jabbar Alam, M., 1986, Tribal unrest in Bihar : Demand for Jharkhand state revived, *New Age* 34(5) February 2, p 8-9.

JHARO

Dubey, R., 1965, Jharo and its people, *Vanyajati* 13(3) July, p 87-02+.

JHOOMING

Barthakur, 1977, Jhooming and its consequences, *Yojana* (Annual Number) 21(1), p 122-123.

JHUMIAS

Banerjee, Asis and **Dasgupta, Malabika**, 1984, Shifting the location of Jhumia villages in Tripura : An empirical study, *Man in India* 64(4) December, p 361-368, bibliography, footnotes, tables.

Dasgupta, Malabika, 1986, Jhumias of Tripura, *Economic and Political Weekly* 21(44-45) 1-8 November, p 1955-1960.

JOBS : RESERVATIONS

Khusro, A.M., 1990, Job reservations : Pro-side, con-side and inside, *Indian Express*, September 13.

Saraf, Pushp, 1990, Job reservation in Railways and accidents, *Indian Express*, September 19.

Solanki, M.S., 1985, Only half of reserved jobs are filled, *Link* 27(36) April 21, p 7-8.

JODHPUR CITY : INDIA : RAJASTHAN

Shyamlal, 1970, Educational development among Bhangis in Jodhpur, *Tribe* 7(1) January, p 26-31, tables.

——, 1973, Sanskritisation and social change among Bhangis in Jodhpur city,

Indian Journal of Social Work 34(1).

JUANG DORMITORIES
See Tribal Dormitories: India: Orissa.

JUANGS
Bose, N.K., 1928, Marriage and kinship among the Juangs, *Man in India* 3(4), p 233-242.
Roy, J.K. and **Roy, B.C.**, 1986, Hunger and physique: Study of the Juang population of Orissa, *Man and Life* 12(1-2) January-June, p 110-112.

JUGIS : INDIA : TRIPURA
Datta, Upali and **Ghosh, G.C.**, 1988, A study of handclasping and armfolding among the Jugi of Tripura, *Man in India* 68(2-3) June-September, p 211-215, bibliography.

JUSTICE FOR TRIBALS
Malhotra, R., 1985, Tribals : Which way justice?, *Mainstream* 23(36) May 4, p 21-23.

JUTI MAKERS/SHOE MAKERS : WOMEN
Harinder Kaur and **Singh, B.P.**, 1989, Juti-making women of Rajasthan in Punjab, *Social Change* 19(3) September, p 23-30.

KACHARIS
Rao, L.N., 1939, The Kacharis of Brahamputra valley Assam, *Rural India* 2(3) September, p 136-139.
Sengupta, Gouranga Gopal, 1959, The Kacharis of Assam, *Indian Folklore* 2(3) July-September, p 226-227.

KAHARS : INDIA : KARNATAKA
Anantha Krishna Iyer, L.K., 1929, The Kahars of Mysore, *Man in India*, 9.

KALADY : INDIA : TRAVANCORE
Velayudhan, R., 1940, A study of social conditions among the Pulayas (Harijans) of Kalady in Travancore state, *Indian Journal of Social Work* 1(3) December, p 393-403, tables.

KALASHS
Ahmed, Akbar, 1986, The lost tribes, *Illustrated Weekly of India* 107(3) 19 January, p 42-43.

KAMAR TRIBE : INDIA : MADHYA PRADESH
Srivastava, Harish C.. 1990, A socio-economic and demographic profile of the Kamar tribe of Madhya Pradesh, *Main in India* 70(2) June, p 101-122.

KAMNAS : INDIA : ANDHRA PRADESH
Deep Kumar, V.S., 1985, A genetic study of Kamna and Kapu caste groups of Andhra Pradesh, *Journal of Indian Anthropological Society* 20(1) March, p 59-65, bibliography.

KANAURAS/KINNARAS
See Kinnauras.

KANDHAS
See Kondhs.

KANTHAPURAM : INDIA

Sivakumar, S.S. and **Sivakumar, Chitra**, 1979, Class and Jati at Asthapuram and Kanthapuram: Some comments towards a structure of interests, *Economic and Political Weekly*, 19, Annual Number, February, p 263-286.

KANWARS : INDIA : MADHYA PRADESH

Mukherjee, D.P., 1985, Skeletal development of tribal children : Kanwar and Oraon of Surguja district M.P., *Journal of Indian Anthropological* Society 20(1) March, p 77-85, bibliography, tables.

—— and **Das, N.K.**, 1985, Age at menarche in tribal girls: The Kanwar and the Oraon of Surguja district M.P., *Journal of Indian Anthropological Society*, 20(2) July, p 153-158, bibliography, tables.

KAPU SAVARAS
See Savaras.

KAPUS : INDIA : ANDHRA PRADESH

Deep Kumar, V.S., 1985, A genetic study of Kamna and Kapu caste groups of Andhra Pradesh, *Journal of Indian Anthropological Society* 20(1) March, p 59-65, bibliography

See also Savaras

KARBIS : INDIA : ASSAM

Dev, A.K., 1985, Affinity of the Karbis of Assam in respect of P.T.C. taste sensitivity, *Indian Journal of Physical Anthropology and Human Genetics* 11(1-2) April-August, p 81-84, bibliography, tables.

KARNATAKA : INDIA

Anon, 1941, Problem of dedication of Harijan girls to prostitution in Karnataka, *Rural India* 4(6) June, p 303-308.

Hegde, Ramakrishna, 1986, Reservation policy in Karnataka, *Monthly Commentary on Indian Economic Conditions* 28(2) September, p 10-13.

See also Geographical Area subdivision under main Descriptor.

KARPOORI FORMULA : RESERVATION

Anon, 1990, CPM favours Karpoori formula, *Hindustan Times*, August, 31.

KASHMIR : INDIA

Khayal, Ghulam Nabi, 1985, The Gujjars of Kashmir: A forgotten community, *Indian Education* 13(6) October, p 1-4.

Pandit, Trilokinath, 1959, The Gujar of Kashmir valley : Some observations on their ecology and social organisation, *Vanyajati* 7(2) April, p 64-71.

See also Jammu and Kashmir.

KATKARI LABOUR

Sathe, Madhusudan Duttatraya, 1988, Katkari labour in charcoal making, *Economic and Political Weekly* 23(34) July 30, p 1565-1567.

KATKARIS

Ferreira, John. V., 1962, The Katkaris: An evaluation of available material, *Journal*

of Social Research, 5(2) September, p 64-70, references.

KAURS
See Mundas.

KAWARS
See also Kanwars.

KAYASTHS : INDIA

Arti Kumari, 1988, A study on the palmar dermatolyphics of the Kayasth of Ranchi, *Man in India* 68(2-3) June-September, p 216-227, bibliography.

Shastri, Raghuvira Mitthulal, 1931, A comprehensive study into the origin and status of the Kayasthas, *Man in India* 11(2) April-June, p 116-159, footnotes.

KEONJHAR DISTRICT : INDIA : ORISSA

Jena, A.C., 1986, Forms of exploitation in tribal areas and their consequences: Some observations in Keonjhar district of Orissa, *Man and Life* 12(3-4) July-December, p 173-180, bibliography.

Rout, Siba Prasad, 1963-1964, Functions of Juang dormitory in Keonjhar district, *Adibasi* 5(2) p 29-34.

KERALA : INDIA

Achuthan, K.R., 1984, The social spectrum of Kerala, *Journal of Kerala Studies* 9(1-4) March-December, p 103-162.

Alexander, K.C., 1967, The problem of the Neo-Christians of Kerala, *Man in India* 47(4) October-December, p 317-330, references, tables.

——, 1968, Changing religious beliefs and practices of the Pulayas of Kerala, *Social Action* 18(5) September-October, p 390-398.

——, 1968, Changing status of Pulaya Harijans of Kerala, *Economic and Political Weekly,* Special Number, July.

D' Monte, Darryl, 1986, Cholanaickans : Homeless in Kerala, *Hindustan Times* (Magazine) August 17, p 5, col 1-6.

Shrikant, L.M., 1960, Evaluation of work of non-official associations in Bombay, Madras and Kerala, *Vanyajati* 8(1) January, p 3-5.

See also Geographical Area subdivison under main Descriptor.

KHAIRWARS : INDIA : MADHYA PRADESH

Sharma, K.K.N., 1989, A note on the distribution of matrimonial distance of the Khairwar tribal population of Surguja District, Madhya Pradesh, *Man in India* 69(3) September, p 267-271.

KHAMPTIS

Duarah, Dwijendra Kumar and **Das, Priya Bala**, 1984, A cross-sectional study of growth in four somatometic characters of the Khampti boys of Arunachal Pradesh, *Resarun* 10(1) Spring-Summer, p 15-24, bibliography, flags, tables.

Kondinyn, Bhikshu, 1981-1982, Monastic social structures in Khampti society, *Journal of the Assam Research Society,* 26, p 33-37, footnotes.

KHANDESH

Khan, G. Ahmed, 1935, The Bhils of Khandesh, *Man in India* 15(2-3) April-September, p 133-143.

KHARIAS/KHERIAS

Banerjee, Hamendra Nath, 1962, Socio-ritual status of the Kharia in the ethnic background of Manbhum, *Bulletin of Cultural Research Institution* 1(2), p 16-28, references, tables.

See also Lodhas.

KHARKHARA PROJECT

Bahadu, F., ed, 1966, Kharkhara Project: Survey of displaced families, *Bulletin of Tribal Research and Training Institute* (Bhopal) 6(1) June, p 1-13, tables.

KHASAS : WOMEN : INDIA : UTTAR PRADESH

Upreti, H.C., 1967, The position of women among Khasas of Kumaon, *Journal of Social Research* 10(1) March, p 37-45, references.

KHASI HILLS : INDIA : MEGHALAYA

Paul, Gemini, 1957, Importance of egg and cock in Khasi and Jaintia hills, *Vanyajati* 5(2) April, p 66-69, references.

KHASI REVIVALIST MOVEMENT

Pant, Mandakini, 1990, Khasi revivalist movement: A sociological analysis, *Vanyajati* 38(1) January, p 6-10.

KHASI SYNTENGS

See Khasis.

KHASIS : INDIA : MEGHALAYA

Bandyopadhyay, S.S. and **Laxmi, G.R.**, 1989, Diet and nutrition of the Khasis of Meghalaya, *Vanyajati* 37(2) April, p 21-24.

KHASIS : WOMEN

Mann, K., 1987, Status of Bhil and Khasi women : A comparative study, *Man and Life* 13(1-2) January-June, p 57-66, bibliography.

KHATRIS : PHYSICAL CHARACTERISTICS

Indera P. Singh and **Kumbnani, H.K.**, 1959, Distribution of papillary patterns on the middle and proximal phalanges of Sindhi Khatris, *Anthropologist* 6(1-2) March-August, p 26-37, references, tables.

KHATRIS : SINDHIS

See Sindhi Khatris.

KHAWAS

Deuri, R.K., 1985, Home brewed liquor of the Khawas, *Resarun* 11(2) Autumn-Winter, p 8-10.

KHERWAR MOVEMENT

Sinha, Surendra Prasad, 1961, Kherwar movement in Hazaribagh district (1870-1880), *Vanyajati* 9(3) July, p98-104.

KHOKRO

Das Gupta, Biman Kumar, 1959, The Pahiras of Khokro, Singhbhum, *Bulletin of Department of Anthropology* 8(2) July, p 85-90, references.

——, 1962, A short ethnographic note on the Pahiras of Khokro, *Vanyajati* 10(3) July, p 110-119, references, tables.

KHUTTO SAVARAS
See Savaras.

KINNAUR : TRIBAL LANGUAGES : INDIA : HIMACHAL PRADESH
Sharma, Bansi Ram, 1984, Dr. Siddheswar Varma's notes on tribal languages of Kinnaur in Himachal Pradesh, *Vishveshranand Indological Journal* 22(1-2) June-December, p 138-148.

KINNAUR : WOMEN
Shashi, S.S., 1973, Women of Kinnaur, *Hindustan Times* (Sunday World), September, 2, p 8, col.1-6.

KINNAUR POLYANDRY
Raha, Manish Kumar and **Commar, Palash Chandra**, 1988, The Kinnaur polyandry and the allocation of paternity, *Man and Life* 14(3-4) July-December, p 147-162.

KINSHIP AND MARRIAGE : IGBO OF NIGERIA
Onwurah, Emeka, 1989, Kinship and marriage among the Igbo of Nigeria, *Sarvaratham*, 14 p 3-12, footnotes.

KINSHIP SYSTEMS : TRIBALS
Mukherjee, Bhabananda, 1961, Comparative study of the kinship systems of six matrilineal tribes, *Eastern Anthropologist* 14(3) September-December, p 216-228, references, tables.

KINSHIP TERMINOLOGY
Karve, Iravati, 1940, Kinship terminology and kinship uses of the Maratha country, *Bulletin of the Deccan College Research Institute* 2(4) p 327-389.

Raha, Manish Kumar and **Commar Palash, Chandra**, 1989, The kinship terms of he Bhantu of Andamans : Structural analysis, *Man in India* 69(4) December, p 374-386.

KISAN CHILDREN : INDIA : ORISSA
Ratha, S.N., and Mahakud, N.K., 1988, The kisan children at work : Data from a West Orissa village, *Man in India* 68(4) December, p 369-379.

KODAGU
Shankara Narayan Rao, N.P., 1985, Identity of the Yeravas of Kodagu, *Quarterly Journal of the Mythic Society* 76(3-4) July-December, p 211-228.

KODAL HILLS
Venkataraman, S.R., 1984, Tribes of Palani and Kodal hills, *Vanyajati* 32(3) July, p 13-15.

KODAVA SOCIETY
Srinivas, M.N., 1985, The Poleyas in the Kodava society, *Journal of Historical Studies* 19, p 75-79, bibliography.

KODHUS
See Kondhs.

KOKRO
See Khokro

KOLES
See Kols

KOLES : GIRLS
Sengupta, Sabuj and **Pathak, S.**, 1988, A study of sexual maturation in the tribal (Koles) girls of Koteswar, Marwa region of Madhya Pradesh, *Man in India* 68(4) December, p 470-472, bibliography, tables.

KOLGHAS
Massive, M.I., 1983, Poverty among the Kolghas of Gujarat, *Journal of the Gujarat Research Society 45(3) July, p 16-31, tables.*
See also Kolis.

KOLI HILLS
Gunasekaran, R., 1988, Changing phase of tribal economy in Koli hills, *Khadi Gramodyog* 35(3) December, p 162-174.

KOLIS
Biswas, D.P., 1989, The Kolis of Gujarat : An ecological variapt, *Vanyajati* 37(2) April, p 25-26.
Chandervarker, Pushker, 1958, Kolis of Tharadari, *Folklore* 1(3) July-September, p 30-33.
Gare, G.M., 1973, Process of social change in the Scheduled Tribes : A case study of immigrant Mahadeo Kolis in Poona City, *Indian Journal of Social Work* 34(2), p 131-139.
Parry, J.P., 1970, The Koli dilemma, *Contributions to Indian Sociology (NS)*, 4, December, p 84-104.

KOLS : EDUCATION : INDIA : UTTAR PRADESH
Hasan, Amir, 1968, A note on education among the Kols of Uttar Pradesh, *Eastern Anthropologist* 21(1) January-April, p 83-86.

KOLS : INDIA : UTTAR PRADESH
Maheshwari, J.K. and **Singh, J.P.**, 1985, Plants used in magico-religious beliefs by the Kols of Uttar Pradesh : A Study, *Folklore* 26(9) September, p 170-173.
Tripathi, R.S., 1989, Agricultural economy of the Kols in Manikpur Block (U.P.), *Vanyajati* 37(3) July, p 3-8.
See also Koles: Girls.

KONDA KAMARAS
Lakshmi, G.R. and **Bandyopadhyay**, 1990, Differential fertility among the Konda Kamara, *Vanyajati* 38(1) January, p 3-5.

KONDARS
See Khairwars.

KONDHAS/KONDHS
Elwin, Verrier, 1944, Notes on a Kondh, *Man in India* 24(1) March, p 40-58, footnotes.
Jena, Krishna Chandra, 1962, The Kondhas of Koraput, *Indian Journal of Social Work* 23(1) April, p 57-61.
Majumdar, B.C., 1932, The Kui or the Kondh people, *Man in India* 12(4) October-December, p 245-252.

Panda, S., 1969, Demography of Kondh village, *Adibasi* 11(3) October, p 27-35, tables.

KONDS

Sharma, J.C. et al, 1985, A study of some of the genetic traits in the Kond tribe of Orissa, *Journal of Indian Anthropological Society* 20(1) March, p 50-58, bibliography, tables.

KONKAN TRADE : INDIA : MAHARASHTRA

Wandrekar, D.N., 1949, Educational progress of the Adivasis in the Konkan trade of Bombay Province, *Eastern Anthropologist* 3(1) September, p 3-7.

KONNIKARS

Zutshi, G.L., 1957, Functions of the Pattapara among the Konnikars, *Vanyajati* 6(2) April, p 84-86.

KORAGAS

Bhat, Vasudev, 1985, Tribal subplan percolates down to Koragas, *Social Welfare* 32(3) June, p 14-15+.

KONTA : INDIA : MADHYA PRADESH

Athavale, M.C. and **Nahatkar, Sunil**, 1983, Evaluation study of tribal area development programme in Konta and Dantewara, Bstar district, Madhya Pradesh, *Cooperative Perspective* 18(3) October-December, p 93-100.

KORAPUT DISTRICT : INDIA : ORISSA

Das, Nityananda, 1960, Changing pattern of a Koraput village, *Vanyajati* 8(2) April, p 65-72.

Das, S.R., et al., 1968, A somatological survey of five tribes in the Koraput district, Orissa, *Bulletin of Anthropological Survey of India* 17(4) October, p 400-422, references, tables.

Jena, Krishna Chandra, 1962, The Kondhas of Koraput, *Indian Journal of Social Work* 23(1) April, p 57-61.

Mohapatra, P.C., 1985, Consumption pattern of Scheduled Tribes : A case study of Koraput district, Orissa, *Vision* 5(2) October-December, p 15-22, bibliography, tables.

Somasundram, A.M., 1949, A note on the Gadabas of Koraput district, *Man in India* 29(1) January-March, p 36-45.

KORKUS : INDIA : UTTAR PRADESH

Fuchs, Stephen, 1988, The Korkus of the Vindhya Hills, *Man in India* 68(2-3) June-September, p 308-309.

KOTRA BHOMAT

Carstairs, Morris, 1954, The Bhils of Kotra Bhomat, *Eastern Anthropologist* 7(3-4) March-August, p 169-181.

KOTTE KOYAS

See Koyas.

KOYAS

Raju, P.S.S., 1988, The religious beliefs of Koyas as described in Koya folk tables, *Eastern Anthropologist* 41(1) January-March, p 99-102.

KSHATRIYAS : EQUATION WITH BRAHMINS

Jain, Girilal, 1988, Kshatriya-Brahmin equation : Historic shift under the Raj, *Times of India*, July 27, p 4, col 3-5.

KSHATRIYAS : INDIA

Gupta, Jaya Dutta, 1959, A study of the Paundra Kshatriyas of West Bengal, *Bulletin of Department of Anthropology* 8(2) JUly, p 109-130, appendix, references.

Rammi Reddi, V. et al, 1986, Palmer transverse ereases among Kshatriyas of Southern Andhra Pradesh, *Indian Journal of Physical Anthropology and Human Genetics* 12(1) January-April, p 75-78, bibliography, tables.

KUIS

See Konds.

KUKI RIANGS

See Riang Kuki Tribe.

KUMAON : INDIA

Upreti, H.C., 1967, The position of women among Khasas of Kumaon, *Journal of Social Research* 10(1) March, p 37-45, references.

KUNAPIPI RITUALS

Mccallum, D. Kent, 1965, Control : The Kunapipi ritual and attendant taboo, *Eastern Anthropologist* 18(2) May, August, p 80-88, references.

KURBAS

Shashi, S.S., 1988, Kurbas : Shepherds of Karnataka, *Mainstream* 26(14) January 16, p 27-28.

KURNOOL SAMITI : INDIA : ANDHRA PRADESH

Meera Reddy V., 1990, TRYSEM programme : A case study In Kurnool Samiti of Andhra Pradesh, *Journal of Rural Development* 9(2) March, p 435-443.

KUTCH : INDIA

Anon, 1955, Welfare work among Scheduled Tribes in Kutch, *Vanyajati* 3(2) April, p 88-89.

KUTTIYA KONDHS

See Kondhs.

L A M P COOPERATIVE SOCIETIES : TRIBALS

Mahalingam, S., 1987, LAMP cooperative societies in tribal India, *Co-operators Bulletin* 30(7) July, p 5-9.

See also Labour Cooperative Societies: Forest.

LAB TO LAND PROGRAMME : TRIBALS

Das, P., et al, 1986, How lab to land programme is helping tribal farmers, *Kurukshetra* 34(4) January-June, p 109-110.

LABOUR : CHARCOAL MAKING

Sathe, Madhusudan Dattatraya, 1988, Katkari labour in charcoal making, *Economic and Political Weekly* 23(3-4) July 30, p 1565-1567.

LABOUR COOPERATIVE SOCIETIES : FOREST

Shrikant, L.M., 1970, Seminar on tribal forest labour cooperatives, *Vanyajati* 18(2) April, p 49-50.

Wandrekar, D.N., 1966, The progress of the movement of the forest labourer's co-operatives, *Vanyajati* 14(4) October, p 165-170.

——, 1967, Forest labour cooperatives or corporations, *Vanyajati* 15(4) October, p 184-187.

See also LAMP Cooperative Societies: Tribals.

LABOUR POWER

Dasgupta, Ranjit, 1986, From peasants and tribesmen to plantation workers : Colonial capitalism of labour power, *Economic and Political Weekly* (Supplement) 21(4) January 25, p 1-p E-10.

LABOUR PROBLEMS : TRIBALS : INDIA : GUJARAT

Naik, J.B., 1949, Labour problems of tribal Gujarat, *Eastern Anthropologies* 3(1) September, p 22-27.

LAC : IMPACT ON TRIBAL

Bhupinder Singh, 1984, Lac and tribals, *Administrator* 29(3) July-September, p 183-190.

LAMBADAS

Prakash Rao, R., 1954, Village organisation and authority among the Lambadas of the Deccan, *Eastern Anthropologist* 8(1) September-November, p 3-12.

Rattord, B. Shyamak Devi, 1984, Class and caste differences among the Lambadas in Andhra Pradesh, *Social Scientist* 12(7) July, p 47-56, bibliography, tables.

LAMBADIS

See Sugalis.

LAND CONTROL : IMPACT ON TRIBALS

Viegas, Philip, 1987, Land control and tribal struggle for survival, *Social Action* 37(4) October-December, p 325-344, footnotes.

LAND ECONOMICS : IMPACT ON WEAKER SECTIONS

Bhuskute, R.V., 1989, Tribals, dalits and government lands, *Economic and Political Weekly* 24(23) June 10, p 1265-1268, tables.

LAND OWNERSHIP STRUCTURE : TRIBAL AREAS

Ramaswamy, V.S., 1985, Land ownership structure in the tribal areas: A study, *Kurukshetra* 33(10) July, p 24-25 +.

LAND OWNING PEASANTS : INDIA : GUJARAT

Desai, Bharati, S., 1982-1983, Channels of mobility used by a land owning peasant caste : An empirical study of the Woras of South Gujarat, *Journal of the Maharaja Sayaji Rao University of Baroda* 31-32(2), p 125-143, bibliography, tables.

LAND PROBLEMS : TRIBALS

Pathy, Jaganath, 1987, Land problems of tribals, *Times of India*, September 9, 10, p 7-8.

LAND REFORMS : TRIBALS

Prashanth, D., 1985, Land reforms and distribution of land among Schedule Tribes in Kerala, *Cochin University Law Review* 9(1-2) March-June, p 213-222.

Roy Burman, B.K., 1989, Society, ecology and land reforms in tribal India, *Indian Journal of Public Administration* 35(1) January-March, p 41.

LAND SYSTEM : TRIBALS

Roy Burman, B.K., 1987, Historical process in respect of communal land system and poverty alleviation among tribals, *Social Action* 37(4) October-December, p 391-420, bibliography, tables.

LANGUAGE DEVELOPMENT : TRIBALS

Sharma, K.R., 1984, A study of language development scholastic achievement and tribal students, *Research Bulletin* 14(1-2) March-June, p 3-21, tables.

LANGUAGES : TRIBAL CHURCHES

Marrison, G.E., 1962, Languages in the tribal churches of North East India, *Religion and Society* 9(4) December, p 72-79.

LANGUAGES AND DIALECTS : TRIBALS

Das, Amal Kumar, 1958, Language and dialects of the tribal of West Bengal, *Vanyajati* 6(3) July, p 130-136.

Mukherjee, Shankarananda, 1964, Sadani : The tribal dialect of the Sundarbans, *Bulletin of Cultural Research Institute* 3(2), p 47-50, references.

See also Tribal Languages

LAOS

See Geographical Area subdivision under main Descriptor.

LAW

Anon, 1986, (Book review), *Indian and Foreign Review* 24(8) February 15, p 26.

Review of the book: **Chatrapati Singh**, 1986, *Common prosperity and common property : India's forests, forest dwellers and the law*, Oxford University Press, Delhi, p 76.

——, 1986, (Book review), *Journal of Indian Law Institute* 28(1) January-March, p 117-121.

Review of the book : **Galanter, Marc**, 1984, *Competing equalities : Law and the backward classes in India*, Oxford University Press, New Delhi, XXV, p 525.

Bakshi, P.M., 1985, Tribal welfare and the law: The prospect, *Cochin University Law Review* 9(1-6) March-June, p 79-86.

Baxi, Upendra, 1989, Historic new law : Protecting SC/ST human rights, *Times of India*, September 6, p 3-5.

Dhagambar, Vasudha, 1986, Tribals and the law, *Indian International Centre Quarterly* 13(3-4) December, p 95-114.

Krishna Iyer, V.R., 1985, Tribal uplift and the rule of law, *Cochin University Law Review* 9(1-2) March-June, p 1-18.

Kulkarni, Sharad, 1985, Adivasis, law and social justice, *Economic and Political Weekly* 20(28) July 13, p 1171-1174.

——, 1986, Adivasis, law and social justice, *Tribal Research Bulletin* 8(2) March, p 1-7, bibliography.

Leelakrishnan, P., et al, 1985, Forest and tribal people : Law and practice, *Cochin University Law Review* 9(1-2) March-June, p 259-270.

Madhava Menon, T., 1985, Law and tribal societies in Kerala, *Cochin University Law Review* 9(1-2) March-June, p 157-172.

Tripathy, G.P., 1985, Scheduled tribes and tribal legislation in Madhya Pradesh, *Cochin University Law review* 9(1-2) March-June, p 105-116.

See also Legislative Measures; Tribal Law.

LAW AND BACKWARD CLASSES

See Other Backward Classes: Law: India.

LEFT PERSPECTIVE

Joseph, M.J., 1988, Class, caste, church and the left, *Economic and Political Weekly* 23(49) December 3, p2573-2574.

Saldonlia, Indra Munshi, 1986, Tribal women in the Warli revolt, 1943-1947 : Class and gender in the Left perspective, *Economic and Political Weekly* (Supplement) 21(17) April 26, pWS-41-WS-52, footnotes.

LEGISLATIVE MEASURES : TRIBAL ECONOMY

Karunakaran, C.K., 1985, Legislative and executive measures for tribal welfare in Kerala, *Cochin University Law Review* 9(1-2) March-June, p 203-212.

Samuel, C.J., 1985, Development of tribal economy : Legislative and executive measures, *Cochin University Law Review* 9(1-2) March-June, p 87-104, footnotes.

LEGITIMISATION : TRIBAL MOVEMENTS

Sengupta, Nirmal, 1988, Reappraising tribal movements : Legitimisation and spread, *Economic and Political Weekly* 23(19) May 7, p 943-945; 23(20) May 14, p 1003-1005; 23(21) May 21, p 1054-1055.

LIBERATION : LINGAYATA CONCEPTION

Mahadevappa, N.G., 1984-85, Implications of the Lingayata (Virasaiva) conception of liberation, *Journal of Karnataka University (Social Science)* 20-21, p 67-80, bibliography.

LIBRARIES : BACKWARD COMMUNITIES

Bhattacharya, Biswanath, 1985, A short note on clubs and libraries of the backward communities, *Bulletin of Cultural Research Institute*, 4, p 53-57, tables.

LIFE STYLES : TRIBALS : INDIA : ORISSA

Parida, Krishan C., 1988, Life style of the Orissan tribes, *Patriot* (Magazine) January 10, p 2, col 1-9.

LINGADHARI KOYAS

See Koyas.

LINGAYATS

Mahadevappa, N.G., 1984-1985, Implications of the Lingayata (Virasaiva) conception of liberation, *Journal of Karnataka University (Social Science)* 20-21, p 67-80, bibliography.

Kusumakar, H., 1986, To be "backward" is good, *Times of India* (Sunday Review) November 9, p 1-8.

LINGAYATS : RITUALS

Bradford, Nicholas J., 1985, From bride-wealth to groom-fee : Transformed marriage customs and socio-economic polarisation among Lingayats, *Contribution*

A bio-social study on the Lodha : A primitive tribal group of West Bengal, *Man and Life* 12 (1-2) January-June, p 47-60, bibliography, tables.

Bhowmick, P.K., 1966, An integrated plan for the development of the Lodhas and other tribals of Midnapur, *Vanyajati* 14(2) April, p 82-89.

LOHARA MUNDAS
See Mundas.

LOHARS
Salunke, N.B. 1988, The Nomadic blacksmiths, *Social Welfare* 35(9) December, p 26-29.

LOHARDGA CONFERENCE (BIHAR)
Anon, 1954, Resolutions passed at the Second Tribal Welfare Conference, Lohardga (Bihar) on 11th, 12th and 13th November, 1953, *Vanyajati* 2(1) January, p 31-32.

LYNGN GAMS
See Khasis.
MADA (MODIFIED AREA DEVELOPMENT APPROACH)
MADA POCKETS : INDIA

Bairagi, K.V., 1987, Modified area development approach pockets (MADA Pockets) and mini modified area development approach pockets (Mini MADA Pockets) clusters based on 1981, *Tribal Research Bulletin* 9(2) March, p 9-11, tables.

Surana, M.B., 1985, Socio-economic survey of tribals in the proposed MADA pocket in Buldhana district, *Tribal Research Bulletin* 7(2) March, p 9-13.

MADHOPUR : INDIA
Cohn, Bernard S., 1959, Madhopur revisited, *Economic Weekly*, July.

MADHYA PRADESH : INDIA
Anon, 1954, Activities conducted under the tribal welfare scheme, Madhya Pradesh during 1953-54, *Vanyajati* 2(2) April, p 64-67.

——, 1954, Note on the progress of the tribal welfare scheme in Madhya Pradesh (From January 1953 — December 1953), *Vanyajati* 2(1) January, p 26-29.

See also Geographical Area subdivison 'Madhya Pradesh' under main Descriptor.

MADIAS
See Gonds

MADRAS : INDIA : TAMIL NADU
Shrikant, L.M., 1960, Evaluation of work of non-official associations in Bombay, Madras and Kerala, *Vanyajati* 8(1) January, p 3-5.

See also Geographical Area subdivision 'Madras' under main Descriptor.

MADRAS PRESIDENCY: INDIA
Radhakrishna, Meena, 1989, The criminal tribes act in Madras Presidency: Implications for itinerant trading communities, *Indian Economic and Social History Review* 26(3) July-September, p 269-295.

See also Tamil Nadu: India.

MADRAS STATE : INDIA
Anon, 1953, Scheme of the Madras State Government for the welfare of the

Scheduled Castes and Scheduled Tribes and other Backward Classes included in the Five Year Plan, *Vanyajati* 1(2) April, p 42-43.
See also Tamil Nadu: India.

MAGICAL SCRIPT
Swaminathan, J., 1985, The magical script, *Link* (Supplement) 27(26) February 3, p 55-63.

MAHALI MUNDAS
See Mundas.

MAHARASHTRA : INDIA
Jhingon, Bela and **Surinder Nath**, 1985, Trends of growth and maturation among the Warlis : A tribal population of Maharashtra, India, *Indian Journal of Physical Anthropology and Human Genetics* 11(1-2) April-August, p 39-55, bibliography and tables.
See also Geographical Area Subdivision 'Maharashtra' under main Descriptor.

MAHARAS
Patwardhan, Sunanda, 1963, Social mobility and conversion and Maharas, *Sociological Bulletin* 17(2) September, p187-202, references.

MAHRAS : INDIA : MADHYA PRADESH : BASTAR
Negi, Raghunath Singh and **Ahmad, S. Hasim**, 1962, The Bhatra, Muria and Mahra of Bastar : A blood group genetic study, *Bulletin of Anthropological Survey of India* 11(3-4), p 201-209, references, tables.

MAIKAL HILLS
Elwin, Verrier, 1942, The duration of marriage among the Aboriginals of the Maikal hills, *Man in India* 22(1) January-March, p 11-12, footnotes.

MALABAR : INDIA
Aiyappan, A, 1937, Social and physical anthropology of Nayadis of Malabar, *Bulletin of Madras Government Museum* 2(4).

MALAPANTARAM TRIBE : INDIA
Sen Gupta, P.N. and **Biswas, S.K.**, 1956, Studies on the diet and nutritional status of the Malapantaram Muthuvan and Ullatan tribes of Travancore, *Bulletin of Department of Anthropology* 5(2), p 9-19, tables.

MALAS : INDIA : ANDHRA PRADESH
Chengal Reddy, P. 1987, Consanguinity and inbreeding load in two Mala populations of Andhra Pradesh, *Man in India* 67(4) December, p 357-363, bibliography, tables.
Govinda Reddy, P., 1987, Effects of consanguineous marriages on fertility and infant mortality among the Mala of Southern Andhra Pradesh, *Indian Journal of Physical Anthropology and Human Genetics* 13(1) January-April, p 43-49, bibliography, tables.
Rathnaiah, K., 1987, The economic organisation of Malas in Chittoor district of Andhra Pradesh: A study, *Folklore* 28(9) September, p 207-215, tables.
See also Reddys.

MALAYALAM KINSHIP

Chattopadhyay, K.P., 1921, Some Malayalam kinship, *Man in India* 1(2), June, p 141-143.

Clamment, John, 1987, Incorporation and assimilation: The aboriginal peoples of Malaysia and letters of modernisation *Journal of Social Economic Studies* 4(2) April-June, p 121-142.

Jain, R.K., 1967, Social stratification and political process in a new nation: Malaysia, *Journal of India Antheopological Society* 2(1) March, p 69-73, references.

MALAYSIA

Clamment, John, 1987, Incorporation and assimilation: The aboriginal peoples of Malaysia and letters of modernisation *Journal of Social Economic Studies* 4(2) April-June, p 121-142.

Jain, R.K., 1967, Social stratification and political process in a new nation: Malaysia, *Journal of Indian Anthropological Society* 2(1) March, p 69-73, references.

See also Geographical Area subdivision under main Descriptor.

MALWA AREA : INDIA

Ahmad, S.H., 1987, The study of phalangeal hair among the Bhil and their allied groups of Malwa area, *Man in India* 67(1), March, p 47-58.

MANAGEMENT TECHNIQUES : TRIBAL AREAS

Singh, K.S., 1990, Environment, technology and management in tribal areas, *Man in India* 70(2) June, p 123-130.

MANBHUM : INDIA

Banerjee, Hamendra Nath, 1962, Socio-ritual status of the Kharia in the ethnic background of Manbhum, *Bulletin of Cultural Research Institute* 1(2) p 16-28, references, tables.

See also South Manbhum.

MANDAL, B.P. : REPORT OF BACKWARD CLASSES COMMISSION

Hoshiar Singh and **Malik, Jagdish Kumar**, 1984, The Mandal Commission Report : A plea for share in power, *Political Science Review* 23(3-4) July-December, p 250-268, bibliography, tables.

Deshpande, Anjali, 1990, Reservations and Mandal report, *Mainstream* 28(44) August 25, p 5 +.

See also Backward Classes Commission, 1979-80, New Delhi.

MANDALA DISTRICT : INDIA : MADHYA PRADESH

Mehta, Shalini, 1988, Role of voluntary and government organisations in tribal welfare : A case study of Mandala district of M.P., *Eastern Anthropologist* 41(1) January-March, p 49-64, tables.

Patel, M.L, 1970, Spatial mobility of unemployed educated tribals of Mandala district, *Vanyajati* 18(2) April, p 70-76, references, tables.

MANIPUR : INDIA

Chakravarti, Manish Ranjan and **Mukherjee, Deba Prasad**, 1962, Dermatoglyphic study on the tribes and castes of Nagaland and Manipur, *Bulletin of Anthropological Survey of India* 11(3-4), p 233-234, tables.

See also Geographical Area, subdivision under main Descriptor.

MANNEDORAS

Suguna, A.V., et al, 1988, The role of descent groups among the Mannedoras, *Man in India* 68(4) December, p 454-458, tables.

MANU : VIEWS ON CASTE

Sharma, Arvind, 1986, Manu on determinants of caste, *Man in India* 66(3) September, p 255-258.

MANU : VIEWS ON VARNA

Chanana, Dev Raj, 1959, The Sudra, the Dasa and Manu, *Indian Journal of Social Work* 20(3) December, p 201-208.

MAPPILA RIOTS, 1896

Malar, K.M., 1987, The Mappila riots of 1896, *Quarterly Review of Historical Studies* 26(4) January-March, p 33-39, bibliography.

MARATHA TOTEMISM

Ferreria, John V., 1964, The problem of Maratha totemism, *Indian Journal of Social Work* 25(2) July, p 135-151, references.

MARATHWARA VILLAGES : INDIA

Anon, 1986, Shivsena enters rural politics: Campaign against Dalits in Marathwara villages, *Economic and Political Weekly* 21(50) December 13, p 2166-2167.

MARIAS

Anon, 1962, The culture studies: A socio-economic survey of Abujhmarh, *Bulletin of Tribal Research Institute* (Chhindwara) 2(2) December, 3(1) June, 1963, p 66-67, references, maps, tables.

Bapat, Nana, 1961, A note on Abujhmarihas of Bastar, *Bulletin of Tribals Research Institute* (Chhindwara) 1(1) June, p 17-18, illustration.

Dube, B.K., 1962-1963, A plan for the culture : The approach to the problem of Abujhmarh, *Bulletin of Tribal Research Institute* (Chhindwara) 2(2) December-June, p 1-4.

Dubey, K.C., 1968, Tikenpal : Some aspects of a Bison Horn Maria village, *Bulletin of Cultural Research Institute* (Chhindwara) 7(1-2), p 66-79, tables.

______, 1969, A note on the Bison Horn Maria Phratries clans and totems, *Eastern Anthropologist* 22(3) September-December, p 371-376.

Elwin, Verrier, 1945, Funerary custom in Bastar State, *Man in India* 25(2) June, p 87-133.

Kurup, A.M. 1963-1964, People of the unknown hills : The Abujmadias, *Vanyajati* 11(1) January, p 38-41; 11(4) October, p 168-176; 12(1) January, p 46-55; 12(2) April, p 67-79; 12(4) October, p 180-189.

Nigam, Raghuvir Sahay, 1961, Marias of Bastar, *Social Service Quarterly* 46(3) January, p 87-88.

Noronha, R.C.V.P., 1962-1963, The culture penetrated: Abujhmarh diary, *Bulletin of Tribal Research Institute* (Chhindwara) 2(2) December; 3(1) June, p 5-21.

Pawar, S.B., 1962-1963, An administrator looks at the culture: A report on Abujhmarh, Tahsil Naraipur, District Bastar, *Bulletin of Tribal Research Institute* (Chhindwara) 2(2) December, 3(1) June, p 22-65.

Satyarthi, Devendra, 1944, In aboriginal India, *Rural India* 7(6) July, p 247-252.

Shesh, S., 1965, Phonology of Abuj Mariya, *Bulletin of Tribal Research and Development Institute* (Bhopal) 5(1-2) June-December, p 35-49, tables.

See also Abuj Marias.

MARITAL LIFE : TRIBALS : INDIA : WEST BENGAL

Khan, N.C., 1969, Some aspects of martial trend among the tribals of West Bengal, *Bulletin of Cultural Research Institute* 8(3-4), p 42-47, tables.

MARKETS : TRIBAL AREA

See Shandies: Tribal Areas: India: Andhra Pradesh, Tribal Markets.

MARRIAGE CUSTOMS : TRIBALS

Oberoi, R.C., 1989, They carry away the bride, *Man in India* 69(4) December, p 403-405.

See also Marriage Systems : Tribals; Mates Acquiring; Matrimonial Distance : Tribals : India : Madhya Pradesh.

MARRIAGE SYSTEMS : TRIBALS

Samanta, R.K. and **Adhikary M.M.**, 1988, Marriage systems among tribals of North-East India : An overview, *Man in India* 68(4) December, p 401-411.

See also Marriage Customs: Tribals; Mates Acquiring : Tribals.

MARRIAGE TRANSACTIONS

Manuel, Moreno, 1989, Marriage transactions among the Pallars of Southern Kongu, Tamil Nadu, *Man in India* 69(1) March, p 13-23.

MARRIAGES : INDIA

Anon, 1984, (Book review), *Indian Quarterly* 40(1) January-March, p 156-160; *Man in India* 64(2) June, 219,221.

Review of the book: **Ostor, Akos**, et al, 1983, *Concepts of person, kinship, caste and marriage in India*, Oxford University Press, New Delhi, xiv, 271 p.

Bose, Dilip Kumar, 1969, On preferential marriage of the tribes of Central India, *Journal of Social Research* 12(2) September, p 106-116, references, tables.

Kannan, C.T., 1961, Intercaste marriage in Bombay, *Sociological Bulletin* 10(2) September, p 53-68, tables.

MARRIAGES : INTERCASTE : INDIA : MAHARASHTRA : BOMBAY

Kannan, C.T., 1961, Intercaste marriage in Bombay, *Sociological Bulletin* 10(2) September, p 53-68, tables.

MARWARIS : INDIA : EASTERN

Goswami, Omkar, 1985, Then came the Marwaris : Some aspects of the changes in the pattern of industrial control on Eastern India, *Indian Economic and Social History Review* 32(3) July-September, p 225-249, bibliography, footnotes.

MARWARIS : SOCIAL LIFE AND CUSTOMS

Agarwala, B.R., 1962, Nature and extent of social change in a mobile commercial community, *Sociological Bulletin* 11(1-2) March-September, p 141-145.

MASKS AND MASQUERADES : BUDDHIST TRIBES : INDIA ARUNACHAL PRADESH

Das, A.K., 1984, Masks and masquerades among the Buddhist tribes of Arunachal Pradesh, *Indian and Foreign Review* 22(10) March 15, p 18-19.

MATERIAL CULTURE : TRIBALS : INDIA : WEST BENGAL

Sarkar, Sabita Ranjan, 1969, Some aspects of material culture of the tribals of West Bengal, *Bulletin of Cultural Research Institute* 8(3-4), p 85-86.

MATES ACQUIRING : TRIBALS : INDIA : BIHAR

Ghosh, B.N., 1967, The ways of acquiring mates in tribal Chotanagpur, *Folklore* 8(11) November, p 403-410, references.

See also Marriage Customs: Tribals; Marriage Systems: Tribals.

MATRILINEAL TRIBES

Mukherjee, Bhabananda, 1961, Comparative study of the kinship systems of six matrilineal tribes, *Eastern Anthropologist* 14(3) September-December, p 216-228, references, tables.

MATRIMONIAL DISTANCE : TRIBALS : INDIA : MADHYA PRADESH

Sharma, K.K.N., 1989, A note on the distribution of matrimonial distance of the Khairwar tribal population of Surguja District, Madhya Pradesh, *Man in India* 69(3) September, p 267-271.

MATURATION : WARLIS : INDIA : MAHARASHTRA

Jhingon, Bela and **Surinder Nath**, 1985, Trends of growth and maturation among the Warlis : A tribal population of Maharashtra, India, *Indian Journal of Physical Anthropology and Human Genetics* 11(1-2) April-August, p 39-45, bibliography, tables.

MAYURBHANJ STATE : INDIA

Acharya, P., 1938, Note on the Dharuas or the Gonds of Mayurbhanj State, *Man in India* 18(2-3) April-September, p 163-167.

MEDICAL MISSION : TRIBALS

Devan, P.K., 1988, A medical mission for the tribals of Wynad, *Social Welfare* 34(11) February, p 9-10.

MEDICINAL HERBS

Sachchidananda, Narayan, 1989, Tribal development through use of medicinal herbs, *Social Welfare* 36(3-4) June-July, p 30-31.

MEDIUM OF INSTRUCTION : TRIBAL STUDENTS

Barla, Anthony, 1965, Medium of instruction for tribal students: Viewpoint, *Indian Education* 4(11) October, p 33-34.

See also Tribal Education.

MEGHALAYA : INDIA

See also Geographical Area subdivision 'Meghalaya' under main Descriptor.

MEMBAS : INDIA : ARUNACHAL PRADESH

Billorey, R.K., 1986, Migration and trade in the North East Frontier of India : The Membas of Arunachal, *Journal of Asiatic Society of Bengal* 28(1) p 56-68, footnotes.

MEMBERS OF PARLIAMENT : INDIA : VIEWS ON RESERVATION

Anon, 1990, Extend reservation to education: MPs, *Patriot*, September 4.

MENARCHE : TRIBAL GIRLS

Mukherjee, D.P. and **Das, N.K.**, 1985, Age at menarche in tribal girls : The Kanwar and the Oraon of Surguja district, M.P., *Journal of Indian Anthropological Society* 20(2) July, p 153-158, bibliography, tables.

MENTAL HEALTH : TRIBALS

Hassan, M.K., 1986, Impact of industrialisation on mental health of tribals, *Social Change* 16(4) December, p 30-33, bibliography, tables.

MEOS

Sharma, S.L. and **Srivastava, R.N.**, 1967, Institutional resistance to induced Islamisation in a convert community: An empiric study in sociology of religion, *Sociological Bulletin* 16(1) March, p 69-80, references.

MESSIANIC MOVEMENTS AND TRIBAL SOLIDARITY

Sinha, Surajit, 1968, Tribal solidarity and messianic movements, *Contributions to Indian Sociology* (NS) December 2, p112-118, references.

METAMORPHOSIS : SOCIAL

Seshadri, H.V., 1987, Ralegana, Sindi : A name for social metamorphosis, *Organiser* 38(40) February, p 10.

MEWASTI BHILS

See also Bhils.

MIDDLE MANAGEMENT : TRIBAL AREAS

Singh, K.M.P., 1984, Tips on training needs and middle management for tribal areas, *Survey* 24(1-2), p 19-25, bibliography.

MIDNAPUR : INDIA : WEST BENGAL

Chaudhuri, Buddhadeb, 1969, An analytical study of witchcraft among the Mundas of Midnapur, *Bulletin of Cultural Research Institute* 8(1-2), p 87-91, references.

MIGRATION : TRIBALS

Buzarbaruah, P.M., 1989, Effects of migration and environment on anthropometric characters of Munda population of Assam: A preliminary observation, *Man in India* 69(3) September, p 292-304.

Naidu, A.R., 1967, Problem of migration of semi-educated tribal boys, *Indian Education* 7(3) February, p 28-36.

MIJIS SAJOLANG : INDIA : ARUNACHAL PRADESH

Datta Chaudhuri, S.S., 1988, Demographic profile of Miji (Sajolang) of Arunachal Pradesh, *Man in India* 68(4) December, p 442-447, bibliography, tables.

MILCH ANIMALS : SUPPLY TO ADIVASIS

Surana, M.B., 1986, Supply of milch animals to Adivasis in Dhule district, *Tribal Research Bulletin* 9(1) September, p 111-115.

MINERALS IN TRIBAL DEVELOPMENT : INDIA : RAJASTHAN

Vaish, Prerana, 1984, Role of mineral in the tribal development of TSP region of Rajasthan, *Tribe* 16(3-4) September-December, p 20-29.

MINERS : INDIA : GOA

Nair, P.K., 1977-78; Welfare scheme for Goa miners, *Social Welfare* 24 (9-10)

December-January, p 71-73.

MINI M A D A POCKETS
See M A D A Pockets.

MINING INDUSTRY : IMPACT ON TRIBALS : INDIA
Srivastava, R.N., 1988, Moving wheels of machine: The impact of mining industralisation of the Bastar tribal region of Central India, *Man and Life* 14(3-4) July-December, p 119-137.

MINOR IRRIGATION : IMPACT ON TRIBAL DEVELOPMENT
Rao, N.V.N. and **Reddy, R.**, 1986, Minor irrigation and tribal development : An empirical study, *Kurukshetra* 34(2) November, p 31-33.

MINORITIES : RIGHTS : INDIA
Heredia, Rudi, 1986, Minority rights and reservation policy : Towards coherence and consistence, *New Frontiers in Education* 16(2) April-June, p 60-63.

MINYONG AREAS : INDIA : ASSAM
Sen Gupta, P.N., 1953, Population studies and living conditions of the tribes in the Padam and Minyong areas of Abor hills, Assam, *Bulletin of Department of Anthropology* 2(1) January, p 91-112, tables.

MIRIS : INDIA : ARUNACHAL PRADESH
Kani, M. and **Bourai, R.A.**, 1985, Aryan tradition among Nishis and Hill Miris of lower Subansiri district, Arunachal Pradesh, *Resarun* 11(2) Autumn-Winter, p 35-38.
See also Hill Miris; Mishings.

MIRZAPUR : TRIBALS : INDIA : UTTAR PRADESH
Srivastava, Rajni, 1983, Some psychological problems of tribals of Mirzapur : A case study, *Indian Educational Review* 18(2) April, p 106-110, tables.

MISHINGS : INDIA : ASSAM
Buzarbaruah, P.M. and **Phookan, M.N.**, 1986, Birth order, mother's age and reproductive wastage among the Mishings of Disangmukh of Sibsagar, Assam, *Indian Journal of Physical Anthropology and Human Genetics* 12(1) January-April, p 43-50, bibliography, tables.
See also Miris.

MISSIONARIES : IMPACT ON ADIVASI CULTURE
Bhagat, Anupdev, 1956, Missionaries, anthropologists and Adivasi culture, *Social Action* 6(11) November, p 457-472, references.

MISSIONARY APPROACH : TRIBAL WELFARE
Vaniker, P.G., 1954, Missionary approach to the tribal welfare, *Indian Journal of Social Work* 14(4) March, p 376-382.

MISSIONARY ZEAL : TRIBAL WELFARE
Das, G.N., 1966, Missionary zeal (with special reference to tribal welfare), *Adibasi* 8(3) October, p 3-7.

MOBILITY
Anon, 1979, Inter-generations mobility among the Scheduled Castes, *Journal of*

Indian Education 5(4) November, p 61.

Desai, Bharti S., 1982-1983, Channels of mobility used by a land owning peasant caste: An empirical study of the Woras of South Gujarat, *Journal of the Maharaja Sayaji Rao University of Baroda* 31-32(2), p 125-143, bibliography, tables.

MODEL COMMUNITY CENTRES : TRIBAL AREAS

Chatterjee, B., 1953, Model community centres in tribal areas, *Indian Journal of Social Work* 14(3) December, p 282-291.

MODERNISATION PROBLEMS : TRIBALS : INDIA

Srivastava, L.R.N., 1969, The problem of modernisation of the tribes of North-East India, *Bulletin of Cultural Research Institute* 8(1-2), p 21-25.

MODIFIED AREA DEVELOPMENT APPROACH POCKETS

See M A D A Pockets.

MONPAS

Dhar, B., 1985, Land tenure system among the Monpas: Conflict and co-existence, *Resarun* 11(2) Autumn-Winter, p 32-34, bibliography.

Durah, D.K., 1985, A study on middle phalangeal hair among the Tagins and Monpas of Arunachal Pradesh, *Resarun* 11(1) Spring-Summer, p 33-41, tables.

_____, 1986, A study on A B C blood groups, P T C taste sensitivity and colour blindness among the Monpas of Arunachal Pradesh, *Resarun* 12(1-2) Spring-Winter, p 36-43, tables.

Dutta, D.K., 1986, Health and hygiene of three villages of Monpas, West Kameng district, *Resarun* 12(1-2) Spring-Winter, p 2-25, tables.

Sen, Biswajit, 1965, The Monpas of Tawang, *Vanyajati* 13(1) January, p 23-26.

See also Tawangs.

MONPAS : ANTHROPOMETRY : INDIA : ARUNACHAL PRADESH

Durah, D.K. and **Sharma, Hem Chandra**, 1979, Hand clasping, armfolding and Earlobe attachment of the Monpas of Kameng, Arunachal, *Resarun* 5(1) Spring-Summer, p 53-61, tables.

MOPLAHS

Malar, K.M., 1987, The Mappila riots of 1896, *Quarterly Review of Historical Studies* 26(4) January-March, p 33-39, bibliography.

MORTUARY PRACTICES : NIGERIA : NORTH EASTERN

Otterbein, Keith F., 1967, Mortuary practices in North-Eastern Nigeria, *Bulletin of Cultural Research Institute* 6(1-2), p 10-18, references, tables.

See also Dead Persons: Disposal of Corpse: India; Funerary Customs: India.

MORUNG ORGANISATION

Aonok, S. Wati, 1956, Morung organisation among the Nokte Nagas, *Vanyajati* 4(2) April, p 73-81, footnotes, illustrations.

MOTHER RIGHTS : MUSLIMS

D'Souza, Victor S. , 1953, Mother right in transition, *Sociological Bulletin* 2(2) September, p 135-142.

MOUASIS

See Korkus.

MUDUGARS/MUDUVANS/MUTHUWANS
See Muthuwan Tribes: India: Travancore.

MUJIS : INDIA : ARUNACHAL PRADESH
Datta Chaudhuri, S.S., 1984, A note on handclasping armfolding and tongue rolling among the Muji of Arunachal Pradesh (India), *Vanyajati* 32(2) April, p 12-13.

MUKHOPADHYAY, BHUDEV : VIEWS ON CASTE SYSTEM
Bhattacharya, Gayatu, 1983-1984, Bhudev Mukhopadhyay and ethnosociology of the caste system: A search for an identity, *Journal of Department of Sociology*, p 53-65, bibliography.

MULIYA SAVARAS
See Savaras.

MULTI PURPOSE TRIBAL BLOCKS
Anon, 1958, Special Multi Purpose Blocks, *Vanyajati* 6(2) April, p 48-51.
——, 1964, The water scarcity problem in Tamia special multipurpose tribal development block, *Bulletin of Tribal Research Training Institute* (Chhindwara) 4(1) June, p 44-49, references, tables.
Verma, Sneh Veena, 1961, Working of the multi-purpose tribal blocks in M.P., *Vanyajati* 9(2) April, p 48-55.

MUNARGAON
Ebnother, Robert, 1966, Munargaon: Its lessons in tribal welfare, *Adibasi* 8(1) April, p 73-84.

MUNDAS
Buzarbaruah, P.M., 1989, Effects of migration and environment on anthropometric characters of Munda population of Assam: A preliminary observation, *Man in India* 69(3) September, p 292-304.
Chaudhauri, Buddhadeb, 1966, Life in a Munda village, *Bulletin of Cultural Research Institute* 5(1-2), p 126-132, tables.
——, 1968, The nature and extent of Munda Hindu interactions, *Bulletin of Cultural Research Institute* 7(1-2) p 154-155, maps, references, tables.
——, 1969, An analytical study of witchcraft among the Mundas of Midnapur, *Bulletin of Cultural Research Institute* 8(1-2), p 87-91, references.
Das Gupta, Samira and **Sarkar, Amitabh**, 1990, A new light on Munda social organisation, *Man in India* 70(2) June, p 195-198.
Dene, Steve, 1985, Religious movement as rite passage: Analysis of the Bisra movement, *Contributions to Indian Sociology* (New Series)19(2) July-December, p 251-268, bibliography.
Mac Naughton, A., 1953, Foreign missions and their work among tribal peoples, *Indian Journal of Social Work* 14(3) December, p 276-81.
Manohar Lal, 1986, The Munda elites: Recruitment, network attitudes, perceptions and role in social transformation, *Sociological Bulletin* 35(2) September, p 152-154.
Patnaik, Nityananda, 1954, The socio-political organisation of the Munda: A study of aculturation, *Vanyajati* 2(2) April, p 46-51.
Srivastava, R.M., and **Kharde, R.L.**, 1983, Traditional beliefs of tribal Mundas associated with cattle husbandry, *Indian Journal of Extension Education* 19(3-4) September-December, p 77-82, reference, tables.

MUNDAS : LANGUAGES AND DIALECTS

Mukerjee, Shankarnanda, 1964, Sadani: The tribal dialect of the Sundarbans, *Bulletin of Cultural Research Institute* 3(2), p 47-50, references.

MUNICIPAL CORPORATIONS

Kamalakar, Jaya, 1988, Ethnic politics in municipal corporations, *Economic and Political Weekly* 23(19) May 7, p 945-946.

MURIAS : INDIA : MADHYA PRADESH : BASTAR

Negi, Raghunath Singh and **Ahmad, S. Hasim**, 1962, The Bhatra, Muria and Mahra of Bastar: A blood group genetic study, *Bulletin of Anthropological Survey of India* 11(3-4), p 201-209, references, tables.

Saha, Swopan S., 1984, Degree of isolation: Reproductive wastage and mortality in a Muria population of Bastar, Madhya Pradesh, *Journal of Indian Anthropological Society* 19(2) July, p 118-124.

MUSLIMS

Lindholm, Charles, 1986, Caste in Islam and the problem of deviant systems: A critique of recent theory, *Contributions to Indian Sociology* (NS) 20(1) January-June, p 61-73, bibliography.

See also Islamisation.

MUSLIMS : KONKANI

D'Souza, Victor S., 1953, Mother right in transition, *Sociological Bulletin* 2(2) September, p 135-142.

MUTHUVAN TRIBE : INDIA : TRAVANCORE

Sen Gupta, P.N. and **Biswas, S.K.**, 1956, Studies on the diet and nutritional status of the Malapantram, Muthuvan and Ullatan tribes of Travancore, *Bulletin of Department of Anthropology* 5(2), p 9-19, tables.

MUTHUWANS/MUDUGARS/MUDUVANS

See also Muthuvan Tribe.

MYTHS AND LEGENDS : TRIBALS : INDIA : ARUNACHAL PRADESH

Batra, N.D., 1985, Myths and legends of Arunachal tribes, *Indian and Foreign Review* 22(10) March 15, p 18-19.

NADIAD

Social Service Quarterly (Periodical), 1926, Untouchables in Nadiad, *Social Service Quarterly* 11(4) April, p 154-155.

See also Geographical Area subdivision under main Descriptor.

NAGALAND : INDIA

Chakravarti, Manish Ranjan and **Mukherjee, Deba Prasad**, 1962, Dermatoglyphic study on the tribes and castes of Nagaland and Manipur, *Bulletin of Anthropological Survey of India* 11(3-4), p 233-234, tables.

Gokhale, A.M., 1989, Village development boards in Nagaland, *Vanyajati* 37(4) October, p 55.

See also Geographical Area subdivision 'Nagaland' under main Descriptor.

NAGAS : INDIA

Paul, Radha Kanta, 1987, The Tangkhuls of Manipur, *Indian Management* 7(5)

April p 50-57.

Shashi, S.S., 1971, The Nagas of North-East India, *Children's Word*, September 19, p 18-20.

———, 1975, The Naga warfare, *Contemporary Social Sciences*, 8, April-June, p 9.

See also Nokte Nagas.

NAHULS

See Korkus.

NAIRS : INDIA : KERALA

Subhashini, A.V., 1987, Tharavads: Kerala's Nair homes, *Indian Management* 7(8) July, p 52-83.

NAKTE NAGAS

See Nokte Nagas

NAMBOODIRIS

Menon, Venu, 1956, Requiem for an era, 1956, *Illustrated Weekly of India* 107(29) 20 July, p 28-29.

NAME TAGS : INDIA : SOUTH

Kusumakar, H., 1985, The name tag tells all in the South, *Times of India* (Sunday Review), September 1, p 1, col 1-8.

NAMES : ETHNOLOGICAL : INDIA : ASSAM

Paul, Gemini, 1956, Origin of certain tribal names pertaining to Assam, *Vanyajati* 4(4) October, p 147-154, references.

NATIONAL CONFERENCE ON PROBLEMS OF SCHEDULED TRIBES, MARCH 31, 1990, NEW DELHI

Paswan, Ram Vilas, 1990, Speech by the Union Minister for Labour and Welfare (at) National Conference on Problems of Scheduled Tribes, 31st March, 1990, *Vanyajati* 36(3) April, p 7-8.

Singh, V.P., 1990, Speech of the Prime Minister (at) National Conference on Problems of Scheduled Tribes, Vigyan Bhavan, New Delhi, 31st March, 1990, *Vanyajati* 38(2) April, p 3-6.

NATIONAL DEBATE : RESERVATION : INDIA

Anon, 1990, National debate on reservation imperative, *Statesman*, September 25.

NATIONAL INTEGRATION : SCHEDULED CASTES AND SCHEDULED TRIBES : INDIA

Bose, Nirmal Kumar, 1968, National integration and the Scheduled Castes and Scheduled Tribes, *Man in India* 48(4) October, p 289-296.

NATIONAL SEMINAR ON NEHRU AND EVOLUTION OF TRIBAL POLICY, SEPTEMBER 20, 1989

Anon, 1989, Report of the National Seminar on Nehru and Evolution of Tribal Policy sponsored by Bhartiya Adamjati Sevak Sangh, *Vanyajati* 37(4) October, p 1-5.

Roy Burman, B.K., 1989, Key Note Address of in the Inaugural Session the National Seminar on Nehru and Evolution of Tribal Policy on 20th September, 1989, *Vanyajati* 37(4) October, p 8-11.

NATIVES: SOCIAL CONDITION

Long, James, 1966, Five hundred questions on subjects requiring investigation in the social condition of the natives, edited with additional notes by Mahadev Prasad Saha, *Folklore* 7(8) August, p 283-329.
Further notes, pt. 1, The proper study of mankind is man 7(12) December 1966, p 456-457; pt. 2 *Bio-Bibliographical data* on J. Long: The father of Indian Sociology by Mahadeva Prasad Saha, 7(72) December, p 458-62, references.

NATIVISTIC MOVEMENTS

See Tribal Uprisings.

NAVAYATS

D'Souza, Victor S., 1953, Mother right in transition, *Sociological Bulletin* 2(2) September, p 135-142.

NAYADIS : INDIA : MALABAR

Aiyappan, A., 1937, Social and physical anthropology of Nayadis of Malabar, *Bulletin of Madras Government Museum* 2(4).

NEHRU, JAWAHARLAL : APPROACH TO TRIBALS

Anon, 1964, How Nehru saw the tribals?, *Vanyajati* 12(3) July, p 122-125.

——, 1989, Homage to Nehru, *Vanyajati* 37(1) January, p 1-2.

Bhupinder Singh, 1989, Nehru's tribal philosophy and tribal India today, *Mainstream* 27(35) May 27, p 46-47.

Sinha, S.P., 1989, Nehru's treatment for tribal development x-rayed, *Vanyajati* 37(4) October, p 39-49.

Trivedi, Harshad R., 1989 Nehru and tribals, *Indian Journal of Public Administration* 35(2) April-June, p 286-291.

Vanyajati (Periodical), 1964, In memoriam: Nehru and the tribes, *Vanyajati* 12(3) July, p 109-110, editorial.

Vidyarthi, L.P., 1966, Nehru's approach to tribal culture, *Vanyajati* 14(4) October, p 170-175, references.

See also National Seminar on Nehru and Evolution of Tribal Policy, September 20, 1989.

NELLITHORAI : TRIBALS

Guruswamy, P.A., 1988, Irula tribes of Nellithorai, *Social Welfare* 34(11) February, p 20-22 +.

NEO BUDDHIST MOVEMENT

See also Caste : Protest/Reform Movements.

NEO CHRISTIANS : INDIA : KERALA

Alexander, K.C., 1967, The problem of the neo-Christians of Kerala, *Man in India* 47(4) October-December, p 317-330, references, tables.

NEPAL

See also Geographical Area subdivision under main Descriptor.

NEPAL : CASTE RELATIONS

Subba, Tanka Bahadur, 1985, Caste relations in Nepal and India, *Social Change* 15(4) December, p 23-26, bibliography.

NETHERLAND

Klin, M.O.L., 1965, Images of the stratification system in the Netherland, *Sociological Bulletin* 14(2) September, p 50-53.

See also Geographical Area subdivision under main Descriptor.

NEWARA CULTURE

Chattopadhyay, P.K., 1925 An essay on the history of Newara culture, *Journal and Proceedings of Asiatic Society of Bengal* (NS) 23(3).

NICOBARESE

See also Hill Tribes; Korkus.

NIGERIA : NORTH EASTERN

Otterbein, Keith F., 1967, Mortuary practices in North-easter Nigeria, *Bulletin of Cultural Research Institute* 6(1-2), p 10-18, references, tables.

NIMADI FOLK SONGS

Upadhyaya, Ram Narain, 1959, The Nimadi folk-songs, *Indian Folklore* 2(4) October-December, p 298-299.

NISHIS : INDIA : ARUNACHAL PRADESH

Chakraborty, S.K., 1989, A brief ethnographic account on the Nishi of Arunachal Pradesh, *Vanyajati* 37(2) April, p 12-20.

Durah, D.K., 1985, Festival of the Nishis of Arunachal Pradesh, *Resarun* 11(2) Autumn-Winter, p 29-31.

Gangwar, A. and **Rama Krishnan, P.S.**, 1987, Agriculture and animal husbandry among the Sulungs and Nishis of Arunachal Pradesh, *Social Action* 37(4) October-December, p 345-372, bibliography, figures, tables.

Kani, M. and **Bourai, R.A.**, 1985, Aryan tradition among Nishis and Hill Miris of lower Subansiri district, Arunachal Pradesh, *Resarun* 11(2) Autumn-Winter, p 35-38.

NOKTE NAGAS

Aonok, S. Wati, 1956, Morung organisation among the Nokte Nagas, *Vanyajati* 4(2) April, p 73-81, footnotes, illustrations.

NOMADIC BLACKSMITHS

See Lohars.

NOMADS

See also Wandering Communities.

NOMADS OF HIMALAYAS

Shashi, S.S., 1988, Gujjars: The Nomads of the Himalayas, *Kurukshetra* 36(4) January, p 13-14.

NON FORMAL EDUCATION

Rout, Upendra Nath, 1978, A new approach to State Non-Formal Education Centre in tribal area for all age groups, *Experiments in Education* 6(4) June, p 60-63.

Swaminathan, Mina, 1982, Needed two evaluations in one non-formal education for women and girls, *Education Quarterly* 34(4) October, p 5-7.

Venkataih, N., 1980, Non-formal education for adult tribal, *Experiments in Education* 8(3) may, p 54-56.

See also Informal Education.

NON GOVERNMENTAL ORGANISATIONS
See Non-Official Associations.

NON OFFICIAL ASSOCIATIONS
Shrikant, L.M., 1960, Evaluation of work of non-official associations in Bombay, Madras and Kerala, *Vanyajati* 8(1) January, p 3-5.

NORTH BALASORE : INDIA
Das, Harish Chandra, 1963-1964, The Sea-fisherman of North Balasore and their way of fishing, *Adibasi* 5(2), p 25-28.

NORTH EAST INDIA
Marrison, G.E., 1962, Languages in the tribal churches of North East India, *Religion and Society* 9(4) December, p 72-79.
Srivastava, L.R.N., 1969, The problem of modernisation of the tribes of North East India, *Bulletin of Cultural Research Institute* 8(1-2), p 21-25.

NORTH SOUTH RELATIONS
Robert, Parkin, 1990, Terminology and alliance in India: Tribal systems and the North-South problem, *Contributions to Indian Sociology* 24(1) January-June, p 61-76.

NORTH WEST INDIA
Mastana, S.S., 1989, Palmar transverse creases among the Lobanas of North-West India, *Man in India* 69(3) September, p 305-309.

NORTHERN INDIA
Khare, R.S., 1970 On hypergamy and progeny rank determination in Northern India, *Man in India* 50(4) October-December, p 350-378, references, tables.
Kudryavtsev, M.K., 1964, On the role of the Jats in Northern India's ethnic history, *Journal of Social Research* 7(1-2) March-September, p 126-135.
Sher, Sher Singh, 1960, Ex-criminal tribes of Northern India need reclassification on more authentic and scientific grounds, *Journal of Social Research* 3(2) September, p 35-92, tables.

NUTRITIVE VALUES : TRIBAL ALCOHOLIC BEVERAGES
Sengupta, P.N., 1956, Studies on the nutritive values of tribal alcoholic beverages, *Bulletin of Department of Anthropology* 5(1) January p 67-80.

NUTRITIONAL PATTERNS : TRIBALS
Sen Gupta, N.K., 1988, A note on the survey and investigation on some physical conditions and nutritional patterns in relation to the tribal people in Singhbhum, *Man in India* 68(4) December, p 473-476.

NUTRITIONAL STATUS : TRIBAL FARMERS : INDIA : BIHAR : CHOTANAGPUR
Singh, B.K., 1989, A Study of nutritional status of tribal farmers in Ranchi district of Chotanagpur in Bihar, *Economic Affairs* 34(1) January-March, p 58-63, tables.

OBC
= Other Backward Classes

OCCUPATION : WEAKER CASTES

Verghese, Alexander V., Education, earning and occupation of weaker castes, *Journal of Higher Education*, 9(3) Spring, p 3873-3881, references.

OCCUPATIONAL ENVIRONMENT : ENDOGAMOUS COMMUNITIES : INDIA : WEST BENGAL

Gangopadhyay, Prodyot and **Kundu, Shampa**, 1988, Familial trend in arterial pressure among few endogamous communities of West Bengal, reared under diverse occupational environment, *Man in India* 68(2-3) June-September, p 235-242, bibliography.

OCCUPATIONAL MOBILITY : SCHEDULED CASTES : INDIA

Amba Rao, U., 1976, Higher education and occupational mobility among the Scheduled Caste youth, *Journal of Higher Education* 1(3) Spring, p 305-314, references, tables.

Jayagopal, R., 1986, Occupational mobility among a special group of Scheduled Castes in Tamil Nadu: A survey, *Indian Journal of Adult Education* 47(1) January, p 8-12.

OCCUPATIONAL PATTERN : SCHEDULED CASTES : INDIA

Forrester, Duncan B., 1975 Initial occupational pattern of Scheduled Castes graduates in India, *New Frontiers in Education* 5(2) May, p 49-65, references, tables.

OCCUPATIONAL STATUS : HARIJANS : INDIA : ORISSA

Kamila, Bana Behari, 1983, Occupational status of parents of Harijan and Tribal Welfare Department high school students of Orissa, *National Journal of Education* 6(1) September, p 56-64, references, tables.

OCCUPATIONAL STRUCTURE : SCHEDULED TRIBES : INDIA

Anon, 1987, (Book review), *Journal of Rural Development* 6(4) July, p 423-426, *National Geographical Journal of India* 33(1) March, p 118-119.
Review of the book: **Singh, R.S.**, 1987, *Changing occupational structure of Scheduled Tribes*, Inter-India Publication, New Delhi, p 291.

ONGE OF LITTLE ANDAMAN

Bose, Savadindu, 1964, Economy of the Onge of Little Andaman, *Man in India* 46(4), p 298-310.

Venkateshan, D., 1988, Innovations and their impact on the Onge of little Andaman, *Man in India* 68(4) December, p 413-423, bibliography.

ORAONS

Bara, David, 1959, Oraon marriage: Social-cultural context, *Sevartham* 14, p 63-73, footnotes.

Bhattacharya, S.K., et al, 1985, The migrant Oraon in the Andaman Islands: Some demographic aspects, *Journal of Indian Anthropological Society* 20(1) March, p 86-92, bibliography, tables.

Bleie, Tone, 1987, Gender relations among Oraons in Bangladesh: Continuity and change, *Economic and Political Weekly* (Supplement) 22(17) April 25, pWS 27-WS-31.

Choudhury, Bhagirathi, 1964, Oraon, *Adibasi* 8(3) January, p 45-50.

Hutton, J.H., 1929, Cultural affinities of the Oraons with the Hill tribes of Assam, *Man in India* 9(1) January-March, p 1-6.

Kar, R.K. and **Sharma J.L.**, 1990, The Oraons of Assam, *Vanyajati* 38(2) April, p 22-32.

Mitra, Mitashree, et al, 1986, A study on some behavioural traits among the Oraons of Twenty Four Parganas, *Indian Journal of Physical Anthropology and Human Genetics* 12(2) May-August, p 155-158, bibliography, tables.

Mukherjee, D.P. and **Das, N.K.**, 1985, Age at menarche in tribal girls: The Kanwar and the Oraon of Surguja dis' 'ct, M.P., *Journal of Indian Anthropological Society* 20(2) July, p 153-158, bibliography, tables.

Mukherjee, D.P., et al, 1985, Skeletal development of tribal children: Kanwar and Oraon of Surguja district (M.P.), *Journal of Indian Anthropological Society* 20(1) March, p 77-85, bibliography, tables.

Nandi, Santibhusan, 1960, Cultural change in an Oraon village, *Vanyajati* 8(1) January, p 12-20.

Pipla, Chumki, et al, 1985, A note on A B O, M N, Rh in (a) blood groups of the Tomang and Oraon tea labourers of the Jalpaiguri district, West Bengal, *Journal of India Anthropological Society* 20(1) March, p 66-70, bibliography.

Suryavanshi, Bhagwan Singh, 1959, Life in the dormitories of the tribal: The Oraons, *Indian Folklore* 2(1) January-May, p 45-47.

ORGANISATIONAL STRUCTURES

Burling, Robbins, 1960, An incipient caste organisation in the Garo hills, *Man in India* 40(4) October-December, p 283-299, references.

Rout, Siba Prasad, 1969, Youth organisation, *Adibasi* 11(1-2) April-July, p 89-95.

ORISSA : INDIA

Acharya, P., 1957-1958, The Puranas: An egg born tribe of Orissa, *Adibasi* 2(1), p 31-34.

Adyappan, A., 1964, Tribal languages of Orissa, *Adibasi* January p 5-6.

Patnaik, Binay Kumar, 1987, Tribles and caste: A case study in an Oriya village, *Man in India* 67(4) December, p 335-351, bibliography.

See also Geographical Area subdivision under main Descriptor.

OTHER BACKWARD CLASSES

Kusumakar, H., 1986, To be "backward" is good. *Times of India* (Sunday Review) November 9, p 11, col 1-8.

Mitra, Chandan, 1989, Moulded in Caste: AJGAR versus the lesser Other Backward Classes, *Times of India*, August 23, p 6, col 3-5.

See also Backward Classes Commission.

OTHER BACKWARD CLASSES : BENEFITS

Dushkin, Lelah, 1979, Backward class benefits and social class in India, 1920-1970, *Economic and Political Weekly*, 14, Annual Number, April, p 661-667.

OTHER BACKWARD CLASSES : CLUBS

Bhattacharya, Biswanath, 1965, A short note on clubs and libraries of the backward communities, *Bulletin of Cultural Research Institute*, 4, p 53-57, tables.

OTHER BACKWARD CLASSES : EDUCATION

Anon, 1987, (Book review), *Journal of Sociological Studies*, January 6, p 187-190.
Review of the book: **Bag, Dulal Chandra**, 1984, *Impact of education on some backward communities of West Bengal*, Calcutta, OPS Publishing, viii, 304 p.

Chitnis, Suma, 1972, Education and equality, *Economic and Political Weekly* 7(31,

32, 33), p 1975-1981.

D'Souza, Claude, 1986, Weaker section of the Indian society and their education, *Social Action* 36(1) January-March, p 13-25.

Educational India (Periodical), 1964, Backwardness, *Educational India* 30 (9) March, p 308-309, editorial.

Gupta, L.P., 1979, A study of personality syndromes and cognitive characteristics of Scheduled Castes, backward classes and non-Scheduled Caste students, *Journal of Higher Education* 4(3) Spring, p 381-387.

Jain, S.P., 1989, Educating backward classes: Role of U.G.C., *Economic Trends* 18(5) April, p 3-6.

Lele, T.P., 1967, A comparative study of the students from different communities, *Educates and Psychology Review* 7(3) July, p 117-124, tables.

Rao, T.S., 1972, Free education for all, *Social Welfare* 19(9) December, p 18-20.

Sharma, R.S., 1985, Developing educational technology for deprived sections of the Indian society, *Bulletin of Non-Normal Education* 3(3) December, p 1-17.

Verghese, Alexander V., 1984, Education, earning and occupation of weaker castes, *Journal of Higher Education* 9(3)`Spring, p 373-381, references.

Verma, B.P. and **Sharma, Keshav**, 1989, A comparative study of locus of control and self-concept of higher, backward and Scheduled Caste students, *Progress of Education* 63(9) April, p 205-208.

Verma, R.P., 1984, Educating the disadvantaged : A few suggestions, *National Journal of Education* 6(2) May, p 1-6, references.

OTHER BACKWARD CLASSES : EDUCATIONAL STATUS

Deshmukh, B.D., 1957, Educational status of the backward communities, *Progress of Education* 32(3) October, p 97-98, letter to editor.

OTHER BACKWARD CLASSES : EMPOWERMENT

Jetley, Surinder, 1968, Transfer of power to a low caste, *Interdiscipline* 5(3) Autumn, p 199-206.

OTHER BACKWARD CLASSES : EQUALISATION

Anon, 1986, (Book review), *Journal of Indian Law Institute* 28(1) January-March, p 117-121.

Review of the book: **Galanter, Marc**, 1984, *Competing equalities : Law and the backward classes in India*, Oxford University Press, New Delhi, 525 p.

Ramaswamy, Uma, 1986, Protection and inequality among backward groups, *Economic and Political Weekly*, 21, May 9, p 399-403.

OTHER BACKWARD CLASSES : ISSUES AND TRENDS

Cheluva Raju, K.H., 1986, Backward classes in India ; Issues and trends, *Indian Journal of Political Science* 47 (4) October-December, p 473-485.

OTHER BACKWARD CLASSES : LAW : INDIA

Anon, 1985, (Book review), *Tribune*, January 12, p 4-8.

Review of the Book : **Galanter, Mare**, 1985, Law and the backward classes in India, Oxford University Press, New Delhi, 525 p.

OTHER BACKWARD CLASSES : LIBRARIES

Bhattacharya, Biswanath, 1965, A short note on clubs and libraries of the backward communities, *Bulletin of Cultural Research Institute*, 4, p 53-57, tables.

OTHER BACKWARD CLASSES : LIVING STANDARDS

Hanumantha Rao, K. and **Sastry, V.S.**, 1990, Levels of living and poverty among social groups in Andhra Pradesh : A cross-section analysis, *Journal of Rural Development* 9(1) January, p 91-105.

OTHER BACKWARD CLASSES : MANDAL COMMISSION

See Backward Classes Commission, 1979-1980.

OTHER BACKWARD CLASSES : PROBLEMS

Anon, 1985, (Book review), *Vision* 4(3) January-March, p 67-69. Review of the book : **Sahoo, B.**, 1985, *The problem of weaker sections*, New Era Publishing, Bhubaneshwar, 248 p.

OTHER BACKWARD CLASSES : PROTEST/REFORM MOVEMENTS

Aziz, Abdul, 1980, The backward class movement in Karnataka, 1918-1929, *Journal of Historical Studies*, 16, p 50-62.

Parvathamma, C., 1986, Role of protest movements in social transformation, *Guru Nanak Journal of Sociology* 7(1) April, p 1-22.

OTHER BACKWARD CLASSES : RECLASSIFICATION

Sher, Sher Singh, 1960, Ex-criminal tribes of Northern India need reclassification on more authentic and scientific grounds, *Journal of Social Research* 3(2) September, p 35-42, tables.

OTHER BACKWARD CLASSES : RESEARCH

Roy, Burman B.K., 1961, A list of research projects with operative significance for welfare of the backward classes (with special reference to West Bengal) *Vanyajati* 9(1) January, p 9-21.

Zutshi, G.L., 1959, Preliminaries regarding applied research among backward classes, *Vanyajati* 7(3) July, p 84-93.

OTHER BACKWARD CLASSES : SOCIAL CHANGE

Blair, Harry W., 1980, Rising kulaks and backward classes in Bihar: Social change in the late 1970s, *Economic and Political Weekly* 15(2) January 12.

Jetley, Surinder, 1968, Transfer of power to a low caste, *Interdiscipline* 5(3) Autumn, p 199-206.

OTHER BACKWARD CLASSES : SOCIAL EQUALITY

Aurora, G.S., Caste and backward classes, *Man in India* 48(4) October-December, p 297-306, footnotes.

Jetley, Surinder, 1968, Transfer of power to a low caste, *Interdiscipline* 5(3) Autumn, p 199-206.

Radhakrishnan, P., 1981, Tamil Nadu backward classes, *Voluntary Action* 27(5-6) November-December, p 65-67 +.

Sinha, Surajit and **Bhattacharya, Ranjit**, 1969, Bhadralok and Chotolok in a rural area of West Bengal, *Sociological Bulletin* 6(2) January, p 104-106, references.

OTHER BACKWARD CLASSES : WELFARE

Abibasi (Periodical), 1965 Defence-cum-production orientation of the programme of backward classes welfare, *Adibasi*, October, p 1-4, editorial.

Anon, 1947, Government drive for uplift of backward classes, *Social Service Quarterly* 33(1) July, p 27-29.

_____, 1953, Scheme of the Madras State Government for the welfare of the

Scheduled Castes and Scheduled Tribes and other backward classes, included in the Five Year Plan, *Vanyajati*, 1(2) April, p 42-43.

——, 1965, Welfare of backward classes: Planning Commission panel discussion, *Vanyajati* 13(2) April, p 39-40 +.

——, 1986, (Book review), *Patriot* November 16, p 4, col 5-7.

Review of the Book : **Biswas, Onell**, 1985, *From justice to welfare*, Intellectual Publishing House, New Delhi, xix, 272 p.

Bajpai, Rajendra Kumari, 1986, National Policy on upliftment of weaker sections, *Secular Democracy* 19 (1-2) January-Fèbruary, p 51-52.

Deva, P.C., 1966, Voluntary organisations and the welfare of backward classes, *Vanyajati* 14(4) October, p 156-164.

Gopala Reddi, B., 1956, Welfare of tribals and other backward classes, *Indian Journal of Social Work* 16(4) March, p 294-296.

Hussain, Syed Khaja Mahboob, 1949, The rural uplift of tribes and backward classes in Hyderabad, Deccan, *Man in India* 29 (3-4) July December, p 185-198.

Nancharaiah, G., 1987, Land reforms and weaker sections : A case study, *Yojana* 31(11) June 16, p 8-13, tables.

OUTCASTES

Ganguly, Swati, 1983-1984, Buddhism, castes and outcastes: A sociological perspective, *Journal of Ancient India History* 14(1-4), p 220-233.

See also Harijans; Untouchables.

OUT OF SCHOOL EDUCATION

See Informal Education; Non Formal Education.

OXYGEN CONSUMPTION : POSTCLIMB EFFECTS : BHUTIAS

Chakraborty, Minakshi, et al, 1984, Post-climb effects on hearing and oxygen consumption at moderate altitude among Bhutia boys, *Journal of Indian Anthropological Society* 19(2) July, p 131-135.

P T C TASTE VARIATION : TRIBALS

Negi, R.S., et al, 1982, PTC taste variation in Bastar (Central India), *Indian Journal of Physical Anthropology and Human Genetics*, 8(1) April, p 41-46, bibliography, tables.

Sudhankar Babu, M., et al, 1984, Variation in taste perception of PTC in two tribal populations of Andhra Pradesh, *Social Welfare* 32(3) June, p 17-19.

PACIFIC

See Geographical Area subdivision under main Descriptor.

PADAM ABORS : GIRLS : ASSOCIATIONS

Gupta, Jaya Dutta, 1960, Ponung or girls association among the Padam Abor in the lower Abor hills, *Bulletin of Anthropological Survey of India* 9(2) July, p 71-73.

PADAM AREAS : INDIA : ASSAM

Sen Gupta, P.N., 1953, Population studies and living conditions of the tribes in the Padam and Minyong areas of Abor hills (Assam), *Bulletin of Department of Anthropology* 2(1) January, p 91-112, tables.

PADARS : INDIA : GUJARAT

Haque, M., 1984 Anthropometry of the Padar of Ranagadh, Gujarat, *Man in India* 64(3) September, p 294-303.

PADDY CULTIVATION : TRIBALS : INDIA : MAHARASHTRA

Pawar, H.S. and **Patel, R.P.**, 1987, Adoption behaviour of the tribal farmers from Surgana taluka (Nasik district) in respect of Paddy cultivation, *Tribal Research Bulletin* 9(2) March, p 15-17.

PADERU SAMITHI : INDIA : ANDHRA PRADESH

Lakshmaiah, T. and **Yadappanavar, Arvind**, 1988, A study of education facilities for tribal students: Problems and impact in Paderu Samithi in Andhra Pradesh, *Man in India* 68(4) December, p 380-400.

PAHADIAS

Thakkar, A.V., 1942, Among Santals and Pahadias, *Rural India* 5(1) January, p 6-8.

PAHIRAS : INDIA : SINGHBHUM

Das Gupta, Biman Kumar, 1959, The Pahiras of Kokro Singhbhum District, *Bulletin of Department of Anthropology* 8(2) July, p 85-90, references.

_____, 1962, A short ethnographic note on the Pahiras of Kokro, *Vanyajati* 10(3) July, p 110-119, references, tables.

PAIJAVANA

Anon, 1984, Paijavana or Pailavaka: A Sudra yogin, *Purana* 26(2) July, p 206-208.

PAILAVAKA

Anon, 1984, Paijavana or Pailavaka: A Sudra yogin, *Purana* 26(2) July, p 206-208.

PAKISTAN

See Geographical Area subdivision under main Descriptor.

PALAMAU TRIBALS

Moulik, T.K., 1987, Palamau tribals: Towards integrated development, *Economic Times*, May 21, p 5, col 3-6.

PALANI HILLS : INDIA

Venkatraman, S.R., 1984, Tribes of Palani and Kodal hills, *Vanyajati* 32(3) July, p 13-15.

PALLARS : INDIA : TAMIL NADU

Manuel, Moreno, 1989, Marriage transactions among the Pallars of Southern Kongu, Tamil Nadu, *Man in India* 69(1) March, p 13-23.

PALLI REDDIES : INDIA : ANDHRA PRADESH

Rami Reddy, V. and **Subhashini, A.B.**, 1984, A B O Blood groups among the Palli Reddies: A Backward caste of Tirupati and others populations of Andhra Pradesh, *Man in India* 64(2) June, p 193-200, bibliography.

PALMAR CREASES/DERMATOLYPHICS

Arti Kumari, 1988, A study on the Palmar dermatolyphics of the Kayasth of Ranchi, *Man in India* 68(2-3) June-September, p 216-227, bibliography

Bhasin, M.K., et al, 1986, Genetic studies of Pangwalas, transhumant and settled Gaddis Palmar dermatoglyphics, *Indian Journal of Physical Anthropology and Human Genetics* 12(1), p 9-28.

Das, R., 1985, A study on variation of Palmar fexion crease among three Assamese castes, *Indian Journal of Physical Anthropology and Human Genetics* 11(3) August-December, p 175-177, bibliography, tables.

Mastana, S.S., 1989, Palmar transverse creases among the Lobanas of North-West India, *Man in India* 69(3) September, p 305-309.

Sengupta, S. and **Dutta, M.N.**, 1985, Palmar main line index and transversality in Wanchos of Arunachal Pradesh, *Resarun* 11(2) Autumn-Winter, p 39-41, bibliography, tables.

PANCHAYAT SYSTEM : INDIA

Sher, Sher Singh, 1959, The Panchayat system of the Sansis of Punjab, *Sociological Bulletin* 8(1) March, p 97-102.

Shrikant, L.M., 1961, Tribal welfare under Panchayati Raj, *Vanyajati* 9(4) October, p 135-144.

Thusu, Kidar Nath, 1965, The panchayat system of the Durwas of Bastar (M.P.), *Man in India* 45(2) April-June, p 134-151, footnotes.

PANCHMAHALS : TRIBAL CHILDREN

Anon, 1985, Profile of a tribal child of Panchmahals, *Social Welfare* 32(3) June, p 28-29.

PANGWALAS/PANGWALS

Bhasin, M.K., et al, 1969, Genetic studies of Pangwalas, transhumant and settled Gaddis Palmer dermatoglyphics *Indian Journal of Anthropology and Human Genetics*, 12(1), p 9-28.

Sharma, Ranbir and **Kamal, Ami Chand**, 1986, Growth of political consciousness: A study of Pangwals tribes of Himachal Pradesh, *Punjab Journal of Politics* 10(1) January-June, p 67-81.

PAPILLARY PATTERNS : SINDHI KHATRIS

Indera P. Singh and **Kumbani, H.K.**, 1959, Distribution of papillary patterns on the middle and proximal phalanges of Sindhi Khatris, *Anthropologist* 6(1-2) March-August, p 26-37, references, tables.

PARASITE PROBLEM

Das, Gananath, 1955-1956, The parasite problem, *Adibasi* 1, p 36-38.

PARENT CHILD RELATIONS : TRIBAL STUDENTS : INDIA

Sowaid, M., et al, 1986, A study of parent child interaction and achievement motivation among tribal high school students, *Journal of Institute of Educational Research* 10(3) September, p 24-27, references.

PARENTAL DEPRIVATION : DENOTIFIED TRIBES : INDIA

Anon, 1982, Effect of parental deprivation on personality adjustment: With special reference to the denotified tribes of U.P., *Indian Educational Review* 17(1) January p 99-109.

Khan, M.A., 1979, Parental deprivation in relations to academic achievement of denotified tribes, *Indian Educational Review* 14(4) October, p 95-98.

Sinha, V., et al, 1976, Parental deprivation in relation to intelligence of denotified tribes, *Asian Journal of Psychology and Education* 1(2) July, p 38-39.

PATELS : INDIA : GUJARAT

Jain, Meenakshi, 1985, The Patels of Gujarat: Story of remarkable rise, *Times of India*, August 3, p 8, col 3-5.

PATTAPARA FUNCTIONS : KONNIKARS

Zutshi, G.L., 1957, Functions of the Pattapara among the Konnikars, *Vanyajati* 6(3) April, p 84-86.

PAUNDRA KSHATRIYAS : INDIA : WEST BENGAL

Gupta, Jaya Dutt, 1959, A study of the Paundra Kshatriya of West Bengal, *Bulletin of Department of Anthropology* 8(2) July, p 109-130, appendix, references.

PAWRAS

See Bhils.

PEASANTRY : TRIBALS

See Tribal Farmers.

PEASANTS : INDIA : GOA

Anon, 1968, Goa peasants on hunger-strike, *People's Democracy* 4(11) March 17, p 5.

PEDAGOGY : TRIBALS

Kundu, Manmatha, 1986, Tribal education in India: An effective pedagogy, *Journal of Indian Education* 12(4) November, p 43-48, references.

See also Tribal Education.

PERIODIC MARKETS : TRIBAL AREAS : INDIA

See Shandies: Tribal Areas: India: Andhra Pradesh.

PHALANGEAL HAIRS

Indera P. Singh and **Kumbani H.K.**, 1959, Distribution of Papillary patterns on the middle and proximal phalanges of Sindhi Khatris, *Anthropologist* 6(1-2) March-August, p 26-37, references, tables.

Negi, R.S., et al, 1962, Distribution of middle phalangeal hair in some Bastar population, *Bulletin of Anthropological Survey of India* 11(3-4), p 175-191, appendix, references, tables.

PHAYENGS : INDIA : MANIPUR

Mayanglambam, Main Babu and **Mayanglambam, Sunit Bala**, 1989 Earlobe attachment and dominant eye among the Phayengs of Manipur, *Man in India* 69(3) September, p 285-291.

——, 1989, Patterns of hand clasping, armfolding and handedness among the Phayengs of Manipur, *Man in India* 69(1) March, p 87-93.

PHONOLOGY : ABUJ MARIYA

Shesh, S., 1965, Phonology of Abuj Mariya, *Bulletin of Tribal Research and Development Institute* (Bhopal) 5(1-2) June-December, p 35-49, table.

PHULE, JOTIRAO : VIEWS ON CASTE

Anon, 1986, (Book review), *India, Past and Present* 3(2), p 315-323.

Review of the book: **O'Hanion, Rosalind**, 1986, *Caste, conflict and ideology: Mahatma Jotirao Phule and low caste protest in nineteenth century*, Western India, Cambridge University Press, Cambridge, 326 p.

PHYSICAL CONDITIONS : TRIBALS : INDIA : SINGHBHUM

Sen Gupta, N.K., 1988, A note on the survey and investigation on some physical conditions and nutritional patterns in relation to the tribal people in Singhbhum,

Man in India 68(4) December, p 473-476.

PLANNING STRATEGY : TRIBAL DEVELOPMENT

Anon, 1985 (Book Review) *Economic Trends* 31(6) March, p 1-4 +; *Financial Express* 9(5) June, p 5-8.
Review of the book : **Patel, M.L.**, 1985, *Planning Strategy for Tribal Development*, Inter-India Publications, New Delhi, 191 p.

PLANTATION WORKERS

Dasgupta, Ranjit, 1986, From peasants and tribesman to plantation workers: Colonial capitalism of labour power, *Economic and Political Weekly* (Supplement) 21(4) January 25, p PE2-PE10.

PNARS

See Khasis.

POLEYAS

Srinivas, M.N., 1985, The Poleyas in the Kodava society, *Journal of Historical Studies* 19, p 75-79, bibliography.

POLICIES : TRIBAL DEVELOPMENT

Tripathi, C.B., 1988, Approaches to tribal development and experience: General policies, administrative approach and personal policies and their implementation: An all India review, *Man in India* 68(4) December, p 335-355.
See also National Seminar on Nehru and Evolution of Tribal Policy, Septermber 20, 1989; Tribal Policy

POLICING : TRIBAL AREAS

Batria, Puran, Policing in tribal areas, *Bulletin of Tribal Research and Development Institute* (Bhopal) 7(1-2) June-December, p 5-18.

POLITICAL ASSESSMENT : RESERVATION : INDIA

Leela Singh, 1984, Job reservation: Political and legal perspective, *Modern Review* 148(9-10) September-October, p 267-274, bibliography.
Malhotra, Inder, 1989, Political commentary: The Yadav and other factors, *Times of India*, August 10, p 6, col 3-5.
Roy, Ashim K., 1985, Anti-reservation movement: A political assessment, *Economic and Political Weekly* 20(32) August 10, p 1343-1344.

POLITICAL CONSCIOUSNESS: TRIBALS : INDIA

Sachchidananda, 1959, Political consciousness in tribal Bihar, *Men in India* 39(4) October-December, p 301-308.
Sahay, B.N. and **Singh, B.K.**, 1970, Political consciousness among the tribals and their representation in gram panchayats, *Vanyajati* 18(1) January, p 12-16, tables.

POLITICAL ECONOMY : TRIBALS

Ghosh, A., 1985, The political economy of development strategy and tribal demography, *Capital* 196(4815) September 30, p 49-52.

POLITICAL INSTITUTIONS : IMPACT ON TRIBAL DEVELOPMENT

Sinha, Rakesh Ranjan, 1967, Traditional political institutions and tribal development, *Vanyajati* 15(3) July, p 135-138.

POLITICAL MOBILISATION

Datta Ray, Sunanda K., 1990, Class into caste: V.P. Singh's political insurance, *Statesman*, September 9.

POLITICAL SOCIOLOGY

Anon, 1985, (Book review), *Social Perspective* 13(3) December, p 204-207. Review of the book: **Alam, Javeed**, 1985, *Domination and Dissent*: Peasant and politics, Culcutta, Mandira.

Kamalakar, Jaya, 1988, Ethnic politics in municipal corporations, *Economic and Political Weekly* 23(19) May 7, p 945-946.

Shah, Ghan Shyam, 1987, Middle class politics: Case of anti-reservation agitation in Gujarat, *Economic and Political Weekly* (AN) 22(19-21) May, p AN155-AN72.

Shyama Nand Singh, 1989, Politics of job reservation, *Mainstream* 27(44) July 29, p 15-20, bibliography, tables.

Sonalkar, Wandana and **Shakir, Moin**, 1987, Caste, politics and development in Maharashtra, *Mainstream* 25(30) April 11, p 25-31, bibliography.

POLUM OF MASSES

Anon, 1988, Polum of the masses, *Times of India*, July 14, p 1-2.

POLYANDROUS PEOPLE : INDIA

Pakrasi, K., 1964, Note on differential sex ratios and polyandrous people in India, *Man in India* 144(2) April-June, p 161-174.

POLYANDROUS SOCIETY : TRIBAL CRIME

Mukherji, Anima, 1950, The pattern of a polyandrous society with particular reference to tribal crime, *Man in India* 39(2-3) April-September, p 56-65.

PONUNG

Gupta, Jaya Dutta, 1960, Ponung or girls association among the Padam Abor in the lower hills, *Bulletin of Anthropological Survey of India* 9(2) July, p 71-73.

POPULATION GROWTH : TRIBALS : INDIA : WEST BENGAL

Das, Amal Kumar and **Banerjee, Swapan Kumar**, 1964, Certain aspects of population growth amongst the tribals of West Bengal, *Bulletin of Cultural Research Institute* 3(1) p 1-14, tables.

See also Tribal Population.

POPULATION STUDIES : TRIBALS : INDIA : ASSAM

Sen Gupta, P.N., 1953, Population studies and living conditions of the tribes in the Padam and Minyong areas of Abor hills (Assam), *Bulletin of Department of Anthropology* 2(1) January, p 91-112. tables.

POVERTY : IMPACT ON SOCIAL BACKWARDNESS

Hasan, Shariful, 1985, Social backwardness is the end result of poverty, *Organiser* 37(1) May 10, p 8.

POVERTY ALLEVIATION : TRIBALS

Karuppaiyan, E., 1989, Issues in poverty alleviation programmes for the tribals, *Social Action* 39(1) January-March, p 72-89, bibliography.

Roy Burman, B.K., 1987, Historical process in aspect of communal land system and poverty alleviation among tribals, *Social Action* 37(4) October-December, p 391-420, bibliography, tables.

POWER STRUCTURE : INDIAN VILLAGES

Anon, 1987, (Book review), *Journal of Social Economic Studies* 4(4) October-December, 387-390.
Review of the book: **Choudhury, Ram Krishna**, 1987, *Caste and power structure in village India*, Inter-India Publications, New Delhi, 178 p.

PRAMALAI KALLARS : INDIA : SOUTHERN

Anon, 1987, (Book review), *Indian Economic Social History Review* 24(3) July-September, p 341-342; *Tribune* (Magazine) September 14, p 5-8.
Review of the book: **Dumont, Louis**, 1988, *A South India subcaste: Social organisation and religion of the Pramalai Kallar*, Oxford University Press, New Delhi, p 634.

Dumont, Louis, 1987, A South Indian sub-caste: Social organisation and religion of the Pramalai Kallar, *Economic Trends* 8(6) February, p 1-4.

PRE SCHOOL CHILDREN : TRIBALS : INDIA : ANDHRA PRADESH

Rao, V.V. Raman, 1984, Impact of supplementary feeding on tribal pre-school children of A.P.: An anthropometric assessment, *Man in India* 64(2) June, p 167-174.

PRIME MINISTER : INDIA : VIEWS ON RESERVATION

Dhar, M.K., 1990, P M commitment to reservation total, *Hindustan Times*, September 1.

PRIMITIVES

Banerjee, Biswanath, 1968, Relation between environment and culture among some Indian primitive communities living in the hills, *Bulletin of Cultural Research Institute* 7(1-2) p 55-61, references.

Guha, P.K., 1988, Shompen: A primitive tribe in transition, *Man in India* 68(4) December, p 465-469.

Hutton, J.H., 1922. Depopulation of primitive communities, *Man in India* 2(4) December, p 220-227, footnotes.

Koppar, D.H., 1956, Primitive tribes of Dharampur, *Journal of Anthropological Society of Bombay* (NS) 10(1) March, p 8-24.

Majumdar, D.N., 1930, The economic background of social institutions in primitive society, *Man in India* 10(2-3) April-September, p 150-166, footnotes.

Mukhiya, Prabhat Kumar, 1960, The primitive people of Orissa, *Vanyajati* 8(4) October, p 140-146.

Nag, D.S., 1954, Education for primitives, *Vanyajati* 2(4) October, p 117-120.

Prasad, R.R., 1986, Role of acculturation in the development of primitive tribes, *Tribal Research Bulletin* 8(2) March, p 8-11 +.

Sanyal, Shubhendu, 1988, Primitive tribes of Bihar: Strategy for development, *Man in India* 68(4) December, p 356-368.

Sirsalkar, P.R., 1985, Primitive tribes: Challenge for development, *Tribal Research Bulletin* 7(2) March, p 7-8.

Somasundram, A.M., 1950, Glimpses into primitive culture of India, *Man in India* 30(4) October-December, p 28-45.

Thakkar, A.V., 1949, Some pressing problems of primitive tribes, *Eastern Anthropologist* 3(1) September, p 1-2.

See also Aborigines; Backward Tribes; Hill Tribes; Scheduled Tribes; Tribes and Tribals.

PROGENY RANK : INDIA : NORTHERN

Khare, R.S., 1970, On hypergamy and progeny rank determination in Northern India, *Man in India* 50(4) October-December, p 350-378, references, tables.

PROHIBITION : SOCIO-ECONOMIC ASPECT

Shrikant, L.M., 1968, Socio-economic aspects of prohibition, *Vanyajati* 16(2) April, p 37-40, 69-70.

PROSTITUTION : HARIJAN GIRLS : INDIA : KARNATAKA

Anon, 1941, Problem of dedication of Harijan girls to prostitution in Karnataka, *Rural India* 4(6) June, p 303-308.

PROTEIN CALORIE INTAKE : TRIBAL STUDENTS

Mohanty, A.K., et al, 1990, Protein calorie intake and growth status of tribal boys in a residential school, *Man in India* 70(2) June, p 144-154.

PROTEST/REFORM MOVEMENTS

Parvathamma, C., 1986, Role of protest movements in social transformation, *Guru Nanak Journal of Sociology* 7(1) April, p 1-22.

See also Anti Brahminism; Caste: Protest/Reform Movements; Tribal Movements.

PSEUDO RAJPUTS

See Rajputs.

PSYCHOANALYSIS

Peter, Prince, 1939, The utility of psycho-analysis in social anthropology, *Indian Journal of Psychology* 14(1) January, p 23-25.

PSYCHOLOGICAL APPROACHES

Gupta, L.P., 1979, A study of personality syndromes and cognitive characteristics of Scheduled Castes, backward classes and non-Scheduled Caste students, *Journal of Higher Education* 4(3) Spring, p 381-387.

Pocock, David E., 1961, Psychological approaches and judgements of reality, *Contributions to Indian Sociology*, October 5, p 44-74.

PSYCHOLOGICAL DEVELOPMENT : TRIBALS : INDIA: RAJASTHAN

Trivedi, H.P., 1986, The T S P area in Rajasthan and its socio-psychological development barriers spectrum, *Rajasthan Economic Journal* 10(1) January, p 53-63, bibliography, tables.

PSYCHOLOGICAL PROBLEMS : TRIBALS : INDIA : UTTAR PRADESH

Srivastava, Rajni, 1983, Some psychological problems of tribals of Mirzapur: A case study, *Indian Educational Review* 18(2) April, p 106-110, tables.

PUBLIC POLICY : TRIBALS : INDIA : TAMIL NADU

Perumal, C.A., and **Padmanabhan**, 1986, Tribals of Tamil Nadu public policy, *Indian Journal of Political Science* 47(4) October-December, p 457-472.

PUBLIC SERVICE DELIVERY SYSTEM : TRIBAL AREAS : INDIA

Basu, Ashok Ranjan, 1985, Improving public service delivery system for tribal population in India: An empirical investigation, *Prashanika* 14(1) January-March, p 1-15.

PUKHTOON TRIBES
See Tribes and Tribals: Pakistan

PULAYAS : INDIA : KERALA
Alexander, K.C., 1967, The problem of the Neo-christians of Kerala, *Man in India* 47(4) October-December, p 317-330, references, tables.
——, 1968, Changing status of Pulaya Harijans of Kerala, *Economic and Political Weekly*, Special Number, July.
Velayudhan R., 1940, A study of social conditions among the Pulays (Harijans) of Kalady in Travancore State, *Indian Journal of Social Work* 1(3) December, p 393-403, tables.
See also Hill Pulayas.

PULAYAS : RELIGIOUS LIFE AND CUSTOMS
Alexander, K.C., 1968, Changing religious beliefs and practices of the Pulayas of Kerala, *Social Action* 18(5) September-October, p 390-398.

PUNJAB : INDIA
Amrit Kaur and **Tarlok Singh**, 1985, Religion education disparity among Scheduled Castes of Punjab, *Indian Journal of Adult Education* 46(4) April, p 7-10 +, tables.
Sher, Sher Singh, 1959, The Panchayat system of the Sansis of Punjab, *Sociological Bulletin* 8(1) March, p 97-102.
See also Geographical Area subdivision 'Punjab' under main Descriptor.

PURANAS
Acharya, P., 1957-1958, The Puranas: An egg-born tribe of Orissa, *Adibasi* 2(1), p 31-34.

PUSHTOON TRIBES
See Tribes and Tribal: Pakistan.

RABARIS : INDIA : KUTCH
Jayaram, K.V., 1986, Rabaris of Kutch, *Economic Trends* 7(5) December, p 6-8.

RAIPUR DISTRICT : INDIA : MADHYA PRADESH
Dube, Krishan Chandra, 1960, Problem of Aboriginal debt in Bhindrawagarh subdivision of the Raipur district (M.P.), *Vanyajati* 8(2) April, p 73-80, tables.

RAJ KOYAS
See Koyas.

RAJA BANSIS
See Rajbansis.

RAJBANSIS
Basu, Swaraj, 1986, A case study of the Rajbansi caste movement in Northern Bengal, 1901-1921, *Quarterly Review of Historical Studies* 26(3) October-December, p 59-61.

RAJAH KOYAS
See Koyas.

RAJASTHAN : INDIA

Chaudhary, N.D., 1975, Educational development among the Scheduled Tribes in Rajasthan, *Education Quarterly* 27(3) October, p 26-30, tables.

Oad, L.K., 1976, Problems of tribal education in Rajasthan, *Journal of Indian Education* 1(6) March, p 53-59.

See also Geographical Area subdivision 'Rajasthan' under main Descriptor.

RAJIV FORMULA : RESERVATION

Anon, 1990, Mishra urges V.P. to accept Rajiv Formula, *National Herald* September 5, p 9, col 5-8.

RAJPUTS

Majumdar, D.N., 1962, Pseudo Rajputs, *Man in India* 6(2-3) June-September, p 152-160, footnotes.

RALEGANA SINDIS

Seshadri, H.V., 1987, Ralegana Sindi: A name for social metamorphosis, *Organiser* 38(40) February 15, p 10.

RAMAKRISHNA PARAMHANS : VIEWS ON CASTE

Mukherjee, Jayasree, 1987, The institution of caste in the eyes of Ramakrishna and Vivekananda, *Quarterly Review of Historical Studies* 27(2) p 22-35, bibliography.

RANG-BANG

Srivastava, R.P., 1953, Rang-Bang in the changing Bhotia life, *Eastern Anthropologist* 6(3-4) March-August, p 190-203, footnotes.

RANK DETERMINATION : INDIA : NORTHERN

Khare, R.S., 1970, On hypergamy and progeny rank determination in Northern India, *Man in India* 50(4) October-December, p 350-378, references, tables.

RASHA KOYAS

See Koyas.

RASKA IMPLICATIONS : TRIBAL EDUCATION

Kundu, M., 1982, Concept of 'Raska' implications for tribal education, *New Frontiers in Education* 12(2) April-June, p 42-46.

RASTOGIS

Rastogi, Sudha, et al, 1984, Finger dermatoglyphics of the Rastogis, *Man in India* 64(3) September, p 286-293.

RECLASSIFICATION OF SCHEDULED TRIBES : INDIA

Roy Burman, B.K., 1966, Questions relating to inclusion in and exclusion from the list of Scheduled Tribes, *Journal of Indian Anthropological Society* 1(1) March, p 7-14, references, illustration.

Sher, Sher Singh, 1960, Excriminal tribes of Northern India need reclassification on more authentic and scientific ground, *Journal of Social Research* 3(2) September, p 35-42, 4 tables.

RED MAN : UNITED STATES OF AMERICA

Mills, J.P., 1923, The lessons of the red man, *Man in India* 3(3-4) September-December, p 217-223, footnotes.

REHABILITATION

Biswas, P.C., 1954, The utility of research for the rehabilitation, *Vanyajati* 2(1) January, p 5-9.

Indra Jeet Singh, 1967, Social rehabilitation and career orientation, *Journal of Social Research* 10(1) March, p 18-21.

See also Tribal Rehabilitation.

RELIGION

Anon, 1987, (Book review), *Indian Journal of Social Work* 47(4) January, p 464-466.

Review of the book: **Gangrade, K.D.**, 1987, *Social work and development role of religion and caste in three Delhi villages*, Northern Book Centre, Delhi, 130 p.

Minz, Nirmal, 1987, Religion, culture and education in the context of tribal aspirations in India, *Journal of Dharma* 12(2) April-June, p 150-164, bibliography, footnote.

Mohapatra, Prashant Kumar, 1970, Leadership and religion, *Adibasi* 11(4) January, p 53-59.

Sharma, S.L. and **Srivastava, R.N.**, 1967, Institutional resistance to induced Islamisation in a convert community: An empirical study in sociology of religion, *Sociological Bulletin* 16(1) March, p 69-80, references.

RELIGION AND RACE : TRIBALS : INDIA

Panchbhai, S.C., 1966, Religion and race as determinants of reference group: A study in stereo types of three Indian tribes, *Indian Journal of Psychology* 41(1) March, p 1-6, references, tables.

RELIGIOUS CRITERION : RESERVATION : INDIA

Kananalkil, Jose, 1986, Secular state and religious criterion for reservation, *Social Action* 36(2) April-June, p 137-148.

RELIGIOUS FESTIVALS : TRIBALS : INDIA : ORISSA

Behura, N.K. and **Misra, K.K.**, 1985, Religious rites and festivals among the tribes of Orissa, *Vision* 4(4)-5(1) April-September, p 66-86, bibliography.

See also Festival: Tribals.

RELIGIOUS FUNCTIONS : CHRISTIANS : INDIA : TRIPURA

Das, Biplas, 1986, The Uchais of Tripura: Some religious functions of the christian groups: *Folklore* 27(8) August, p 171-176, bibliography.

RELIGIOUS MOVEMENTS : INDIA

Dene, Steve, 1985, Religious movement as rite of passage : Analysis of the Birsa movement, *Contributions to Indian Sociology* (NS) 19(2) July-December, p 251-268, bibliography.

RELIGIOUS RITES : TRIBALS : INDIA : ORISSA

Behura, N.K. and **Misra, K.K.** 1985, Religious rites and festivals among the tribes of Orissa, *Vision* 4(4)-5(1) April-September, p 66-86, bibliography.

REPRESSION OF TRIBALS : INDIA : BIHAR

Jabbar Alam, M., 1987, CPI condemns Bihar repression of tribals, *New Age* 35(48) November 29, p 6.

Kalathill, Mathew, 1984, Repression of tribals, *Economic and Political Weekly* 19(36) September 8, p 1562.

REPTILES : TRIBAL AREAS : INDIA : MADHYA PRADESH

Joseph, A.N.T., 1989, Ethnozoology of reptiles in relation to health care among tribals in Madhya Pradesh, *Social Action* 39(4) October-December, p 405-422.

RESEARCH AND DEVELOPMENT

Anon, 1966, Research on tribal welfare, *Vanyajati* 14(2) April, p 53-54.

Biswas, P.C., 1954, The utility of research for the rehabilitation, *Vanyajati* 2(1) January, p 5-9.

Das, Amal Kumar, 1955, The role of research in tribal welfare, *Vanyajati* 13(3) July, p 118-122.

Kochar, V.K., 1967, Objectification of research process in social anthropology, *Indian Journal of Social Work* 27(4) January, p 387-392, references.

Raghaviah, V., 1989, Research on tribal welfare, Rishabdev, *Vanyajati* 37(1) January, p 10-11.

Saraf, Samarendra, 1969, Tribal unrest: An urgent research problem, *Bulletin of Cultural Research Institute* 8(1-2), December, p 32-37, Footnotes, references.

Srivastava S.K., 1969, Current trends in social anthropological research in India, *Journal of Social Sciences* 2(2) July, p 107-115, references.

Surana, M.B., 1987, Research designs for evaluation of tribal development programme, *Tribal Research Bulletin* 9(2) March, p 5-8, bibliography.

Yadav, S.K., 1983, Research review on implementation of educational schemes of Scheduled Castes, *Indian Educational Review* 18 (3) July, p 12-22, references.

Vidyarthi, L.P., 1966, Social anthropological researches in India: Some preliminary observation, *Journal of Social Research* 9(1).

——, 1972, Needed urgent research for Fifth Five Year plan for tribal Bihar, *Research Journal of Ranchi University*, 8, December.

Yadav, S.K., 1963, Research review on implementation of educational schemes of Scheduled Castes, *Indian Economic Review* 18(3) July, p12-22, references.

Zutshi, G.L., 1959, Preliminaries regarding applied research among backward classes, *Vanyajati* 7(3) July, p 84-93.

See also Study Teams: Tribal Welfare; Tribal Development: Research Projects: India.

RESERVATION ISSUES

Abraham, A.S., 1985, Anti-reservation protest: Growing clout of backward classes, *Times of India*, March 1, p 8.

——, 1985, Caste war in Gujarat: Wider objectives of agitation, *Times of India* 14, p 6.

——, 1985, Going beyond reservations: Framework for a wider policy, *Times of India*, April 20, p 8.

——, 1985, Turmoil over reservations: Backward classes in full cry, *Times of India*, April 12, p 8.

——, 1986, Backward class quota: Forming a national consensus, *Times of India* 19(8) September 19, p 8.

——, 1986, Goodbye to modernism: Warring over reservations, *Times of India*, August 6, p 8, col 3-5.

Anon, 1985, Govt. staff in Gandhinagar strike work, *Times of India*, May 1, p 1, col 7-8.

——, 1985, Gujarat: Threat of fresh agitation, *New Age*, November 24, p 2.

——, 1985, (Book Review), *National Herald* 2 (5) October 20, p 5; *Patriot*, November 3, p 4.

Review of the book: **Mehta, Haroobhai** and **Patel, Hasmukh**, 1985, *Dynamics of Reservation Policy*, Patriot Publishing, New Delhi, 320 p.

———, 1985, (Book review), *Patriot* May 12, p 4.

Review of the book: **Desai, I.P.**, et al, 1985, *Caste, caste-conflict and reservations*, Janata Publication, Delhi, viii, 218 p.

———, 1985, A cynical ploy, *Times of India*, January 17, p 8.

———, 1985, Gujarat accord, *Times of India*, July 22, p 8.

———, 1985, Gujarat caste war, *Times of India*, April 17, p 8.

———, 1985, Gujarat government accepts agitators' demands, *Times of India*, April 20, p 1 +.

———, 1985, Reverse discrimination defended, *Link* 27 (36) April 21, p 12.

———, 1985, Statesmanship leads to disaster, *Times of India* (Sunday Review) April 28, p 1 +.

———, 1985, A thorny problem, *Times of India*, March 7, p 8.

———, 1986, (Book review), *India Quarterly* 42(1) January-March, p 103-105; *Link* 28 (25) January 26, p 109-111; *Patriot*, March 9, p 4; *Sunday Statesman*, March 11, p 11; *Tribune*, April 27, p 11.

Review of the book: **Mehta, Haroobhai** and **Patel, Hasmukh**, 1985, *Dynamics of Reservation Policy*, Patriot Publishing, New Delhi, 320 p.

———, 1986, (Book Review), *Indian Express* (Magazine) August 31, p 5.

Review of the book: **Anon**, 1986, *Scenario of the 7 per cent*, Cenemart Foundation, New Delhi, 2 vols.

———, 1986, Mr. Hegde surrenders, *Times of India*, October 9, p 8.

———, 1986, Policy of reservation: A symposium, *Parlance* 9 (11) August p 10-21.

———, 1987, (Book review), *Times of India* (Sunday review), March 8, p vi.

Review of the book: **Sandanshi, D.N.**, 1987, *Reservations for social justice*, Current Law Publishing.

———, 1990, All party meet to discuss reservations, *Hindustan Times*, August 31.

———, 1990, Extent reservation to education: MPs, *Patriot*, September 4.

———, 1990, Job reservations for backward classes, *Patriot*, September 3.

———, 1990, National debate an reservation imperative, *Statesman*, September 1.

———, 1990, Reservations are necessary, *Tribune*, September, 3, p 6.

———, 1990, Reservation doesn't mean mediocrity, *Times of India*, September 3.

———, 1990, Reservation partisan, *Tribune*, August 18.

———, 1990, Teachers front back reservation, *National Herald*, September 4, p 3, col 2-3.

Athre, H.V.R., 1980, Reservation policy, *Mysore Economic Review* 65 (1) January, p 1-3.

Bakshi, P.M., 1985, Reservations for backward classes: Some reflections, *Journal of Indian Law Institute* 27 (2) April-June, p 318-335.

Bakshi, Rajni, 1985, Will the movement spread? *Indian Express*, May 5, p 8.

Baxi, Upendra, 1985, Reflections on reservation crisis in Gujarat, *Mainstream* 23 (41) June 8, p 15-22; 23 (42) June 14, p 20-25, 23 (43) June 22, p 20-24.

Bhattacharjea, 1990, Anti-reservation stir: Skirting the basic issue, *Mainstream* 28 (46) September 8, p 3 +.

Bommai, S.R., 1990, Quota for weaker sections must, *Indian Express*, September 9.

Chopra, Pran, 1989, Casting a deadly bait, *Indian Express*, August 1, p 1 +.

Deshpande, Anjali, 1990, Reservations and Mandal report, *Mainstream* 28 (44) August 25, p 5 +.

Dhagambar, Vasudha, 1985, Reservation: Missing the wood for the trees, *Mainstream* 23 (36) May 4, p 5-6.

Dhar, M.K., 1990, PM commitment to reservation total, *Hindustan Times*, September 1.

Dhawan, Shiv, 1985, Reservations: A critique of social justice, *Patriot* (Magazine), August 4, p 1.

Guru, Gopal, 1984, Reservations and the Sanskritisation of Scheduled Castes: Some theoretical aspects, *Sociological Bulletin* 33 (1-2) March-September, p 29-38, bibliography.

——, 1985, Politics of reservations: A class approach, *Social Change* 4 (3) April-June, p 131-139, bibliography.

Hanumanta Rao, K., 1990, Job reservations for backward classes, *Mainstream* 28 (46) September 8, p 6.

Hasan, Shariful, 1985, Social-backwardness is the end result of poverty, *Organiser* 37 (1) May 19, p 8.

Hedge, Ramakrishna, 1986, Reservation policy in Karnataka, *Monthly Commentary on Indian Economic Conditions* 28 (2) September, p 10-13.

——, 1990, Hedge for economic criteria, *Indian Express*, September 19, p 9.

Heredia, Rudi, 1986, Minority rights and reservation policy: Towards coherence and consistence, *New Frontiers in Education* 16 (2) April-June, p 60-63.

Hoshiar Singh and **Malik, Jagdish Kumar**, 1984, The Mandal Commission report: A plea for share in power, *Political Science Review* 23 (3-4) July-December, 250-268, bibliography, tables.

Jain, Deepa, 1985, Should reservation policy be continued?, *Radical Humanist* 49 (1) April, p 25-28.

Kananaikil, Jose, 1986, Secular state and religious criterion for reservation, *Social Action* 36 (2) April-June, p 137-148.

Khusro, A.M., 1990, Job reservations: Pro-side, con-side and inside, *Indian Express*, September 13.

Kothari, Milap, 1990, What price reservation, *Hindustan Times*, September 6.

Leela Singh, 1984, Job reservation: Political and legal perspective, *Modern Review* 148 (9-10) September-October, p 267-274, bibliography.

Limay, Madhu, 1990, Reservations, *Hindustan Times*, September 10.

Makwana, Yogendra, 1985, Reservation: Does it promote class war, *Link* 27 (36) April 21, p 9-11.

Manohara Prasad, N., 1986, The great reservation divide, *Social Action* 36 (2) April-June, p 212-219.

Mathew, P.M., 1988, Caste reservations: A critique, *Social Change* 18 (2) June, p 93-99, bibliography.

Mehta, Dhawal, 1985, Anti-reservation agitation in Gujarat, *Radical Humanist* 49 (4) July, p 25-31.

Mishra, K.K., 1985, The Dalits reply back, *Link* 27 (36) April 21 p 13.

Nehru, B.K., 1988, Do we still need reservations, *Indian Education* (Magazine) April 17, p 1, col 1-6.

Nehru, Jawaharlal, 1990, Nehru was against quota in services, *Indian Express*, September 19.

Pandya, Dinakar, 1985, Defeated castests on rampage, *Link* 27 (33) March 31, p 21-27.

Paranjape, H.K., 1985, New look at reservations: Other ways to better opportunities, *Times of India*, June 6, p 8; June 7, p 8.

Parmanand Singh, 1987, Preventing exploitative acquisition of reservation benefits through adoption strategem, *Journal of Indian Law Institute* 29 (1) January-March, p 100-109, footnotes.

——, 1987, Reservation reality and the Constitution: Current crisis in India, *Cochin University Law Review* 11 (3-4) September-December, p 284-318.

Paswan, Ram Vilas, 1990 Reservation won't lead to mediocrity, *Patriot*, September 3.

Patwardhan, Vidya and **Palshikar, Vasant**, 1990, Are educational reservations a waste?: The result of a survey, *Janata*, 45, Annual Number, p 35-39.

Pinto, Marina, 1980-1981, Reservation policy in India, *Journal of the University of Bombay* 19 (53), p 65-82, table.

Rajaiah, B., 1982, Reservations in higher education and jobs, *Educational Review* 88 (3) March, p 55-58.

Ravnathan, K.V., 1990, Reservations: Lessons from experience, *Indian Express*, September 7.

Roy, Ashim K., 1985, Anti-reservation movement: A political assessment, *Economic and Political Weekly*, 20 (32) August 10, p 1343-1344.

Saksena, N.S., The reservation issue: A possible basis for consensus, *Times of India*, May 3, p 3-5.

Seerval, H.M., 1985, Reservation in education and public service, *Monthly Commentary on Indian Economic Conditions* 27 (1) August, p 79-86.

Saraf, Pushp, 1990, Job reservation in Railways and accidents, *Indian Express*, September 19.

Shah, A.M., 1990, Reservations: Double talk on castes, *Hindustan Times*, September 7.

Shah, Ghan Shyam, 1985, Caste, class and reservation, *Economic and Political Weekly* 20 (3) January 19, p 132-136, footnotes.

——, 1987, Middle class politics: Case of anti-reservation agitation in Gujarat, *Economic and Political Weekly*, Annual Number, 22 (19-21) May, pAN155-AN172.

Sheth, D.L., 1985, The great reservation debate, *Indian Express* (Magazine) May 12, p 1 +; *Sarvodaya* 33 (1-2) July-August, p 9-19.

——, 1986, The problem of reservations: Economic backwardness ow social injustice ? *Indian Journal of Adult Education* 47 (5) May, p 9-15; 47 (6) June, p 4-7 + ; 47 (7) July, p 14-21 ; 50 (1) April, p 9-14 ; 50 (2) May, p 13-19.

——, 1987, Reservation policy revisited, *Economic and Political Weekly* 22 (46) November 14, p 1957-1962, footnotes.

Shyama Nand Singh, 1986, Reservation controversy in Andhra Pradesh, *Mainstream* 25 (2) September 20, p 2-5 +, tables.

——, 1989, Politics of job reservation, *Mainstream* 27 (44) July 29, p 15-20, bibliography, tables.

Solanki, M.S., 1985, Only half of reserved jobs are filled, *Link* 27 (36) April 21, p 7-8.

Sundaresh, Aruna, 1989, Constitution law and reservations, *New Frontiers in Education* 16 (2) April-June, p 33-40.

Suri, Dona, 1985, Reservations: Arc they still valid ? *Tribune*, April 14, p 1.

Thirupati Rao, U., 1987, Job reservation policy in India, *Educational Review* 93 (2) February, p 29-31.

Vaid, Minnie, 1985, Gujarat is going the way of Assam, *Illustrated Weekly of India* 106 (8) June 30, p 36-37.

Verma, B.R., 1985, Rationale of reservations, *National Herald* (Sunday Herald)

August 11, p 1 +.

Viswam, S., 1985, The reservation conundrum, *Mainstream* 23 (35) April 27, p 3-5 +.

Yagnik, Achyut and **Desai, Harshad**, 1985, The wages of populism, *Illustrated Weekly of India* 106 (8) June 30, p 38-39.

See also Educational Reservations.

RESERVATION POLICY : INDIA

Athre, H.V.R., 1980, Reservation policy, *Mysore Economic Review*, 65 (1) January, p 1-3.

Pinto, Marina, 1980-1984, Reservation policy in India, *Journal of the University of Bombay* 49 (53), p 65-82, table.

See also Reservation Issues; Rights and Reservation Policy: Minorities: India.

RESIDENTIAL SCHOOLS : TRIBAL AREAS

Bapat, N.V., 1968, Residential school in tribal areas, *Vanyajati* 16(4) October, p 154-159.

Mohanty, A.K., et al, 1990, Protein calorie intake and growth status of tribal boys in a residential school, *Man in India* 70(2) June, p 144-154.

RESTAURANT FACILITIES : HARIJANS : INDIA

Social Service Quarterly (Periodical), 1934, Admission of Harijans to public restaurants, *Social Service Quarterly* 19(4) April, p 159-160 , editorial.

REVITALISATION MOVEMENTS : TRIBALS : INDIA

Jay, Edward, 1961, Revitalisation movements in tribal India, *Journal of Social Research* 4(1-2) March-September, p 282-315, references.

See also Tribal Movements.

REVOLTS : ADIVASIS : INDIA

Parulekar, Godavari, 1986, Saga of the Warli Adivasis revolt, *People's Democracy* 10(9) March 2, p 5 +.

RIANGS

Mukherjee, Bhabananda, 1959, The Riang, *Bulletin of Department of Anthropology* 8(1) January, p 1-107, illustrations, references.

_____, 1959, Trends of changes in the Riang culture since independence, *Bulletin of Department of Anthropology* 8(2) July, p 103-108.

Som, J.K., 1988, Transformation of Riang economy in the context of rubber plantation industry: A micro study in Tripura, *Man in India* 68 (2-3) June-September, p 145-166, bibliography, tables.

Thusu, Kidar Nath, 1962, The Riang agricultural practices, *Bulletin of Anthropological Survey of India* 11(3-4), p157-174, appendix, references.

RIDGE COUNT : FINGER PATTERNS : WANCHOS : INDIA : ARUNACHAL PRADESH

Sengupta, S. and **Dutta, M.N.**, 1985, A note on ridge count of finger patterns of the Wanchos of Arunachal Pradesh, *Resarun* 11(2) Autumn-Winter, p 23-26, bibliography, tables.

RIGHTS AND RESERVATION POLICY : MINORITIES : INDIA

Heredia, Rudi, 1986, Minority rights and reservation policy: Towards coherence and consistence, *New Frontiers in Education* 16(2) April-June, p 60-63.

RIGVEDA

Chapekar, N.G., 1952, Traces of totemism in the Rigveda, *Sociological Bulletin* 1(2) September, p 95-98.

RISLEY : VIEWS ON TRIBES AND CASTES

Bandyopadhyay, Sekhar, 1985, The Raj, Risley and the tribes and the castes of Bengal, *India Past and Present* 2(1), p 41-52, footnotes.

ROHTAS DISTRICT : INDIA

Jabbar Alam, M., 1986, Terror against tribals in Rohtas district, *New Age* 34(9) March 2, p 8 +.

ROMANTICISM : TRIBALS

Suryavanshi, Bhagwan Singh, 1959, Romances in the tribals: A living page from the life of the tribals, *Indian Folklore* 2(3) July-September, p 223-225.

ROMAS

Shashi, S.S., 1983, Romas still cherish old memories, *Statesman* March 21, p 8.

See also Gypsies.

ROPE MAKING : TRIBALS

Sao, Suman, et al, 1985, A model of tribal industrial growth: Case study of rope-making, *Man and Life* 11(3-4) July-December, p 207-220, bibliography, tables.

RORSCHACH EFFECT : HARIJANS

Shanker, Prem, 1968, Education and Rorschach affective factors of the Harijans, *Psychological Review* 4(2) July, p 95-100, references, tables.

RURAL COMMUNITY

Mehta, B.H., 1958, Towards a casteless rural community, *Indian Journal of Adult Education* 19(3) October, p 40-46.

RURAL DEVELOPMENT : TRIBAL AREAS

Anon, 1985, (Book review), *Social Action* 35(1) January-March, p 95-98.

Review of the book: **Pachauri, S.K.**, 1984, *Dynamics of Rural Development in tribal areas*. Concept Publishing Company, New Delhi, xiv, 262 p.

RURAL HOUSING : SCHEDULED CASTES : INDIA : ANDHRA PRADESH

Prasad Rao, C.R., 1989, Rural housing among Scheduled Caste in two districts of Andhra Pradesh: A comparison of parameters and predictors, *Vanyajati* 37(4) October, p 76-89.

RURAL MARKETS : TRIBALS

Anon, 1964, Tribal Market: A pilot survey, *Bulletin of Tribal Research and Development Institute* (Chhindwara) 4(2) December, p 33-108, references tables.

See also Shandies: Tribal Areas: India: Andhra Pradesh; Tribal Markets.

SACRED CHIEFS : INDIA : ASSAM

Mills, J.P., 1949, The sacred chiefs of Assam, *Man in India* 23(3) p 149-151.

SADANI DIALECT : TRIBALS : INDIA : SUNDARBANS

Mukherjee, Sankarananda, 1964, Sadani: The tribal dialect of the Sundarbans, *Bulletin of Cultural Research Institute* 3(2), p 47-50, references.

SAHARS
See Saoras.

SANSIS
Sher, Sher Singh, 1959, The Panchayat system of the Sansis of Punjab, *Sociological Bulletin* 8(1) March, p 97-102.
——, 1962, A demographic study of Sansis, *Vanyajati* 10(4) October, p 145-160, references, tables.

SANSKRITISATION : SCHEDULED CASTES : INDIA
Guru, Gopal, 1984, Reservations and the sanskritisation of Scheduled Castes: Some theoretical aspects, *Sociological Bulletin* 33(1-2) March-September, p 29-38, bibliography.
Shyam Lal, 1973, Sanskritisation and social change among Bhangis in Jodhpur city, *Indian Journal of Social Work* 34(1).

SANTAL REBELLION, 1855
Culshaw, W.J. and **Archer, W.G.**, 1945, The Santal Rebellion, *Man in India* 25(4) December, p 218-239, footnotes.

SANTALS
Archer, W.G., 1987, Tribal law and justice: A report on the Santal, *Man in India* 67(1) March, p 81-86.
Bhattacharya, Subhendu Shekhar, 1962, Santal songs: Different types, *Bulletin of Cultural Research Institution* 1(2), p 54-61.
Bodding, P.O., 1925, The Santal medicine, *Memoirs of the Asiatic Society of Bengal* 10(2).
Chakraborty, Falguni, 1985, Making of plough: A case study of rational adaptation of technology among the Santals, *Man in India* 65(3) September, p 246-260.
Chaudhuri, A.B., 1986, Witch killings among Santals, *Social Change* 16(1) March, p 69-70.
Choudhuri, Uma, 1955, A comparison of Santal mental test reactions in rural and urban areas, *Bulletin of the Department of Anthropology* 4(1), p 67-68.
Das, Harish Chandra, 1964, Santal, *Adibasi* January, p 65-68.
Das Gupta, Pranab Kumar, 1964, Impact of industrialisation of tribal life, *Bulletin of Anthropological Survey of India* 13(1-2) January-June, p 85-106, tables.
Duyber, Edward, 1982, Economic change and the Santals of West Bengal, *Bengal Past and Present* 101(1-2) January-December, p 61-78.
Kavalackata, Thomas, 1985, The killing of Santal tribals, *Social Action* 35(3) July-September, p 278-283.
Kochar, V.K., 1964, Profile of a tribal village, *Vanyajati* 12(2) April, p 80-95, references, tables.
——, 1966, Village organisation among the Santals, *Bulletin of Cultural Research Institute* 5(1-2), p 11-19, references, tables.
Lal Bahadur Singh, et al, 1985, Authoritarianism and intolerance of ambiguity in Santals: An appraisal, *Man in India* 65(3) September, p 234-245, bibliography.
——, 1986, Modes of parental discipline among Santals and Hindus: among Santals and Hindus: Assessment across communities, *Indian Journal of Social Work* 47(3) October, p 315-322, bibliography, tables.
Mahapatra, Sitakant, 1987, Modernisation and ritual: Identity and changes in Santal society, *indian Economic and Social History Review* 24(4) October-December, p 441.

Mukherjee, Charulal, 1943, The Santal in a changing civilisation, *Indian Journal of Social Work* 4(2) September, p 171-181.

Ojha, Hardev and **Rajiv Singh**, 1987, Sex difference in social attitudes of Santal high school students, *Asian Journal of Psychology and Education* 19(5-6), p 40-43, tables, bibliography.

——, 1988, Santal music, *National Centre for the Performing Arts Quarterly Journal* 17(1) March, p 45-47.

Onkar Prasad, 1985, Structural and technological constraints in the development of the Santal music and dance, *Man in India* 65(2) June, p 177-86, bibliography.

Oraons, Martin, 1959, A tribe in search of a great tradition: The emulation-solidarity conflict, *Man in India* 39(2) April-June, p 108-114, references.

Ouyker, Edward, 1987, Tribal guerrillas: The Santals of West Bengal and the Naxalite movement, *Indian Economic and Social History Review* 24(4) October-December, p 436-437.

Ray, Mainmarji, 1988, Ethnic difference intelligence, *Indian Education Review* 23(2) April, p 114-119, bibliography.

Roy, U.K., et al, 1985, To be with Santals, *Man and Life* 11(3-4) July-December, p 226-27.

Sen, Gopi Nath, 1983, Life and culture of the Santals, *Modern Review* 147(7-8), July-August, p 214-222.

——, 1984, Patriotic lyrics of the Santals, *Modern Review* 148(3-4) March-April, p 100-11.

Sen, Suchibrata, 1984, The Santals of Jungle Mahals : An agrarian history, 1793-1861, *Indian Archaeology* 33(2) July-December, p 86-88.

——, 1985, The Santals of Jungle Mahals, *Times of India*, February 24, p I, col 1-4.

Shashi, S.S., 1988, Santhals in Naxalite movement, *Mainstream*, November 12, p 60.

Sinha, Surajit, 1968, Tribal solidarity and messianic movements, *Contribution to Indian Sociology (NS)*, 2, December, p 112-118, references.

Som, Sujit, 1983, Incidence of mild digital hair among the Santal of Orissa, *Vanyajati* 31 (3) July, p 23-27.

Swain, Laxmidhar, 1985, Santal tribes : Infant feeding practices, *Social Welfare* 32(3) June, p 22-23.

Thakkar, A.V., 1942, Among Santals and Pahadias, *Rural India* 5(1) January, p 6-8.

SANTALS : TRIBAL GOVERNMENT

Kochar, V.K., 1966, Village organisation among the Santals, *Bulletin of Cultural Research Institute* 5(1-2) p 11-19, references, tables.

SAORA

Bhupinder Singh, 1985, The Saora highlanders : Leadership and development, *Indian Economic and Social History Review* 22(2) April-June, p 220-221; *Journal of Rural Development* 4(2) March, p 354-355.

Das, Nityananda, 1959, A note on the markets in the Saora land of Orissa, *Vanyajati* 7(3) July, p 98-103.

Sahu, R.S. and **Baral, J.K.**, 1987, Leadership and socio-political change of tribes of Orissa, Saoras, *Vision* 6(3-4) January-June, p 57-69, bibliography.

SAORIAS

Bainbridge, R.B., 1907, The Saorias and the Rajmahal Hills, *Memoirs of the Asiatic*

Society of Bengal 2(4).

SARORA FITURIS

Elwin, Verrier, 1945, Sarora Fituris, *Man in India* 25(4) December, p 254-257, footnotes.

SATNAM PANTHA

Parganiha, B.L., 1967, The Satnami movement, *Journal of Social Research* 10(1) March, p 1 +.

SATNAMI MOVEMENT

See Satnam Pantha.

SAURAS

See Saora; Saorias.

SAVANTVATI

Social Service Quarterly (Periodical), 1938, Harijans in Savantvati, *Social Service Quarterly* 24(3) January, p 129-130, editorial.

SAVARAS

Kar, R.K., 1989, The Savaras of Assam, *Vanyajati* 37(2) April, p 5-11.

Ray, H.M., 1988, Savara: The snake charmer, *Man in India* 68(4) December, p 438-487.

SCAVENGERS : INDIA : HIMACHAL PRADESH

Thakur, D.S., et al, 1989, Socio-economic conditions of scavengers in Himachal Pradesh, *Social Change* 19(3) September, p 42-55.

See also Bhangies; Scavenging Labours; Sweepers.

SCAVENGER'S LIVING CONDITIONS ENQUIRY COMMITTEE, BOMBAY

Patel, Leela, 1954, A review of the report of the Scavenger's Living Conditions Enquiry Committee, State of Bombay, *Social Service Quarterly* 29(4) April, p 102-106.

SCAVENGING LABOURS : INDIA : MAHARASHTRA : BOMBAY

Bhalerao, Shanta, 1936, The scavenging and halakhore labour of Bombay : Some impressions, *Social Service Quarterly* 22(1) July, p 11-14.

See also Scavengers; Sweepers.

SCHEDULED AREAS : TRIBALS : INDIA : MADHYA PRADESH

Anon, 1965, Indebtedness among the tribal people of the scheduled areas of Madhya Pradesh, *Bulletin of Tribal Research and Development Institute* (Bhopal) 5(1-2) June-December, p 1-18, tables.

SCHEDULED AREAS AND SCHEDULED TRIBES COMMISSION

Anon, 1962, Recommendations of the Dhebar Commission and their implementation, *Vanyajati* 10(4) October, p 127-129.

——, 1962, Report of Scheduled Areas and Scheduled Tribes Commission: Summary of recommendations, *Vanyajati* 10(1) January, p 35-40.

SCHEDULED CASTES : CHILDREN : INDIA

Srivastava, Jai Prakash, 1954, Aggressiveness in Scheduled Caste children, *Education* 33(4) April, p 16-19; 33(5) May, p 10-13.

SCHEDULED CASTES : INDIA

Amba Rao, V., 1976, Higher education and occupational mobility among the Scheduled Caste youth, *Journal of Higher Education* 1(3) Spring, p 305-314, references, tables.

Amar Dev and **Banerjee Guha, S.**, 1989, Socio-economic condition of the Scheduled Castes in India : A geographical analysis, *National Geographical Journal of India* 35(Part 2) June, p 129-139.

Amrit Kaur and **Tarlok Singh**, 1985, Regional educational disparity among Scheduled Castes of Punjab, *Indian Journal of Adult Education* 46(4) April, p 7-10 +, tables.

Anon, 1979, Inter-generations mobility among the Scheduled Castes, *Journal of Indian Education* 5(4) November, p 61.

——, 1981, (Book review), *Education Quarterly* 33(3) July, p 48-49.
Review of the book: **Aikara, Jacob**, 1981, *Scheduled Castes and higher education : A study of college students in Bombay*, Dastane Rama Chand, Pune, 112 p.

——, 1984, (Book review) *Economic and Political Weekly* 21(23) June 7, p 1011-1012; *Indian Economic and Social History Review* 23(2) April-June, p 233-234.
Review of the book : **Khare, R.S.**, 1983, *The untouchables as himself : Ideology, identity and pragmatism among the Lucknow chambers*, Cambridge University Press, Cambridge, 189 p.

——, 1984, (Book review), *Indian Journal of Public Administration* 32(1) January-March, p 216-217.
Review of the book : **Ghosh, S.K.**, 1986, *Protection of Minorities and Scheduled Castes*, Ashish Publishing House, New Delhi, 181 p.

——, 1985, (Book review), *Indian Economic and Social History Review* 23(4) October-December, p 442-443.
Review of the book : **Ghosh, S.K.**, 1986, *The Scheduled Castes in modern Indian politics : Their emergence as political power*, Munshiram Manoharlal, New Delhi, xi, 355 p.

——, 1985, Uplift of Scheduled Castes, *Haryana Review* 19(9) September, p 16-18.

——, 1986, (Book review), *Indian Archives* 35(1) January-June, p 99-101, *Patriot*, January, p 1-3.
Review of the book : **Gupta, S.K.**, 1986, *The Scheduled Castes in modern Indian politics : Their emergence as a political power*, Munshiram Manoharlal, New Delhi, p 355.

——, 1986, (Book review), *Education Quarterly* 38(2) Summer, p 51-52.
Review of the book : **Parvathamma, C.**, 1986, *New horizons and Scheduled Castes*, Ashish Publishing House, New Delhi, p 184.

——, 1989, (Book review), *Man in India* 69(3) September, p 313-316.
Review of the book : **Nandu Ram**, 1989, *The mobile Scheduled Castes : Rise of a new middle class*, Hindustan Corporation (India), Delhi, p 137 + xx.

Beteille, Andre, 1985, Head count of Harijans : Patterns of regional distribution, *Times of India* March 21, p 6, col 3-5.

Bose, A.B., 1970, Educational development among Scheduled Castes, *Man in India* 50(3) July-September, p 209-239, references, tables.

Chaddha, Kumkum, 1987, Entry barred, *Hindustan Times* (Magazine), July 12, p 1, col 1-6 +.

Chandana, R.C., 1989, Spatial dimensions of Scheduled Castes in India, *Tribune* (Magazine), September 2, p 1-6.

Chandramohan Reddy, T., 1987, Status of Scheduled Castes in rural power structure : An analysis, *Man in India* 67(4) December, p 372-382, bibliography, tables.

Chaturvedi, Arun Kumar, 1986, Harijan students of Uttar Pradesh, *Social Welfare* 33(1) April, p 30-31.

Chitnis, Suma, 1975, Education of the Scheduled Castes, *Journal of Higher Education* 1(2) Autumn, p 167-178, tables.

Dang, Satyapal, 1974, Plight of women sweepers, *Mainstream* 12(50).

Dollu, Venkateshwarlu, 1987, Psychological conflict between Harijans and upper class, middle class, caste Hindus : A study in Andhra Pradesh (India), *Sociological Bulletin* 36(1) March, p 77-98.

Forrester, Duncan B., 1975, Initial occupational pattern of Scheduled Castes graduates in India, *New Frontiers in Education* 5(2) May, p 49-65, references, tables.

Gupta, L.P., 1978, A study of personality syndromes and cognitive characteristics of Scheduled Castes, backward classes and non-Scheduled Caste students, *Journal of Higher Education* 4(3) Spring, p 381-387.

Guru, Gopal, 1984, Reservations and the sanskritisation of Scheduled Castes : Some theoretical aspects, *Sociological Bulletin* 33(1-2) March-September, p 29-38, bibliography.

Hadimani, R.N., et al, 1985, Sericulture as a leverage of social mobility among Scheduled Castes in rural areas : A case study of a non-sericulturist village in Karnataka, *Journal of Institute of Economic Research* 20(1-2), p 27-37.

Jain, Meenakshi, 1987, Religious world of Harijans : Different from Brahminical order, *Times of India* 9(6) July, p 3-5.

Jayagopal, R., 1986, Occupational mobility among a special group of Scheduled Castes in Tamil Nadu : Survey, *Indian Journal of Adult Education* 47(1) January, p 8-12.

Jayaram, N., 1986, Can law save Scheduled Castes? *Mainstream* 24(37) May 17, p 15-48 +.

Juyal, P.D., 1986, Some demographic variables influencing the attitude of Scheduled Caste towards the measures adopted for their welfare : An empirical study, *Progress of Education* 61(4-5) November-December, p 85-88, references.

Kalam, Mohammad Abdul 1984, Conversions and protective discrimination, *Bulletin of Christian Institute of Islamic Studies* 7(3-4) July-December, p 26-34, bibliography.

Kananaikil, Jose, 1986, Religion, culture and power : The case of the Scheduled Castes in India, *Religion and Society* 33(2) June, p 27-32.

Karlekar, Malavika, 1975, Higher education and Scheduled Castes, *Journal of Higher Education* 1(2) Autumn, p 179-87, references, tables.

Khurana, G., 1979-80, Educational facilities for Scheduled Castes, *Education Quarterly* 31(3-4) October-January, p 31-35.

Lal, Shiva Kumar, 1975, Scheduled Caste college students in Rajasthan, *Journal of Higher Education* 1(2) Autumn, p 244-250, references.

Lancy, Lobo, 1989, Conversion, emigration and social mobility of an ex-Scheduled Caste from Central Gujarat, *Social Action* 39(4) October-December, p 423-437.

Majeed, A. and **Ghosh, E.S.K.**, 1989, Affective syndrome crisis in Scheduled Castes, *Vanyajati* 37(4) October, p 90-94.

Mehra, Savita, et al, 1984, Status improvement of Scheduled Castes in Haryana, *Haryana Review* 18(7) July, p 164.

Misra, Ajay M., et al, 1983, A study of attitude towards learning of science among Scheduled Caste students, *Journal of Education and Psychology* 41(3) October, p 112-116.

Mohanty, Rabindra K., 1984, Scheduled Castes as 'minorities', *Mainstream* 23(18) December 29, p 27-29.

Nancharaiah, G., 1989, Scheduled Castes as agricultural labourers, *Social Change* 19(3) September, p 31-41.

———, 1990, The changing position of Scheduled Castes as agricultural labourers in the labour market, *Social Action* 40(2) April-June, p 172-183.

Narayana Reddy, G., 1984, Scheduled Castes movement, *Voluntary Action* 27(5-6) November-December, p 68-69 +.

Pandian, M.S.S., 1985, State Christianity and Scheduled Castes, *Economic and Political Weekly* 20(42) October 19, p 1776-1777.

Pathak, Bindeshwar, 1989, Caste is their only crime, *Times of India* (Sunday Review) July 3, p 1-8.

Prasad, R.R., 1986, Change and continuity among the Scheduled Caste leather workers of Uttar Pradesh, *Journal of Rural Development* 5(6) November, p 605-628.

Prasad Rao, C.R., 1989, Rural housing among Scheduled Castes in two districts of Andhra Pradesh : A comparison of parameters and predictors, *Vanyajati* 37(4) October, p 76-89.

Premi, Kusum K., 1974, Educational opportunities for the Scheduled Castes : Role of protective discrimination in equalisation, *Economic and Political Weekly* 9(45-46) November, p 1902-1910.

———, 1976, Educational problems of Scheduled Castes in Punjab, *Journal of Indian Education* 1(6) March, p 44-52, tables.

———, 1984, Educational equality and economic opportunities : A comparative study of Scheduled Castes and non-Scheduled Castes, *Journal of Higher Education* 9(3) Spring, p 363-372, references, tables.

Ramaswamy, Uma, 1974, Scheduled Caste in Andhra : Some aspects of social change, *Economic and Political Weekly* 9(20) July 20, p 1153-1158.

———, 1974, Self identity among Scheduled Castes : A study of Andhra, *Economic and Political Weekly* 9(47) November 23, p 1959-1964.

Ravindranathan, M.N., 1981, Educational problems of Scheduled Castes, *Educational Review* 87(4) April, p 69-74.

Roy Chowdhury, Bidyut Kumar, 1963, Comparative study of the progress of secondary education among the Scheduled Castes and Scheduled Tribes of West Bengal, *Bulletin of Cultural Research Institute* 2(1), p 40-52, appendix, tables.

Satyanarayana, B.S., 1982, Educational problems of Scheduled Caste college students in Karnataka, *Journal of Higher Education* 7(3) Spring, p 253-260, bibliography, footnote, tables.

Shakir, Moin, 1974, Scheduled Caste : Beyond the system, *Economic and Political Weekly* 9(16) April 20, p 629-631.

Sharma, Govaid P., 1984, Trends in the study of Scheduled Castes, *Indian Anthropologist* 14(2) December, p 119-131, bibliography.

Sharma, S.K., 1987, Hopes for Harijans, *Haryana Review* 21(10) October, p 17-18.

Shekharappa, Veera, 1984, Labour in an unorganised sector : Rural Scheduled Castes women, *Vision* 4(2) October-December, p 4-14, bibliography, tables.

Singh, Y.P., 1986, Housing programme for Scheduled Castes in U.P., *Kurukshetra* 34(8) May, p 4-7.

Sivadasan Pillai, K., 1988. Equality of educational opportunity and the Scheduled Castes. *Progressive Education Herald* 3(1) October, p 40-42.

Sood, Renu, 1980-81, Role of achievement anxiety, alleviation and value discrepancy in academic achievement of Scheduled Caste students, *Journal of Higher Education* 6(1-3), p 117-122, references, tables.

Subramanian, K.S., 1987, Violence against Scheduled Castes in India: An overview, problems, prospects, *Man and Development* 9(1) March, p 26-42.

Subrahamanyam, S., 1986, Problems of school dropouts : A study with special reference to Scheduled Castes and Scheduled Tribes in Andhra Pradesh, *Education Quarterly* 38(3) Autumn, p 28-32.

Sudama, G.R. and **Thiagarajan, A.P.**, 1981, Enrolment of the Scheduled Castes in general colleges : A case study of Tamil Nadu, *Experiment in Education* 9(4) June, p 63-69, tables.

——, 1982, Academic difficulties of college youth : A case study of the Scheduled Castes, *Indian Education* 12(5-6) August-September, p 23-29.

Swaminathan, M.S., 1982, Educational development of the Scheduled Castes, *Journal of Indian Education* 8(1) May, p 40-58, tables.

Thiagarajan, A.P., 1981, A study of the Scheduled Caste students in some secondary schools of Tamil Nadu, *Indian Education* 11(5) August, p 22-26, tables.

Tripathi, C.B., 1987, Development of Scheduled Caste women, *Journal of Social Economic Studies* 4(4) October-December.

Venkataramana, M., et al, 1989, Housing patterns in Scheduled Castes of Andhra Pradesh : A micro-empirical study, *Vanyajati* 37(4) October, p 62-75.

Verma, B.P. and **Sharma, Keshav**, 1989, A comparative study of locus of control and self concept of higher, backward and Scheduled Caste students, *Progress of Education* 63(9) April, p 205-208.

Yadav, S.K., 1982, A study of the Scheduled Castes awareness about the schemes for their educational progress, *Indian Educational Review* 17(1) January, p 85-93.

——, 1983, Research review on implementation of educational schemes of Scheduled Castes, *Indian Educational Review* 18(3) July, p 112-122, references.

SCHEDULED CASTES : INDIA : ANDHRA PRADESH

Dollu, Venkateshwarlu, 1987, Psychological conflict between Harijans and upper class, middle class caste Hindus : A study in Andhra Pradesh (India), *Sociological Bulletin* 36(1), p 77-98.

Prasad Rao, C.R., 1989, Rural housing among Scheduled Castes in two districts of Andhra Pradesh : A comparison of parameters and predictors, *Vanyajati* 37(4) October, p 76-89.

Subrahamanyam, S., 1986, Problems of school dropouts : A study with special reference to Scheduled Castes and Scheduled Tribes in Andhra Pradesh, *Education Quarterly* 38(3) Autumn, p 28-32.

Venkataramana, M., et al, 1989, Housing pattern in Scheduled Castes of Andhra Pradesh : A micro-empirical study, *Vanyajati* 37(4) October, p 62-75.

SCHEDULED CASTES : INDIA : GUJARAT

Lancy, Lobo, 1989, Conversion, emigration and social mobility of an ex-Scheduled Castes from Central Gujarat, *Social Action* 39(4) October-December, p 423-437.

SCHEDULED CASTES : INDIA : HARYANA

Mehra, Savita, et al, 1984, Status improvement of Scheduled Castes in Haryana, *Haryana Review* 18(7) July, p 167.

SCHEDULED CASTES : INDIA : KARNATAKA

Hadimani, R.N., et al, 1985, Sericulture as a leverage of social mobility among Scheduled Castes in rural areas : A case study of a non-sericulturist village in Karnataka, *Journal of Institute of Economic Research* 20(1-2), p 27-37.

Satyanarayana, B.S., 1982, Educational problems of Scheduled Caste college students in Karnataka, *Journal of Higher Education* 7(3) Spring, p 253-260.

SCHEDULED CASTES : INDIA : MAHARASHTRA : BOMBAY

Anon, 1981, (Book review), *Education Quarterly* 33(3) July, p 48-49.
Review of the book : **Aikara, Jacob**, 1981, *Scheduled Castes and higher education : A study of college students in Bombay*, Dastane Rama Chand, Pune, 112 p.

SCHEDULED CASTES : INDIA : PUNJAB

Amrit Kaur and **Tarlok Singh**, 1985, Regional educational disparity among Scheduled Castes of Punjab, *Indian Journal of Adult Education* 46(4) April, p 7-10 +, tables.

Premi, Kusum K., 1976, Educational problems of Scheduled Castes in Punjab, *Journal of Indian Education* 1(6) March, p 44-52, tables.

SCHEDULED CASTES : INDIA : TAMIL NADU

Jayagopal, R., 1986, Occupational mobility among a special group of Scheduled Castes in Tamil Nadu : Survey, *Indian Journal of Adult Education* 47(1) January, p 8-11.

Sudama, G.R. and **Thiagarajan, A.P.**, 1981, Enrollment of the Scheduled Castes in general colleges : A case study of Tamil Nadu, *Experiments in Education* 9(4) June, p 63-69, tables.

Thiagarajan, A.P., 1981, A study of the Scheduled Caste students in some secondary schools of Tamil Nadu, *Indian Education* 11(5) August, p 22-26.

SCHEDULED CASTES : INDIA : UTTAR PRADESH

Chaturvedi, Arun Kumar, 1986, Harijan students of Uttar Pradesh, *Social Welfare* 33(1) April, p 30-31.

Prasad, R.R., 1986, Change and continuity among the Scheduled Caste leather workers of Uttar Pradesh, *Journal of Rural Development* 5(6) November, p 605-628.

Singh, Y.P., 1986, Housing programme for Scheduled Castes in U.P., *Kurukshetra* 24(8) May, p 4-7.

SCHEDULED CASTES : INDIA : UTTAR PRADESH : LUCKNOW

Anon, 1984, (Book review), *Economic and Political Weekly* 21(23) June 7, p 1011-1012; *Indian Economic and Social History Review* 23(2) April-June, p 233-234.
Review of the book : **Khare, R.S.**, 1983, *The untouchable as himself : Ideology, identity and pragmatism among Lucknow Chamars*, Cambridge University Press, Cambridge, p 189.

SCHEDULED CASTES : INDIA : WEST BENGAL

Roy Chowdhury, Bidyut Kumar, 1963, Comparative study of the progress of secondary education among the Scheduled Castes and Scheduled Tribes of West Bengal, *Bulletin of Cultural Research Institute* 2(1), p 40-52, appendix, tables.

SCHEDULED CASTES : WOMEN : INDIA

Dang, Satyapal, 1974, Plight of women sweepers, *Mainstream* 12(50).

Shekarappa, Veera, 1984, Labour in an unorganised sector : Rural Scheduled Caste women, *Vision* 4(2), October-December, p 4-14, bibliography, tables.

Tripathi, C.B., 1987, Development of Scheduled Caste women, *Journal of Social Economic Studies* 4(4) October-December.

SCHEDULED CASTES AND SCHEDULED TRIBES : ATROCITIES : INDIA

Abraham, A.S., 1985, Violence against Harijans : Integral part of rural change, *Times of India*, August 16, p 6, col 3-5.

——, 1988, Massacre in Jehanabad : Looking for a scapegoat, *Times of India*, August 19, p 4, col 3-5.

Anirudh Prasad, 1985, People's perception of the atrocities committed on Harijans in Bihar, *Journal of Social and Economic Studies* (New Series) 2(1) January-March, p 105-125.

Anon, 1986, Atrocities on the Scheduled Castes, *Social Action* 36(2) April-June, p 201-211.

D'Mello, Bernard, 1987, Arwal massacre : Report of People's Tribunal, *Economic and Political Weekly* 22(35) August 29, p 1486-1487.

Mohanty, Rabindra K., 1988, Dynamics of atrocities on Scheduled Castes in rural India, *Indian Journal of Social Work* 49(1) January, p 51-66.

Rai, Lagan, 1988, Murder most foul, *Times of India* (Sunday Review), January 17, p 6, col 1-5.

Singh, R.G., 1986, Atrocities on tribals, *Khadi Gramodyog* 32(7) April, p 358-361, table.

Subramanian, K.S., 1987, Behind rural violence, *Mainstream* 25(45) July 25, p 19-25.

Tavleen Singh, 1988, Murder and mayhem in Jehanabad, *Indian Express* 4(1) September 4, p 1, col 1-8.

SCHEDULED CASTES AND SCHEDULED TRIBES: BIBLIOGRAPHY: INDIA

Anon, 1986, Annotated bibliography, *Social Action* 36(2) April-June, p 220-225.

SCHEDULED CASTES AND SCHEDULED TRIBES : CHILDREN : INDIA

Srivastava, Jai Prakash, 1954, Aggressiveness in Scheduled Caste children, *Education*, 33(4) April, p 16-19; 33(5) May, p 10-13.

Thakur, Laxmi and **Nathawat, S.S.**, 1987, Cognitive performance of Scheduled Caste children, *Educational Review*, 93(7) July, p 113-116, bibliography, tables.

SCHEDULED CASTES AND SCHEDULED TRIBES : CONVERSION TO CHRISTIANITY

Sunil, K.P., 1989, Children of a lesser God, *Illustrated Weekly of India* 110(26) June 25, p 36-39.

SCHEDULED CASTES AND SCHEDULED TRIBES : CONVERSION TO SIKHISM

Trivedy, Shikha, 1989, A matter of faith, *Illustrated Weekly of India* 110 (25) June 18, p 42-45.

SCHEDULED CASTES AND SCHEDULED TRIBES : EDUCATION : INDIA

Adiseshiah, Malcolm, S., 1975, Scheduled Castes and Tribes in higher education in Tamil Nadu, *Journal of Higher Education* 1(2) Autumn, p 241-244.

Aggarwal, R.B., 1989, Educating backward classes : Role of UGC, *Economic Trends* 18(5) April, p 3-6.

Aggarwal, Yash, 1987, Some aspects of educational development among the Scheduled Caste population in India, *Journal of Education Planning and Administration* 1(2) April, 137-164, bibliography, figures, tables.

Alam, Khurshid, 1987, Educational aspirations and drop-out factors among Scheduled Castes, *Indian Journal of Community Guidance Service* 4(1) January, p 25-31, bibliography, tables.

Ameerjan, M.S., 1979, A comparative study of academic achievement of the Scheduled Castes and tribes students of agriculture, *Journal of Education and Psychology* 37(2) July, p 121-129, references, tables.

——, 1984, Background variables of the Scheduled Caste and Tribe college students : A comparative study, *Indian Educational Review* 19(2) April, p 28-36.

—— and **Thimappa, M.S.**, 1986, Academic achievement of the Scheduled Caste and Tribe students: An analysis, *Journal of Education and Psychology* 44(1) April, p 29-35, bibliography.

Amrit Kaur and **Tarlok Singh**, 1985, Regional education disparity among Scheduled Castes of Punjab, *Indian Journal of Adult Education* 46(4) April, p 7-10 +, tables.

Anon, 1981, (Book review), *Education Quarterly* 39(4) Winter, p 49-50.

Review of the book : **Goyal, B.R.**, 1981, *Educating Harijans*, The Academic Press, Gurgaon, xvii, p 129.

——, 1985, (Book review), *Social Change* 15(1) March, p 57; *Sunday Statesman* 23(11) June, p 4-5.

Review of the book : **Siddiqui, M.K.A.**, 1985, *Educating a backward minority*, Abidi Publication, Calcutta.

——, 1986, (Book review), *Education Quarterly* 38(2) Summer, p 51-52; *Journal of Rural Development* 5(1) January, p 124.

Review of the book : **Parvathamma C.** and **Satyanarayana**, 1984, *New horizons and Scheduled Castes*, Ashish Publishing House, New Delhi, vii, 184 p.

Azad, J.L., 1976, Education of Scheduled Castes and Scheduled Tribes, *Journal of Indian Education* 1(6) March, p 23-28.

Bennur, C.S., 1967, Education and prejudice, *Progress of Education* 41(8) March, p 294-298 +.

Bhupinder Singh, 1985, Perspectives on adult education programme for Scheduled Tribes, *Man and Development* 7(1) March, p 65-72.

Bose, A.B., 1970, Educational development among Scheduled Castes, *Man in India* 50(3) July-September, p 209-239, references, tables.

——, 1970, Caste prejudice and children, *Progress of Education* 41(10-11) May-June, p 392-393, letter to editor.

——, 1970, Education and prejudice : A perversity? *Progress of Education* 41(9) April, p 345-46, letter to editor.

Chitnis, Suma, 1975, Education of the Scheduled Castes, *Journal of Higher Education* 1(2) Autumn, p 167-178, tables.

Desai, Haribhai G. and **Uchat, D.A.**, 1981, Self-concept of Harijan student and attitudes of other students towards them, *Indian Educational Review* 16(3) July, p 44-50.

D'Souza, Claude, 1986, Weaker sections of the Indian society and their education, *Social Action* 36(1) January-March, p 13-25.

Educational India (Periodical), 1964, Backwardness, *Educational India* 30(9) March, p 308-309, editorial.

Gopinatharao, C., 1986, Residential schools for weaker sections : A study, *ASCI Journal of Management* 15(2) March, p 303-325.

Goyal, B.R., 1975, Education of the under-privileged under the 10 + 2 + 3 scheme, *Journal of Indian Education* 1(1) May, p 69-74.

Gupta, L.P., 1979, A study of personality syndromes and cognitive characteristics of Scheduled Castes, backward classes and non-Scheduled Caste students, *Journal of Higher Education* 4(3) Spring, p 381-387.

Heredia, Rudi, 1986, Minority rights and reservation policy : Towards coherence and consistence, *New Frontiers in Education* 16(2) April-June, p 60-63.

Horsey, Anita, 1981, Conditions of Scheduled Castes and Tribes, *New Frontiers in Education* 11(2) April-June, p 1-36, references.

Jain, S.P., Backward classes : Problems of education, *Times of India*, July 13, p 4, col 3-5.

Juyal, P.D., 1986, Some demographic variables influencing the attitude of Scheduled Caste towards the measures adopted for their welfare : An empirical study, *Progress of Education*, 61(4-5) November-December, p 85-88, references.

Kamila, Bana Behari, 1983, Occupational status of parents of Harijan and Tribal Welfare Department high school students of Orissa, *National Journal of Education* 6(1) September, p 56-64, references, tables.

———, 1985-1986, A study of attitude of students towards school of Harijans and Tribal Welfare Department high school of Orissa, *Journal of Education and Psychology* 43(3-4) October-January, p 187-92, references.

Karlekar, Malavika, 1975, Higher education and the Scheduled Castes, *Journal of Higher Education* 1(2) Autumn, p 179-187, references, tables.

Khurana, G., 1979-1980, Educational facilities for Scheduled Castes, *Education Quarterly* 31(3-4) October-January, p 31-35.

Kirpal, Vinay, et al, 1985, Scheduled Caste and Tribe students in higher education : A study of Article 117, *Economic and Political Weekly* 20(29) July 20, p 1238-1248, table.

Kunnukal, Thomas, 1986, Education for the weaker section, *Social Action* 36(1) January-March, p 1-12.

Lal, Shiva Kumar, 1975, Scheduled Caste college students :. Rajasthan, *Journal of Higher Education* 1(2) Autumn, p 244-250, references.

Lele, T.P., 1967, A comparative study of the students from different communities, *Education and Psychology Review*, 7(3) July, p 117-124, tables.

Malhotra, P.L., 1986, Social disadvantage, education and development in India, *Social Change* 16(2-3) June-September, p 41-51, bibliography, tables.

Masilamani, S., 1986, Educational achievement of Scheduled Caste : Sex bias and a case study of "Chakkiliyara" of Chinnathadagam village, *Social Action* 36(2) April-June, p 149-165.

Menon, P.S.K., 1975, Post metric scholarship for Scheduled Caste and Scheduled Tribe students, *Journal of Higher Education* 1(2) Autumn, p 263-266.

Misra, Ajay M., et al, 1983, A study of attitude towards learning of science among Scheduled Caste students, *Journal of Education and Psychology* 41(3) October, p 112-116.

Nandu Ram, 1986, Socio-structural variants and higher education among the

Scheduled Castes and Tribes, *Social Action* 36(2) April-June, p 166-182.

Om Prakash, 1980, Educational attainment of children in the sweeper community at AIIMS campus : An exploratory study, *Indian Educational Review* 15(4) October, p 97-103.

Pandey, Balaji, 1986, Education development among Scheduled Castes, *Social Scientist* 14(2-3) February-March, p 59-68.

Pareek, M., 1987, A comparative study of the relationship between intelligence and socio-economic status between GI and Scheduled Caste/Scheduled Tribe students, *Educational Review* 93(12) December, p 213-215.

Parikh, Y.O., 1982-1983, Education and incidence of poverty among Scheduled Castes, *Journal of Maharaja Sayajirao University of Baroda* 31-32(2), p 53-59, tables.

Prasad, L.M., 1986, Educational policy for Scheduled Castes and Tribes and its implementation, *Indian Journal of Public Administration* 32(4) October-December, p 908-932.

Premi, Kusum K., 1984, Educational equality and economic opportunities : A comparative study of Scheduled Castes and non-Scheduled Castes, *Journal of Higher Education* 9(3) Spring, p 363-372, references, tables.

Rajaiah, B., 1982, Reservations in higher education and jobs, *Educational Review* 88(3) March, p 55-58.

Ramaswamy, Uma, 1985, Education and inequality, *Economic and Political Weekly* 20(36) September 7, p 1523-1528.

Rastogi, S.P., 1978, Attitudes and beliefs of Harijan students, *Journal of Higher Education* 4(2) Autumn, p 251-258.

——, 1980, The impact of Constitutional provision upon the uplift of Harijans, *Indian Educational Review* 15(4) October, p 76-80.

Ravindranathan, M.N., 1981, Educational problems of Scheduled Castes, *Educational Review* 87(4) April 1981, p 69-74.

Rice, Marion J., 1980, Harijan wasti, *Progress of Education* 55(2) September, p 51-57

Roy Chowdhry, Bidyut Kumar, 1963, Comparative study of the progress of secondary education among the Scheduled Castes and Scheduled Tribes of West Bengal, *Bulletin of Cultural Research Institute* 2(1), p 40-52, appendix, notes, tables.

Sangameswara Rao, D., 1988, Reservations in admissions to educational institutions *vis-a-vis* equality of opportunity, *Progressive Educational Herald* 3(1) October, p 46-48.

Satyanarayana, B.S., 1982, Educational problems of Scheduled Caste college students in Karnataka, *Journal of Higher Education* 7(3) Spring p 253-260. references, tables.

Sharma, K.R., 1983, Scheduled Tribes and equality of educational opportunity, *Indian Education* 12(10) January, p 10-13.

Sharma, R.S., 1985, Developing educational technology for deprived sections of the Indian society, *Bulletin of Non-formal Education* 3(3) December, p 1-17.

Sheth, D.L., 1986, The problem of reservations : Economic backwardness or social injustice, *Indian Journal of Adult Education* 47(5) May, p 9-15; 47(6) June, p 4-7 +; 47(7) July p 14-21.

Sood, Renu, 1980-1981, Role of achievement anxiety, alleviation and value discrepancy in academic achievement of Scheduled Caste students, *Journal of Higher Education*, 6(1-3) p 117-122, references, tables.

Subrahmanyam, S., 1986, Problems of school dropouts: A study with a special references to Scheduled Castes and Scheduled Tribes in Andhra Pradesh, *Education Quarterly* 38(3) Autumn, p 28-32.

Sudama, G.R. and **Thiagarajan, A.P.**, 1981, Enrolment of the Scheduled Castes in general colleges : A case study of Tamil Nadu, *Experiments in Education* 9(4) June, p 63-69, tables.

——, 1982, Academic difficulties of college youth : A case study of the Scheduled Castes, *Indian Education* 12(5-6) August-September, p 23-29.

Sundaresh, Aruna, 1986, Constitution law and reservations, *New Frontiers in Education* 16(2), p 33-40.

Swaminathan, M.S., 1982, Educational development of the Scheduled Castes, *Journal of Indian Education* 8(1) May, p 40-45, tables.

Thakur, Laxmi and **Nathawat, S.S.**, 1987, Cognitive performance of Scheduled Caste children, *Educational Review* 93(7) July, p 113-116, bibliography, tables.

Thiagarajan, A.P., 1981, A study of the Scheduled Caste students in some secondary schools of Tamil Nadu, *Indian Education* 11(5) August, p 22-26, tables.

——, 1987, Educational progress of Scheduled Castes, *Experiments in Education* 15(5) May, p 94-96.

Varma, R.P., 1984, Educating the disadvantaged : A few suggestions, *National Journal of Education*, 6(2) May p 1-6, references.

Verghese, Alexander V., 1984, Education, earning and occupation of weaker castes, *Journal of Higher Education*, 9(3) Spring, p 373-381, references.

Yadav, S.K., 1982, A study of the Scheduled Castes awareness about the schemes for their educational progress, *Indian Educational Review* 17(1), January 1982, p 85-93.

——, 1983, Research review on implementation of educational scheme of Scheduled Castes, *Indian Educational Review* 18(3) July, p 112-122, references.

See also Tribal Education.

SCHEDULED CASTES AND SCHEDULED TRIBES : EDUCATION : INDIA : ANDHRA PRADESH

Subrahmanyam, S., 1986, Problems of school dropouts: A study with a special reference to Scheduled Castes and Scheduled Tribes in Andhra Pradesh, *Education Quarterly* 38(3) Autumn, p 28-32.

Yadav, S.K., 1988, Educational wastage amongst Scheduled Castes : A research review, *Indian Educational Review* 23(1) January, p 90-98, bibliography.

SCHEDULED CASTES AND SCHEDULED TRIBES : EDUCATION : INDIA : BOMBAY

See Scheduled Castes and Scheduled Tribes : Education : India : Maharashtra : Bombay.

SCHEDULED CASTES AND SCHEDULED TRIBES : EDUCATION : INDIA : DELHI

Om Prakash, 1980, Educational attainment of children in the sweeper community at AIIMS campus : An exploratory study, *Indian Educational Review* 15(4) October, p 97-103.

SCHEDULED CASTES AND SCHEDULED TRIBES : EDUCATION : INDIA : KARNATAKA

Satyanarayana, 1982, Educational problems of Scheduled Caste college students in Karnataka, *Journal of Higher Education* 7(3) Spring, p 253-260, references, tables.

SCHEDULED CASTES AND SCHEDULED TRIBES : EDUCATION : INDIA : MAHARASHTRA : BOMBAY

Aikara, Jacob, 1981, Scheduled Castes and higher education : A study of college student sin Bombay, Dastane Ramachand & Co., Pune, 112 p, *Educational Quarterly* 33(3) July, p 48-49, book review.

Deshmukh, B.D., 1957, Educational status of the backward communities, *Progress of Education* 32(3) October, p 97-98, letter to editor.

Ramanamma, A. and **Bambawala, U.**, 1985, Education among Scheduled Castes, Scheduled Tribes and others in Maharashtra, *Cochin University Law Review* 9(1-2) March-June, p 129-148.

SCHEDULED CASTES AND SCHEDULED TRIBES : EDUCATION : INDIA : ORISSA

Kamila, Bana Behari, 1983, Occupational status of parents of Harijan and Tribal Welfare Department high school students of Orissa, *National Journal of Education* 6(1) September p 56-64, references, tables.

——, 1985-86, A study of attitude of students toward school of Harijans and Tribal Welfare Department high school of Orissa, *Journal of Education and Psychology* 43(3-4) October-January, p 187-92, references.

SCHEDULED CASTES AND SCHEDULED TRIBES : EDUCATION : INDIA : PUNJAB

Amrit Kaur and **Tarlok Singh**, 19885, Regional educational disparity among Scheduled Castes of Punjab, *Indian Journal of Adult Education* 46(4) April, p 7-10 +, tables.

Premi, Kusum K., 1976, Educational problems of Scheduled Castes in Punjab, *Journal of Indian Education* 1(6) March, p 44-52, tables.

SCHEDULED CASTES AND SCHEDULED TRIBES : EDUCATION : INDIA : RAJASTHAN

Lal, Shiva Kumar, 1975, Scheduled Caste college students in Rajasthan, *Journal of Higher Education*, 1(2) Autumn, p 244-250, references.

SCHEDULED CASTES AND SCHEDULED TRIBES : EDUCATION : INDIA : TAMIL NADU

Adiseshiah, M.S., 1975, Scheduled Castes and Tribes in higher education in Tamil Nadu, *Journal of Higher Education* 1(2) Autumn, p 241-244.

Sudama, G.R. and **Thiagarajan, A.P.**, 1981, Enrolment of the Scheduled Castes in general colleges : A case study of Tamil Nadu, *Experiments in Education* 9(4) June, p 63-69, tables.

Thiagarajan, A.P., 1981, A study of the Scheduled Caste students in some secondary schools of Tamil Nadu, *Indian Education* 11(5) August, p 22-26, tables.

SCHEDULED CASTES AND SCHEDULED TRIBES : EMPLOYMENT : INDIA :

Amba, Rao U., 1976, Higher education and occupational mobility among the Scheduled Caste youth, *Journal of Higher Education* 1(3) Spring, p 305-314, references, tables.

Anon, 1979, Inter-generations mobility among the Scheduled Castes, *Journal of Indian Education* 5(4) November, p 61.

Forrester, Duncan B., 1975, Initial occupational pattern of Scheduled Castes graduates in India, *New Frontiers in Education* 5(2) May, p 49-65, references, tables.

Jayagopal, R., 1986, Occupational mobility among a special group of Scheduled Castes in Tamil Nadu : A survey, *Indian Journal of Adult Education* 47(1) January, p 8-12.

SCHEDULED CASTES AND SCHEDULED TRIBES : INDIA

Anand, 1987, Some thought to ponder for our Harijan brothers, *Organiser* 39(15) September 13, p 8-9.

Anon, 1986, Cross opportunitism, *Times of India*, July 18, p 8, col. 1-2.

_____, 1987, (Book review), *Journal of Education Planning and Administration* (2) April, p 256-259.

Review of the book : **Hanumantha Rayappa P.**, and **Mutharayappa, R.**, 1986, *Backwardness and welfare of Scheduled Castes and Scheduled Tribes in India*, Ashish Publishing House, New Delhi, 121 p.

_____, (Book review), 1987, *Social Change* 17(3) September, p 97-99.

Review of the book : **Roy, Ramashrey** and **Singh, V.B.**, 1987, *Between two worlds : A study of Harijan elites*, Discovery Publishing House, Delhi, 176 p.

_____, 1988, (Book review), *Legal News and Views* 2(3) March, p 5-6.

Review of the book : **Khosla, Dinesh**, 1987, *Myth and reality of the protection of civil rights law : Study of untouchability in rural India*, Hindustan Publishing, Delhi, 190 p.

_____, 1988, Polum of the masses, *Times of India*, July 14, p 4, col. 1-2.

_____, 1988, To enter god's house, *Times of India*, August 13, p 6, col. 1-2.

_____, 1989, (Book review), *Indian Express* (Magazine), March 5, p 5 col 1-3.

Review of the book : **Shimta, Prabhati Mukherjee**, 1988, *Beyond the four varnas : The untouchables in India*, Indian Institute of Advance Studies, Shimla.

_____, 1989, (Book review), *Tribune*, January 29, p 2, col 1-2.

Review of the book : **Premi, Kusum**, 1989, *Scheduled Castes and Scheduled Tribes in industrial training institutes*, Vikas Publishing, New Delhi, 134 p.

Balgopal, K., 1987, Karamchedu : Second anniversary, *Economic and Political Weekly* 22(33) 15 August, p 1378-1381.

Baxi, Upendra, 1989, Historic new law : Protecting SC/ST man rights, *Times of India*, September 15, p 3-6, Col 3-5.

Bhatnagar, Damyanti, 1986, Possibilities of social change in the context of the attitude of bureaucratic personnel towards Scheduled Castes and Scheduled Tribes, *Journal of Sociological Studies*, January 5, p 150-160, bibliography, tables.

Bhatt, Raj N., 1989, Multani kinship Organisation : An investigation, *Man in India* 69(4) December, p 387-392.

Jain, Meenakshi, 1986, The politics of consensus : Jagjivan Ram and the Harijans, *Times of India*, July 29, p 8, Col 3-5.

Naidu, J. M., 1989, Further data on colour blindness among Andhra population, *Main in India* 69(4) December, p 413-415.

Kulkarni, S. D., 1974, Scheduled Caste and Scheduled Tribes: Problems and policies, *Economic and Political Weekly* 9(42), p 1775-1778.

Makwana, M. H., 1988 , The untouchables : An overview, *Vision* 6(1-2), p 45-52, bibliography.

Man Mohan, 1987, In search of equality, *Hindustan Times* (Magazine) September 27, p 1, col 1-6.

Menon, Venu, 1988, Conflict in the cathedral, *Illustrated Weekly India* 109(32) August 7, p 20-21.

Munirathna Naidu, K., 1985, Development of SCs and STs : An assessment, *Economic Trends* 19(5) October, p 3-6.

Narayana, K. V., et al, 1987, Socio-economic status of Sheduled Castes and Tribes : A study, *Kurukshetra* 35(8) May, p 18-21.

Prasad, Chandra Bhan, 1988, Poverty elimination and untouchability, *Mainstream* 26(25) April 2, p 17 +.

Prasad, L. M., 1987, Voluntary agencies for development of Scheduled Castes and Scheduled Tribes : Their role and function, *Indian Journal of Public Administration* 33(3) July-September, p 588-612, bibliography.

Ramotra, K. C., 1988, Scheduled Castes literacy in the North Western India : A spatial perspective, *National Geographer* 23(2) December, p 147-155.

Rohini, A and **Reddy, G. G.**, 1986, Harijans and Girijans of Andhra Pradesh : An application of analysis of variance in the study of fertility, mortality and family planning, *Indian Journal of Physical Anthropology and Human Genetics* 12(3) September-December, p 203-212, bibliography, tables.

Saini, B. R., 1981, Scope of Articles 15(4) and 16(4) of the Constitution of India, *Kurukshetra Law Journal* 10, p 53-61.

Satya Raju, R., 1986, Role of government in Scheduled Tribes development, *Kurukshetra* 34(4) January, p 21-24.

Sinha, R. K., 1984, Alienation among Scheduled Castes in an urban setting, *Indian Journal of Social Research* 25(2) August, p 151-161.

See also Backward Classes

SCHEDULED CASTES AND SCHEDULED TRIBES : INDIA : ANDHRA PRADESH

Prabhakar Rao, A., 1985, Harijan batting in Andhra, *Link* 28(2) August 18, p 25-27.

Ramachandra Raju, D., 1985, Protective laws in scheduled areas of Andhra Pradesh, *Economic and Political Weekly* 9(1-2) March-June, p 149-156.

Ramamurthy, B., 1986, Caste and occupational mobility among the Harijans in Andhra village, *Folklore* 27(2) February, p 36-38.

—— and **Subbarayudu, L**, 1985, Community relationship and power structure in an Andhra village among the Harijans, *Folklore* 26(12) December, p 233-236.

See also Malas; Sriramula, Bandi.

SCHEDULED CASTES AND SCHEDULED TRIBES : INDIA : HARYANA

Mehra, Savita et al, 1984, Status improvement of Scheduled Caste in Haryana, *Haryana Review* 18(7) July, p 16+

SCHEDULED CASTES AND SCHEDULED TRIBES : INDIA : GUJARAT

Kalathil, Mathew, 1985, Repression of Scheduled Castes and Tribes in Broach, *Economic and Political Weekly* 20(7) February 16, p 265-267.

SCHEDULED CASTES AND SCHEDULED TRIBES : INDIA : MAHARASHTRA

Anon, 1985, (Book review), *India Quarterly* 41(1) January-March, p 182-184.

Review of the book : **Deshpande, Vasant**, 1983, *Struggle of the deprived for development : The Mhaisal untouchables*, Dastane, Ramachandra and Company, Pune, 168 p.

Bairagi, K. V., 1987, Modified area development approach pockets (MADA pockets) and mini modified area development approach pockets (Mini-MADA pockets) clusters based on 1981, *Tribal Research Bulletin* 9(2) March, p 9-11, tables.

SCHEDULED CASTES AND SCHEDULED TRIBES : INDIA : ORISSA

Baboo, Balgovind, 1986, Cognition and structure : Explaining the 'exploitation' of an untouchable in Orissa, *Eastern Anthropologist* 39(3) July-September, p 187-195.

SCHEDULED CASTES AND SCHEDULED TRIBES : INDIA : PUNJAB

Sidhu, S. and **Sidhu, L. S.**, 1987, The impact of age at menarche and age at "marriage" on fertility among Scheduled Caste women of Punjab, *Guru Nanak Journal of Sociology* 8(2) October, p 41-46, bibliography, tables.

SCHEDULED CASTES AND SCHEDULED TRIBES : INDIA : SOUTHERN

Deliege, Robert, 1989, Job mobility among the brickmakers of South India, *Man in India* 69(1) March 3, p 42-63.

See also Scheduled Castes and Scheduled Tribes: India: Tamil Nadu.

SCHEDULED CASTE AND SCHEDULED TRIBES : INDIA : TAMIL NADU

Anon, 1987, Tamil Nadu violence, *Times of India*, September 19, p 6 Col 1-2.

Dorairaj, S., 1985, AIADMK's balancing tactics, *Link* 27(37) April 28, p 12-13.

Jayagopal, R., 1986, Occupational mobility among a special group of Scheduled Castes in Tamil Nadu : A survey, *Indian Journal of Adult Education* 47(1) January, p 8-12.

See also Schedule Castes and Scheduled Tribes: India: Southern.

SCHEDULED CASTES AND SCHEDULED TRIBES : NATIONAL INTEGRATION : INDIA

Bose, Nirmal Kumar, 1968, National integration and the Scheduled Castes and Scheduled Tribes, *Man in India* 48(4) October-December p 289-96.

SCHEDULED CASTES AND SCHEDULED TRIBES: OCCUPATIONS: INDIA

See Scheduled Castes and Scheduled Tribes : Employment : India.

SCHEDULED CASTES AND SCHEDULED TRIBES : RESERVATION ISSUES

See Reservation Issues.

SCHEDULED TRIBES : INDIA

Anon, 1953, Scheme of the Bihar State Government submitted to the Government of India under Article 275 of Constitution of India for the uplift of Scheduled Tribes during 1952-1953, *Vanyajati* 1(3) July, p 72-74.

——, 1953, Scheme in Bombay Government, sanctioned for 1952-53 for Scheduled Tribes under Act 275 of the Constitution, *Vanyajati* 1(4) October, p 101-102.

——, 1953, Schemes in West Bengal sanctioned for 1952-53 for Scheduled Tribes under act 275 of the Constitution, *Vanyajati* 1(4) October, p 103-104.

——, 1960, Progress of Scheduled Tribes during 1957-59, *Vanyajagi* 7(2) April, p 41-43 +.

——, 1962, Report of Scheduled Areas and Scheduled Tribes Commission: Summary of recommendations, *Vanyajati* 19(1), p 35-40.

——, 1987 (Book review), *Journal of Rural Development* 6(4) July, p 423-426; *National Geographical Journal of India* 33(1) March, p 118-119.

Review of the Book : **Singh, R. S.**, 1987, *Changing Occupational Structure of Scheduled Tribes*, Inter-India Publication, New Delhi, 291 p.

Bose, A. B., 1970, Problems of educational development of Scheduled Tribes, *Man in India* 50(1) January-March, p 26-50, references, tables.

Chaudhry, N. D., 1975, Educational development among the Scheduled Tribes in Rajasthan, *Education Quarterly* 27(3) October, p 26-30, tables.

Das, Amal Kumar, 1962, Scheduled Tribes or West Bengal : A panoramic picture, *Bulletin of Cultural Research Institute* 1(1), p 35-56, illustrations.

Karve, Iravati, 1958, Social education of the Scheduled Tribes, *Vanyajati* 5(4) October, p 164-169.

Khurana, G., 1978, Approach to education of Scheduled Tribes, *Education Quarterly* 30(1) April, p 17-23, tables.

Leuva, K. K., 1964, Impact of constitutional safeguards on the Scheduled Tribes, *Journal of Social Research* 7(1-2) March-September, p 62-69.

Mohapatra, P. C., 1985, Consumption pattern of Scheduled Tribes : A case study of Koraput district, Orissa, *Vision* 5(2) October-December, p 15-22, bibliography, tables.

Nag, Narendra Gopal, 1970, Implication of cultural and demographic factors on the socio-political trends among Scheduled Tribes, *Vanyajati* 18(2) April, p 51-58, references, tables.

Paswan, Ram Vilas, 1990, Speech by the Union Minister for Labour and Welfare (at) National Conference on Problems of Scheduled Tribes, 31st March 1990, *Vanyajati* 38(2) April, p 7-8.

Prashant, D., 1985, Land reforms and distribution of land among Scheduled Tribes in Kerala, *Cochin University Law Review* 1(2) March-June, p 213-222.

Roy Burman, B. K., 1958, Problem of family planning among the Scheduled Tribes of West Bengal, *Vanyajati* 6(4) October, p 160-64.

———, 1966, Questions relating to inclusion in and exclusion from the list of Scheduled Tribes, *Journal of Indian Anthropological Society* 1(1) March, p 7-14, references, illustration.

Roy Chowdhury, Bidyut Kumar, 1963, Comparative study of the progress of secondary education among the Scheduled Tribes of West Bengal, *Bulletin of Cultural Research Institute* 2(1) p 40-52, appendix, notes, tables.

Sanyal, Shubhendu, 1987, An appraisal of the major problems of Scheduled Tribes in India : With particular reference to Bihar, *Man in India* 67(4) December, p 404-423, bibliography, tables.

Shah, P. G., 1956, The use of multi-purpose employment co-operative societies for the Scheduled Tribes of India, *Vanyajati* 4(1) January, p 29-31.

Sharma, K. R., 1983, Scheduled Tribes and equality of educational opportunity, *Indian Education* 12(10) January, p 10-13.

Sharma, V. S., 1958, The Scheduled Tribes of Himachal Pradesh and their problems, *Vanyajati* 6(3) July, p 117-122.

Shrikant, L. M., 1966, Measures proposed for the spread of education amongst the Scheduled Tribes, *Vanyajati* 14(3) July, p 133-138, tables.

Singh, V. P., 1990, Speech of the Prime-Minister (at) National Conference on Problems of Scheduled Tribes, Vigyan Bhavan, New Delhi, 31st March 1990, *Vanyajati* 38(2) April, p 3-6.

Tripathi, G. P., 1985, Scheduled Tribes and tribal legislation in Madhya Pradesh, *Cochin University Law Review* 9(1-2) March-June, p 105-116.

Vanyajati (Periodical), 1984, Scheduled Tribes and 1981 Census figures, *Vanyajati* 32(3) April, p 1-4, editorial.

Venkataraman, S. R., 1951, The Scheduled Tribes, *Social Service Quarterly* 36(4), p 114-117, tables.

See also Denotified Tribes.

SCHOLASTIC ACHIEVEMENT : TRIBAL STUDENTS

Sharma, K. R., 1984, A study of language development scholastic achievement and tribal students, *Research Bulletin* 14(1-2) March-June, p 3-21, tables.

See also Academic Achievements.

SCHOLASTIC BACKWARDNESS : TRIBAL CHILDREN

Ramchandra Rao, A., 1966, Scholastic backwardness in tribal children, *Indian Education* 5(6) May, 20-25.

See also Educational Backwardness: Tribal Students.

SCHOOLING : HARIJANS : INDIA

Raymond, L., 1952, Harijans at school, *Social Action* 1(1) March, p 398-12.

SCIENCE : STUDY AND TEACHING : SCHEDULED CASTES

Misra, Ajay M., et al, 1983, A study of attitude towards learning of science among Scheduled Caste students, *Journal of Education and Psychology* 41(3) October, p 112-116.

SCIENTIFIC PROGRESS : TRIBALS

Sanganna, Toyaka, 1964, Tribal culture and its preservation and scientific development, *Adibasi*, 6 January, p 3-4.

SCOUTING : TRIBALS

Bapat, N. V., 1959, Scouting among tribals, *Vanyajati* 7(3) July, p 82-83.

SEA FISHERMAN

Das, Harish Chandra, 1963-1964, The sea-fisherman of North Balasore and their way of fishing, *Adibasi* 5(2), p 25-28.

SECULAR STATE : RESERVATION CRITERION

Kananalkil, Jose, 1986, Secular state and religious criterion for reservation, *Social Action* 36(2) April-June, p 137-148.

SEMI NOMADISM

Kapoor, A. K., et al, 1990, Semi-Nomadism and transhumance in Central Himalayas : A pragmatic perspective, *Man in India*, 70(1) March, p 47-60.

SEMINAR ON BRAHAMANS IN EARLY TAMILAHAM, 1959, MADRAS

Anon, 1965, Brahamans in early Tamilaham, *Bulletin of Institute of Traditional Culture*, Part II, 1965, p 275-317.

SEMINAR ON CASTEISM AND REMOVAL OF UNTOUCHABILITY, 1955, DELHI

Nanavatty, Mehar C., 1955, Seminar on casteism and untouchability : A review, *Indian Journal of Adult Education* 16(4) December, p 41-50.

SEMINAR ON IMPACT OF MODERN FORCES ON TRIBES AND CASTES IN INDIA

Bage, S. K., 1964, Seminar on impact of modern forces on Tribes and castes in India : Welcome address, *Journal of Social Research* 7(1-2) March-September, p 12-14.

SEMINAR ON SOCIO-ECONOMIC PROBLEMS OF SCHEDULED TRIBES

Anon, 1984, Recommendations of the Seminar on socio-economic problems of Scheduled Tribes, *Vanyajati* 32(3) July, p 1-4.

SEMINAR ON TRIBAL FOREST LABOUR COOPERATIVES

Shrikant, L. M., 1970, Seminar on tribal forest labour cooperatives, *Vanyajati* 18(2) April, p 49-50.

SEMINAR ON THE TRIBAL SITUATION IN INDIA, SIMLA

Sanwal, R. D., 1969, Seminar on the tribal situation in India, Simla, *Sociological Bulletin* 18(2) September.

SEMINAR ON TRIBAL WELFARE, 1956, CHHINDWARA

Anon, 1956, Seminar on tribal welfare at Chhindwara, *Vanyajati* 4(3) July, p 1-59.

SERF LABOUR

Sivaswamy, K.G., 1984, Serf labour among the Aboriginals, *Indian Journan of Social Work* 8(4) March, p 310-319.

SEROLOGICAL STATUS : CASTES AND TRIBES : INDIA : GUJARAT

Majumdar, D. N. and **Kishen, K.**, 1948, Serological status of caste and tribes of central Gujarat, *Eastern Anthropologist* 2(2) December, p 92-97.

SEX DIFFERENCES IN CREATIVITY : TRIBALS : INDIA : MEGHALAYA

Dutta, Gitika, 1982, Sex differences in creativity among the tribe of Meghalaya, *Journal of Institute of Educational Research* 6(2) May, p 23-26, references, tables.

SEXUAL DIMORPHISM : HIGH ALTITUDE POPULATION

Sidhu, L. S., et al, 1985, Sexual dimorphism, physique and body composition of adult Bhotia : A high altitude population, *Indian Anthropologist* 15(2) December, p 115-126, bibliography.

SHAH BANO

Ganguli, Amulya, 1990, Divide and lose : Mandal in Shah Bano's wake, *Statesman*, September 5.

SHANDIES : TRIBAL AREAS : INDIA : ANDHRA PRADESH

Krishna Rao, Murali I., 1989, Marketing in tribal economy : A study with special reference to Shandies (Periodic Markets) in Tribal belt of Sriakulam district of Andhra Pradesh, *Vanyajati* 37(1) January, p 9.

See also Rural Market: Tribals; Tribal Markets.

SHADAS

See Bhotiya.

SHAVARAS : INDIA : WEST BENGAL

Devi, Mahasveta, 1985, The Shavara tribal of West Bengal, *Economic and Political Weekly* 20(35) 31 August, p 1476-1469.

SHEPHERDS : INDIA : KARNATAKA

Shashi, S. S., 1988, Kurbas : Shepherds of Karnataka, *Mainstream* 26(1) January 16, p 27-28.

SHIFTING CULTIVATION

Vishwa Mohan, 1964, Ramnants of shifting cultivation, *Eastern Anthropologist* 17(1) January-April, p 31-38, references.

SHIV SENA

Anon, 1986, Shiv sena enters rural politics : Campaign against Dalits in Marathwara villages, *Economic and Political Weekly* 21(50) December 13, p 2166-2167.

SHOMPEN TRIBE

Guha, P. K., 1988, Shompen : A primitive tribe in transition, *Man in India* 68(4) December, p 465-469, tables.

SICKLE CELL TRAIT : INDIA : GUJARAT

Choubisa, S.L., 1990, Sickle cell traits in Damor tribe of Dungalpur district, Southern Rajasthan, *Man in India*, 70(4) December, p 454-458.

Negi, R.S., 1968, Sporadic occurrence of sickle-cell trait in penninsular Gujarat, *Bulletin of Anthropological Survey of India* 17(4) October, p 379-381, tables.

SICKLING

Buchi, Ernst C., 1955, Is sickling a wedded trait?, *Anthropologist* 21(1) March, p 25-29, references.

SIDDIS

Pal, Bulbul, 1986, Rooted in an African past, *Indian Education* (Mag) 5(3) January, p 5-8.

SIHAVAS

Keswani, Raaj Kumar, 1987, The Survivors, *Illustrated Weekly of India* 107(46) 23 November, p 20-23.

SIKKIM : INDIA

Subba, Tanka Bahadur, 1984, Caste and agrarian structure : A study in hill Darjeeling and Sikkim, *Man in India* 64(1) March, p 59-68, bibliography.

SIKLIGARS

Sher, Sher Singh, 1963, Demography of Sikligars, *Vanyajati* 11(2) April, p 79-81, tables.

SIMILLPAL

Krishna, Sumi, 1985, In the heart of Simillpal, *Hindustan Times* (Magazine), August 4, p 1, col 1-8.

SINDHI KHATRIS

Indera P. Singh, and **Kumbani, H. K.**, 1959, Distribution of papillary patterns on the middle and proximal phalanges of Sindhi Khatris, *Anthropologist* 6(1-2) March-August, p 26-37, references, tables.

SINDIS : RALEGANA

See Relegana Sindis.

SINGH V. P. : VIEWS ON RESERVATION

Datta Ray, Sunanda K., 1990, Class into Caste : V.P. Singh's political insurance, *Statesman*, September 9.

SINGHBHUM : INDIA : WEST BENGAL

Sen Gupta, N. K., 1988, A note on the survey and investigation on some physical conditions and nutritional patterns in relation to the tribal people in Singhbhum, *Man in India* 68(4) December, p 473-476.

SIRAHA : INDIA : MADHYA PRADESH : BASTAR

Pandey, N. N., 1961, Changing status of the 'Siraha' in a Bastar village, *Vanyajati* 9(2) April, p 55-57.

SITAMARHI PARLIAMENTARY CONSTITUENCY : INDIA

Jha, Amar Kumar, 1987, Caste-politics interactions : Process and consequences : A case study of Sitamarhi parliamentary constituency, *Journal of Social Economic Studies* 4(3) July-September, p 211-228.

SKELETAL DEVELOPMENT : TRIBAL CHILDREN : INDIA : MADHYA PRADESH

Mukherjee, D. P., 1985, Skeletal development of tribal children : Kanwar and Oraon of Surguja district (M.P.), *Journal of Indian Anthropological Society* 20(1) March, p 77-85, bibliography, tables.

SNAKE CHARMARS

Ray, H. M., 1988, Savara : The snake charmar, *Man in India* 68(4) December, p 438-487.

SOCIAL ARTICULATION : INDIA : BIHAR

Das, Arvind N., 1984, Class in itself, caste for itself : Social articulation in Bihar, *Economic and Political Weekly* 19(37) September 15, p 1616-1619.

SOCIAL BACKWARDNESS

Hasan, Shariful, 1985, Social backwardness is the end result of poverty, *Organiser* 37(1) May 19, p 8.

SOCIAL BEHAVIOUR : WAGHERS : INDIA : GUJARAT

Bajpai, Geeta, 1983, Economic determinants of social behaviour : A case study of the Waghers of Gujarat in the second half of the nineteenth century, *Journal of the Gujarat Research Society* 45(3) July, p 32-41, bibliography, footnotes.

SOCIAL CHANGE : ASIA : SOUTH EAST

Rao, M. S. A., 1964 Social change in South-East Asia, *Sociological Bulletin* 13(1) March, p 22-32, references.

SOCIAL CHANGE : TRIBALS

Ahuja, Ram, 1969, Tribal leadership and social change, *Indian Journal of Social Research* 10(3) December, p 198-203, references.

Gunasekaran, R., 1988, Social change among tribals : A study, *Kurukshetra* 36(4) January, p 9-12.

Rao, G. R. S., 1966, Process of industrialisation and direction of social changes in tribal society, *Journal of Social Research,* September 21, p 65-69.

Sachchidananda, 1988, Economic development, education and social change in Arunachal Pradesh, *Man in India* 65(1) March, p 33-57.

SOCIAL CLASSES

Fonseca, A., 1958, A new social class, *Social Action* 8(1) January, p 15-23.

Hodges, Donald C., 1961, Classical economics and Marx's theory of social class, *Indian Journal of Social Research* 2(2) July, p 91-95, references.

Lallemand, A., 1953, Social classes, *Social Action* 2(12) March p 382-387.

Mohan, Raj Pal, 1985, Social class : A Review, *Indian Sociological Bulletin* 2(4) July, p 226-227, references.

Pal, Roma and **Dixit, Ashok K.**, 1984, Social class and marital status as correlates of modernisation, *Asian Journal of Psychology and Education* 14(1-4), p 25-33, bibliography.

SOCIAL CLASSES : EVALUATION

Panday, Ram Newaj, 1966, Development of a questionnaire for social class evaluation, *Indian Psychological Review* 3(1), p 53-56, references.

SOCIAL CLASSES : INDIA

Bulsara, J. F., 1959, Implications of a casteless and classless, society, *Journal of Anthropological Society of Bombay* (NS) 11(1), p 43-60.

Dushkin, Lelah, 1979, Backward class benefits and social class in India, 1920-1970, *Economic and Political Weekly* 14, AN, April, p 661-667.

Jetley, Surinder, 1968, Transfer of power to a low caste, *Interdiscipline* 5(3) Autumn, p 199-206.

Sayanna, V. V., 1950 , The social class structure and its influence on rural economy with special reference to the prestige classes in rural society, *Rural India* 13(5) June p 198-200.

Social Service Quarterly (Periodical), 1952, The abolition of caste distinctions, *Social Service Quarterly* 37(1) July, p 10-12, editorial.

SOCIAL CLASSES : INDIA : ANCIENT

Verma, O. P., Determinants of status in ancient India, *Journal of Bihar Puravid Parishad*, 3, p 87-90.

SOCIAL CLASSES : INDIA : GUJARAT

Naik, T. B., 1957, Social status in Gujarat, *Eastern Anthropologist* 10(3-4) March-August, p 173-181, footnotes.

SOCIAL CLASSES : INDIA : PUNJAB

D'Souza, Victor S., 1969, Measurement of rigidity-fluidity dimension of social stratification in six Indian villages, *Sociological Bulletin* 18(1) March, p 35-49, references, tables.

SOCIAL CLASSES : INDIA : RAJASTHAN

Sharma, K. L., 1950, Changing class stratification in rural Rajasthan, *Man in India* 50(3) July-September, p 257-268, references.

Srivastava, Sahab Lal, 1950, Stratification and etiquette in village communities, *Man in India*, 50(3) July-September, p 269-279.

SOCIAL CLASSES : INDIA : WEST BENGAL

Sinha, Surajit and **Bhattacharya, Ranjit**, 1969, Bhadralok and Chhotolok in a rural area of West Bengal, *Sociological Bulletin* 6(2) January, p 104-106, references.

SOCIAL CLASSES : MALAYSIA

Jain, R. K., 1967, Social stratification and political process in a new nation : Malaysia, *Journal of Indian Anthropological Society*, 2(1) March, p 69-73, references.

SOCIAL CLASSES : NETHERLANDS

Klein, M. O. L., 1965, Images of the stratification system in the Netherlands, *Sociological Bulletin* 14(2) September, p 50 53.

SOCIAL CLASSES : UNITED KINGDOM

Bernard, Thomas L., 1969, Implications of social class factors in contemporary English secondary education, *India Sociological Bulletin* 6(2) January, p 104-106, references.

SOCIAL CONDITIONS : NATIVES

Long, James, 1966, Five hundred questions on subjects requiring investigation in the social condition of the natives, edited with additional notes by Mahadev Prasad Shah, *Folklore* 7(8) August, p 283-329.

SOCIAL CONTEXT : TRIBAL EDUCATION

Shah, Vimal P. and **Patel, Tara**, 1986, Social context of tribal education, *Education Quarterly* 38(2) Summer, p 49-51.

SOCIAL DEVELOPMENT : TRIBAL AREAS

Deogaonkar, Warora S. G., 1989, Role of voluntary agencies and tribal institutions in social and ecological developments in tribal area, *Vanyajati* 37(4) October, p 32-38.

Sachchidananda, 1989, Role of voluntary agencies in social and ecological developments in tribal areas, *Vanyajati* 37(4) October, p 26-32.

SOCIAL DISORGANISATION : TRIBALS : INDIA : BIHAR

Anon, 1985, (Book Review) *Contributions to Indian Sociology* (NS) 20(1) January-June, p 155-158; *Sociological Bulletin* 33(1-2) March-September, p 152-154.

Review of the book : **Sachchidananda** and **Mandal, B. B.**, 1985, *Industrialisation and the Social Disorganisation* : A study of tribals in Bihar, Concept Publishing Company, New Delhi, 164 p.

SOCIAL EDUCATION

Anon, 1954, Social education for the tribals, *Vanyajati* 2(4) October, p 107-109.

——, 1957, Social education for tribal areas, *Indian Journal of Social Work*, 18(2) September, p 136-139.

——, 1958, Social education and casteism, *Indian Journal of Adult Education* 19(3) October, p 1-2.

Das, Gananath, 1967, The programme of social education for backward tribals, *Adibasi* 8(4) January, p 5-6.

Karve, Iravati, 1958, Social education of the Scheduled Tribes, *Vanyajati* 5(4) October, p 164-169.

Nanavatty, Meher C., 1958, Casteism and social education : Role of the social education, *Indian Journal of Adult Education* 19(3) October, p 47-51.

SOCIAL ENGINEERING

Das, G. N., 1964, Culture contact and social engineering, *Adibasi*, November, p 19-22.

SOCIAL FORESTRY : TRIBAL AREAS

Roy Burman, J. J., 1990, Environmental management in tribal areas through social forestry, *Vanyajati* 38(1) January, p 26-32.

SOCIAL GROUPS

See Social Classes.

SOCIAL GROUPS : INDIA : ANDHRA PRADESH

Hanumantha Rao, K. and **Sastry, K. V. S.**, 1990, Levels of living and poverty among social groups in Andhra Pradesh : A cross-section analysis, *Journal of Rural Development* 9(1) January, p 91-105.

SOCIAL INJUSTICE

Sheth, D. L., 1986, The problem of reservations : Economic backwardness or social injustice, *Indian Journal of Adult Education* 47(5) May, p 9-15; 47(6) June, p 4-7 + ; 47(7) July, p 14-21.

See also Social Justice.

SOCIAL INSTITUTIONS : PRIMITIVE SOCIETY

Majumdar, D. N., 1930, The economic background of social institutions in primitive society, *Man in India* 10(2-3) April-September, p 105-166, footnotes.

SOCIAL JUSTICE

Dhawan, Shiv, 1985 Reservations : A critique of social justice, *Patriot* (Magazine), August 4, p 1, col 5-8.

Kulkarni, Sharad, 1985, Adivasis, law and social justice, *Economic and Political Weekly* 20(28) July 13, p 1171-1174.

——, 1986, Adivasis, law and social justice, *Tribal Research Bulletin* 8(2) March, p 1-7, bibliography.

See also Social Injustice.

SOCIAL MOBILITY

Anon, 1984 (Book review), *Hindustan Times* (Magazine), January 6, p 8, col 1-6. Review of the book : **Dev, Bimal J.** and **Lahri, Dilip K.**, 1985, *Cosmogony of caste and social mobility in Assam*, Mittal Publication, Delhi, p 183.

——, 1959, Inter-ethnic relation and social mobility movements among some tribes and castes of Eastern and Central India, 1900-1959, *Bulletin of Department of Anthropology* 8(2) July, p 9-130.

Banerjee, Hemendra Nath, 1989, Reconsideration of the principles of social stratification viewed through class-caste distinction : Social mobility in India : A sociological approach, *Man in India* 69(4) December, p 393-402.

Hadimani, R. N. et al, 1985, Sericulture as a leverage of social mobility among Scheduled Castes in rural areas : A case study of a non-sericulturist village in Karnataka, *Journal of the Institute of Economic Research* 20(1-2), p 27-35.

Mukherjee, Bhabananda, 1968, Tends of social mobility movement, *Journal of Indian Anthropological Society* 3(1-2) March-September, p 121-129.

Patwardhan, Sunanda, 1968, Social mobility and conversion of Maharas, *Sociological Bulletin* 17(2) September, p 187-202, references.

SOCIAL PHENOMENA : CASTEISM

Anon, 1958, Casteism as a social phenomenon, *Indian Journal of Adult Education* 19(3) October, p ii.

SOCIAL SCIENCES

Bose, Nirmal Kumar, 1955-1956, The use of social science, *Adibasi* 1, p 5-6.

SOCIAL SPECTRUM : INDIA : KERALA

Achyuthan, K. R., 1984, The social spectrum of Kerala, *Journal of Kerala Studies* 9(1-4) March-December, p 103-162.

SOCIAL STRATIFICATION : ASIA : SOUTH EAST

Rao. M. S. A., 1964, Social stratification and social change in South-East Asia, *Sociological Bulletin* 13(1) March, p 22-32, references.

SOCIAL STRATIFICATION : INDIA

Ahmed, Saghir, 1970, Social stratification in Punjabi villege, *Contributions to Indian Sociology* (NS) 4, December, 105-125.

Banerjee, Hemendra Nath, 1989, Reconsideration of the principles of social stratification viewed through class-caste distinction : Social mobility in indian : A sociological approach, *Man in India* 69(4) December, p 393-402.

D'Souza, Victor S., 1969, Measurement of rigidity-fluidity dimension of social stratification in six Indian villages, *Sociological Bulletin 18(1)* March, p 35-49, references, tables.

Gupta, Shiv K., 1984, The significance of social stratification in Harijan community, *Indian Journal of Social Work* 45(2) July, p 175-187, bibliography.

Ouden, J. H. B., Den, 1979, Some stratification as expressed through language : A case study of a South Indian village, *Contributions to Indian*, Sociology, NS 13, January-June, p 33-59.

Sharma, K. L., 1950, Changing class stratification in rural Rajasthan, *Man in India*, 50(3) July-September, p 257-268, references.

Srivastava, Sahab Lal, 1950, Stratification and etiquette in village communities, *Man in India* 50(3) July-September, p 269-279.

SOCIAL STRATIFICATION : NETHERLAND

Klein, M. O. L., 1965, Images of the stratification system in the Netherlands, *Sociological Bulletin* 14(2) September, p 50-53.

SOCIAL STRUCTURE : TRIBALS

Naik, Shukadeb and **Sharma, A. K.**, 1985, Social structure and family planning : A case study of two tribal villages, *Journal of Family Welfare* 32(1) September, p 50-58, bibliography.

SOCIAL TRANSFORMATION

Parvathamma, C., 1986, Role of protest movements in social transformation, *Guru Nanak Journal of Sociology* 7(1) April, p 1-22.

Roy Burman, B. K., 1968, Some dimensions of transformation of tribal societies in India, *Journal of Social Research* 11(1) March, p 88-94; *Vanyajati* 17(1) January, p 1-4 +.

SOCIO-CULTURAL BARRIERS : INDIA : BIHAR

Akhwari, N., 1958, Socio-cultural barriers to rural change in an East Bihar Community, *Eastern Anthropologist* 11(3-4), p 212-219.

SOCIO-CULTURAL MORES : TRIBALS : INDIA : BANSWARA

Nagdo, B. L., 1988, Socio-cultural mores and high fertility among tribes in Banswara, *Social Welfare* 34(11) February, p 14-15 +.

SOCIO-ECONOMIC ASPECT OF PROHIBITION

Shrikant, L. M., 1968, Socio-economic aspects of prohibition, *Vanyajati* 16(2) April, p 37-40; 69-70.

SOCIO-ECONOMIC CHARACTERISTICS : TRIBALS : INDIA : HIMACHAL PRADESH

Amar Dev and **Banerjee Guha, Swapna**, 1986, Tribes in Himachal **Pradesh** : Socio-economic characteristics, *National Geographical Journal of India* **32(4)** December, p 281-286.

SOCIO-ECONOMIC CONDITIONS : SCHEDULED CASTES : INDIA

Amar Dev and **Banerjee Guha, S.**, 1980, Socio-economic condition of the Scheduled Castes in India : A geographical analysis, *National Geographical Journal of India* 35(Part 2) June, p 129-139.

SOCIO-ECONOMIC DEVELOPMENT : TRIBALS

Laxmaiah, T., 1984, Socio-economic development of tribals, *Mainstream* 23(18) December, p 21-22.

SOCIO-ECONOMIC IMPLICATIONS OF GUINEA WORM DISEASE : TRIBALS

Vyas, N. N. and **Chaudhary, N. D.**, 1983, The socio-economic implications of Guinea worm : A disease in tribal setting, *Tribe* 15(1-2) March-June, p 15-26.

SOCIO-ECONOMIC PROBLEMS : SCHEDULED TRIBES : INDIA

Anon, 1984, Recommendations of the Seminar on socio-economic problems of Scheduled Tribes, *Vanyajati* 32(3) July, p 1-4.

SOCIO-ECONOMIC PROFILE : TRIBALS : INDIA : TAMIL NADU

Sripal, K. B. and **Knight, A. John**, 1986, Socio-economic profile of tribal of Tamil Nadu, *Kurukshetra* 34(4) January, p 35-37.

SOCIO-ECONOMIC STATUS : TRIBAL CHILDREN

Krishna Kumari, P., et al, 1986, Study of creative abilities of tribal children in relation to their sex and socio-economic status, *Journal of Institute of Educational Research* 10(1) January, p 1-4, references.

SOCIO-ECONOMIC SURVEYS : TRIBAL AREAS : INDIA : BULDBANA

Surana, M. B., 1985, Socio-economic survey of tribals in the proposed M.A.D.A. pocket in Buldbana district, *Tribal Research Bulletin* 7(2) March, p 9-13.

SOCIOLOGICAL CONSTRAINTS : TRIBAL DEVELOPMENT : INDIA : MADHYA PRADESH

Paul, S. P. and **Baghel, A. S.**, 1987, Sociological constraints and attitude to development of tribal farmers in the tribal areas of M. P., *Journal of Rural Development* 6(2) March, p 197-210.

SOCIOLOGICAL PROBLEMS : TRIBAL EDUCATION

Srivastava, Rajni, 1982, Sociological problems in tribal education : A case study, *Indian Educational Review* 17(3) July, p 110-113.

SOCIO-POLITICAL ORGANISATION : MUNDAS

Patnaik, Nityananda, 1954, The socio-political organisation of the Munda : A study of acculturation, *Vanyajati* 2(2) April, p 46-51.

SOCIO-PSYCHOLOGICAL CORRELATES : TRIBALS

Chakrabarti, A.K., et al, 1984, Socio-psychological correlates in the adoption of health innovations among tribals within intensive service zone of primary health centre, *Health and Population* 7(1) January-March, p 72-83, bibliography.

Verma, Ram Swaroop, 1985, Socio-psychological makeup of Tharu and Boksa adolescents, *Bhartiya Shiksha Shodh Patrika* 4(2) July-December, p 27-33.

SOCIO-RELIGIOUS LIFE : TRIBALS : INDIA

Anon, 1968, A study on the socio-religious life of tribals in Gudvella area, Bolangir

Quarterly, 11(1) July, p 28-29, editorial.

SOUTH INDIA

Anon, 1987, (Book review), *Indian Economic and Social History Review* 24(3) July-September, p 341-342; *Tribune* (Magazine), September 14, p 5-8.
Review of the book : **Dumont, Louis**, 1986, *A South Indian subcaste : Social organisation and religion of the Pramalai Kallar*, Oxford University Press, New Delhi, 634 p.

Assayag, Jackie, 1989, Women-Goddess, Women distress, Yallama Goddess devoties in South India (Karnataka), *Man in India* 69(4) December p 359-373.

Bhargava, G.S., 1986-1987, Caste war in South India, *Janata*, 41(25) November 30, p 7-8, 41(27) January 4, p 5-6.

Kusumakar, H., 1985, The name-tag tells all in the South, *Times of India* (Sunday Review), September 1, p 1, col. 1-8.

Social Service Quarterly (Periodical) 1930, Socio-economic reconstruction among hill tribes in the South, *Social Service Quarterly* 16(4) April, p 153-154, editorial.

See also Andhra Pradesh, Kerala, Tamil Nadu.

SOUTH MANBHUM

Sinha, Surajit, 1959, Bhumij-Kshatriya social movement in South Manbhum, *Bulletin of Department of Anthropology* 8(2) July, p 9-32, references.

See also Manbhum.

SPATIAL ASPECTS : TRIBAL CULTURE

Vyas, N.N., 1984, Some spatial aspects of tribal culture and development, *Tribe* 16(3-4) September-December, p 1-6.

SPATIAL MOBILITY : TRIBALS : INDIA

Patel, M.L., 1970, Spatial mobility of unemployed educated tribals of Mandla district, *Vanyajati* 18(2) April, p 70-76, references, tables.

SRIRAMULY, BANDI

Ramaswamy, Gita, 1989, Pen-portrait : Bandi Sriramuly, *Main Stream* 27(39) 24 June, p 23-24.

STARVATION : TRIBALS

Jabbar Alam, M., 1985, Tribal starving to extinction, *New Age* 33(25) June 23, p 5.

STATISTICAL ANALYSIS : TRIBAL EDUCATION : INDIA : BIHAR

Sinha, H.K., 1960, Tribal education in Bihar : A preliminary statistical analysis, *Journal of Social Research* 3(1) March, p 85-92, references, tables.

STATUS : CLASS AND CASTE : INDIA : SOUTHERN

Driver, Edwin D., 1982, Class, caste and status summation in urban South India, *Contributions to Indian Sociology* (NS) 16(2) July-December, p 226-253.

STATUS AND ROLE OF WOMEN : TRIBALS

Garg, B.M., 1960, Status of women in tribal communities in India, *Indian Journal of Social Work* 21(2) September, p 191-197.

Jahagirdar, M.P., 1988, The status and role of women in a tribal community, *Man in India* 68(4) December, p 424-430.

STUDENTS

Anon, 1981, (Book review); *Education Quarterly* 33(3) July, p 48-49.
Review of the book: **Aikara, Jacob**, 1981, *Scheduled Castes and higher education : A study of college students in Bombay*, Dastane Ramachandra and Co., Pune; $12p,

Ameerjan, M.S., 1979, A comparative study of academic achievement of the Scheduled Castes and Tribe students of agriculture, *Journal of Education and Psychology* 37(2) July, p 121-129, references, tables.

——, 1984, Background variables of the Scheduled Caste and Tribe college students : A comparative study, *Indian Educational Review* 19(2) April, p 28-36.

Desai, Haribhai G. and **Uchat, D.A.**, 1981, Self-concept of Harijan students and attitudes of other students towards them, *Indian Educational Review* 16(3) July, p 44-50.

Dhruv, P.R., 1968, The tribal students of Madhya Pradesh, *Vanyajati* 16(3) July, p 97-99.

Ganguly, J.B., 1970, Tribal Students between tradition and modernity, *Educational Miscellany* 7(1-2) July-September, p 61-69.

Kamila, Bana Behari, 1983, Occupational status of parents of Harijan and Tribal Welfare Department high school students of Orissa, *National Journal of Education* 6(1) September, p 56-64, references, tables.

——, 1985-1986, A study of attitude of students towards school of Harijans and Tribal Welfare Department high school of Orissa, *Journal of Education and Psychology* 43(3-4) October-January, p 187-192, references.

Lal, Shiva Kumar, 1975, Scheduled Caste college students in Rajasthan, *Journal of Higher Education* 1(2) Autumn, p 244-250, references.

Lele, T.P., 1967, A comparative study of the students from different communities, *Education and Psychology Review* 7(3) July, p 117-124, tables.

Menon, P.S.K., 1975, Post-metric scholarship for Scheduled Caste and Scheduled Tribe students, *Journal of Higher Education* 1(2) Autumn, p 263-266.

Misra, Ajay M., et al, 1983, A study of attitude towards learning of science among Scheduled Caste students, *Journal of Education and Psychology* 41(3) October, p 112-116

Rastogi, S.P., 1978, Attitudes and beliefs of Harijan students, *Journal of Higher Education*, 4(2) Autumn, p 251-258.

Satyanarayana, B.S., 1982, Educational problems of Scheduled Caste college students in Karnataka, *Journal of Higher Education* 7(3) Spring, p 256-260, references, tables.

Sharma, K.R., 1977, Specific problems of tribal students in non-tribal schools, *Education Quarterly* 28(4) January, p 30-32.

——, 1983, A study of educational backwardness of tribal students, *Education Quarterly* 35(2) April, p 33-38.

Sood, Ram, 1980-81, Role of achievement anxiety, alienation and value discrepancy in academic achievement of Scheduled Caste students, *Journal of Higher Education* 6(1-3), p 117-122, references, tables.

Sowaid, M., et al, 1986, A study of parent child interaction and achievement motivation among tribal high school students, *Journal of Institute of Educational Research* 10(3) September, p 24-27, references.

Subrahmanyam, S., 1985-86, A study of attitude of students towards school of Harijans and Tribals Welfare Department high school of Orissa, *Journal of Education and Psychology* 43(3-4) October-January, p 187-192, references.

Thiagarajan, A.P., 1981, A study of the Scheduled Caste students in some secondary schools of Tamil Nadu, *Indian Education,* 11(5) August, p 22-26, tables.
See also Tribal Students.

STUDENTS : COMPARATIVE STUDY

Verma, B.P. and **Sharma, Keshav**, 1989, A comparative study of locus and control and self-concept of higher, backward and Scheduled Caste students, *Progress of Education* 63(9) April, p 205-208.

STUDY TEAMS : TRIBAL WELFARE

Anon, 1959, The study team and tribal welfare, *Vanyajati* 7(4) October, p 115-118, references.

——, 1967, Study team on tribal development programmes, *Vanyajati* 15(1) January, p 45-52.
See also Research and Development; Tribal Studies.

SUB PLAN PROGRAMME

See Tribal Sub Plan.

SUDRAS : INDIA

Anon, 1984, Paijavana or Pailavaka : A Sudra Yogin, *Purana* 26(2) July, p 206-208.

Chanana, Dev Raj, 1959, The Sudra, the Dasa and Manu, *Indian Journal of Social Work* 20(3) December, p 201-208.

Sharma, R.S., 1984, Sudras in ancient India, *Journal of the Institute of Economic Research* 19(2) July, p 32-33.

SUGALIS

Kusuma, A., 1988, Infant feeding practices among Sugalis, *Social Welfare* 35(8) November, p 7 +.

Ramachandra Reddy, M. and **Chengal Reddy, P.**, 1989, Fertility behaviour in the Sugalis of Chittoor district, Andhra Pradesh, *Health and Population* 9(4) October-December, p 205-217.

SULUNGS : INDIA : ARUNACHAL PRADESH

Gangwar, A. and **Rama Krishnan, P.S.**, 1987, Agriculture and animal husbandry among the Sulungs and Nishish of Arunachal Pradesh, *Social Action* 37(4) October-December, p 345-372, bibliography, figures, tables.

SUNDARBANS : INDIA : WEST BENGAL

Mukherjee, Sakarananda, 1964, Sadani : The tribal dialect of the Sundarbans, *Bulletin of Cultural Research Institute* 3(2), p 47-50, references.

SUNDARGARH DISTRICT : INDIA : ORISSA

Anon, 1967, A summary of the study on impact of industrialisation on the tribals of Sundargarh district, *Adibasi* 8(4) January, p 46-51.

SURGANA TALUKA : INDIA

Pawar, H.S. and **Patil, R.P.**, 1987, Adoption behaviour of the tribal farmers from Surgana taluka (Nasik district) in respect of paddy cultivation, *Tribal Research Bulletin* 9(2) March, p 15-17.

SURGUJA DISTRICT : INDIA : MADHYA PRADESH

Mukherjee, D.P., and **Das, N.K.**, 1985, Age at menarcghe in tribal girls; The Kanwar and the Oraon of Surguja district, M.P., *Journal of Indian Anthropological Society*, 20(2) July, p153-158, bibliography, tables.

Mukherjee, D.P., et al, 1985, Skeletal development of tribal children : Kanwar and Oraon of Surguja district (M.P.), *Journal of Indian Anthropological Society* 20(1) March, p 77-85, bibliography, tables.

Sharma, K.K.N., 1989, A note on the distribution of matrimonial distance of the Khaiwal tribal population of Surguja district, Madhya Pradesh, *Man in India* 69(3) September, p 267-271, bibliography, tables.

SURVEYS : EDUCATIONAL RESERVATION

Patwardhan, Vidya and **Palshikar, Vasant**, 1990, Are educational reservations a waste?: The results of a survey, *Janata*, 45, Annual Number, p 35-39.

SURVIVAL STRATEGY : TRIBALS

Viegas, Philip, 1987, Land control and tribal struggle for survival, *Social Action* 37(4) October-December, p 325-344, footnotes.

See also Extinction: Tribal struggle for Survival.

SUTHARS COMMUNITY : INDIA : RAJASTHAN

Choubisa, S.L., et al, 1987, Abnormal haemoglobin, thalassaemia and G-6 P D deficiency genews in the Suthar community of Southern Rajasthan, *Indian Journal of Physical Anthropology and Human Genetics* 13(1) January-April, p 9-16, bibliography, tables.

SWANGLAS : INDIA

Chowdhary, A.K., 1988, P T C taste sensitivity and colour blindness among Bodh and Swangla of Lahaul, *Man in India* 68(7) December, p 448-453, bibliography, tables.

SWEEPERS : INDIA

Anon, 1918, The temper of work: A day service, *Social Service Quarterly* 3(4) April, p 192-195.

Mehta, Vaikunth L., 1941, Harijans and municipalities, *Social Service Quarterly* 28(2) October, p 41-48.

See also Bhangis; Scavengers.

SWEEPERS : INDIA : DELHI

Om Prakash, 1980, Educational attainment of children in the Sweeper community of A I I M S campus : An exploratory study, *Indian Educational Review* 15(4) October, p 97-103.

SWEEPERS : INDIA : MAHARASHTRA : BOMBAY CITY

Bhalerao, Shanta, 1936, The scavenging and halakhore labour of Bombay : Some impressions, *Social Service Quarterly* 22(1) July, p 11-14.

Thakkar, A.V., 1918, Disabilities of municipal sweepers in Bombay, *Social Service Quarterly* 3(3) January, p 120-124.

SWEEPERS : INDIA : ORISSA : BHUBANESHWAR

Debi, Kiranbala, 1966, Sweepers and scavengers in Bhubaneshwar, *Adibasi* 8(3) October, p 35-41.

SWEEPERS : INDIA : UTTAR PRADESH : LUCKNOW

Gupta, S.C. and **Prasad B.G.**, 1964, A socio-medical survey of sweepers and their families in Lucknow Municipal Corporation, *Indian Journal of Social Work* 24(4) January, p 289-296.

——, 1965, A note on the living and working conditions of the sweeper community in Lucknow, *Eastern Anthropologist* 18(3) September-December, p 117-185, references, tables.

SYLVAN AREAS

Mehta, B.H., 1962, Youth organisations in Sylvan areas, *Indian Journal of Adult Education* 23(10) October, p 38-40.

SYNTENGS

See also Khasis.

TADP

= Tribal Area Development Plan

TRYSEM

= Training of Rural Youth for Self Employment

TSP

= Tribal Sub Plan

TRYSEM PROGRAMME : INDIA : ANDHRA PRADESH

Meera Reddy, V., 1990, TRYSEM programme : A case study in Kurnool Samiti of Andhra Pradesh, *Journal of Rural Development* 9(2) March, p 435-443.

TSP AREAS : INDIA : RAJASTHAN

Trivedi, H.V., 1986, The T S P area in Rajasthan and its socio-psychological development barriers spectrum, *Rajasthan Economic Journal* 10(1) January, p 53-63, bibliography, tables.

Vaish, Prerana, 1984, Role of mineral in the tribal development of T S P region of Rajasthan, *Tribe* 16(3-4) September-December, p 20-29.

See also Tribal Sub Plan.

TABOOS

Mc Callum, D. Kent, 1965, Consensus and control : The Kunapipi ritual and attendant taboo, *Eastern Anthropologist* 18(2) May-August, p 80-88, references.

TADVI BHILS

See Bhils.

TAGINS : INDIA : ARUNACHAL PRADESH

Durah, D.K., 1985, A study on middle phalangeal hair among the Tagins and Monpas of Arunachal Pradesh, *Resarun* 11(1) Spring-Summer, p 33-41, tables.

TALWADA ASHRAM SCHOOL : INDIA : MAHARASHTRA

Apte, J.S., 1960, Talwada Ashram School : An experiment in tribal education, *Vanyajati* 8(2) April, p 81-82.

TAMANGS : INDIA : WEST BENGAL

Piplai, Chumki, et al, 1985, A note on A B O, M N, Rh and in (a) blood groups of the Tamang and Oraon tea labourers of Jalpaiguri district, West Bengal, *Journal*

observations, *Anthropos*, 71, p 868-877.

TEA LABOURERS : TRIBALS : INDIA : WEST BENGAL

Piplai, Chumki, et al, 1985, A note on A B O, M N, Rh and in (a) blood groups of the Tamang and Oraon tea labourers of the Jalpaiguri district, West Bengal, *Journal of Indian Anthropological Society* 20(1) March, p 66-70, bibliography, tables.

TEA PLANTATION INDUSTRY : TRIBAL LABOURERS

Dasgupta, Pranab Kumar and **Khan, Iar Ali**, 1985, Impact of tea plantation industry on the life of tribal labourers, *Man and Life* 12(1-2) January-June, p 109-110.

TEACHERS : VIEWS ON RESERVATION

Anon, 1990, Teachers Front back reservation, *National Herald*, September 4, p 3, col 2-3.

TEACHERS IN TRIBAL AREAS

Prasada Rao, D.L. and **Venkata Rao, P.**, 1983, Problems of teachers working in tribal areas, *Educational Review* 89(8) August, p 139-141.

TECHNICAL EDUCATION : TRIBALS

Roy Chowdhry, K.P., 1957, Technical education for tribals, *Vanyajati* 5(2) April, p 87-93.

See also Tribal Education.

TECHNICAL TRAINING : ADIVASI YOUTHS

Patil, H.G., 1957, A scheme for technical training of Adivasi youths, *Vanyajati* 5(3) July, p 150-154, tables.

See also Technical Education: Tribals.

TECHNOLOGY : TRIBAL AREAS

Singh, K.S., 1990, Environment, technology and management in tribal areas, *Man in India* 70(2) June, p 123-130

TECHNOLOGY TRANSFER

Roy Burman, B.K., 1989, Technology transfer to tribal areas, *Mainstream* 27(44) July 29, p 23-27.

TEMPLE ENTRY BILL

Lele, P.R., 1934, The Temple Entry Bill, *Social Service Quarterly* 19(3) January, p 109-112.

TEMPLE ENTRY PROCLAMATION : INDIA : MALABAR

Social Service Quarterly (Periodical), 1937, Temple Entry Proclamation, *Social Service Quarterly* 22(3) January, p 116-119, editorial.

TEMPLE ENTRY SATYAGRAHA

Social Service Quarterly (Periodical), 1929, Temple entry satyagraha, *Social Service Quarterly* 15(2) October, p 57-58, editorial.

TEMPLE FUNCTIONARIES : INDIA : KARNATAKA

Goswami, B.B. and **Morab, S.G.**, 1988, Tribes and castes as temple functionaries in the temples of Karnataka, *Man in India* 68(1) March, p 61-69.

TERMINOLOGY AND ALLIANCE : TRIBALS

Robert, Parking, 1990, Terminology and alliance in India: Tribal systems and the North-South problems, *Contributing to Indian Sociology* 24(1) January-June, p 61-76.

TERRORISM AGAINST TRIBALS : INDIA : ROHTAS

Jabbar Alam, M., 1986, Terror against tribals in Rohtas district, *New Age* 34(9) March 2, p 8 +.

THAILAND

Madge, Charles, 1958, Caste and community in India and Thailand : A contract, *Indian Journal of Adult Education* 19(3) October, p 13-15.

THAKKAR BAPPA : ROLE

Kaujalgi, H.S., 1941, Thakkar Bappa meets the Harijans, *Rural India* 4(3) March, p 147-148.

THAKURS : INDIA : GUJARAT

Pandey, Ashok K. and **Nigam, Sushma**, 1985, A study of tongue rolling and tongue folding among Thakurs of village Shobhasan (Gujarat, India), *Indian Journal of Physical Anthropology and Human Genetics* 11(1-2) April-August, p 67-70, bibliography, tables.

THARADARI : INDIA

Pushker, Chanderverker, 1958, Kolis of Tharadari, *Folklore* 1(3) July-September, p 30-33.

THARAVADS

Subashini, A.V., 1987, Tharavads : Kerala's Nair homes, *Indian Management* 7(8) July, p 52-63.

THARIA RANIGUNGE COAL FIELD AREA, CALCUTTA

Anon, 1981, (Book Review), *Man in India* 67(1) March, p 89-90.
Review of the book: **Banerjee, Sukumar**, 1981, *Impact of Industrialisation on the tribal population of Tharia Ranigunge Coal Field area*, Calcutta, Anthropological Survey of India, 160 p.

THARUS

Govila, J.P., 1959, The Tharus of Tarai and Bhabhar, *Indian Folklore* 2(3) July-September, p 228 +.

Hu, C.T., 1957, Marriage by exchange among the Tharus with a geneological case study, *Eastern Anthropologist* 10 (1), pp 662-684.

Jha, Amiya, 1986, In outsider country, *Hindustan Times* (Magazine) March 2, p 4, col. 1-8.

Roy Choudhry, P.C., 1952, The Tharus, *Man in India* 32(4) October-December, p 246-250.

Srivastava, Om Prakash, 1960, Tharus in Balampur Tahsil, *Vanyajati*, 8(1) January, p 28-30.

Verma, Ram Swaroop, 1985, Socio-psychological makeup of Tharu and Boksa adolescents, *Bhartiya Shiksha Shodh Patrika* 4(2) July-December, p 27-33.

THEOLOGICAL PERSPECTIVES : TRIBALS

Exem, A. Van, 1987, The tribe : God's own people : A theological perspective,

Sevartham 12, p 45-64, footnotes.

TIBETANS
See also Bhotiyas.

TIKIRIA KONDHS
See Kondhs.

TIRAP DISTRICT : INDIA : ARUNACHAL PRADESH
Dutta, P.C., 1978, Social organisation of the Wanchos of Tirap district, Arunachal Pradesh, *Resarun* 4(1) January-March, p 14-34.

TIRUPATI : INDIA : ANDHRA PRADESH
Rami Reddy, V. and **Subhashini, A.B.**, 1984, A B O blood groups among the Palli Reddies : A backward caste of Tirupati and other populations of Andhra Pradesh, *Man in India* 64(2) June, p 193-200, bibliography.

TODAS
Anon. 1954, the Todas, *Social Service Quarterly* 39(4) April, p 97-102.
Peter, R.H. Prince, 1953, The problem of Toda survival, *Vanyajati* 1(3) July, p 59-68.
Venkatraman, S.R., 1954, The Todas, *Vanyajati* 2(3) July, p 82-85.
——, 1959, Some problems of tribal welfare work, *Social Service Quarterly* 44(3) January, p 77-82.

TOMARAS
Phogat, Silak Ram, 1984, The original home of Tomaras : A new interpretation, *Journal of Haryana Studies* 16 (1-2), p 16-20, bibliography

TOTEMISM
Buredkar, M.P., 1940, Totemism among the Gods, *Man in India* 20(3) July-September, p 114-143; 20(4) October-December, p 268-269, footnotes, tables.
Chapekar, N.G., 1952, Traces of totemism in the Rigveda, *Sociological Bulletin* 1(2) September, p 95-98.
Ferreira, John V., 1964, The problems of Maratha totemism, *Indian Journal of Social Work* 25(2) July, p 135-151, references.
——, 1967, Towards integral man through integral anthropology, *Sociological Bulletin* 16(2) September, p 77-93.
See also Totems.

TOTEMS
Dubey, K.C., 1969, A note on the Bison-Horn Maria Dharatries, Claus and totems, *Eastern Anthropologist* 22(3) September-December, p 371-376.
See also Totemism.

TOTOS
Majumdar, Bimalendu, 1986, Culture change among the Totos, *Man and Life* 12 (1-2) January-June, p 77-78, bibliography.

TOWNSHIPS AND TRIBALS
Thakur, Devendra, 1984, Township and its impact on tribal urbanisation, *Monthly Commentary on Indian Economic Conditions* 26(3) October, p 7-10.

TRADE PATTERNS : LAOS : NORTHERN

Halpern, Joel Martin, 1958-1959, Trade patterns in Northern Laos, *Eastern Anthropologist* 12(2) December-February, p 119-124.

TRADERS : CRIMINAL TRIBES : INDIA : TAMIL NADU

Radhakrishna, Meena, 1989, The Criminal Tribes Act in Madras Presidency: Implications for intinerant trading communities, *Indian Economic and Social History Review* 26(3) July-September, p 269-295.

TRADITIONAL BELIEFS : TRIBALS

Srivastava, R.M. and **Kharde, R.L.**, 1983, Traditional beliefs of tribal Mundas associated with cattle husbandry, *Indian Journal of Extension Education* 19(3-4) September-December, p 77-82, references, tables.

See also Traditions and Customs: Tribals.

TRADITIONS AND CUSTOMS : TRIBALS : INDIA

Rajyalakshmi, P. and **Geervani, P.**, 1988, Tribal people : Traditions, Customs and attitudes related to food and dietary practices : A case study of Vizianagram district, Andhra Pradesh, *Indian Journal of Social Work* 49(1) January, p 45-50.

Sirkar, R.H., 1968, Women in tribal India through custom and traditions, *Folklore* 9(12) December, p 458-467, references.

See also Traditions Beliefs: Tribals.

TRADITIONS AND CUSTOMS : TRIBALS : INDIA : NORTH EAST

Roy Burman, J.J., 1990, Tribal tradition and modern development in North-East India, *Vanyajati* 38(2) April, p 9-13.

TRAINING : TRIBAL WELFARE WORKERS

Anon, 1955, Training of social workers in tribal areas, *Vanyajati* 3(3) July, p 95-98.

——, 1957, The need for training for tribal welfare work, *Vanyajati* 2(2) January, p 39-42.

——, 1961, Training of tribal welfare workers, *Vanyajati* 9(3) July, p 87-89.

Gare, G.M., 1985, Need of training of workers in tribal development, *Tribal Research Bulletin* 7(2) March, p 5-6.

Karva, S.P., 1986, Training tribal youth, *Tribal Research Bulletin* 9(1) September, p 28-29.

TRAINING NEEDS : TRIBAL AREAS

Singh, K.M.P., 1984, Tips on training needs and middle management for tribal areas, *Survey* 24(1-2), p 19-25, bibliography.

TRAINING OF RURAL YOUTH SELF EMPLOYMENT

See TRYSEM

TRANSFORMATION : TRIBAL SOCIETIES : INDIA

Roy Burman, B.K., 1968, Some dimensions of transformation of tribal societies in India, *Journal of Social Research* 9(1), p 88-94.

See also Tribal Transformation.

TRANSHUMANCE : NOMADS

Kapoor, A.K., et al, 1990, Semi nomadism and transhumance in central Himalayas : A pragmatic perspective, *Man in India* 70(1) March, p 47-60.

TRAVANCORE STATE : INDIA

Velayudhan, R., 1940, A study of social-conditions among the Pulayas (Harijans) of Kalady in Travancore State. *Indian Journal of Social Work* 1(3) December, p 393-403, tables.

See also Geographical Area subdivision under main Descriptor.

TRIBAL ADMINISTRATION

Bhupinder Singh, 1985, Tribe administration : A critique, *Indian Journal of Public Administration* 31(3) July-September, p 879-901.

Paul, Gemini, 1957, Anthropology and Tribal administration, *Vanyajati* 5(1) January, p 4-11.

TRIBAL AFFAIRS

Anon, 1955, Conference on tribal affairs, *Vanyajati* 3(1) January, p 1-3.

TRIBAL AREAS

Aiyappan, A., 1965, A case for intensification of the development of tribal areas, *Adibasi*, July, p 47-52.

Anon, 1957, Social education for tribal areas, *Indian Journal of Social Work* 18(2) September, p 136-139.

—— 1966, A study of the tribal people and tribal areas of Madhya Pradesh, *Bulletin of Tribal Research and Development Institute* (Bhopal) 6(2) December, p 3-176.

——, 1985, (Book review), *Social Action* 35(1) January-March, p 95-98.
Review of the book : **Pachauri, S.K.**, 1984, *Dynamics of Rural Development in Tribal Areas*, Concept Publishing Company, New Delhi, xiv, 262 p.

——, 1986 (Book review), *Southern Economist* 24(23) April 1, p 26-27.
Review of the book : **Pachauri, S.K.**, 1984, *Dynamics of Rural Development in Tribal Areas*, Concept Publishing, New Delhi, xiv, 262 p.

Athavale, M.C. and **Nahatkar, Sunil**, 1983, Evaluation study of tribal area development programme in Konta and Dantewara, Bastar district, M.P., *Cooperative Perspective* 18(3) October-December, p 93-100.

Banerjee, S.P., 1961, Crimes in tribal areas, *Bulletin of Tribal Research and Development Institute* (Chhindwara) 1(2) December, p 4-8.

Batria, Puran, 1960, Policing in tribal areas, *Bulletin of Tribal Research and Development Institute* (Bhopal) 7(1-2) June-December, p 5-18.

Chatterjee, B., 1953, Model community centres in tribal areas, *Indian Journal of Social Work* 14(3) December, p 282-291.

Chatterjee, Bishwa B., 1970, Functional literacy for family planning in tribal areas, *Indian Journal of Adult Education* 31(1) January, p12-13+ tables.

Das, A.K., 1965, Prospects of fish culture in tribal area, *Man in India* 45(4) October-December, p 316-321, references.

Dayal, L., 1984, Industrialisation in tribal areas, *Bihar Journal of Public Administration* 1(1) Spring, p 62-64.

Deogaonkar, Warora S.G., 1989, Role of voluntary agencies and tribal institutions in social and ecological development in tribal areas, *Vanyajati* 37(4) October, p 32-38.

Jabbar Alam, M., 1986, Injecting communalism into tribal areas, *New Age* 34(39) September 28, p 11.

Jena, A.C., 1986, Forms of exploitation in tribal areas and their consequences : Some observations in Keonjhar district of Orissa, *Man and Life* 12(3-4)

July-December, p 173-180, bibliography.

Kashli, N. Singh and **Rama Shankar Singh**, 1984, Levels of regional and tribal development in tribal areas : Are they identical, *National Geographical Journal of India* 30(1) March, 1-12, appendix, tables.

Mehta, B.H., 1962, Social experiments in extension projects : the Balvadi in tribal areas, *Indian Journal of Social Work* 23(1) April, p 53-56.

——, 1966, Forestry and tensions in tribal area, *Journal of Social Research* 9(2) September, p 10-25.

Minz, Nirmal, 1962, Impact of traditional religions and modern secular ideologies in the tribal areas of Chotanagpur, *Religion and Society* 9(4) December, p 46-56.

Pant, S.P. and Baghal, A.S., 1987 Sociological constraints and attitude to development of tribal farmers in the tribal areas of M.P., *Journal of Rural Development* 6(2) March, p 197-210.

——, 1989, Elements of development plan for tribal area farmers of Madhya Pradesh, *Journal of Rural Development* 8(1) p 71-78.

Pathy, Jaganath, 1987, The agrarian situation in tribal areas, *Journal of Social Studies* 4(2) April-June, p 143-162.

Prasad Rao, D.L., and **Venkata Rao, P.**, 1983, Problems of teachers working in tribal areas, *Educational Review* 89(8) August, p 139-141.

Rajagopal, 1986, Agricultural labourers in tribal areas, *Kurukshetra* 34(4) January, p 17-18 +.

Ramaswamy, V.S., 1985, Land ownership structure in the areas: A study, *Kurukshetra* 33(10) July, p 24-25 +.

Roy Burman, J.J., 1990, Environmental management in tribal areas through social forestry, *Vanyajati* 38(1) January, p 26-32.

Sachchidananda, 1989, Role of voluntary agencies in social and ecological development in tribal areas, *Vanyajati* 37(4) October, p 26-31.

Satish Kumar, 1985, Development in tribal areas : An overview, *Link* (Supplement) 27(26) February 3, p 13-18, tables.

Sharma, Suryanarayan, 1985, Accent on tribal area development, *Commerce* 151(3873) August 17, p 325-326.

Shyam Manohar, 1964, Education in tribal areas with employment bias, *Indian Education* 3(10) September, p 18-24.

Singh, K.M.P., 1984, Tips on training needs and middle management for tribal areas, *Survey* 24(1-2), p 19-25, bibliography.

Singh, K.S., 1990, Environment, technology and management in tribal areas, *Man in India* 70(2) June, p 123-130.

Tarlok Singh, 1966, Education in tribal areas, *Folklore* 7(10) October, p 397-401.

Uday Bhaskar Reddy, I. and **Chattopadhyay, R.N.**, 1985, Industrialising tribal areas: Boon or banne, *Yojana* 39(5) March 16, p 18-20.

Vyas, Ambalal, 1970, How backward the tribal areas of Orissa state are? *Vanyajati* 18(3) July, p 131-133, tables.

TRIBAL ART

Anon, 1986, Home of tribal art, *Link* (Supplement) 28(30) March 2, p 35-36.

Aryan, Subhashini, 1985, Tribal art of India, *Indian and Foreign Review* 22(19) July 31, p 23-26.

TRIBAL ASPIRATIONS : INDIA

Minz, Nirmal, 1986, Religion and culture as power in the context of tribal aspirations in India, *Religion and Society* 33(2) June, p 45-54.

TRIBAL AUTONOMY

Anon, 1985, Three years of tribal autonomous comment, *People's Democracy* 9(12) March 24, p 7-8.

Bhattacharjee, P.K., 1987, New horizon of tribal autonomy and tribal development in Tripura, *Journal of North-East India Council* 11(1) April, p 33-42.

TRIBAL BIBLIOGRAPHY

Anon, 1988, (Book review), *Man in India* 68(2-3) June-September, p 305. Review of the book : **Gour, P.N.**, ed., 1988, *Bihar Tribal Bibliography*, Patna Library Publication, Patna, 135 p.

TRIBAL BLOCKS

Anon, 1960, Special tribal blocks, *Vanyajati* 8(4) October, p 129-131+.

TRIBAL CHILDREN

Anon, 1985, Profile of a tribal child of Panchmahals, *Social Welfare* 32(3) June, p 28-29.

Krishna Kumari, P., et al, 1986, Study of creative abilities of tribal children in relation to their sex and socio-economic status, *Journal of Institute of Educational Research* 10(1) January, p 1-4, references.

Mukherjee, D.P., 1985, Skeletal development of tribal children : Kanwar and Oraon of Surguja district (M.P.), *Journal of Indian Anthropological Society* 20(1) March, p 77-78, bibliography, tables.

Venkataraman, S.R., 1963, The life of the aboriginal child, *Social Service Quarterly* 48(4) April, p 105-109.

TRIBAL CHILDREN : ANTHROPOMETRY : INDIA : MADHYA PRADESH

Mukherjee, D.P., 1985, Skeletal development of tribal children : Kanwar and Oraon of Surguja district (M.P.), *Journal of Indian Anthropological Society* 20(1) March, p 77-85, bibliography, tables.

Rao, V.V. Raman, 1984, Impact of supplementary feeding on tribal pre-school children of A.P.: An anthropometric assessment, *Man in India* 64(2), June, p 167-174.

TRIBAL CHILDREN : NUTRITION : INDIA : ANDHRA PRADESH

Rao, V.V. Raman, 1984, Impact of supplementary feeding on tribal pre-school children of A.P.: An anthropometric assessment, *Man in India* 64(2), June, p 167-174.

TRIBAL COMMUNICATION : INDIA : ARUNACHAL PRADESH

Gurubasve, K.S., 1985, Tribal communications in Arunachal Pradesh, Gowda, *Resarun* 11(2) Autumn-Winter, p 25-26.

Majumdar, Aurobindo, 1985, Tribal communication : A case study of Arunachal Pradesh, *Vidura* 22(4) August, p 195-200.

TRIBAL COMMUNITIES

Moasosang, P., 1964, Social and cultural changes in the tribal communities today and the responsibility of the churches, *Religion and Society*, 9(4) December, p40-45.

Reddy, G.P., 1984, Tribal communities in india : A struggle for identity, *Parlance* 8(2-3) November-December, p 13-20.

Volchock, B. Ya, 1964, The interaction on caste and tribal communities in Central India, *Journal of Social Research* 7(1-2) March-September, p 104-112.

references.
See also Tribal Community and Women.

TRIBAL COMMUNITY AND WOMEN
Jahagirdar, M.P., 1988, The status and role of women in a tribal community, *Man in India* 68(4) December, p 424-430.

TRIBAL COOPERATIVE SOCIETIES
See also Cooperative Movement: Tribals; Cooperatives: Tribals.

TRIBAL COOPERATIVE SOCIETIES : INDIA
Shah, P.G., 1956, The use of multi-purpose employment co-operative societies for the Scheduled Tribes of India, *Vanyajati* 4(1) January, p 29-31.
Shrikant, L.M., 1967, Co-operative movement among the tribal, *Vanyajati* 15(1) January-October, p 1-154.

TRIBAL COOPERATIVE SOCIETIES : INDIA : ANDHRA PRADESH
Shrikant, L.M., 1967, Co-operative movement among tribals: Andhra Pradesh Scheduled Tribes Co-operative Finance Development Corporation, *Vanyajati* 15(2) April, p 94-97, tables.

TRIBAL COOPERATIVE SOCIETIES : INDIA : MADHYA PRADESH
Anon, 1966, A short note on the working of the co-operative movement for benefit of tribal district of Raigarh (Madhya Pradesh), *Vanyajati* 14(1) January, p 40-43.
Shrikant, L.M., 1967, Co-operative movement among tribal, III: The Madhya Pradesh State Tribal Co-operative Development Corporation Limited, Bhopal, *Vanyajati* 15(3) July, p 101-108, tables.

TRIBAL COOPERATIVE SOCIETIES : INDIA : MAHARASHTRA
Apte, J.S., 1960, Co-operative movement among the tribals of district Thana, Bombay State, *Vanyajati* 8(3) July, p 102-104.

TRIBAL CRIME
Batria, P., 1963, Crime and witchcraft among the tribes of Madhya Pradesh, *Bulletin of Tribal Research and Development Institute* (Chhindwara) 3(1), p 21-29, references, tables.
Mukherjee, Anima, 1950, The pattern of a polyandrous society with particular reference to tribal crime, *Man in India* 30(2-3) April-September, p 56-65.
See also Crime: Tribal Areas.

TRIBAL CRISIS : INDIA : TRIPURA
Das Gupta, Barun, 1987, Background to Tripura tribal crisis, *Mainstream* 25(16) January 3, p 4-6.

TRIBAL CULTURE
Acharjee, Ranjeet Kumar, 1986, The tribals of Tripura : Their culture and religion, *Prabuddha Bharata* 91(3) March, p 149-159.
Anon, 1990, (Book review), *Man in India* 70(2) June, p 199-201. Review of the book : **Bhasin, Veena**, 1980, *Ecology, culture and change: Tribals of Sikkim Himalayas*, Inter-India Publications, p 407+22, photoplates.
Banerjee, Biswanath, 1968, Relation between environment and culture among some Indian primitive communities living in the hills, *Bulletin of Cultural Research Institute* 7(1-2), p 55-61, references.

Bose, Nirmal Kumar, 1964, Change in tribal cultures before and after Independence, *Man in India* 44(1) January-March, p 1-10.

Das, Gananath,, 1967, Tribal culture and democracy, *Adibasi* 9(3) October, p 31-35.

Hans, A.B.D., 1986, Tribal culture and education's response : Search for a model of education for the tribal people, *New Frontiers in Education* 16(1) January-March, p 1-147, appendix.

Kurup, A.M., 1962, Glimpses of life and culture of the tribes of Madhya Pradesh, *Vanyajati* 10(4) October, p 139-145.

Majumdar, D.N., 1939, Tribal cultures and acculturation, *Man in India* 19(2-3) April-September, p 99-172.

Minz, Nirmal, 1987, Religion, culture and education in the context of tribal aspirations in India, *Journal of Dharma* 12(2) April-June, p 150-164 bibliography, footnotes.

Mohanty, Gopinath, 1964, Fading outlines in tribal culture, *Adibasi*, January, p 25-38.

Nag, Narendra Gopal, 1970, Implication of cultural and demographic factors on the socio-political trends among Scheduled Tribes, *Vanyajati* 18(2) April, p 51-58, references, tables.

Nandi, Shanti Bhushan, 1960, Cultural change in an Oraon village, *Vanyajati* 8(1) January, p 12-20.

Nongbri, T., 1989, Some reflections on culture and development among the tribes, *Vanyajati* 37(4) October, p 20-25.

Prasad, B.R., 1985, Tribal culture development, *Administrator* 30(4) October-December, p 347-355, bibliography.

Sachchidananda, 1958, Study of culture change in tribal Bihar, *Adibasi* 3(2) May-June, p 11-16.

Sanganna, Toyaka, 1964, Tribal culture and its preservation and scientific development, *Adibasi*, January, p 3-4.

Shah, P.G., 1952, Culture synthesis in India, *Journal of Anthropological Society of Bombay* (NS) 6(2) September, p 62-65.

Sinha, Surajit, 1957, Tribal cultures of peninsular India as a dimension of little tradition in the study of Indian civilisation : A preliminary statement, *Man in India* 37(2) April-June, p 93-118, references.

Somasundram, A.M., 1950, Glimpses into primitive culture of India, *Man in India* 30(4) October-December, p 28-45.

Vidyarthi, L. P., 1966, Nehru's approach to tribal culture, *Vanyajati* 14(4) October, p 170-175, references.

Vyas, N.N., 1984, Some spatial aspects of tribal culture and development, *Tribe* 16(3-4) September-December, p 1-6.

TRIBAL DELINQUENCY

Kunda, C.L., 1969, Intelligence and tribal delinquency, *Indian Journal of Applied Psychology* 6(1) January, p 29-30, references, tables.

TRIBAL DEMOGRAPHY

Ghosh, A., 1985, The political economy of development strategy and tribal demography, *Capital* 196(4815) September 30, p 49-52.

See also Demographic Characteristics: Tribals; Population Growth: Tribals: India: West Bengal; Tribal Population.

TRIBAL DEVELOPMENT

Adibasi (Periodical), 1967, (Editorial), *Adibasi* 9(2) July, p 1-3, editorial.

Adiseshiah, W., 1958, Tribal welfare, *Social Action* 8(5-6) May-June, p 201-208.

Anon, 1955, Conference on Tribal Affairs, *Vanyajati* 3(1) January, p 1-3.

——1955, Unreal, *Social Action* 5(5-6) May-June , p 193-194.

——, 1966, Research on tribal welfare, *Vanyajati* 14(2) April, p 53-54.

——, 1961, New frontier in social welfare and tribal development, *Vanyajati* 9(4) October, p 133-135 +.

——, 1985, A new thrust to tribal development, *Andhra Pradesh* 28(10) August, p 7-9.

——, 1985 (Book review), *Economic Trends* 31(6) March, p 1-4 + ; *Financial Express* June 9, p 5, col 5-8.
Review of the book : **Patel, M.L.**, 1985, *Planning strategy for tribal development*, Inter-India Publication, New Delhi, 191 p.

——, 1985, (Book review), *Indian Journal of Political Studies*, December 9, p 119-20.
Review of the book : **Basu, R.**, 1985, *Tribal development programme and administration*, National Book Organisation, New Delhi, 322 p.

——, 1986, (Book review), *Indian Express* (Magazine) March 9, p 5, col 4-7.
Review of the book : **Raizada, Ajit**, 1986, *Tribal development in Madhya Pradesh: A planning perspective*, Inter-India Publication, New Delhi.

Banerjee, B.G., 1984, On development and tribal development, *Tribal Research Bulletin* 7(1) September, p 9-11 +.

Bhattacharjee, P.R., 1987, New horizon of tribal autonomy and tribal development in Tripura, *Journal of North-East India Council* 11(1) April, p 33-42.

Bhattacharya, S.N, 1987, Tribal development since Independence, *Kurukshetra* 35(10) July, p34-38.

Bhowmick, P.K., 1987, Voluntary effort in tribal development : The Bidisa experiment, *Journal of Social Economic Studies* 4(2) April-June, p 175-186.

Bhupinder Singh, 1984, Tribal development in retrospect and prospect : Sixth Plan mid-term appraisal, *Indian Journal of Public Administration* 30(4) October-December, p 1064-1081, tables.

Bodade, V. N., et al, 1988, Tribals and demonstrations for tribal development, *Indian Farming* 38(8) November, p 39-40.

Bose, S. C., 1986, Planning for tribal development, *Yojana* 30(5) March 16, p 21-23, tables.

Brij Raj Singh and Thapar, Rajiv, 1985, Forestry and tribal development, *Link* (Supplement) 27(26) February 3, p 24-28.

Chauhan, Indira, 1988, Tribal development administration in M. P., *Eastern Anthropologist* 41(1) January-March, p 87-92.

Das, Gananath, 1967, Tribal welfare methodology, *Adibasi* 9(1) April, p 10-13.

Deogaonkar, Warora S. G., 1989, Role of voluntary agencies and tribal institutions in social and ecological developments in tribal areas, *Vanyajati* 37(4) October, p 32-38.

Dey, P. C., 1987, Tribal development : An economic anthropological approach, *Vision* 6(3-4) January-June, p 33-40, bibliography.

Gangadharan, K. A., 1985, Tribal welfare and development in Kerala, *Cochin University Law Review* 9(1-2) March-June, p 173-188.

Gare, G. M., 1955, Need of training of workers in tribal development, *Tribal Research Bulletin* 7(2) March, p 5-6.

Goswami, Atul, 1984, Tribal development with special references to *North-East India, Social Scientist* 12(8) August, p 55-60, footnotes.

Gupta, Dipankar, 1986, Tribal development in a West Bengal district, *Economic and Political Weekly* 21(1) January 4, p 35-45.

Gupta, Ram Pratap and Sunil, 1986, Madhya Pradesh : Development of tribals, *Economic Times*, December 8, p 3, col 1-5.

Hussain, Monirul, 1987, Tribal movement for autonomous state in Assam, *Economic and Political Weekly* 22(32) August 8, p 1329-32.

Jha, Raghunath, 1986 Adult education and tribal development, *Mainstream* 24(50) August 16, p 35-36 +.

Kashi, N. Singh and **Ramashankar Singh**, 1984, Levels of regional and tribal development in tribal areas : Are they identical, *National Geographical Journal of India* 30(1) March, p 1-12, appendix, tables.

Lakshminarayana, 1986, Tribal development in Maharashtra, *Tribal Research Bulletin* 9(1) September, p 1-10, bibliography.

Mahalingam, S., 1988, Tribal development programmes: a review, *Kurukshetra* 36(4) January, p 4-8.

Mathur, V. K., 1966, Modernity : The nexus of tribal development, *Adibasi* 8(3) October, p 17-22.

Mathur, Vijay Kumar, 1967, Indicators of tribal development, *Adibasi* 8(4) January, p 41-45.

———. 1967, The traditional modern continuum : An assumption in tribal development, *Journal of Social Research* 19(2) September, p 11-25.

Mehta, B. H., 1957, Tribal welfare and forest economy, *Indian Journal of Social Work* 18(3) December, p 155-161.

Mukhopadhyay, Lipi and **Mukhopadhyay, Durgadas**, 1989, Tribal development administration, *Social Welfare* 36(3-4), p 26-29.

Naryana Reddy, G., 1983, Approach to tribal development : An overview, *Tribe* 15(1-2) March-June, p 1-14.

Nongbri, T., 1989, Some reflections on culture and development among the tribes, *Vanyajati* 37(4) October, p 20-25.

Prasad, R. R., 1988, Tribal development in India : Strategies and programmers *Journal of Rural Development* 7(1) January, p 81-103, bibliography, tables.

Qamar, Ahsan, 1987, Tribal development strategy needs rethinking, *Yojana* 31(5) March, 16, p 18-22, tables.

Raghaviah, V., 1989, Research on tribal welfare, *Vanyajati* 37(1) January p 10-11.

Ramachandra Raj, G., 1984, Problems and prospects of tribal development in Kerala, *Journal of Kerala Studies* 9(1-4) March-December, p 275-278.

Rao, N. V., and **Ram Reddy, R.**, 1986, Minor irrigation and tribal development : An empirical study, *Kurukshetra* 34(2) November, p 31-33.

Raval, Indubhai B., 1964, Sociology of tribal economic development, *Indian Journal of Social Work* 25(1) April, p 43-51, tables.

Roy Burman, B. K., 1960., Basic concepts of tribal welfare and tribal integration, *Journal of Social Research* 3(2) September, p 16-24.

———, 1985, Issues in tribal development, *Mainstream* 23(19) January 5, p 11-14 +; 23(20) January 12, p 20-22.

———, 1986, Institutional finance and tribal development, *Mainstream* 24(20) January 18, p 16-22.

Sachchidananda, 1989, Role of voluntary agencies in social and ecological development in tribal areas, *Vanyajati* 37(4) October, p 26-31.

Sachindra Narayan, 1989, Tribal development through use of medicinal herbs, *Social Welfare* 36(3-4) June-July, p 30-31.

Sharma, B. D., 1979, Tribal development : The concept and the frame, *Journal of Indian Education* 7(2) July, p 70.

——, 1985, Administration for tribal development, *Journal of Social and Economic Studies* (NS) October-December, p 361-379.

Sinha, Rakesh Ranjan, 1967, Traditional political institutions and tribal development, *Vanyajati* 15(3) July, p 135-138.

Sinha, S. P., 1989, Nehru's testament for tribal x-rayed, *Vanyajati* 37(4) October, p 39-49.

Srivastava, O. M., 1978, Continuing education and tribal development : The role of colleges near tribal areas, *Indian Journal of Adult Education* 39(4) April, p 15-20.

Tripathi, C. B., 1988, Approaches to tribal development and experience : General policies, administrative approach and personnel policies and their implementation: An all India review, *Man in India* 68(4) December, p 335-355.

Tripathi, Premananda, 1985, Administration for tribal development : An analytical review, *Indian Journal of Public Administration* 31(3) July-September, p 870-878.

Vaish, Prerana, 1984, Role of mineral in the tribal development of TSP region of Rajasthan, *Tribe* 16(3-4) September-December, p 20-29.

Vidyarthi, L. P., 1976, Tribal development in independent India and its future, *Man in India* 56(1) p 172-183.

See also Tribal welfare; Subdivision "Economic Conditions" and "Social Conditions" under names of tribes, e.g., Bhils : Economic Conditions; Birhors : Social conditions.

TRIBAL DEVELOPMENT : INDIA

Adibasi (Periodical), 1965, Defence-cum-production orientation of the programme of backward classes welfare, *Adibasi*, October, 1965, p 1-4, editorial

Aiyappan, A., 1965, A case for intensification of the development of tribal areas, *Adibasi*, July, p 47-52.

Anon, 1954, The need for training for tribal welfare work, *Vanyajati* 2(2) January, p 39-42.

——, 1955, Scheduled Tribes and their welfare, *Vanyajati* 3(4) October, p 143-146.

——, 1955, Training of social workers in tribal areas, *Vanyajati* 3(3) July, p 95-98.

——, 1955, Welfare work among Scheduled Tribes in Kutch; *Vanyajati* 3(2) April, p 88-89.

——, 1956, Scheduled Tribes under Five Year Plans, *Vanyajati* 4(4) October, p 97-99 +

——, 1957, Life membership scheme for tribal welfare work, *Vanyajati* 5(4) October, p 161-163.

——, 1957, Need for life workers for tribal welfare, *Vanyajati* 5(3) July, p 155-156.

——, 1957, Social reconstruction among Adivasis, *Vanyajati* 5(3) July, p 111-114.

——, 1958, Special multi purpose tribal blocks, *Vanyajati* 5(2) April, p 48-51.

——, 1959, The study team and tribal welfare, *Vanyajati* 7(4) October, p 115-118, references.

——, 1960, On the march of progress, *Vanyajati* 8(1) January p 1-2+.

——, 1960, Problems of Adivasi and suggestions to solve them, *Vanyajati* 3(4) October, 1955, p 176-177.

——, 1960, Progress of Scheduled Tribes during 1957-59, *Vanyajati* 7(2) April, p 41-43 +.

——, 1960, Special tribal blocks, *Vanyajati* 8(4) October, p 129-131+.

——, 1967, Study team on tribal development programmes, *Vanyajati* 15(1) January, p 45-52.

——, 1961, A Christian approach to tribal communities in India today, *Religion and Society* 8(3) September, p 60-83.

——, 1961, New frontier in social welfare and tribal development, *Vanyajati* 9(4) October, p 133-135 +.

——, 1961, Training of tribal welfare workers, *Vanyajati* 9(3) July, p 87-89 +.

——, 1965, Report of the Planning Committee of the B.A.J. Sevak Sing on 4th Five Year Plan on tribal welfare, *Vanyajati* 13(2) April, p 79-84.

——, 1965, Welfare of backward classes : Planning Commission Panel discussion, *Vanyajati* 13(2) April, p 39-40 +.

Bage, S. K., 1965, Anthropologists and tribal administration, *Journal of Social Research* 8(1) March, p 11-16.

Bhagat, Anupdev, 1956, Missionaries, anthropologists, and Adivasi culture, *Social Action* 6(11) November, p 475-472, references.

Biswas, P. C., 1954, The utility of research for the rehabilitation *Vanyajati* 2(1) January, p 5-9.

Bose, Nirmal Kumar, 1957, Anthropology and tribal welfare, *Man in India* 37(3) July-September, p 169-181.

——, 1964, Change in tribal cultures before and after Independence, *Man in India* 44(1) January-March, p 1-10.

——, 1969, The tribal situation, *Main in India* 19(3) July-September, p 217-223.

Bryce, L. Winifred, 1962, Revolution and the tribal peoples, *Bulletin of Tribal Research and Development Institute* (Chhindwara) 2(1) June, p 15-18.

Chatterjee, B., 1953, Model community centres in tribal areas, *Indian Journal of Social Work* 14(3) December, p 282-291.

Chattopadhyay, K. P., 1949, The tribal problem and its solution, *Eastern Anthropologist* 3(1) September, p 15-21, references.

——, 1952, Conference for tribal welfare at Delhi, *Man in India* 32(3) July-September, p 167-169.

Chinchalkar, J. H., 1970, Welfare of tribal women, *Vanyajati* 18(1) January, p 37-40.

Das, Amal Kumar, 1965, The role of research in tribal welfare, *Vanyajati* 13(3) July, p 118-122.

Das, G. N., 1966, Inaccessibility, *Adibasi*, 8(2) July p 62-64.

——, 1966, Missionary zeal (with special reference to tribal welfare), *Adibasi* 8(3) October, p 3-7.

Das, Gananath, 1964 Evolution in tribal policy, *Adibasi* January, p 21-24.

Das, T. C., 1960, A scheme for tribal welfare, *Journal of Social Research* 3(2) September, p 93-112.

Dave, P. C., 1966, Voluntary organisations and welfare of backward classes, *Vanyajati* 14(4) October, p 156-164.

Deb, P. C., 1961, Change in tribal society, *Religion and Society* 8(3) September, p 84-89.

Dube, S. C., 1960, Approaches to the tribal problem in India, *Journal of Social Research* 3(2) September, p 11-15.

——, 1949, Some aspect of tribal problem, *Eastern Anthropologist* 3(1) September, p 28-35.

Garg, B. M., 1960, Status of women in tribal communities in India, *Indian Journal of Social Work* 21(2) September, p 191-197.

Gopala Reddy, B., 1956, Problems of tribal people, *Vanyajati* 4(1) January, p 46-48.

——, 1956, Welfare of tribals and other backward classes, *Indian Journal of Social Work* 16(4) March, p 294-296.

Gopichand, 1956, Welfare of socially handicapped tribes, *Indian Journal of Social Work* 16(4) March, p 296-300.

Grigson, W. V., 1946, The Aboriginal in the future India, *Man in India* 26(2) June, p 81-96, footnotes.

Heda, H. C., 1955, One aspect of planning : Bringing backward areas forward, *Vanyajati* 3(4) October, p 174-176.

Indra Jeet Singh, 1967, Social rehabilitation and career orientation, *Journal of Social Research* 10(1) March, p 18-21.

Journal of Social Research (Periodical), 1960, Editorial by L. P. Vidyarthi, *Journal of Social Research* 3(2) September, p 1-2, editorial.

Kalelkar, Kaka, 1955, The Adivasis and their needs, *Vanyajati* 3(2) April, p 73-77.

Khan, M. Rafiq, 1970, Introduction, *Interdiscipline* 7(4) Winter, p 1-5.

Kurup, A. M., 1970, A scheme for need based tribal development and welfare, *Vanyajati* 18(3) July, p 105-108.

Lala, Arjun, 1956, Welfare of tribes including ex-criminal tribes, *Indian Journal of Social Work* 16(4) March, p 300-305.

Mangla, A. P., 1970, Levels of living and problems of tribal welfare, *Vanyajati* 18(2) April, p 59-60.

Mathur, V. K., 1967, The traditional continuum : An assumption in tribal development, *Journal of Social Research* 10(2) September, p 11-25.

Mehta, B. H., 1959, Tribal welfare and forest economy, *Journal of Social Research* 2(1-2) March-September, p 72-81.

——, 1962, Social experiments in extension projects; The Balvadi in tribal areas, *Indian Journal of Social Work* 23(1) April, p 53-56.

——, 1963, Social work and tribal welfare. *Social Work Forum* 1(4) October, p 7-13.

Minendra Nath, 1960, A hint on the survey of a tribe for economic and social improvement, *Vanyajati* 8(3) July, p 97-101.

Mohapatra, Kulamani, 1964, Approaching the tribal people for welfare, *Adibasi* January, p 7-16.

Nair, S. P., 1960, Problems in tribal housing, *Vanyajati* 8(2) April, p 48-50.

Panda, Satyananda, 1962, Implications of tribal welfare policy in India, *Vanyajati* 10(1) January, p 12-16.

Pande, B. M., 1968, Development schemes as a factor of change in tribal areas, *Journal of Social Research*, 11(2) September, p 33-57, references, tables.

Patel, G. D., 1968, Problems of tribal development, *Bulletin of Cultural Research Institute* 7(1-2), p 5-10.

Raghaviah, V., 1956, How to approach the Adivasi, *Vanyajati* 4(1) January, p 31-38.

Rajendra Prasad, 1955, Adivasis and our duty to them, *Vanyajati* 3(4) October, p 147-148.

Rao, G. R. S., 1966, Process of industrialisation and direction of social change in tribal society, *Journal of Social Research* 9(2) September, p 65-69.

Raval, Indubhai B., 1961, Tribal community development survey, *Indian Journal of Social Work* 21(4) March, p 369-371.

Roy Burman, B. K., 1961, Perspective of tribal welfare, *Bulletin of Tribal Research* *and Development Institute* (Chhindwara) 1(1) June, p 12-16.

Sachchidananda, 1960, Community development in tribal areas, *Journal of Social Research* 3(2), September, p 49-56.

——, 1964, Community development and the tribals, *Journal of Social Research* 7(1-2) March-September, p 70-78, tables.

Sahu, L. N., 1956, Social service among hill tribes, *Vanyajati* 4(4) October, p 140-142, illustrations.

——, 1961, The aboriginal : From symbolic to individual life, *Vanyajati* 9(4) October, p 149-150.

Saksena, R. N., 1964, The changing tribes of India, *Journal of Social Research* 7(1-2) March-September, p 15-28, references.

Sanganna, Toyaka, 1963-1964, The new dimension and approach of tribal welfare, *Adibasi* 5(2), p 3-4.

Sen, Jyoti, 1966, Problems in tribal transformation, *Man in India* 46(4) October-December, p 319-330.

Shrikant, L. M., 1953, Tribal social welfare, *Indian Journal of Social Work* 14(3) December, p 292-295.

——, 1954, Tribal welfare, *Indian of Journal of Social Work* 14(4) March, p 360-366.

——, 1956, Some suggestions for constructive workers in scheduled areas, *Vanyajati* 4(2) April, p 58-59, references.

——, 1956, Tribal welfare in West India, *Vanyajati* 4(4) October, p 100-102.

——, 1957, Social service among the tribals, *Vanyajati* 5(2) April, p 54-57.

——, 1960, Evaluation of work of non-official associations in Bombay, Madras and Kerala, *Vanyajati* 8(1) January, p 3-5.

——, 1961, Tribal welfare under Panchayat Raj; *Vanyajati* 9(4) October, p 136-144.

——, 1962, Tribal welfare with special reference to the tribal development blocks, *Indian Journal of Social Work* 22(4) March, p 379-385.

——, 1964, Tribal problems and publicity, *Vanyajati* 12(4) October, p 159-160.

——, 1968, Tribal development blocks (community development blocks), *Vanyajati* 16(4) October, p 119-122 +.

——, 1969, Tribal development blocks, *Vanyajati* 17(?) April, p 35-36+.

Srivastava, L. R. N., 1966, The problem of integration of the tribal, *Indian Journal Social Work* 27(1) April, p 51-57.

——, 1968, Plans and programmes of social education for the tribal people, *Bulletin of Cultural Research Institute* 7(1-2), p 39-50.

Somasundaram, A. M., 1947, Segregation or assimilation, *Man in India* 27(1) March, p 66-73.

Suresh Singh, 1966, Development schemes as a factor of change in tribal area, *Journal of Social Research* 11(2) September, p 52-64.

Thakkar, A. V., 1949, Some pressing problems of primitive tribes, *Eastern Anthropologist* 3(1) September, p 1-2.

Vaniker, P. G., 1954, Missionary approach to the tribal welfare, *Indian Journal of Social Work* 14(4) March, p 376-382.

Verma, Sneh Veena, 1961, Working of the multi-purpose tribal blocks in M. P., *Vanyajati* 9(2) April, 1961, p 48-55.

Vidyarthi, Lalit P., 1957, Anthropology, authority and tribal welfare, *Eastern Anthropologist* 11(1) September-November, p 14-24, references.

——, 1959, Anthropology and administration in India, *Journal of Social Research*

2(1-2) March-September, p 59-71, references.

Vimal Chandra, 1965, Key to tribal development, *Vanyajati* 13(4) October, p 143-45.

Vinoba Bhave, 1958, Tribal welfare workers and their role in gramdan work, *Vanyajati* 6(4) October, p 143-145 +.

Wadia, A. R., 1966, A note on the tribals and the Government, *Journal of Anthropological Society of Bombay* (NS) 12(1), p 12-14.

Wilkinson, T. S., 1961, Isolation, assimilation and integration in their historical perspective, *Religion and Society* 8(3) September, p 13-25.

Zutshi, G. L., 1959, Preleminaries regarding applied research among backward classes, *Vanyajati* 7(3) July, p 85-93.

See also Bhil Seva Mandal; Bhumijan Seva Mandal; Dandakaranya Project; Detribalisation; Scheduled Areas and Scheduled Tribes Commission; Seminar on Tribal Welfare, 1956, Chhindwara; Tribal Welfare Conference, 1953, Ranchi; Sub-divisions "Economic Condition", "Social Condition" under names of tribes, e.g., Bhils : Economic Conditions; Birhors : Social Condition.

TRIBAL DEVELOPMENT : INDIA : ANDHRA PRADESH

Bose, Nirmal Kumar, 1964, Integration of tribes in Andhra Pradesh, *Man in India* 44(2) January-March, p 97-104.

Shrikant, L. M., 1959, Evaluation of tribal welfare work in Nellore district (Andhra Pradesh), *Vanyajati* 7(4) October, p 124-126, illustration.

TRIBAL DEVELOPMENT : INDIA : ANDHRA PRADESH : HYDERABAD

Anon, 1954, Welfare of Hyderabad tribes, *Indian Journal of Social Work* 15(1) June, p 59-60.

Husain, Syed Khaja Mahboob, 1949, The rural uplift of tribes and backward classes in Hyderabad, Deccan, *Man in India* 29(3-4) July-December, p 185-198.

TRIBAL DEVELOPMENT : INDIA : ASSAM

Anon, 1953, A plea for intensive non-official work in Assam, *Vanyajati* 1(3) July, p 49-51.

———, 1953, Scheme of the Assam State Government for the welfare of Scheduled Tribes, included in the Five Year Plan, *Vanyajati* 1(3) July, p 71-72.

Moasosang, P., 1962, Social and cultural changes in the tribal communities today and the responsibility of the churches, *Religion and Society* 9(4) December, p 40-45.

Pakyntein, E. H., 1962, Change in the life of the tribal communities of Assam, *Religion and Society* 9(4) December, p 15-39.

Pugh, B. M., 1961, Christianity and the tribal communities of Assam, *Religion and Society* 8(3) September, p 46-52, appendix.

TRIBAL DEVELOPMENT : INDIA : BIHAR

Anon, 1953, Schemes of the Bihar State Government submitted to the Government of India under Article 275 of Constitution of India for the uplift of Scheduled Tribes during 1952-1953, *Vanyajati* 1(3) July, 1953, p 72-74.

Clump, C. C., 1953, Village uplift, *Social Action* 3(8) November, p 288-293.

Jaiswal, N. K., Khan, A. K., and **Shanber, Jai**, 1969, Attitude towards agricultural development among tribal and non-tribal people *Man in India* 49(3) July-September, p 267-280, tables.

See also Tribal Welfare Conference, 1953, Lohardga.

TRIBAL DEVELOPMENT : INDIA : BIHAR : CHOTANAGPUR

Minz, Nirmal, 1962, Impact of traditional religions and modern secular ideologies in the tribal areas of Chotanagpur, *Religion and Society* 9(4) December, p 46-56.

Roy, Sarat Chandra, 1946, The Aborigines of Chotanagpur : Their proper status in the reformed Constitution, *Man in India* 26(2) June, p 120-136.

TRIBAL DEVELOPMENT : INDIA : GUJARAT

Raval, Indubhai B., 1962, Tribal community development survey, *Social Work Review* 9 July, p 48-46.

TRIBAL DEVELOPMENT : INDIA : GUJARAT : KUTCH

Kuruwa, U. J., 1955, Welfare work among Scheduled Tribes in Kutch, *Vanyajati* 3(2) April, p 88-89.

TRIBAL DEVELOPMENT : INDIA : HIMACHAL PRADESH

Sharma, V. S., 1958, The Scheduled Tribes of Himachal Pradesh and their problems, *Vanyajati* 6(3) July, p 117-122.

TRIBAL DEVELOPMENT : INDIA : HIMALAYAN AREAS

Das, A. K., Basic approach for welfare activities in the Himalayas, *Adibasi* 11(3) October, p 42-48.

TRIBAL DEVELOPMENT : INDIA : KARNATAKA

Rachappa, B., 1965, Hill tribes of Mysore State and welfare work among them, *Vanyajati* 3(3) July, p 119-123.

TRIBAL DEVELOPMENT : INDIA : MADHYA PRADESH

Anon, 1954, Activities conducted under the tribal welfare scheme, Madhya Pradesh during 1953-54, *Vanyajati* 2(2) April, p 64-67.

——, 1954, Note on the progress of the tribal welfare scheme in Madhya Pradesh (from January 1953 December 1953), *Vanyajati* 2(1) January, p 26-29.

——, 1969, Socio-economic survey of tribal development blocks, *Bulletin of Tribal Research and Development Institute* (Bhopal) 7(1-2) January-December, p 33-189, tables.

Bahadur, F., 1965, Socio-Economic survey of tribal development blocks in M. P., *Bulletin of Tribal Research and Development Institute* (Bhopal) 5(1-2) June-December, p 28-34, appendix.

Bapat, N. V., 1953, Bondar: A unique tribal welfare centre in M. P., *Vanyajati* April, p 38-40.

Buch, M. N., Land improvement and agricultural development in tribal areas: Lack of motivation, *Bulletin of Research and Development Institute* (Bhopal) 7(1-2) June-December, p 1-4.

Kurup, A. M., 1970, Towards a methodology for tribal welfare research, *Bulletin of Tribal Research and Development Institute* (Bhopal) 8(1-2) June-December, p 13-18.

Mathur, K. S., 1960, Some problems of tribal rehabilitation in M. P., *Journal of Social Research* 3(2) September, p 113-120.

Mehta, B. H., 1962, Youth organistions in Sylan areas, *Indian Journal of Adult Education* 23(10) October, p 38-40.

Shukla, Ravi Shankar, 1955, Tribal welfare work in Bastar district (M.P.), *Vanyajati* 3(2) April, p 78-80.

See also Kharkhara Project; Marias.

TRIBAL DEVELOPMENT : INDIA : MAHARASHTRA

Anon, 1947, Government drive for uplift of backward classes, *Social Service Quarterly* 33(1) July, p 27-29.

——, 1953, Scheme in Bombay Govt., sanctioned for 1952-53 for Scheduled Tribes under Article 275 of the Constitution, *Vanyajati* 194) October, p 101-102.

Bhadrapur, K. B., 1942, Uplift work amongst hill tribes in Kolaba district, *Rural India* 5(11) November, p 502-506, tables.

Thomas, C., 1964, Tribal welfare in Maharashtra State, *Social Action*, April, p 179-184.

TRIBAL DEVELOPMENT : INDIA : MANIPUR

Ram Ratan, 1967, Emergent leadership and development in a tribal village, *Adibasi* 9(2) July, p 35-43.

TRIBAL DEVELOPMENT : INDIA : MYSORE

See Tribal Development: India: Karnataka

TRIBAL DEVELOPMENT : INDIA : NORTH EAST FRONTIER AGENCY

Shrikant, L. M., 1963, Welfare work in NEFA area, *Vanyajati* 11(4) October, p 145-46 +.

TRIBAL DEVELOPMENT : INDIA : ORISSA

Das, G. N., 1965, The adibasis of Orissa and their welfare, *Vanyajati* 5(2) April, p 74-82, references.

——, 1965, Tribal welfare and some special aspects of tribal development blocks, *Adibasi*, July, p 7-14.

——, 1966, Some more reflections on tribal welfare, *Adibasi* 8(1) April, p 67-72.

Ebnother, Robert, 1966, Munargaon its lessons in tribal welfare, *Adibasi* 8(1) April, p 73-84.

Mohapatra, K., 1964, Action programme on economic projects among the Gonds of Orissa, *Adibasi*, November, p 23-28.

Rout, Jnanendra Kumar, 1964, Tribal welfare in Orissa, *Adibasi*, p 17-20.

Sanganna, Toyaka, 1966, Tribal problems of Orissa, *Adibasi* 8(2) July, p 2-8.

TRIBAL DEVELOPMENT : INDIA : RAJASTHAN

Singh, R. R., A new approach to tribal welfare, *Vanyajati* 16(3) July, p 100-109.

TRIBAL DEVELOPMENT : INDIA : TAMIL NADU : MADRAS

Anon, 1953, Scheme of the Madras State Government for the welfare of the Schedule Castes and Scheduled Tribes and other backward classes, included in the Five Year Plan, *Vanyajati* 1(2) April, p 42-43.

Social Service Quarterly (Periodical), 1930, Socio-economic reconstruction among hill tribes in thea South, *Social Service Quarterly* 16(4) April, p 153-54, editorial.

Venkatraman, S. R., 1969, Tribal development block, Yercaud : An impression, *Social Service Quarterly* 54(3) January, p 77-79.

TRIBAL DEVELOPMENT : INDIA : VINDHYA PRADESH

Anon, 1954, Tribal welfare work in Vindhya Pradesh, *Vanyajati* 2(2) April, p 67-69.

Chaturvedi, K. C., 1955, Welfare of Scheduled Castes and Scheduled Tribes in Vindhya Pradesh, *Vanyajati* 3(3) July, p 128-131.

TRIBAL DEVELOPMENT : INDIA : WEST BENGAL

Anon, 1953, Schemes in West Bengal sanctioned for 1952-53 for Scheduled Tribes under Article 275 of the Constitution, *Vanyajati* 1(4) October, p 103-104.

Bhowmick, P. K., 1966, An integrated plan for the development of the Lodhas and other tribals of Midnapur, *Vanyajati* 14(2) April, p 82-89.

Das, Amal Kumar, 1962, Scheduled Tribes of West Bengal : A panoramic picture, *Bulletin of Cultural Research Institute* 1(1), p 35-56, illustration.

TRIBAL DEVELOPMENT : OFFICIALS AND EMPLOYEES : INDIA

Mathur, Vijay Kumar, 1967, Training for tribal development *Adibasi* 9(3) October, p 26-30.

Misra, Somnath, 1967, Qualifications for tribal welfare work, *Adibasi* 8(4) January, p 3-5.

TRIBAL DEVELOPMENT : RESEARCH PROJECTS : INDIA

Burman, B. K., 1961, A list of research projects with operative significance for welfare of the backward classes (with special reference to West Bengal) *Vanyajati* 9(1) January, p 9-21.

See also Research and Development; Study Teams: Tribal Welfare.

TRIBAL DEVELOPMENT AREAS

See Tribal Development Blocks.

TRIBAL DEVELOPMENT BLOCKS

Anon, 1964, The water scarcity problem in Tamia special multipurpose tribal development blocks, *Bulletin of Tribal Research Training Institute* (Chhindwara) 4(1) June, p 44-49, references, tables.

——, 1969, Socio-economic survey of tribal development blocks, *Bulletin of Tribal Research and Development Institute* (Bhopal) January-December, p 33-189, tables.

Bahadur, F., 1965, Socio-economic survey of tribal development blocks in M.P., *Bulletin of Tribal Research and Development Institute* (Bhopal) 5(1-2) June-December, p [illegible]-34, appendix.

Das, G. N., 1965, Tribal welfare and some aspects of tribal development blocks, *Adibasi*, July, p 7-14.

Shrikant, L. M., 1962, Tribal welfare with special reference to the tribal development blocks, *Indian Journal of Social Work* 22(4) March, p 379-385; *Vanyajati* 10(1) January, p 4-12.

——, 1969, Tribal development blocks, *Vanyajati* 17(2) April, p 35-36.

Shyam Manohar, 1968, A new deal for tribal development blocks, *Indian Education* 7(9) August, p39-45.

Venkataraman, S. R., 1969, Tribal development blocks, Yercaud : An impression, *Social Service Quarterly* 54(3) January, p 77-79.

TRIBAL DEVELOPMENT PROGRAMME

Surana, M.B., 1987, Research designs for evaluation of tribal development programme, *Tribal Research Bulletin* 9(2) March, p 5-8, bibliography.

TRIBAL DIALECTS

See Languages and Dialects : Tribals; Sadani Dialect: Tribals: India: Sundarbans; Subdivision "Languages and Dialects" under names of tribes, e.g., Mundas : Languages and Dilects; Tribal Languages.

TRIBAL DORMITORIES : INDIA

Majumdar, D.N., 1930, The economic background of social institutions in primitive society, *Man in India* 10(2-3) April-September, p 150-166, footnotes.

Srivastava, R.P., Rang-Bang in the changing Bhotia life, *Eastern Anthropologist* 6(3-4) March-August, p 190-203, footnotes.

Suryavanshi, Bhagwan Singh, 1959, Life in the dormitories of the tribals: The Oraons, *Indian Folklore* 2(1) January-May, p 45-47.

Zutshi, G.L., 1957, Functions of the Pattapara among the Konnikars, *Vanyajati* 6(2) April, p 84-86.

TRIBAL DORMITORIES : INDIA : ASSAM

Gupta, Jaya Dutta, 1960, Ponung or girls association among the Padam Abor in the lower Abor hills, *Bulletin of Anthropological Survey of India* 9(2) July, p 71-73.

TRIBAL DORMITORIES : INDIA : EASTERN

Maitra, Sunilranjan, 1970, Bachelor's dormitories of the tribes of Eastern India, *Bulletin of Anthropological Survey of India* 19(2) April p 61-65, references.

TRIBAL DORMITORIES : INDIA : NORTH EAST FRONTIER AGENCY

Aonok, S. Wati, 1956, Monung organisation among the Nokte Nagas, *Vanyajati* 4(2) April, p 73-81, footnotes, illustrations.

Nair, P. Thankappan, 1967, Ladies club of NEFA, *Vanyajati* 15(1) January, p 9-14.

TRIBAL DORMITORIES : INDIA : ORISSA

Das, Nityananda, 1955-1956, Dormitory: A dying tribal institution, *Adibadi* 1, p 19-21.

Rout, Siba Prasad, 1963-1964, Functions of Juang dormitory in Keonjhar district, *Adibasi* 5(2), p 29-34.

TRIBAL ECONOMIC DEVELOPMENT : SOCIOLOGICAL ASPECT

Raval, Indubhai B., 1964, Sociology of tribal economic development, *Indian Journal of Social Work* 25(1) April, p 43-51, tables.

See also Tribal Development.

TRIBAL ECONOMY

Anon, 1985, (Book review), *Tribune*, June 15, p 4, col 3-4.
Review of the book : **Shah, Ghanshyam**, 1985, *Economic differentiations and tribal economy*, Ajanta Publication, Delhi, 152 p.

Bose, Savadindu, 1964, Economy of the Onge of Andaman, *Man in India* 46(4), p 298-310.

Gaikwad, John S., 1986, Role of minor forest produce in tribal economy, *Tribal Research Bulletin* 8(2) March, p 12-16.

Gunasekaran, R., 1988, Changing phase of tribal economy in Kolli hills, *Khadi Gramodyog* 35(3) December, p 162-174.

Kumar, B. Das, 1986, Development of the tribal economy : A spatial approach, *Kurukshetra* 34(4) January, p 13-14 +.

Kunhaman, M., 1985, The tribal economy of Kerala : An intra-regional analysis, *Economic and Political Weekly* 29(1) March 16, p 466-474.

Mehta, B.H., 1959, Tribal welfare and forest economy, *Journal of Social Research* 2(1-2) March-September, p 72-81.

Samuel, C.J., 1985, Development of tribal economy : Legislative and executive measures, *Cochin University Law Review* 9(1-2) March-June, p 87-104, footnotes.

Srivastava, R.M. a. **l Kharde, R.L.**, 1984 Tribal economy : An analytical view, *Tribal Research Bulletin* 7(1) September, p 12-15.

Zutshi, G.L., 1961, Place of forests in tribal economy, *Vanyajati* 9(1) January, p 32-35.

TRIBAL EDUCATION

Pawar, S.S. and **Bhuvanedran, P.**, 1988, Tribal education : A study in M.P.S.S., *Kurukshetra* 36(4) January, p 18-21.

——, 1988, Tribal education in the West Zone of M.P., *Social Welfare* 34(11) February, p 4-5.

Rajni Kanth, G. and **Suman Chandra, K.**, 1988, Education of tribals : The role of tribal political organisation, *Man in India* 68(4) December p 459-464.

Sharma, A.G., 1951, Eradication of illiteracy among aborigines, *Educational India* 17(7) January, p 216-218.

Sharma, Khem Raj, 1990, Cultural effects on education of the tribals, *Vanyajati* 37(1) January, p 14-16.

See also Medium of Instructions: Tribals; names of Coferences, Seminars, e.g., National Seminar on Tribal Education, 1965, Udaipur; Pedagogy: Tribals; Residential Schools: Tribal Areas; Technical Education: Tribals

TRIBAL EDUCATION : AUSTRALIA

Anon, 1954, Aboriginal education in Australia, *Education Review* 60(4) April, p 57-76

——, 1965, School on wheels for aborigines in Northern territory, *Education* 44(10) October, p 26-28.

TRIBAL EDUCATION : INDIA

Ahmad, Aijazuddin and **Nuna, Sheel Chand**, 1987, Tribal education : Shadows of an uncertain future, *Journal of Education Planning and Administration* 1(2) April, p 90-170, bibliography, footnotes, tables.

Anon, 1952, Education of the underprivileged, *Indian Journal of Social Work* 13(3) December, 1952, p 175-181.

——, 1957, Social education for tribal areas, *Indian Journal of Social Work* 18(2) September, p 136-139.

——, 1954, Social education for the tribals *Vanyajati* 2(4) October, p 107-109.

——, 1966, Education Commission, Government of India : Questionnaire on the education of the backward classes, *Vanyajati* 14(3) July, p 139-144.

——,1984, (Book review), *Journal of Education Planning and Administration* 1(2) April, p 252-255.

Review of the book ; **Patel, Tara**, 1987, *Development education among tribal women*, Mittal Publication, New Delhi, 198 p.

——, 1986, (Book review), *Tribune* April 13, p 11, col 5-8.

Review of the book: **Patel, Tara**, 1986, *Development of education among tribal women*, Mittal Publication, Delhi, 18 p.

——, 1986, Tribal culture and education's response : Search for a model of education for the tribal people, *New Frontiers in Education* 166(1) January-March p 1-47, appendix.

Azad, J.L., 1976, Education of Scheduled Castes and Scheduled Tribes, *Journal of Indian Education* 1(6) March, p 23-28.

Bapat, N.V., 1962, Education of the Aborigines: From the Presidential address to the Aborigines Education Section at the last All India Education Conference, *Educational Review* 68(7) July, p 161-165

——, 1964, A few thoughts on tribal education, *Vanyajati* 12(4) October,

p 190-194.

——, 1968, Residential school in tribal areas, *Vanyajati* 16(4) October, p 154-159.

Bapat, Nana, 1961, Tribal education: A problem, *Vanyajati* 9(1) January, p 37-39.

Barla, Anthony, 1965, Medium of instruction for tribal students: Viewpoint, *Indian Education* 4(11) October, p 33-34.

Basu, Minendra Nath, 1961, Suggestions for the educational plan of the Aboriginal peoples of India, *Vanyajati* 9(3) July, p 123-126.

——, 1963, Anthropology in tribal education, *Bulletin of Cultural Research Institute* 2(1), p 22-27.

Bhowmick, P. K., 1967, Ways of educated the tribals, *Adibasi* 9(1) April, p 29-39, illustrations, references.

Biswas, P. C., 1955, Anthropology and tribal education, *Vanyajati* 3(2) April, p 81-83.

Bose, A. B., 1970, Problems of educational development of Scheduled Tribes, *Man in India* 50(1) January-March, p 26-50, refereces, tables.

Bose, Nirmal Kumar, 1966, Some suggestions on tribal education, *Folklore* 7(2) February, p 47-51.

Chattopadhyay, K. P., 1953, Tribal education, *Man in India* 33(1) January-March, p 1-18, appendix.

Choudhary, K., 1987, Education or real boon to tribal youth, *Times of India* 13(5), p 7-8.

Choudhary, N. D., 1987, Anganwadi workers in a tribal belt, *Social Welfare* 34(7) October, p 14-15 +, tables.

Das, G. N., 1963-1964, Some aspects of tribal education, *Adivasi* 5(2), p 21-24.

Das, Gananath, 1967, The programme of social education from backward tribals, *Adibasi* 8(4) January, p 56.

——, 1967, Tribal education : Transition from orthodox education towards education for modernity, *Adibasi* 9(2) July, p 21-27.

Das, N., 1958, Glimpses of aborigines education, *Vanyajati* 6(3) July, p 122-129.

——, 1968-1969, Priorities for tribal education, *Adibasi* 103(3-4) October-January, p 1-10.

Das Gupta, Narendra Kumar, 1959, Tribal language and education, *Man in India* 39(1) January-March, p 61-64.

Dutta, S.C., 1983, Educational programme for tribal population : An alternative strategy, *Indian Journal of Adult Education* 44(4) April, p 11-14.

Ganguly, J. B., 1970, Tribal students between tradition and modernity, *Educational Miscellany* 7(1-2) July-September, p 61-69.

Hans, A. B. D., 1986, Tribal culture and education response : Search for a model of education for the tribal people, *New Frontiers in Education* 16(1) January-March, p 1-47, appendix.

Johanna, M., 1965, Integration of school education activities in tribal girls schools, *Social Action* 15(11) November, p 1167-1170.

Karve, Iravati, 1958, Social education of the Scheduled Tribes, *Vanyajati* 5(4) October, p 164-169.

Khurana, G., 1978, Approach to education of Scheduled Tribes, *Education Quarterly* 30(1) April, p 17-23, tables.

Kundu, C.L., 1968, Education of de-notified tribes, *Progress of Education* 42(10-12) May-June, p351-354.

Kundu, M., 1981, Preparing 'readers' for tribal adult learners: Some viable topics, *Indian Journal of Adult Education* 42(9) September, p 21-24, references.

——, 1982, Concept of 'Raska' implications for tribal education, *New Frontiers in Education* 12(2) April-June, p 42-46.

Kurup, A. M., 1968, Extent and problems of tribal education, *Vanyajati* 16(2) April, p 55-59.

Madan, T. N., 1952, Education of tribal India, *Eastern Anthropologist* 5(4) June-August, p 179-182.

Mehta, B. H., 1969, Education of tribal women and girls, *Education Quarterly* 21(1) April, p 44-46.

Minendra Nath, 1958, The role of anthropology in the education of the Aborigines in India, *Adibasi* 3(2) May-July, p 1-8.

Minz, Nirmal, 1982, Higher education in the tribal context, *New Frontiers in Education* 12(1) January-March, p 50-53.

Mukherjee, P. K., 1961, The aim of tribal education, *Vanyajati* 9(1) January, p 26-28.

Nag, D. S., 1954, Education for primitives, *Vanyajati* 2(4) October, p 117-120.

Naidu, A. R., 1967, Problems of migration of semi-educated tribals boys, *Indian Education* 6(3) February, p 28-36.

Naik, T. B., 1950, How to educate aboriginals, *Indian Journal of Social Work* 11(2) September, p 172-180.

Narain Prasad, 1961, Primary education among the Adivasis, *Vanyajati* 9(4) October, p 161-162.

Nair, S. P., 1960, Cultural change and social education in tribal area, *Vanyajati* 8(4) October, p 163-165.

Panda, Premananda, 1988, Barriers to educational development in tribal areas, *Journal of Adult Education* 49(3) July-September, p 79-83, bibliography.

Panda, Subash Chandra, 1983, A study of school climate of the secondary school of selected tribal districts of Orissa, *Vision* 3(1-2) July-December, p 75-84, tables.

Patil, H. G., 1957, A scheme for technical training of Adivasi youths, *Vanyajati* 5(3) July, p 150-154, tables.

Prasad, S., 1971, Modern education among the tribes of Bihar in second half of he 19th century, *Man in India* 41(94) p 364-394.

——, 1975, Implication of the 10 + 2 + 3 pattern for the education of tribal children, *Journal of Indian Education* 1(1) May, p 75-79.

Prasad Rao, D. L., and **Venkata Rao**, P., 1983, Problems of teacher working in tribal areas, *Educational Review* 59(8) August, p 139-141.

Raj, Hilda, 1952, Education of Adibasis, *Eastern Anthropologist* 5(4) June-August, p 174-178.

Ramachandra Naidu, A., 1966, Informal education among tribals, *Vanyajati* 14(4) October, p 183-191.

Rao, G. S., 1979, Literacy for tribals, *Indian Journal of Adult Education* 440(4) April, p 1-4, references.

Ravindranathan, M. N., 1983, The problem of cultural integration of the tribals education as the chief instrument of change, *Education Quarterly* 35(4) October, p 20-24.

Roy Burman, B. C., 1987, Pattern of tribal education status of research and sociological dimensions for projecting the future, *Journal of Education Planning and Administration* 1(2) April, p 126-136.

Roy Chowdhry, K. P., 1957, Technical education for tribals, *Vanyajati* 5(2) April, p 87-93.

Sen Gupta, S. C., 1966-1967, Tribal education : Present position and future progress, *Indian Education* 6(1-2) December-January, p 37-62, tables.

Shah, Vimal P. and **Patel, Tara**, 1986, Social context of tribal education, *Education Quarterly* 38(2) Summer, p 49-51.

Shamsuddin, 1966, Gholeng school : Adivasis heaven, *Education of India* 33(4) October, p 123-126, illustration.

Sharma, A. C., 1949, Illiteracy of aborigines in India, *Educational Review* 55(4) April, p 67-69.

——, 1950, Report of the aborigines Education Section, *Journal of Education India* 16(10) April, p 286-287.

——, 1951, Education io tribal women and girls, *Education Quarterly* 21(1) April, p 44-46.

Sharma, K. R., 1977, Specific problems of tribal students in non-tribal schools, *Education Quarterly* 28(4) January, p 30-32.

——, 1983, A study of educational backwardness of tribal students, *Education Quarterly* 35(2) April, p 33-38.

——, 1984, A study of language development scholastic achievement and tribal students, *Research Bulletin* 14(1-2) March-June, p 3-21, tables.

Shaw, Biswanath, 1958-1959, Vocational education in the Ashram Schools, *Adibasi* 3(3-4) August-January, p 31-34.

Shrikant, L. M., 1966, Education Commission and backward classes, *Vanyajati* 14(3) July, p 95-98.

——, 1966, Measures proposed for the spread of education amongst the Scheduled Tribes, *Vanyajati* 14(3) July, p 133-138, tables.

Shrivastava, O. M., 1978, Continuing education and tribal development : The role of colleges near tribal areas, *Indian Journal of Adult Education* 39(4) April, p 15-20.

Shyam Manohar, 1964. Education in tribal areas with employment bias, *Indian Education* 3(10) September, p 18-24.

——, 1968, A new deal for tribal development blocks, *Indian Education*, 7(9) August, p 39-45.

Sirsalkar, P. R., 1984, Evaluation of Ashram Schools managed by the voluntary agencies in Maharashtra State, *Tribal Research Bulletin* 7(1) September, p 7-8.

Sowaid, M., 1986, A study of parent child interaction and achievement motivation among tribal high school students, *Journal of Institute of Educational Research* 10(3) September, p 44-27, references.

Srivastava, B. N., 1966, Education Commission and tribal education, *N I E Journal* 1(2) November, p 78-82.

Srivastava, Rajni, 1982, Sociological problems in tribal education: A case study, *Indian Educational Review* 17(3) July, p 110-113.

Sundarasen V. V. and **Subha Reddy, B. N.**, 1982, Equality for tribals : The role of education, *Experiments in Education* 9(12) February, p 213-215.

Tarlok Singh, 1966, Education in tribal areas, *Folklore* 7(10) October, p 397-401.

Thakkar, A. V., 1945, Education among tribal people, *Social Service Quarterly* 32(1), p 1-4.

Venkatraman, S. R., 1950, Education of the Aborigines, *Educational Review* 56(7) July, p 129-132; 56(8) August, p 150-152.

——, 1962, Education of Aborigines, *Social Service Quarterly* 47(4) April, p 119-126.

——, 1964, Education as a basic factor in tribal welfare, *Social Service Quarterly* 48(3) January, p 88-92.

Vyas, A., 1957, Why this emphasis on vocational bias in education in Ashrams?, *Adibasi* 2(1), p 45-49.

Wilkinson, T. S., 1962, Reorientation of tribal education, *Social Action* 12(4) April, p 202-207.

See also Scheduled Castes and Scheduled Tribes: Education; subdivision 'Education' under names of individual tribal groups, e.g., Kols : Education.

TRIBAL EDUCATION : INDIA : ANDHRA PRADESH

Ahuja, G. C., 1980, Educational wastage and stagnation among tribal children, *Journal of Indian Education* 6(1) May, p 58-70, references, tables.

Digumari, 1984, Educational problems of tribal children of forest and hill areas, *Experiments in Education* 12(11) March, p 15-18.

Krishna Kumari, P., et al, 1986, Study of creative abilities of tribal children in relation to their sex and socio-economic status, *Journal of Institute of Educational Research* 10(1) January, p 1-4, references.

Kundu, Manmatha, 1986, Tribal education in India : An effective pedagogy, *Journal of India Education* 12(4), November, p 43-48, references.

Reddy, G. P., 1970, Causes of wastage in tribal education of Andhra Pradesh, *Vanyajati* 18(3) July, p 109-120, references, tables.

Rout, Upendra Nath, 1978, A new approach to State Non-formal Education Centre in tribal area for all age groups, *Experiments. in Education* 6(4) June, p 60-63.

Sharma, K. R., 1984, Tribal students and role of schools, *Primary Teacher* 9(4) October, p 11-13.

Venkataih, N., 1980, Non-formal education for adult tribals, *Experiments in Education* 8(3) May, p 54-56.

TRIBAL EDUCATION : INDIA : BIHAR

Sachchidananda, 1964, Tribal education in Bihar, *Vanyajati* 12(1) January, p 3-6.

Sinha, H. K., 1960, Tribal education in Bihar : A preliminary statistical analysis, *Journal of Social Research* 3(1), March, p 85-92, references, tables.

Vidyarthi, L. P., 1955, Education in tribal Bihar, *Man in India* 35(1) January-March, p 39-45.

TRIBAL EDUCATION : INDIA : GUJARAT

Anon, 1986, (Book review), *Social Action* 36(1) January, March, p 120-122. Review of the book : **Shah, Ghanshyam**, et al, 1985, *Tribal Education in Gujarat*, Ajanta Publication, New Delhi, 143 p.

Punalekar, S. P., 1985, Tribal education in Gujarat, *Mainstream* 23(39) May 25, p 20-23, bibliography, tables.

Shah, Vimal, 1966, Tribal education in Gujarat, *Vanyajati* 14(3) July, p 109-112.

TRIBAL EDUCATION : INDIA : MADHYA PRADESH

Dhruw, P. R., 1968, Tribal students of Madhya Pradesh, *Vanyajati* 16(3) July, p 97-99.

Kulshrestha, Shivendra Kumar, 1979, Self-situational deprivations in the schools adjustment of tribal children, *Journal of Indian Education* 5(2) July, p 41-47.

Maurya, R. D., 1985, Education for tribals in M P : Problems and prospects, *Kurukshetra* 33(39) May 25, p 20-23, bibliography, tables.

TRIBAL EDUCATION : INDIA : MAHARASHTRA

Apte, J. S., 1960, Talwada Ashram School : An experiment in tribal education, *Vanyajati* 8(2) April, p 81-82.

Coelho, C. P., 1952, A new approach to Adivasi education, *Progress of Education* 27(12) July, p 340-344.

Jha, S K. and **Barde, H. R.**, 1984, The second change education for the tribals of Vidarbha, *Progress of Education* 58(11) June, p 270-272.

Nanal, V. M., 1961, Education of the Adivasis in Thana District, *Progress of Education* 35(12) July, p 382-386, 36(1) August, p 19-24 +.

Parasnis, N. R., 1958, The problem of the education of the Aboriginal tribes (Adiwasis) in the Thana District, Bombay State, *Progress of Education* 32(8) March, p 254-259; 32(9) April, p 316-328.

Reddy, L. R., 1952, The problem of Adivasi education, *Progress of Education* 27(5) December, p 135-138.

——, 1953, The education of the Adivasis, *Progress of Education* 27(9) April, p 258-261.

Wandrekar, D. N., 1949, Educational progress of the Adiwasis in the Konkan trade of Bombay Province, *Eastern Anthropologist* 3(1) September, p 3-7.

TRIBAL EDUCATION : INDIA : MEGHALAYA

Dutta, Gitika, 1982, Sex differences in creativity among the tribe of Meghalaya, *Journal of Institute of Education Research* 6(2) May, p 23-26, references, tables.

TRIBAL EDUCATION : INDIA : ORISSA

Kar, P., 1966, Educational survey of some Adivasi villages of Orissa, *Adibasi* 8(1) April, p 49-52.

Mohanty, Jagannath, 1966, Sole problems in tribal education in Orissa and their solutions, *Adibasi* 8(2) October, p 32-34.

Mohapatra, Kulamani, 1966, Primary education in tribal languages : Problems and prospects, *Adibasi* 8(2) July, p 48-55.

Panda, Subash Chandra, 1988, A study of the secondary schools climate in selected tribal ditricts of Orissa, *Progress of Education* 62(7) February, p 158-162.

Vyas, Ambalal, 1963, 15 years progress of tribal education in Orissa, *Vanyajati* 11(2) April, p 51-54.

TRIBAL EDUCATION : INDIA : RAJASTHAN

Chaudhry, N. D., 1975, Educational development among the Scheduled Tribes in Rajasthan, *Education Quarterly* 27(3) October, p 26-30, tables.

Oad, L. K., 1976, Problems of tribal education in Rajasthan, *Journal of Indian of Education* 1(6) March, p 53-59.

TRIBAL EDUCATION : INDIA : UTTAR PRADESH

Chatterjee, B. B., 1970, Functional literacy for family planning in tribal areas, *Indian Journal of Adult Education* 31(1) January, p 12-13 +

Khan, M. A., 1979, Parental deprivation in relations to academic achievement of denotified tribes, *Indian Educational Review* 14(4) October, p 95-98.

TRIBAL EDUCATION : INDIA : WEST BENGAL

Mukherjee, D. P., 1970, A concept of tribal education in West Bengal, *Vanyajati* 18(1) January, p 31-34, references.

Roy Chowdhury, Bidyut Kumar, 1964, Factors regarding tribal education in West Bengal, *Bulletin of Cultural Research Institute* 3(2), p 26-40, appendix, references, tables.

Soren, Bhabatosh, 1969, A few words concerning literacy drive in the tribal communities, *Bulletin of Cultural Research Institute* 8(1-2), p 5-7

TRIBAL EDUCATION : RESEARCH : INDIA

Ravindranathan, M. N., 1981, Perspectives of research in tribal education, *Experiments in Education* 9(1) March, p 15-18; 9(2) April, p 21-26.

TRIBAL EXPLOITATION

See Exploitation of Tribals.

TRIBAL FARMERS

Amar Singh and **Suraj Singh**, 1981, Training needs of tribal farmers, *Indian Journal of Extension Education* 17(3-4) September-December, p 81-88, tables.

Anon, 1983, (Book review), *State and Society* 6(1) January-March, p 76-80.

Review of the book : **Pathy, Jagannath**, 1983, *Tribal peasantry : Dynamics of development*, Inter-India Publications, New Delhi, 233 p.

——, 1984, (Book review), *Society and Change* 4(1) October-December, p 74-77.

Review of the book : **Pathy, Jagannath**, 1983, *Tribal peasantry : Dynamics of development*, Inter-India Publications, New Delhi, 233 p.

Bajaj, S. S., 1985, Role of information sources in the adoption of I R S paddy by tribal farmers, *Tribal Research Bulletin* 7(2) March, p 17-19.

Chakravarty, M. I., 1989, Economic analysis of employment, income and consumption pattern of tribal farmers, *Journal of Rural Development* 8(1) January, p 97-108, tables.

Das, P., et al, 1988, How lab to land programme is helping tribal farmers, *Kurukshetra* 34(4) January-June, p 109-110.

Paul, S.P. and **Baghel, A.S.**, 1987, Sociological constraints and attitude to development of tribal farmers in the tribal areas of M.P., *Journal of Rural Development* 6(2) March, p 197-210.

——, 1989, Elements of a development plan for tribal area farmers of Madhya Pradesh, *Journal of Rural Development* 8(1) January, p 71-78.

Pawar, H.S. and **Patil, R.P.**, 1987, Adoption behaviour of the tribal farmers from Surgana taluka (Nashik district) in respect of paddy cultivation, *Tribal Research Bulletin* 9(2) March, p 15-17.

Prasada Rao, D. L. and **Venkata Rao, P.**, 1984, Are they right in blaming tribals : A view point on tribal-forest relations, *Vanyajati* 32(3) July, p 17-21.

Singh, B.K., 1989, A study of nutritional status of tribal farmers in Ranchi district of Chotanagpur in Bihar, *Economic Affairs* 34(1) January March, p 58-63, tables.

TRIBAL FESTIVALS

See Festivals: Tribals: India.

TRIBAL GIRLS

See also Tribal Women.

TRIBAL GIRLS : EDUCATION

Johanna, M., 1965, Integration of school education activities in tribal girls schools, *Social Action* 15(11) November, p 1167-1170.

Mehta, B. H., 1969, Education of tribal women and girls, *Education Quarterly* 21(1) April, p 44-46.

TRIBAL GENUS

Anon, 1988, The neglect of the tribal genus, *Tribune*, July 24, p 1, col 1-8,

TRIBAL GOVERNMENT

See also Tribals and Government; subdivision, 'Tribal Government', under names of

TRIBAL LABOURERS

Das Gupta, Pranab Kumar and **Khan, Iar Ali**, 1985, Impact of tea plantation industry on the life of tribal labourers, *Man and Life* 12(1-2) January-June, p 109-110.

TRIBAL LANGUAGES

Aiyappan, H., 1964, Tribal languages of Orissa, *Adibasi*, January, p 5-6.

Das Gupta, Narendra Kumar, 1959, Tribal language and education, *Man in India* 39(1) January-March, p 61-64.

Mohapatra, Kulamani, 1966, Primary education in tribal languages : Problems and prospects, *Adibasi* 8(2) July, p 48-55.

Sharma, Bansi Ram, 1984, Dr. Siddheswar Varma's notes on tribal languages of Kinnaur in Himachal Pradesh, *Vishveshvaranand Indological Journal* 22(1-2) June-December, p 138-148.

See also Languages and Dialects: Tribals; Subdivision 'Languages and Dilects' under names of tribes, e.g., Mundas: Languages and Dilects.

TRIBAL LAW

Anon, 1986, (Book review) *Tribune* (Magazine), September, 7, p 2, col 6-8. Review of the book : **Archer, W. G.**, 1986, *Tribal law and justice*, Concept Publishing Company, New Delhi, 741 p.

Archer, W. G., 1987, Tribal law and justice : A report on the Santal, *Man in India* 67(1) March, p 81-86.

Tripathy, G. P., 1985, Scheduled Tribes and tribal legislation in Madhya Pradesh, *Cochin University Law Review* 9(1-2) March-June, p 105-116.

See also Law.

TRIBAL LEADERS

Kulkarni, R. R. and **Borkar, S. T.**, 1986, Tribal leaders and their role in agricultural development, *Tribal Research Bulletin* 8(2) March, p 17-20.

See also Bhanjdeo, Pravin Chandre; Birsa Bhagwan; Tribal Leadership.

TRIBAL LEADERSHIP

Ahjua, Ram, 1969, Tribal leadership and social change, *Indian Journal of Social Research* 10(3) December, p 198-203, references.

Das, Amal Kumar, 1963, Leadership : Its role in ancient India and among the tribals, *Bulletin of Cultural Research Institute* 1(3), p 1-7, references.

Mohapatra, Prashant Kumar, 1970, Leadership and religion, *Adibasi* 11(4) January, p 53-59.

Sinha, Surajit, 1968, Tribal solidarity and messianic movements, *Contributions to Indian Sociology (NS)* 2 December, p 112-118, references.

TRIBAL LEADERSHIP : INDIA : ASSAM

Mills, J. P., 1949, The sacred chief of Assam, *Man in India* 23(2), p 149-151.

TRIBAL LEADERSHIP : INDIA : BIHAR

Sinha, A. C., 1967, Leadership in a tribal society, *Man in India* 47(3) July-September, p 222-227, references.

See also Birsa Bhagwan.

TRIBAL LEADERSHIP : INDIA : MADHYA PRADESH

Bhouraskar, K. M., 1962, Dynamics of leadership in a tribal village, *Bulletin of Tribal Research and Development Institute* (Chhindwara) 2(1) June, p 1-14,

———, 1988, Santal music, National Centre for the Performing Arts, *Quarterly Journal* 17(1) March, p 45-47.

TRIBAL NAMES

Paul, Gemini, 1956, Origin of certain tribal names pertaining to Assam, *Vanyajati* 4(4) October, p 147-154, references.

TRIBAL PEASANTRY

See Tribal Farmers.

TRIBAL PEOPLES : WELFARE

Mac Naughton, A., 1953, Foreign missions and their work among tribal peoples, *Indian Journal of Social Work* 14(3) December, p 276-281.

Mohapatra, Kulamani, 1964, Approaching the tribal people for welfare, *Adibasi*, January, p 7-16.

See also Tribal Welfare.

TRIBAL POLICY

Das, Gananath, 1964, Evolution of tribal policy, *Adibasi* January, p 21-24.

See also Policies: Tribal Development; National Seminar on Nehru and Evolution of Tribal Policy, September 20, 1989.

TRIBAL POPULATION

Mehta, B. H., 1953, Historical background of tribal population, *Indian Journal of Social Work* 14(3) December, p 236-244.

Sarkar, S. S., 1958, The tribal population in West Bengal, *Man in India* 38(1) January-March, p 60-64, tables.

See also Demographic Charateristics: Tribals; Population Growth: India: West Bengal.

TRIBAL PROBLEMS

Chattopadhyay, K. P., 1949, The tribal problem and is solution, *Eastern Anthropologist* 3(1) September, p 15-21, references.

Dube, S. C., 1959, Some aspect of tribal problem, *Eastern Anthropologist* 3(1) September, p 28-35.

———, 1960, Approaches to the tribal problem in India, *Journal of Social Research* 3(2) September, p 11-15.

Roy Burman, B. K., 1989, Critical approach to tribal problems, *Mainstream* 27(42) July 15, p 12-14.

Sanganna, Toyaka, 1966, Tribal problems of Orissa, *Adibasi* 8(2) July, p 2-8.

See also Housing Problems: Tribals.

TRIBAL PROSPERITY

Patnaik, J. B., 1986, Towards tribal prosperity, *Link* (Supplement) 28(30) March 2, p 24-28.

TRIBAL PROTECTION : INDIA : KARNATAKA

Continho, V. B., 1985, Tribal protection in Karnataka : An appraisal, *Cochin University Law Review* 9(1-2) March-June, p 117-128.

TRIBAL REHABILITATION : INDIA : MADHYA PRADESH

Mathur, K. S., 1960, Some problems of tribal rehabilitation in M.P., *Journal of Social Research* 3(2) September, p 113 120.

TRIBAL REVOLTS
See Revolts: Adivasis: India; Tribes and Tribals Revolts.

TRIBAL REVOLUTIONS
See also Revolts: Tribal Movements; Tribal Unrest; Tribal Uprising; Adivasis: India.

TRIBAL REVOLUTIONS : INDIA : MADHYA PRADESH : BASTAR
Naskar, Santosh K. and **Naskar, Indrani**, 1989, Pre-independent tribal revolution in Bastar : A historical analysis, *Vanyajati* 37(2) April p 30-34.

TRIBAL SITUATION : INDIA : WEST BENGAL
Bhowmick, P. K., 1985, Tribal situation in West Bengal, *Indian Anthropologist* 15(1) June, p 1-19.

TRIBAL SOCIETY
Deb, P. C., 1961, Change in tribal society, *Religion and Society* 8(3) September, p 84-89.
Madhava Menon, T., 1985, Law and tribal societies in Kerala, *Cochin University Law Review* 9(1-2) March-June, p 157-172.
Rao, G. R. S., 1966, Process of industrialisation and direction of social changes in tribal society, *Journal of Social Research* 21(2) September, p 65-69.
Roy Burman, B. K., 1968, Some dimensions of transformation of tribal societies in india, *Journal of Social Research* 9(1) p 88-94.
———, 1970, Socio-political processes in India and integration of the tribal societies, *Vanyajati* 18(1) January, p 6-14.
Sinha, A. C., 1967, Leadership in a tribal society, *Man in India* 47(3) July-September, p 222-227, references.

TRIBAL SOLIDARITY
Sinha, Surajit, 1968, Tribal solidarity and messianic movements, *Contributions to Indian Sociology* (NS) December, 2, p 112-118, references.
See also Solidarity Conflicts: Tribals.

TRIBAL STRUGGLE FOR SURVIVAL
Viegas, Philip, 1987, Land control and tribal struggle for survival, *Social Action* 37(4) October-December, p 325-344, footnotes.
See also Survival Strategy: Tribals.

TRIBAL STUDENTS
Ganguli, J. B., Tribal students between tradition and modernity, *Educational Miscellany* 7(1-2) June-September, p 61-69.
Sharma, K. R., 1984, Tribal students and role of schools, *Primary Teacher* 9(4) October, p 11-13.

TRIBAL STUDIES
Aurora, G. S., 1985, Tribal studies, *Contributions to Indian Sociology* (NS) 19(2) July-December, p 359-365.
See also Study Teams: Tribal Welfare.

TRIBAL SUB PLAN
Anon, 1987, Tribal sub-plan programme, *Times of India*, (Magazine), January 22, p 11, col 1-8 +.
Nayar, P. K. B., 1985, Tribal sub-plan of Kerala : A critical appraisal, *Cochin*

University Law Review 9(1-2) March-June, p 189-202.

Pramod Kumar and **Sood, Atul**, 1985, Tribal sub-plan : A critical appraisal, *Link* (Supplement) 27(26) February, 3, p 48-54, tables.

See also TSP Areas.

TRIBAL TRADITION

See Traditions and Customs: Tribals.

TRIBAL TRANSFORMATION

Mukhopadhyay, Rajatsubhra, 1984, Dilemma of tribal transformation: The case of Chenchus, *Vanyajati* 32(2) April, p 19-24.

Sen, Jyoti, 1966, Problem in tribal transformation, *Man in India* 46(4) October-December, p 319-330.

See also Transformation: Tribal Societies: India.

TRIBAL UNREST

Das Gupta, Malabika, 1985, Tribal unrest in Tripura : An alternative view, *Economic and Political Weekly* 20(1) January 5, p 38-40.

Jabbar Alam, M., 1986, Tribal unrest in Bihar : Demand for Jharkhand State revived, *New Age* 34(5) February 2, p 8-9.

Saraf, Samarendra, 1969, Tribal unrest : An urgent research problem, *Bulletin of Cultural Research Institute* 8(1-2) December, p 32-37, footnotes.

See also Tribal Movements; Tribal Uprisings; Tribal Revolutions: India: Madhya Pradesh: Bastar.

TRIBAL UPRISINGS

See also Kherwar Movement; Nativistic Movements; Santal Rebellion, 1855;Sarora Finuris; Tribal Movements, Tribal Unrest; Tribal Revolutions: India: Madhya Pradesh: Bastar.

TRIBAL UPRISINGS : INDIA

Saraf, Samarendra, 1969, Tribal unrest : An urgent research problem *Bulletin of Cultural Research Institute* 8(1-2), December, p 32-37, footnotes, references.

Sinha, Surendra Prasad, 1961, Kherwar movement in Hazaribagh district (1870-1880), *Vanyajati* 9(3) July, p 98-104.

Von Furer-Haimendorf, Christoph, 1945, Aboriginal rebellions in the Deccan, *Man in India* 25(4) December, p 208-217.

TRIBAL UPRISINGS : INDIA : TAMIL NADU : MADRAS

Elwin, Verrier, 1945, Sarora Finuris, *Man in India* 25(4) December, p 254-257, footnotes.

TRIBAL URBANISATION

Thakur, Devendra, 1984, Township and its impact on tribal urbanisation, *Monthly Commentary on Indian Economic Conditions* 26(3) October, p 7-10.

See also Urbanisation: Impact on Tribal Habitats.

TRIBAL WELFARE

Anon, 1954, Activities conduced under the tribal welfare scheme. Madhya Pradesh during 1953-1954, *Vanyajati* 2(2) April, p 64-67.

——, 1954, Note on the progress of the tribal welfare scheme in Madhya Pradesh (from January 1953-December 1953), *Vanyajati* 2(1) January, p 26-29.

——, 1954, Tribal welfare work in Vindhya Pradesh, *Vanyajati* 2(2) April, p 67-68.

——, 1956, Seminar on tribal welfare at Chhindwara, *Vanyajati* 4(3) July, p 1-59.

——, 1957, Life membership scheme for tribal welfare work, *Vanyajati* 5(4) october, p 161-163.

——, 1957, Need for life workers for tribal welfare, *Vanyajati* 5(3) July, p 155-156.

——, 1959, The study team and tribal welfare, *Vanyajati* 7(4) October, p 115-116, references.

——, 1961, Training of tribal welfare workers, *Vanyajati* 9(3) July, p 87-89 +.

Bakshi, P. M., 1985, Tribal welfare and the law : The prospect, *Cochin University Law Review* 9(1-6) March-June, p 79-86.

Bose, Nirmal Kumar, 1957, Anthropology and tribal welfare, *Man in India* 37(3) July-September, p 169-181.

Gangadharan, K. A., 1985, Tribal welfare and development in Kerala, *Cochin University Law Review* 9(1-2) March-June, p 173-188.

Kamila, Bana Behari, 1983, Occupational status of parents of Harijan and Tribal Welfare Department high school students of Orissa, *National Journal of Education* 6(1) September, p 56-65, references, tables.

Karunakaran, C. K., 1985, Legislative and executive measures or tribal welfare in Kerala, *Cochin University Law Review* 9(1-2) March-June, p 203-212.

Krishnan, P. G., 1985, Constitution and tribal welfare, *Cochin University Law Review* 9(1-2) March-June, p 49-66.

Mangla, A. P., 1970, Levels of living and problems of tribal welfare, *Vanyajati* 18(2) April, p 59-60.

Mehta, B. H., 1957, Tribal welfare and forest economy, *Indian Journal of Social Work* 18(3) December, p 155-161.

——, 1959, Tribal welfare and forest economy, *Journal of Social Research* 2(1-2) March-September, p 72-81.

——, 1963, Social work and tribal welfare, *Social Work Forum* 1(4) October, p 7-13.

Mehta, Shalini, 1988, Role of voluntary and government organisation in tribal welfare : Case study of Mandala district of M.P., *Eastern Anthropologist* 41(1) January-March, p 49-64, tables.

Raghaviah, V., 1989, Research on tribal welfare, *Vanyajati* 37(1) January, p 10-11.

Roy Burman, B. K., 1960, Basic concepts of tribal welfare and tribal integration, *Journal of Social Research* 3(2) September, p 16-24.

Sharma, B. D., 1985, Tribal welfare legislation and enforcement, *Cochin University Law Review* 9(1-2) March-June, p 19-47.

Shrikant, L. M., 1959, Evaluation of tribal welfare work in Nellore district (Andhra Pradesh), *Vanyajati* 7(4) October, p 124-126, illustration.

Shukla, Ravi Shankar, 1955, Tribal welfare work in Bastar district (M.P.), *Vanyajati* 3(2) April, p 78-80.

Venkataraman, S. R., 1959, Some problems of tribal welfare work, *Social Service Quarterly* 44(3) January, p 77-82.

——, 1964, Education as a basic factor in tribal welfare, *Social Service Quarterly* 49(3) January, p 88-92.

Vidyarthi, L. P., 1957, Anthropology, authority and tribal welfare in India, *Eastern Anthropologist*, 11(1).

See also Tribal Development; Tribal Peoples: Welfare

TRIBAL WELFARE CENTRES : INDIA : MADHYA PRADESH

Bapat, N. V., 1953, Bondar : a unique tribal welfare centre in M.P., *Vanyajati* 1(2) April, p 38-40.

TRIBAL WELFARE CONFERENCE, 1st, 1952, DELHI

Anon, 1955, Conference on tribal affairs, *Vanyajati* 3(1) January, p 1-3.

TRIBAL WELFARE CONFERENCE, 2nd, 1953, LOHARDAGA

Anon, 1954, Resolutions passed at the Second Tribal Welfare Conference, Lohardaga (Bihar) on 11th, 12th and 13th November, 1953, *Vanyajati* 2(1) January, p 31-32.

Shah, P. G., 1954, The Second Tribal Welfare Conference, 11th, 12th, and 13 November, 1953, *Journal of Anthropological Society Bombay* (NS) 8(1) March, p 76-79.

Wadia, A. R., 1953, Tribal Welfare Conference, Lohardaga, Bihar, *Indian Journal of Social Work* 14(2) December, p 296-300.

TRIBAL WELFARE CONFERENCE, 3rd, 1955, JAGDALPUR

Anon, 1955, Resolutions passed at the Third Tribal Welfare Conference held at Jagdalpur (M.P.) on 13th 14th and 15th March, 1955, *Vanyajati* 3(2) April, p 84-85.

——, 1955, Tribal Welfare Conference, *Main in India* 35(2) April-June, p 146-148.

TRIBAL WELFARE CONFERENCE, 5th, 1959, BORDI

Anon, 1959, The Tribal Welfare Conference at Bordi, *Social Service Quarterly* 44(3) January, p 72-77.

Venkataraman, S. R., 1959, The Tribal Welfare Conference at Bordi, *Vanyajati* 7(1), p 29-35.

TRIBAL WELFARE CONFERENCE, 6th, 1960, OCTACAMUND

Anon, 1960, Resolution passed at the Sixth Tribal Welfare Conference, Octacamund, *Vanyajati* 8(3) July, p 124-26.

TRIBAL WELFARE CONFERENCE, 10th, 1968, BORDI

Anon, 1969, Brief report of the Tenth All India Tribal Welfare Conference, *Vanyajati* 17(1) January, p 28-33.

TRIBAL WELFARE FIELD WORKER'S SEMINAR

Bhouraskar, K. M., 1961, The First Tribal Welfare Field Worker's Seminar, *Bulletin of Tribal Research and Development Institute* (Chhindwara) 1(2) December, p 1-3.

TRIBAL WOMEN

See also Tribal Girls: Education; Tribal Dormitories; subdivision 'Women' under names of tribes, e.g., Khasas: Women: India: Uttar Pradesh.

TRIBAL WOMEN : INDIA

Brij Mohan, 1961, Status of women in tribal communities in India, *Vanyajati* 10(2) April, p 60-66.

Chinchalkar, J. H., 1970, Welfare of tribal women, *Vanyajati* 18(1) January, p 37-40.

Garg, B.M., 1960, Status of women in tribal communities is India, *Indian Journal of Social Work* 21(2) September, p 191-197.

Jahagirdar, M.P., 1988, The states and role of women in a tribal community, *Man in India* 68(4) December 4.

Mann, K., 1987, Status of Bhil and Khasi women : A comparative study, *Man and Life* 13(1-2) January-June, p 57-66, bibliography

Mehta, B. H., 1969, Education of tribal women and girls, *Education Quarterly* 21(1)

April, p 44-46.

Menon, Geeta, 1987, Tribal women : Victims of the development process, *Social Action* 37(4) October-December, p 373-390, bibliography, tables.

Naskar, Santosh K., 1989, Status of tribal women in Bastar, *Vanyajati* 37(3) July, p 16-20.

Rose, J. A., The changing picture of the life of young tribal girls, *Religion and Society* 8(3) September, p 53-59.

Saldonlia, Indra Munshi, 1986, Tribal women in the Warli revolt : 1945-1947 : Class and gender in the Left perspective, *Economic and Political Weekly* (Supplement) 21(17) 26 April, p Ws41-52, footnotes.

Sarkar, R.M., 1968, Women in tribal India through custom and traditions, *Folklore* 9(12) December, p 458-467, references.

Shashi, S. S., 1986, Tribal women of India, *Kurukshetra* 34(4) January, p 15-16.

Upreti, H.C., 1967, The position of women among Khasas of Kumaon, *Journal of Social Research* 10(1) March, p 37-45, references.

TRIBAL WOMEN : INDIA : ANDHRA PRADESH

Ramalingaswami, Prabha, 1986, Impact of social change on health problems of tribal women, *Society and Change* 16(2-3) June-September, p 100-103, bibliography, tables.

Rohini, A., 1987, Some demographic trends among the tribal women of Andhra Pradesh, *Man and Life* 13(1-2) January-June, p 91-96, bibliography, tables.

TRIBAL WOMEN : INDIA : MADHYA PRADESH : BASTAR

Naskar, Santosh K., 1989, Status of tribal women in Bastar, *Vanyajati* 37(3) July, p 16-20.

TRIBAL YOUTH

Bhuriya, Mahipal, 1985, Tribal youth : Bringing them into the national mainstream, *Vivekananda Kendra Patrika* 14(2) August, p 35-42.

Jitendra Mohan and Narendra Kumar, 1980, A study of social and personal problems of tribal youth, *Asian Journal of Psychology and Education* 6(1) January, p 5-8.

Karva, S.P., 1986, Training tribal youth, *Tribal Research Bulletin* 9(1) September, p 28-29.

TRIBAL YOUTH : INDIA

Rout, Siba Prasad, 1969, Youth organisation, *Adibasi* 11(1-2) April-July, p 89-95.

TRIBAL YOUTH : INDIA : ORISSA

Das, Gananath, 1967, Tribal culture and democracy, *Adibasi* 9(3) October, p 31-35.

TRIBAL YOUTH DORMITORIES

See Tribal Dormatories.

TRIBALISATION

Chauhan, R. R., 1966, Tribalisation, *Tribe* 2(1-2), p 5-11.

Sen Gupta, A. K., 1967, Hindustation and tribalisation : Two cases studies, *Folklore* 8(1-2) December, p 433-438, references.

See also Detribalisation.

TRIBALS

Anon, 1960, Dandakaranya and the tribals, *Vanyajati* 8(2) April, p 41-43.

——, 1961, A essay in migration, *Social Action* 11(12) December, p 575-576+.

Joseph, A.N.T., 1989, Ethnozoology of reptiles in relation to health care among tribals in Madhya Pradesh, *Social Action* 39(4) October-December, p 405-422.

See also Tribes and Tribals.

TRIBALS AND GOVERNMENT

Wadia, A.R., 1966, A note on the tribals and the government, *Journal of Anthropological Society of Bombay* (NS) 12(1), p 12-14.

See also Tribal government; Tribes and Tribals.

TRIBES AND TRIBALS

See also Aborigines; Criminal Tribes; Gypsies; Tribal Peoples: Wellfare.

TRIBES AND TRIBALS : ABILITY TESTING : INDIA : TRIPURA

Chatterjee, Neera, 1965, A comparison of performance of tribal and non-tribal boys of Tripura (India) on five performance tests, *Journal of Psychological Research* 9(3) September, p 151-158, references tables.

TRIBES AND TRIBALS : ASIA : SOUTHEAST

Kingdon-Ward, F., 1946, What of the tribes, *Man in India* 26(2) June, p 110-119.

TRIBES AND TRIBALS : AUSTRALIA

McCallum, D. Kent, 1965, Control : The Kunapipi ritual and attendant taboo, *Eastern Anthropologist* 18(2) May-August, p 80-88, references.

TRIBES AND TRIBALS : BANGLADESH

Khan, M.Q., 1985, Tribal survival in Chittagang hill tracts of Bangladesh, *Man in India* 65(1) March, p 58-74, bibliography.

Mukhopadhyay, Sunil K., 1987, The exodus, *Illustrated Weekly of India* 108(8) February 22, p 30-31.

See also Oraons; Santals; Tribes and Tribals : India : West Bengal.

TRIBES AND TRIBALS : BIBLIOGRAPHY : INDIA

Anon, 1962, Bibliography, *Social Action* 12(4) April, p 199-201.

Barange, B. G., 1963, An annotated bibliography on tribal indebtedness, *Bulletin of Tribal Research and Development Institute* (Chhindwara) 3(1) June, p 60-66.

TRIBES AND TRIBALS : BIBLIOGRAPHY : INDIA : BIHAR

Anon, 1988, (Book Review), *Man in India* 68(2-3) June-September, p 305.

Review of the book: **Gour, P. N.**, ed., 1988, *Bihar tribal bibliography*, Patna Library, Patna, 135 p.

TRIBES AND TRIBALS : BIBLIOGRAPHY : INDIA : MADHYA PRADESH

Barange, B. G., 1963, An annotated bibliography on tribal indebtedness, *Bulletin of Tribal Research and Development Institute* (Chhindwara) 3(1) June, p 60-66.

TRIBES AND TRIBALS : BURMA

Kindon-Ward, F., 1946, What of the tribes, *Man in India* 26(3) June, p 110-119.

TRIBES AND TRIBALS : CENSUS : INDIA : WEST BENGAL

See Population Growth: Tribals: India: West Bengal; Tribal Population.

TRIBES AND TRIBALS : CHILDREN

See Tribal Children.

TRIBES AND TRIBALS : CLUBS

See Tribes and Tribals : Societies and Clubs.

TRIBES AND TRIBALS : DEFINITION

Naik, T. B., 1964, What is a tribe?: Conflicting definitions, *Bulletin of Tribal Research and Training Institute* (Chhindwara) 4(1) June, p 1-13.

Sanganna, Toyaka, 1964, Problems of definition, *Adibasi* November, p 15-18.

TRIBES AND TRIBALS : DIET

See Tribes and Tribals : Food : Nutrition.

TRIBES AND TRIBALS : ECONOMIC CONDITIONS : INDIA : MADHYA PRADESH

Barange, B. G., 1963, An annotated bibliography on tribal indebtedness, *Bulletin of Tribal Research and Development Institute* (Chhindwara) 3(1) June, p60-61.

TRIBES AND TRIBALS : ECONOMIC CONDITIONS : INDIA : ORISSA

Das, Gananath, 1955-1956, The parasite problem, *Adibasi*, 2, p 36-38.

TRIBES AND TRIBALS : ECONOMIC CONDITIONS : INDIA : WEST BENGAL

Banerjee, Swapan Kumar, 1963, Role of handicrafts in tribal economy, *Bulletin of Cultural Research Institute* 1(3), p15-19, references.

TRIBES AND TRIBALS : EDUCATION

See Tribal Education.

TRIBES AND TRIBALS : FOOD : NUTRITION

Debi, Kiranbala, 1990, Necessity of adequate diet for tribal students *Adibasi* 8(1) April, p 61-66.

See also Diet and Nutritional Studies: Tribals

TRIBES AND TRIBALS : HEALTH AND HYGIENE

Anon, 1986, (Book review), *Panjab University Research Bulletin (Arts)* 18(1) April, p 221-223.

Review of the book : **Chaudhuri, Buddhadeb**, 1986, *Tribal health: Socio cultural dimensions*, Inter-India Publication, New Delhi, 350 p.

——, 1988, (Book review), *Indian Economic Social History Review* 25(1) January-March, p 107-109; *Indian History Review* 11(1-2) July-January p 259-260.

Review of the book : **Singh, K. S.**, 1985, *Tribal society in India : An anthropo-historical perspective*, Manohar Publication, New Delhi, 327 p.

TRIBES AND TRIBALS : HISTORY : INDIA

Archer, Mildred, 1947, Early records of Indian tribes, *Man in India* 26(1) March, p 39-43.

Chetan Singh, 1988, Conformity and conflict : Tribes and the agarian system of Mughal India, *Indian Economic Social History Review* 25(3) July-September p 314-340.

Parulekar, Godavari, 1986, Saga of the Warli Adivasis revolt, *People's Democracy* 10(2) March 2, p 5+.

Zaidi, Sunita, 1989, The Mughal state and tribes in seventeenth century Sind, *Indian Economic and Social History Review*, 26(3) July to Septermber, p 343-362.

TRIBES AND TRIBALS : INDEBTEDNESS

See Tribes and Tribals : Economic Conditions.

TRIBES AND TRIBALS : INDIA

Adiseshiah, W. C., 1958, Tribal welfare, *Social Action* 8(5-6) May-June, p 201-208.

Anon, 1959, Inter-ethnic relation and social mobility movements among some tribes and castes of Eastern and Central India 1900-1959, *Bulletin of Department of Anthropology* 8(2) July, p 9-130.

——, 1964, How Nehru saw the tribals?, *Vanyajati*, 12(3) July 1, p 122-125.

——, 1981, (Book review) *Man in India* 67(1) March, p 89-90.
Review of the book: **Banerjee, Sukumar**, 1981, *Impact of industrialisation on the tribal population of Tharia Ranigunge Coal Field Area*, Calcutta, Anthropological Survey of India, 160 p.

——, 1982, (Book review), *Sunday Statesman*, August 27, p 13, col 1-5.
Review of the book : **Anderson, Robert**, and **Huber, Walter**, 1982, *The hour of the fex*, Sage Publications New Delhi.

——, 1983, (Book review), *State and Society* 6(1) January-March, p 76-80.
Review of the book: **Jaganath Pathy**, 1983, *Tribal peasantry: Dynamics of development*. Inter-India Publications, New Delhi, 233 p.

——, 1984, (Book Review), *Contribution to Indian Sociology* (New Series) 18(1) January-June, p 141-142.
Review of the book : **Von Furer-Hamendorf, Christoph**, 1982, *Tribes of India: The struggle for survival*. Oxford University Press, New Delhi, 325 p.

——, 1984, Recommendations of the Seminar on socio-economic problems of Scheduled Tribes, *Vanyajati* 32(3) July, p 1-4.

——, 1985, (Book review), *Economic and Political Weekly* 20(41) October 12, p 1739-1740.
Review of the book : **Singh, K. S.**, ed., 1985, *Tribal movements in India*, Manohar Pub., New Delhi, 405p, 2 vols.

——; 1985, (Book review), *Frontiers in Education* March 10, p 5, col 5-6; *National Herald*, March 21, p 7, col 1-4; *Indian Journal of Political Studies*, December 9, p 119-120.
Review of the book : **Basu, R.**, 1985, *Tribal development programmes and administration*, National Book Organisation, New Delhi, 322 p.

——, 1985, (Book review), *Indian Journal of Public Administration* 32(4) October-December, p 1110-1112.
Review of the book : **Pamecha, Renuka**; 1985, *Elite in a tribal society*, Printwell Pub., Jaipur, 223 p.

——; 1985, (Book review), *Indian Journal of Public Administration* 33(2) April-June, p 368-370.
Review of the book : **Basu, Ashok K**; 1985, *Tribal development programmes and administration in India*, National Book Organisation, New Delhi, 322 p.

——, 1985, (Book review), *Patriot*, November 14, p 4, col 4-7.
Review of the book : **Chaubey, N.P.**, ed; 1983, *Tribal techniques, social organisation and development : Disruption and alternatives*, IASS, Allahabad, 206 p.

——, 1985, (Book review), *Rajasthan Economic Journal* 9(1) January, p 67-68.
Review of the book : **Trivedi, Hari Vallabh**; 1985, *Economic development of tribes in India*, Himanshu Publication, Udaipur, 195 p.

——, 1985, (Book review), *Sarvartham* 13, p 130-131.
Review of the book : **Singh, K. S.**, 1985, *Tribal society in India*, Manohar Pub, New Delhi, 327 p.

——, 1985, (Book review), *Social Action* 35(1) January-March, p 95-98.

Review of the book : **Pachauri, S. K.**, 1984, *Dynamics of rural development in tribal areas*, Concept Publishing Company, New Delhi, xiv, 262 p.
——, 1985, (Book review), *Social Scientist* 13(5) May, p 68-71.
Review of the book : **Pathy, Jaganath**, 1985, *Tribal peasantry : Dynamics of development*, Inter-India Publications, New Delhi.
——, 1985, The poor have no vice, *Hindustan Times* (Magazine) September, 1, p 5, col. 1-8.
——, 1986, (Book review), *Economic and Political Weekly* 21(4) January 25, p 161-163.
Review of the book : **Singh, K. S.**, 1985, *Tribal Society in India*, Manohar Pub., New Delhi, 327 p.
——, 1986, (Book review), *Folklore* 27(6) June, p 130.
Review of the book : **Chaudhuri, Buddhadeb**, ed, 1986, *Tribal health : Socio-cultural dimensions*, Inter-India Publications, New Delhi, 130 p.
——, 1986, (Book Review), *New Quest*, 56, March-April, p 127-128.
Review of the book : **Mahapatra, Sitakant**, 1986, *The awakened wind : The oral poetry of the Indian tribes*, Vikas Publication, New Delhi, 322 p.
——, 1986, (Book review), *Tribune* (Magazine), September 7, p 2, col 6-8.
Review of the book : **Archer, W. G.**, 1986, *Tribal law and Justice*, Concept Publishing Company, New Delhi, xxxvi, 741 p.
——, 1986, (Book review), *Yojana* 30(8) May 1, p 34.
Review of the book : **Joshi, Ramasharan**, 1986, *Flight of the tribals : Tribes : Islands of deprivation*, National Book Shop, Delhi, xvi, 196 p.
——, 1986, (Book Review), *Indian Express* (Magazine) August 31, p 4, col 1-5.
Review of the book : **Anon**, 1986, *Scenario of the 7 percent*, Cenemart Foundation, New Delhi, 2 vols.
——, 1987, (Book review), *Contribution to Indian Sociology* (NS) 22(1) January-June, p 116-118, *Social Scientist* 10(2) February, p 60-66.
Review of the book : **Hardiman, David**, 1987, *The coming of Devi : Adivasi assertion in Western India*, Oxford University Press, New Delhi, 248 p.
——, 1987, (Book review), *Journal of Rural Development* 6(4) July 87, p 423-426; *National Geographical Journal of India* 33(1) March, p 118-119.
Review of the book : **Singh, R. S.**, 1987, *Changing occupational structure of Scheduled Tribes*, Inter-India Publication, New Delhi, 291 p.
——, 1987, (Book review), *Mainstream* 25(31) April 18, p 22-23.
Review of the book : **Basu, N. G.**, 1987, *Forest and tribals*, Manisha Granthalaya, Calcutta, 203 p.
——, 1987, (Book review), *Man in India* 67(1) March, p 74-77.
Review of the book : **Chakrabarty**, et al, 1985, *Agrarian situations in India*, Anthropological Survey of India, Calcutta, 2 vols.
——, 1987, (Book review), *Tribune* March 15, p 11, col 7-8.
Review of the book : **Maheshwari Prasad**, ed, 1987, *Tribals : Their environment and culture*, Amar Prakashan, Delhi, 344 p.
——, 1987, Caused are the dispossessed, *Link* 29(36) 12 April, p 408.
——, 1987, Displacement of tribals due to location of Centre State Projects : Problems and related issues, *Tribal Research Bulletin* 9(2) March, p 21-26, bibliography.
——, 1988 (Book review), *Economic and Political Weekly* 23(4) January 23, p 148; *Patriot*, January, 31, p 4, col 3-7.
Review of the book : **Basu, N. C.**, 1987, *Forest and tribals*, Manisha Granthalaya,

Calcutta, vi, 196 p.

——, 1988, (Book review), *Sarvartham*, 13, p 126-128.
Review of the book : **Prasad, M.**, ed, 1988, *Tribes: Their environment and culture*, Amar Prakashan, Delhi, xv, 344 p.

——, 1988, (Book review), *Social Scientist* 16(2) February, p 60-66.
Review of the the book : **Hardiman, David**, 1988, *The coming of Devi : Adivasi assertion in Western India*, Oxford University Press, Delhi, 248 p.

——, 1988 (Book review), *Times of India* (Sunday Review), January 10, p 1+.
Review of the book : **Maheshwari Prasad**, 1988, *Tribes : Their environment and culture*, Amar Prakashan, Delhi.

——, 1988, Workshop on tribal development, *Mainstream*, 26(35) June 11, p 27-28 +.

Aryan, Subhashini, 1985, Tribal art of India, *Indian and Foreign Review* 22(19) 31 July, p 23-26.

Assayag, Jackie, 1989, Women-Goddess, women-distress Yellamma Goddess devotees in South India (Karnataka), *Man in India* 69(4) December, p 359-373.

Aurora, G. S., 1968, Caste and backward classes, *Man in India* 48(4) October-December, p 297-306, footnotes.

——, 1985, Tribal studies, *Contribution to Indian Sociology* (New Series) 19(2) July-December, p 359-365.

Ayyangar, M. A., 1964, Impact of modern forces on the tribes and castes in India, *Journal of Social Research* 7(1-2) March-September, p 1-6.

Bage, S. K., 1964, Seminar on impact of modern forces on tribes and castes in India : Welcome address, *Journal of Social Research* 7(1-2) March-September, p 12-14.

Bailey, F. G., 1961, Tribe and Caste in India, *Contributions to Indian Sociology*, 5, October, p 7-19.

Bajaj, S. S., et al, 1985, Role of information sources in the adoption I R S paddy by tribal farmers, *Tribal Research Bulletin* 7(2) March, p 17-19.

Bakshi, P. M., 1985, Tribal welfare and the law : The prospect, *Cochin University Law Review* 9(1-6) March-June, p 79-86.

Banerjee, B. G., 1984, On development and tribal development, *Tribal Research Bulletin* 7(1) September, p 9-11 +.

Banerjee, Biswanath, 1968, Relation between environment and culture among some Indian primitive communities living in the hills, *Bulletin of Cultural Research Institutes* 7(1-2) p 55-61, references.

Basu, Ashok Ranjan, 1985, Improving public service delivery system for tribal population in India : An empirical investigation, *Prashashnika* 14(1) January-March, p 1-15, bibliography.

Basu, Minendra Nath, 1963, Anthropological approach to the tribal peoples of India, *Vanyajati* 11(1) January, p 4-8.

——, 1964, Property and inheritance among the primitives, *Bulletin of Cultural Research Institute* 3(2), p 7-12.

——, 1965, The concept of soul among the tribal folk of India, *Bulletin of Cultural Research Institute* 4(1), p 5-8.

Batria, Puran, 1962, Accidental deaths among tribes, *Bulletin of Tribal Research and Development Institute* (Chhindwara) 2(1), p 43-48.

Baxi, Upendra, 1989, Historic new law : Protecting SC/ST human rights, *Times of India*, September 6, p 3-5.

Bhageshwar Singh and **Reddy, N. K.**, 1982, A plea for demogenetic studies of numerically small and large tribes, *Indian Journal of Physical and Human Genetics* 8(1) April, p 67-70, bibliography.

Bhattacharyya, Debasish and **Chattopadhyay, R. N.**, 1987, Housing problems of dislocated tribals in industrial areas and a step towards solutions, *Man in Life* 13(1-2) January-June, p 49-55, bibliography.

Bhattacharya, S. N., 1987, Tribal development since Independence, *Kurukshetra* 35(10) July, p 34-38.

Bhowmick, P. K., 1987, Voluntary effort in tribal development : The Bidisa experiment, *Journal of Social Economic Studies* 4(2) April-June, p 175-186.

Bhupinder Singh, 1984, Lac and tribals, *Administrator* 29(3) July-September p 183-190.

——, 1984, Tribal development in retrospect and prospect : Sixth Plan mid term appraisal, *Indian Journal of Public Administration* 30(4) October-December, p 1064-1081, tables.

——, 1985, Tribal administration : A critique, *Indian Journal of Public Administration* 31(3) July-September, p 879-909.

——, 1989, Nehru's tribal philosophy and tribal India today, *Mainstream* 27(35) 27 May, p 46-47.

Bhuriya, Mahipal, 1985, Tribal youth : Bringing them into the national mainstream, *Vivekananda Kendra Patrika* 1(2) August, p 35-42.

Bhuskute, R. V., Tribals, Dalits and Government lands, *Economic and Political Weekly* 24(23) 10 June, p 1265-1268, tables.

Bodade, V. N., et al, 1988, Tribals and demonstrations for tribal development, *Indian Farming* 38(8) November, p 39-40.

Bose, Dilip Kumar, 1969, On preferential marriage of the tribes of Central India, *Journal of Social Research* 12(2) September, p 106-116, references, tables.

Bose, Nirmal Kumar, 1968, National integration and the Scheduled Castes and Scheduled Tribes, *Man in India* 48(4) October-December, p 289-296.

Brij Mohan, 1961, Status of women in tribal communities in India, *Vanyajati* 10(2) April, p 60-66.

Chakrabarti, A. K., et al, 1984, Socio-psychological correlater in the adoption of health innovations among tribals within intensive service of primary health centre, *Health and Population* 7(1) January-March, p 72-83, bibliography.

Chakraborty, Bhabatosh, 1985, Upholding the cause of the tribals, *National Herald* (Sunday Herald) April 21, p 1, col 3-6 +.

Chakravarty, M. I., 1989, Economic analysis of employment, income and consumption pattern of tribals farmers, *Journal of Rural Development* 8(1) January, p 97-108, tables.

Chattopadhyay, K. P., 1954, A short note on cultivation among tribal folk in India, *Vanyajati* 2(4) October, p 110-112.

Chaudhary, Maitreyi, 1987, Class analysis in a collage society; A cluster theoretic approach, *Economic and Political Weekly* 22(49) December 5, p 2121-2126.

Chauhan, R.R., 1966, Tribalisation, *Tribe* 2(1-2), p 5-11.

Choubey, Bindo Kumar, 1985, More efforts needed to uplift tribals, *Times of India*, February 27, p 8, col 7-8.

Danda, Ajit K., 1988, Tribes in India, *Man in India* 68(4) December, p 313-334.

Das, A. K., 1965, Prospects of fish culture in tribal area, *Man in India* 45(5) October-December, p 316-321, reference.

Das, N., 1968-1969, Methods of social anthropology: An study of tribes in India, *Adibasi* 10(3-4) October-January, p 40-50, references.

Das, Nityananda, 1963, Tribes : Their problems and administration of tribal areas, *Vanyajati* 11(3) July, p 106-25.

Das, P., et al, 1986, How lab to land programme are helping tribal farmers, *Kurukshetra* 34(4) January-June, p 109-110.

Das, T. C., 1962, Nature and extent of social change in tribal society of Eastern India, *Sociological Bulletin* 11(1-2) March-September, p 221-238, tables.

Das, Victor, 1989, Tribals of Jharkhand and the question of their survival, *Social Action* 39(4) October-December, p 438-443.

Das Gupta, P. K., 1964, Impact of industrialisation on tribal life, *Bulletin of the Anthropological Survey of India* 13, p 85-106.

Das Gupta, Pranab Kumar and **Khan, Iar Ali**, 1985, Impact of tea plantation industry on the life of tribal labourers, *Man and Life* 12(1-2) January-June, p 109-111.

Das Gupta, Ranjit, 1986, From peasants and tribesman to plantation workers : Colonial capitalism of labour power, *Economic and Political Weekly* (Supplement) 21(4) January 25, p PE2-PE-10.

Dhagambar, Vasudha, 1986, Tribals and the law, *India International Centre Quarterly* 13(3-4) December, p 95-114.

Dhebar, U. N., 1970, Weaker sections of the community, *Interdiscipline* 7(4) Winter, p 27-31.

Dubey, K. C., 1969, Tribal legends and customs and tribal history, *Vanyajati* 17(2) April, p 46-48.

Eastern Anthropologist (Periodical), 1969, Tribal identity, *Eastern Anthropologist* 22(2) May-August, p 135-139, editorial.

Ehrenfels, U. R., 1962, Gifts of Aboriginality, *Journal of Social Research* 5(2) September, p 71-80.

Elwin, Verrier, 1942, Do we really want to keep them in a zoo?, *Indian Journal of Social Work* 2(4) March, p 438-448.

Exem, A. Van, 1987, The tribe : God's own people : A theological perspective, *Sevartham*, 12, p 45-64, footnotes.

——, 1988, Tribal forever : The cachatology of the Sarna, *Sevartham*, 13, p 27-42, footnotes.

Fatima, Johra, 1986, Tribals who do not know how to measure weights, space and times, *Patriot* (Magazine) August 3, p 1, col 5-6.

Fox, Richard G., 1969, Professional primitives : Hunters and gather of nuclear South Asia, *Man in India* 49(2) April-June, p 139-160, bibliography, footnotes.

Gare, G.M., 1955, Need of training of workers in tribal development, *Tribal Research Bulletin* 7(2) March, p 5-6.

——, 1984, Voluntary agencies in tribal areas : Their roles and functional types, *Tribal Research Bulletin* 7(1) September, p 5-6 +.

Garg, B. M., 1960, Status of women in tribal communities in India, *Indian Journal of Social Work* 21(2) September, p 191-197.

Ghosh, A., 1985, The political economy of development strategy and tribal demography, *Capital* 196(4815) September 30, p 49-52.

Guha, K., 1960, Tribal handicrafts in India, *Vanyajati* 8(3) July.

Gunasekaran, R., 1988, Social change among tribals : A study, *Kurukshetra* 36(4) January, p 9-12.

Hans, Dilbar, 1962, The rediscovery of the tribal personality in the new context, *Religion and Society* 9(4) December, p 5-14.

Hemant Kumar, 1970, Characteristics of tribes in India, *Vanyajati* 18(2) April,

p 65-69.

Hutton, J. H., 1922, Dopopulation of primitive communities, *Man in India* 2(4), December, p 220-227, footnotes.

Jahagirdar, M. P., 1988, The status and role of women in a tribal community, *Man in India* 68(4) December, p 424-430.

Jaiswal, N. K., Khan, A. S. and **Jai Shankar**, 1969, Attitudes towards agricultural development among tribal and non-tribal people, *Man in India* 49(3), p 267-281.

Jha, Raghunath, 1986, Adult education and tribal development, *Mainstream* 24(50) August 16, p 35-36 +.

Jitendra Mohan and **Narendra Kumar**, 1980, A study of social and personal problems of tribal youth, *Asian Journal of Psychology and Education* 6(1) January, p 5-8.

Kalathill Mathew, 1984, Repression of tribals, *Economic and Political Weekly* 19(36) September 8, p 1562.

Kanekar, P. G., 1942, Isolation or assimilation ? *Social Service Quarterly* 28(3) January, p 97-115.

Kar, R. K., 1970, A tribe in the context of tea industry in India : Some preliminary observations, *Anthropos*, 71, p 868-877.

Karuppaiyan, E., 1989, Issues in poverty alleviation programmes for the tribals, *Social Action* 39(1) January-March, p 72-89, bibliography.

Kaul, S. K., 1955, Adivasis and Indian army, *Vanyajati* 3(1) January, p 23-25.

Knabe, Wolfang K., 1983, The role of sociology and anthropology in solving problems of Indian tribals, *Development Policy and Administration Review* 9(1-2) January-December, p 15-23.

Kodanda Rao, P., 1954, Liquor and the aboriginals, *Indian Journal of Social Work* 14(4) March, p 382-385.

Krishna Iyer, V. R., 1985, Tribal uplift and the rule of law, *Cochin University Law Review* 9(1-2) March-June, p 1-8.

Krishnan, P. G., 1985, Constitution and tribal welfare, *Cochin University Law Review* 9(1-2) March-June, p 49-66.

Kulkarni, M. G., 1985, Economic development of tribal people, *Tribal Research Bulletin* 7(2) March.

Kulkarni, Sharad, 1985, Adivasis, law and social justice, *Economic and Political Weekly* 20(28) July 13, p 1171-1174.

——, 1987, Forest legislation and tribals : Comments on Forest Policy Resolution, *Economic and Political Weekly* 22(50) December 12, p 2143-2148.

Kumar, B. Das, 1986, Development of the tribal economy : A spatial approach, *Kurukshetra* 34(4) January, p 13-14 +.

Kuthiala, S. K., 1969, Demographic characteristics of tribal population in India, *Indian Sociological Bulletin* 7(1) October, p 57-58, references.

Lahiri, Kuntala, 1990, Will the Birhor survive modernisation?, *Geographical Review of India* 52(1) March, p 99-101.

Lakshmaiah, T., 1984, Socio-economic development of tribals, *Mainstream* 23(18) December 29, p 21-22.

Lakshmi Devi, 1985, Tribal world after 1947, *Social Welfare* 32(3) June, p 20-21.

Leelakrishnan, P., et al, 1985, Forest and tribal people : Law and practice, *Cochin University Law Review* 9(1-2) March-June, p 259-270.

Leuva, K. K., 1964, Impact of constitutional safeguards on the Scheduled Tribes, *Journal of Social Research* 7(1-2) March-September, p 62-69.

Long, James, 1966, Five hundred questions on subjects requiring investigation in the social condition of the natives, edited with additional notes by **Mahadev Prasad**, *Folklore* 7(8) August, p 283-329.

Mahalingam, S., 1987, LAMP cooperative societies in tribal India, *Co-operators Bulletin* 30(7) July, p 5-9.

——, 1988, Tribal development programmes : A review, *Kurukshetra* 36(4) January, p 4-8.

Maheshwari, J. K., 1987, Tribal ecosystem : An over view, *Tribal Research Bulletin* 9(2) March, p 1-4 +.

Majumder, D. N., 1929, Sex and sex control in primitive society, *Man in India* 9(4) December, p 251-266.

——, 1939, Tribal cultures and acculturation, *Man in India* 19(2-3) April-September, p 99-172.

——, 1949, The changing canvas of tribal life, *Eastern Anthropologist* 3(1) September, p 40-47.

Malhotra, R., 1985, Tribals : Which way justice ? *Mainstream* 23(36) May 4, p 21-23.

Man in India (Periodical), 1988, Tribes of India, *Man in India* 68(4) December, editorial.

Mani, S. B., 1964, Bows and arrows in tribal India, *Vanyajati* 12(1) January, p 40-50, references.

Marrison, G. E., 1962, Languages in the tribal churches of North East India, *Religion and Society* 9(4) December, p 72-79.

Mastana, S. S., 1989, Palmar transverse creases among the Lobanas of North-West India, *Man in India* 69(3) September, p 305-309.

Mehta, B. H., 1949, The problem of Aborigines, *Indian Journal of Social Work* 10(2) September.

——, 1953, Historical background of tribal population, *Indian Journal of Social Work* 14(3) December, p 236-244.

——, 1966, Forestry and tensions in tribal area, *Journal of Social Research* 9(2) September, p 10-25.

Memoria, C. B., 1957, Tribes in India; Their civil and social conditions, *Indian Journal of Social Work* 18(2) September, p 115-124, tables.

Menon, P. S. K., 1986, Programme of tribal development under Seventh Plan, *Tribal Research Bulletin* 8(2) March, p 21-22.

Minz, Nirmal, 1985, Anthropology and the deprived, *Religion and Society* 32(4) December, p 3-19, bibliography.

——, 1986, Religion and culture as power in the context of tribal aspiration in India, *Religion and Society* 33(2) June, p 45-54.

——, 1987, Religion, culture and education in the context of tribal aspirations in India, *Journal of Dharma* 12(2) April-June, p 150-164, bibliography, footnotes.

——, 1987, A theological interpretation of the tribal reality in India, *Religion and Society* 34(4) December, p 71-85.

Mitra, Ashok, 1988, Tribal exploitation : An overview, *Main Stream* 26(33) May 28, p 32-34.

Mohanty, A. K., et al, 1990, Protein calorie intake and growth status of tribal boys in a residential school, *Man in India* 70(2) June p 144-154.

Mohanty, Gopinath, 1964, Fading outlines in tribal culture, *Adibasi* January, p 25-38.

Mukherji, Anima, 1950, The pattern of a polyandrous society with particular reference to tribal crime, *Man in India* 39(2-3) April-September, p 56-65.

Mukherjee, Bhabananda, 1961, Comparative study of he kinship systems of six matrilineal tribes, *Eastern Anthropologist* 14(3) September-December, p 216-228, references, tables.

Mukhopadhyay, Lipi and **Mukhopadhyay, Durgadas**, 1989, Tribal development administration, *Social Welfare* 36(3-4) June-July, p 26-29.

Nag, Narendra Gopal, 1970, Implication of cultural and demographic factors on the socio-political trends among Scheduled Tribes, *Vanyajati* 18(2) April, p 51-58, references, tables.

Naik, T. B., 1964, What is a tribe : Conflicting definitions, *Bulletin of Tribal Research and Training Institute* (Chhindwara) 4(1) June, p 1-13.

Narayana, K. V., 1985, Tribals in rural development, *Kurukshetra* 34(2) November, p 7-8 +.

Narayana Reddy, G., 1983, Approaches to tribal development : An overview, *Tribe* 15(1-2) March-June, p 1-14.

Naresh Kumar, 1985, Cooperatives for tribals, *Social Welfare* 32(3) June, p 30-32.

Nehru, Jawahar Lal, 1953, Right approach to tribal peoples, *Indian Journal of Social Work* 14(3) December, p 231-235.

——, 1955, Place of Adivasis in our national life, *Vanyajati* 3(2) April, p 55-57.

——, 1964, Speeches delivered on various occasions, *Vanyajati* 12(3) July, p 127-144.

Oberoi, R. C., 1989, They carry away the bride, *Man in India* 9(4) December, p 403-405.

Oraon, Kartik, 1964, Tribes and tribalism of India, *Journal of Social Research* 7(1-2) March-September, p 36-52, references.

Panchbhai, S. C., 1966, Religion and race as determinants of reference group : A study in stereo types of three Indian tribes, *Indian Journal of Psychology* 41(1) March, p 1-6, references, tables.

——, 1967, The levels of regional and national identification and intergroup relations among Harijans and Adivasis, *Journal of Indian Anthropological Society* 2(1) March, p 27-40, references.

Paswan, Ram Vilas, 1990, Speech by the Union Minister for Labour and Welfare (at) National Conference on problems of Scheduled Tribes, 31st March, 1990, *Vanyajati* 38(2) April, p 7-8.

Pathy, Jaganath, 1987, The agrarian situation in tribal areas, *Journal of Social Economic Studies* 4(2) April-June, p 143-162.

——, 1989, The idea of tribe and the Indian scene, *Man in India* 69(4) December, p 346-358.

Paul, Gemini, 1957, Anthropology and tribal administration, *Vanyajati* 5(1) January, p 4-11.

——, 1957, Importance of egg and cock in Khasi and Jaintia hills, *Vanyajati* 5(2) april, p 66-69, references.

Prasad, R. R., 1985, Tribal culture development, *Administrator* 30(4) October-December, p 347-355, bibliography.

——, 1988, Tribal development in India : Strategies and programmes, *Journal of Rural Development* 7(1) January, p 81-103, bibliography, tables.

Prasada Rao, D. L. and **Venkata Rao, P.**, 1984, Are they right in blaming tribals: A view point on tribal-forest relations, *Vanyajati* 32(3) July, p 17-21.

Raha, Manish Kumar, 1963, Forest in tribal life, *Bulletin of Cultural Research Institute* 2(1), p 56-61, footnotes.

Rangaya, D., 1955, Memorandum submitted to the Backward Classes Commission on behalf of the Bhartiya Adamjati Sevak Singh, Delhi, *Vanyajati* 3(1) January, p 33-39.

Rao, E. N. B. and **Girja Shankar, K.**, 1986, Tribals : Are they better off, *Kurukshetra* 34(4) January, p 30-32.

Rao. G. R. S., 1966, Process of industrialisation and direction of social changes in tribal society, *Journal of Social Research,* September 21(2), p 65-69.

Rao, N. V. N. and **Ram Reddy, R.**, 1986, Minor irrigation and tribal development : An empirical study, *Kurukshetra* 34(2) November, p 31-33.

Ray, Baren, 1989, The tribal problem in India : Some remarks, *Vanyajati* 37(4) October, p 50-54.

Reddy, G. P., 1984, Tribal communities in India : A struggle for identity, *Parlance* 8(2-3) November-December, p 13-20.

Robert, Parkin, 1990, Terminology and alliance in India: Tribal system and the north-south problem, *Contributions to Indian Sociology* 24(1) January-June, p 61-76.

Roy Burman, B. K., 1954, A note on the taxonomy of the tribals with special references to Bengal, *Vanyajati* 2(3) July, p 86-91.

——, 1958-1959, Problem of integration of the tribals in Indian Society, *Adibasi* 3(3-4) August-January, p 9-16.

——, 1961, Meaning and process of tribal integration in a democratic society, *Sociological Bulletin* 10(1) March, p 27-40, references.

——, 1965, Cultural factors in economic development and technological change in tribal areas, *Journal of Social Research* 8(1) March, p 21-32; *Vanyajati* 13(3) July, p 102-113.

——, 1966, Questions relating to inclusion in and exclusion from the list of Scheduled Tribes, *Journal of India Anthropological Society* 1(1) March, p 7-14, references, illustrations.

——, 1966, Structure of bridge and buffer communities in the border areas, *Man in India* 46(2) April-June, p 103-107.

——, 1968, Some dimensions of transformation of tribal societies in India, *Journal of Social Research* 11(1) March, p 88-94.

——, 1969, Some dimensions of transformation of tribal societies in India, *Vanyajati* 17(1) January, p 1-4 +;

——, 1970, Social-political processes in India and integration of the tribal societies, *Vanyajati* 18(1) January, p 6-11.

——, 1970, Tentative framework of an integrated tribal policy, *Inter discipline* 7(4) Winter, p 48-52.

——, 1985, Issues in tribal development, *Mainstream* 23(19) January 5, p 11-14 +; 23(20) January 12, p 20-22.

——, 1987, Historical process in respect of communal land system and poverty alleviation among tribals, *Social Action* 37(4) October-December, p 391-420, bibliography, tables.

——, 1987, Tribals in a global perspective, *Journal of Social Economic Studies* 4(2) April-June, p 95-120.

——, 1989, Critical approach to tribal problems, *Mainstream* 27(42) 15 July, p 12-14.

——, 1989, Society, ecology and land reform in tribal India, *Indian Journal of Public Administration* 35(1) January-March, p 41.

——, 1989, Technology transfer to tribal areas, *Mainstream* 27(44), July 29, p 22-27.

——, 1989, The tribal problems in India : Some remarks, *Vanyajati* 37(4) October, p 50-54.

Roy Burman, J. J., 1990, Environmental management in tribal areas through social forestry, *Vanyajati* 38(1) January, p 26-32.

Sachchidananda, 1959, Political consciousness in tribal Bihar, *Man in India* 39(4) October-December, p 301-308.

——, 1978, Social structure and status and mobility patterns : The case study of tribal women, *Man in India* 58(1) January-March, p 1-12.

Sachindra Narayan, 1989, Tribal development through use of medicinal verbs, *Social Welfare* 36(3-4) June-July, p 30-31.

Sahu, Laxminarayan, 1957, We and the Aboriginals, *Vanyajati* 5(1), p 30-32.

——, 1959, My experiences of work among the hill tribes of India, *Vanyajati* 7(2) April p 49-52.

——, 1961, The problem of the Indian and Aboriginal population, *Vanyajati* 10(2) April, p 70-73.

Samuel, C.J., 1985, Development of tribal economy : Legislative and executive measures, *Cochin University Law Review* 9(1-2) March, June p 87-104, footnotes.

Sanganna, Toyaka, 1984, Problems of definition, *Adibasi* November, p 15-18.

Sanwal, R. D., 1969, Seminar on the tribal situation in India, Simla, *Sociological Bulletin* 18(2) September, p 175-181.

Sanyal, Shubhendu, 1987, An appraisal of the major problems of Scheduled Tribes in India : With particular reference to Bihar, *Man in India* 67(4) December, p 404-423, bibliography, tables.

Saraf, Samarendra, 1969, Tribal unrest : An urgent research problem *Vanyajati* 17(3-4), July-October, p 118-122.

Sarkar, Haribishnu, 1951, Disposal of the dead at the Indus Valley and its survival among the Aboriginal peoples of India, *Man in India* 31(1) January-March, p 23-32 references, tables.

Sarkar, R. M., 1968, Women in tribal India through customs and traditions, *Folklore* 9(12) December, p 458-467, references.

Sarkar, S. S., 1957-1958, Anthropology and tribal welfare, *Adibasi* 2(1), p 6-8.

Satyanarayana, T. V., 1986, Cheaper foodgrains for tribals, *Indian and Foreign Review* 23(16) June 16, p 8-9.

——, 1986, Subsidised foodgrains for tribals, *Yojana* 30(7) April 16, p 19-20.

Sen, Sachin, 1964, Impact of modern forces on castes and tribes, *Journal of Social Research* 7(1-2) March-September, p 113-118.

Sen Gupta, A. K., 1967, Hinduisation and tribalisation: Two case studies, *Folklore* 8(12) December, p 433-438, references.

Sengupta, Nirmal, 1988, Reappraising tribal movements legitimisation and spread, *Economic and Political Weekly* 23(19) May 7, p 943-945; 23(20) May 14, p 1003-1005; 23(21) May 21, p 1054-1055.

Sengupta, P. N., 1956, Studies on the nutritive values of tribal alcoholic beverages, *Bulletin of Department of Anthropology* 5(1) January, p 67-80.

Shah, U. M., 1984, Cooperatives and tribals, *Tribe* 16(3-1) September-December, p 7-19.

——, 1986 Co-operatives and tribals, *Khadi Gramodyog* 31(7) April 9, p 314-322; *Kurukshetra* 34(4) January, p 4-8; *Gramodyog,* 33(3) December, p 158-165.

Shahabuddin, Syed, 1987, New approach to tribal Indian, *Janata* 42(16) October 4, p 7-8.

Sharma, B. D., 1979, Tribal development : The concept and the frame, *Journal of*

Indian Education 7(2) July, p 70.

——, 1985 Administration for tribal development, *Journal of Social and Economic Studies* (New Series) 2(4) October-December, p 361-379.

——, 1985, Tribal welfare legislation and enforcement, *Cochin University Law Review* 9(1-2) March-June, p 19-47.

Sharma, O. P., Literacy trends : Selected tribes vis-a-vis mother tongue, *Economic Times*, January 20, p 5, col. 3-6.

Shastri, Lal Bahadur, 1965, Serve tribals in a dedicated spirit, *Vanyajati* 13(1) January, p 1-2.

Shrikant, L. M., 1968, Socio-economic aspects of prohibition, *Vanyajati* 16(2) April, p 37-40; 69-70.

Shrivastava, Aruna, 1986, Tribals habitats under the impact to urbanisation and industrialisation, *Man and Life* 12(1-2) January-June, p 69-76, bibliography.

Shyam Chaudhuri, N. K., 1952, The enumeration and treatment of tribe in the Indian Census : A study in retrospect, *Man in India* 32(3) July-September, p 160-166, tables.

Singh, K. M. P., 1984, Tips on training needs and middle management for tribals areas, *Survey* 24(1-2), p 19-25, bibliography.

Singh, K. S., 1990, Environment, technology and management in tribal areas, *Man in India* 70(2) June, p 123-130.

Singh, V. P., 1990, Speech of the Prime-Minister (at) National Conference on problems of Scheduled Tribes, Vigyan Bhavan, New Delhi, 31st March, 1990, *Vanyajati* 38(2) April, p 3-6.

Sinha, Surajit, 1957, Tribal cultures of peninsular India as a dimension of little tradition in the study of Indian civilisation : A preliminary statement, *Man in India* 37(2) April-June, p 93-118, references.

——, 1965, Tribe-caste and tribe-peasant continuum in Central India, *Man in India* 45(1) January-March, p 57-83, references, tables.

Sinha, V., et al, 1976, Parental deprivation in relation to intelligence of denotified tribes, *Asian Journal of Psychology and Education* 1(2) July, p 38-39.

Sirsalkar, P. R., 1985, Primitive tribes : Challenge for development, *Tribal Research Bulletin* 7(2) March, p 7-8.

Sivaswamy, K. G., 1948, Serf labour among the Aboriginals, *Indian Journal of Social Work* 8(4) March, p 310-319.

Somasundram, A. M., 1950, Glimpses into primitive culture of India, *Man in India* 30(4) October-December, p 28-45.

Srivastava, R. M., and **Kharde, R. L.**, 1983, Traditional beliefs of tribal Mundas associated with cattle husbandry, *Indian Journal of Extension Education* 19(3-4) September-December, p 77-82, references, tables.

Srivastava, Shakuntala, 1961, A note on the question of dress for the tribals : (with an apology to Dr. Verrier Elwin), *Sociological Bulletin* 10(2) September, p 42-45.

Suryavanshi, Bhagwan Singh, 1959, Romances in the tribals : A living page from the life of the tribals, *Indian Folklore* 2(3) July-September, p 223-225.

Synghal, S., 1984, Integrated tribal development projects, *Kurukshetra* 32(12) September, p 6-8 +.

Thakur, Devendra, 1984, Township and its impact on tribal urbanisation, *Monthly Commentary on India Economic Conditions* 26(3) October, p 7-10.

Tribune (Newspaper), 1988, The neglect of the tribal genius, *Tribune*, July 24, p 1, col. 1-8, editorial

Tripathi, C. B., 1988, Approaches to tribal development and experience, *Man in*

India 68(4) December, p 335-355.

Tripathi, Premananda, 1985, Administration for tribal development : An analytical review, *Indian Journal of Public Administration* 31 (3) July-September, 870-878.

Trivedi, Harshad R., 1989, Nehru and tribals, *Indian Journal of Public Administration* 35(2) April-June, p 286-291.

Udaya Bhaskara Reddy I. and **Chattopadhyay, R. N.**, 1986, Industrializing tribal areas: Boon or banne, *Yojana* 30(5) March 16, p 18-20.

Vanyajati (Periodical), 1964, In memorium : Nehru and the tribes, *Vanyajati* 12(3) July, p 109-110, editorial.

Varma, S.C., 1959, Problems of drinking in the primitive tribes, *Eastern Anthropologist* 12(4) June-August, p 252-256.

Venkatraman, S. R., 1951, The Scheduled Tribes, *Social Service Quarterly* 36(4) April, p 114-117, tables.

——, 1967, Social welfare and exercise of human :ights regarding tribes, *Social Service Quarterly* 53(2) October, p 54-58.

Vidyarthi, L. P., 1957, Anthropology, authority and tribal welfare in India, *Eastern Anthropologist* 11(1).

——, 1963, Approach to tribal integration in India, *Vanyajati* 11(2) April, p 47-50.

——, 1966, Nehru's approach to tribal culture, *Vanyajati* 14(4) October, p 170-175, references.

——, 1966, Social anthropological researches in India : Some preliminary observations, *Journal of Social Research* 9(1).

——, 1968, Cultural change in the tribes of modern India, *Journal of Social Research*, 11(1) March, p 1-36, tables.

——, 1972, Needed urgent research for Fifth Five Year Plan for tribal Bihar, *Research Journal of Ranchi University*, Docombor 8.

——, 1976, Tribal development in independent India and its future, *Main in India* 56(1) p 172-183.

Viegas, Philip, 1987, Land control and tribal struggle for survival, *Social Action* 37(4) October-December p 325-344 footnotes.

Von Furer-Haimendorf, Christoph, 1971, Tribes and Hindu society, *Contributions to Indian Sociology*, New Series, 5, December, p 24-33.

Vyas, N. N., 1968, Economic aspect of tribal life, *Rural India* 31(6) July-August, p 216-218, tables.

——, 1984, Some spatial aspects of tribal culture and development, *Tribe* 16(3-4) September-December, p 1-6.

——, and **Chaudhary, N.D.**, 1983, The socio-economic implications of Guinea worm : A disease in tribal setting, *Tribe* 15(1-2) March-June, p 15-26.

Wandrekar, D. N., 1966 Tackling the problem of the poverty of the Adivasis, *Vanyajati* 14(3) July, p 99-108.

Wilkinson, T. S., 1962, Isolation, assimilation and integration in their historical perspectives, *Bulletin of Tribal Research and Development Institute* (Chhindwara) 2(1) June, p 19-28.

Zutshi, G. L., 1961, Place of forests in tribal economy, *Vanyajati* 9(1) January, p 32-36.

See also Anthropology : Socio Cultural Approach; Clans and Clan System; Criminal Tribes; Detribalisation; Economics : Primitive; Forest Cooperative Societies; Indian Aborigines Friends Society; Kinship Systems: Tribals; Nehru, Jawaharlal: Approach to Tribals; Scheduled Castes and Scheduled Tribes : India; Totemism; Tribal Cooperative Societies; Tribal Development; Tribal Government; Tribal

Leadership; Tribal Uprisings; Tribes and Tribals : Bibliography : India; Tribes and Tribals : History : India; under name of tribes, e.g., Ahoms, etc.

TRIBES AND TRIBALS : INDIA : ANCIENT

Mukherjee, D., 1984, A review of Audumbara coin, *Indian Museum Bulletin*, 19, p 66-68.

Prasad, R. R., 1986, Role of acculturation in the development of primitive tribes, *Tribal Research Bulletin* 8(2) March, p 8-11 +

See also Audumbaras.

TRIBES AND TRIBALS : INDIA : ANDAMAN AND NICOBAR ISLANDS

Agarwal, H. N., 1965, A B O blood groups in Andaman Islands, *Bulletin of Anthropological Survey of India* 14(1-2) January-June, p 59-60, tables.

Bhupinder Singh, 1989, Between two worlds: Five ancient tribal groups of Andaman and Nicobar Islands, *Vanyajati* 37(2) April, p 1-4.

De, P. K., 1985, The vanishing tribals of Andaman Islands, *Social Welfare* at (12) March, p 17-19 +.

Majumdar, Nabendu Datta, 1955, Aboriginal peoples of the Andaman and Nicobar Islands, *Vanyajati* 3(4) October, p 149-150.

Nigam, R. C., 1960, Little known tribes of Andaman Islands : Their problems and prospects, *Vanyajati* 8(1-3) January-July, p 5-97.

Pandit, T. N., 1985, The tribal and the non-tribal in Andaman Islands : A historical perspective, *Journal of Indian Anthropological Society* 10(2) July, p 111-131, bibliography, tables.

Raha, Manish Kumar and **Coomar, Palash Chandra**, 1989, The kinship terms of the Bhantu of Andamans : structural analysis, *Man in India* 68(4) December, p 374-386.

Sarkar, S. S., Blood groups from the Andaman and Nicobar Islands, *Bulletin of Department of Anthropology* 1(1) January, p 25-30, illustrations, references.

Sinha, A. K., 1986, Chotanagpur tribals of Baratang Island : A brief note, *Journal of Social Research*, 29, September, p 73-79.

Shrikant, L. M., 1961, Scheduled Tribes of Andaman and Nicobar Islands : Their conditions and needs, *Vanyajati* 9(3) July, p 90-98.

See also Oraons; Shompen Tribe.

TRIBES AND TRIBALS : INDIA : ANDHRA PRADESH

Anon, 1985, A new thrust to tribal development, *Andhra Pradesh* 28(10) August, p 7-9.

Amar Singh and **Suraj Singh**, 1981, Training needs of tribal farmers, *Indian Journal of Extension Education* 17(3-4) September-December, p 81-88, tables.

Balagopal, K., 1987, A total of arson, *Economic and Political Weekly* 22(29) January 18, p 1169-1171.

Fernades, Walter, 1989, Andhra move to deprive tribals of land, *Social Action* 39(3) July-September, p 308-315, bibliography.

Mohan Rao, K., The ceremonial friendship among the tribal people of Andhra Pradesh, *Man in India* 68(1) March, p 93-104.

Prasada Rao, P. D., 1959, Tribal people of Araku Valley, Vishakapatnam, *Vanyajati* 7(3) July, p 103-105.

Rajyalakshmi, P. and **Geervani, P.**, 1988, Tribal people : Traditions, customs and attitudes related to food and dietary practices: A case study of Vizianagram district, Andhra Pradesh, *Indian Journal of Social Work* 49(1) January, p 45-50.

Ramaswamy, V. S., 1985, Land ownership structure in the tribal areas: A study, *Kurukshetra* 33(9-10) July, p 24-25 +.

Rayudu, C. S., 1985, New milestones in Andhra Pradesh, *Social Welfare* 32(3) June, p 17-19.

Reddy, G. P., 1969, The role of liquor in the culture of the tribes of Andhra Pradesh and its economic implications, *Vanyajati* 17(2) April, p 37-45, tables.

Shankraiah, A. and **Ghanshyam Das, O.**, 1985, P D S in a tribal village, *Kurukshetra* 34(3) December, p 30-32 +.

Somasekhar, A., 1987, Tribal development in Andhra Pradesh : Certain issues, *Man and Life* 13(1-2) January-June, p 67-76, bibliography.

Sudhakar Babu, M., et al, 1984, Variation in taste perception PTC in two tribal populations of Andhra Pradesh, *Indian Anthropologist* 14(1) June, p 63-68, bibliography.

Sujatha, K., Inequality in educational development of tribes : A case study of Andhra Pradesh, *Journal of Educational Planning and Administration* 1(2) April, p 108-125, bibliography, tables.

Suryanarayana, C. and **Chiranjeevi Rao, V.** 19 Marketing in tribal areas, *Indian Journal of Commerce* 38(3) July-September, p 132-140, tables.

Times of India (Newspaper), 1987, A new approach, *Times of India*, September 14, p 6, col. 1-2, editorial.

See also Chenchus; Kshatriyas; Koyas; Malas; Mannedoras; Sriramuly, Bandi; Sugalis; Yanadies.

TRIBES AND TRIBALS : INDIA : ANDHRA PRADESH : HYDERABAD

Gaffoor, Khaja Abdul, 1954, The future of Hyderabad Adivasis, *Vanyajati* 2(3), p 91-94.

Husain, Syed Khaja Mahboob, 1951, Tribal inheritance, *Man in India* 31(2) April-June, p 84-87.

TRIBES AND TRIBALS : INDIA : ARUNACHAL PRADESH

Anon, 1988 (Book review), *Teacher Today* 28(2) October-December, p 124-125. Review of the book : **Thankappan Nair, P.**, 1985, *Tribes of Arunachal Pradesh*, Spectrum Publications, Guwahati, 319 p.

Bachi, R. N., 1979, Family system and inheritance of property among the tribes of Arunachal, *Resarun* 5(1) Spring-Summer, p 38-41, bibliography.

Batra, N. D., 1985, Myths and legends of Arunachal tribes, *Indian and Foreign Review* 22(10) 15 March, p 18-19.

Das, A. K., 1984, Masks and masquerades among the Buddhist tribes of Arunachal Pradesh, *Indian and Foreign Review* 22(10) 15 March, p 18-19.

Gangwar, A. and **Ramakrishanan, P.S.**, 1987, Agriculture and animal husbandry among the Sulungs and Nishis of Arunachal Pradesh, *Social Action* 37(4) October-December p 345-372, bibliography, figures, tables.

Gurubasve, K. S., 1985, Tribal communication in Arunachal Pradesh, Gowda, *Resarun* 1192) Autumn-Winter, p 25-26.

Majumdar, Aurobindo, 1985, Tribal communication : A case study of Arunachal Pradesh, *Vidura* 22(4) August, p 195-200.

Nair, P. Thankappan, 1985, Tribes of Arunachal Pradesh, *Teacher Today* 28(2) October-December, p 124-125.

Sachchidananda, 1988, Economic development, education and social change in Arunachal, *Man in India* 65(1) March, p 33-57.

See also Adis; Bangnis; Bokars; Boris; Gallongs; Hrussos; Khamptis; Khawas;

Lisus; Membas; Mijis; Miris; Monpas; Nishis; Tagins; Wanchos.

TRIBES AND TRIBALS : INDIA : ASSAM

Anon, 1990, (Book review), *Man in India* 70(2) June, p 206-209.

Review of the book: **Paul, M. C.**, 1989, *Dimensions of tribal movements in India : A study of Udayachal in Assam Valley*, Inter-India Publications, New Delhi, p 107.

Burling, Robbins, 1960, A incipient caste organisation in the Garo hills, *Man in India* 40(4) October-December, p 283-299, references.

Buzarbarua, P. M., 1989, Effects of migration and environment on anthropometric characters of Munda population of Assam: A preliminary observation, *Man in India* 69(3) September, p 292-304.

Elwin, Varrier, 1961, The beauty of tribal Assam, *Folklore* 2(4) July-August, p 209-222.

Hussain, Monirul, 1987, Tribal movement for autonomous state in Assam, *Economic and Political Weekly* 22(32) 8 August, p 1329-1332.

Hutton, J. H., 1929, Cultural affinities of the Oraons with the Hill tribes of Assam, *Man in India* 9(1) January-March, p 1-6.

Kar, R. K. and **Sharma, J. L.**, 1990, The Oraons of Assam, *Vanyajati* 38(2) April, p 22-32.

Kingdon-Ward, F., 1946, What of the tribes ? *Man in India* 26(2) June, p 110-119.

Mitra, Mrinal K., et al, 1985, Some observations on rural indebtedness, *Rajasthan Economic Journal* 9(2) July, p 62-74, bibliography.

Mukherjee, Deba Prasad, 1963, Variation in defective colour vision among some tribes of Assam, *Bulletin of Anthropological Survey of India* 12(1-2) January-June, p 39-42, references, tables.

Pugh, B. M., 1961, Christianity and the tribal communities of Assam, *Religion and Society* 8(3) September, p 46-52, appendix.

Sen Gupta, P. N., 1953, Population studies and living conditions of the tribes in the Padam and Minyong areas of Abor hills (Assam), *Bulletin of Department of Anthropology* 2(1) January, p 91-112, tables.

Thakkar, A. C., 1941, Census of Assam tribals, *Man in India* 21(40 October-December, p 243-247.

See also Bodos; Hill Tribes; Karbis; Mishings.

TRIBES AND TRIBALS : INDIA : BIHAR

Amar Kumar Singh, et al, 1987, The myth of the healthy tribal, *Social Change* 17(1) March, p 3-23, bibliography, figures, tables.

——, 1988, Tribal attitudes to the tribals and non-tribals in South Bihar, *Social Change* 18(2) June, p 3-27, bibliography, tables

Anon, 1985, (Book review) *Management and Labour Studies* 10(1) January, p 46-47.

Review of the book : **Biswas, R. K.**, et al, 1985, *Industries face to face with tribal people : The case of Chotanagpur in Bihar*, Ranchi, NIPM, 66 p.

——, 1985, Industry, police, carpet-baggers run amuck in Chotanagpur, *Link* 21(50) 21 July, p 4-9.

——, 1985, Industry takes away Adivasi land, gives jobs to outsiders, *Link* 27(50) July 21, p 10-15.

——, 1985, (Book review), *Contribution to Indian Sociology* (New Series) 20(1) January-June, p 155-158; *Sociological Bulletin* 33(1-2) March-September, p 152-154.

Review of book : **Sachchidananda and Mandal, B. B.**, 1985, *Industrialisation* *and the social disorganisation : A study of tribals in Bihar*, **Concept Publishing** Company, New Delhi, 164 p.

_____, 1987, For a democratic solution to problems of Bihar tribals, *New Age* 35(43) October 25, p 9.

_____, 1987, Tribal sub-plan programme, *Times of India* (Magazine) January 22, p`11, col. 1-8 +, tables.

Bahuguna, Sunderlal, 1990, INTACH Seminar on problems facing tribals and launching of Chipko movement in Chotanagpur, held at the Grove, Hazaribagh on October 22 and 23, *Man in India* 70(1) March, p 96-70.

Chakravarti, M. R., et al, 1985, Environmental hazards in reproduction performance among Chotanagpur tribals, South Bihar, India, *Journal of Indian Anthropological Society* 20(2) July, p 137-144, bibliography, tables.

Das, Arvind N., 1985, Bihar society in perspective : Roots of regional imbalance, *Times of India*, October 24, p 8, col 3-5; October 25, p 8, col 7-8.

Dayal, L., 1984, Industrialisation in tribal areas, *Bihar Journal of Public Administration* 1(1) Spring, p 62-64.

Ghosh, B. N., 1967, The ways of acquiring mates in tribal Chotanagpur, *Folklore* 8(11) November, p 403-410, references.

Guglani, P. L., 1986, A probe into tribal farming in Bihar, *Kurukshetra* 34(4) January, p 25-26.

Hassan, M. K., 1986, Impact of industrialisation on mental health of tribals, *Social Change* 16(4) December, p 30-33, bibliography, tables.

Jabbar Alam, M., 1985, Tribals starving to extinction, *New Age* 33(25) June, 23, p 5.

_____, 1986, Injecting communalism into tribal areas, *New Age* 34(39) 28 September, p 11.

_____, 1986, Terror against tribals in Rohtas district, *New Age* 34(9) March, 2, p 8 +.

_____, 1986, Tribal unrest in Bihar : Demand for Jharkhand State revived, *New Age* 34(5) February 2, p 8-9.

_____, 1987, CPI condemns Bihar repression of tribals, *New Age*, 35(48) November, 29, p 6.

Jay, Edward 1961, Revitalisation movements in tribal India, *Journal of Social Research* 4(1-2) March-September, p 282-315, references.

Kashi N. Singh and **Rama Shankar Singh**, 1984, Levels of regional and tribal development in tribal areas : Are they identical, *National Geography Journal of India* 30(1) March, p 1-12, appendix, tables.

Moulik, T. K., 1987, Palamau tribals : Towards integrated development, *Economic Times* May 21, p 5, col. 3-6.

Mukhopadhyay, Durgadas, 1980, Tribals in Bihar, *Indian and Foreign Review* 23(16) June 15, p 15 +.

Qamar, Ahsan, 1987, Tribal development strategy needs rethinking, *Yojana* 31(5) March 16, p 18-22, tables.

Rajendran, C. P., 1988, Women power, *Illustrated Weekly of India* 107(32) August 7, p 40-41.

Sachchidananda, 1955, Class and caste in tribal Bihar, *Man in India* 35(3) July-September, p 195-202.

Sahay, B. N. and **Singh, B K.**, 1969, Representation of tribals in gram panchayats, *Journal of Social Research* 12(2) September, p 130-136, references, tables.

_____, 1970, Political consciousness among the tribals and their representation in gram panchayats, *Vanyajati* 18(1) January, p 12-16, tables.

Sahu, Chaturbhuj and **Dayal N.**, 1985, Cerunmen types among tribal population of Bihar, *Indian Journal of Physical Anthropology and Human Genetics* 11(1-2) April-August, p 95-98, bibliography, tables.

Sanyal, Shubhendu, 1988, Primitive tribes of Bihar : Strategy for development, *Man in India* 68(4) December, p 356-368, bibliography.

Sao, Suman, et al, 1985, A model of tribal industrial growth : Cases study of rope making, *Man and Life* 11(3-4) July-December, p 207-220, bibliography, tables.

Shaileshwar Prasad, 1960, Where tribes and casts meet : Some preliminary observations, *Journal of Social Research* 3(2) September, p 132-144, references, tables.

Sinha, H. S. P. and **Ranjan, R.**, 1981, An analysis of tribal loanees in repayment of loans, *Indian Journal of Extension Education* 17(3-4) September-December, p 54-65, references, tables.

Sinha, S. C., et al., 1969, The concept of Diku among the tribes of Chotanagpur, *Man in India* 49(2) April-June, p 121-138, references

Srivastava, R. M. and **Kherde, R. L.**, 1984, Tribal economy : An analytical view, *Tribal Research Bulletin* 7(1) September, p 12-15.

Thakur, Devendra, 1985, Bihar tribals share benefits of green revolution, *Link* 28(19) December 15, p 26-27; *Monthly Commentary on Indian Economic Conditions* 27(4) November, p 7-9.

Vidyarthi, L. P., 1964, The changing face of tribal Bihar: Some preliminary observations on the concept of detribalisation, *Journal of Social Research* 7(1-2) March-September, p 53-61, references.

See also Ho Tribes Women; Mundas; Santals; Tharus.

TRIBES AND TRIBALS : INDIA : BIHAR : BIBLIOGRAPHY

Anon, 1988, (Book review), *Man in India* 68(2-3) June-September, p 305.
Review of the book : **Gour, P. N.**, ed., 1988, *Bihar Tribal Bibliography*, Patna Library Pub., Patna, 135 p.

TRIBES AND TRIBALS : INDIA : BIHAR : CHOTANAGPUR

Chakravarti, M. R., et al, 1988, Environmental hazards in reproduction performance among Chotanagpur tribals, South Bihar, India, *Journal of Indian Anthropological Society* 20(2) July, p 137-140, bibliography, tables.

Ekka, P., 1962, The Adivasis of Chotanagpur : How will they adjust to the modern world : *Social Action* 12(4) April, p 188-189, tables.

Ghosh, B. N., 1967, The ways of acquiring mate in tribal Chotanagpur *Folklore* 8(11) November, p 403-410, references.

Singh, B. K., 1989, A study of nutritional status of tribal farmers in Ranchi district of Chotanagpur in Bihar, *Economic Affairs* 34(1) January-March, p 58-63, tables.

Sinha, S. C., **Sen, Jyoti** and **Panchbhai, Sudhir**, 1969, The concept of Diku among the tribes of Chotanagpur, *Man in India* 49(2) April-June, p 121-139, references.

TRIBES AND TRIBALS : INDIA : BIHAR : JAMSHEDPUR

Sharma, T. R., 1962, A tribal community in an industrial context: A case study in Jamshedpur city, *Journal of Social Research* 5(1) March, p 114-123, references, tables.

TRIBES AND TRIBALS : INDIA : CENTRAL PROVINCES

Baduri, Manindra Bhusan, 1941, The Aboriginal tribes of the Udaipur State (C. P.), *Man in India* 21(2-3) April-September, p 92-126, footnotes.

Elwin, Verrier, 1942, The duration of marriage among the Aboriginals of the Maikal hills, *Man in India* 22(1) January-March, p 11-21, footnotes

TRIBES AND TRIBALS : INDIA : DECCAN

Dube, S. C., 1950, Inter-tribal relations : A study, *Man in India* 30(2-3) April-September, p 73-80.

TRIBES AND TRIBALS : INDIA : GUJARAT

Anon, 1985, (Book review), *Tribune* 15(4) June, p 3-4.
Review of the book : **Shah, Ghanshyam**, 1985, *Economic differentiations and tribal economy*, Ajanta Publication, Delhi, 152 p.

——— 1985, Profile of a tribal child of Panchmahals, *Social Welfare* 32(3) June, p 28-29.

———, 1986, (Book review), *Social Action* 36(1) January-March, p 120-122.
Review of the book : **Shah, Ghanshyam**, 1985, *Tribal education in Gujarat*, Ajanta Publication, New Delhi, 152 p.

Chanderverker, Pushker, 1961, A scheme for Folk Culture Institute in Gujarat, *Folklore* 2(5) September-October, p 318-322.

Das, Biswaroop, 1986, Submerging tribal belt in Gujarat, *State and Society* 6(1) January-March, p 24-52, footnotes.

Desai, Ambudhal, T. and **Kulkarni, K. M.**, 1988, From tribal villages of North Gujarat, *Annals of National Association of Geographers India* 8(1) June, p 23-30.

Desai, Anjana P., 1985, On perceiving problems of rural development, *Deccan Geographer* 23(1) January-June, p 95-102, bibliography, tables.

Desai, A. T. and **Kulkarni, K. M.**, 1988, Four tribal villages of North Gujarat, *Annals of the National Association of Geographers, India* 8(1) June, p 23-30.

Krishnan, Jairam, 1986, The Chotta Udepur experiment, *Economic Trends* (Supplement) 16(11) March, p 1-4.

———, 1988, Adivasi upsurge at Dharol, *Economic Times* January 17, p 3, Col. 1-6.

Naik, T. B., 1949, Labour problems of tribal Gujarat, *Eastern Anthropologist* 3(1) September, p 22-27.

———, 1950-1951, Aboriginals of Gujarat, *Eastern Anthropologist*, 4(1) September-November, p 42-51.

Negi, R. S., 1968, Sporadic occurrence of Sickle-Cell trait in peninsular Gujarat, *Bulletin of Anthropological Survey of India* 17(4) October, p 379-381, tables.

Patel, Ashok A. and **Patel, M. R.**, 1987, Gujarat and its tribals, *Kurukshetra* 35(5) February, p 13-14.

Patel, Harbans, 1985, Why tribal girls stay away : A case study in Gujarat, *Mainstream* 24(3) October 26, p 26-28, tables.

Shah, Ghanshyam, 1985, Economic differential and tribal identity: A case study of Chaudhries, *Perspectives in Education* 1(2) April, p 129-131.

See also Ahoms; Kolghas; Koragas; Padas; Rabaris; Siddis; Waghers; Warlis.

TRIBES AND TRIBALS : INDIA : HIMACHAL PRADESH

Amar Dev and **Banerjee Guha, Swapna**, 1986, Tribes in Himachal Pradesh : Socio-economic characteristics, *National Geographical Journal of India* 32(4) December, p 281-286.

Sharma, Bansi Ram, 1984, Dr. Siddheswar Varma's notes on tribal languages of Kinnaur in Himachal Pradesh, *Vishveshvaranand Indological Journal* 22(1-2) June-December, p 138-148.

Sharma, H. R., et al, 1987, Pattern of income, consumption and employment,

Economic Affairs 32(2) June, p 81-88, appendix, tables.
See also Kinnaurs; Pangwalas.

TRIBES AND TRIBALS : INDIA : HIMALAYAN REGION

Kapoor, A. K., et al, 1990, Semi-Nomadism and Transhumance in Central Himalayas : A pragmatic perspective, *Man in India* 70(1) March, p 47-60.

TRIBES AND TRIBALS : INDIA : JAMMU AND KASHMIR

See Bodhs; Swanglas.

TRIBES AND TRIBALS : INDIA : KARNATAKA

Continho, V. B., 1985, Tribal protection in Karnataka : An appraisal, *Cochin University Law Review* 9(1-2) March-June, p 117-128.

Goswami, B. B. and **Morab, S. G.**, 1988, Tribes and casts and functionaries in the temples of Karnataka, *Man in India* 68(1) March, p 61-69.

Kurian, K. V., 1985, The ex-criminal tribes of North Karnataka : A study, *Quarterly Journal of Mythic Society* 16(3-4) July-December, p 366-377.

See also Hakkipikkis; Soligas.

TRIBES AND TRIBALS : INDIA : KERALA

Anon, 1984, (Book review), *Man and Life* 10(1-2) January-June, p 107-109. Review of the book : **Anantha Krishna Iyer, L. K.**, 1981, *The tribes and castes of Cochin*, Cosmo Publications, Delhi, 3 vols.

——, 1985, The exploitation of Kerala tribals, *Link* 28(4) September 1, p 16-18.

——, 1988, Kerala shows the way, *Times of India*, August 2, p 4, col 1-2.

Bose, S. C., 1986, Planning for tribal development, *Yojana* 80(5) March 16, p 21-23, tables.

Devan, P. K., 1988, A medical mission for the tribals of Wynad, *Social Welfare* 34(11) February, p 9-10.

Gangadharan, K. A., 1985, Tribal welfare and development in Kerala, *Cochin University Law Review* 9(1-2) March-June, p 173-188.

Karunakaran, C. K., 1985, Legislative and executive measures for tribal welfare in Kerala, *Cochin University Law Review* 9(1-2) March-June, p 203-212.

Kunhaman, M., 1985, The tribal economy of Kerala : An intra regional analysis, *Economic and Political Weekly* 20(11) March 16, p 466-474.

Luiz, A. A. D., 1958 Tribes of Kerala : Move tribes to rural areas, *Vanyajati* 6(1) January, p 39-41.

Madhava Menon, T., 1985, Law and tribal societies in Kerala, *Cochin University Law Review* 9(1-2) March-June, p 157-172.

Mathew, K. J., 1986, We are the slaves of the lords of the hill, We are the slaves of the lords of the field, *Religion and Society* 33(2) June, p 55-68.

Nayar, P. K. B., 1985, Tribal sub-plan of Kerala : Critical appraisal, *Cochin University Law Review* 9(1-2) March-June, p 189-202.

Prashant, D., 1985, Land reforms and distribution of land among Scheduled Tribes in Kerala, *Cochin University Law Review* (1-2) March-June, p 213-222.

Ramachandra Raj, G., 1984, Problems and prospects of tribal development in Kerala, *Journal of Kerala Studies* 9(1-4) March-December, p 275-278.

Sankara Narayan, A. S. and **Lakshmanan, K. K.**, 1987, A tribal festival in Attappady, Kerala : An aspect of worship of nature as God, *Folklore* 28(10) October, p 235-236.

See also Cholanaickans; Uralies.

TRIBES AND TRIBALS : INDIA : MADHYA PRADESH

Anon, 1964, Economic organisation of the tribes of Madhya Pradesh, *Bulletin of Tribal Research and Development Institute* (Chhindwara) 4(2) December, p 1-32, tables.

———, 1964, The water scarcity problem in Tamia special multipurpose tribal development block, *Bulletin of Tribal Research Training and Development Institute* (Chhindwara) 4(1) June, p 44-49, references, tables.

———, 1965, Indebtedness among the tribal people of the scheduled areas of Madhya Pradesh, *Bulletin Tribal Research and Development Institute* (Bhopal) 5(1-2) June-December, p 1-18, tables.

———, 1966, A study of the tribal people and tribal areas of Madhya Pradesh, *Bulletin of Tribal Research and Development Institute* (Bhopal) 6(2) December, p 3-176.

———, 1985, (Book review), *Economic Trends* 31(6) March, p 1-4+; *Financial Express* 9(5) June, p 5-8.

Review of the book : **Patel, M.L.**, 1985, *Planning strategy for tribal development*, Inter-India Publication, New Delhi, p 191.

———, 1986, (Book review), *Indian Express* (Magazine) March 9, p 5, col 4-7.

Review of book : **Raizada, Ajit**, 1986, *Tribal Development in Madhya Pradesh: A Planning Perspective*, Inter-India Publication, New Delhi.

———. 1989, Uneasy quiet, *Illustrated Weekly of India* 110(36) September 3, p 20-23.

Athavale, M.C. and **Nahatkar, Sunil**, 1983, Evaluation study of tribal area development programme is Konta and Dantwara, Bastar district, Madhya Pradesh, *Co-operative Perspective* 18(3) October-December, p 93-100.

Banerjee, S. P., 1961, Crimes in tribal areas, *Bulletin of Tribal Research and Development Institute* (Chhindwara) 1(2) December, p 4-8.

Bapat, N. V., 1959, Scouting among tribals, *Vanyajati* 7(3) July, p 82-83.

Barange, B. G., 1963, An annotated bibliography on tribal indebtedness, *Bulletin of Tribal Research and Development Institute* (Chhindwara) 3(1) June, p 60-66.

Batria, P., 1983, Crime and witchcraft among the tribes of Madhya Pradesh, *Bulletin of Tribal Research and Development Institute* (Chhindwara) 3(1) June, p 21-29, references, tables.

———, 1969, Policing in tribal areas, *Bulletin of Tribal Research and Development Institute* (Bhopal) 7(1-2) June-December, p 5-18.

Brij Raj Singh and **Thapar, Rajiv**, 1985, Bastar : Impact of change : A viewpoint, *Link* (Supplement) 27(26) February 3, p 34-37, tables.

——, 1985, Forestry and tribal development *Link*, (Supplement) 27(26) February 3, p 24-28.

Chaturvedi, K. C., 1957, Vindhya's tribals in new Madhya Pradesh, *Vanyajati* 5(1) January, p 39-41, references

Chauhan, Indira, 1988, Tribal development administration in Madhya Pradesh, *Eastern Anthropologist* 41(1) January-March, p 87-92.

Despande, W.R., et al, 1988, Travails of the tribals of Jhabua, *Indian Farming* 38(8) November, p 33-35.

Dhruw, P. R., 1968, The tribal students of Madhya Pradesh, *Vanyajati* 16(3) July, p 97-99.

Dube, Krishna Chandra, 1960, Problem of Aboriginal debt in Bhindranawagarh subdivision of the Raipur district (M.P.), *Vanyajati* 8(2) April, p 73-80, tables.

Dube, S.C., 1948, Arrow marriage, *Eastern Anthropologist* 2(1) September,

p 22-26.

Ghosal, S.L., 1986, Tribal Jhabua in transition : Some factors, *Kurukshetra* 34(4) January, p 27-29 +.

Gupta, Ram Pratap and **Sunil**, 1985, Madhya Pradesh : Development of tribals, *Economic Trends* 8(3), p 1-5.

Jarial, Gurpal Singh, 1984, Creativity as a prediction of entrepreneurial success among tribals, *Experiments in Education* 11(12) February, p 110-114, references.

Joseph, A.N.T., 1989, Ethnozoology of reptiles in relation to health care among tribals in Madhya Pradesh, *Social Action* 39(4) October-December, p 405-422.

Kurup, A. M., 1962, Glimpses of life and culture of the tribes of Madhya Pradesh, *Vanyajati* 1(4) October, p 139-145.

Mehta, Shalini, 1983, Role of voluntary and government organisations in tribal welfare : A case study of Mandala district of Madhya Pradesh, *Eastern Anthropologist* 41(1) January-March, p 49-64, tables.

Mukherjee, D.P., 1985, Skeletal development of tribal children : Kanwar and Oraon of Surguja district (M.P.), *Journal of Indian Anthropological Society* 20(1) March, p 77-85, bibliography, tables.

——— and **Das, N.K.**, 1985, Age at menarche in tribal girls : The Kanwar and the Oraon of Surguja district, M.P., *Journal of Indian Anthropological Society* 20(2) July, p 153-158, bibliography, tables.

Naskar, Santosh K., 1989, Status of tribal women in Bastar, *Vanyajati* 37(3) July, p 16-20.

——— and **Naskar, Indrani**, 1989, Pre-Independence tribal revolution in Bastar : A historical analysis, *Vanyajati* 37(2) April, p 30-34.

Negi, Raghunath Singh et al, 1962, Distribution of middle phalangeal hair in some Bastar population, *Bulletin of Anthropological Survey of India* 11(3-4) p 175-191, appendix, references, tables.

Negi, Raghunath Singh and **Ahmad, S. Hasim**, 1962, The Batra, Muria and Mahra of Bastar : A blood group genetic study, *Bulletin of Anthropological Survey of India* 11(3-4), 201-209, references, tables.

Negi, R.S. et al, 1982, P T C taste variation in Bastar (Central India), *Indian Journal of Physical Anthropology and Human Genetics* 8(1) April, p 41-46, bibliography, tables.

Pandey, N. N., 1961, Changing status of the 'Siraha' in a Bastar village, *Vanyajati* 9(2) April, p 55-57.

Parte, Swaroop Singh, 1970, Tribes of Bastar and their forest rights, *Vanyajati* 18(2) April, p 77-83.

Paul, S.P. and **Baghel, A.S.**, 1987, Sociological constraints and attitude to development of tribal farmers in the tribal areas of Madhya Pradesh, *Journal of Rural Development* 6(2) March, p 197-21.

———, 1989, Elements of a development plan for tribal area farmers of Madhya Pradesh, *Journal of Rural Development* 8(1) January, p 71-78.

Pawar, S.S. and **Bhuvanendran, P.**, 1988, Tribal education : A study in M.P.S.S., *Kurukshetra* 36(4) January, p 18-21.

———, 1988, Tribal education in the West Zone of Madhya Pradesh, *Social Welfare* 34(11) February, p 4-5.

Pramod Kumar and **Sood, Atul**, 1985, Tribal sub-plan : A critical appraisal, *Link* (Supplement) 27(26) February 3, p 48-54, tables.

Pramod Kumar and **Yadav, Bhupender** 1985, *Link* (Supplement) 27(26) February 3, p 7-12.

Rajagopal, 1986, Agricultural labourers in tribal areas, *Kurukshetra* 34(4) January, p 17-18+.

Satish Kumar, 1985, Development in tribal areas : An overview, *Link* (Supplement) 27(26) February 3, p 13-18, table.

Shamsuddin, 1988, Glimpses of Bastar, *Social Welfare* 34(11) February, p 2-3.

——, 1989, The tribal world of Bastar, *Social Welfare* 35(10) January p 17-20.

Sharma, J.C., 1970, Convergence and divergence of dermatoglyphic traits in human populations based on a study of the four tribal groups of Bastar, *Eastern Anthropologist* 23(1) January-April, p 17-35.

Sharma, K.K.N., 1989, A note on the distribution of matrimonial distance of the Khairwar tribal population of Surguja District, Madhya Pradesh, *Man in India* 69(3) September, p 267-271.

Sharma, K.N., 1969, Development planning for M.P. tribes, *Bulletin of Tribal Research and Development Institute* (Bhopal) 7(1-2) June-December, p 19-25; *Journal of Social Research* 12(1) March, p 93-99.

Sharma, Suryanarayan, 1985, Accent on tribal area development, *Commerce* 151(3873) August 17, p 325-326.

Shashi, S.S., 1971, The Baigas of Madhya Pradesh, *Children's World*, October 10, p 18.

Srivastava, R.N., 1988, Moving wheels of machine: The impact of mining industrialisation of the Bastar tribal region of Central India, *Man and Life* 14(3-4) July-December, p 119-137.

Srivastava, Ratish, 1984, Tribals of Madhya Pradesh and Forest Bill of 1980, *Man in India* 64(3) September, p 320-327.

Swaminathan T., 1985, The magical script, *Link* (Supplement) 27(26) February 3, p 55-63.

Tripathi, G.P., 1985, Scheduled Tribes and tribal legislation in Madhya Pradesh, *Cochin University Law Review* 9(1-2) March-June, p 105-116.

Tripathy, Sangam, 1989, A silent revolution of forest dwellers and a tribals, *Janata* 44(7) April, p 15-16.

Varma, S. C., 1961, Tribal problems, *Bulletin of Tribal Research Institute* (Chhindwara) 1(2) December, p 16-18.

Vishwa Mohan, 1964, Remnants of shifting cultivation, *Eastern Anthropologist* 17(1) January-April, p 31-38, references.

Yadav, Bhupender, 1985, Growing up in wilderness, *Link* (Supplement) 27(26) February 3, p 19-23.

—— and **Nasharan Singh, G.**, 1985, Tribals : Myth and Reality, *Link* (Supplement) 27(26) February 3, p 48-54, tables.

See also Bhainas; Bhatras; Bhils; Dhurwas; Dorlas; Koles; Korkus; Murias; Sihavas.

TRIBES AND TRIBALS : INDIA : MAHARASHTRA

Anon, 1987, Using the violence bogey against the Left, *Economic and Political Weekly* 22(34) August 22, p 1437-1438.

Chinai, Rupa, 1986, Adivasis : Conflicts within the circle of life, *Indian Express* (Magazine) March 9, p 3, col 1-8.

Gaikwad, John S., 1986, A demographic profile of tribals in Maharashtra state, *Tribal Research Bulletin* 9(1) September, p 16-27 +.

——, 1986, Role of minor forest produce in tribal economy, *Tribal Research Bulletin* 8(2) March, p 12-16.

——, 1987, Transformation of economy of the tribal cultivators through the electric motor pumps, *Tribal Research Bulletin* 9 (2) March, p 18-20.

Karva, S.P., 1986, Training tribal youth, *Tribal Research Bulletin* 9 (1) September, p 28-29.

Kulkarni, R.R. and **Bolkar, S.T.**, 1986, Tribal leaders and their role in agricultural development, *Tribal Research Bulletin* 8(2) March, p 17-20.

Kulkarni, Sharad, 1986, Adivasis, law and social justice, *Tribal Research Bulletin* 8(2) March, p 1-7, bibliography.

Lakshminarayana, 1986, Tribal development in Maharashtra, *Tribal Research Bulletin* 9(1) September, p 1-10, bibliography.

Pawar, H.S. and **Patil, R.P.**, 1987, Adoption behaviour of the tribal farmers from Surgana Taluka (Nasik district) in respect of paddy cultivation, *Tribal Research Bulletin* 9(2) March, p 15-17.

Ramachandran, Janani, 1988, The Warli tribal community: Economic realities and the Warli's view point. *Annals of the National Association of Geographers, India*, 8(2) December, p 1-9.

Sathe, Madhusudan Dattatraya, 1988, Katkari labour in Charcoal making. *Economic and Political Weekly* 23(34) July 30, p 1565-1567.

Surana, M.B., 1985, Socio-economic survey of tribals in the proposed M.A.D.A. pocket in Buldbana district, *Tribal Research Bulletin* 7(2) March, p 9-13.

———, 1986, Supply of milch animals to Adivasis in Dhule district, *Tribal Research Bulletin* 9(1) September, p 11-15.

———, 1987, Research designs for evaluation of tribal development programme, *Tribal Research Bulletin* 9(2) March, p 5-8, bibliography.

Times of India (Newspaper), 1989, Tribals short charged, *Times of India*, May 11, p 4, col 1-2, editorial.

See also Warlis.

TRIBES AND TRIBALS : INDIA : MAHARASHTRA : BOMBAY

Koppar D.M., 1956, Primitive tribes of Dharampur, *Journal of Anthropological Society of Bombay*(NS) 10(1) March, p 8-24.

TRIBES AND TRIBALS : INDIA : MANIPUR

Chakravarti, Manish Ranjan and **Mukherjee, Deba Prasad**, 1962, Dermatoglyphic study on the tribes and castes of Nagaland and Manipur, *Bulletin of Anthropological Survey of India* 11(3-4). p 233-234, tables.

Mayanglambam, Mani Babu and **Mayanglambam, Suniti Bala**, 1989, Earlobe attachment and dominant eye among the Phayengs of Manipur, *Man in India* 69(3) September, p 285-291.

———, 1989, Patterns of hand clasping, arm folding and handedness among the Phayengs of Manipur; *Man in India* 69(1) March, p 87-93.

See also Nagas; Tangkhul; Taraos.

TRIBES AND TRIBALS : INDIA : MEGHALAYA

See also Hajongs.

TRIBES AND TRIBALS : INDIA : MID INDIA

Ishtiaque, M., 1989, Changing patterns of linguistic identity among the Austric speaking tribes in Mid-India, *National Geographical Journal of India* 35 (Part 2) June, p 140-152.

TRIBES AND TRIBALS : INDIA : NORTH EASTERN

Anon, 1986, (Book Review), *Contributions of Indian Sociology* (New series) 20(1) January-June, p 155-156.

Review of the book : **Mishra S.N.**, 1985, *Tribal economic transformation : The North East Indian pattern*, Tokyo, Institute of Development, Economics, p 11.

Gangwar, A.K., 1990, Tribals and forests of North-Eastern India : Strategies for sustainable development, *Vanyajati* 38(2) April, p 14-21.

Gangmumei, Kabui, 1989, Tribes in North-East India in historical perspective The emerging pattern and the perspective for the future, *Vanyajati* 37(4) October, p 12-19.

Goswami, Atul, 1984, Tribal development with special reference to North-East India, *Social Scientist* 12(8) August, p 55-60, footnotes.

Ramakrishnan, P.S., 1985, Tribal man in the humid tropics of the North East, *Man in India* 65(1) March, p 1-32, bibliography, tables.

Roy Burman, B.K., 1986, Institutional finance and tribal development, *Mainstream* 24(20) January 18 p 16-22.

——, 1989, Problems and prospects of tribal development in North-East India, *Economic and Political Weekly* 24(13) April, p 693-697.

Roy Burman, J.J., 1990, Tribal tradition and modern development in North-East India, *Vanyajati* 38(2) April, p 9-13.

Samanta, R.K. and **Adhikary, M.M.**, 1988, Marriage systems among tribals of North-East India : An overview, *Man in India* 68(4) December, p 401-412.

TRIBES AND TRIBALS : INDIA : NORTH EAST FRONTIER AGENCY

Anon, 1958, NEFA highlanders, *Indian Folklore* 1(1) January-March, p 85-88, illustrations.

Kingdon-Ward, F., 1946, What of the tribe, *Man in India* 26(3) June, p 110-119.

Minyong and **Pangi**, 1954, Investigations into the dietary habits of the Aboriginal tribes of Abor hills (North East Frontier), Part 2, *Bulletin of Department of Anthropology* 3(2) July, p 155-173; Part 3, *Bulletin of Department of Anthropology* 4(2) July, 1955, p 69-95.

Srivastava, L.R.N., 1966, Hair style, head dress and their social significance among some of the tribes of North-East Frontier of India, *Bulletin of Cultural Research Institute* 5(1-2), p 110-125, footnotes references.

Von Furer-Haimendorf, Christoph, 1949, Anthropology and administration in the tribal areas of the North-East Frontier, *Eastern Anthropologist* 3(1) September, p 8-14.

TRIBES AND TRIBALS : INDIA : ORISSA

Aiyappan, A., 1964, Tribal languages of Orissa, *Adibasi*, January, p 5-6.

Anon, 1964, Tribal ethnography of Orissa, *Adibasi*, January, p 41 + illustration.

——, 1967, A summary of the study on impact of industrialisation on the tribals of Sundargarh district, *Adibasi* 8(4) January, p 46-51.

——, 1968, A study on the socio-religious life of tribals in Gudvella area, Bolangir district, *Adibasi* 9(4) January, p 3-30.

——, 1986, All round growth at Chatikhona, *Link* (Supplement) 28(30) March 2, p 20-21.

——, 1986, Bring them to school, *Link* (Supplement) 28(30) March 2, p 33-34.

——, 1986, Bringing tribal into the mainstream, *Link* (Suupplement) 28(30) March 2, p 29-32.

——, 1986, Home of tribal art, *Link* (Supplement) 28(30) March 2, p 35-36.

——, 1986, Into the future, *Link* 28(30) March 2, p 37-40.

Baboo, Balgovind, 1986, Economic exchanges in a tribal village, *Man in India* 66(2) June, p 151-65.

Bebura, N.K. and **Misra, K.K.**, 1985, Rcligions rites and festivals among the tribes of Orissa, *Vision* 4(4) - 5(1) April-September, p 66-86, bibliography.

Bose, Nirmal Kumar, 1955-1956, The use of social science, *Adibasi*, 1, p 5-6.

Das, Anirudha, 1968, Impact of Christianity on the tribals in Orissa: The historical background, *Adibasi* 10(1) April, p 87-99.

Das, Nityananda, 1960, Changing pattern of a Koraput village, *Vanyajati* 8(2) April, p 65-72.

Das, S.R., Mukherjee, D.P. and **Sastry, D.B.**, 1968, A somatological survey of five tribes in the Koraput district, Orissa, *Bulletin of Anthropological Survey of India* 17(4) October, p 400-422, references, tables.

Dinbandhu, Mahal, 1985, The role of Tribal Development Cooperative Corporation of Orissa Limited for the development of tribals, *Tribal Research Bulletin* 7(2) March, p 20-23.

——, 1985, The Tribal Development Cooperative Corporation of Orissa, *Cooperative Perspective* 20(3) October-December, p 42-46.

Jena, A. C., 1986, Forms of exploitation in tribal areas and their consequences : Some observations in Keonjhar district of Orissa, *Man and Life* 12(3-4) July-December, p 173-180, bibliography.

Jena, Krishna Chandra, 1959, The Adivasis of Orissa, *Rural India* 22(1) January, p 39-40.

Kamila, Bana Behari, 1983, Occupational status of parents of Harijans and Tribal Welfare Department high school students of Orissa, *National Journal of Education* 6(1) September, p 56-64, references, tables.

Krishna, Sumi, 1985, In the heart of Simillpal, *Hindustan Times* (Magazine) August 4, p 1, col 1-8.

Mahatab, H.K., 1957-1958, Our Adibasi problem, *Adibasi* 2(1) p 1-2.

Mishra, Satish, 1986, A silver of hope for Adivasis, *Link* (Supplement) 28(30) March 2, p 4-19.

Mohapatra, P. C., 1985, Consumption pattern of Scheduled Tribes : A case study of Koraput district, Orissa, *Vision* 5(2) October-December, p 15-22, bibliography, tables.

Mukhiya, Prabhat Kumar, 1960, The primitive people of Orissa, *Vanyanati* 8(4) October, p 140-146

Panda, Subash Chandra, 1984, Impediments to education of tribals of Orissa, *Vanyajati* 32(4) October, p 7-13.

Parida, Krishan, C., 1988, Life style of the Orissan tribes, *Patriot* (Magazine) January 10, p 2, col 1-9.

Pathy, Jaganath, 1987, Land problems of tribals, *Times of India,* September 10, p 6, col 7-8.

Patnaik, Binay Kumar, 1987, Tribe and Case: A case study in an Orissa village, *Man in India* 67(4) December, p 335-351, bibliography.

Patnaik, J. B., 1986, Towards tribal prosperity, *Link* (Supplement) 28(30) March 2, p 24-28.

Patnaik, K. M., 1987, Industrialisation for accelerating development in a tribal setting, *Vision* 6(3-4) January, p 52-56.

Sahu, L.N., 1958, The problem of Aborigines, *Vanyajati* 6(4) October, p 170-173.

Sahu, Laxminarayan, 1955-1956, Thc problem of the Aboriginals, *Adibasi*, 1, p 16-18.

Sanganna, Toyaka, 1964, Tribal culture and its preservation and scientific development, *Adibasi* January, p 3-4.

Sarkar, S.S, 1957, Finger prints of Orissan Aborigines, *Man in India* 37(3) July-September, p 182-191, tables.

Soren, Sonaram, 1955-1956, Social and cultural problems of the Adibasis in Orissa, *Adibasi*, 1, p 1-4.

Times of India (Newspaper), 1985, Disgrace abounding, *Times of India*, August 5, p 8 col 1-2, editorial.

Vyas, Ambalal, 1970, How backward the tribal areas of Orissa State area?, *Vanyajati* 18(3) July, p 131-133, tables.

See also Bondas; Juangs; Konds; Lodhas; Santals; Saoras; Tribes and Tribals: Economic Condition: India: Orissa.

TRIBES AND TRIBALS : INDIA : ORISSA : ECONOMIC CONDITION

See Tribes and Tribals : Economic Condition : India : Orissa.

TRIBES AND TRIBALS : INDIA : RAJASTHAN

Anon, 1983, (Book review), *Sociological Bulletin* 32(2) September, p 224-227. Review of the book : **Vyas, N. N.** and **Mann, R. S.**, 1983, *Disease, culture contact and tribals*, MLV Tribal Research and Training Institute, Udaipur, 14, 86p.

——, 1983, Cultural contacts, *Sociological Bulletin* 32(2) September, p 224-227.

——, Health and hygiene, *Sociological Bulletin* 32(2) September, p 224-227.

Mann, R. S. and **Mann, K.**, 1986, Social implications of acculturation in tribal Rajasthan, *Journal of Social Research*, September 29, p 42-50.

Nagdo, B. L., 1988, Socio-cultural mores and high among tribes in Banswara, *Social Welfare* 34(11) February, p 14-15 +.

Sebastian, M. K. and **Bhandari, M. M.**, 1984, Cultivation of wild plants for the uplift of tribals in the forest areas of Rajasthan, *Tribe* 16(3-4) September, p 30-35, bibliography.

Shyamlal, 1986, Socio-religious movements among the tribals of Banswara district, Rajasthan, *Man and Life* 12(3-4) July-December, p 159-172, bibliography.

Swaminathan, Srilata, 1987, Endless night in Dabi Pada, *Indian Express* (Magazine) January 25, p 4, col 1-8.

Talesara, Rajendra, 1984, Agricultural development among tribals : Issue and aspects, *Prashanika* 13(1) January-March, p 27-33.

Trivedi, H. V., 1986, The T S P area in Rajasthan and its socio-psychological development barriers spectrum, *Rajasthan Economic Journal* 10(1) January, p 53 63, bibliography, tables.

Vaish, Prerana, 1984, Role of mineral in the tribal development of TSP region of Rajasthan, *Tribe* 16(3-4) September-December, p 20-29.

See also Bhils; Gadia Lohars; Garasias; Suthars.

TRIBES AND TRIBALS : INDIA : SIKKIM

Anon, 1990, (Book review), *Man in India* 70(2) June, p 199-201.

Review of the book : **Bhasin, Veena,** 1989, *Ecology, culture and change : Tribals of Sikkim Himalayas*, Inter-India Publications, p 407 +, photoplates.

Subba, Tanka Bahadur, 1988, Tribal handicrafts of Sikkim : A profile, *Man in India* 68(4) December, p 431-441, bibliography.

TRIBES AND TRIBALS : INDIA : SINGHBHUM

Sen Gupta, N. K., 1988, A note on the survey and investigation on some physical conditions and nutritional patterns in relation to the tribal people in Singhbhum, *Man in India* 68(4) December, p 473-476.

TRIBES AND TRIBALS : INDIA : SUNDARBANS

Mukherjee, Shankarananda, 1969, Folklore of the Sundarban tribes, *Bulletin of Cultural Research Institute* 8(1-2), p 97-100.

Sil, Ajit Kumar, 1990, Adaptation of the migrant Oraon in their present habitat in Sundarbans, *Geographical Review of India* 52(1) March, p 89-90.

TRIBES AND TRIBALS : INDIA : TAMIL NADU

Gunasekaran, R., 1988, Changing phase of tribal economy in Kolli hills, *Khadi Gramodyog* 35(3) December, p 162-174.

Manuel, Moreno, 1989, Marriage transactions among the Pallars of Southern Kongu, Tamil Nadu, *Man in India* 69(1) March, p 13-23.

Perumal, C. A. and **Padmanabhan**, 1986, Tribals of Tamil Nadu Public Policy, *Indian Journal of Political Science* 47(4) October-December, p 457-472.

Rajagopalan, K. R. and **Bhagvandas, M.**, 1987, Kudu-Kudu-P-Paik-Karans *Folklore* 28(12) December, p 283-286, bibliography.

Sripal, K. B. and **Knight, A. John**, 1986, Socio-economic profile of tribals of Tamil Nadu, *Kurukshetra* 34(4) January, p 35-37.

Venkatraman, S. R., 1984, Tribes of Palani and Kodal hills, *Vanyajati* 32(3) July, p 13-15.

See also Trulas; Villis.

TRIBES AND TRIBALS : INDIA : TAMIL NADU : MADRAS

Buchi, E. C., 1955, Is sickling a wedded trait, *Anthropologist* 2(1) March, p 25-29, references.

TRIBES AND TRIBALS : INDIA : TRAVANCORE

Bose, Uma, 1952, Blood groups of the tribes of Travancore, *Bulletin of Department of Anthropology* 1(1) January, p 19-24, references, ables.

Krishna Iyer, L. A., 1945, The Hill-tribes of 'Travancore, *Man in India* 25(3) September, p 194-198.

Ray, Sachin, 1955, Distribution of ABO, MN blood groups and the ABH secretor among the tribes of Central and Northern Travancore, *Man in India* 35(1) January-March, p 57-65, illustrations, references, tables.

Sen Gupta, P. N. and **Biswas, S. K.**, 1956, Studies ion the diet and nutritional status of the Malpantaram, Muthuvan and Ullatan tribes of Travancore, *Bulletin of Department of Anthropology* 5(2) p 9-16, tables.

TRIBES AND TRIBALS : INDIA : TRIPURA

Acharjee, Ranjeet Kumar, 1986, The tribals of Tripura : Their culture and religion, *Prabuddha Bharata* 91(3), p 149-159.

Anon, 1985, Three years of tribal autonomous comment. *People's Democracy* 9(12) March, 24, p 7-8.

Barma, Thakur Jitendra Mohan Dev, 1958, Origin of Tripura and its people, *Vanyajati* 6(3) July, p 108-116, tables.

Bhattacharjee, P. R., New horizon of tribal autonomy and tribal development in Tripura, *Journal of North East India Council* 11(1) April, p 33-42.

Das Gupta, Barun, 1987, Background to Tripura tribals crisis, *Mainstream* 25(16) January p 4-6.

Das Gupta, Malabika, 1985, Tribal unrest in Tripura : An alternative view, *Economic and Political Weekly* 20(1) January 5, p 38-40.

Ganguly, J. B., 1986, Tripura tribals and mainstream : Tripura politics, *Asian Studies* 4(2) April, p 1-19.

See also Jugis; Jhumias; Riangs; Tribes and Tribals: Ability Testing: India; Tripura; Uchais

TRIBES AND TRIBALS : INDIA : UTTAR PRADESH

Anon, 1982, Effect of parental deprivation on personality adjustment with special reference to the denotified tribes of U.P., *Indian Educational Review* 17(1) January, p 99-109.

——, 1985, (Book review); *Co-operative Perspective* 20(1) April-June, p 45-46. Review of the book : **Hasan, Amir**, 1982, *Meet the Uttar Pradesh tribes*, Academic Press, Gurgaon, 107 p.

Dubey, R., 1965, Tharo and its people, *Vanyajati* 13(3) July, p 87-92+.

Majumdar, D. N., 1950, Experiment in tribal life, *Indian Journal of Social Work* 10(4) March, p 281-292.

——, 1959, The light that failed, *Journal of Social Research* 2(1-2) March-September, p 90-97.

Mathur, K. S., 1951-1952, Sorcery and witchcraft among the tribes of Dudhi, *Eastern Anthropologist* 5(2-3) December-May, p 79-86.

Srivastava, Rajni, 1983, Some psychological problems of tribals of Mirzapur : A case study, *Indian Educational Review* 18(2) April, p 106-110, tables.

Verma, Ram Swaroop, 1985, Socio-psychological make up of Tharu and Boksa adolescents, *Bhartiya Shiksha Shodh Patrika* 4(2) July-December, p 27-33.

See also Bhotiyas; Kols.

TRIBES AND TRIBALS : INDIA : WEST BENGAL

Anon, 1986-1988, Castes and tribes in economic transition : A regional study, *Arthaniti*, 25, p 46-64.

Banerjee, Swapan Kumar, 1963, Land alienation : Causes and effects thereof on tribal economy, *Bulletin of Cultural Institute* 2(2), p 19-22.

Basu, Sunil Kumar, 1969, A note on important festivals among the major tribals of West Bengal, *Bulletin of Cultural Research Institute* 8(3-4) p 17-33, tables.

Bhattacharya, Biswanath, 1965, A short note on clubs and libraries of the backward communities, *Bulletin of Cultural Research Institute*, 4, p 53-57, tables.

Bhowmick, P. K., 1985, Tribal situation in West Bengal, *Indian Anthropologist* 15(1) June, p 1-19.

Bose, Sukla, 1985, Caste, tribe and female labour participation, *Social Change* 15(2) June, p 15-20, bibliography, tables.

Das, Amal Kumar, 1958, Language and dialects of the tribals of West Bengal, *Vanyajati* 6(3) July, p 130-136.

——, 1962, Influence of the city life on educated tribals, *Bulletin of Cultural Research Institute* 1(2), p 69-78, tables.

——, 1963, Social system : A cross cultural analysis, *Bulletin of Cultural Research Institute* 2(2), p 1-10.

——, and **Banerjee, Swapan Kumar**, 1963, The 'family' of tribals of West Bengal : Static and dynamic aspects of composition, *Bulletin of Cultural Research Institute* 2(1) p 12-21.

——, 1964, Certain aspects of population growth amongst the tribals of West Bengal, *Bulletin of Cultural Research Institute* 3(1), p 1-14, tables.

Das, Harish Chandra, 1963-1964, The sea-fisherman of North Balasore and their way of fishing, *Adibasi* 5(2), p 25-28.

Gangopadhyay, Prodyot and **Kundu, Shampa**, 1988, Familial trend in arterial pressure among few endogamous communities of West Bengal reared under

diverse occupational environment, *Man in India* 68(2-3) June-September, p 235-242, bibliography.

Gupta, Dipankar, 1986, Tribal development in a West Bengal district, *Economic and Political Weekly* 21(1) January 4, p 35-45.

Khan, N. C., 1969, Some aspects of marital trend among the tribals of West Bengal, *Bulletin of Cultural Research Institute* 8(3-4), p 42-47, tables.

Mukherjee, Bhabananda, 1968, Trends of social mobility movement, *Journal of Indian Anthropological Society* 3(1-2) March-September, p 121-129.

Piplai, Chumki, et al, 1985, A note on ABO, MN, RH and in (a) blood groups, of the Tamang and Oraon tea labourers of the Jalpaiguri district, West Bengal, *Journal of Indian Anthropology Society* 20(1) March, p 66-70, bibliography, tables.

Roy Burman, B. K., 1958, Problem of family planning among the Scheduled Tribes of West Bengal, *Vanyajati* 6(4) October, p 160-164.

Sarkar, Sabita Ranjan, 1969, Some aspects of material culture of the tribals of West Bengal, *Bulletin of Cultural Research Institute* 8(3-4) p 85-86.

Sen, Gopi Nath, 1983, Some socio-religious aspects of the tribal people of West Bengal, *Modern Review* 147(3-4) March-April, p 81-86.

Sengupta, N. K., 1988, A note on the survey and investigation on some physical conditions and nutritional patterns in relation to the tribal people in Singhbhum, *Man in India* 68(4) December, p 473-476, tables.

See also Bauls; Lodhas; Santals; Shavaras; Totos; Tribes and Tribals : Economic Condition: India: West Bengal.

TRIBES AND TRIBALS : ISLANDS OF THE PACIFIC

Hutton, J. H., 1924, Assam and the Pacific, *Man in India* 4(1-2) March-June, p 1-13, footnotes.

TRIBES AND TRIBALS : LAOS

Halpern, Joel Martin, 1958-1959, Trade patterns in Northern Laos, *Eastern Anthropologist* 12(2) December-February, p 119-124.

TRIBES AND TRIBALS : LIBRARIES

Bhattacharya, Biswanath, 1965, A short note on clubs and libraries of the backward communities, *Bulletin of Cultural Research Institute*, 4, p 53-57, tables.

TRIBES AND TRIBALS : MALASIYA

Clamment, John, 1987, Incorporation and assimilation : The Aboriginal peoples of Malaysia and letters of modernisation, *Journal of Social Economic Studies* 4(2) April-June, p 121-142.

TRIBES AND TRIBALS : NIGERIA

Otterbein, Keith F., 1967, Mortuary practices in North-Eastern Nigeria, *Bulletin of Cultural Research Institute* 6(1-2), p 10-18, references, tables.

Onwurah, Emeka, 1989, Kinship and marriage among the Igbo of Nigeria, *Sarvartham*, 14, p 3-12, footnotes.

TRIBES AND TRIBALS: NORTH EAST FRONTIER AGENCY

See Tribes and Tribals : India : North East Frontier Agency.

TRIBES AND TRIBALS: NUTRITION

See Tribes and Tribals: Food: Nutrition.

TRIBES AND TRIBALS : PAKISTAN

Anon, 1986, Zia's punitive strike on Pushtoon tribes, *New Age* 34(5) February 2, p 13.

TRIBES AND TRIBALS : PSYCHOLOGICAL ASPECT

Kundu, C. L., 1969, Intelligence and tribal delinquency, *Indian Journal of Applied Psychology* 6(1) January, p 29-30, references, tables.

TRIBES AND TRIBALS : RESEARCH : INDIA

Anon, 1968-1969, An address in Census conference of 1969, *Adibasi* 10(3-4) October-January, p 51-56.

TRIBES AND TRIBALS : REVOLT : INDIA

Ghosh, S. K., 1990, Tribal revolt in India, *Hindustan Times*, Magazine Section, November 18, p 13.

TRIBES AND TRIBALS : SOCIETIES AND CLUBS : INDIA

Bhattacharya, Biswanath, 1965, A short note on clubs and libraries of the communities, *Bulletin of Cultural Research Institute* 4, p 53-57, tables.

Nair, P. Thankappan, 1967, Ladies club of NEFA, *Vanyajati* 15(1) January p 9-14.

TRIBES AND TRIBALS : UNITED STATES OF AMERICA

Mills, J. P., 1923, The lessons of the red man, *Man in India* 3(3-4) September-December, p 217-223, footnotes.

TRIPURA : INDIA

Acharjee, Ranjeet Kumar, 1986, The tribals of Tripura : their culture and religion, *Prabudha Bharata*, 91(3) March, p 149-159.

Das, Biplas, 1986, The Uchais of Tripura : Some religious functions of the Christian groups, *Folklore* 27(8) August, p 171-176, bibliography.

Das Gupta, Malabika, 1986, Jhumias of Tripura, *Economic and Political Weekly* 21(44-45) November 1-8, p 1955-1960.

Datta, Upali and **Ghosh, G.C.**, 1988, A study of hand clasping and armfolding among the Jugi of Tripura, *Man in India* 68(2-3) June-Septermber, p 211-215, bibliography.

See also Geographical Area susdivision 'Tripura' under main Descriptor.

UDAIPUR STATE : INDIA

Baduri, Manindra Bhusan, 1941, The Aboriginal tribes of the Udaipur State (C. P.), *Man in India* 21(2-3) April-September, p 92-126, footnotes.

See also Geographical Area subdivision under main Descriptor.

UCHAIS : INDIA : TRIPURA

Das, Biplas, 1986, The Uchais of Tripura : Some religious functions of the Christian groups, *Folklore* 27(8) August, p 171-176.

UDAYACHAL : INDIA : ASSAM

Anon, 1990; (Book review), *Man in India* 70(2) June, p 206-209.

Review of the book : **Paul, M. C.**, 1989, *Dimensions of tribal movements in India : A study of Udayachal in Assam Valley*, Inter-India Publications, New Delhi, p 107, Rs. 95.

ULLATAN TRIBE : INDIA : TRAVANCORE

Sen Gupta, P. N. and **Biswas, S. K.**, 1956. Studies on the diet and nutritional status of the Malapantaram, Muthuvan and Ullatan tribes of Travancore, *Bulletin of Department of Anthropology* 5(2), p 9-19, tables.

UNDERPRIVILEGED PERSONS : EDUCATION

Anon, 1952, Education of The under-privileged, *Indian Journal of Social Work* 13(3) December, 1952, p 175-181.

Goyal, B. R., 1975, Education of the under-privileged under the 10+2+3 scheme, *Journal of Indian Education* 1(1) May, p 69-74.

UNITED KINGDOM

See Geographical Area subdivision under main Descriptor.

UNIVERSALS OF CULTURE

Mukherjee, Radhakamal. 1965, Unities and universals of culture, *Eastern Anthropologist* 18(1) January-April, p 1-11. references.

UNTOUCHABILITY : INDIA

Anon, 1932. The curse of untouchability, *Social Service Quarterly* 18(2) October, p 64-65.

——, 1955, Seminar on casteism and removal of untouchability, *Indian Journal of Social Work* 16(3) December, p 203-206.

Barve, V.N., 1942. A call from the downtrodden, *Social Service Quarterly* 28(4) April, p 145-147.

Chatterjee, Ramananda, 1933, A fundamental right, *Social Service Quarterly* 18(4) April, p 125.

Ganesan, Sangu, 1955, The root cause of untouchability, *Rural India* 18(11-12) November-December, p 406-407.

Jagjivan Ram, 1958, Casteism and untouchability : An analysis, *Indian Journal of Adult Education* 19(3) October, p 33-37.

Jhaveri, Krishnalal, 1933. The uplift of the harijans, *Social Service Quarterly* 18(4) April, p 126-127.

Kalelkar, Kaka, 1958, Casteism and untouchability : An analysis, *Indian Journal of Adult Education*, 19(3) October, p 33-37.

Lele, P.R., 1933. Worthy of the forgiveness untouchability : Changed angle of vision, *Social Service Quarterly* 18(3) January, p 83-86.

Majumdar, P.L., 1933, The problem of untouchability, *Social Service Quarterly* 18 (4) April, p 130-131.

Malkani, N.R., 1970. A hereditary proletariat, *Interdiscipline* 7(4) Winter, p 32-36.

Nanavatty, Meher C., 1955, Seminar on casteism and untouchability : A review, *Indian Journal of Adult Education* 16(4) December, p 41-50.

Nargokar, V.S., 1969, Removal of untouchability : Goals and attainments, *Indian Journal of Social Work* 30(3) October, p 189-201.

Nilkanth, Vidhya Ramanbhai, 1933. Untouchability : The supposed mainstay of Hindu religion, *Social Service Quarterly* 18 (4) April, p 127-129.

Prasad, R.R., 1986, Untouchability and measures for its eradication, *Gandhi Marg* 8(8) November, p 492-505.

Rajagopalachari, C., 1933. A denial of religion, *Social Service Quarterly* 18(4) April, p 124.

Rastogi, S.P., 1980, The impact of Constitutional provision upon the uplift of

Harijans, *Indian Educational Review* 15(4) October, p 76-80.

Sachchidananda, 1970, Untouchability and Gandhi, *Interdiscipline* 7(4) Winter, p 37-47, references.

Seshadri, H.V., 1987, Ralegana Sindi : A name for social metamorphosis, *Organiser* 38(40) 15 February, p 10.

Wadia, A.P 1958, Casteism and untouchability : An analysis, *Indian Journal of Adult Education* 19(3) October, p 28-33.

See also Bhangis; Bombay Harijan Temple Worship Act; Depressed Classes Institute, Bombay; Gandhi, Mohandas Karamchand : Views on Untouchability; Harijans; Seminar on Casteism and Removal of Untouchability, 1955, Delhi; Temple Entry Bill; Temple Entry Proclamation : India: Malabar.

UNTOUCHABILITY : INDIA : GUJARAT

Social Service Quarterly (Periodical), 1926, Untouchables in Nadiad, *Social Service Quarterly* 11(4) April, p 154-155.

UNTOUCHABILITY : INDIA : KARNATAKA

Radetotad, N.K., 1966, Caste hierarchy among the untouchables of Dharwar, *Eastern Anthropologist* 19(3) September-December, p 205-214, references, tables.

Ramu, G.N., 1968, Untouchability in rural areas, *Indian Journal of Social Work* 29(2) July, p 147-155, tables.

UNTOUCHABILITY : INDIA : MAHARASHTRA : BOMBAY

Anon, 1933, Anti-untouchability campaign, *Social Service Quarterly* 18(4) April, p 131-142.

Social Service Quarterly (Periodical), 1920, Temple entry satyagraha, *Social Service Quarterly* 15(2) October, p 57-58, editorial.

UPLIFT : WEAKER SECTIONS : INDIA

Bhadrapur, K.B., 1942, Uplift work amongst hill tribes in Kolaba district, *Rural India* 5(11) november, p 502-506, tables.

Chobey, Bindo Kumar, 1985, More efforts needed to uplift tribals, *Times of India*, February 27, p 8, col 7-8.

Husain, Syed Khaja Mahboob, 1949, The rural uplift of tribes and backward classes in Hyderabad, Deccan, *Man in India* 29 (3-4) July-December, p 185-198.

Jhaveri, Krishnalal, 1933, The uplift of the Harijans, *Social Service Quarterly* 18(4) April, p 126-127.

Krishna Iyer, V.R., 1985, Tribal uplift and the rule of law, *Cochin University Law Review*, 9(1-2) March-June, p 1-18.

Rastogi, S.P., 1980, The impact of Constitutional provision upon the uplift of Harijans, *Indian Educational Review* 15(4) October, p 76-80.

Sebastian, M.K. and **Bhandari, M.M.**, 1984, Cultivation of wild plants for the uplift of tribals in the forest areas of Rajasthan, *Tribe* 16(3-4) September, p 30-35, bibliography.

See also Welfare: Weaker Sections: India.

UPPER CASTES : INDIA

Anon, 1967, On minimising social distance existing between the upper castes and Harijans, *Interdiscipline* 4(4) Winter, p 316-321, reference.

URALIES

Prakasham, M.S., 1988, The social world of Uralies, *Social Welfare* 34(11) February, p 7-8.

URALS : INDIA : TRAVANCORE

Mukherjee, Bhabananda, 1952, Marriage customs and kinship organisation of the Ural of Travancore, *Bulletin of Department of Anthropology*, 1(2) July, p 37-54, appendix, tables.

URBANISATION : IMPACT ON TRIBAL HABITATS

Shrivastava, Aruna, 1986, Tribals habitats under the impact of urbanisation and industrialisation, *Man and Life* 12(1-2) January-June, p 69-76, bibliography.

See also : Tribal Urbanisation.

UTTARKHAND : INDIA

Sah, Nirmal K., 1986, A tribe in transition : Bhotiyas of Uttar Khand, *Asian Studies* 4(2) April, p 20-27.

UTTAR PRADESH : INDIA

Hasan, Amir, 1968, A note on education among the Kols of Uttar Pradesh, *Eastern Anthropologist* 21(1) January-April, p 83-86.

See also Geographical Area subdivision 'Uttar Pradesh' under main Descriptor.

VANYAJATI

See Tribes and Tribals.

VARNA SAMKARA : INDIA : ANCIENT

Kalidas, Raju, 1984, Varna samkara in ancient India, *Quarterly Journal of Mythic Society* 75(4) October-December, p 374-387.

VASAVAS/VASAVES

See Bhills.

VIDARBHA : INDIA

Jha, S.K. and **Barde, H.R.**, 1984, The Second change education for the tribals of Vidarbha, *Progress of Education* 58(11) June, p 270-272.

VILLAGE ORGANISATIONS AND AUTHORITY : LAMBADAS

Prakash Rao, R., 1954, Village organisation and authority among the Lambadas of the Deccan, *Eastern Anthropologist* 8(1) September-November, p 3-12.

VILLIES

Venkataraman, S.R., 1984, Villies of Chingleput district, *Vanyajati* 32(2) April, p 5-11.

VINDHYA : INDIA

Chaturvedi, K.C., 1957, Vindhya's tribals in new Madhya Pradesh, *Vanyajati* 5(1) January, p 39-41, references.

VINDHYA HILLS : INDIA

Fuchs, Stephen, 1988, The Korkus of the Vindhya Hills, *Man in India* 68(2-3) June-September, p 308-309.

VINDHYA PRADESH : INDIA

Anon, 1954, Tribal welfare work in Vindhya Pradesh, *Vanyajati* 2(2) April, p 67-69.

VIOLENCE

Anon, 1987, Rural violence in Bihar, *Link* 29(49), July 12, p 17-20.

——, 1987, Using the violence bogey against the Left, *Economic and Political Weekly* 22(34) August 22, p 1437-1438.

Das, Arvind N., 1985, Growing violence in Bihar : Social roots of the cult of the gun, *Times of India* 21(8) November, p 3-5.

Pathy, Suguna, 1987, Caste, and violence : An appraisal, *Teacher Politics* 13(2), p 61-75, bibliography.

VIRA SAIVAS

See Lingayats.

VIVEKANANDA : VIEWS ON CASTE

Mukherjee, Jayasree, 1987, The institution of caste in the eyes of Ramakrishna and Vivekananda, *Quarterly Review of Historical Studies* 27(2), p 22-35, bibliography.

VIZIANAGRAM DISTRICT : INDIA : ANDHRA PRADESH

Rajyalakshmi, P. and **Geervani, P.**, 1988, Tribal people: Traditions, customs and attitudes related to food and dietary practices: A Case study of Vizianagram district, Andhra Pradesh, *Indian Journal of Social Work* 49(1) January, p 45-50.

VOCATIONAL EDUCATION

Shaw, Biswanath, 1958-1959, Vocational education in the Ashram Schools, *Adibasi* 3(3-4) August-January, p 31-34.

Vyas, A., 1957-1958, Why this emphasis on vocational bias in education in Ashrams? *Adibasi* 2(1), p 45-49.

VOKKALIGAS

Kusumakar, H., 1986, To be 'backward' is good, *Times of India* (Sunday Review) November 9, p 11, col 1-8.

VOLUNTARY ORGANISATIONS : ROLE IN WELFARE OF WEAKER SETIONS

Dave, P.C., 1966, Voluntary organisations and welfare of backward classes, *Vanyajati* 14(4) October, p 156-64.

Deogaonkar Warora, S.G., 1989, Role of voluntary agencies and tribal institutions in social and ecological development in tribal areas, *Vanyajati* 37(4) October, p 32-38.

Mehta, Shalini, 1988, Role of voluntary and government organisations in tribal welfare : A case study of Mandala district of M.P., *Eastern Anthropologist* 41(1) January-March, p 49-64, tables.

Sachchidananda, 1989, Role of voluntary agencies in social and ecological development in tribal areas, *Vanyajati* 37(4) October, p 26-31.

See also Non Official Associations.

VOLUNTARY WORK : TRIBAL WELFARE

Bhowmick, P.K., 1987, Voluntary effort in tribal development : The Bidisa experiment, *Journal of Social Economic Studies* 4(2) April-June, p 175-186.

VORAS : INDIA : GUJARAT

Desai, Bharati S., 1982-1983, Channels of mobility used by a landowning peasant caste : An empirical study of the Woras of South Gujarat, *Journal of the Maharaja Sayajirao University of Baroda* 31-32(2) p 125-143, bibliography, tables.

WAGHERS : INDIA : GUJARAT

Bajpai, Geeta, 1983, Economic determinants of social behaviour : A case study of the Waghers of Gujarat in the second half of the nineteenth century, *Journal of the Gujarat Research Society* 45(3) July, p 32-41, bibliography, footnotes.

——, 1985, Economic determinants of social behaviour : A case study of the Waghers of Gujarat in the second half of nineteenth century, *India, Past and Present* 2(1), p 31-40, footnotes.

WANCHO LANGUAGE : INDIA : ARUNACHAL PRADESH

Das Gupta, K., 1979, A note on the Wancho language of Arunachal Pradesh, *Resarun* 5(1) Spring-Summer, p 25-37, bibliography.

WANCHOS : ANTHROPOMETRY : INDIA : ARUNACHAL PRADESH

Sengupta, S. and **Dutta, M.N.**, 1985, A note on ridge count of finger patterns of the Wanchos of Arunachal Pradesh, *Resarun* 1(2) Autumn-Winter, p 23-26, bibliography, tables.

——, 1985, Palmar main line index and transversality in Wanchos of Arunachal Pradesh, *Resarun* 11(2) Autumn-Winter, p 39-41, bibliography, tables.

WANCHOS : INDIA : ARUNACHAL PRADESH

Das Gupta, K., 1979, A note on the Wancho language of Arunachal Pradesh, *Resarun* 5(1) Spring-Summer, p 25-37, bibliography.

Dutta, P.C., 1978, Social organisation of the Wanchos of Tirap district, Arunachal Pradesh, *Resarun* 4(1) January-March, p 14-35.

WANDERING COMMUNITIES

Sarkar, R.M., 1984, Conflict compromise and dispersity unity oriented life philosophy of a wandering community, *Indian Museum Bulletin* 19, p 48-55.

See also Gypsies; Lohars; Nomads of Himalayas; Romas.

WARLI REVOLT

Parulekar, Godavari, 1986, Glorious saga of the Warli Adivasis revolt, *People's Democracy* 10(8) February 23, p 6-7.

——, Saga of the Warli Adivasis, *People's Democracy* 10(9) March 2, p 51.

Saldonlia, Indra Munshi, 1986, Tribal women in the Warli revolt 1945-1947 : Class and gender in the Left perspective, *Economic and Political Weekly* (Supplement) 21(17) April 26, p Ws41-Ws52, footnotes.

WARLIS : INDIA

Jhingon, Bela and **Surinder Nath**, 1985, **Trends** of growth and maturations among the Warlis : A tribal population of Maharashtra, India, *Indian Journal of Physical Anthropology and Human Genetics* 11(1-2) April-August, p 39-45, bibliography and tables.

Mondal, S.K. and **Malhotra, R.**, 1984, Agrarian stratification among the Warlis of Gujarat : An observation, *Tribe* 16(3-4) September-December, p 36-43.

See also Warli Revolt.

WASTAGE : TRIBAL EDUCATION : INDIA : ANDHRA PRADESH

Reddy, G.P., 1970, Causes of wastage in tribal education of Andhra Pradesh, *Vanyajati* 18(3) July, p 109-20, references, tables.

WATER SCARCITY : TRIBAL AREAS

Anon, 1964, The water scarcity problem in Tamia Special Multipurpose Tribal Development Block, *Bulletin of Tribal Research Training Institute* (Chhindwara) 4(1) June, p 41-49, references, tables.

WEAKER SECTIONS

Bommai, S.R., 1990, Quota for weaker sections must, *Indian Express*, September 9.

Dhebar, U.N., 1970, Weaker sections of the community, *Interdiscipline* 7(4) Winter, p 27-31.

Verghese, Alexander V., 1984, Education, earning and occupation of weaker castes, *Journal of Higher Education* 9(3) Spring, p 373-381.

See also Uplift: Weaker Sections: India; Welfare: Weaker Section: India.

WEAVERS : INDIA

Umeshrao, 1939, The Weavers of India, *Rural India* 1(7) May, p 419.

WELFARE : WEAKER SECTIONS : INDIA

Anon, 1954, Welfare of Hyderabad tribes, *Indian Journal of Social Work* 15(1) June, p 59-60.

——, 1965, Welfare of backward classes : Planning Commission Panel discussion, *Vanyajati* 13(2) April, p 39-40+

Juyal, P.D., 1986, Some demographic variables influencing the attitude of Scheduled Caste towards the measures adopted for their welfare : An empirical study, *Progress of Education* 61(4-5) November-December, p 85-88, references.

See also Tribal People: Welfare; Tribal Welfare; Uplift: Weaker Sections: India.

WEST BENGAL : INDIA

Anon, 1953, Scheme in West Bengal sanctioned for 1952-53 for Scheduled Tribes under Artical 275 of the Constitution, *Vanyajati* 1(4) October, p 101-102.

Devi, Mahasveta, 1985, The Shavara tribal of West Bengal, *Economic and Political Weekly* 20(35) August 31, p 1476-1489.

Gupta, Jaya Dutta, 1959, A study of the Paundra Kshatriya of West-Bengal, *Bulletin of Department of Anthropology* 8(2) July, p 109-30, appendix, references.

Roy Chowdhury, Bidyut Kumar, 1963, Comparative study of the progress of secondary education among the Scheduled Tribes of West-Bengal, *Bulletin of Cultural, Research Institute* 2(1), p 40-52, appendix, notes, tables.

Sarkar, S.S., 1958, The tribal population in West Bengal, *Man in India* 38(1) January-March, p 215-16.

See also Geographical Area subdivision under main **Descriptor**.

WEST INDIA

Shrikant, L.M., 1956, Tribal welfare in West India, *Vanyajati* 4(4) October, p 100-102.

See also Geographical Area subdivision 'India : West' under main Descriptor.

WILD PLANTS : INDIA : RAJASTHAN

Sebastian, M.K. and **Bhandari, M.M.**, 1984, Cultivation of wild plants for the uplift

of tribals in the forest areas of Rajasthan. *Tribe*, 16(3-4) September, p 30-35, bibliography.

WITCHCRAFT : TRIBALS

Batria, P., 1963, Crime and witchcraft among the tribes of Madhya Pradesh, *Bulletin of Tribal Research Institute* (Chhindwara) 3(1) June, p 21-29.

Chaudhuri, Buddhadeb, 1969, An analytical study of witchcraft among the Mundas of Midnapur, *Bulletin of Cultural Research Institute* 8(1-2), p 87-91, references.

Mathur, K.S., 1951-1952, Sorcery and witchcraft among the tribes of Dudhi, *Eastern Anthropologist* 5(2-3) December-May, p 79-86.

WOMEN : GODDESS : INDIA : KARNATAKA

Assayag, Jackie, 1989, Women-Goddess, Women-distress Yellamma Goddess devotees in South India (Karnataka), *Man in India* 69(4) December, p 359-373.

WOMEN : TRIBALS

See Triabl Women.

WORAS

Desai, Bharti S., 1982-1983, Channels of mobility used by a landowning peasant caste : Am empirical study, *Journal of the Maharaja Sayajirao University of Baroda* 31-32(2), p 125-143, bibliography, tables.

WORKERS : TRIBAL WELFARE

Gare, G.H., 1985, Need of Training of workers in tribal development, *Tribal Research Bulletin* 7(2) March, p5-6.

WYNAD

Devan, P.K., 1988, A medical mission for the tribals of Wynad, *Social Welfare* 34(11) February, p 9-10.

YADAVS

Malhotra, Inder, 1989, Political commentary : The Yadav and other factors, *Times of India*, August 10, p 6, col 3-5.

YALMOS

See Bhotias.

YANADIS

Agrawal, Binod C., et al, 1984, Determinants of cultural adaptation in the process of change : A case of Yanadi, *Man in India* 64(2) June, p 133-142.

Gurumurthy, G., 1985, Marriage patterns, age at marriage and fertility behaviour among Yanadis : A study of tribal community in Andhra Pradesh, *Health and Population* 8(4) October-December, p 235-236, bibliography, tables.

——, 1988, Socio-economic status and fertility among Yanadi women, *Social Welfare* 34(11) February, p 11-13+

Reddy, A.P., 1984, Ethnographic note about the Yanadi tribe of Andhra Pradesh, *Vanyajati* 32(2) April, p 14-18.

Shaik, Abdul Azeez Saheb and **Shaik, Gousia Begum**, 1990, Struggle against starvation : A study of the Yanadi food getting techniques, *Man in India* 70(2) June, p 169-184.

YELLAMMA GODDESS : INDIA : KARNATAKA

Assayag, Jackie, 1989. Women-Goddess. Women distress Yellamma Goddess devotees in South-India (Karnataka). *Man in India* 69(4) December, p 359-373.

YENADIS

See Yanadis.

YENITY KONDHS

See Kondhs.

YERAVAS

Shankara Narayan Rao, N.P., 1985. Identity of the Yeravas of Kodagu. *Quarterly Journal of the Mythic Society* 76(3-4) July-December, p 211-228.

YERCAUD

Venkatraman, S.R., 1969. Tribal development block, Yercaud : An impression. *Social Service Quarterly* 54(3) January, p 77-79.

YOUTH ORGANISATIONS : SYLVAN AREAS

Mehta, B.H., 1962. Youth organisations in Sylvan areas. *Indian Journal of Adult Education* 23(10) October, p 38-40.

YOUTHS : TRIBALS

See Tribal Youth.

ZAMINDARI ABOLITION

Saxena, N.C., 1985. Caste and Zamindari abolition in U.P., *Mainstream* 23(42) June 15. p 15-19. tables.

FOUR

AUTHOR APPROACH

Abraham, A.S., 1985, Anti-reservation protest : Growing clout of backward classes, *Times of India*, March 1, p 8.

——, 1985, Caste war in Gujarat : Wider objectives of agitation, *Times of India*, June 14, p 6.

——, 1985, Going beyond reservations : Framework for a wider policy, *Times of India*, April 20, p 8.

——, 1985, Gujarat Caste War, *Times of India*, April 17, p 8, col 1-2.

——, 1985, Turmoil over reservations : Backward classes in full cry, *Times of India*, April 12, p 8.

——, 1985, Violence against Harijans : Integral part of rural change, *Times of India*, August 10, p 6, col 3-5.

——, 1986, Backward class quota : Farming a national consensus, *Times of India*, September 19, p 8, col 3-5.

——, 1986, Goodbye to modernism : Warring over reservations, *Times of India*, August 1, p 3-5.

——, 1988, Massacre in Jehanabad : Looking for a scapegoat, *Times of India*, August 19, p 4, col 3-5.

——, 1990, OBC forces in full cry : Bid for power in perpetuity, *Times of India*, September 4, p 8, col 2-4.

Acharjee, Ranjeet Kumar, 1986, The tribals of Tripura : Their culture and religion, *Prabuddha Bharata* 91 (3) March, p 149-159.

Acharya, P., 1938, Note on the Dharuas or the Gonds of Mayurbhanj State, *Man in India* 18(2-3) April-September, p 163-167, footnotes.

——, 1957-58, The Puranas : An egg-born tribe of Orissa, *Adibasi* 2(1), p 31-34.

Achyuthan, K.R., 1984, The social spectrum of Kerala, *Journal of Kerala Studies* 9(1-4) March-December, p 103-162.

Adibasi (Periodical), 1965, Defence-cum-production orientation of the programme of backward classes welfare, *Adibasi*, October, p 1-4, editorial.

Adiseshiah, Malcolm S., 1975, Scheduled Castes and Tribes in higher education in Tamil Nadu, *Journal of Higher Education* 1 (2) Autumn, p 241-244.

Adiseshiah, W., 1958, Tribal welfare, *Social Action* 8(5-6) May-June, p 201-208.

Agarwal, B.R., 1962, Nature and extent of social change in a mobile commercial community, *Sociological Bulletin* 11 (1-2) March-September, p 141-145.

Aggarwal, Yash, 1987, Some aspects of educational development among the Scheduled Caste population in India, *Journal of Education Planning and Administration* 1 (2) April, 137-164, bibliography, figures, tables.

Agrawal, Binod, C., et al, 1984, Determinants of cultural adaptation in the process of change : A case of Yanadi, *Man in India* 64(2) June, p 133-142.

Note: See also **ADDED ENTRIES in Chapter Five.**

Agrawal, H.N., 1965, A B O blood groups in Andaman Islands, *Bulletin of Anthropological Survey of India* 14(1-2) January-June, p 59-60, tables.

Agrawal, S.P., 1975, Castes, communities and tribes in India, *Contemporary Social Sciences* 4(8) April-June, p 5-6; 4(9) July-September, p 5-6.

Ahmad, Aijazuddin and **Nuna, Sheel Chand**, 1987, Tribal education shadows of an uncertain future, *Journal of Education Planning and Administration* 1(2) April, p 90-107, bibliography, footnotes, tables.

Ahmad, Akbar, 1986, The lost tribes, *Illustrated Weekly of India* 107(3) January 19, p 42-43.

Ahmad, S.H., 1987, The study of phalangeal hair among the Bhil and their allied groups of Malwa area, *Man in India* 67(1) March, p 47-58.

Ahmed, Imtiaz, 1972, For a Sociology of India, *Contributions to Indian Sociology*, New Series, December 6, p 172-177.

Ahmed, Saghir, 1970, Social stratification in Punjabi village, *Contributions to Indian Sociology*, New Series, 4, December, p 105-125.

Ahuja, G.C., 1980, Educational wastage and stagnation among tribal children, *Journal of Indian Education* 6(1) May, p58-70, references, tables.

Ahuja, Ram, 1969, Tribal leadership and social change, *Indian Journal of Social Research* 10(3) December, p 198-203, references.

Aiyappan, A., 1937, Social and physical anthropology of Nayadis of Malabar, *Bulletin of Madras Government Museum* 2(4).

——, 1964, Tribal languages of Orissa, *Adibasi*, January, p 5-6.

——, 1965, A case for intensification of the development of tribal areas, *Adibasi*, July, p 47-52.

Akhilesh Kumar, 1988, Genesis of caste riots in Bihar, *Mainstream* 26(21) March 5, p 25-26.

Akhwari, N., 1958, Socio-cultural barriers to rural change in an East Bihar community, *Eastern Anthropologist* 11(3-4), p 212-219.

Alam, Khurshid, 1987, Educational aspirations and drop-out factors among Scheduled Castes, *Indian Journal of Community Guidance Service* 4(1) January, p 25-31, bibliography, tables.

Alexander, K.C., 1967, The problem of the Neo-christians of Kerala, *Man in India* 47(4) October-December, p 317-330, references, tables.

——, 1968, Changing religious belief and practices of the Pulayas of Kerala, *Social Action* 18(5) September-October, p 390-398.

——, 1988, Changing status of Pulaya Harijans of Kerala, *Economic and Political Weekly*, Special Number, July.

Amar Dev and **Banerjee-Guha, Swapna**, 1986, Tribes in Himachal Pradesh : Socio-economic characteristics, *National Geographical Journal of India* 32(4) December, p 281-286.

——, 1989, Socio-economic condition of the Scheduled Castes in India : A geographical analysis, *National Geographical Journal of India* 35(2) June.

Amar Kumar Singh, 1988, Tribal attitude to the tribals and non-tribals in South Bihar, *Social Change* 18(2) January, p 3-27, bibliography, tables.

——, et al, 1987, The myth of the healthy tribal, *Social Change* 17(1) March, p 3-23, bibliography, figures, tables.

Amar Singh and **Suraj Singh**, 1981, Training needs of tribal farmers, *Indian Journal of Extension Education* 17(3-4) September-December, p 81-88, tables.

Amba Rao, U., 1976, Higher education and occupational mobility among the Scheduled Caste youth, *Journal of Higher Education* 1(3) Spring, p 305-314, references, tables.

Ameerjan, M.S., 1979, A comparative study of academic achievement of the Scheduled Caste and tribe students of agriculture, *Journal of Education and Psychology* 37(2) July, p 121-129, references, tables.

——, 1984, Background variables of the Scheduled Caste and Tribe college students : A comparative study, *Indian Educational Review* 19(2) April, p 28-36.

—— and **Thimappa, M.S.**, 1988, Academic achievement of the Scheduled Caste and Tribe students : An analysis, *Journal of Education and Psychology* 44(1) April, p 29-35, bibliography.

Amrik Singh, 1990, Mandal Commission : Educational impact, *Times of India*, August 18.

Amrit Kaur and **Tarlok Singh**, 1985, Regional education disparity among Scheduled Castes of Punjab, *Indian Journal of Adult Education* 46(4) April, p 7-10 +, tables.

Anand, 1987, Some thoughts to ponder for our Harijan brothers, *Organiser* 39(15) September 13, p 8-9.

Anantha Krishna Iyer, L.K., 1929, The Kahars of Mysore, *Man in India*, 9.

Anirudh Prasad, 1985, People's perception of atrocities committed on Harijans in Bihar, *Journal of Social and Economic Studies* (New Series) 2(1) January-March, p 105-125.

Anon, 1918, The temper of work : A day service, *Social Service Quarterly* 3(4) April, p 192-195.

——, 1932, The course of untouchability, *Social Service Quarterly* 18(2) October, p 64-65.

——, 1933, Anti-untouchability campaign, *Social Service Quarterly* 18(4) April, p 131-142.

——, 1934, Admission of Harijans to public restaurants, *Social Service Quarterly* 19(4) April, p 159-160, editorial.

——, 1938, Admission of Harijans to Hindu temples, *Social Service Quarterly* 24(1) July, p 39-41.

——, 1941, Problem of dedication of Harijan girls to prostitution in Karnataka, *Rural India* 4(6) June, p 303-308.

——, 1942, Appeal for help : Bhumijan Seva Mandal, *Rural India* 5(8) August, p 348-352.

——, 1945-46, Chowdwar Harijan Conference, *Social Service Quarterly* 32(2) October, p 61-64; 33(1) July, p 12-21.

——, 1947, Government drive for uplift of backward classes, *Social Service Quarterly* 33(1) July, p 27-29.

——, 1952, Education of the underprivileged. *Indian Journal of Social Work* 13(3) December, p 175-181.

——, 1953, A plea for intensive non-official work in Assam, *Vanyajati* 1(3) July, p 49-51.

——, 1953, Scheme in Bombay Government sanctioned for 1952-53 for Scheduled Tribes under Article 275 of the Constitution, *Vanyajati* 1(4) October, p 101-102.

——, 1953, Scheme in West Bengal sanctioned for 1952-53 for Scheduled Tribes under Article 275 of the Constitution, *Vanyajati* 1(4) October, p 103-104.

——, 1953, Scheme of the Assam State Government for the welfare of Scheduled Tribes, included in the Five Year Plan, *Vanyajati* 1(3) July, p 71-72.

——, 1953, Schemes of the Bihar State Government submitted to the Government of India under Article 275 of Constitution of India for the uplift of Scheduled Tribes during 1952-1953, *Vanyajati* 1(3) July, p 72-74.

——, 1953, Scheme of the Madras State Government for the welfare of the Scheduled Castes and Scheduled Tribes and Other Backward Classes, included in the Five Year Plan, *Vanyajati* 1(2) April, p 42-43.

——, 1954, Aboriginal education in Australia, *Indian Educational Review* 60(4) April, p 57-76.

——, 1954, Activities conducted under the tribal welfare scheme, Madhya Pradesh during 1953-1954, *Vanyajati* 2(2) April, p 64-67.

——, 1954, Note on the progress of the tribal welfare scheme in Madhya Pradesh (from January 1953 — December 1953), *Vanyajati* 2(1) January, p 26-29.

——, 1954, On the different aspects or levels in Hinduism, *Contributions to Indian Sociology*, April 3, p 40-54.

——, 1954, Resolutions passed at the Second Tribal Welfare Conference, Lohardga (Bihar) on 11th, 12th and 13th November, 1953, *Vanyajati* 2(1) January, p 31-32.

——, 1954, Social education for the tribals, *Vanyajati* 2(4) October, p 107-109.

——, 1954, The need for training for tribal welfare work, *Vanyajati* 2(2) January, p 39-42.

——, 1954, The Todas, *Social Service Quarterly* 39(4) April, p 97-102.

——, 1954, Tribal welfare work in Vindhya Pradesh, *Vanyajati* 2(2) April, p 67-69.

——, 1954, Welfare of Hyderabad Tribes, *Indian Journal of Social Work* 15(1) June, p 59-60.

——, 1955, Conference on Tribal Affairs, *Vanyajati* 3(1) January, p 1-3.

——, 1955, Resolutions passed at the Third Tribal Welfare Conference held at Jagdalpur (M.P.) on 13th, 14th and 15th March, 1955, *Vanyajati* 3(2) April, p 84-85.

——, 1955, Scheduled Tribes and their welfare, *Vanyajati* 3(4) October, p 143-146.

——, 1955, Seminar on casteism and removal of untouchability, *Indian Journal of Social Work* 16(3) December, p 203-206.

——, 1955, Training of social workers in tribal areas, *Vanyajati* 3(3) July, p 95-98.

——, 1955, Tribal Welfare Conference, *Man in India* 35(2) April-June, p 146-148.

——, 1955, Unreal, *Social Action* 5(5-6) May-June, p 193-194.

——, 1955, Welfare work among Scheduled Tribes in Kutch, *Vanyajati* 3(2) April, p 88-89.

——, 1956, Scheduled Tribes under the Five Year Plans, *Vanyajati* 4(4) October, p 97-99 +.

——, 1956, Seminar on tribal welfare at Chhindwara, *Vanyajati* 4(3) July, p 1-59.

——, 1957, Life membership scheme for tribal welfare work, *Vanyajati* 5(4) October, p 161-63.

——, 1957, Need for life workers for tribal welfare, *Vanyajati* 5(3) July, p 155-156.

——, 1957, Social education for tribal areas, *Indian Journal of Social Work* 18(2) September, p 136-139.

——, 1957, Social reconstruction among Adivasis, *Vanyajati* 5(3) July, p 111-114.

——, 1958, Casteism as a social phenomenon, *Indian Journal of Adult Education* 19(3) October, p 11.

——, 1958, NEFA highlanders, *Indian Folklore* 1(1) January-March, p 85-88, illustrations.

——, 1958, Social education and casteism, *Indian Journal of Adult Education* 19(3) October, p 1-11.

——, 1958, Special multi-purpose tribal blocks, *Vanyajati* 5(2) April, p 48-51.

——, 1959, The study team and tribal welfare, *Vanyajati* 7(4) October 7(4) October, p 115-118, references.

—— 1959, The Tribal Welfare Conference at Bordi, *Social Service Quarterly* 44(3) January, p 72-77.

——, 1959, Inter-ethnic relation and social mobility movements among some tribes and castes of Eastern and Central India, 1900-1959, *Bulletin of Department of Anthropology* 8(2) July, p 9-130.

——, 1960, Dandakaranya and the tribals, *Vanyajati* 8(2) April, p 41-43.

——, 1960, On the march of progress, *Vanyajati* 8(1) January, p 1-2+.

——, 1960, Problems of Adivasi and suggestions to solve them, *Vanyajati* 3(4) October, p 176-177.

——, 1960, Progress of Scheduled Tribes during 1957-59, *Vanyajati* 7(2) April, p 41-43 +.

——, 1960, Resolutions passed at the Sixth Tribal Welfare Conference, Otacamund, *Vanyajati* 8(3) July, p 124-126.

——, 1960, Special tribal blocks, *Vanyajati* 8(4) October, p 120-131.

——, 1961, A Christian approach to tribal communities in India today, *Religion and Society* 8(3) September, p 60-83.

——, 1961, An essay in migration, *Social Action* 11(12) December, p 575-76 +.

——, 1961, Dhurwas of Bastar, *Bulletin of Tribal Research Institute* (Chhindwara) 1(1) June, p 19-69.

——, 1961, New frontier in social welfare and tribal development, *Vanyajati* 9(4) October, p 133-135 +.

——, 1961, Training of tribal welfare workers, *Vanyajati* 9(3) July, p 87-89 +.

——, 1962, Bibliography, *Social Action* 12(4) April, p 199-201.

——, 1962, Recommendations of the Dhebar Commission and their implementation, *Vanyajati* 10(4) October, p 127-129.

——, 1962, Report of Scheduled Areas and Scheduled Tribes Commission : Summary of recommendations, *Vanyajati* 10(1) January, p 35-40.

——, 1962, The culture studies (A socio-economic survey of Abujhmarh), *Bulletin of Tribal Research Institute* (Chhindwara) 2(2) December, 3(1) June, 1963, p 66-67, references, maps, tables.

——, 1964, A note on locality in relation to descent, *Contributions to Indian Sociology*, March 7, p 71-76.

——, 1964, Economic organisation of the tribes of Madhya Pradesh, *Bulletin of Tribal Research and Development Institute* (Chhindwara) 4(2) December, p 1-32, tables.

——, 1964, How Nehru saw the tribals, *Vanyajati* 12(3) July, p 122-125.

——, 1964, The water scarcity problem in Tamia special multipurpose tribal development block, *Bulletin of Tribal Research and Development Institute* (Chhindwara) 4(1) June, p 44-49, references, tables.

——, 1964, Tribal Market: A pilot survey, *Bulletin of Tribal Research and Development Institute* (Chhindwara) 4(2) December, p 33-108, references, tables.

——, 1965, Brahmans in early Tamilaham, *Bulletin of Institute of Traditional Culture*, Part II, p 275-317.

——, 1965, Indebtedness among the tribal people of the scheduled areas of Madhya Pradesh, *Bulletin of Tribal Research and Development Institute* (Bhopal) 5(1-2) June-December, p 1-18, tables.

——, 1965, Report of the Planning Committee of the B.A.J. Sevak Sangh on Fourth Five Year Plan on tribal welfare, *Vanyajati* 13(2) April, p 79-84.

——, 1965, Schools on wheels for Aborigines in Northern territory, *Education* 44(10) October, p 26-28.

——, 1965, Welfare of backward class : Planning Commission Panel discussion, *Vanyajati* 13(2) April, p 39-40 +.

——, 1966, A short note on the working of the co-operative movement for benefit of tribal district of Raigarh (Madhya Pradesh), *Vanyajati* 14(1) January, p 40-43.

——, 1966, A study of the tribal people and tribal areas of Madhya Pradesh, *Bulletin of Tribal Research and Development Institute* (Bhopal) 6(2) December, p 3-176.

——, 1966, Education Commission, Government of India : Questionnaire on the education of the backward classes, *Vanyajati* 14(3) July, p 139-144.

——, 1966, Research on tribal welfare, *Vanyajati* 14(2) April, p 53-54.

——, 1967, A summary of the study on impact of industrialisation on the tribals of Sundargarh district, *Adibasi* 8(4) January, p 46-51.

——, 1967, On minimising social distance existing between the upper castes and Harijans, *Interdiscipline* 4(4) Winter, p 316-321, references.

——, 1967, Study team on tribal development programmes, *Vanyajati* 15(1) January p 45-52.

——, 1968, A study on the socio-religious life of tribals in Gudvella area, Bolangir district, *Adibasi* 9(4) January, p 3-30.

——, Goa peasants on hunger-strike, *People's Democracy* 4(11) March 17, p 5.

——, 1968-1969, An Address in Census Conference of 1969, *Adibasi* 10(3-4) October-January, p 51-56.

——, 1969, Brief report of the Tenth All India Tribal Welfare Conference, *Vanyajati* 17(1) January, p 28-33.

——, 1969, Socio-economic survey of tribal development blocks, *Bulletin of Tribal Research and Development Institute* (Bhopal) 7(1-2) January-December, p 33-189, tables.

——, 1969, The outsider : The dilemma of the Harijan, *Social Action* 19(3) July-September, p 249-253.

——, 1969, Tribal ethnography of Orissa, *Adibasi*, January, p 41 +, illustration.

——, 1979, Inter-generations mobility among the Scheduled Castes, *Journal of Indian Education* 5(4) November, p 61.

——, 1980 (Book Review), *Contemparary Social Sciences*.
Review of the book: **Mac, M.R.**, 1980, Select Bibliography on Scheduled Castes, Centre for Social Studies, Surat, 225 p.

——, 1981, (Book review), *Education Quarterly* 39(4) Winter, p 49-50.
Review of the book : **Goyal, B.R.**, 1981, *Educating Harijans*, Academic Press, Gurgaon, xvii, 129 p.

——, 1981, (Book review), *Education Quarterly* 33(3) July, p 48-49.
Review of the book : **Aikara, Jacob**, 1981, Scheduled Castes and higher education : A study of college students in Bombay, Dastane Ramchandra and Co., Pune, 112 p.

——, 1982, (Book review), *Progress of Education* 56(8) March, p 200-201, *Quest in Education* 19(1) January, p 90-94.

Review of the book : **Goyal, B.R.**, 1981, Educating Harijans, Academic Press (India), Gurgaon, 129 p.

——, 1982, (Book review), *Sunday Statesman*, August 27, p 13, col 1-5.
Review of the book : **Anderson, Robert S.** and **Huber, Walter**, 1982, The hour of the fex, Sage Publications, New Delhi.

——, 1982, Effect of parental deprivation on personality adjustment : With special reference to the denotified tribes of U.P., *Indian Educational Review* 17(1) January, p 99-109.

——, 1982-83, (Book review), *Indian History Review* 9(1-2) July-January, p 297-298.
Review of the book : **Mukherjee, A.B.**, 1980, *Chamars of Uttar Pradesh : A study in social geography*, Inter-India Publication, New Delhi, 155 p.

——, 1983, (Book review), *Annals of the National Association of Geographers, India*·3(1) June, p 76-77.
Review of the book : **Mukherjee, A.B.**, 1980, *The chamars of Uttar Pradesh*, Inter-India Publications, New Delhi, 155 p.

——, 1983, (Book review), *Sociological Bulletin* 32(2) September, p 224-227.
Review of the book : **Vyas, N.N.** and **Mann, R.S.**, 1983, *Disease, culture, contact and tribals*, MLV Tribal Research and Training Institute, Udaipur, p 14-86.

——, 1983, (Book review), *State and Society* 6(1) January-March, p 76-80.
Review of the book : **Pathy, Jaganath**, 1983, *Tribal peasantry : Dynamics of development*, Inter-India Publications, New Delhi, 233 p.

——, 1983, Cultural contacts, *Sociological Bulletin* 32(2) September, p 224-227.

——, 1983, Health and hygiene, *Sociological Bulletin* 32(2) September, p 224-227.

——, 1984, (Book review), *Contributions to Indian Sociology* (New Series) 18(1) January-June, p 141-142.
Review of the book : **Von Furer-Haimendorf, Christoph**, 1982, *Tribes of India : The struggle for survival*, Oxford University Press, New Delhi.

——, 1984, (Book review), *Economic and Political Weekly* 21(23) June 7, p 1011-1012; *Indian Economic and Social History Review* 23(2) April-June, p 233-234.
Review of the book : **Khare, R.S.**, 1983, *The untouchable as himself : Ideology, identity and pragmatism among the Lucknow Chamars*, Cambridge University Press, Cambridge, 189 p.

——, 1984, (Book review), *Economic Times* 30(6) December, p 1-4.
Review of the book : **Brass, Paul R.**, 1983, *Caste faction and party in Indian Politics*, Chanakya Publication, Delhi, 339 p.

——, 1984, (Book review), *India Quarterly* 40(1) January-March, p 156-160 : *Man in India* 64(2) June, p 219-221.
Review of the book : **Ostor, Akos**, et al, 1983, *Concepts of person, kinship, caste and marriage in India*, Oxford University Press, New Delhi, xiv, 271 p.

——, 1984, (Book review), *Man and Life* 10(1-2) January-June, p 107-109.
Review of the book : **Anantha Krishna Iyer, L.K.**, 1981, *The tribes and castes of Cochin*, Cosmo Publications, New Delhi, 3 vols.

——, 1984, (Book review), *Man in India* 64(4) December, p 440-44.
Review of the book: **Varma S.C.**, 1978, *The Bhil kills*, Kunj Publishing House, Delhi, 1978.

——, 1984, (Book review), *Society and Change* 4(1) October-December, p 74-77.
Review of the book : **Pathy, Jaganath**, 1983, *Tribal peasantry : Dynamics of development*, Inter-India Publications, New Delhi, 233 p.

——, 1984, Paijavana or Pailavaka : A Sudra Yogin, *Purana* 26(2) July, p 206-208.

——, 1984, Recommendations of the Seminar or socio-economic problem of Scheduled Tribes, *Vanyajati* 32(3) July, p 1-4.

——, 1985, (Book review), *Contributions to Indian Sociology* (New Series) 20(1) January-June, p 155-158; *Sociological Bulletin* 33(1-2) March-September, p 152-154.
Review of the book : **Sachchidananda** and **Mandal, B.B.**, 1985, *Industrialisation and the social disorganisation : A study of tribals in Bihar*, Concept Publishing Company, New Delhi, 164 p.

——, 1985, (Book review), *Co-operative Perspective* 20(1) April-June, p 45-46.
Review of the book : **Hasan, Amir**, 1982, *Meet the Uttar Pradesh Tribes*, Academic Press, Gurgaon, 107 p.

——, 1985, (Book review), *Economic and Political Weekly* 20(41) October 12, p 1739-1740.
Review of the book : **Singh, K.S.**, ed., 1985, *Tribal movements in India*, Manohar Publications, New Delhi, 405 p, 2 vols.

——, 1985, (Book review), *Economic Trends* 31(6) March, p 1-4 +; *Financial Express* 9(5) June, p 5-8.
Review of the book : **Patel, M.L.**, 1985, *Planning strategy for tribal development*, Inter-India Publication, New Delhi, 191 p.

——, 1985, (Book review), *Hindustan Times* (Magazine) January 6, p viii, col 1-6.
Review of the book : **Dey, Bimal J.** and **Lehri, Dilip K.**, 1984, *Cosmogony of caste and social mobility in Assam*, Mittal Publications, Delhi, 183 p.

——, 1985, (Book review), *Hindustan Times* (Magazine), August 8, p 6-8.
Review of the book : **Rajagopal, Indhu**, 1985, *The tyranny of caste: The non-Brahmin movement and political development in South India*, Vikas Publication, New Delhi, 195 p.

——, 1985, (Book review), *India Quarterly* 41(1) January-March, p 182-184.
Review of the book : **Deshpande, Vasant**, 1983, Struggle of the deprived for development : The Mhaisal untouchables, Dastane, Ramachandra and Company, Pune, 168 p.

——, 1985, (Book review), *Indian Economic and Social History Review* 23(4) October-December, p 442-443.
Review of the book : **Gupta, S.K.**, 1986, *The Scheduled Castes in modern Indian politics : Their emergence as political power*, Munshiram, New Delhi, xi, 355 p.

——, 1985, (Book review), *Indian Journal of Political Studies*, 9 December, p 119-120.
Review of the book : **Basu, R.**, 1985, *Tribal development programmes and administration*, National Book Organisation, New Delhi, 322 p.

——, 1985, (Book review), *Indian Journal of Public Administration* 32(4) October-December, p 1110-1112.
Review of the book : **Pamecha, Renuka**, 1985, *Elite in a tribal society*, Printwell Pub., Jaipur, 223 p.

——, 1985, (Book review), *Journal of Social Research*, September 29, p 80-81; *Man in India* 68(4) December, p 471-478; *Sarvartham* 13, p 128-130.
Review of the book : **Sahay, K.N.**, et al, 1985, *Change of tribal identity in Chotanagpur : A study of conversion from one tribal group to the other*, Kishor Vidya Niketan, Varanasi, 91 p.

——, 1985, (Book review), *Management and Labour Studies* 10(1) January, p 46-47.

Review of the book : **Biswas, R.K.**, et al, 1985, *Industries face to face with tribal people : The case of Chotanagpur in Bihar*, NIPM, Ranchi, 66 p.

——, 1985, (Book review), *National Herald*, October 20, p 5, col 2-5, *Patriot*, November 3, p 4.

Review of the book : **Mehta, Haroobhai** and **Patel, Hasmukh**, 1985, *Dynamics of reservation policy*, Patriot Publishing, New Delhi, 320 p.

——, 1985, (Book review), *Patriot*, May 12, p 4, col 1-4.

Review of the book : **Desai, I.P.**, et al, 1985, *Caste, caste-conflict and reservations*, Janata Publication, Delhi, viii, 218 p.

——, 1985, (Book review), *Patriot*, November 24, p 4, col 4-7.

Review of the book : **Chaubey, N.P.**, ed., 1983, *Tribal techniques, Social organisation and development : Disruption and alternatives*, IASS, Allahabad, 206 p.

——, 1985, (Book review), *Perspective in Education* 10(5) March, p 5-6; *National Herald*, March 21, p 7, col 1-4.

Review of the book : **Joshi, Ramasharan**, 1985, *Tribals: Islands of deprivation*, National Book Shop, Delhi, 196 p.

——, 1985, (Book review), *Sarvartham* 13, p 130-131.

Review of the book : **Singh, K.S.**, 1985, *Tribal society in India*, Manohar Pub., New Delhi, 327 p.

——, 1985, (Book review), *Social Action* 35(1) January-March, p 95-98.

Review of the book : **Pachauri, S.K.**, 1984, *Dynamics of rural development in tribal areas*, Concept Publishing Company, New Delhi, xiv, 262 p.

——, 1985, (Book review), *Social Change* 15(1) March, p 57; *Sunday Statesman* 23(11) June, p 4-5.

Review of the book : **Siddiqui, M.K.A.**, 1985, *Educating a backward minority*, Abidi Publication, Calcutta.

——, 1985, (Book review), *Social Perspective* 13(3) December, p 204-207.

Review of the book : **Alam, Javeed**, 1985, *Domination and dissent: Peasant and politics*, Calcutta, Mandira.

——, 1985, (Book review), *Social Scientist* 13(5) May, p 68-71.

Review of the book : **Pathy, Jaganath**, 1983, *Tribal peasantry : Dynamics of development*, Inter-India Publications, New Delhi.

——, 1985, (Book review), *Times of India* February 24, p 1, col 1-4.

Review of the book : **Sen, Suchibrata**, 1985, *The Santals of Jungle Mahals*, Ratna Prakashan, Calcutta.

——, 1985, (Book review), *Tribune*, January 12, p 3-4.

Review of book: **Galanter, Marc**, 1984, *Law and the backward classes in India*, Oxford University Press, New Delhi, 525 p.

——, 1985, (Book review), *Tribune*, June 15, p 4, col 3-4.

Review of the book : **Shah, Ghanshyam**, 1985, *Economic differentiations and tribal economy*, Ajanta Publication, Delhi, 152 p.

——, 1985, (Book review), *Vision* 4(3) January-March, p 67-69.

Review of the book : **Saboo, B.**, 1985, *The problem of weaker sections*, New Era Publishing, Bhubaneshwar, 248 p.

——, 1985, Caste war in Gujarat : Wider objectives of agitation, *Times of India*, June 14, p 6.

——, 1985, A cynical ploy, *Times of India*, January 17, p 8, col 1-2.

——, 1985, The exploitation of Kerala tribals, *Link* 28(4) September 1, p 16-18.

——, 1985, Going beyond reservations : Framework for a wider policy, *Times of India*, April 20, p 8.
——, 1985, Govt. staff in Gandhinagar strike work, *Times of India* May 1, p 1 +.
——, 1985, Gujarat : Threat of fresh agitation, *New Age*, November 24, p 2.
——, 1985, Gujarat accord, *Times of India*, July 22, p 8.
——, 1985, Gujarat caste war, *Times of India*, April 17, p 8.
——, 1985, Gujarat Government accepts agitators' demands, *Times of India*, April 20, p 1 +.
——, 1985, Industry, police, carpet-baggers run amuck in Chotanagpur, *Link* 21(50) July 21, p 4-9.
——, 1985, Industry takes away Adivasi land, gives jobs to outsiders, *Link* 27(50) July 21, p 10-15.
——, 1985, A new thirst to tribal development, *Andhra Pradesh* 28(10) August, p 7-9.
——, 1985, The poor have no voice, *Hindustan Times* (Magazine) September 1, p 5, col 1-8.
——, 1985, Profile of a tribal child of Panchmahals, *Social Welfare* 32(3) June, p 28-29.
——, 1985, Reverse discrimination defended, *Link* 27(36) April 21, p 12.
——, 1985, Stuntmanship leads to disaster, *Times of India* (Sunday Review) April 28, p 1 +.
——, 1985, A thorny problem, *Times of India*, March 7, p 8.
——, 1985, Three years of tribal autonomous comment, *People's Democracy* 9(12) March 24, p 7-8.
——, 1985, Turmoil over reservations : Backward classes in full cry, *Times of India*, April 12, p 8.
——, 1985, Uplift of Scheduled Castes, *Haryana Review* 19(9) September, p 16-18.
——, 1985-1986, Castes and tribes in economic transition : A regional study, *Arthaniti* 25, p 46-64.
——, 1986, All round growth at Chatikhona, *Link* (Supplement) 28(30) March 2, p 20-21.
——, 1986, Annotated bibliography, *Social Action* 36(2) April-June, p 220-225.
——, 1986, Atrocities on the Scheduled Castes, *Social Action* 36(2) April-June, p 201-211.
——, 1986, Backward class quota : Farming a national consensus, *Times of India* 19(8) September 19, p 8.
——, 1986, Bondas opt for development, *Link* (Supplement) 28(30) March 2, p 22-23.
——, 1986, (Book review), *Contributions to Indian Sociology* (New Series) 20(1) January-June, p 155-156.
Review of the book : **Mishra, S.N.**, 1985, *Tribal economic transformation : The North East Indian pattern*, Institute of Development Economics, Tokyo, 81 p.
——, 1986, (Book review), *Economic and Political Weekly* 2(4) January-March 25, p 161-163.
Review of the book : **Singh, K.S.**, 1985, *Tribal society in India*, Manohar Pub., New Delhi, 327 p.
——, 1986, (Book review), *Economic Times* 30(6) December, p 1-4.
Review of the book : **Brass, Paul R.**, 1983, *Caste faction and party in Indian politics*, Chanakya Publication, Delhi, 339 p.

——, 1986, (Book review), *Education Quarterly* 38(2) Summer, p 51-52; *Journal of Rural Development* 5(1) January, p 124.
Review of the book : **Parvathamma, C.**, 1986, *New horizons and Scheduled Castes*, Ashish Publishing House, New Delhi, 184 p.

——, 1986, (Book review), *Education Quarterly* 38(2) Summer, p 49-51; *Social Action* 36(1) January-March, p 122-124.
Review of the book : **Shah, Vimal P.** and **Patel, Tara**, 1985, *Social contacts of tribal education*, Concept Publishing Company, New Delhi, xii, 212 p.

——, 1986, (Book review), *Financial Express*, February 2, p 5, col 5-8.
Review of the book : **Sharma, Madan Lal** and **Dak, T.M.**, eds., 1985, *Caste and class in agrarian society : Dynamics of rural development*, Ajanta Publications, Delhi, 256 p.

——, 1986, (Book Review), *Folklore* 27(6) June, p 130.
Review of the book : **Chaudhuri, Buddhadeb**, 1986, *Tribal health : Socio-cultural dimensions*, Inter-India Publication, New Delhi, 350 p.

——, 1986, (Book review), *India Past and Present* 3(2), p 315-323.
Review of the book : **O'Hanion, Rosalind**, 1986, *Caste, conflict and ideology : Mahatma Jatirao Phule and low caste protest in nineteenth century Western India*, Cambridge University Press, Cambridge, 320 p.

——, 1986, (Book review), *India Quarterly* 42(1) January-March, p 103-105; *Patriot*, March, 9, p 4, col 4-7; *Sunday Statesman*, March 9, p 11, col 1-5; *Tribune*, April 27, p 11, col 5-8.
Review of the book : **Mehta, Haroobhai** and **Patel, Hasmukh**, 1985, *Dynamics of reservation policy*, Patriot Publishing, New Delhi, 320 p.

——, 1986, (Book review), *Indian and Foreign Review* 24(8) February 15, p 26.
Review of the book : **Chatrapati Singh**, 1986, *Common prosperity and common property : India's forests, forest dwellers and the law*, Oxford University Press, Delhi.

——, 1986, (Book review), *Indian Archives* 35(1) January-June, p 99-101.
Review of the book : **Gupta, S.K.**, 1986, *The Scheduled Castes in modern Indian politics : Their emergence as political power*, Manohar Pub., New Delhi, 355 p.

——, 1986, (Book review), *Indian Express* (Magazine) March 9, p 5, col 4-7.
Review of the book : **Raizada, Ajit**, 1986, *Tribal development in Madhya Pradesh: A planning perspective*, Inter-India Publication, New Delhi.

——, 1986, (Book review), *Indian Express*, June 29, p 5, col 4-8.
Review of the book : **Aggarwal, Pratap**, 1986, *Halfway to equality*, Manohar Pub. New Delhi.

——, 1986, (Book review), *Indian Express* (Magazine), August 31, p 4, col 1-5.
Review of the book : **Anon**, 1986, *Scenario of the 7 per cent*, Cenemart Foundation, New Delhi, 2 vols.

——, 1986, (Book review), *Indian Journal of Social Work* 47(2) July, p 237-238.
Review of the book : **Sinha, Sachchidananda**, 1982, *Caste system: Myth reality challenge*, Intellectual Publication, New Delhi, 236 p.

——, 1986, (Book review), *Journal of Indian Law Institute* 28(1) January-March, p 117-121.
Review of the book : **Galanter, Marc**, 1984, *Competing equalities : Law and the backward classes in India*, Oxford University Press, New Delhi, 525 p.

——, 1986, (Book review), *New Quest*, 56, March-April, p 127-128.
Review of the book: **Mahapatra, Sitakant**, 1986, *The awakened wind: The oral poetry of the Indian tribes*, Vikas Publication, New Delhi, 322 p.

——, 1986, (Book review), *Panjab University Research Bulletin* (Arts) 18(1) April, p 221-223.
Review of the book : **Chaudhuri, Buddhadeb**, ed., 1986, *Tribal health : Socio-cultural dimensions*, Inter-India Publication, New Delhi, 350 p.

Anon, 1986, (Book review), *Patriot*, January, p 1-3.
Review of the book : **Gupta, S.K.**, 1986, *The Scheduled Castes in modern Indian polities : Their emergence as a politics power*, Munshi Ram, New Delhi, 355 p.

——, 1986, (Book review), *Patriot*, February 4, p 4-7.
Review of the book : **Brass, Paul R.**, 1983, *Caste faction and party in Indian politics*, Chanakya Publication, Delhi, 323 p.

——, 1986, (Book review), *Patriot*, October 19, p 4, col 1-4.
Review of the book : **Das, S.T.**, 1980, *Tribal life of North Eastern India*, Gian Publishing, New Delhi, 321 p.

——, 1986, (Book review), *Patriot*, November, 16, p 4, col 5-7.
Review of the book : **Biswas, Onell**, 1985, *From justice to welfare*, Intellectual Publishing House, New Delhi, xix, 272 p.

——, 1986, (Book review), *Social Action* 36(1) January-March, p 120-122.
Review of the book : **Shah, Ghanshyam**, et al, 1985, *Tribal education in Gujarat*, Ajanta Publication, New Delhi, 143 p.

——, 1986, (Book review), *Southern Economist* 24(23) April, p 26-27.
Review of the book : **Pachauri, S.K.**, 1984, *Dynamics of rural development in tribal areas*, Concept Publishing Company, New Delhi, xiv, 262 p.

——, 1986, (Book review), *Tribune*, April 13, p 11, col 5-8.
Review of the book : **Patel, Tara**, 1986, *Development of education among tribal women*, Mittal Publication, Delhi, 198 p.

——, 1986, (Book review), *Tribune* (Magazine), September 7, p 2, col 6-8.
Review of the book : **Archer, W.G.**, 1986, *Tribal law and justice*, Concept Publishing Company, New Delhi, xxxvi, 741 p.

——, 1986, (Book review), *Yojana* 30(8) May 1, p 34.
Review of the book : **Joshi, Ramasharan**, 1986, *Flight of the tribals : Tribes : Islands of deprivation*, National Book Shop, Delhi, xvi, 196 p.

——, 1986, Bring them to school, *Link* (Supplement) 28(30) March 2, p 33-34.

——, 1986, Bring tribal into the mainstream, *Link* (Supplement) 28(30) March 2, p 29-32.

——, 1986, Caste politics, *Economic Trends* 4(5) June, p 1-2.

——, 1986, Cross opportunism, *Times of India*, July 18, p 8, col 1-2.

——, 1986, Goodbye to modernism : Warring over reservations, *Times of India*, August 1, p 8.

——, 1986, Home of tribal art, *Link* (Supplement) 28(30) March 2, p 35-36.

——, 1986, Into the future, *Link* 28(30) March, p 37-40.

——, 1986, Mr. Hegde surrenders, *Times of India*, October 9, p 8, col 1-2.

——, 1986, Policy of reservation : A symposium, *Parlance*, August, p 10-21.

——, 1986, Shiv Sena enters rural politics : Campaign against Dalits in Marathwara villages, *Economic and Political Weekly* 21(50) December 13, p 2166-2167.

——, 1986, Tribal culture and education's response : Search for a model of education for the tribal people, *New Frontiers in Education* 16(1) January-March, p 1-47, appendix.

——, 1986, Zia's punitive strike on Pushtoon tribes, *New Age* 34(5) February 2, p 13.

——, 1987, (Book review), *Contributions to Indian Sociology* (New Series) 21(1) January-June, p 248-249.
Review of the book : **Das Gupta, Satadal**, 1986, *Caste, kinship and community : Social system of a Bengal Caste*, Madras University Press, Madras, xii, 291 p.

——, 1987, (Book review), *Contribution to Indian Sociology* (NS) 22(1) January-June, p 116-118; *Social Scientist* 16(2) February, p 60-66.
Review of the book : **Hardiman, David**, 1988, *The coming of Devi : Adivasi assertion in Western India*, Oxford University Press, New Delhi, 248 p.

——, 1987, (Book review), *Economic and Political Weekly* 22(26) June 27, p 1030-1031.
Review of the book : **Srinivas, M.N.**, 1987, *The dominant caste and other essays*, Oxford University Press, New Delhi, ix, 195 p.

——, 1987, (Book review), *Indian Economic Social History Review* 24(3) July-September, p 341-342; *Tribune* (Magazine) September 14, p 5-8.
Review of the book : **Dumont, Louis**, 1986, *A South Indian subcaste : Social organisation and religion of the Pramalai Kallar*, Oxford University Press, New Delhi, 634 p.

——, 1987, (Book review), *Indian Express* (Magazine) January 10, p 8, col 6-8.
Review of the book : **Fernades, Walter** and **Menon, Geeta**, 1987, *Tribal women and forest economy*, Indian Social Institute, New Delhi.

——, 1987, (Book review), *Indian Journal of Social Work* 47(4) January, p 464-466.
Review of the book : **Gangrade, K.D.**, 1986, *Social work and development : Role of religion and caste in three Delhi villages*, Northern Book Centre, Delhi, 130 p.

——, 1987, (Book review), *Journal of Education Planning and Administration* 1(2) April, p 256-259.
Review of the book : **Hanumantha Rayappa, P.** and **Mutharayappa, R.**, 1986, *Backwardness and welfare of Scheduled Castes and Scheduled Tribes in India*, Ashish Publishing House, New Delhi, 121 p.

——, 1987, (Book review), *Journal of Education Planning and Administration* 1(2) April, p 252-255.
Review of the book : **Patel, Tara**, 1986, *Development of education among tribal women*, Mittal Publications, New Delhi, 198 p.

——, 1987, (Book review), *Journal of Rural Development* 6(4) July 7, p 423-426; *National Geographical Journal of India* 33(1) March, p 118-119.
Review of the book : **Singh, R.S.**, 1987, *Changing occupational structure of Scheduled Tribes*, Inter-India Publication, New Delhi, 291 p.

——, 1987, (Book review), *Journal of Sociological Studies*, January 6, p 187-190.
Review of the book : **Bag, Dulal Chandra**, 1984, *Impact of education on some backward communities of West Bengal*, OPS Publishing, Calcutta, viii, 304 p.

——, 1987, (Book review), *Mainstream* 25(3) April 18, p 22-23.
Review of the book : **Basu, N.G.**, 1987, *Forest and tribals*, Manisha Granthalaya, Calcutta, 203 p.

——, 1987, (Book review), *Man in India* 67(1) March, p 74-77.
Review of the book : **Chakrabarty**, et al, 1985, *Agrarian situation in India*, Anthropological Survey of India, Calcutta, 2 vols.

——, 1987, (Book review), *Social Change* 17(3) September, p 97-99.
Review of the book : **Roy, Ramashray** and **Singh, V.B.**, 1987, *Between two worlds : A study of Harijan elites*, Discovery Publishing House, Delhi, 176 p.

——, 1987, (Book review), *Times of India* (Sunday review) March 8, p 6.

Review of the book : **Sundanshi, D.N.**, 1987, *Reservations for social justice*, Current Law Publishing.

——, 1987, (Book review), *Times of India* (Sunday review) March 15, p 1-5.

Review of the book : **Gould, Herald A.**, 1987, *The Hindu caste system : The sacralisation of a social order*, Chanakya Publication, Delhi.

——, 1987, (Book review), *Tribune*, March 15, p 11, col 7-8.

Review of the book : **Maheshwari Prasad**, ed.; 1987, *Tribals: Their environment and culture*, Amar Prakashan, Delhi, 344 p.

——, 1987, A class of rights, *Hindustan Times* (Magazine) June 21, p 1-5 +.

——, 1987, Class war in Bihar, *Hindustan Times* (Magazine) June 21, p 1-6.

——, 1987, Cursed are the dispossessed, *Link* 29(36) April 12, p 4-8.

——, 1987, Displacement of tribals due to location of Centre State projects : Problems and related issues, *Tribal Research Bulletin* 9(2) March, p 21-26, bibliography.

——, 1987, Economy of a border region : The Bhotiyas of Kumaon, *Link* 29(45) June 14, p 17-20.

——, 1987, For a democratic solution to problems of Bihar tribals, *New Age* 35(43) October 25, p 9.

——, 1987, Is there a cure for Bihar? *Hindustan Times* (Magazine) June 7, p 1-3.

——, 1987, Rural violence in Bihar, *Link* 29(49) July 12, p 17-20.

——, 1987, Tamil Nadu violence, *Times of India*, September 19, p 6, col 1-2.

——, 1987, Tribal sub-plan programme, *Times of India* (Magazine), January 22, p 11, col 1-8 +, tables.

——, 1987, Using the violence bogey against the Left, *Economic and Political Weekly* 22(34) August 22, p 1437-1438.

——, 1988, (Book review), *Contributions to Indian Sociology* (New Series) 22(1) January-June, p 116-118.

Review of the book : **Hardiman, David**, 1987, *The coming of the Devi : Adivasi assertion in Western India*, Oxford University Press, New Delhi, xii, 248 p.

——, 1988, (Book review), *Economic and Political Weekly* 23(4) January 23, p 148; *Patriot*, January 31, p 4, col 3-7.

Review of the book : **Basu, N.G.**, 1987, *Forests and tribals*, Manisha Granthalaya, Calcutta, vi, 196 p.

——, 1988, (Book review), *Economic and Political Weekly* 23(42) October 15, p 2165.

Review of the book : **Shukla, Hiralal**, 1987, *Dictionary of tribal languages : Historical comparative*, B.R. Publishing, Delhi, 330 p.

——, 1988, (Book review), *Hindustan Times* (Magazine) August 28, p 1-4.

Review of the book : **Shah, A.M.** and **Desai, I.P.**, 1988, *Division and hierarchy : An overview of caste in Gujarat*, Hindustan Publication Corporation, Delhi, 150 p.

——, 1988, (Book review), *Indian Economic Social History Review* 25(1) January-March, p 107-109; *Indian History Review* 11(1-2) July-January, p 259-260.

Review of the book : **Singh, K.S.**, 1985, *Tribal society in India : An anthropo-historical perspective*, Manohar Pub., New Delhi, 327 p.

——, 1988, (Book review), *Legal News and Views* 2(3) March, p 5-6.

Review of the book : **Khosla, Dinesh**, 1987, *Myth and reality of the protection of civil rights law : Study of untouchability in rural India*, Hindustan Publishing, Delhi, 190 p.

——, 1988, (Book review), *Man in India* 68(2-3) June-September, p 305.

Review of the book : **Gour, P.N.**, ed., 1988, *Bihar tribal bibliography*, Patna Library Publishing, Patna, 135 p.

——, 1988, (Book review), *Man in India* 68(2-3) June-September, p 308-309.

Review of the book : **Roy, Kanchan**, 1988, *The Korkus of the Vindhya hills*, Inter-India Publications, New Delhi, 443p, maps, tables, plates.

——, 1988, (Book review), *Sarvartham* 13, p 126-128; *Times of India* (Sunday review) January 10, p 1 +.

Review of the book : **Maheshwari Prasad**, 1988, *Tribes: Their environments and culture*, Amar Prakashan, Delhi, 344 p.

——, 1988, (Book review), *Social Scientist* 16(2) February p 60-66.

Review of the book : **Hardiman, David**, 1988, *The coming of the Devi : Adivasi assertion in Western India*, Oxford University Press, Delhi.

——, 1988, (Book review), *Social Scientist* 16(4) April, p 64-67.

Review of the book : **Sukumaran, M.K.** 1987, *Tribal economy in transition*, Inter-India Publication, New Delhi.

——, 1988, Caste in Bihar's political mould, *Times of India*, February 9, p 2-5 +.

——, 1988, Castes and tribes in economic transition : A regional study, *Arthaniti*, 25, p 46-63.

——, 1988, Kerala shows the way, *Times of India*,, August 2, p 4, col 1-2.

——, 1988, Polum of the masses, *Times of India*, July 14, p 4, col 1-2.

——, 1988, They enter god's house, *Times of India*, August 13, p 6, col 1-2.

——, 1988, Workshop on tribal development, *Mainstream* 26(35) June 11, p 27-28 +.

——, 1989, Ashram schools, *Vanyajati* 37(3) July, p 1-2.

——, 1989, (Book review), *Economic Times* 5(6) February, p 1-4.

Review of the book : **Nancharaiah, Gummadi**, 1989, *Land and caste*, Himalayan Publishing House, Bombay, 112 p.

——, 1989, (Book review), *Indian Express* (Magazine) March 5, p 5 col 1-3.

Review of the book: **Mukherjee, Shimtam Prabhati**, 1989, *Beyond the four varnas : The untouchables in India*, Indian Institute of Advance Studies, Shimla.

——, 1989, (Book review), *Man in India* 69(3) September, p 313-316.

Review of the book : **Nandu Ram**, 1989, *The Mobile Scheduled Castes : Rise of a new middle class*, Hindustan Corporation (India), Delhi, p 137 +.

——, 1989, (Book review), *Patriot*, April 9, p 3-6.

Review of the book : **Jain, S.K.**, 1989, *Castes and politics in Bihar*, Common Health Publication, New Delhi, 134 p.

——, 1989, (Book review), *Tribune*, January 29, p 2, col 1-2.

Review of the book : **Premi, Kusum K.**, 1989, *Scheduled Castes and Scheduled Tribes in industrial training institutes*, Vikas Publishing, New Delhi, 134 p.

——, 1989, Homage to Nehru, *Vanyajati*, 37(1), January 1, p 1-2.

——, 1989, Ranga's murder raises many questions, *Times of India* (Section II) February 20, p 2-6 +.

——, 1989, Report of the National Seminar on Nehru and Evolution of Tribal Policy sponsored by Bhartiya Adamjati Sevak Sangh, *Vanyajati* 37(4) October, p 1-5.

——, 1989, Uneasy quiet, *Illustrated Weekly of India* 110(36) September 3, p 20-23.

——, 1990, Advani assails, V.P. on minorities quota, *Hindustan Times*, September 2.

——, 1990, Advani assails, V.P. on Muslim quota, *Times of India*, September 2.

——, 1990, Agreement on four-point, says Upendra, *National Herald*, September 4, p 1, col 1.

——, 1990, Ahir and Gujjars 'left alone', *Statesman*, September 7.

——, 1990, All party meet not a failure : N.F., *Hindustan Times*, September 5, p 24, col 4.

——, 1990, All party meet to discuss reservations, *Hindustan Times*, August 31.

——, 1990, Anger of the elite? *Statesman*, Septermber 7.

——, 1990, Anti-Mandal stir: No decision on Delhi rally, *Times of India*, September 9.

——, 1990, Anti quota stir hits grain trade, *Times of India*, September 8.

——, 1990, Anti quota stir spreads, four filled in Patna violence, *Times of India*, September 5, p 1, col 1-2.

——, 1990, Anti quota stir toll rises to 7 in Orissa, *Statesman*, September 3, p 1, col 3-5, p 7, col 5.

——, 1990, Anti reservation stir in Bihar : Situation needs mature handling, *Patriot*, September 1.

——, 1990, Anti reservation stir unabated : 4 killed in Orissa police firing, *Times of India*, September 2.

——, 1990, Army alerted in Baroda : Curfew in three cities, *Hindustan Times*, September 6.

——, 1990, Army alerted in Simla, *Hindustan Times*, September 8, p 1 +, col 5-7.

——, 1990, Army called out in Kangra district : H.P. rejects Mandal report, *Times of India*, September 7.

——, 1990, B.J.P. against quota for minorities, says Advani, *Hindustan Times*, September 3, p 1 col 4.

——, 1990, B.J.P., CPM for talks with students, *Tribune*, September 7.

——, 1990, B.J.P. flays Govt. on job quota issue, *Hindustan Times*, September 9.

——, 1990, B.J.P. for 50 per cent as quota limit, *Hindustan Times*, September 1.

——, 1990, B J P-Left call for economic criterion, *Times of India*, August 18.

——, 1990, Backward quota a forward step, *Hindustan Times*, September, 7.

——, 1990, Backwardness won't go by playing patty politics; V.P.S. ebstinacy will divide India; Plea for uplift of poorest of poor : Rajiv in marathon L S speech, *National Herald*, September 7.

——, 1990, Bandh no way to do it, say traders, *Hindustan Times*, September 7.

——, 1990, Basu calls for modification, *Indian Express*, September 1.

——, 1990, Be your own light, *Tribune* August 19.

——, 1990, Beyond mere palliatives, *Hindu*, September 9.

——, 1990, Bill on job quota for SC, ST on anvil, *Hindustan Times*, September 3, p 18, col 1-2.

——, 1990, Bommai warns of bloodshed, *Tribune*, September 9.

——, 1990, (Book review), *Man in India* 70(2) June, p 199-201.
Review of the book : **Bhasin, Veena**, 1989, *Ecology, culture and change : Tribals of Sikkim Himalayas,* Inter-India, Publications, p 407 +, photoplates.

——, 1990, (Book review), *Man in India* 70(2) June, p 206-209.
Review of the book : **Paul, M.C.**, 1989, *Dimensions of tribal movements in India : A study of Udayachal in Assam Valley*, Inter-India Publication, New Delhi, p 107.

——, 1990, CPM favours Karpoori formula, *Hindustan Times*, August 31.

——, 1990, CPM view on quota against its policy, *Times of India*, September 2.

——, 1990, Cabinet not split over quota : V.P., *Times of India*, September 5.

——, 1990, Carrying the can, *Times of India*, September 5, p 8, col 1.

———, 1990, Caste not basis, says V.P. Singh, *Hindu*, September 7.
———, 1990, Cauldron of caste tensions, *Hindu*, September 4, p 8, col 3-6.
———, 1990, Central order on job reservation, *Hindustan Times*, August 19, p 12, col 5-8.
———, 1990, Centre accepts states plea, *Times of India*, September 3.
———, 1990, Chakha Jam plan washed away, *Hindustan Times*, September 8, p 5, col 2-5.
———, 1990, A challenge to political parties, *National Herald*, September 2.
———, 1990, Congress (I) flays govt. move on quota, *Indian Express*, September 5, p 9, col 1-5.
———, 1990, Congress to boycott all-party meet, *Hindustan Times*, September 3, p 1, col 1-3, p 18, col 1-2.
———, 1990, Consensus eludes all party meet; Cong. leaders attend; Govt. stand rigid, *Hindustan Times*, September 4, p 1, col 1-4.
———, 1990, DUTA Chief's bid to scuttle discussion condemned, *Hindu*, September 2.
———, 1990, DUTA split over Mandal report, *Times of India*, September 2.
———, 1990, Dalit Christians allege bias, *Hindustan Times*, August 18, p 5, col 5-8.
———, 1990, Dalit Christians demands SC status, *Times of India*, August, 18.
———, 1990, Dalit Christians want SC status, privileges, *Hindu*, August 18.
———, 1990, Decision on Mandal report hasty : Dhawan, *Tribune*, September 9.
———, 1990, Decision on quota hasty : NF leader, *Times of India*, September 9.
———, 1990, Delhi incident-free, but stir continues, *Hindu*, September 2.
———, 1990, Divided they stand, *Tribune*, September 5, p 6, col 1-2.
———, 1990, Do not destroy country : Dinesh, *Hindustan Times*, September 6.
———, 1990, Don't take a hasty decision on quota, Left tells V.P., *National Herald*, September 5, p 1, col 1.
———, 1990, Double talk on castes, *Hindustan Times*, September 7.
———, 1990, End the drift, *Hindustan Times*, September 7.
———, 1990, Expert disagrees with Mandal report, *Hindustan Times*, September 1.
———, 1990, Extend reservation to education: MPs, *Patriot*, September 4.
———, 1990, Farmers blast quota policy, *Hindustan Times*, September 9.
———, 1990, Fire spreads, *National Herald*, September 8, p 6, col 1-2.
———, 1990, Firing in Bihar; stir spreads to South, *Times of India*, August 19.
———, 1990, Five die in Bihar anti-quota stir, *Indian Express*, September 5, p 9, col 1-4.
———, 1990, Five lakh likely to attend Anti Mandal Forum rally, *National Herald*, September 4, p 3, col 2.
———, 1990, Forum asks students to go back to classes, *Hindustan Times*, September 1.
———, 1990, Fresh violence in Bihar, Haryana, *Hindustan Times*, September 6.
———, 1990, From crisis to crisis : The unmaking of the Singh Government, *Probe India*, 11(7) September, p 8-12.
———, 1990, Full speed backwards by P.M., *Times of India*, September 4, p 8, col 3-4.
———, 1990, Govt. has put students fate in jeopardy : Aiyer, *National Herald*, September 4, p 3-5.
———, 1990, Govt. pulled up for not tabling report, *Tribune*, September 7.
———, 1990, Govt. urged to seek apex courts advice, *Hindu*, September 8.
———, 1990, Gujarat coalition in fresh row, *Patriot*, September 8.

——, 1990, Gujarat 'no' to Mandal report, *Statesman*, September 5, p 1, col 7-8.

——, 1990, Gujjar leader assails report, *Indian Express*, September 5 p 16, col 1-3.

——, 1990, Haryana observes complete bandh, *Times of India*, September 1.

——, 1990, Haryana panel on backward classes, *Hindustan Times*, September 9.

——, 1990, High living, plain thinking : Mandalised metropolitan mind, *Times of India*, September 5, p 8, col 2-4.

——, 1990, How a tragedy is enacted, *Indian Express*, September 5, p 8, col 1.

——, 1990, The impasse continues, *National Herald*, September 6.

——, 1990, In a bind of sports, *Hindu*, September 5, p 8, col 1.

——, 1990, Injustice will be legalised, *Indian Express*, September 8, p 5, col 6-7.

——, 1990, Irony of the Mandal: Meenakshi Jain, *Indian Express*, September 3, p 8, col 3-6.

——, 1990, Is shoe-shining that shameful? *Times of India*, Septembuer 9.

——, 1990, JNU students join anti quota stir, *Times of India* August 19.

——, 1990, Janata party opposes Mandal report, *National Herald*, September 3, p 11, col 5.

——, 1990, Job quota ends Manu's legacy, *Statesman*, September 8.

——, 1990, Job reservations for backward classes, *Patriot*, Septermber 3.

——, 1990, Kanshi Ram assails V.P. on Mandal, *Hindustan Times*, September 6.

——, 1990, List of castes delayed, *Times of India*, September 9.

——, 1990, Lung power keeps pot boiling, *Hindustan Times*, September 7.

——, 1990, Mandal : Champion of backward classes? *Indian Express*, August 19, p 1, col 1-5; p 9, col 1.

——, 1990, Mandal : Myth of merit and equity, *Times of India*, September 4, p 8, col 6-7.

——, 1990, Mandal mania and social justice, *Indian Express*, September 5, p 8 col 2-5.

——, 1990, Mandal not relevant to Orissa, says J.B. Patnaik, *National Herald*, September 3, p 12, col 2.

——, 1990, Mandal panel report: Harves of headcounts in caste politics, *Link*, 33(4) September 2, p 4-5.

——, 1990, Mandal report not to be imposed on States : V.P., *Indian Express*, September 2.

——, 1990, Mandal report scientific : Gill, *Hindustan Times*, September 6.

——, 1990, The Mandal trap, *Hindustan Times*, September 1.

——, 1990, A messiah always in the news, *Times of India*, September 9.

——, 1990, Minority govt. arrogance, *Tribune*, September 4, p 6, col 2-4.

——, 1990, Mishra urges V.P. to accept Rajiv Formula, *National Herald*, September 5, p 9, col 5-8.

——, 1990, More politics than jobs, says Rajiv, *Hindustan Times*, September 8, p 1, col 1-2; p 10.

——, 1990, NF allies may seek changes in Mandal, *National Herald*, September 2.

——, 1990, NF Parliamentary Party boo; implementation, *Indian Express*, September 4, p 1, col 2-4 and p 9, col 5.

——, 1990, National debate on reservation imperative, *Statesman*, September 1.

——, 1990, Need for dialogue, *Indian Express*, September 6.

——, 1990, Need, not caste, *Times of India*, September 8.

——, 1990, Need to redefine backwardness, *National Herald*, September 1.

——, 1990, Nehru for Lohia? *National Herald*, August 24.

———, 1990, No compromises on Mandal : Mulayam, *National Herald*, September 3, p 11, col 2-3.
———, 1990, No confrontation with States : V.P., *Times of India*, September 2.
———, 1990, No consensus on Mandal report, Cong. attends all party meet, *Times of India*, September 4, p 1, col 3-4; p 16, col 2.
———, 1990, No legal hurdles to job quota, *Hindustan Times*, August 19, p 1, col 1.
———, 1990, No plan to change quota formula : Nayanar, *Indian Express*, September 8, p 14, col 1-4.
———, 1990, No way to consensus, *Patriot*, September 5.
———, 1990, Not by closure, *Patriot*, September 3.
———, 1990, Not by violence, *Times of India*, August 18.
———, 1990, Not without a consensus, *Hindustan Times*, September 5, p 14, col 1.
———, 1990, Now it is caste fanaticism, *Hindustan Times*, September 8, p 5, col 1-3.
———, 1990, Omens in Gujarat, *Times of India*, September 6.
———, 1990, One killed in U P firing, *Times of India*, September 4, p 1, col 5-7; p 16, col 3.
———, 1990, Orissa asks for Central forces, *Hindustan Times*, September 2.
———, 1990, Orissa firing toll 6; agitation continues in many States, *Indian Express*, September 3, p 1, col 6-8; p 12, col 3-5.
———, 1990, PM dividing nation on caste lines : Rajiv, *Times of India*, September 9.
———, 1990, PM urged to defuse crisis, *Hindustan Times*, September 7.
———, 1990, Patnaik orders probe into firing, *Patriot*, September 4.
———, 1990, Pointless polemics, *Patriot*, September 8.
———, 1990, Politicians viewpoint, *Hindustan Times*, September 9.
———, 1990, The politics of pell mell, *Hindustan Times*, September 2.
———, 1990, Professors oppose job quota, *Hindustan Times*, August 18, p 1, col 4; p 22, col 1.
———, 1990, Pro-quota men set for rally, *Hindustan Times*, September 6.
———, 1990, Pro-quota rally a damp squid, *Indian Express*, September 8, p 1, col 5-7; p 9, col 1.
———, 1990, Pro-quota youth rally today, *National Herald*, September 4, p 3, col 5-6.
———, 1990, Protest against Mandal report, *Tribune*, September 3, p 7, col 2-5.
———, 1990, Quota a hasty step : NF leader, *Hindustan Times*, September 9.
———, 1990, Quota created caste divide in muslims, says Mishra, *National Herald*, September 9.
———, 1990, Quota for OBC ad hoc solutions, *National Herald*, September 3, p 12, col. 3-4.
———, 1990, Quota for OBCs in education also sought, *Hindustan times*, September 4, p 1, col 5.
———, 1990, Quota should be avaited of once only, *Indian Express*, September 8, p 3, col 4-6.
———, 1990, Quota stir spreads to many areas, *Hindustan Times*, September 7.
———, 1990, Rain God is anti Mandal : Paswan, *Hindustan Times*, September 8, p 1, col 11.
———, 1990, Rajiv urges exhautive paper, *Times of India*, September 4, p 16, col. 1.
———, 1990, Reservations are necessary, *Tribune*, September 3, p 6, col. 3-5.
———, 1990, Reservations doesn't mean mediocrity, *Times of India*, September 3.
———, 1990, Reservation partisan, *Tribune*, August 8.
———, 1990, Reservation won't lead to mediocrity : Paswan, *Patriot*, September 3.

———, 1990, Rift in Bihar Cong-I over quota issue, *Indian Express*, September 7.
———, 1990, Right to work demand, *National Herald*, September 7, p 3, col. 2-4.
———, 1990, Road, rail traffic disrupted, *Times of India*, August 24.
———, 1990, Schools closed in three States, *Times of India*, September 9.
———, 1990, Shared warning on stir, *Hindustan Times*, September 3, p 18, col. 2-4.
———, 1990, Sikkim also rejects report, *Times of India*, September 8.
———, 1990, Sikkim to benefit by Mandal report, *Times of India*, September 7.
———, 1990, Slamming the doors, *Indian Express*, September 8, p 8, col. 1-2.
———, 1990, Society's supplements, *Hindustan Times*, September 2.
———, 1990, Statement on extension of reservation policy, *Mainstream*, 28(46) September 8, p 2.
———, 1990, States of unrest, *Statesman*, September 8.
———, 1990, Storm round the corner, *Link*, 33(4) September 2, p 7-8.
———, 1990, Students block roads in Haryana towns, *Hindustan Times*, September 1.
———, 1990, Students burn Mandal report, *Statesman*, August 18.
———, 1990, Students clear warning, *Hindustan Times*, September 2.
———, 1990, Students get farmer's support, *Hindustan Times*, September 5, p 1, col. 4-7.
———, 1990, Students must join talks : Bommai, *Times of India*, September 4, p 4-6.
———, 1990, 27 per cent but for whom: Rajeev Dhawan, *Patriot*, September 7.
———, 1990, 28 injured in clashes, *Hindustan Times*, September 4, p 1, col. 1-3.
———, 1990, Talk to youth, Advani tells govt., *Indian Express*, September 5, p 9, col 6.
———, 1990, The talks fail, *National Herald*, September 5, p 6, col. 1.
———, 1990, Teachers front back reservation, *National Herald*, September 4, p 3, col. 2-3.
———, 1990, This is not collectivism, *National Herald*, September 4, p 6 col. 1.
———, 1990, Tikait not to lead anti quota agitation, *Times of India*, August 18.
———, 1990, Toll figure inflated, Says Bihar C.M., *Hindu*, September 6, p 4, col. 2-5.
———, 1990, Top Cong. leaders held in Orissa, *Hindustan Times*, September 5, p 1, col. 1-2.
———, 1990, Troops patrol M P towns, *Times of India*, September 8.
———, 1990, Two injured in DU clash, *Times of India*, September 7.
———, 1990, U P C C Chief flays quota policy, *National Herald*, September 3, p 9, col. 4.
———, 1990, Uncharacteristics calm; Political compulsions, *Hindu*, September 9.
———, 1990, Undertaking democracy right, *Hindu*, September 4.
———, 1990, The unmaking of the Indian Union, *Indian Express*, September 3, p 1, col. 1-4.
———, 1990, Upendra claim absurd, *National Herald*, September 5, p 1, col. 2.
———, 1990, V P : No going back on rights of minorities, *Tribune*, September 3, p 1, col. 7-8.
———, 1990, V P asks NF MPs to explain Mandal report to people, *Hindustan Times*, September 8, p 1, Col. 2-3.
———, 1990, V P dares Cong. to reverse decision, *Hindustan Times*, September 6.
———, 1990, V P gets backing of State J D Chiefs, *National Herald*, September 3, p 1, col, 4-5.
———, 1990, V P revised agenda, *Tribune*, September, 4, p 1, col. 2-5.
———, 1990, V P Singh in a hind, *Patriot*, September 4.

——, 1990, V P working to divide nation on caste lines : Rajiv, *Hindustan Times*, September 7.
——, 1990, V P wrote to CMs before decision, *Hindustan Times*, September 2.
——, 1990, V P's bid to score over Devi, Mishra, *National Herald*, August 19, p 4, col. 3-8.
——, 1990, V P's challenge to Cong-I, *Indian Express*, September 6.
——, 1990, V P's other storm-trooper, *Tribune*, September 7.
——, 1990, V. P. Singh warns Pakistan, *Democratic World* 19(6) February 11, p 7.
——, 1990, V.P. Singh's strategy, *Democratic World* 19(11) March 18, p 10.
——, 1990, Vacancies for the OBCs, *Democratic World* 19(37) September 16, p 4.
——, 1990, Vajpayee hails all party meet on quota, *National Herald*, September 3, p 12, col. 1.
——, 1990, Virtual collapse of administration, *Democratic World* 19(45) November 1, p 8.
——, 1990, Violence in more States : Cuttack curfew extended, *Hindustan Times*, September 1.
——, 1990, Violence mars bandh in Delhi, 214 rounded up, *Hindustan Times*, September 7.
——, 1990, Violence unabated in Orissa, *Link* 33(4) September 2, p 8-9.
——, 1990, Wages of silence, *Indian Express*, August 25.
——, 1990, Walkout by BJP, CPI, CPM, *Tribune*, September 4, p 1, col. 6-8.
——, 1990, A way out of caste war, *Tribune*, September 3, col. 1-2.
——, 1990, What has Hershman disclosed? *Democratic World* 19(3) January 21, p 9-10.
——, 1990, What is the basis of the Rajiv's optimism, *Democratic World* 19(3) January 21, p 8-9.
——, 1990, When VPS stands up, *Mainstream* 28(48) September 22, p 1-2.
——, 1990, Will a compromise on Ram temple work ? *Democratic World* 19(41) October 14, p 10.
——, 1990, Will Devil Lal rejoin as Deputy P.M. ? *Democratic World* 19(3) P 5-7.
——, 1990, Who is to do it ? *Hindustan Times*, September 7.
——, 1990, Woes of Mandal beneficiaries, *Tribune*, September 6.
——, 1990, Wrong move, *Indian Express*, September 6.
Aonok, S. Wati, 1956, Morung organisation among the Nokte nagas, *Vanyajati* 4(2) April, 73-81, footnotes, illustrations.
Appadurai, A., 1974, Right and Left-hand castes in South India, *Indian Economic and Social History Review* 11(2-3), p 216-260.
Apte, J.S., 1960, Co-operative movement among the tribals of district Thana, Bombay State, *Vanyajati* 8(3) July, p 102-105.
——, 1960, Talwada Ashram School: An experiment in tribal education, *Vanyajati* 8(2) April, p 81-82.
Archer, Mildred, 1947, Early records of Indian tribes, *Man in India* 27(1) March, p 39-43.
Archer, W.G., 1987, Tribal law and justice : A report on the Santal, *Man in India* 67(1) March, p 81-86.
Arti Kumari, 1988, A study on the palmar dermatolyphics of the Kayasth of Ranchl, *Man in India* 68(2-3) June-September, p 216-227, bibliography.
Aryan, Subhashini, 1985, Tribal art of India, *Indian and Foreign Review* 22(19) 31 July, p 23-26.

Assayag, Jackie, 1989, Women-Goddess, Women-distress, Yellamma Goddess devotes in South India (Karnataka), *Man in India* 69(4) December, p 359-373.

Athavale, M.C. and **Nahatkar, Sunil**, 1983, Evaluation study of tribal area development programme in Konta and Dantewara, Bastar district, Madhya Pradesh, *Co-operative Perspective* 18(3) October-December, p 93-100.

Athre, H.V.R., 1980, Reservation policy, *Mysore Economic Review* 65(1) January, p 1-3.

Aurora, G.S., 1968, Caste and backward classes, *Man in India* 48(4) October-December, p 297-306, footnotes.

——, 1985, Tribal studies, *Contribution to Indian Sociology* (New Series) 19(2) July-December, p 359-365.

Ayrookuzheil, A.M. Abrahi, 1985, Religion : A way of salvation or an ideology of oppression ? *Religion and Society* 32(1) March, p 3-23, footnotes, tables.

Ayyanger, M.A., 1964, Impact of modern forces on the tribes and castes in India, *Journal of Social Research* 7(1-2) March-September, p 1-6.

Azad, J.L., 1976, Caste prejudice and children, *Progress of Education* 41(10-11) May-June, p 392-93, letter to Editor.

——, 1976, Education and prejudice : A perversity ? *Progress of Education* 41(9) April, p 345-46, letter to Editor.

——, 1976, Education of Scheduled Castes and Scheduled Tribes, *Journal of Indian Education* 1(6) March, p 23-28.

Aziz, Abdul, 1980, The backward class movement in Karnataka, 1918-1929, *Journal of Historical Studies* 16, p 50-62.

Baboo, Balgovind, 1986, Economic exchanges in a tribal village, *Man in India* 66(2) June, p 151-165.

——, 1986, Cognition and structure : Explaining the 'exploitation' of an untouchable in Orissa, *Eastern Anthropologist* 39(3) July-September, p 187-195.

Bachi, R.N., 1979, Family system and inheritance of property among the tribes of Arunachal, *Resarun* 5(1) Spring-Summer, p 38-41, bibliography.

Badhwar, Inderjeet, 1990, Mandal Commission: Dividing to rule, *India Today*, September 15.

Baduri, Manindra Bhusan, 1941, The Aboriginal tribes of the Udaipur State (C.P.), *Man in India* 21(2-3) April-September, p 92-126.

Bagchi, Tilak, et al, 1986, Ecology of some aspects of protein in energy malnutrition : A bio-social study on the Lodha : A primitive tribal group of West Bengal, *Man and Life* 12(1-2) January-June, p 47-60, bibliography, tables.

Bage, S.K., 1964, Seminar on impact of modern forces on tribes and castes in India : Welcome address, *Journal of Social Research* 7(1-2) March-September, p 12-14.

——, 1965, Anthropologists and tribal administration, *Journal of Social Research* 8(1) March, p 11-16.

Bahadur, F., 1965, Socio-economic survey of tribal development blocks in M.P., *Bulletin of Tribal Research and Development Institute* (Bhopal) 5 (1-2) June-December, p 28-34, appendix.

——, ed, 1966, Kharkhara Project: Survey of displaced families, *Bulletin of Tribal Research and Institute* (Bhopal) 6(1) June, p 1-13, tables.

Bahuguna, Sunderlal, 1990, INTACH Seminar on problems facing tribals and launching of Chipko movement in Chotanagpur, held at the Grove, Hazaribagh on October 22 and 23, *Man in India* 70(1), p 96-97.

Bailey, F.G., 1961, Tribe and caste in India, *Contributions to Indian Sociology*, October 5, p 7-19. Comments by **Dumont, Louis**, December 6, 1962, p 120-122.

Bainbridge, R.B., 1907, The Saorias and the Rajmahal Hills, *Memoirs of the Asiatic Society of Bengal* 2(4).

Bairagi, K.V., 1987, Modified area development approach pockets (MADA pockets) and mini-modified area development approach pockets (Mini-MADA pockets) clusters based on 1981, *Tribal Research Bulletin* 9(2) March, p 11, tables.

Bajaj, S.S., et al, 1985, Role of information sources in the adoption I R S paddy by tribal farmers, *Tribal Research Bulletin* 7(2) March, p 17-19.

Bajpai, Geeta, 1983, Economic determinants of social behaviour : A case study of the Waghers of Gujarat in the second half of the nineteenth century, *Journal of the Gujarat Research Society* 45(3) July, p 32-41, bibliography, footnotes.

——, 1985, Economic determinants of social behaviour : A case study of the Waghers of Gujarat in the second half of the nineteenth century, *India Past and Present* 2(1), p 31-40, footnotes.

Bajpai, Rajendra Kumari, 1986, National policy on upliftment of weaker sections, *Secular Democracy* 19(1-2) January-February, p 51-52.

Bakshi, P.M., 1985, Reservations for backward classes: Some reflections, *Journal of Indian Law Institute* 27(2) April-June, p 318-335.

——, 1985, Tribal welfare and the law : The prospect, *Cochin University Law Review* 9(1-6) March-June, p 79-86.

Bakshi, Rajni, 1985, Will the movement spread? *Indian Express*, May 5, p 8.

Balagopal, K., 1987, Karamchedu : Second anniversary, *Economic and Political Weekly* 22(33) August 15, p 1378-1381.

——, 1987, A tale of arson, *Economic and Political Weekly* 22(29) July 18, p 1169-71.

Bandyopadhyay, S.S. and **Laxmi, G.R.**, 1989, Diet and nutrition of the Khasis of Meghalaya, *Vanyajati* 37(2) April, p 21-24.

——, 1985, The Raj, Risley and the tribes and the castes of Bengal, *India Past and Present* 2(1) p 41-52, footnotes.

Bandhyopadhyay, Sekhar, 1985, Caste in the perception of the Raj : A note on the evolution of colonial sociology of Bengal, *Bengal Past and Present* 105(1-2) January-December, p 58-80, bibliography, footnotes.

Banerjee, A.R. and **Chowdhuri, Lipi**, 1988, Caste exogamy and Clan-Gotra endogamy in the contemporary Bangalee society, *Man in India* 64(4) December, p 361-368, bibliography, footnotes, tables,

Banerjee, B.G., 1984, On development and tribal development, *Tribal Research Bulletin* 7(1) September, p 9-11 +.

Banerjee, Biswanath, 1965, An outline of background, theory and methods of socio-cultural anthropology, *Bulletin of Cultural Research Institute*, p 44-52, references.

——, 1968, Relation between environment and culture among some Indian primitive communities living in the hills, *Bulletin of Cultural Research Institute* 7(1-2), p 55-61, references.

Banerjee, Hemendra Nath, 1962, Socio-ritual status of the Kharia in the ethnic background of Manbhum, *Bulletin of Cultural Research Institute* 1(2) p 16-28, references, tables.

——, 1989, Reconsideration of the principles of social stratification viewed through class-caste distinction : Social mobility in India : A Sociological approach, *Man in India* 69(4) December, p 393-402.

Banerjee, S.P., 1961, Crimes in tribal areas, *Bulletin of Tribal Research and Development Institute* (Chhindwara) 1(2) December, p 4-8.

Banerjee, Sukumar, 1981, Impact of industrialisation on the tribal population of Tharia Ranigunj Coal Filed area, *Anthropological Survey of India*, 160 p; *Man in India* 67(1) March, p 89-90.

Banerjee, Swapan Kumar, 1963, Land alienation : Causes and effects thereof on tribal economy, *Bulletin of Cultural Research Institute* 2(2), p 19-22.

——, 1963, Role of handicrafts in tribal economy, *Bulletin of Cultural Research Institute* 1(3), p 15-19, references.

Bannerji, Asis and **Dasgupta, Malabika**, 1984, Shifting the location of Jhumia villages in Tripura: An empirical study, *Man in India* 64(4) December, p 361-368, bibliography, footnotes, tables.

Bapat, N.V., 1953, Bondar : A unique tribal welfare centre in M.P., *Vanyajati* 1(2) April, p 38-40.

——, 1959, Scouting among tribals, *Vanyajati* 7(3) July, p 82-83.

——, 1962, Education of the Aborigines, *Indian Educational Review* 68(7) July, p 161-165. [From the Presidential address to the Aborigines Education Section at the last All India Education Conference.]

——, 1964, A few thoughts on tribal education, *Vanyajati* 12(4) October, p 190-194.

——, 1968, Residential school in tribal areas, *Vanyajati* 16(4) October, p 154-159.

Bapat, Nana, 1961, A note on Abujmarihas of Bastar, *Bulletin of Tribal Research Institute* 1(1) June, p 17-18, illustration.

——, 1961, Tribal education : A problem, *Vanyajati* 9(1) January, p 37-39.

Bara, David, 1989, Oraon marriage : Socio-cultural context, *Sevartham* 14, p 63-73, footnotes.

Baral, J.K. and **Gaju, R.S.**, 1987, Leadership and socio-political change of tribes of Orissa, *Vision* 6(3-4) January-June, p 57-69, bibliography.

Barange, B.G., 1963, An annotated bibliography on tribal indebtedness, *Bulletin of Tribal Research and Development Institute* (Chhindwara) 3(1) June, p 60-66.

Barla, Anthony, 1965, Medium of instruction for tribal students : Students viewpoint, *Indian Education* 4(11) October, p 33-34.

Barma, Jitendra Mohan Dev, 1958, Origin of Tripura and is people, *Vanyajati* 6(3) July, p 108-116, tables.

Barthakur, 1977, Jhooming and its consequences, *Yojana* (Annual Number) 21(9), p 122-123.

Barua, Saumitra, 1985, Red green colour blindness and earlobe attachment among the Hajongs of Meghalaya (India), *Indian Journal of Physical Anthropology and Human Genetics* 11(3) August-December, p 151-154, bibliography, tables.

Barve, V.N., 1942, A call from the downtrodden, *Social Service Quarterly* 28(4) April, p 145-147.

Basham, A.L., 1963, Some reflections on Dravidians and Aryans, *Bulletin of Institute of Traditional Cultures*, Part II, p 225-234.

Basu, Ashok Ranjan, 1985, Improving public service delivery system for tribal population in India : An empirical investigation, *Prashasnika* 14(1) January-March, p 1-15, bibliography.

Basu, Minendra Nath, 1961, Suggestions for the educational plan of the Aboriginal peoples of India, *Vanyajati* 9(3) July, p 123-126.

——, 1963, Anthropological approach to the tribal peoples of India, *Vanyajati* 11(1) January, p 4-8.

——, 1963, Anthropology in tribal education, *Bulletin of Cultural Research Institute* 2(1), p 22-27.

——, 1964, Property and inheritance among the primitives, *Bulletin of Cultural Research Institute* 3(2), p 7-12.

——, 1965, The concept of soul among the tribal folk of India, *Bulletin of Cultural Research Institute* 4(1) p 5-8.

Basu, Sunil Kumar, 1969, A note on important festivals among the major tribals of West Bengal, *Bulletin of Cultural Research Institute* 8(3-4) p 17-33, tables.

Basu, Swaraj, 1986, A case study of the Rajbansi caste movement in Northern Bengal, 1901-1921, *Quarterly Review of Historical Studies*, 26(3) October-December, p 59-61.

Batra, N.D., 1985, Myths and legends of Arunachal tribes, *Indian and Foreign Review* 22(10) March 15, p 18-19.

Batria, P., 1962, Accidental deaths among tribes, *Bulletin of Tribal Research and Development Institute* (Chhindwara) 2(1), p 43-48.

——, 1963, Crime and witchcraft among the tribes of Madhya Pradesh, *Bulletin of Tribal Research and Development Institute* (Chhindwara) 3(1) June, p 21-29, reference, tables.

Batria, Puran, 1969, Policing in tribal areas, *Bulletin of Tribal Research and Development Institute* (Bhopal) 7(1-2) June-December, p 5-18.

Baxi, Upendra, 1985, Reflections on reservation crisis in Gujarat, *Mainstream* 23(43) June 8, p 15-22; 23(42) June 14, p 20-25; 23(43) June 22, p 20-24.

—— 1989, Historic new law : Protecting SC/ST humans rights, *Times of India*, September, 15, p 6, col 3-5.

Behura, N.K. and **Misra, K.K.**, 1985, Religious rites and festivals among the tribes of Orissa, *Vision* 4(4); 5(1) April-September, p 66-86, bibliography.

Bennur, C.S., 1967, Caste prejudice and children, *Progress of Education* 41(10-11) May-June, p 392-93, letter to editor.

——, 1967, Education and prejudice, *Progress of Education* 41(8) March, p 294-98 +.

Bernard, Thomas L., 1969, Implications of social class factors in contemporary English secondary education, *Indian Sociological Bulletin* 6(2) January, p 104-106, references.

Berraman, Gerald D., 1971, Brahmanical view of caste, *Contributions to Indian Sociology*, New Series, December 5, p 16-23.

Beteille, Andre, 1985, Head count of Harijans : Pattern of regional distribution, *Times of India*, March 21, p 6, col 3-5.

Bhadra, Ranjit K., 1979, Rural class structure in post-independence Assam, *Economic and Political Weekly* 14(4) January 27, p 165-167.

Bhadrapur, K.B., 1942, Uplift work amongst hill tribes in tribes in Kolaba district, *Rural India* 5(11) November, p 502-506, tables.

Bhagat, Anupdev, 1956, Missionaries, anthropologists and Adivasi culture, *Social Action* 6(11) November, p 457-472, references.

Bhageshwar Singh and **Reddy, N.K.**, 1982, A plea for demogenetic studies of numerically small and large tribes, *Indian Journal of Physical and Human Genetics* 8(1) April, p 67-70, bibliography.

Bhalerao, Shanta, 1936, The scavenging and halakhore labour of Bombay : Some impression, *Social Service Quarterly* 22(1) July, p 11-14.

Bhardwaj, A.N., 1956, The problem of Gujar tribe, *Vanyajati* 4(4) October, p 124-126, illustration.

Bhargava, G.S., 1986-87, Caste war in South India, *Janata* 41(25) November 30, p 5-7; 41(26) December 21, p 7-8; 41(27) January 4, p 5-6.

Bhasin, M.K., et al, 1986, Genetic studies of Pangwalas, transhumant and settled Gaddis Palmar dermatoglyphics, *Indian Journal of Physical Anthropology and Human Genetics* 12(1), p 9-28.

Bhaskara Rao, Digumarti, 1984, Educational problems of tribal children of forest and hill areas, *Experiments in Education* 12(11) March, p 15-18.

Bhat, Vasudev, 1985, Tribal sub-plan percolates down to Koragas, *Social Welfare*, 32(3) June, p 14-15 +.

Bhatia, Prem, 1990, A mostly unread document, *Tribune*, September 7.

Bhatnagar, Damyanti, 1986, Possibilities of social change in the context of the attitude of bureaucratic personnel towards Scheduled Castes and Scheduled Tribes, *Journal of Sociological Studies*, January 5, p 150-160, bibliography, tables.

Bhatt, G.S., 1954, The Chamar of Lucknow, *Eastern Anthropologist* 8(1) September-November, p 27-41, footnotes.

——, 1964, Sociology and anthropology in India and the West, *Journal of Social Research* 7(1-2) March-September, p 143-152, references.

Bhatt Raj, N., 1989, Multani kinship organisation : An investigation, *Man in India* 69(4) December, p 387-392.

Bhattacharjea, 1990, Anti-reservation stir : Skirting the basic issue, *Mainstream* 28(46) September 8, p 3 +.

Bhattacharjea, P.R., 1987, New horizon of tribal autonomy and tribal development in Tripura, *Journal of North East India Council* 11(1) April, p 33-42.

Bhattacharya, Biswanath, 1965, A short note on clubs and libraries of the backward communities, *Bulletin of Cultural Research Institute*, 4, p 53-57, tables.

Bhattacharya, Debasish and **Chattopadhyay, R.N.**, 1987, Housing problems of dislocated tribals in industrial areas and a step towards solution, *Man in India* 13(1-2) January-June, p 49-55, bibliography.

Bhattacharya, Gayatri, 1983-1984, Bhumdev Mukhopadhyay and ethnosociology of the caste system : A search for an identity ? *Journal of Department of Sociology*, p 53-55, bibliography.

Bhattacharya, S., 1975, Linguistic convergence in the Dravido-Munda culture area, *International Journal of Dravidian Linguistics* 4(2), p 199-214.

—— and **D' Almeida, Fleur**, 1986, The caste system and discrimination in historical perspective, *New Frontiers Education* 16(2) April-June, p 25-32, bibliography.

Bhattacharya, S.K., et al, 1985, The migrant Oraon in the Andaman Islands : Some demographic aspects, *Journal of Indian Anthropological Society* 20(1) March, p 86-92, bibliography, tables.

Bhattacharya, S.N., 1987, Tribal development since Independence, *Kurukshetra* 35(10) July, p 34-38.

Bhattacharya, Subhendu Shekhar, 1962, Santal songs: Different types, *Bulletin of Cultural Research Institution* 1(2), p 54-61.

Bhouraskar, K.M., 1961, The First Tribal Welfare Field Workers Seminar, *Bulletin of Tribal and Development Institute* (Chhindwara) 1(2) December, p 1-3.

——, 1962, Dynamics of leadership in a tribal village, *Bulletin of Tribal Research and Development Institute* (Chhindwara) 2(1) June, p 1-14, references.

Bhowmick, P.K., 1966, An integrated plan for the development of the Lodhas and other tribals of Midnapur, *Vanyajati* 14(2) April, p 82-89.

——, 1967, Ways to educate the tribals, *Adibasi* 9(1) April, p 29-39, Illustration, references.

——, 1985, Social organisation of the Chenchus: A gathering hunting tribe of Andhra Pradesh, *Journal of Asiatic Society* (Bengal) 27(3), p 35-78, bibliography, tables.

——, 1985, Tribal situation in West Bengal, *Indian Anthropologist* 15(1) June, p 1-19.

——, 1987, Voluntary effort in tribal developemt: The Bidisa experiment, *Journal of Social Economic Studies* 4(2) April-June, p 175-186.

Bhupinder Singh, 1984, Lac and tribals, *Administrator* 29(3) July-September, p 183-190.

——, 1984, Tribal development in retrospect and prospect: Sixth Plan mid term appraisal, *Indian Journal of Public Administration* 30(4) October-December p 1064-1081, tables.

——, 1985, Perspectives on adult education programmes for Scheduled Tribes, *Man and Development* 7(1) March, p 65-72.

——, 1985, The Saora highlanders: Leadership and development, *Indian Economic and Social History Review* 22(2) March, p 354-355.

——, 1985, Tribal administration : A critique, *Indian Journal of Public Administration* 31 (3) July-September, p 879-909.

——, 1989, Between two worlds : Five ancient tribal groups of Andaman and Nicobar Islands, *Vanyajati* 37(2) April, p 1-4.

——, 1989, Nehru's tribal philosophy and tribal India today, *Mainstream* 27(35) May, 27, p 46-47.

Bhuriya, Mahipal, 1985, Tribal youth : Bringing them into the national mainstream *Vivekananda Kendra Patrika* 14(2) August, p 35-42.

Bhuskute, R.V., 1989, Tribals, Dalits and Government lands, *Economic and Political Weekly* 24(23) June 10, p 1265-1266, tables.

Billorey, R.K., 1986, Migration and trade in the North East Frontier of India : The Mombas of Arunachal, *Journal of Asiatic Society* (Bengal) 28(1), p 56-68, footnotes.

Bishei, Ulrich, 1983, The dominant caste and its landscape expression in Indian villages, *Geographic Review of India* 45(40) December, p 34-47, bibliography.

Biswas, D.P., 1989, The Kolis of Gujarat : An ecological variant, *Vanyajati* 37(2) April, p 25-26.

Biswas, P.C., 1954, The utility of research for the rehabilitation, *Vanyajati* 2(1) January, p 5-9.

——, 1955, Anthropology and tribal education, *Vanyajati* 3(2) April, p 81-83.

Blair, Harry W., 1980, Rising kulaks and backward classes in Bihar : Social change in the late 1970s, *Economic and Political Weekly* 15(2) January 12, p 64-74.

Bleie, Tone, 1987, Gender relations among Oraons in Bangladesh: Continuity and change, *Economic and Political Weekly* (Supplement) 22(17) April 25, p WS31.

Bodade, V.N., et al, 1988, Tribals and demonstrations for tribal development, *Indian Farming* 38(8) November, p 39-40.

Bodding, P.O., 1925, The Santal medicine, *Memoirs of the Asiatic Society of Bengal* 10(2).

Bommai, S.R., 1990, Quota for weaker sections must, *Indian Express*, September 9.

Borgohain, H., 1986, A tour to Payum : The Bori land, *Resarun* 12(1-2) Spring-Winter, p 14-19, bibliography.

Bose, A.B., 1970, Educational development among Scheduled Castes, *Man in India* 50(3) July-September, p 209-239, references, tables.

——, 1970, Problems of educational development of Scheduled Tribes, *Man in India* 50(1) January-March, p 26-50, references, tables.

Bose, Dilip Kumar, 1969, On preferential marriage of the tribes of Central India, *Journal of Social Research* 12(2) September, p 106-116, references, tables.

Bose, J.K., 1938, Ordeals among the Garos, *Man in India* 18(2-3) April-September, p 174-176.

Bose, N.K., 1928, Marriage and kinship among the Juangs, *Man in India* 3(4), p 233-242.

——, 1955-1956, The use of social science, *Adibasi*, 1, p 5-6.

——, 1957, Anthropology and tribal welfare, *Man in India* 37(3) July-September, p 169-181.

——, 1962, Some observations on industrialisation and its effects on tribal life, *Man in India* 42(1) January-March, p 5-9.

——, 1964, Change in tribal cultures before and after Independence, *Man in India* 44(1) January-March, p 1-10.

——, 1964, Integration of tribes in Andhra Pradesh, *Man in India* 44(2) January-March, p 97-104.

——, 1966, Some suggestions on tribal education, *Folklore* 7(2) February, p 47-51.

——, 1968, National integration and the Scheduled Castes and Scheduled Tribes, *Man in India* 48(4) October-December, p 289-296.

——, 1969, The tribal situation, *Man in India* 9(3) July-September, p 217-223.

Bose, S.C., 1986, Planning for tribal development, *Yojana* 30(5) March 16, p 21-23, tables.

Bose, Savadindu, 1964, Economy of the Onge of Andaman, *Man in India* 46(4) p 298-310.

Bose, Sukla, 1985, Caste tribe and female labour participation, *Social Change* 15(2) June, p 15-20, bibliography, tables.

Bose Uma, 1952, Blood groups of the tribes of Travancore, *Bulletin of Department of Anthropology* 1(1) January, p 19-24, references, tables.

Bougle C., 1958, The essence and reality of the caste system, *Contributions to Indian Sociology*, 2, April, p 7-30.

Bradford, Nicholas J., 1985, From bride-wealth to groom-fee: Transformed marriage customs and socio-economic polarisation among Lingayats, *Contribution to Indian Sociology* (New Series), 19(2) July-December, p 269-302, bibliography

Brij Mohan, 1961, Status of woman in tribal communities in India, *Vanyajati* 10(2) April, p60-66.

Brij Raj Singh and **Thapar, Rajiv**, 1985, Baster: Impact of change: A viewpoint, *Link* (Supplement) 27 (26) February 3, p 34-37, tables.

Bryee, L. Winifred, 1962, Revolution and the tribal peoples, *Bulletin of Tribal Research and Development Institute* (Chhindwara) 2(1) June, p 15-18.

Buch, M.N., 1969, Land improvement and agricultural development in tribal areas: Lack of motivation , *Bulletin of Tribal Research and Development Institute* (Bhopal) 7(1-2) June-December, p 1-4.

Buchi, Ernst C., 1955, Is sickling a wedded trait?, *Anthropologist* 2(1) March, p 25-29, references.

——, 1969, Caste and race in South India, *Anthropologist* (Special Volume), p 61-67, references.

Bulsara, Jal F., 1958, 'Gnyati-Bandan' or caste barriers: What are they? *Indian Journal of Adult Education* 19(3) October, p 5-12+.

——, 1959, Implications of a casteless and classless society, *Journal of Anthropological Society of Bombay* (NS) 11(1), p 43-60.

——, 1969, Thoughts on approaches to the study of man and society, *Journal of Anthropological Society of Bombay* (NS) 14(2), p 109-124.

Buradkar, M.P., 1940, Totemism among the Gonds, *Man in India* 20(3) July-September, p 114-143; 20(4) October-December, p 268-269, footnotes, tables.

——, 1947, The clan organisation of the Gonds, *Man in India* 27(2) June, p 127-136, footnotes.

Burling, Robbins, 1960, An incipient caste organisation in the Garo hills, *Man in India* 40(4) October-December, p 283-299, references.

Business India (Periodical), 1990, Risking the Mandal Report, *Business India*, September 3-16, editorial.

Buzarbaruah, P.M., 1989, Effects of migration and environment on anthropometric characters of Munda population of Assam : A preliminary observation, *Man in India* 69(3) September, p 292-304.

—— and **Phookan, M.N.**, 1986, Birth order, mother's age and reproductive wastage among the Mishings of Disangmukh of Sibsagar, Assam, *Indian Journal of Physical Anthropology and Human Genetics* 12(1) January-April, p 43-50, bibliography, tables.

Campbell, J., 1956, Ethnography of India, *Journal of Asiatic Society of Bengal*, 35.

Carstairs, Morris, 1954, The Bhils of Kotra Bhomat, *Eastern Anthropologist* 7(3-4) March-August, p 169-181.

Chaddha, Kumkum, 1987, Entry barred, *Hindustan Times* (Magazine) July 12, p 1, col 1-6 +.

Chakrabarti, A.K. et al, 1984, Socio-psychological correlater in the adoption of health innovations among tribals within intensive service of primary health centre, *Health and Population* 7(1) January-March, p 72-83, bibliography.

Chakraborty, Bhabatosh, 1985, Upholding the cause of the tribals, *National Herald* (Sunday Herald) April 21, p 1, col. 3-6 +.

Chakraborty, Falguni, 1985, Making of plough : A case study of rational adaptation of technology among the Santals, *Man in India* 65(3) September, p 246-260.

Chakraborty, Minakshi, et al, 1984, Post-climb effects on hearing and oxygen consumption at moderate altitude among Bhutia boys, *Journal of Indian Anthropological Society* 19(2) July, p 131-135.

Chakraborty, S.K., 1989, A brief ethnographic account on the Nishi of Arunachal Pradesh, *Vanyajati* 37(2) April, p 12-20.

Chakravarthi, M.R., et al, 1988, Environmental hazards in reproduction performance among Chotanagpur tribals, South Bihar, India, *Journal of Indian Anthropological Society* 20(2) July, p 137-140 bibliography, tables.

Chakravarti, Manish Ranjan and **Mukherjee, Deba Prasad**, 1962, Dermatoglyphic study on the tribes and castes of Nagaland and Manipur, *Bulletin of Anthropological Survey of India* 11(3-4), p 233-234, tables.

Chakravarty, M.I., 1989, Economic analysis of employment, income and consumption pattern of tribal farmers, *Journal of Rural Development* 8(1) January, p 97-108, tables.

Chanana, Dev Raj, 1959, The Sudra, the Dasa and Manu, *Indian Journal of Social Work* 20(3) December, p 201-208.

Chandana, R.C., 1989, Spatial dimensions of Scheduled Castes in India, *Tribune* (Magazine) September 2, p 1-6.

Chanderverker Pushker, 1958, Kolis of Tharadari, *Folklore* 1(3) July-September, p 30-33.

——, 1961, A scheme for Folk-culture Institute in Gujarat, *Folklore* 2(5) September-October, p 318-322.

Chandramohan Reddy, T., 1987, Status of Scheduled Castes in rural power structure : An analysis, *Man in India* 67(4) December, p 372-382, bibliography, tables.

Channa, V.C., 1984, From childhood to youth : The learning process amongst the Aggarwals of the city of old Delhi, *Indian Anthropologist* 14(1) June, p 23-39, bibliography.

Chapekar, N.G., 1952, Traces of totemism in the Rigveda, *Sociological Bulletin* 1(2) September, p 95-98.

Chatterjee, B., 1953, Model community centres in tribal areas, *Indian Journal of Social Work* 14(3) December, p 282-291.

Chatterjee, Bishwa B., 1970, Functional literacy for family planning in tribal areas, *Indian Journal of Adult Education* 31(1) January, p 12-13 +. tables.

Chatterjee, Neera, 1965, A comparison of performance of tribal and non-tribal boys of Tripura (India) on five performance tests, *Journal of Psychological Research* 9(3) September, p 151-158, references, tables.

Chatterjee, Raj, 1990, First things first, *Tribune*, September 7.

Chatterjee, Ramanada, 1933, A fundamental right, *Social Service Quarterly* 18(4) April, p 125.

Chattopadhyay, Gouranga, 1960, Application of anthropology to administration : Case studies in rural and tribal areas, *Journal of Social Research* 3(1) March, p 48-54, references.

Chattopadhyay, K.P., 1921, Some Malayalam kinship, *Man in India* 1(2), June, p 141-143.

——, 1925, An essay on the history of Newar culture, *Journal and Proceedings of Asiatic Society of Bengal* (NS) 23(3).

——, 1949, The tribal problem and its solution, *Eastern Anthropologist* 3(1) September, p 15-21 references.

——, 1952, Conference for tribal welfare at Delhi, *Man in India* 32(3) July-September, p 167-169.

——, 1953, Tribal education, *Man in India* 33(1) January-March, p 1-18, appendix.

——, 1954, A short note on cultivation among tribal folk in India, *Vanyajati* 2(4) October, p 110-112.

Chattopadhyay, Prasanta Kumar, 1950, Some physical studies among the Gujars of Delhi, *Man in India* 50(2) April-June, p 185-188, references.

Chaturvedi, Arun Kumar, 1986, Harijan students of Uttar Pradesh, *Social Welfare* 33(1) April, p 30-31.

Chaturvedi, K.C., 1955, Welfare of Scheduled Castes and Scheduled Tribes in Vindhya Pradesh, *Vanyajati* 3(3) July, p 128-131.

—— 1957, Vindhya's tribals in new Madhya Pradesh, *Vanyajati* 5(1) January, p 39-41, references.

Chaturvedi, K.N. and **Mishra, R.C.**, 1988, Children spontaneous recall in relation to their caste group affiliation, *Indian Journal of Community Guidance Service* 5(2) May, p 23-30, bibliography, tables.

Chaudhary, N.D., 1987, Anganwadi workers in a tribal belt, *Social Welfare* 34(7) October, p 14-15 +. tables.

Chaudhuri, A.B., 1986, Witch killings among Santals, *Social Change* 16(1) March, p 69-70.

Chaudhuri, Buddhadeb, 1966, Life in a Munda village, *Bulletin of Cultural Research Institute* 5(1-2), p 126-132, tables.

——, 1968, The nature and extent of Munda Hindu interactions, *Bulletin of Cultural Research Institution* 7(1-2) p 154-165, maps, references, tables.

——, 1969, An analytical study of witchcraft among the Mundas of Midnapur, *Bulletin of Cultural Research Institute* 8(1-2) p 87-91, references.

Chaudhuri, Maitreyi, 1987, Class analysis in a village society: A cluster theoretic approach, *Economic and Political Weekly* 22(49) December 5, p 2121-2126.

Chaudhury, N.D., 1975, Educational development among the Scheduled Tribes in Rajasthan, *Education Quarterly* 27(3) October, p 26-30, tables.

Chauhan, Devraj, 1990, Educational occupational levels of SCs, STs, *Mainstream* 28(42) August, 11, p 15-20.

Chauhan, Indira, 1988, Tribal development administration in Madhya Pradesh, *Eastern Anthropologist* 41(1) January-March, p 87-92.

Chauhan, R.R., 1966, Tribalisation, *Tribe* 2(1-2), p 5-11.

Chengal Reddy, P., 1987, Consanguinity and inbreeding load in two Mala populations of Andhra Pradesh, *Man in India* 67(4) December, p 357-363, bibliography, tables.

Chetan Singh, 1988, Conformity and Conflict: Tribes and the agrarian system of Mughal India, *Indian Economic and Social History Review*, 25(3) July-September, p314-340.

Chinai, Rupa, 1985, Fighting for a cultural identity, *Indian Express* (Magazine) September 22, p 3, col. 1-8.

——, 1986, Adivasis: Conflicts within the circle of life, *Indian Express* (Magazine) March 9, p 3, col 1-8.

Chinchalkar, J.H., 1970, Welfare of tribal women, *Vanyajati* 18(1) January, p 37-40.

Chitnis, Suma, 1972, Education and equality, *Economic and Political Weekly* 7, (31,32 and 33), p 1970-1981.

——, 1975. Education of the Scheduled Castes, *Journal of Higher Education* 1(2) Autumn, p 167-78, tables.

Chopra, Pran, 1989, Casting a deadly bait, *Indian Express* (Magazine) August 1, p 1 +.

Choubey, Bindo Kumar, 1985, More efforts needed to uplift tribals, *Times of India*, February 27, p 8, col 7-8.

Choubisa, S.L., 1990, Sickle cell traits in Damor tribe of Dungarpur district, Southern Rajasthan, *Man in India* 70(4) December, p 454-458.

——, et al, 1987, Abnormal haemoglobin, thalassaemia and G-6 PD deficiency genews in the Suther community of Southern Rajasthan, *indian Journal of Physical Anthropology and Human Genetics* 13(1) January-April, p 9-16, bibliography, tables.

Choudhary, Kameshwar, 1988, Caste in politics: A rejoinder, *Times of India*, August 12, p 6, col. 7-8.

Choudhary, Ram Krishna, 1987, Achievement orientation and career pattern of rural Jat youth in a Haryana village, *Journal of Social Studies*, January 6, p 123-130, bibliography.

Choudhuri, Uma, 1955, A comparison of Santal mental test reactions in rural and urban areas, *Bulletin of the Department of Anthropology* 4(1), p 67-68.

Choudhury, Bhagwathi, 1964, Oraon, *Adibasi* January, p 45-50.

Chowdhury, A.K., 1988, P T C taste sensitivity and colour blindness among Bodh and Swangla of Lahaul, *Man in India* 68(7) December, p 448-453. bibliography, tables.

Clamment, John, 1987, Incorporation and assimilation : The Aboriginal peoples of Malaysia and letters of modernisation, *Journal of Social Economic Studies* 4(2) April-June, p 121-142.

Clump, C.C., 1953, Village uplift, *Social Action* 3(8) November, p 288-239.

Coelho, E.P., 1952, A new approach to Adivasi education, *Progress of Education* 27(12) July, p 340-344.

Cohn, Bernard S., 1959, Madhopur revisited, *Economic Weekly*, July.

Continho, V.B., 1985, Tribal protection in Karnataka : An appraisal, *Cochin University Law Review* 9(1-2) March-June, p 117-128.

Corbridge, S., 1989, Tribal politics, finance and the State : The Jharkhand India, 1900-1980, *Ethnic and Racial Studies*, April 12, p 174-207, bibliography, map.

Culshaw, W.J. and **Archer, W.G.**, 1945, The Santal rebellion, *Man in India* 25(4) December, p 218-239, footnotes.

Danda, Ajit K., 1988, Tribes in India, *Man in India* 68(4) December, p 313-334.

Dang, Satyapal, 1974, Plight of women sweepers, *Mainstream* 12(50)

Das, A.K., 1965, Prospects of fish culture in tribal areas, *Man in India* 45(4) October-December, p 316-321, references.

——, 1969, Basic approach for welfare activities in the Himalayas, *Adibasi* 11(3) October, p 42-48.

——, 1984, Macko and masquerades among the Buddhist tribes of Arunachal Pradesh, *Indian and Foreign Review* 22(10) March 15, p 18-19.

Das, Amal Kumar, 1958, Language and dialects of the tribals of West Bengal, *Vanyajati* 6(3) July, p 130-136.

——, 1962, Influence of city life on educated tribals, *Bulletin of Cultural Research Institute* 1(2), p 69-78, tables.

——, 1962, Scheduled Tribes of West Bengal : A panoramic picture, *Bulletin of Cultural Research Institute* 1(1) p 35-56, illustration.

——, 1963, Leadership : Its role in ancient India and among the tribals, *Bulletin of Cultural Research Institute* 1(3), p 1-7, references.

——, 1963, Social system : A cross cultural analysis, *Bulletin of Cultural Research Institute* 2(2), p 1-10.

——, 1965, The role of research in tribal welfare, *Vanyajati* 13(3) July, p 118-122.

—— 1966, Special problems in tribal transformation : Industrialisation as a means of such transformation, *Bulletin of Cultural Research Institute* 5 (1-2), p 5-10, references.

——and **Banerjee, Swapan Kumar**, 1963, The family of tribal of West Bengal : Static and dynamic aspects of composition, *Bulletin of Cultural Research Institute* 2(1), p 12-21.

——, 1964, Certain aspects of population growth amongst the tribals of West Bengal, *Bulletin of Cultural Research Institute* 3(1), p 1-14, tables.

Das, Anirudha, 1968, Impact of Christianity on the tribals in Orissa: The historical background, *Adibasi* 10(1) April, p 87-99.

Das, Arvind N., 1984, Class in itself, caste for itself : Social articulation in Bihar, *Economic and Political Weekly* 19(37) September 14, p 1616-1619.

——, 1985, Bihar society in perspective : Roots of regional imbalance, *Times of India*, October 24, p 8, col 3-5; October 25, p 8, col 7-8.

——, 1985, Growing violence in Bihar : Social roots of the cult of the gun, *Times of India*, November 21, p 8, col 3-5.

——, 1987, Bihar disinformation : Caste killings and naxalite alibi, *Mainstream* 25(40) June 20, p 7-10.

Das, Biplas, 1986, The Uchais of Tripura : Some religious functions of the Christian groups, *Folklore* 27(8) August, p 171-176.

Das, Biswaroop, 1986, Submerging tribal belt in Gujarat, *State and Society* 6(1) January-March, p 24-52, footnote.

Das, G.N., 1955-1956, The parasite problem, *Adibasi*, 1, p 36-38.

——, 1957, The Adibasis of Orissa and their welfare, *Vanyajati* 5(2) April, p 74-82, references.

——, 1963-64, Some aspects of tribal education, *Adibasi* 5(2), p 21-24.

——, 1964, Culture contact and social engineering, *Adibasi* 6(3) November p 19-22.

——, 1965, Tribal welfare and some special aspects of tribal development blocks, *Adibasi* 7(2) July, p 7-14.

——, 1966, Inaccessibility, *Adibasi* 8(2) July, p 62-64.

——, 1966, Missionary zeal (with special reference to tribal welfare), *Adibasi* 8(3) October, p 3-7.

——, 1966, Some more reflections on tribal welfare, *Adibasi*, 8(1) April, p 67-72.

Das, Gananath, 1964, Evolution of tribal policy, *Adibasi*, January, p 21-24.

——, 1967, The programme of social education for backward tribals, *Adibasi* 8(4) January, p 56.

——, 1967, Tribal culture and democracy, *Adibasi* 9(3) October, p 31-35.

——, 1967, Tribal education: Transition from orthodox education towards education for modernity), *Adibasi* 9(2) July, p 21-27.

——, 1967, Tribal welfare methodology, *Adibasi* 9(1) April p 10-13.

Das, Harish Chandra, 1963-64, The sea-fisherman of North Balasore and their way of fishing, *Adibasi* 5(2), p 25-28.

——, 1964, Santal, *Adibasi* 6(1) January, p 65-68.

Das, Manmatha Nath, 1955-56, Dormitory : A dying tribal institution, *Adibasi*, 1, p 19-21.

——, 1956, Female infanticide among the Bedees and the Chouhans : Motives and modes, *Man in India* 36(4) October-December, p 261-266.

Das, Nityananda, 1958, Glimpses of Aborigines education, *Adibasi* 3(1) February-April, p 31-40; *Vanyajati* 6(3) July, p 122-129.

——, 1959, A note on the markets in the Saora land of Orissa, *Vanyajati* 7(3) July, p 98-103.

——, 1960, Changing pattern of a Koraput village, *Vanyajati* 8(2) April, p 65-72.

——, 1963, Tribes : Their problems and administration of tribal areas, *Vanyajati* 11(3) July, p 106-125.

——, 1967, The Hill Kharia of Simplipal Hills: A study of an isolated food gathering community, *Adibasi* 9(2) July, p 44-49.

——, 1968-69, Methods of social anthropology and study of tribes in India, *Adibasi* 10(-4) October-January, p 40-50, references.

——, 1968-69, Priorities for tribal education, *Adibasi* 10(3-4) October-January, p 1-10.

Das, P., et al, 1986, How lab to land programme are helping tribal farmers, *Kurukshetra* 34(4) January-June, p 109-110.

Das, R., 1985, A study on variation of palmar fexion crease among three Assamese castes, *Indian Journal of Physical Anthropology and Human Genetics* 11(3) August-December, p 175-177, bibliography, tables.

Das, S.R., et al, 1968, A somatological survey of five tribes in the Koraput district, Orissa, *Bulletin of Anthropological Survey of India* 17(4) October, p 400-422, references, tables.

Das, T.C., 1960, Assimilation, integration, acculturation, *Journal of Social Research* 3(2) September, p 6-10.

——, 1960, A scheme for tribal welfare, *Journal of Social Research* 3(2) September, p 93-112.

——, 1962, Nature and extent of social change in tribal society of Eastern India, *Sociological Bulletin* 11(1-2) March-September, p 221-238, tables.

Das, Veena, 1968, A sociological approach to the caste Puranas, *Sociological Bulletin* 17(2) September, p 141-164, references.

—— and **Uberoi, Jit Singh**, 1971, Elementary structure of caste, *Contributions to Indian Sociology*, New Series 5, December, p 33-43.

Das, Victor, 1989, Tribals of Jharkhand and the question of their survival, *Social Action* 39(4) October-December, p 438-443.

Das Gupta, Barun, 1987, Back ground to Tripura tribal crisis, *Mainstream* 25(16) January 3, p 4-6.

Das Gupta, Biman Kumar, 1959, The Pahiras of Khokro, Singhbum district, *Bulletin of Department of Anthropology* 8(2) July, p 85-90, references.

——, 1962, A short ethnographic note on the Pahiras of Khokro, *Vanyajati* 10(3) July, p 110-119, references, tables.

Das Gupta, K., 1979, A note on the Wancho language of Arunachal Pradesh, *Resarun* 5(1) Spring-Summer, p 25-37, bibliography.

Das Gupta, Malabika, 1985, Tribal unrest in Tripura : An alternative view, *Economic and Political Weekly* 20(1) January 5, p 38-40.

——, 1986, Jhumias of Tripura, *Economic and Political Weekly* 21(44-45) November, 1-8, p 1955-1960.

Das Gupta, Narendra Kumar, 1959, Tribal language and education, *Man in India* 39(1) January-March, p 61-64.

Das Gupta, Pranab Kumar, 1964, Impact of industrialisation of tribal life, *Bulletin of Anthropological Survey of India* 13(1-2) January-June, p 85-106, tables.

—— and **Khan, Iar Ali**, 1985, Impact of tea plantation industry on the life of tribal labourers, *Man and Life* 12(1-2) January-June, p 109-110.

Das Gupta, Ranjit, 1986, From peasants and tribesmen to plantation workers : Colonial capitalism of labour power, *Economic and Political Weekly* (Supplement) 21(4) January p 2-10.

Das Gupta, Samira and **Sarkar, Amitabh**, 1990, A new light on Munda social organisation, *Man in India* 70 (2) June, p 195-198.

Datta, Upali and **Ghosh, G.C.**, 1988, A study of handclasping and armfoldings among the Jugi of Tripura, *Man and Life* 68(2-3) June-September, p 211-215, bibliography

Datta Chaudhuri, S.S., 1984, A note on hand clasping, armfolding and tongue rolling among the Muji of Arunachal Pradesh (India) *Vanyajati* 32(2) April, p 12-13.

——, 1988, Demographic profile of Miji population: Sajolang of Arunachal Pradesh, *Man in India* 68(4) December, p 442-447, bibliography, tables.

Datta Ray, Sunanda K., 1990, Class into caste : V.P. Singh's political insurance, *Statesman*, September 9.

Dave, P.C., 1966, Voluntary organisations and welfare of backward classes, *Vanyajati* 14(4) October p 156-164.

Dayal, L., 1984, Industrialisation in tribal areas, *Bihar Journal of Public Administration* 1(1) Spring, p 62-64.

De, P.K., 1985, The vanishing tribals of Andaman Islands, *Social Welfare* 31(12) March, p 17-19 +.

Deb, P.C., 1961, Change in tribal society, *Religion and Society* 8(3) September, p 84-89.

Debi, Kiranbala, 1966, Necessity of adequate diet for tribal students, *Adibasi* 8(1) April, p 61-66.

——, 1966, Sweepers and scavengers in Bhubaneshwar, *Adibasi* 8(3) October, p 35-41.

Deep Kumar, V.S., 1985, A genetic study of Kamna and Kapu caste groups of Andhra Pradesh, *Journal of Indian Anthropological Society* 20(1) March, p 59-65, bibliography.

Deliege, Robert, 1989, Job mobility among the brickmakers of South India, *Man in India* 69(1) March, p 42-63.

Dene, Steve, 1985, Religious movement as rite passage: Analysis of the Birsa movement, *Contributions to Indian Sociology* (New Series) 19(2) July-December, p 251-268, bibliography.

Deogaonkar, Warora S. G., 1989, Role of voluntary agencies and tribal institutions in social and ecological development in tribal areas, *Vanyajati* 37(4) October, p 32-38.

Desai, Ambudharl T. and **Kulkarni, K. M.**, 1988, Four tribal villages of North Gujarat, *Annals of the National Association of Geographers India* 8(1) June, p 23-30.

Desai, Anjana P., 1985, On perceiving problems of rural development, *Deccan Geographer* 23(1) January-June, p 95-102, bibliography, tables.

Desai, Bharati S., 1982-1983, Channels of mobility used by a landowning peasant caste : An empirical study of the Woras of South Gujarat, *Journal of the Maharaja Sayajirao University of Baroda* 31-32(2), p 125-143, bibliography, tables.

Desai, Haribhai G. and **Uchat, D. A.**, 1981, Self concept of Harijan student and attitude of other students towards tem, *Indian Educational Review* 16(3) July, p 44-50.

Deshmukh, B. D., 1957, Educational status of the backward communities, *Progress of Education* 32(3) October, p 97-98, letter to editor.

Deshpande, Anjali, 1990, Reservations and Mandal report, *Mainstream* 28(44) August 25, p 5+.

Deuri, R. K., 1985, Home brewed liquor of the Khawas, *Resarun* 11(2) Autumn-Winter, p 8-10.

Dev, A. K., 1985, Affinity of the Karbis of Assam in respect of P T C taste sensitivity, *Indian Journal of Physical Anthropology and Human Genetics* 11(1-2) April-August, p 81-84, bibliography, tables.

Devan, P. K., 1988, A medical mission for the tribals of Wynad, *Social Welfare* 34(11) February, p 9-10.

Devi, Mahasveta, 1985, The Shavara tribal of West Bengal, *Economic and Political Weekly* 20(35) August 31, p 1476-1468.

——, 1988, Story of Agna Panna, *Economic and Political Weekly*, 23(42) October 15, p 2151-2152.

Dey, P. C., 1987, Tribal development : An economic anthropological approach, *Vision* 6 (3-4) January-June, p 33-40, bibliography.

Dhagambar, Vasudha, 1985, Reservation : Missing the wood for the trees, *Mainstream* 23(36) May 4, p 5-6.

——, 1986, Tribals and the law, *India International Centre Quarterly* 13(3-4) December, p 95-114.

Dhar, B., 1985, Land tenure system among the Monpas: Conflict and co-existence, *Resarun* 11(2) Autumn-Winter, p 32-34, bibliography.

Dhar, M. K., 1990, PM commitment to reservation total, *Hindustan Times*, September 1.

Dhawan, Harmohan, 1990, Text of Harmohan Dhawan's letter to P M, *National Herald*, September 9.

Dhawan, Shiv, 1985, Reservations : A critique of social justice, *Patriot* (Magazine) August 4, p 1.

Dhebar, U. N., 1979, Weaker sections of the community, *Interdiscipline* 7(4) Winter, p 27-31.

Dhruw, P. R., 1968, The tribal students of Madhya Pradesh, *Vanyajati* 16(3) July, p 97-99.

Dinbandhu, Mahal, 1985, The role of Tribal Development Cooperative Corporation of Orissa Limited for the development of tribals, *Tribal Research Bulletin* 7(2) March, p 20-23.

——, 1985, the Tribal Development Cooperative Corporation of Orissa, *Cooperative Perspective* 20(3) October-December, p 42-46.

Divakar, P. and **Yengneshwar V.**, 1986, Tusser culture and tribal development, *Kurukshetra* 34(4) January, p 19-20 +.

D'Mello, Bernard, 1987, Arwal massacre : Report of people's tribal, *Economic and Political Weekly* 22(35) August 29, p 1486-1487.

D'Monte, Darryl, 1986, Cholanaickanas : Homeless in Kerala, *Hindustan Times* (Magazine) August 17, p 5, col 1-6.

Dollu, Venkateshwarlu, 1987, Psychological conflict between Harijans and upper class, middle class, caste Hindus : A study in Andhra Pradesh (India), *Sociological Bulletin* 36(1) March, p 77-78.

Dorairaj, S., 1985, AIADMK's balancing tactic, *Link* 27(37) April 28, p 12-13.

Driver, Edwin D., 1982, Class, caste and 'Status Summations' in urban South India, *Contributions to Indian Sociology*, New Series, 16(2) July-December, p 226-253.

D'Souza, Claude, 1986, Weaker sections of the Indian society and their education, *Social Action* 36(1) January-March, p 13-25.

D'Souza, Victor S., 1953, Mother right in transition, *Sociological Bulletin* 2(2) September, p 135-142.

——, 1969, Measurement of rigidity-fluidity dimension of social stratification in six Indian villages, *Sociological Bulletin* 18(1) March, p 35-49, reference, tables.

Dube, B. K., 1962-1963, A plan for the culture: The approach to the problem of Abujmarh, *Bulletin of Tribal Research Institute* (Chhindwara) 2(2) December-June, p 1-4.

Dube, Krishna Chandra, 1960, Problem of Aboriginal debt in Bhindranawagarh subdivision of the Raipur district (M.P.), *Vanyajati* 8(2) April, p 73-80, tables.

Dube, Leela, 1970, The craft of social anthropology, *Eastern Anthropologist* 23(3) September-December, p 285-297.

Dube, S.C., 1948, Arrow marriage, *Eastern Anthropologist* 2(1) September, p 22-26.

——, 1949, Some aspect of tribal problem, *Eastern Anthropologist* 3(1) September, p 28-35.

——, 1950, Inter-tribal relations : A Study, *Man in India* 30(2-3) April-September, p 73-80.

——, 1955, Methods and problems of social anthropology in India, *Anthropologist* 2(1) March, p 21-24.

——, 1960, Approach to the tribal problem in India, *Journal of Social Research* 3(2) September, p 11-15.

——, 1987, Tribes and development : Human aspects of Bodhghat, *Times of India*, May 11, p 6, col. 3-5.

——, 1990, Against fratricidal caste war, *Mainstream* 28(46) September 8, p 4-5.

——, 1990, A retrograde fetish, *Hindustan Times*, September 3, p 11, col. 2-5.

Dubey, K. C., 1968, Tikanpal : Some aspects of a Bison-Horn Maria village, *Bulletin of Cultural Research Institute* 7(1-2), p 66-79, tables.

——, 1969, A note on the Bison-Horn Maria Dhratries clans and totems, *Eastern Anthropologist* 22(3) September-December, p 371-376.

——, 1969, Tribal legends and customs and tribal history, *Vanyajati* 17(2) April, p 46-48.

——, 1970, The Dorlas of Bhopalpatnam, Bastar district, *Bulletin of Tribal Research and Development Institute* (Bhopal) 8(1-2) June-December.

Dubey, R., 1965, Jharo and its people, *Vanyajati* 13(3) July, p 87-92.

Dubey, S. N., 1964, Celebration of Diwali among the Gonds of Tamia, *Bulletin of Tribal Research and Training Institute* (Chhindwara) 4(1) June, p 37-43.

Dumont, Louis, 1987, A South Indian sub-caste : Social organisation and religion of the Pramali Kallar, *Economic Trends* 8(6) February, p 1-4.

——, and **Pocock, D.**, 1958, Hocart: On caste religion and power, and Bougle: The essence and reality of the caste system, *Contributions to Indian Sociology*, 2, April, p 7-30.

Durah, D. K., 1985, Festival of the Nishis of Arunachal Pradesh, *Resarun* 11(2) Autumn-Winter, p 29-31.

——, 1985, A study on middle phalangeal heir among the Tagins and Monpas of Arunachal Pradesh, *Resarun* 11(1) Spring-Summer, p 33-41, tables.

——, 1986, A study on A B O blood groups, P T C taste sensitivity and colour blindness among the Monpas of Arunachal Pradesh, *Resarun* 12(1-2) Spring-Winter, p 36-43, tables.

Durah, Dwijendra Kumar and **Das, Priya Bala**, 1984, A cross-sectional study of growth in four somatomatic characters of the Khampti boys of Arunachal Pradesh, *Resarun* 10(1) Spring-Summer, p 15-24, bibliography, flags, tables.

Dushkin, Lelah, 1970, Backward class benefits and social class in India, 1920-1970, *Economic and Political Weekly* 14, Annual Number, April, p 661-667.

Dutta, D. K., 1979, A little known tribe of Tirap, *Resarun* 5(1) Spring-Summer, p 61-67.

——, 1984, An ethnographic note on the Lisus of Gandhigram, Tirap district, *Resarun* 10(2) Autumn-Winter, p 28-44.

——, 1986, Health and hygiene of three villages of Monpas, West Kaneng district, *Resarun* 12(1-2) Spring-Winter, p 20-25, tables.

Dutta, Dipak K., 1984, Dances of the Hrussos, *Resarun* 10(1) Spring-Summer, p 38-40.

Dutta, Gitika, 1982, Sex differences in creativity among the tribe of Meghalaya, *Journal of Institute of Educational Research* 6(2) May, p 23-26, references, tables.

Dutta, P. C., 1978, Social organisation of the Wanchos of Tirap district, Arunachal Pradesh, *Resarun* 4(1) January-March, p 14-35.

Dutta, S. C., 1983, Educational programme for tribal population : A alternative strategy, *Indian Journal of Adult Education* 44(4) April, p 11-14.

Duyber, Edward, 1982, Economic change and the Santals of West Bengal, *Bengal Past and Present* 101(1-2) January-December, p 61-78.

Eastern Anthropologist (Periodical), 1969, Tribal identify: *Eastern Anthropologist* 22(2) May-August, p 135-139, editorial.

Ebnother, Robert, 1966, Munargaon: Its lessons in tribal welfare, *Adibasi* 8(1) April, p 73-84.

——, 1967, Traditionalism or modernity in development, *Adibasi* 9(1) April, p 59-61.

Educational India (Periodical), 1964, Backwardness, *Educational India* 30(9) March, p 308-309, editorial.

Ehrenfels, U. R., 1958, Example and responsibility : Two acculuration problems, *Indian Journal of Social Work* 19(2) June, p 143-149.

—— 1959, Anthropology and traditional cultures, *Indian Journal of Social Work* 19(4) March, p 323-324.

——, 1962, Gifts of Aboriginality, *Journal of Social Research* 5(2) September, p 71-80.

Ekka, P., 1962, The Adivasis of Chotanagpur : How will they adjust to the modern world?, *Social Action* 12(4) April, p 188-189, tables.

Elwin, Verrier, 1942, Do we really want to keep them in a zoo?, *Indian Journal of Social Work* 2(4) March, p 438-448.

——, 1942, The duration of marriage among the Aboriginals of the Maikal hills, *Man in India* 22(1) January-March, p 11-21, footnotes.

——, 1942, Reply on the problem of culture contact, to *Isolation or assimilation*, by P. G. Kanekar, *Social Service Quarterly* 28(4) April, 147-152.

——, 1944, Notes on a Kondh, *Man in India* 24(1) March, p 40-58, footnotes.

——, 1945, Bhumijan Seva Mandal, *Rural India* 8(3) March, p 72-73.

——, 1945, Funerary custom in Bastar State, *Man in India* 25(2) June, p 87-133.

——, 1945, Sarora Fituris, *Man in India* (4) December, p 254-257, footnotes.

——, 1961, The beauty of tribal Assam, *Folklore* 2(4) July-August, p 209-222.

Exem, A. Van, 1987, The tribe : God's own people : A theological perspective, *Sevartham* 12, p 45-64, footnotes.

——, 1988, Tribal forever : The Cachatology of the Sarna, *Sevartham*, 13, p 27-42, footnotes.

Father, P. and **Gisbert, S. J.**, 1951, Sociology's debt to anthropology, *Journal of Anthropological Society of Bombay* (NS) 6(1) March, p 1-13, references.

Fatima, Johra, 1986, Tribals who do not know how to measure weights, space and times, *Patriot* (Magazine) August 3, p 1, col. 5-6.

Fernades, Walter, 1989, Andhra move to deprive tribals of land, *Social Action* 39(3) July-September, p 308-315, bibliography.

Ferreira, John V., 1962, The Katkaris : An evaluation of available material, *Journal of Social Research* 5(2) September, p 64-70.

——, 1964, Ethnology and history, *Sociological Bulletin* 13(1) March, p 1-11, references.

——, 1964, The problem of Maratha totemism, *Indian Journal of Social Work* 25(2) July, p 135-151, references.

——, 1967, Towards integral man through integral anthropology, *Sociological Bulletin* 16(2) September, p 77-93.

——, 1969, Applied anthropology in India, *Journal of Anthropological Society of Bombay* (NS) 14(1), p 15-25, references.

Fonseca, A., 1958, A new social class, *Social Action* 8(1) January, p 15-23.

Forrester, Duncan B., 1975, Initial occupational pattern of Scheduled Castes graduates in India, *New Frontiers in Education* 5(2) May, p 49-65, references, tables.

Fox, Richard G., 1969, Professional primitives : Hunters and gatherers of nuclear Sough Asia, *Man in India* 49(2) April-June, p 139-160, references.

Fuchs, Stephen, 1969 A royal saviour of the Bastar tribals, *Journal of Anthropological Society of Bombay* (NS) 14(1), p 36-50, references.

——, 1988, The Korkus of the Vindhya Hills, *Man in India* 68(2-3) June-September, p 308-309.

Gaffoor, Khaja Abdul, 1954, The future of Hyderabad's Adivasis, *Vanyajati* 2(3) July, p 91-94.

Gaikwad, John S., 1986, A demographic profile of tribals in Maharashtra State, *Tribal Research Bulletin* 9(1) September, p 16-27 +.

——, 1986, Role of minor forest produce in tribal economy, *Tribal Research Bulletin* 8(2) March, p 12-16.

——, 1987, Transformation of economy of tribal cultivators through the electric motor pumps, *Tribal Research Bulletin* 9(2) March, p 18-20.

Gandhi, Rajiv, 1990, More politics than jobs, *Hindustan Times* September 8.

Ganesan, Sangu, 1955, The root cause of untouchability, *Rural India* 18(11-12) November-December, p 406-407.

Gangadharan, K. A., 1985, Tribal welfare and development in Kerala, *Cochin University Law Review* 9(1-2) March-June, p 173-188.

Gangmumei Kabui, 1989, Tribes in North-East India in historical perspective : The emerging pattern and the perspective for the future, *Vanyajati* 37(4) October, p 12-19.

Gangopadhyay, Prodyot and **Kundu, Shampa**, 1988, Familial trend in arterial pressure among few endogamous communities of West Bengal reared under diverse occupational environment, *Man in India* 68(2-3) June-September, p 235-242, bibliography.

Ganguli, Amulya, 1990, Divide and lose : Mandal in Shah Bano's wake, *Statesman*, September, 5, p 6, col. 4-6.

Ganguly, J. B., 1970, Tribal students between tradition and modernity, *Educational Miscellany* 7(1-2) June-September, p 61-69.

——, 1986, Tripura tribals and mainstream : Tripura politics, *Asian Studies* 4(2) April, p 1-19.

Ganguly, Swati, 1983-1984, Buddhism, castes and outcastes : A sociological perspective, *Journal of Ancient Indian History* 14(1-4), p 220-223.

Gangwar, A. and **Ramakrishnan, P. S.**, 1987, Agriculture and animal husbandry among the Sulungs and Nishis of Arunachal Pradesh, *Social Action* 37(4) October-December, p 345-372, bibliography, figures, tables.

Gangwar, A. K., 1990, Tribals and forests of North-Eastern India : Strategies for sustainable development, *Vanyajati* 38(2) April, p 14-21.

Gani, H. A., 1990, Dalit unity, *Janata*, 45, Annual Number, p 41 +.

Gare, G. M., 1955, Need of training of workers in tribal development, *Tribal Research Bulletin* 7(2) March, p 5-6.

——, 1973, Process of social change in the Scheduled Tribes : A case study of immigrant Mahadeo Kolis in Poona city, *Indian Journal of Social Work* 3(2), p 131-139.

——, 1984, Voluntary agencies in tribal areas : Their roles and functional types, *Tribal Research Bulletin* 7(1) September, p 5-6 +.

Garg, B. M., 1960, Status of women in tribal communities in India, *Indian Journal of Social Work* 21(2) September, p 191-197.

Garg, R. K., 1990, For development sans divisions, *Patriot*, September 5.

Gayre, G. R., 1956, The significance and usefulness of cultural anthropology to ethnological studies, *Vanyajati* 4(1) January, p 18-28, illustrations.

Ghosal, S. L., 1986, Tribal Jhabua in transition : Some factors, *Kurukshetra* (34) January, p 27-29 +.

Ghosh, A., 1985, The political economy of development strategy and tribal demography, *Capital* 196(4815) September 30, p 49-52.

Ghosh, B. N., 1967, The ways of acquiring mates in tribal Chotanagpur, *Folklore* 8(11) November, p 403-410, bibliography; *Vanyajati* 15(4) October, p 169-175, references.

Ghosh, Kishalay, 1986, Tribal education : An appraisal, *Social Action* 36(1) January-March, p 54-69, bibliography, tables.

Ghosh, S. K., 1990, Tribal revolt in India, *Hindustan Times*, (Magazine Section), November 18, p 13.

Ghurye, G. S., 1943, A note on cross cousin marriage and rural organisation, *Journal of University of Bombay* 5(1), p 88-90.

——, 1952, Social Change in Maharashtra, part I, *Sociological Bulletin*, 1.

——, 1964, Social Change in Maharashtra, part II, *Sociological Bulletin*, 3.

Gill, M. S. and **Singh, A. M.**, 1989, Reactionary dissent by case Hindu employees, *Social Change* 19(3) September, p 16-22.

Gisbert, P., 1961, Culture as the central interest of anthropology, *Journal of Anthropological Society of Bombay* (NS) 11(2), p 1-10.

——, 1962, Cultural change among he tribals, *Social Action* 12(4) April, p 179-187.

Gladstone, J. W., 1985, Caste, religion and people's movements in Kerala with particular reference to South Kerala, *Religion and Society* 32(1) March, p 24-35, footnotes.

Goel, N. P., et al, 1986, Changes in socio-economic status of the Scheduled Caste population in rural Rajasthan : 1961-1981, *Rajasthan Economic Journal* 10(1) January, p 65-73, bibliography, tables.

Gohain, B. C., 1974, Agricultural organisation among the Abor, *Bulletin of the Department of Anthropology* 3(2).

Gokhale, A. M., 1989, Village development boards in Nagaland, *Vanyajati* 37(4) October, p 55.

Gopala Reddi, B., 1956, Problem of tribal people, *Vanyajati* 4(1) January, p 46-48.

——, 1956, Welfare of tribals and other backward classes, *Indian Journal of Social Work* 16(4) March, p 294-296.

Gopala Sarana, 1961, Professor Majumdar and anthropology of Indian religion, *Journal of Social Research* 4(1-2) March-September, p 1-12, references.

——, 1970, Anthropology of Indian civilisation, *Journal of Indian Anthropological Society* 5(1-2) April-October, p 31-39, references.

Gopichand, 1956, Welfare of socially handicapped tribes, *Indian Journal of Social Work* 16(4) March, p 296-300.

Gopinatharao, C., 1986, Residential schools for weaker sections : A study, *ASCI Journal of Management* 15(2) March, p 303-325.

Goswami, Atul, 1984, Tribal development with special reference to North-East India, *Social Scientist* 12(8) August, p 55-60, footnote.

Goswami, B. B. and **Morab, S. G.**, 1988, Tribes and castes as functionaries in the temples of Karnataka, *Man in India* 68(1) March, p 61-69.

Goswami, Omkar, 1985, Then came the Marwaris : Some aspects of the changes in the pattern of industrial control on Eastern India, *Indian Economic and Social Review* 22(3) July-September, p 225-249, bibliography, footnote.

Govila, J. P., 1959, The Tharus of Tarai and Bhabar, *Indian Folklore* 2(3) July-September, p 228 +.

Govinda Reddy, P., 1987, Effects of consanguineous marriages on fertility and infant mortality among the Mala of Southern Andhra Pradesh, *Indian Journal of Physical Anthropology and Human Genetics* 13(1) January-April, p 43-49, bibliography, tables.

Goyal, B. R., 1975, Education of the under-privileged under the 10 + 2 + 3 scheme, *Journal of Indian Education* (1) May, p 69-74.

Greenfield, Sydney M., 1984, Social anthropology and economic theory : Their place in study and policy formulation in the new nations, *Indian Sociological Bulletin* 1(4) July, p 24-31, references.

Grigson, W. V., 1946, The Aboriginal in the future India, *Man in India* 26(2) June, p 81-96, footnotes.

Guglani, P. L., 1986, A probe into tribal farming in Bihar, *Kurukshetra* 34(4) January, p 25-26.

Guha, K., 1960, Tribal handicrafts in India, *Vanyajati* 8(3) July, p 117-123.

Guha, P. K., 1989, Shompen : A primitive tribe in transition, *Man in India* 68(4) December, p 465-469, tables.

Gulati, Leela, 1975, Female work participation : A study of Inter-State differences, *Economic and Political Weekly* 10(1-2) January, p 35-42.

Gulati, R. K., 1970, Biological and cultural affinities : An interpretation, *Eastern Anthropologist* 23(3) September-December, p 235-242.

Gunasekaran, R., 1988, Changing phase of tribal economy in Koli hills, *Khadi Gramodyog* 35(3) December, p 162-174.

——, 1988, Social change among Tribals : A study, *Kurukshetra* 36(4) January, p 9-12.

Gupta, Dipankar, 1981, Caste, infrastructure and super structure: A critique, *Economic and Political Weekly* 16(51) December, p 2039-2104.

——, 1984, Continuous hierarchies and discreet castes, *Economic and Political Weekly* 19(46) November 17, p 1955-1958; 19(47) November 24, p 2003-2005; 19(48) December 1, p 2049-1053, bibliography.

——, 1986, Tribal development in a West Bengal district, *Economic and Political Weekly* 21(1) January, p 35-45.

Gupta, Jaya Dutta, 1959, A study of the Paundra Kshatriya of West Bengal, *Bulletin of Department of Anthropology* 8(2) July, p 109-30, appendix, references.

——, 1960, Ponung or girls association among the Padam Abor in the lower Abor hills, *Bulletin of Anthropological Survey of India* 9(2) July, p 71-73.

Gupta, L. P., 1979, A study of personality syndromes and cognitive characteristics of Scheduled Castes, backward classes and non-Scheduled Caste students, *Journal of Higher Education* 4(3) Spring, p 381-387.

Gupta, Ram Pratap and **Sunil**, 1986, Madhya Pradesh : Development of tribals, *Economic Times*, December 8, p 3, col 1-5 +.

Gupta, S. C. and **Prasad, B. G.**, 1964, A socio-medical survey of sweepers and their families in Lucknow Municipal Corporation, *Indian Journal of Social Work* 24(4) January, p 289-296.

——, 1965, A note on the living and working conditions of the sweeper community in Lucknow, *Eastern Anthropologist* 18(3) September-December, p 117-185, references, tables.

Gupta, Shiva K., 1984, The significance of social stratification in Harijan community, *Indian Journal of Social Work* 45(2) July, p 175-187, bibliography.

Guru, Gopal, 1985, Casteism in the South, *Mainstream* 23(47) July 20, p 20-22, bibliography.

——, 1985, Politics of reservations : A class approach, *Social Change* 4(3) April-June, p 131-139, bibliography.

——, 1984, Reservations and the Sanskritisation of Scheduled Castes : Some theoretical aspects, *Sociological Bulletin* 33(1-2) March-September, p 29-38, bibliography.

Gurubasve, K. S., 1985, Tribal communication in Arunachal Pradesh, Gowda *Resarun* 11(2) Autumn-Winter, p 25-26.

Gurumurthy, G., 1985, Marriage patterns, age at marriage and fertility behaviour among Yanadis : A study of tribal community in Andhra Pradesh, *Health and Population* 8(4) October-December, p 235-236, bibliography, tables.

——, 1988, Socio-economic status and fertility among Yanadi women, *Social Welfare* 34(11) February, p 11-13 +.

Guruswamy, P. A., 1988, Irula tribes of Nellithoral, *Social Welfare* 34(11) February, p 20-22 +.

Hadimani, R. N., et al, 1985, Sericulture as a leverage of social mobility among Scheduled Castes in rural areas : A case study of a non-sericulturist village in Karnataka, *Journal of the Institute of Economic Research* 20(1-2) p 27-37.

Halpern, Joel Martin, 1958-1959, Trade patterns in Northern Laos, *Eastern Anthropologist* 12(2) December-February, p 119-124.

Hans, A. B. D., 1986, Tribal culture and education's response : Search for a model of education for the tribal people, *New Frontiers in Education* 16(1) January-March, p 1-47, appendix.

Hans, Dilbar, 1962, The rediscovery of the tribal personality in the new context, *Religion and Society* 9(4) December, p 5-14.

Hanumantha Rao, K., 1990, Job reservations for backward classes, *Mainstream* 28(46) September 8, p 6.

—— and **Sastry, K. V. S.**, 1990, Levels of living and poverty among social groups in Andhra Pradesh : A cross section analysis, *Journal of Rural Development* 9(1) January, p 91-105.

Haque, M., 1984, Anthropometry of the Padar of Ranagadh, Gujarat, *Man in India* 64(3) September, p 294-303.

——, 1984, A note on earlobe attachment of the Bhil of Dungarpur, Rajasthan, *Vanyajati* 32(4), p 20-22.

Harinder Kaur and **Singh, B. P.**, 1989, Juti-making women of Rajasthan in Punjab, *Social Change* 19(3) September, p 23-30.

Hasan, Amir, 1968, A note on education among the Kols of Uttar Pradesh, *Eastern Anthropologist* 21(1) January-April, p 83-86.

Hasan, Shariful, 1985, Social-backwardness is the end result of poverty, *Organiser* 37(1) May 19, p 8.

Hassan, M. K., 1986, Impact of industrialisation on mental health of tribals, *Social Change* 16(4) December, p 30-33, bibliography, tables.

Hazara, Durgades, 1959, The Dorla of Bastar, *Bulletin of Department of Anthropology* 8(2) July, p 75-84, references.

Heda, H. C., 1955, One aspect of planning : Bringing backward areas forward, *Vanyajati* 3(4) October, p 174-176.

Hegde, Ramakrishna, 1986, Reservation policy in Karnataka, *Monthly Commentary on Indian Economic Conditions* 28(2) September, p 10-13.

——, 1990, Hegde for economic criteria, *Indian Express*, September 19, p 9.

Hemant Kumar, 1970, Characteristics of tribes in India, *Vanyajati* 18(2) April, p 65-69.

Herédia, Rudi, 1986, Minority rights and reservation policy : Towards coherence and consistence, *New Frontiers in Education* 16(2) April-June p 60-63.

Hindustan Times (Newspaper), 1990, The Mandalmess, *Hindustan Times*, September 19, editorial

——, 1990, Time for second thoughts, *Hindustan Times*, September 13, editorial.

Hiralal, 1922, Aborigines of Central India, *Man in India* 2(1-2) March-June, p 12-32.

Hocart, A.M., 1958, A.M. Hocart views on caste, religion and power, *Contributions to Indian Sociology*, 2, p 45-63.

Hodges, Donald, C., 1961, Classical economics and Marx's theory of social class, *Indian Journal of Social Research* 2(2) July, p 91-95, references.

Hodson, K.C., 1962, Cultural anthropology, *Man in India* 6(2-3) June-September, p 84-89.

Holmstrom, Mark, 1972, Caste and status in an Indian city, *Economic and Political Weekly* 7(15) April, 8, p 769-774.

Horsey, Anita, 1981, Conditions of Scheduled Castes and Tribes, *New Frontiers in Education* 11(2) April-June, p 1-36, references.

Hoshiar Singh and **Malik, Jagdish Kumar**, 1984, The Mandal Commission report : A plea for share in power, *Political Science Review* 23(3-4) July-December, p 250-268, bibliography, tables.

Hu, C. T., 1956-57, Marriage by exchange among the Tharus with a geneological case study, *Eastern Anthropologist*, Vol. 10(2) December-February, p 116-129, tables.

Husain, Syed Khaja Mahboob, 1949, The rural uplift of tribes and backward classes in Hyderabad, Deccan, *Man in India* 29(3-4) July-December, p 185-198.

——, 1951, Tribal inheritance, *Man in India* 31(2) April-June, p 84-87.

Hussain, Monirul, 1987, Tribal movement for autonomous state in Assam, *Economic and Political Weekly* 22(32) August 8, p 1329-1332.

Hutton, J. H., 1922, Depopulation of primitive communities, *Man in India* 2(4) December, p 220-227, footnotes.

——, 1924, Assam and the Pacific, *Man in India* 4(1-2) March-June, p 1-13, footnotes.

——, 1929, Cultural affinities of the Oraons with the hill tribes of Assam, *Man in India* 9(1) January-March, p 1-6.

Indera P. Singh and **Kumbani, H. K.**, 1959, Distribution of papillary patterns of the middle and proximal phalanges of Sindhi Khatris, *Anthropologist* 6(1-2) March-August, p 26-37, references, tables.

India Today (Periodical), 1990, Policy reservations, *India Today*, September 15, editorial.

Indra Deva and **Srirama**, 1989, Varnashrama and the industrialisation of violence, *Radical Humanist* 53(1) April, p 21-23, bibliography.

Indra Jeet Singh, 1967, Social rehabilitation and career orientation *Journal of Social Research* 10(1) March, p 18-21, references.

Ishtiaque, M., 1989, Changing patterns of linguistic identify among the Austric speaking tribes in Mid-India, *National Geographical Journal of India*, 35(part 2) June, p 140-152.

Jabbar Alam, M., 1985, Tribals starving to extinction, *New Age* 33(25) June, 23, p 5.

——, 1986, Injecting communalism into tribal areas, *New Age* 34(3) September 20, p 11.

——, 1986, Terror against tribals in Rohtas district, *New Age* 34(9) March 2, p +.

——, 1986, Tribal unrest in Bihar : Demand for Jharkhand state revived, *New Age* 34(5) February 2; p 8-9.

——, 1987, CPI condemns Bihar repression of tribals, *New Age* 35(48) November 29, p 6.

Jagjivan Ram, 1958, Casteism and untouchability : An analysis, *Indian Journal of Adult Education* 19(3) October, p 33-37.

Jahagirdar, M.P., 1988, The status and role of women in a tribal community, *Man in India* 68(4) December, p 424-430.

Jain, Deepa, 1985, Should reservation policy be continued ? *Radical Humanist* 49(1) April, p 25-28.

Jain, Girilal, 1987, Intra-Hindu conflicts : Main sources of turbulence, *Times of India*, June 17, p 3-5.

——, 1988, Kshatriya-Brahmin equation : Historic shift under the Raj, *Times of India*, July 27, p 3-5.

Jain, Meenakshi, 1985, Anti-Brahminism by another name, *Times of India*, September 4, p 5, col 7-8.

——, 1985, Coping with dominant castes : Ignored aspect of Mrs. Gandhi's politics, *Times of India*, June 17, p 8, col 7-8; June 18, p 8, col 7-8; June 19, p 6, col 7-8.

——, 1985, Failure of Indira strategy : Backward castes support not enough, *Times of India* July 13, p 8, col 3-5.

——, 1985, Rise of a political caste in Gujarat, *Times of India*, July 8, p 7-8.

——, 1985, The Patels of Gujarat : Story of remarkable rise, *Times of India*, August 3, p 3-5.

——, 1986, The politics of consensus : Jagjivan Ram and the Harijans, *Times of India*, July 29, p 8, col 3-5.

——, 1987, Religious world of Harijans : Different from Brahminical order, *Times of India*, July 9, p 6, col 3-5.

——, 1990, The plight of Brahmins, *Indian Express*, September 18.

Jain, R.K., 1967, Social stratification and political process in a new nation : Malaysia, *Journal of Indian Anthropological Society* 2(1) March p 69-73, references.

Jain, S.P., Backward classes : Problem of education, *Times of India*, July 13, p 4 col. 3-5.

——, 1971, Religion and caste ranking in a North Indian town, *Sociological Bulletin* 20(2) p 134-144.

——, 1989, Educating backward classes: Role of UGC, *Economic Trends* 18(5) April 5, p 3-6.

Jaiswal, N.K., et al, 1969, Attitude towards agricultural development among tribal and non-tribal people, *Man in India* 49(3) July-September, p 267-280, tables.

Janardhan Rao, B., 1987, Land alienation in tribal areas, Warangal *State and Society* 7(3-4) July-December, p 75-77.

Jarial, Gurpal Singh, 1984, Creativity as a prediction of entrepreneurial success among tribals, *Experiments in Education* 11(12) February p 110-114, references.

Jay, Edward J., 1959, The anthropologist and tribal welfare : Hill Maria : A case study, *Journal of Social Research* 2(2), p 82-89, references.

——, 1961, Revitalisation movements in tribal India, *Journal of Social Research* 4(1-2) March-September, p 282-315, references.

Jayagopal,R., 1986, Occupational mobility among a special group of Scheduled Castes in Tamil Nadu : A survey, *Indian Journal of Adult Education* 47(1) January, p 8-12.

Jayaram, K.V., 1986, Rabaris of Kutch, *Economic Trends* 7(5) December, p 6-8.

——, 1986, They carry on the tradition, *Economic Trends* 27(4) April, p 1-5.

Jayaram, N., 1986, Can law save Scheduled Castes? *Mainstream* 24(37) May 17, p 15-18 +.

Jena, A.C., 1986, Form of exploitation in tribal areas and their consequences : Some observations in Keonjhar district of Orissa, *Man and Life* 12(3-4) July-December, p 173-180, bibliography.

Jena, Kishna Chandra, 1959, The Adivasis of Orissa, *Rural India* 22(1) January, p 39-40.

——, 1962, The Kondhas of Koraput, *Indian Journal of Social Work* 23(1) April, p 57-61.

Jetley, Surinder, 1968, Transfer of power to a low caste, *Interdiscipline* 5(3) Autumn, p 199-206.

Jha, Amar Kumar, 1987, Caste-politics interactions : Process and consequences : A case study of Sitamarhi parliamentary constituency, *Journal of Social Economic Studies* 4(3) July-September, p 211-228.

Jha, Amiya, 1986, In outsider country, *Hindustan Times* (Magazine), March 2, p 4, col. 1-8.

Jha, Jata Shankar, 1979, Some unpublished records relating to the caste movement in Bihar, *Journal of Bihar Puravid Parishad* 3, p 208-222.

Jha, Raghunath, 1986, Adult education and tribal development, *Mainstream* 24(50) August 16, p 35-36 +.

Jha, S.K. and **Barde, H.R.**, 1984, The second change education for the tribals of Vidarbha, *Progress of Education* 58(11) June, p 270-272.

Jhaveri, Krishnalal M., 1933, The uplift of the Harijans, *Social Service Quarterly* 18(4) April, p 126-127.

Jhingon, Bela and **Surinder Nath**, 1985, Trends of growth and maturation among the Warlis: A tribal population of Maharashtra, India, *Indian Journal of Physical Anthropology and Human Genetics* 11(1-2) April-August, p 39-45, bibliography and tables.

Jitendra Mohan and **Narendra Kumar**, 1980, A study of social and personal problems of tribal youth, *Asian Journal of Psychology and Education* 6(1) January, p 5-8.

Johanna, M., 1965, Integration of school education activities in tribal girls schools, *Social Action* 15(11) November, p 1167-1170.

Joseph, A.N.T., 1989, Ethnozoology of reptiles in relation to health care among tribals in Madhya Pradesh, *Social Action* 39(4) October-December, p 405-422.

Joseph, M.J., 1988, Class, caste, church, and the Left, *Economic and Political Weekly* 23(49) December 3, p 2573-2574.

Juyal P.D., 1986, Some demographic variables influencing the attitude of Scheduled Caste towards in measures adopted for their welfare : An empirical study, *Progress of Education* 61(4-5) November-December p 85-88, bibliography, references, tables.

Kailash, 1990, Workshop structure of children: A case study of Jhabua district in Madhya pradesh, *Geographical Review of India* 52(1) March, p 69-76.

Kalam, Mohammad Abdul, 1984, Conversions and protective discrimination, *The Bulletin of Christian Institute of Islamic Studies* 7(3-4) July-December, p 36-34, bibliography.

Kalathil, Mathew, 1984, Repression of tribals, *Economic and Political Weekly* 19(36) September 8, p 1562.

——, 1985, Repression of Scheduled Castes and tribes in Broach, *Economic and Political Weekly* 20(7) February 16, p 265-267.

Kalelkar, Kaka, 1955, The Adivasis and their needs, *Vanyajati* 3(2) April, p 73-77.

——, 1958, Casteism and untouchability : An analysis, *Indian Journal of Adult Education*, 19(3) October, p 33-37.

Kalidas, Raju, 1984, Varna Saṃkara in ancient India, *Quarterly Journal of Mythic Society* 75(4) October-December, p 374-387.

Kamalakar, Jaya, 1988, Ethnic politics in municipal corporations, *Economic and Political Weekly* 23(19) May 7, p 945-946.

Kamila, Bana Behari, 1983, Occupational status of parents of Harijan and Tribal Welfare Department high school students of Orissa, *National Journal of Education* 6(1) September, p 56-64, references, tables.

——, 1985-1986, A study of attitude of students towards school of Harijan and Tribal Welfare Department high school of Orissa, *Journal of Education and Psychology* 43(3-4) October-January, p 187-192 references.

Kananaikil, Jose , 1986, Religion, culture and power : The case of the Scheduled Castes in India, *Religion and Society* 33(2) June, p 27-32.

——,1986, Secular state and religious criterion for reservation, *Social Action* 36(2) April-June, p 137-148.

Kanekar, P.G., 1942, Isolation or assimilation? *Social Service Quarterly* 28(3) January, p 97-115.

Kani, M. and **Bourai, R.A.**, 1985, Aryan tradition among Nishis and Hill Miris of lower Subansiri district, Arunachal Pradesh, *Resarun* 11(2) Autumn-Winter, p 35-38.

Kannan, C.T., 1961, Intercaste marriage in Bombay, *Sociological Bulletin*, 10(2) September, p 53-68, tables.

Kapoor, A. K., et al, 1990 Semi-Nomadism and Transhumance in Central Himalayas : A pragmatic perspective, *Man in India* 70(1) March, p 47-60.

Kar, P., 1966, Educational survey of some Adivasi village of Orissa, *Adibasi* 8(1) April, p 49-52.

Kar, R.K., 1970, A tribe in the context of tea industry in India : Some preliminary observations, *Anthropos*, 71, p 868-877.

——, 1989, The Savars of Assam, *Vanyajati* 37(2) April, p 5-11.

——, 1990, The peoples of North East India : An appraisal, *Vanyajati* 38(1) January, p 11-19.

—— and **Sharma, J.L.**, 1990, The Oraons of Assam, *Vanyajati* 38(2) April, p 22-32.

Karlekar, Hiranmay, 1990, Undermining India, *Indian Express*, August 25.

Karlekar, Malavika, 1975, Higher education and the Scheduled Castes, *Journal of Higher Education* 1(2) Autumn, p 179-87, references, tables.

Karunakaran, C.K., 1985, Legislative and executive measures for tribal welfare in Kerala, *Cochin University Law Review* 9(1-2) March-June, p 203-212.

Karuppaiyan, E., 1989, Issues in poverty alleviation programme for the tribals, *Social Action* 39(1) January-March, p 72-89, bibliography.

Karva, S.P., 1986, Training tribal youth, *Tribal Research Bulletin* 9(1) September, p 28-29.

Karve, Iravati, 1940, Kinship terminology and kinship uses of the Maratha country, *Bulletin of the Deccan College Research Institute* 2(4) p 327-389.

——, 1958, Social education of the Scheduled Tribes, *Vanyajati* 5(4) October, p 164-169.

Kashi N. Singh and **Rama Shankar Singh**, 1984, Levels of regional and tribal development in tribal areas : Are they identical, *National Geographical Journal of India* 30(1) March, p 1-12, appendix, tables.

Kaujalgi, H.S., 1941, Thakkar Bappa meets the Harijans, *Rural India* 4(3) March, p 147-148.

Kaul, S.K., 1955, Adivasis and Indian army, *Vanyajati* 3(1) January, p 23-25.

Kavalackata, Thomas, 1985, The killing of Santal tribals, *Social Action* 35(3) july-September, p 278-283.

Keswani, Raaj Kumar, 1987, The survivors, *Illustrated Weekly of India* 107(46) November 23, p 20-23.

Khan, A.H., 1956, The study of community in social studies, *Educational Forum* 1(1) January, p 9-11.

Khan, G. Ahmed, 1935, The Bhils of Khandesh, *Man in India* 15(2-3) April-September, p 133-143.

Khan, M.A., 1979, Parental deprivation in relations to academic achievement of denotified tribes, *Indian Educational Review* 14(4) October, p 95-98.

Khan, M.Q., 1985, Tribal survival in Chittagang hill tracts of Bangla Desh, *Man in India* 65(1) March, p 58-74, bibliography.

Khan, M. Rafiq, 1970, introduction, *Interdiscipline* 7(4) Winter, p 1-5.

Khan, M.Y., 1990, Kinship in the Gadabas of Bastar, *Man in India* 70(2) June, 192-194.

Khan, Masood Ali, 1987, Indologist on Gypsies affinity to India, *New Age* 35(40) October 4, p 14.

Khan, N.C., 1969, Some aspects of marital trend among the tribals of West Bengal, *Bulletin of Cultural Research Institute* 8(3-4), p 42-47, tables.

Khanna, H.R., 1990, Weakening the roots, *Hindustan Times* September 8.

Khare, R.S., 1970, On hypergamy and progeny rank determination in Northern India, *Man in India* 50(4) October-December, p 350-378, references, tables.

Khayal, Ghulam Nabi, 1985, The Gujjars of Kashmir : A forgotten community, *Indian Express* (Magazine) October 13, p 6, col 1-4.

Khurana, G., 1978, Approach to education of Scheduled Tribes, *Education Quarterly* 30(1) April, p 17-23, tables.

——, 1979-80, Educational facilities for Scheduled Castes, *Education Quarterly* 31(3-4) October-January, p 31-35.

Khushwant Singh, 1990, Mandal mess, *Hindustan Times* September 8.

Khusro, A.M., 1990, Job reservations : Pro-side, con-side and inside, *Indian Express*, September 13.

Kingdon-Ward, F., 1946, What of the tribes?, *Man in India* 26(2) June, p 110-119.

Kirpal, Vinay, et al, 1985, Scheduled Caste and Scheduled Tribe students in higher education : A study of Article 117, *Economic and Political Weekly* 20(29) July 20, p 1238-1248, tables.

Kishwar, Madhu, 1987, Toiling without rights : Ho women of Singhbum, *Economic and Political Weekly* 22(3) January 17, p 95-101 ; 22(4) January 24, p 149-155 ; 22(5) January 31, p 194-200.

Klein, M.O.L., 1965, Images of the stratification system in the Netherlands,*Sociological Bulletin* 14(2) September, p 50-53.

Knabe, Wolfgang K., 1983, The role of sociology and anthropology in solving problems of Indian tribals, *Development Policy and Administration Review* 9(1-2) January-December, p 15-23.

Kochar, V.K., 1964, Profile of a tribal village, *Vanyajati* 12(2) April, p 80-95, references, tables.

——, 1966, Village organisation among the Santals, *Bulletin of Cultural Research Institute* 5(1-2), p 11-19, references, tables.

——, 1967, Objectification of research process in social anthropology, *Indian Journal Social Work* 27(1) January, p 387-392, references.

Kodanda Rao, P. 1942, Directed assimilation: Regoinder to 'Isolation or assimilation, by P.G. Kanekar; *Social Service Quarterly* 29(1) July, p 4-8.

——, 1954, Liquor and the Aboriginals, *Indian Journal of Social Work* 14(4) March, p 382-385.

Kodinyn, Bhikshu 1981-82, Monastic social structures in Khampti society, *Journal of the Assam Research Society* 26, p 33-37, footnotes.

Koppar, D.H., 1956, Primitive tribes of Dharampur, *Journal of Anthropological Society Bombay* (NS) 10(1) March, p 8-24.

Koppers, W., 1938-40, My Central Indian expedition, *Man in India* 20(3) July-September, p 178-81.

Kothari, Milap, 1990, What price reservation?, *Hindustan Times*, September 6.

Kothari, Rajni, 1990, Meaning of Mandal, *Hindustan Times* September 24, p 13,

Krishan Kumar, 1984, The traditional economic life of the Bokars, *Resarun* 10(1) Spring-Summer, p 5-15; 10(2) Autumn-Winter, p 7-16.

Krishna, Sumi, 1985, In the heart of Simillpal, *Hindustan Times* (Magazine), August 4, p 1, col. 1-8.

Krishna Iyer, L.A., 1945, The hill-tribes of Travancore, *Man in India* 25(3) September, p 194-198.

Krishna Iyer, V.R., 1985, Tribal uplift and the rule of law, *Cochin University Law Review* 9(1-2) March-June, p 1-18.

Krlshna Kumari, P., et al, 1986, Study of creative abilities of tribal children in relation to their sex and socio-economic status. *Journal of Institute of Educational Research* 10(1) January, p 1-4, references.

Krishna Nandan Prasad, 1990 Incidence of bilingualism among the Ho tribes of Chotanagpur, *Man in India* June, p 155-168.

Krishna Rao, Murali I., 1989, Marketing in tribal economy : A study with special reference to Shandies (periodic markets) in tribal belt of Srikakulam district of Andhra Pradesh, *Vanyajati* 37(1) January, p 9.

Krishnan, Jairam, 1986, The Chotta Udepur experiment, *Economic Trends* (Supplement) 16(11) March, p 1-4.

——, 1988, Adivasi upsurge at Dharol, *Economic Times* January 17, p 3, col. 1-6.

Krishnan, P.G., 1985, Constitution and tribal welfare, *Cochin University Law Review* 9(1-2) March-June, p 49-66.

Kudryavtsev, M.K., 1964, On the role of the Jats in Northern India's ethnic history, *Journal of Social Research* 7(1-2) March-September, p 126-135, references.

Kulkarni, M.G., 1985, Economic development of tribal people, *Tribal Research Bulletin* 7(2) March.

Kulkarni, R.R. and **Borkar, S.T.**, 1986, Tribal leaders and their role in agricultural development, *Tribal Research Bulletin* 8(2) March p 17-20.

Kulkarni, S.D., 1974, Scheduled Caste and Scheduled Tribes, problems and policies, *Economic and Political Weekly* 9(42), p 1775-1178.

Kulkarni, Sharad, 1985, Adivasis, law and social justice, *Economic and Political Weekly* 20(28) July 13, p 1171-1174.

——, 1986, Adivasis, law and social justice, *Tribal Research Bulletin* 8(2) March, p 1-7, bibliography.

——, 1987, Forest legislation and tribals : Comments on Forest Policy Resolution, *Economic and Political Weekly* 22(50) December 12, p 2143-2148.

Kulshrestha, Shivendra Kumar, 1979, Self situational deprivations in the school adjustment of tribal children, *Journal of Indian Education* 5(2) July, p 41-47.

Kumar, B. Das, 1986, Development of the tribal economy : A spatial approach, *Kurukshetra* 34(4) January, p 13-14 +.

Kumar, K., 1955, Traditional beverage of the Gallongs of Arunachal Pradesh, *Resarun* 11(2) Autumn-Winter, p 4-7.

——, 1985, The Pailobos, *Man and Life* 11(3-4) July-December, p 224-226.

Kundu, C.L., 1968, Education of de-notified tribes, *Progress of Education* 42(10-11) May-June, p 351-354.

——, 1969, Intelligence and tribal delinquency, *Indian Journal of Applied Psychology* 6(1) January, p 29-30, references, tables.

Kundu, M., 1981, Preparing 'readers' for tribal adult learners: Some viable topics, *Indian Journal of Adult Education* 42(9) September, p 21-24, references.

——, 1982, Concept of 'Raska' implications for tribal education, *New Frontiers in Education* 12(2) April-June, p 42-46.

Kundu, Manmatha, 1986, Tribal education in India : An effective pedagogy, *Journal of Indian Education* 12(4) November, p 43-48, references.

Kundu, N.N., 1985, Tribal fair : A source of acquiring a mate : A study of Garasia : A scheduled tribe of Rajasthan, *Folklore* 26(5) May, p 91-94.

Kunhaman, M., 1985, The tribal economy of Kerala : An intra-regional analysis, *Economic and Political Weekly* 20(11) March 16, p 466-474.

Kunnukal, Thomas, 1986, Education for the weaker section, *Social Action* 36(1) January-March, p 1-12.

Kurian, K.V., 1985, The ex-criminal tribes of North Karnataka : A study, *Quarterly Journal of Mythic Society* 16(3-4) July-December, p 366-377.

Kurup, A.M., 1962, Glimpses of life and culture of the tribes of Madhya Pradesh, *Vanyajati* 10(4) October, p 139-145.

——, 1963-1964, People of the unknown hills : The Abujhmadias, *Vanyajati* 11(1) January, p 38-41; 11(4) October, p 168-176; 12(1) January, p 46-55; 12(2) April, p 67-79; 12(4) October, p 180-189.

——1963, Impact of industrialisation on tribal life, *Vanyajati* 11(2) April, p 71-75.

——, 1968, Extent and problems of tribal education, *Vanyajati* 16(2) April, p 55-59.

——, 1970, A scheme for need based tribal development and welfare, *Vanyajati* 18(3) July, p 105-108.

——, 1970, Towards a methodology for tribal welfare research, *Bulletin of Tribal Research and Development Institute* (Bhopal) 8(1-2) June-December, p 13-18.

Kuruwa, U.J., 1955, Welfare work among Scheduled Tribes in Kutch, *Vanyajati* 3(2) April, p 88-89.

Kusuma, A., 1988, Infant feeding practices among Sugalis, *Social Welfare* 35(8) November, p 7 +.

Kusumakar, H., 1985, The name tag tells all in the south, *Times of India* (Sunday Review) September, 1, p 1, col. 1-8

——, 1986, To be backward is good, *Times of India* (Sunday Review) November 9, p 11 col. 1-8.

Kuthiala, S.K., 1969, Demographic characteristics of tribal population in India, *Indian Sociological Bulletin* 7(1) October, p 57-68, references.

Lahiri, Kuntala, 1990, Will the Birhor survive modernisation, *Geographical Review of India* 52(1) March, p 99-101.

Laiq, Jawid, 1988, Ethnopolitical issues in South-East Asia, *Economic and Political Weekly* 23(18) April 30, p 909-917.

Lakshmaiah, T., 1984, Socio-economic development of tribals, *Mainstream* 23(18) December 29, p 21-22.

Lakshmi Devi, 1985, Tribal world after 1947, *Social Welfare* 32(3) June, p 20-21.

Lakshmi, G.R. and **Bandyopadhyay**, 1990, Differential fertility among the Konda Kamara, *Vanyajati* 38(1) January, p 3-5.

Lakshmaiah, T. and **Yadappanavar, Arvind**, 1988, A survey of educational facilities for tribal students : Problems and impacts in Paderu Samithi in Andhra Pradesh, *Man in India* 68(4) December, p 350-400, bibliography.

Lakshminarayana, 1986, Tribal development in Maharashtra, *Tribal Research Bulletin* 9(1) September, p 1-10, bibliography.

Lal, Shiva Kumar, 1975, Scheduled Caste college students in Rajasthan, *Journal of Higher Education* 1(2) Autumn, p 244-50, references.

Lal Bahadur Singh, et al, 1985, Authoritarianism and intolerance of ambiguity in Santals: An appraisal, *Man in India* 65(3) September, p 234-245, bibliography.

——, 1986, Modes of parental discipline among Santals and Hindus : Assessment across communities, *Indian Journal of Social Work* 47(3) October, p 315-322, bibliography, tables.

Lala, Arjun, 1956, Welfare of tribes including ex-criminal tribes, *Indian Journal of Social Work* 16(4) March, p 300-305.

Lallemand, A., 1953, Social classes, *Social Action* 2(12) March p 382-387.

Lancy, Lobo, 1989, Conversion, emigration and social mobility of an ex-Scheduled Caste from central Gujarat, *Social Action* 39(4) October-December, p 423-437.

Leela Singh, 1984, Job reservation: Polittical and legal perspective, *Modern Review* 148(9-10) September-October, p267-274, bibliography.

Leelakrishnan, P., et al, 1985, Forest and tribal people : Law and practice, *Cochin University Law Review* 9(1-2) March-June, p 259-70.

Lele, P.R., 1933, Worthy of the forgiveness untouchability : Changed angle of vision, *Social Service Quarterly* 18(3) January, p 83-86.

——, 1934, Harijan Sevak Sangh, *Social Service Quarterly* 20(2) October, p 60-63.

——, 1934, The Temple Entry Bill, *Social Service Quarterly* 19(3) January, p 109-112.

Lele, T.P., 1967, A comparative study of the students from different communities, *Education and Psychology Review* 7(3) July, p 117-124.

Leuva, K.K., 1964, Impact of Constitutional safeguards on the Scheduled Tribes, *Journal of Social Research* 7(1-2) March-September, p 62-69.

Limay, Madhu, 1990 Reservations, *Hindustan Times*, September 10.

Lindholm, Charles, 1986, Caste in Islam and the problem of deviant systems : A critique of recent theory, *Contributions to Indian Sociology* (New Series) 20(1) January-June, p 61-73, bibliography.

Long, James, 1966, Five hundred questions on subjects requiring investigation in the social condition of the natives, edited with additional notes by **Mahadev Prasad Saha**, *Folklore* 7(8) August, p 283-329.

Further Notes, pt 1, The proper study of mankind is man. 7(12) December, 1966 p 456-457; pt 2, Bio-bibliographical data: The father of Indian Sociology, by **Mahadev Prasad Saha**, p 450-62, reference.

Luiz, A.A.D., 1958, Tribes of Kerala: Move tribes to rural areas *Vanyajati* 6(1) January, p 39-41.

Mac Dougalle, John, 1979, Dominant castes or rich peasant? *Economic and Political Weekly* 14(12-13) March 24, p 625-634.

Mac Naughton, A., 1953, Foreign missions and their work among t[illegible] peoples, *Indian Journal of Social Work* 14(3) December, p 276-281.

Madan, T.N., 1952, Education of tribal-India, *Eastern Anthropologist* 5(4) June-August, p 179-182.

——, 1971, On the nature of caste in India : A review symposium on Louis Demont's Homo Hierarchichus, *Contributions to Indian Sociology*, (New Series) 5, December, p 1-13.

——, 1971, On understanding caste, *Economic and Political Weekly* 6(3-4) August 21, p 1805-1808.

Madge, Charles, 1958, Caste and community in India and Thailand : A contrast, *Indian Journal of Adult Education* 19(3) October, p 13-15.

Madhara Rau, M.S., 1940, A Harijan conference and its lessons, *Social Service Quarterly* 26(1) July, p 14-19.

Madhava Menon, T., 1985, Law and tribal societies in Kerala, *Cochin University Law Review* 9(1-2) March-June, p 157-172.

Mahadevappa, N.G., 1984-85, Implications of the Lingayata (Virasaiva) conception of liberation, *Journal of Karnataka University* (Social Science) 20-21, p 67-80, bibliography.

Mahalingam, S., 1987, LAMP cooperative societies in tribal India, *Co-operators Bulletin* 30(7) July, p 5-9.

——, 1988, Tribal development programme: A review, *Kurukshetra* 36(4) January, p 4-8.

Mahapatra, Sitakant, 1987, Modernisation and ritual : Identity and changes in Santal society, *Indian Economic and Social History Review* 24(4) October-December, p 441.

Mahatab, H.K., 1957-58, Our Adibasi problem, *Adibasi* 2(1), p 1-2.

Maheshwari, J.K., 1987, Tribal ecosystem : An over view, *Tribal Research Bulletin* 9(2) March, p 1-4 +.

—— and **Singh, J.P.**, 1985, Plants used in magico-religious beliefs by the Kols of Uttar Pradesh: A study, *Folklore* 26(9) September, p 170-173.

Maiji, Amba Shankar, U., 1936, The Bhil Seva Mandal, Dohad, *Social Service Quarterly* 21(3) January, p 92-94.

Maitra, Sunilranjan, 1970, Bachelor's dormitories of the tribes of Eastern India, *Bulletin of Anthropological Survey of India* 19(2) April, p 61-65, references.

Maity, Sachindra Kumar, 1960 Note on caste in ancient India, *Man in India* 40(1) January-March, p 65-67, references.

Majeed, A. and **Ghosh, E.S.K.**, 1989, Affective syndrome crisis in Scheduled Castes, *Vanyajati* 37(4) October, p 90-94.

Majumdar, Aurobindo, 1985, Tribal communications : A case study of Arunachal Pradesh, *Vidura* 22(4) August, p 195-200.

Majumdar, B.C., 1932, The Kui or the Kondh people, *Man in India* 12(4) October-December, p 245-252.

Majumdar, Bimalendu, 1986, Culture change among the Totos, *Man and Life* 12(1-2) January-June, p 77-87, bibliography.

Majumdar, D.N., 1926, Pseudo Rajputs, *Man in India* 6(2-3) June-September, p 152-168, footnotes.

——, 1929, Sex and sex control in primitive society, *Man in India* 9(4) December, p 251-266.

——, 1930, The economic background of social institutions in primitive society, *Man in India* 10(2-3) April-September, p 150-166, footnotes.

——, 1939, Tribal cultures and acculturation, *Man in India* 19(2-3) April-September, p 99-172.

——, 1949, The changing canvas of tribal life, *Eastern Anthropologist* 3(1) September, p 40-47.

——, 1950, Experiment in tribal life, *Indian Journal of Social Work* 10(4) March, p 281-292.

——, 1951, Anthropology under glass, *Journal of the Anthropological Society of Bombay*(NS) 5 (1) March,

——, 1956-1957, What the sociologists can do, what they must do, how they can do and how they should do it, *Eastern Anthropologist* 10(2) December-February, p 130-143.

——, 1959, The light that failed, *Journal of Social Research* 2(1-2) March-September, p 90-97.

—— and **Kishen, K.**, 1948, Serological status of caste and tribes of central Gujarat, *Eastern Anthropologist* 2(2) December, p 92-97.

Majumdar, Nabendu Datta, 1955, Aboriginal peoples of the Andaman and Nicobar Islands, *Vanyajati* 3(4) October, p 149-150.

Majumdar, P.L., 1933, The problem of untouchability, *Social Service Quarterly* 18(4) April, p 130-131.

Makwana, M.H., 1988, The untouchables : An overview, *Vision* 6(1-2) 45-52, bibliography.

Makwana, Yogendra, 1985, Reservation : Does it promote class war, *Link* 27(36) April 21, p 9-11.

Malar, K.M., 1987, The Mappila riots of 1896, *Quarterly Review of Historical Studies* 26(4) January-March, p 33-39, bibliography.

Malhotra, Inder, 1989, Political commentary : The Yadav and other factors, *Times of India*, August 10, p 3-5.

Malhotra, K.C. and **Sen Gupta, B.**, 1985, Absolute and fluctuating asymmetry of digital ridge counts among Hatkars of Maharashtra, *Man in India* 65(2) June, p 139-153, bibliography, tables.

Malhotra, P.L., 1986, Social disadvantage, education and development in India,*Social Change* 16(2-3) June-September, p 41-51, bibliography, tables.

Malhotra, R., 1985, Tribals : Which way justice? *Mainstream* 23(26) May 4, p 21-23.

Malik, Neena,1979, Helping Harijans in Haryana, *Haryana Review* 13(2) February, p 6 +.

Malkani, N.R., 1970, A hereditary proletariat, *Interdiscipline* 7(4) Winter, p 32-36.

Man in India (Periodical), 1988, Tribes of India, *Man in India* 68(4) December, editorial.

Man Mohan, 1987, In search of equality, *Hindustan Times* (Magazine), September 27, p 1, col. 1-6.

Mandal, S.K. and **Malhotra, R.**, 1984, Agrarian stratification among the Warlis of Gujarat: An observation, *Tribe* 16(3-4) September-December, p 36-43.

Mangla, A.P., 1970, Levels of living and problems of tribal welfare, *Vanyajati* 18(2) April, p 59-60.

Mani, S.B., 1964, Bows and arrows in tribal India, *Vanyajati* 12(1) January, p 40-45, references.

Mann, K., 1987, Status of Bhil and Khasi women : A comparative study, *Man and Life* 13(1-2) January-June, p 57-66, bibliography.

Mann, R.S., 1985, Hakkipikki : Trapper and seller, *Man and Life* 11(3-4) July-December, p 221-224.

—— and **Mann, K.**, 1986, Social implications of acculturation in tribal Rajasthan, *Journal of Social Research*, September 29, p 42-50.

Manohar Lal, 1986, The Munda elites : Recruitment, network attitudes perceptions and role in social transformation, *Sociological Bulletin* 35(2) September, p 125-154.

Manohar Prasad, N., 1986, The great reservation divide, *Social Action* 36(2) April-June, p 212-219.

Mannuel, Moreno, 1989, Marriage transactions among the Pallars of Southern Kongu, Tamil Nadu,*Man in India* 69(1) March, p 13-23.

Marrison, G.E., 1962, Language in the tribal churches of North East India, *Religion and Society* 9(4) December, p 74-79.

Marya, R.D., 1985, Education for tribals in Madhya Pradesh : Problems and prospects, *Kurukshetra* 33(4) January, p 28-32.

Masavi, M.I., 1983, Poverty among the Kolghas of Gujarat, *Journal of the Gujarat Research Society* 45(3) July, p 16-31, tables.

Mascarenhas, Antonio, 1984, Conversion : Coercion or conviction ? *Goa Today* 19(1) August, p 31-35.

Mascarenhas, Lambart, 1985, Castes and integration, *Goa Today* 19(7) February, p 12-13.

Masilamani, S., 1986, Educational achievement of Scheduled Caste : Sex bias and a case study of Chakkiliyara of Chinnathdaga village, *Social Action* 36(2) April-June, p 149-165.

Mastana, S.S., 1989, Palmar transverse creases among the Lohanas of North-West India, *Man in India* 69(3) September, p 305-309.

Mathew, K.J., 1986, We are the slaves of the lords of the hill, We are the slaves of the lords of the field, *Religion and Society* 33(2) June, p 55-68.

Mathew, P.M., 1988, Caste reservations : A critique, *Social Change* 18(2) June, p 93-99, bibliography.

Mathur, K.S., 1951-52, Sorcery and witchraft among the tribes of Dudhi, *Eastern Anthropologist* 5(2-3) December-May, p 79-86.

——, 1960, Some problems of tribal rehabilitation in M.P., *Journal of Social Research* 3(2) September, p 113-120.

Mathur, V.K., 1966, Modernity : The nexus of tribal development, *Adibasi* 8(3) October, p 17-22.

——, 1967, Indicators of tribal development, *Adibasi* 8(4) January, p 41-45.

——, 1967, The traditional-modern continuum : An assumption in tribal development, *Journal of Social Research* 10(2) September, p 11-25.

——, 1967, Training for tribal development, *Adibasi* 9(3) October, p 26-30.

Mavalankar, Damodar K., 1987, Castes in India, *Theosophist* 108(8) May, p 327-330.

Mayanglambam, Mani Babu and **Mayanglambam, Suniti Bala**, 1989, Earlobe attachment and dominant eye among the Phayengs of Manipur, *Man in India* 69(3) September, p 285-291.

——, 1989, Patterns of hand clasping, armfolding and handedness among the Phayengs of Manipur, *Man in India* 69(1) March, p 87-93.

Mc Callum, D. Kent., 1965, Consensus and control : The Kunapipi ritual and attendant taboo, *Eastern Anthropologist* 18(2) May-August, p 80-88.

Mc Gilvary, B. Dennis, ed, 1985, Caste ideology and interaction, *Man in India* 65(2) June, p 192-195.

Medge, Charles, 1958, Caste and Community in India and Thailand : A contrast, *Indian Journal of Adult Education* 19(3) October, p 13-15.

Meera Reddy, V., 1990 TRYSEM programme : A case study in Kurnool Samiti of Andhra Pradesh, *Journal of Rural Development* 9(2) March, p 435-443.

Meerwarth, A.M., 1989, The Andamanese, Nicobarese and Hill tribes of Assam, *Marg* 40(4), p 90-91.

Mehra, Savita, et al, 1984, Status improvement of Scheduled Castes in Haryana, *Haryana Review* 18(7) July, p 16 +.

Mehta, B.H., 1949, The problem of Aborigines, *Indian Journal of Social Work* 10(2) September, p 87-93.

——, 1953, Historical background of tribal population, *Indian Journal of Social Work* 14(3) December, p 236-244.

——, 1957, Tribal welfare and forest economy, *Indian Journal of Social Work* 18(3) December, p 155-161.

——, 1958, Towards a casteless rural community, *Indian Journal of Adult Education* 19(3) October, p 40-46.

——, 1959, Tribal welfare and forest economy, *Journal of Social Research* 2(1-2) March-September, p 72-81.

——, 1962, Social experiments in extension projects : The Balvadi in tribal areas, *Indian Journal of Social Work* 23(1) April, p 53-56.

——, 1962, Youth organisations in Sylvan areas, *Indian Journal of Adult Educations* 23(10) October, p 38-40.

——, 1963, Social work and tribal welfare, *Social Work Forum* 1(4) October, p 7-13.

——, 1966, Forestry and tensions in tribal area, *Journal of Social Research* 9(2) September, p 10-25.

——, 1966, The heterogeneous character of clan based societies with special references to Gonds of the Central Indian highlands, *Journal of Anthropological Society of Bombay* (NS) 12(1), p 50-70.

——, 1969, Education of tribal women and girls, *Education Quarterly* 21(1) April, p 44-46.

——, 1985, Gonds of the Central Indian highlands, *Indian Journal of Social Work* 46(2) July, p 299-301.

Mehta, Dhawal, 1985, Anti-reservation agitation in Gujarat, *Radical Humanist* 49(4) July, p 25-31.

Mehta, Manubhai N., 1938, The Bhils of the Gwalior State, *Man in India* 18(4) October-December, p 264-284.

Mehta, Shalini, 1988, Role of voluntary and government organisations in tribal welfare : A case study of Mandala district of Madhya Pradesh, *Eastern Anthropologist* 41(1) January-March, p 49-64, tables.

Mehta, Vaikunth L., 1941, Harijans and municipalities, *Social Service Quarterly* 28(2) October, p 41-48.

Mehtab, H.K., 1957-58, Our Adibasi problem, *Adibasi* 2(1) p 1-2.

Memoria, C.B., 1957, Tribes in India : Their civil and social conditions, *Indian Journal of Social Work* 18(2) September, p 115-124, tables.

Menon, Geeta, 1987, Tribal women : Victims of the development process, *Social Action* 37(4) October-December, p 373-390, bibliography, tables.

Menon, P.S.K., 1975, Post-matric scholarship for Scheduled Caste and Scheduled Tribe students, *Journal of Higher Education* 1(2) Autumn p 263-266.

——, 1986, Programme of tribal development under Seventh Plan, *Tribal Research Bulletin* 8(2) March, p 21-22.

Menon, Venu, 1986, Requiem for an era, *Illustrated Weekly of India* 107(29) July 20, p 28-29.

——, 1988, Conflict in the cathedral, *Illustrated Weekly of India* 109(32) August, p 20-21.

Meulder, E., 1954, The missionary approach to Aboriginal welfare, *Indian Journal of Social Work* 14(4) March p 366-375.

Mills, J.P., 1923, The lessons of the Red Man, *Man in India* 3(3-4) September-December, p 217-223, footnotes.

——, 1949, The sacred chiefs of Assam, *Man in India* 2(3) p 149-151.

Minendra Nath, 1958, The role of anthropology in the education of the Aborigines in India, *Adibasi* 3(2) May-July, p 1-8.

——, 1960, A unit on the survey of a tribe for economic and social improvement, *Vanyajati* 8(3) July, p 97-101.

Minyong and **Pangi**, 1954, Investigation into the dietary habits of the Aboriginal tribes of Abor hills (North-East Frontier), *Bulletin of Department of Anthropology* 3(2) July, p 158-173; 4(2) July, 1955, p 69-95.

Minz, Nirmal, 1962, Impact of traditional religions and modern secular ideologies in the tribal areas of Chotanagpur, *Religion and Society* 9(4) December, p 46-56.

——, 1964, Property and inheritance among the primitives, *Bulletin of Cultural Research Institute* 3(2) p 7-12.

——, 1982, Higher education in the tribal context, *New Frontiers in Education* 12(1) January-March, p 50-53.

——, 1985, Anthropology and the deprived, *Religion and Society* 32(4) December, p 3-19, bibliography.

——, 1986, Religion and culture as power in the context of tribal aspiration in India, *Religion and Society* 33(2) June, p 45-54.

——, 1987, Religion, culture and education in the context of tribal aspirations in India, *Journal of Dharma* 12(2) April-June p 150-164, bibliography, footnote.

——, 1987, A theological interpretation of the tribal reality in India, *Religion and Society* 34(4) December, p 71-85.

Minz, P.S.K., 1986, Programme of tribal development under Seventh Plan, *Tribal Research Bulletin* 8(2) March, p 21-22.

Mishra, Girish, 1987, Agrarian violence in Bihar, *Mainstream* 25(39) June 13, p 6-8.

Mishra, K.K., 1985, The Dalits reply back, *Link* 27(36) April 21, p 13.

——, 1985, Harijans challenge the upper castes: Singhpur tragedy, *Link* 28(6) September 15, p 13-14.

Mishra, Satish, 1986, A silver of hope for Adivasis, *Link* (Supplement) 28(30) March 2, p 4-19.

Mishra, Sudhanshu, 1990, Most party leaders keep aloof, *Link* 33(4) September 2, p 6-7.

Misra, Ajay M., et al, 1983, A study of attitude towards learning of science among Scheduled Caste students, *Journal of Education Psychology* 41(3) October, p 112-116.

Misra, Kamal K., 1985, Life and development in Bonda hills of South Orissa, *Social Welfare* 32(3) June, p 12-13.

Misra, L.S., 1985, The community practices of informal social controls in rural India, *Indian Journal of Criminology* 13(2) July, p 96-102, tables.

Misra, P.K., 1963, A note on an organised effort to bring a change in the caste status by the charmakars, *Bulletin of Anthropological Survey of India* 12(1-2) January-June, p 127-128.

Misra, Somanath, 1967, Qualifications for tribal welfare work, *Adibasi* 8(4) January, p 3-5.

Mitkong, N., 1984, The Binnyat offering in Solung festival of the Adis, *Resarun* 10(2) Autumn-Winter, p 45-50.

——, 1985, Customary laws of adoption and property inheritance of the Adis, *Resarun* 11(1) Spring-Summer, p 27-32.

——, 1985, Customs and laws of widow inheritance of the Adis, *Resarun* 11(2) Autumn-Winter, p 14-24.

——, 1986, Role of intergroup relations in communal harmony among the Adis, *Resarun* 12(1-2) Spring-Winter, p 9-13.

Mitra, Ajay M., et al, 1983, A study of attitude towards learning of science among Scheduled Caste students, *Journal of Education and Psychology* 41(3) October, p 112-116.

Mitra, Ashok, 1988, Tribal exploitation: An overview, *Mainstream* 26(33) May 28, p 32-34.

Mitra, Chandan, 1989, Moulded in caste : AJGAR versus the lesser OBCs, *Times of India*, August 23, p 3-5.

Mitra, Mitashree, et al, 1986, A study on some behavioural traits among the Oraons of Twenty Four Parganas, *Indian Journal of Physical Anthropology and Human Genetics* 12(2) May-August, p 155-158, bibliography, tables.

Mitra, Mrinal K., et al, 1985, Some observations on rural indebtedness, *Rajasthan Economic Journal* 9(2) July, p 62-74, bibliography.

Mitra, Sarat Chandra, 1921, Types of cultural theory, *Man in India* 1(3) September, p 240-261, footnotes.

Moasosang, P., 1962, Social and cultural changes in the tribal communities today and the responsibility of the churches, *Religion and Society* 9(4) December, p 40-45.

Mohan, Raj Pal, 1965, Social class : A review, *Indian Sociological Bulletin* 2(4) July, p 226-227, references.

Mohan Rao, K., 1988, The ceremonial friendship among the tribal people of Andhra Pradesh, *Man in India* 68(1) March, p 93-104.

Mohanty, A.K., et al, 1990, Protein calorie intake and growth status of tribal boys in a residential school, *Man in India* 70(2) June, p 144-154.

Mohanty, Gopinath, 1964, Fading outlines in tribal culture, *Adibasi* January, p 25-38.

Mohanty, Jagannath, 1966, Some problems in tribal education in Orissa and their solutions, *Adibasi* 8(3) October, p 32-34.

Mohanty, Rabindra K., 1984, Scheduled Castes as minorities *Mainstream* 23(18) December 29, p 27-29.

——, 1988, Dynamics of atrocities on Scheduled Castes in rural India, *Indian Journal of Social Work* 49(1) January, p 51-66.

Mohapatra, K., 1964, Action programme on economic projects among the Gonds of Orissa, *Adibasi*, November, p 23-28.

Mohapatra, Kulamani, 1958, The changing status of Harijans in a village of Cuttack district, *Adibasi* 3(2) May-July, p 26-30.

——, 1964, Approaching the tribal people for welfare, *Adibasi*, January, p 7-16.

——, 1966, Primary education in tribal languages: Problem and prospects, *Adibasi* 8(2) July, p 48-55.

Mohapatra, P.C., 1985, Consumption pattern of Scheduled Tribes : A case study of Koraput district, Orissa, *Vision* 5(2) October-December, p 15-22, bibliography, tables.

Mohapatra, Prashant Kumar, 1970, Leadership and religion, *Adibasi* 11(4) January, p 53-59.

Mondal, S.K. and **Malhotra R.**, 1984, Agrarian stratification among the Warlis of Gujarat : An observation, *Tribe* 16(3-4) September-December, p 36-43.

Moulik, T.K., 1987, Palamau tribals : Towards integrated development, *Economic Times*, May 21, p 5, col. 3-6.

Mukherjee, Anima, 1950, The pattern of a polyandrous society with particular reference to tribal crime, *Man in India* 3(2-3) April-September, p 56-65.

Mukherjee, Bhabananda, 1952, Marriage customs and kinship organisation of the Ural of Travancore, *Bulletin of Department of Anthropology* 1(2) July, p 37-54, appendix, tables.

——, 1957, Garo family, *Eastern Anthropologist* 11(1), September-November, p 25-30, references.

——, 1959, The Riang, *Bulletin of Department of Anthropology* 8(1) January, p 1-107, illustration, references.

——, 1959, Trends of changes in the Riang culture since Independence, *Bulletin of Department of Anthropology* 8(2) July, p 103-108.

——, 1961, Comparative study of the kinship systems of six matrilineal tribes, *Eastern Anthropologist* 14(3) September-December, p 216-227, references, tables.

——, 1966, Social anthropology and its roles, *Vanyajati* 14(2) April, p 78-81.

——, 1968, Trends of social mobility movement, *Journal of Indian Anthropological Society* 3(1-2) March-September, p 121-129.

Mukherjee, Charulal, 1943, The Santals in a changing civilisation, *Indian Journal of Social Work* 4(2) September, p 171-181.

——, 1990, Social Anthropology and its roles, *Vanyajati* 37(1) January, p 17-21.

Mukherjee, D., 1984, A review of Audumbara coin, *Indian Museum Bulletin* 19, p 66-68.

Mukherjee, D.P., 1970, A concept of tribal education in West Bengal, *Vanyajati* 18(1) January, p 31-34, references.

——, 1985, Skeletal development of tribal children : Kanwar and Oraon of Surguja district, M.P., *Journal of Indian Anthropological Society* 20(1) March, p 77-85, bibliography, tables.

—— and **Das, N.K.**, 1985, Age at menarche in tribal girls : The Kanwar and the Oraon of Surguja district, M.P., *Journal of Indian Anthropological Society* 20(2) July, p 153-158, bibliography, tables.

Mukherjee, Deba Prasad, 1963, Variation in defective colour vision among some tribes of Assam, *Bulletin of Anthropological Survey of India* 12(1-2) January-June, p 39-42, references, tables.

Mukherjee, Jayasree, 1987, The institution of caste in the eyes of Ramakrishna and Vivekananda, *Quarterly Review of Historical Studies* 27(2), p 22-35, bibliography.

Mukherjee, P.K., 1961, The aim of tribal education, *Vanyajati* 9(1) January, p 26-28.

Mukherjee, Radhakamal, 1965, Unities and universals of culture, *Eastern Anthropologist* 18(1) January-April, p 1-11, references.

Mukherjee, Sankarananda, 1964, Sadani : The tribal dialect of the Sundarbans, *Bulletin of Cultural Research Institute* 3(2), p 47-50, references.

——, 1969, Folklore of the Sundarban tribals, *Bulletin of Cultural Research Institute* 8(1-2), p 97-100.

Mukhiya, Prabhat Kumar, 1960, The primitive people of Orissa, *Vanyajati* 8(4) October, p 140-146.

Mukhopadhyay, Durgadas, 1980, Tribals in Bihar, *Indian and Foreign Review* 23(16) June 15, p 15 +.

Mukhopadhyay, Lipi, and **Mukhopadhyay, Durgadas**, 1989, Tribal development administration, *Social Welfare* 36(3-4) June-July, p 26-29.

Mukhopadhyay, Rajatsubhra, 1984, Dilemma of tribal transformation: The case of Chenchus, *Vanyajati* 32(2) April, p 19-24.

Mukhopadhyay, Sunil K., 1987, The exodus, *Illustrated Weekly of India* 108(8) February 22, p 30-31.

Munirathna Naidu, K., 1985, Development of SCs and STs : An assessment, *Economic Trends* 19(5) October, p 3-6.

Muthamma, C.B., 1990, Change the system, *Hindustan Times* September 21.

Nadkarni, V.C., 1975, Devadasis : Married to God and Mammon, *Illustrated Weekly of India*, December 14.

Nag, D.S., 1954, Education for primitives, *Vanyajati* 2(4) October, p 117-120.

Nag, Narendra Gopal, 1970, Implication of cultural and demographic factors on the socio-political trends among Scheduled Tribes, *Vanyajati* 18(2) April, p 51-58, references, tables.

Nagdo, B.L., 1988, Socio-cultural mores and high fertility among tribes in Banswara, *Social Welfare* 34(11) February, p 14-15 +.

Naidu, A.R., 1967, Problem of migration of semi-educated tribal boys, *Indian Education* 6(3) February, p 28-36.

Naidu, J.M., 1989, Further data on colour blindness among Andhra population, *Man in India* 69(4) December, p 413-415.

Naik, Shukadeb and **Sharma, A.K.**, 1985, Social structure and family planning : A case study of two tribal villages, *Journal of Family Welfare* 32(1) September, p 50-58, bibliography.

Naik, T.B., 1949, Labour problems of tribal Gujarat, *Eastern Anthropologist* 3(1) September, p 22-27.

——, 1950, How to educate Aboriginals, *Indian Journal of Social Work* 11(2) September, p 172-180.

——, 1950-1951, Aboriginals of Gujarat, *Eastern Anthropologist* 4(1) September-November, p 42-51.

——, 1957, Social status in Gujarat, *Eastern Anthropologist* 10(3-4) March-August, p 173-181, footnotes.

——, 1964, What is a tribe : Conflicting definitions, *Bulletin of Tribal Research and Training Institute* (Chhindwara) 4(1) June, p 1-13.

——, 1965, Gond leadership, *Adibasi*, July, p 19-28.

Nair, P.K.,1977-1978, Welfare scheme for Goa miners, *Social Welfare* 24(9-10) December-January, p 71-73 +.

Nair, P. Thankappan, 1960, Cultural change and social education in tribal area, *Vanyajati* 8(4) October, p 163-165.

——, 1967, Ladies club of NEFA, *Vanyajati* 15(1) January, p 9-140.

——, 1985, Tribes of Arunachal Pradesh, *Teacher Today* 28(2) October-December, p 124-125.

Nair, S.P., 1960, Problems in tribal housing, *Vanyajati* 8(2) April, p 48-50.

Nanal, Y.M., 1961, Education of the Adivasis in Thana district, *Progress of Education* 35(12) July, p 382-386; 36(1) August, p 19-24.

Nanavatty, Meher C., 1955, Seminar on casteism and removal of untouchability : A review, *Indian Journal of Adult Education* 16(4) December, p 41-50.

——, 1958, Casteism and social education : Role of the social education, *Indian Journal of Adult Education* 19(3) October, p 47-51.

Nancharaiah, G., 1987, Land reforms and weaker sections : A case study, *Yojana* 31(11) June, 16, p 8-13, tables.

——, 1989, Scheduled Castes as agricultural labourers, *Social Change* 19(3) September, p 31-41.

Nandi, Santi Bhushan, 1960, Cultural change in an Oraon village, *Vanyajati* 8(1) January, p 12-20.

Nandu Ram, 1986, Socio-structural variants and higher education among the Scheduled Castes and Tribes, *Social Action* 36(2) April-June, p 166-182.

Narahari, S., 1990, The Challa : An ethnographic account, *Vanyajati* 38(1) January, p 20-23.

——, 1990, The changing position of Scheduled Castes as agricultural labourers in the labour market, *Social Action* 40(2) April-June, p 172-183.

Narain Prasad, 1961, Primary education among the Adivasis, *Vanyajati* 9(4) October, p 161-162.

Narayana, K.V., 1985, Tribals in rural development, *Kurukshetra* 34(2) November, p 7-8.

——, et al, 1987, Socio-economic status of Scheduled Castes and Tribes : A study, *Kurukshetra* 35(8) May, p 18-21.

Narayana Reddy, G., 1983, Approaches to tribal development : An overview, *Tribe* 15(1-2) March-June, p 1-14.

——, 1984, Dominant caste and social interaction in a Karnataka village, *Social Change* 14(4) December, p 25-30, bibliography, tables.

——, 1984, Scheduled Castes movement, *Voluntary Action* 27(5-6) November-December, p 68-69 +.

Naresh Kumar, 1985, Cooperatives for tribals, *Social Welfare* 32(3) June, p 30-32.

Nargolkar, V.S., 1969, Removal of untouchability : Goals and attainments. *Indian Journal of Social Work* 30 (3) October, p 189-201.

Naskar, Santosh K., 1989, Status of tribal women in Bastar, *Vanyajati* 37(3) July, p 16-20,

—— and **Naskar, Indrani**, 1989, Pre-Independent tribal revolution in Bastar : A historical analysis, *Vanyajati* 37(2) April, p 30-34.

Nautiyal, K.C. and **Sharma, Y.D.**, 1980, Equalisation of educational opportunities for Scheduled Castes and Scheduled Tribes, National Council of Educational Research and Training, New Delhi, *Journal of Indian Education* 6(1) May, p 78-79.

Navlakha, Surendra Kumar, 1959, The authority structure among the Bhumij and Bhils : A study of historical causations, *Eastern Anthropologist* 13(1) September-November, p 27-40.

Nayar, P.K.B., 1985, Tribal sub-plan of Kerala : A critical appraisal, *Cochin University Law Review* 9 (1-2) March-June, p 189-202.

Negi, D.B., 1990, Jajmani relations in tribal world : A study of Kinnaura tribes, *Man in India* 70(2) June, p 131-143.

Negi, R.S., 1962, Distribution of middle phalangeal hair in some Bastar population, *Bulletin of Anthrcpological Survey of India* 11(3-4) p 175-191, appendix, references, tables.

——, 1968, Sporadic occurrence of sickle-cell trait in penninsular Gujarat, *Bulletin of Anthropological Survey of India* 17(4) October, p 379-381, tables.

——, et al, 1982, P T C taste variation in Bastar (Central India), *Indian Journal of Physical Anthropology and Human Genetics* 8(1) April, p 41-46, bibliography, tables.

Negi, Raghunath Singh and **Ahmad, S. Hasim**, 1962, The Bhatra, Muria and Mahra of Bastar : A blood group genetic study, *Bulletin of Anthropological Survey of India* 11(3-4), 201-209, references, tables.

Nehru, B.K., 1988, Do we still need reservations?, *Indian Express* (Magazine) April 17, p 1, col. 1-6.

Nehru, Jawaharlal, 1953, Right approach to tribal peoples, *Indian Journal of Social Work* 14(3) December, p 231-235.

——, 1955, Place of Adivasis in our national life (Inaugural address delivered in Hindi at 3rd Tribal Welfare Conference held at Jagdalpur, 1955), *Vanyajati* 3(2) April, p 55-57.

——, 1964, Speeches delivered on various occasions, *Vanyajati* 12(3) July, p 127-144.

——, **1990, Nehru was against quota in services,** ***Indian Express*****, September 19.**

Nigam, R.C., 1960, Little known tribes of Andaman Island : Their problems and prospects, *Vanyajati* 8(1) January, p 5-11; 8(2) April, p 44-47, 8(3) July p 90-97.

Nigam, Raghuvir Sahay, 1961, Marias of Bastar, *Social Service Quarterly* 46(3) January, p 87-88.

Nilkanth, Vidhya Ramanbhai, 1933, Untouchability: The supposed mainstay of Hindu religion, *Social Service Quarterly* 18(4) April, p 127-129.

Nongbri, T., 1989, Some reflections on culture and development among the tribes, *Vanyajati* 37(4) October, p 20-25.

Noronha, R.C.V.P., 1962-1963, The culture penetrated: Abujhmarh diary, *Bulletin of Tribal Research Institute* (Chhindwara) 2(2) December; 3(1) June, p 5-31.

Oad, L.K., 1976, Problems of tribal education in Rajasthan, *Journal of Indian Education* 1(6) March, p 53-59.

Oberoi, R.C., 1989, They carry away the bride, *Man in India* 69(4) December, p 403-405.

Ojha, Hardev and **Rajiv Singh**, 1987, Sex difference in social attitudes of Santal high school students, *Asian Journal of Psychology and Education* 19(5-6), p 40-43, tables, bibliography.

Om Prakash, 1980, Educational attainment of children in the sweeper community at AIIMS campus : An exploratory study, *Indian Educational Review* 15(4) October, p 97-103.

Onkar Prasad, 1985, Structural and technological constraints in the development of the Santal music and dance, *Man in India* 65(2) June, p 177-186, bibliography.

——, 1988, Santal music, *National Centre for the Performing Arts Quarterly Journal* 17(1) March, p 45-47.

Onwurah, Emeka, 1989, Kinship and marriage among the Igbo of Nigeria, *Sarvartham*, 14, p 3-12, footnotes.

Oommen, T.K., 1970, The concept of dominant caste : Some queries, *Contributions to Indian Sociology*, (New Series), 4, December, p 73-83.

Oraon, Kartik, 1964, Tribes and tribalism of India, *Journal of Social Research* 7(1-2) March-September, p 36-52, references.

Oraons, Martin, 1959, A tribe in search of a great tradition : The emulation-solidarity conflict, *Man in India* 39(2) April-June, p 108-114, references.

Otterbein, Keith F., 1967, Mortuary practices in North-eastern Nigeria, *Bulletin of Cultural Research Institute* 6(1-2), p 10-18, illustrations, references, tables.

Ouden, J.H.B. Den, 1979, Some stratification as expressed through language : A case study of a South Indian village, *Contributions of Indian Sociology*, (New Series) 13, January 1, June, p 33-59.

Ouyker, Edward, 1987, Tribal guerrillas: The Santals of West Bengal and Naxalite movement, *Indian Economic and Social History Review* 24(4) October-December, p 436-437.

Paddiash, G. and **Reddy, G.G.**, 1982, Finger dermatoglyphics of the Gadaba, *Indian Journal of Physical Anthropology and Human Genetics* 8(1) April, p 57-62, bibliography, tables.

Pakrasi, K., 1964, Note on differential sex ratios and polyandrous people in India, *Man in India* 44(2) April-June p 161-174.

Pakyntein, E.H., 1962, Changes in the life of the tribal communities of Assam, *Religion and Society* 9(4) December, p 15-39.

Pal, Bulbul, 1986, Rooted in an African past, *Indian Express* (Mag) January 5, p 3, col 5-8.

Pal, Roma and **Dixit, Ashok K.**, 1984, Social class and marital status as correlates of modernisation, *Asian Journal of Psychology and Education* 14(1-4), p 25-33, bibliography.

Panchbhai, S.C., 1966, Religion and race as determinants of references group: A study in stereo types of three Indian tribes, *Indian Journal of Psychology* 41(1) March, p 1-6, references, tables.

——, 1967, The levels of regional and national identification and intergroup relations among Harijans and Adivasis, *Journal of Indian Anthropological Society* 2(1) March, p 75-83, references, tables.

Panda, Premananda, 1988, Barriers to educational development in tribal areas, *Indian Journal of Adult Education* 49(3) July-September, p 79-83, bibliography.

Panda, Satyananda, 1962, Implications of Tribal Welfare Policy in India, *Vanyajati* 10(1) January, p 12-16.

——, 1969, Demography of Kondh village, *Adibasi* 11(3) October, p 27-35, tables.

Panda, Subash Chandra, 1983, A study of school climate of the secondary schools of selected tribal districts of Orissa, *Vision* 3(1-2) July-December, p 75-84, tables

——, 1984, Implements to education of tribals of Orissa, *Vanyajati* 32(4) October, p 7-13.

——, 1988, A study of the secondary school climate in selected tribal districts of Orissa, *Progress of Education* 62(7) February, p 158-162.

Panday, Ram Newaj, 1966, Development of a questionnaire for social class evaluation, *Indian Psychological Review* 3(1) p 53-56, references.

Pande, B.M., 1968, Development schemes at a factor of change in tribal areas, *Journal of Social Research* 11(2) September, p 33-57, references, tables.

Pandey, Ashok K. and **Nigam, Sushma**, 1985, A study of tongue rolling and tongue folding among Thakurs of village Shobhasan (Gujarat, India), *Indian Journal of Physical Anthropology and Human Genetics* 11(1-2) April-August, p 67-70, bibliography, tables.

Pandey, Balaji, 1986, Educational development among Scheduled Castes, *Social Scientist* 14(2-3) February-March, p 59-68.

Pandey, N., 1961, Changing status of the Siraha in a Bastar village, *Vanyajati* 9(2) April, p 55-57.

Pandian, M.S.S., 1985, State, christianity and Scheduled Castes, *Economic and Political Weekly* 20(42) October 19, p 1776-1777.

Pandit, T.N.,1960, Demographic study of a Gujar village, *Anthropologist* 7(1-2) March-August, p 1-6, references, tables.

——, 1985, The tribal and non-tribal in Andaman Islands : A historical perspective, *Journal of Indian Anthropological Society* 10(2) July, p 111-131, bibliography, tables.

Pandit, Trilokinath, 1959, The Gujar of Kashmir valley : Some observations on their ecology and social organisation, *Vanyajati* 7(2) April, p 64-71.

Pandya, Dinakar, 1985, Defeated casteists on rampage, *Link* 27 (33) March 31. p 21-27.

Pant, Mandakini, 1990, Khasi Revivalist Movement : A sociological Analysis, *Vanyajati* 38(1) January, p 6-10.

Pant, Rashmi, 1987, The cognitive status of caste in colonial ethnography : A review of some literature on the North West Province and Oudh, *Indian Economic Social History Review* 24(2) April-June, p 145-162.

Paranjape, H.K., 1985, New look at reservations : Other ways to better opportunities, *Times of India*, June 6, p 8; 7(8) June, p 8.

Parasnis, N.R., 1958, The problem of the education of the Aboriginal tribes (Adivasis) in the Thana district, Bombay State, *Progress of Education* 32(8) March, p 254-259, ; 32 (9) April, p 316-328, references.

Pardesi, Ghanshyam, 1986, The Taraos : Threatened with extinction, *Indian Express* (Magazine) August 17, p4, col 1-8.

Pareek, M., 1987, A comparative study of the relationship between intelligence and socio-economic status between G I and Scheduled Caste/Scheduled Tribe students, *Educational Review* 93(12) December, p 213-215.

Parganiha, B.L., 1967, The Satnami movement, *Journal of Social Research* 10(1) March, p 1 +.

Parida, Krishan C., 1988, Life style of the Orissan tribes, *Patriot* (Magazine) January 10, p 2, col. 1-9.

Parikh, Y.O., 1982-1983, Education and incidence of poverty among Scheduled Castes, *Journal of Maharaja Sayajirao University of Baroda* 31-32(2), p 53-59, tables.

Parmanand Singh, 1987, Preventing exploitative acquisition of reservation benefits through adoption stratagem, *Journal of Indian Law Institute* 29(1) January-March, p 100-109, footnote.

——, 1987, Reservations reality and the Constitution: Current crisis in India, *Cochin University Law Review* 11(3-4) September-December, p 284-318.

Parry, J.P., 1970, The Koli dilemma, *Contribution to Indian Sociology* (NS) December, 4 p 84-104.

Parte, Swaroop Singh, 1970, Tribes of Bastar and their forest rights, *Vanyajati* 18(2) April, p 77-83.

Parulekar, Godavari, 1986, Glorious saga of the Warli Adivasis revolt, *People's Democracy* 10 (8) February 23, p 6-7.

——, 1986, Saga of the Warli Adivasis revolt, *People's Democracy* 10(9) March 2, p 5 +.

Parvathamma, C., 1986, Role of protest movements in social transformation, *Guru Nanak Journal of Sociology* 7(1) April, p 1-22.

——, 1986, Should caste be a basis for recognising backwardnesses, *Guru Nanak Journal of Sociology* 7(2) October, p 89-101, bibliography, table.

Paswan, Ram Vilas, 1990, Reservation won't lead to mediocrity, *Patriot*, September 3.

——,1990, Speech by the Union Minister for Labour and Welfare (at) National Conference on Problems of Scheduled Tribes, 31st March, *Vanyajati* 38(2) April, p 7-8.

Patel, Ashok A. and **Patel, M.R.**, 1987, Gujarat and its tribals, *Kurukshetra* 35(5) February, p 13-14.

Patel, G.D., 1968, Problems of tribal development, *Bulletin of Cultural Research Institute* 7(1-2) p 5-10.

Patel, Harbans, 1985, Why tribal girls stay away : A case study in Gujarat, *Mainstream* 24(3) October 26, p 26-28, tables.

Patel, Leela, 1954, A review of the report of the Scavenger's Living Conditions Enquiry Committee, State of Bombay, *Social Service Quarterly* 39(4) April, p 102-106.

Patel, M.L., 1970, Spatial mobility of unemployed educated tribals of Mandala district, *Vanyajati* 18(2) April, p 70-76, references, tables.

Pathak, Bindeshwar, 1989, Caste is their only crime, *Times of India* (Sunday Review), July 3, p 1-8.

Pathy, Jaganath, 1987, The agrarian situation in tribal areas, *Journal of Social Economic Studies* 4(2) April-June, p 143-162.

——, 1987, Land problems of tribals, *Times of India*, September 10, p 6, col. 7-8.

——, 1989, The idea of tribe and the Indian seene, *Man in India* 69(4) December, p 346-358.

Pathy, Suguna, 1987, Caste, class and violence : An appraisal, *Teaching Politics* 13(2) p 61-75, bibliography.

Patil, H.G., 1957, A scheme for technical training of Adivasi youths, *Vanyajati* 5(3) July, p 150-154, tables.

Patnaik, Binay Kumar, 1987, Tribe and caste : A case study in an Oriya village, *Man in India* 67(4) December, p 335-351, bibliography.

Patnaik, J.D., 1986, Towards tribal prosperity, *Link* (Supplement) 28(30) March 2, p 24-28.

Patnaik, K.M., 1987, Industrialisation for accelerating development in a tribal setting, *Vision* 6(3-4) January, p 52-56.

Patnaik, Nityananda, 1954, The socio-political organisation of the Munda : A study of acculturation, *Vanyajati* 2(2) April, p 46-51.

Patwardhan, Sunanda, 1968, Social mobility and conversion of Maharas, *Sociological Bulletin* 17(2) September, p 187-202, references.

Patwardhan, Vidya and **Palshikar, Vasant**, 1990, Are educational reservations a waste? : The results of a survey, *Janata*, 45, Annual No., p 35-39.

Paul, Gemini, 1956, Origin of certain tribal names pertaining to Assam, *Vanyajati* 4(4) October, p 147-154, references.

——, 1957, Anthropology and tribal administration, *Vanyajati* 5(1) January, p 4-11.

——, 1957, Importance of egg and cock in Khasi and Jaintia hills, *Vanyajati* 5(2) April, p 66-69, references.

Paul, Radha Kanta, 1987, The Tangkhuls of Manipur, *Indian Management* 7(5) April, p 50-57.

Paul, S.P. and **Baghel, A.S.**, 1987, Sociological constraints and attitude to development of tribal farmers in the tribal areas of Madhya Pradesh, *Journal of Rural Development* 6(2) March, p 197-210.

Pawar, H.S. and **Patil, R.P.**, 1987, Adoption behaviour of the tribal farmers from Surgana Taluka (Nasik district) in respect of paddy cultivation, *Tribal Research Bulletin* 9(2) March, p 15-17.

Pawar, S.B., 1962-1963, An administrator looks at the culture A report on Abujhmarh, Tahsil Naraipur, district Bastar, *Bulletin of Tribal Research Institute* (Chhindwara) 2(2)-3(1) December-June (combined issue), p 22-65.

Pawar, S.S. and **Bhuvanedran, P.**, 1988, Tribal education : A study in M.P.S.S., *Kurukshetra* 36(4) January, p 18-21.

——, 1988, Tribal education in the West Zone of Madhya Pradesh, *Social Welfare* 34(11) February, p 4-5.

Perumal, C.A., and **Padmanabhan**, 1986, Tribals of Tamil Nadu Public Policy, *Indian Journal of Political Science* 47(4) October-December, p 457-472.

Peter, Prince, 1939, The utility of psycho-analysis in social anthropology, *Indian Journal of Psychology* 14(1) January, p 23-25.

——, 1953, The problems of Tola survival, *Vanyajati* 1(3) July, p 59-68.

Phogat, Silak Ram, 1984, The original home of Tomaras : A new interpretation, *Journal of Haryana Studies* 16(1-2), p 16-20, bibliography.

Pinto, Marina, 1980-1984, Reservation policy in India, *Journal of the University of Bombay* 49(53), p 65-82, tables.

Piplai, Chumki, et al, 1985, A note on ABO, MN, RH, and in (a) blood groups of the Tamang and Oraon tea labourers of the Jalpaiguri district, West Bengal, *Journal of Indian Anthropology Society* 20(1) March, p 66-70, bibliography, tables.

Pocock, David F., 1961, Psychological approaches and judgements of reality, *Contributions to Indian Sociology*, October 5, p 44-74.

Porte, Swaroop Singh, 1970, Tribes of Bastar and their forest rights, *Vanyajati* 18(2) April, p 77-83.

Prabhakar Rao, A., 1985, Harijan baiting in Andhra, *Link* 28(2) August 18, p 25-27.

Pradhan, H. Prasad, 1979, Caste and class in Bihar, *Economic and Political Weekly* 14, Annual Number, February, p 481-484.

Prakash Rao, R., 1954, Village organisation and authority among the Lambadas of the Deccan, *Eastern Anthropologist* 8(1) September-November, p 3-12.

Prakashan, M.S., 1988, The social world of Uralics, *Social Welfare* 34(11) February, p 7-8.

Pramanik, Paramananda, 1964, Stool making industry of wicker-work in rural Bengal, *Folklore* 5(12) December, p 454-458, illustration.

Pramod Kumar and **Sood, Atul**, 1985, Tribal sub-plan : A critical appraisal, *Link* (Supplement) 27(26) February 3, p 48-54, tables.

_____, and **Yadav, Bhupinder**, 1985, *Link* (Supplement) 27(26) February 3, p 48-54, tables.

Prasad, Chandra Bhan, 1988, Poverty elimination and untouchability, *Mainstream* 26(25) April 2, p 17 +.

Prasad, L.M., 1986, Educational policy for Scheduled Castes and Scheduled Tribes and its implementation, *Indian Journal of Public Administration* 32(4) October-December, p 908-932.

_____, 1987, Voluntary agencies for development of Scheduled Castes and Scheduled Tribes : Their role and function, *Indian Journal of Public Administration* 33(3) July-September, p 588-512, bibliography.

Prasad, R.R., 1985, Tribal culture development, *Administrator* 30(4) October-December, p 347-355, bibliography.

_____, 1986, Change and continuity among the Scheduled Caste leather workers of Uttar Pradesh, *Journal of Rural Development* 5(6) November, p 605-628.

_____, 1986, Role of acculturation in the development of primitive tribes, *Tribal Research Bulletin* 8(2) March, p 8-11 +.

_____, 1986, Untouchability and measures for its eradication, *Gandhi Marg* 3(8) November, 492-505.

_____, 1988, Tribal development in India : Strategies and programme, *Journal of Rural Development* 7(1) January, p 81-103, bibliography, tables.

Prasad, S., 1971, Modern education among the tribes of Bihar in second half of the 19th century, *Man in India* 41(4) p 364-394.

_____, 1975, Implications of the 10+2+3 pattern for the education of tribal children, *Journal of Indian Education* 1(1) May, p 75-79.

Prasad Rao, C.R., 1989, Rural housing among Scheduled Castes in two districts of Andhra Pradesh : A comparison of parameters and predictors, *Vanyajati* 37(4) October, p 76-89.

Prasad Rao, D.L. and **Venkata Rao, P.**, 1983, Problems of teachers working in tribal areas, *Educational Review* 59(8) August, p 139-141.

_____, 1984, Are they right in blaming tribals?: A view point on tribal-forest relations, *Vanyajati* 32(3) July, p 17-21.

Prasad Rao, P.D., 1959, Tribal people of Araku Valley, Visakhapatnam, *Vanyajati* 7(3) July, p 103-105.

Prashanth, D., 1985, Land reforms and distribution of land among Scheduled Tribes in Kerala, *Cochin University Law Review* 9(1-2) March-June, p 213-222.

Premi, Kusum K., 1974, Educational opportunities for the Scheduled Castes : Role of protective discrimination in equalisation, *Economic and Political Weekly* 9(45-46) November, p 1902-1910.

——, 1976, Educational problems of Scheduled Castes in Punjab, *Journal of Indian Education* 1(6) March, p 44-52, tables.

——, 1984, Educational equality and economic opportunities : A comparative study of Scheduled Castes and non-Scheduled Castes, *Journal of Higher Education* 9(3) Spring, p 368-372, bibliography, tables.

Pugh, B.M., 1961, Christianity and the tribal communities of Assam, *Religion and Society* 8(3) September, p 49-52, appendix.

Punalekar, S.P., 1985, Tribal education in Gujarat, *Mainstream* 23(39) May 24, p 20-23, bibliography, tables.

Puri, Rajender, 1990, Mandal: A way out, *Hindustan Times*, September 11.

Quamar, Ahsan, 1987, Tribal development strategy needs rethinking, *Yojana* 31(5) March 16, p 18-22, tables.

Rachappa, B., 1955, Hill tribes of Mysore state and welfare work among them, *Vanyajati* 3(3) July, p 119-123.

Radetotad, N.K., 1966, Caste hierarchy among the untouchables of Dharwar, *Eastern Anthropologist* 19(3) September-December, p 205-214, references, tables.

Radhakrishna, Meena, 1989, The criminal Tribes Act in Madras Presidency : Implications for itinerant trading communities, *Indian Economic and Social History Review* 26(3) July-September, p 269-295.

Radhakrishna, P., 1984, Tamil Nadu backward classes, *Voluntary Action* 27(5-6) November-December, p 65-67 +.

Raghviah, V., 1956, How to approach the Adivasi?, *Vanyajati* 4(1) January, p 31-38.

——, 1989, Research on tribal welfare, *Vanyajati* 37(1) January, p 10-11.

Raha, Manish Kumar, 1963, Forest in tribal life, *Bulletin of Cultural Research Institute* 2(1) , p 56-61, footnotes.

——, 1966, The Garos, *Bulletin of Cultural Research Institute* 5(1-2) p 26-35, references, tables.

——and **Coomar, Palash Chandra**, 1988, The Kinnaura polyandry and the allocation of paternity, *Man and Life* 14(3-4) July-December, p 147-162.

——, 1989, The kinship terms of the Bhantu of Andamans : Structural analysis, *Man in India* 69(4) December, p 374-386.

Rahu, R.S. and **Baral, J.K.**, 1987, Leadership and socio-political change of tribes of Orissa Saoras, *Vision* 6(3-4) January-June, p 57-69, bibliography.

Rai, Lagan, 1988, Murder most foul, *Times of India* (Sunday Review), January, 17, p 3, col. 1-5.

Raj, Hilda, 1952, Education of Adivasis, *Eastern Anthropologist* 5(4) June-August, p 174-178.

Rajagopal, 1986, Agriculture labourers in tribal areas, *Kurukshetra* 34(4) January, p 17-18.

Rajagopalacharl, C., 1933, A denial of religion, *Social Service Quarterly* 18(4) April, p 124.

Rajagopalan, K.R. and **Bhagvandas, M.**, 1987, Kudu Kudu-P-Paik-Karans, *Folklore* 28(12) December, p 283-288, bibliography.

Rajaiah, B., 1982, Reservations in Higher education and jobs, *Educational Review* 88(3) March, p 55-58.

Rajappa, S., 1990, Tamil Nadu for it, rest of South quiet, *Statesman*, September 4.

Rajendra Prasad, 1955, Adivasis and our duty to them, *Vanyajati* 3(4) October, p 147-148.

Rajendran, C.P., 1988, Women power, *Illustrated Weekly of India* 107(32) August 7, p 40-41.

Rajni Kanth, G. and **Suman Chandra, K.**, 1988, Education of tribals : The role of tribal political organisation, *Man in India* 68(4) December, p 459-464.

Rajpal Singh, 1989, Rise of the Jat power, *Tribune* (Magazine), April 9, p 3-6.

Raju, P.S.S., 1988, The religious beliefs of Koyas as described in Koya folk tables, *Eastern Anthropologist* 41(1) January-March, p 99-102.

Raju Cheluva, K.H., 1986, Backward classes in India : Issues and trends, *Indian Journal of Political Science* 47(4) October-December, p 473-485.

Rajyalakshmi, P. and **Geervani, P.**, 1988, Tribal people: Traditions, customs and attitudes related to food and dietary practices : A case study of Vizianagram district, Andhra Pradesh, *Indian Journal of Social Work* 49(1) January, p 45-50.

Rakhshit, Hirendra K., 1970, Language, culture and race in South India, *Journal of Indian Anthropological Society* 5 (1-2) April-October, p 205-232 appendix.

Ram Ratan, 1967, Emergent leadership and development in a tribal village, *Adibasi* 9(2) July, p 35-43.

Ram Sagar Singh, 1986, Caste consciousness identity and protest : A sociological analysis of neo-Buddhist movement in India, *Journal of Social Studies*, January 5, p 161-180, bibliography.

Rama Badri, 1990, Connotation of merit, *Hindustan Times*, September 4, p 11, col. 6-7.

Ramachandra Raj, G., 1984, Problems and prospects of tribal development in Kerala, *Journal of Kerala Studies* 9(1-4) March-December, p 275-278.

Ramchandra Rao, A., 1966, Scholastic backwardness in tribal children, *Indian Education* 5(6) May, p 20-25.

Ramachandra Raju, D., 1985, Protective laws in scheduled areas of Andhra Pradesh, *Economic and Political Weekly* 9(1-2) March-June, p 149-156.

Ramachandra Reddy, M. and **Chengal Reddy, P.**, 1986, Fertility behaviour in the Sugalis of Chittoor district, Andhra Pradesh, *Health and Population* 9(4) October-December, p 205-217.

——, 1989, Family planning behaviour in the Sugalis of Andhra Pradesh, *Vanyajati* 37(1) January, p 3-8.

Ramachandran, Janani, 1988, The Warli tribal community: Economic realities and the Warli's view point, *Annals of the National Association of Geographers, India* 8(2) December, p 1-9.

Ramachandran, R., et al, 1986, Caste and consciousness : An invested pyramid, *Indian Journal of Social Work* 47(3) October, p 243-253, tables.

Ramadas, G., 1931, The Gadabas, *Man in India* 11(2) April-June, p 160-173.

Ramaiah, A., 1990, Mandal Commission's recommendations : A critical view, *Mainstream* 28(43) August 18, p 19-20 +.

Ramakrishnan, P.S., 1985, Tribal man in the humid tropics of the North East, *Man in India* 65(1) March, p 1-32, bibliography, tables.

Ramalingaswami, Prabha, 1986, Impact of social change on health problems of tribal women, *Society and Change* 16(2-3) June-September, p 100-103, bibliography, tables.

Ramamurthy, B., 1986, Caste and occupational mobility among the Harijans in Andhra village, *Folklore* 27(2) February, p 36-38.

—— and **Subbarayudu, L.**, 1985, Community relationship and power structure in an Andhra village among the Harijans, *Folklore* 26(12) December, p 233-236.

Ramanamma, A. and **Bambawala, U.**, 1985, Education among Scheduled Castes, Scheduled Tribes and others in Maharashtra, *Cochin University Law Review* 9(1-2) March-June, p 129-148.

Ramanathan, K.V., 1990, Lessons from experience, *Indian Express*, September 7.

Ramaswamy, Gita, 1989, Pen-portrait : Bandi Sriramuly, *Mainstream* 27(39) Júne 24, p 23-24.

Ramaswamy, Uma, 1974, Scheduled Caste in Andhra : Some aspects of social change, *Economic and Political Weekly* 9(20) July 20, p 1153-1158.

——, 1974, Self identity among Scheduled Castes : A study of Andhra, *Economic and Political Weekly* 9(47) November 23, p 1959-64.

——, 1985, Education and inequality, *Economic and Political Weekly* 20(36) September 7, p 1523-1528.

——, 1986, Protection and inequality among backward groups, *Economic and Political Weekly* 21(9) May 1, p 399-403.

Ramaswamy, V.S., 1985, Land ownership structure in the tribal areas: A study, *Kurukshetra* 33(10) July, p 24-25 +.

Ramchandra Naidu, A., 1966, Informal education among tribals, *Vanyajati* 14(4) October, p 183-191.

Rammi Reddy, V. and **Subhashini, A.B.**, 1984, A B O blood groups among the Palli Reddies : A backward caste of Tirupati and other populations of Andhra Pradesh, *Man in India* 64(2) June, p 193-200, bibliography.

——, et al, 1989, Palmer transverse creases among Kshatriyas of Southern Andhra Pradesh, *Indian Journal of Physical Anthropology and Human Genetics* 12(1) January-April, p 75-78, bibliography, tables.

Ramotra, K.C., 1988, Scheduled Castes literacy in the North Western India : A spatial perspective, *National Geographer* 23(2) December, p 147-155.

Ramu, G.N., 1968, Untouchability in rural areas, *Indian Journal of Social Work* 29(2) July, p 147-155, tables.

Ranadive, B.T., 1979, Caste class and property relations, *Economic and Political Weekly* 14, Annual Number, February, p 337-348.

Rangaya, D., 1955, Memorandum submitted to the Backward Classes Commission on behalf of the Bhartiya Adamjati Sevak Sangh, Delhi, *Vanyajati* 3(1) January, p 33-39.

Ranjan, Sudhanshu, 1988, Bihar killings in retrospect, *Mainstream* 26(21) March 5, p 27-29.

Rao, E.N.B. and **Girja Shankar, K.**, 1986, Tribals : Are they better off, *Kurukshetra* 34(4) January, p 30-32.

Rao, G.R.S., 1966, Process of industrialisation and direction of social changes in tribal society, *Journal of Social Research*, 9, September, p 65-69.

Rao, G.S., 1979, Literacy for tribals, *Indian Journal of Adult Education* 40(4) April, p 1-4, references.

Rao, L.N., 1939, The Kacharis of Brahampulra valley, Assam, *Rural India* 2(3) September, p 136-139.

Rao, M.S.A., 1964, Social stratification and social change in South-East Asia, *Sociological Bulletin* 13(1) March, p 22-32, references.

Rao, N.V.N. and **Ram Reddy, R.**, 1986, Minor irrigation and tribal development : An empirical study, *Kurukshetra* 34(2) November, p 31-33.

Rao, T.S., 1972, Free education for all, *Social Welfare* 19(9) December, p 18-20.

Rao, V.K.R.V., 1966, Social change and the tribal culture, *Journal of Social Research* 9(2) September, p 1-9.

Rao, V.V. Raman, 1984, Impact of supplementary feeding on tribal pre-school children of A.P.: An anthropometric assessment, *Man in India* 64(2) June, p 167-174.

Rastogi, S.P., 1978, Attitudes and beliefs of Harijan students, *Journal of Higher Education* 4(2) Autumn, p 251-58.

——, 1980, The impact of constitutional provision upon the uplift to Harijans, *Indian Educational Review* 15(4) October, p 76-80.

Rastogi, Sudha, et al, 1984, Finger dermatoglyphics of the Rastogis, *Man in India* 64(3) September, p 286-293.

Rath, R., 1986, Educational problems of disadvantaged tribal children, *Vivekananda Kendra Patrika* 15(2) August, p 75-82.

Ratha, S.N. and **Mahakud, N.K.**, 1988, The Kisan children at work : Data from a West Orissa village, *Man in India* 68(4) p 369-379.

Rathnaiah, K., 1987, The economic organisation of Malas in Chittoor district of A.P. : A study, *Folklore* 28(9) September, p 207-215, tables.

Rattord, B., Shyamak Devi, 1984, Class and caste differences among the Lambadas in Andhra Pradesh, *Social Scientist* 12(7) July, p 47-56, bibliography, tables.

Raval, Indubhai B., 1961, Tribal community development survey, *Indian Journal of Social Work* 21(4) March, p 369-371.

——, 1962, Tribal community development survey, *Social Work Review*, 9, July, p 43-46.

——, 1964, Sociology of tribal economic development, *Indian Journal of Social Work* 25(1) April, p 43-51, tables.

Ravindranathan, M.N., 1981, Educational problems of Scheduled Castes, *Educational Review* 87(4) April, p 69-74,

——, 1981, Perspectives of research in tribal education, *Experiments in Education* 9(1) March, p 15-18 : 9 (2) April, p 21-26.

——, 1983, The problem of cultural integration of the tribals: Education as the chief instrument of change, *Education Quarterly* 35(4) October, p 20-24.

Ravnathan, K.V., 1990, Reservations : Lessons from experience, *Indian Express*, September 7.

Ray, Baren, 1989, The tribal problem in India : Some remarks, *Vanyajati* 37(4) October, p 50-54.

Ray, H.M., 1988, Savara : The snake charmer, *Man in India* 68(4) December, p 438-487.

Ray, Mainmarji, 1988, Ethnic difference in intelligence, *Indian Education Review* 23(2) April, p 114-119, bibliography.

Ray, P.C., 1951, Difference in concrete intelligence among Jaunsaries, *Journal of Asiatic Society*, 17, p 45-52.

——, 1951, Differences in concrete intelligence among the Bhils of Central India, *Indian Journal of Psychology* 26(1-4), p 73-77, tables.

———, 1953, Maze Test performance of Bhils of Central India, *Bulletin of Department Anthropology* 2(1) p 83-90.

———, 1955, The tensional feelings among the Abors and Gallongs indicated by Rorschach Techniques, *Indian Journal of Psychology* 30(1-2) p 95-103.

———, 1957, Effect of culture-contact on the personality structure, *Bulletin of Department of Anthropology* 6(2).

Raymond, L., 1952, Harijans at school, *Social Action* 1(12) March, p 398-412.

Rayudu, C.S., 1985, New milestones in Andhra Pradesh, *Social Welfare* 32(3) June, p 17-19.

Reddi, L.R., 1952, The problem of Adivasi education, *Progress of Education* 25(5) December, p 135-138.

———, 1953, The education of the Adivasis, *Progress of Education* 27(9) April, p 258-261.

Reddy, A.P., 1984, Ethnographic note about the Yanadi tribe of Andhra Pradesh, *Vanyajati* 32(2) April, p 14-18.

Reddy, G.P., 1969, The role of liquor in the culture of the tribes of Andhra Pradesh and its economic implications, *Vanyajati* 17(2) April, p 37-45, tables.

———, 1970 Causes of wastage in tribal education of Andhra Pradesh, *Vanyajati* 18(3) July, p 109-120, references, tables.

———, 1984, Tribal communities in India : A struggle for identity, *Parlance* 8(2-3) November-December, p 13-20.

Reddy, N.S., 1973, Caste in a tribal society : The formative process, *Contributions to Indian Sociology*, (New Series), 7, p 159-167.

Rice, Marion J., 1980, Harijan wasti, *Progress of Education* 55(2) September p 51-57.

Robert, Parkin, 1990, Terminology and alliance in India: Tribal systems and the North-South problem *Contributions to Indian Sociology* 24(1) January-June, p 61-76.

Roberts, Michael, 1984, Caste feudalism in Sri Lanka : A critique through the Asokan persons and European contrasts, *Contributions to Indian Sociology* (New Series) 19(2) July-December, p 189-217.

Rohini, A., 1987, Some demographic trends among the tribal women of Andhra Pradesh, *Man and Life* 13(1-2) January-June, p 91-96, bibliography, tables.

——— and **Reddy, G.G.**, 1986, Harijans and Girijans of Andhra Pradesh: An application of analysis of variance in the study of fertility, mortality and family planning, *Indian Journal of Physical Anthropology and Human Genetics* 12(3) September-December, p 203-212, bibliography, tables.

Rose, J.A., 1961, The changing picture of the life of young tribal girls, *Religion and Society* 8(3) September, p 53-59.

Rout, Jnanendra Kumar, 1964, Tribal welfare in Orissa, *Adibasi*, January, p 17-20.

Rout, Siba Prasad, 1963-64, Functions of Juang dormitory in Keonjhar district, *Adibasi* 5(2), p 29-34.

———, 1969, Youth organisation, *Adibasi* 11(1-2) April-July, p 89-95.

Rout, Upendra Nath, 1978, A new approach to State Non-formal Education Centre in tribal area for all age groups, *Experiments in Education* 6(4) June, p 60-63.

Roy, Ashim K., 1985, Anti-reservation movement : A political assessment, *Economic and Political Weekly* 20(32) August 10, p 1343-1344.

Roy, J.K. and **Roy, B.C.**, 1986, Hunger and physique-study of the Juang population of Orissa, *Man and Life* 12(1-2) January-June, p 110-112.

Roy, S.C., 1921, Anthropological research in India, *Man in India*, 1.

Roy, Sachin, 1955, Distribution of A B O , M N blood groups and the A B H secretor among the tribes of Central and Northern Travancore, *Man in India* 35(1) January-March, p 57-65, illustration, references, tables.

——, 1958, Hunting and fishing among the Adi, *Vanyajati* 6(2) p 140-152.

Roy, Sarat Chandra, 1934-1938, Caste, race and religion in India, *Man in India* 14(1) January-March, p 39-63; 14(2) April-June, p 75-220; 14(3-4) July-December, p 71-311; 17(3) June-September, p 147-176; 17(4) October-December, p 212-254; 18(2-3) April-September, p 85-105, footnotes.

——, 1946, The aboligines of Chatanagpur: Their proper status in the refermed constitution, *Man in India* 26(2) June, p 120-136.

Roy, U.K., et al, 1985, To be with Santals, *Man and Life* 11(3-4) July-December, p 226-227.

——, 1987, Pattern of tribal education, status of research and sociological dimensions for projecting the future, *Journal of Education Planning and Administration* 1(2) April, p 126-136, bibliography.

Roy Burman, B.K., 1954, A note on the taxonomy of the tribals with special reference to Bengal, *Vanyajati* 2(3) July, p 86-91.

——, 1958, (Letter to the editor regarding "The tribal population in West Bengal, by S.S. Sarkar" and reply by S.S. Sarkar), *Man in India* 38(3) June-September, p 215-216.

——, 1958, Problem of family planning among the Scheduled Tribes of West Bengal, *Vanyajati* 6(4) October, p 160-164.

—— 1958-59, Problem of integration of the tribals in Indian society, *Adibasi* 3(3-4) August-January, p 9-16.

——, 1960, Basic concepts of tribal welfare and tribal integration, *Journal of Social Research* 3(2) September, p 16-24.

——, 1961, A list of research projects with operative significance for welfare of the backward classes (with special reference to West Bengal, *Vanyajati* 9(1) January, p 9-21.

——, 1961, Meaning and process of tribal integration in a democratic society, *Sociological Bulletin* 10(1) March, p 27-40, references.

——, 1961, Perspective of tribal welfare, *Bulletin of Tribal Research and Development Institute* (Chhindwara) 1(1) June, p 12-16.

——, 1965, Cultural factors in economic development and technological change in tribal areas, *Journal of Social Research* 8(1) March, p 21-32.

——, 1965, Cultural factors in economic development and technological change in tribal India, *Vanyajati* 13(3) July, p 102-113.

——, 1966, Questions relating to inclusion in and exclusion from the list of Scheduled Tribes, *Journal of Indian Anthropological Society* 1(1) March, p 7-14, illustrations, references.

——, 1966, Structure of bridge and buffer communities in the border areas, *Man in India* 46(2) April-June, p 103-107.

——, 1967, Area approach to the socio-economic development of tribal communities, *Adibasi* 9(2) July, p 16-20.

——, 1968, Some dimensions of transformation of tribal societies in India, *Journal of Social Research* 11(1) March, p 88-94,

——, 1969, Some dimensions of transformation of tribal societies in India, *Vanyajati* 17(1) January, p 1-4 +.

——, 1970, Family planning from the point of view of cultural anthropology, *Indian Journal of Social Work* 30(4) January, p 343-353, references.

——, 1970, Socio-political processes in India and integration of the tribal societies, *Vanyajati* 18(1) January, p 6-11.

——, 1970, Tentative framework of an integrated tribal policy, *Inter-discipline* 7(4) Winter, p 48-52.

——, 1985, Issues in tribal development, *Mainstream* 23(19) January, 5, p 11-14 + ; 23(20) January 12, p 20-22.

——, 1986, Institutional finance and tribal development, *Mainstream* 24(20) January 18, p 16-22.

——, 1987, Historical process in respect of communal land system and poverty alleviation among tribals, *Social Action* 37(4) October-December, p 391-420, bibliography, tables.

——, 1987, Tribals in a global perspective, *Journal of Social Economic Studies* 4(2) April-June, p 95-120.

——, 1989, Critical approach to tribal problems, *Mainstream* 27(42) July 15, p 12-14.

——, 1989, Key note address : The National Seminar on Nehru and Evolution of Tribal Policy, in the inaugural session on 20th September, 1989, *Vanyajati* 37(4) October, p 8-11.

——, 1989, Problems and prospects of tribal development in North-East India, *Economic and Political Weekly* 24 (13) April 1, p 693-697.

—— 1989, Society, ecology and land reform in tribal India, *Indian Journal of Public Administration* 35(1) January-March, p 41.

——, 1989, Technology transfer to tribal areas, *Mainstream* 27(44) July 29, p 23-27.

——, 1990, Burman questions 1931, Census, *Hindustan Times* September 18.

Roy Burman, J.J., 1990, Environmental management in tribal areas through social forestry, *Vanyajati* 38(1) January, p 26-32.

——, 1990, Tribal tradition and modern development in North-East India, *Vanyajati* 38(2) April, p 9-13.

Roy Choudhary, P.C., 1952, The Tharus, *Man in India* 32(4) October-December, p 246-250.

Roy Chowdhury, Bidyut Kumar, 1963, Comparative study of the progress of secondary education among the Scheduled Castes and Scheduled Tribes of West Bengal, *Bulletin of Cultural Research Institute* 2(1), p 40-52, appendix, tables.

——, 1964, Factors retarding tribal education in west Bengal, *Bulletin of Cultural Research Institute* 3(2), p 26-40, appendix, references, tables.

Sachchidananda, 1954, Birsa : An Adivasi fighter for freedom, *Vanyajati* 2(4) October, p 120-124.

——, 1954, Economic cooperation in tribal India, *Man in India* 34(3) July-September, p 220-224.

——, 1955, Class and caste in tribal Bihar, *Man in India* 35(3) July-September, p 195-202.

——, 1958, Study of culture change in tribal Bihar, *Adibasi* 3(2) May-July, p 11-16.

——, 1959, Political consciousness in tribal Bihar, *Man in India* 39(4) October-December, p 301-308.

——, 1960, Community development in tribal areas, *Journal of Social Research* 3(2), September, p 49-56.

——, 1964, Community development and the tribals, *Journal of Social Research* 7(1-2) March-September, p 70-78, tables.

——, 1964, Tribal education in Bihar, *Vanyajati* 12(1) January, p 3-6.

——, 1965, Directed change among the Birhor, *Eastern Anthropologist* 18(3) September-December, p 172-176, references.

——, 1970, Untouchability and Gandhi, *Inter-discipline* 7(4) Winter, p 37-47, references.

——, 1978, Social structure and status and mobility pattern : The case study of tribal women, *Man in India* 58(1) January-March, p 1-12.

——, 1988, Economic development, education and social change in Arunachal Pradesh, *Man in India* 65(1) March, p 33-57.

——, 1989, Role of voluntary agencies in social and ecological development in tribal areas, *Vanyajati* 37(4) October, p 26-31.

Sah, B.L., 1985, Change and stagnation go together in Kumayun, Himalaya, *Social Welfare* 32(3) June, p 5-7 +.

Sah, Nirmal K., 1986, A tribe in transition : Bhotiyas of Uttarkhand, *Asian Studies* 4(2) April, p 20-27.

Saha, Mahadev Prasad, 1966, M.J. Long: The father of Indian Sociology, *Folklore* 7(8) August, p 450-462.

Saha, Swopan S., 1984, Degree of Isolation : Reproductive wastage and mortality in a Muria population of Bastar, Madhya Pradesh, *Journal of Indian Anthropological Society* 19(2) July, p 118-124.

Sahay, B.N. and **Singh, B.K.**, 1969, Representation of tribals in gram panchayats, *Journal of Social Research* 12(2) September, p 130-136, references, tables.

——, 1970, Political consciousness among the tribals and their representation in gram panchayats, *Vanyajati* 18(1) January, p 12-16, tables.

Sahu, Chaturbhaj and **Dayal, N.**, 1985, Cerumen types among tribal population of Bihar, *Indian Journal of Physical Anthropology and Human Genetics* 11(1-2) April-August, p 95-98, bibliography, tables.

Sahu, L.N., 1954, The Gadabas, *Vanyajati* 2(2) April, p 61-63.

Sahu, Laxminarayan, 1955-1956, The problem of the Aboriginals, *Adibasi*, 1, p 16-18.

——, 1956, Social service among Hill tribes, *Vanyajati* 4(4) October, p 140-142, illustrations.

——, 1957, We and the Aboriginals, *Vanyajati* 5(1) January, p 30-32.

——, 1957-1958, The Gadabas, *Adibasi* 2(1) p 27-30.

——, 1958, The problem of Aborigines, *Vanyajati* 6(4) October, p 170-173.

——, 1959, My experiences of work among the hill tribes of India, *Vanyajati* 7(2) April, p 49-52.

——1961, The Aboriginal from symbolic to individual life, *Vanyajati* 9(4) October, p 149-150.

——, 1961, The problem of the Indian and Aboriginal population, *Vanyajati* 10(2) April, p 70-73.

Sahu, R.S. and **Baral, J.K.**, 1987, Leadership and socio-political change of tribes of Orissa, Saoras, *Vision* 6(3-4) January-June, p 57-69, bibliography.

Saini, B.R., 1984, Scope of Articles 14(4) and 16(4) of the Constitution of India, *Kurukshetra Law Journal*, 10, p 53-61.

Saksena, R.N., 1964, The changing tribes of India, *Journal of Social Research* 7(1-2) March-September, p 15-28, references.

Saksena, N.S., 1958, The reservation issue : A possible basis for consensus, *Times of India*, May 3, p 3-5.

key-in-start here JOSHI

Saldonlia, Indra Munshi, 1986, Tribal women in the Warli revolt, 1945-1947 : Class and gender in the Left perspective, *Economic and Political Weekly* (Supplement) 21(17) April, 26, Ws p 41-52, footnotes.

Salunke, N.B., 1988, The Nomadic blacksmiths, *Social Welfare* 35(9) December, p 26-29.

Samanta, R.K. and **Adhikary, M.M.**, 1988, Marriage systems among tribals of North-East India : An overview, *Man in India* 68(4) December, p 401-412.

Samuel, C.J., 1985, Development of tribal economy : Legislative and executive measures, *Cochin University Law Review* 9(1-2) March-June, p 87-104, footnotes.

Sangal, P.S., 1990, Re-examination of criteria necessary, *National Herald*, September 9.

Sangameswara Rao, D., 1988, Reservations in admissions to educational institutions *vis-a-vis* equality of opportunity, *Progressive Educational Herald* 3(1) October, p 46-48.

Sanganna, Toyaka, 1963-64, The new dimension and approach of tribal welfare, *Adibasi* 5(2), p 3-4.

——, 1964, Problems of definition, *Adibasi*, November, p 15-18.

——, 1964, Tribal culture and its preservation and scientific development, *Adibasi*, January, p 3-4.

——, 1966, Tribal problems of Orissa, *Adibasi* 8(2) July, p 2-8.

Sanghvi, L.D., 1969, Perspectives for study of racial origins in India, *Anthropologist* (Special Volume), p 69-73.

Sangwan, K.S., 1986, Harijan legislators : Awareness and role performance, *Guru Nanak Journal of Sociology* 7(2) October, p 79-88, bibliography, tables.

Sankaranarayan, A.S. and **Lakshmanan, K.K.**, 1987, A tribal festival in Attappady, Kerala : An aspect of worship of nature as God, *Folklore* 28(10) October, p 235-236.

Sanwal, R.D., 1969, Seminar on the tribal situation in India, Simla, *Sociological Bulletin* 18(2) September, p 175-181.

Sanyal, B.S., 1987, Can they live outside in conflict with the mother society?, *Organiser* 39(11) August 9, 8-9.

Sanyal, Shubhendu, 1987, An appraisal of the major problems of Scheduled Tribes in India : With particular reference to Bihar, *Man in India* 67(4) December, p 404-423, bibliography, tables.

——, 1988, Primitive tribes of Bihar : Strategy for development, *Man in India* 68(4) December, p 356-368, bibliography.

Sao, Suman, et al, 1985, A model of tribal industrial growth : Case study of rope making, *Man and Life* 11(3-4) July-December, p 207-220, bibliography, tables.

Saraf, Pushp, 1990, Job reservation in Railways and accidents, *Indian Express*, September 19.

Saraf, Samarendra, 1969, Tribal unrest : An urgent research problem, *Bulletin of Cultural Research Institute* 8(1-2), December, p 32-37, references; *Vanyajati* 17(3-4), July-October, p 118-122.

Saran, Soubhagyalaxmi, 1986, Caste in modern setting, *Vision* 5(3-4) January-June, p 56-61.

Sardesai, Rajdeep, 1990, Mandal fails to agitate Maharashtra, *Times of India*, September 1.

Sarkar, Haribishnu, 1951, Disposal of the dead at the Indus Valley and its survival among the Aboriginal people of India, *Man in India* 31(1) January-March, p 23-32, references, tables.

Sarkar, Jayanta, 1985, Antithetical activities of the Bhaina in local social hierarchy, *Journal of Indian Anthropological Society* 20(1) March, p 32-42, bibliography, tables.

Sarkar, R.M., 1968, Women in tribal India through custom and traditions, *Folklore* 9(12) December, p 458-467, references.

——, 1984, Conflict, compromise and diversity unity oriented life philosophy of a wandering community, *Indian Museum Bulletin* 19, p 48-55.

Sarkar, S.S., 1952, Blood groups from the Andaman and Nicobar Islands, *Bulletin of Department of Anthropology* 1(1) January, p 25-30, references, tables.

——, 1957, Finger prints of Orissan Aborigines, *Man in India* 37(3) July-September, p 182-191, references, tables.

——, 1957-1958, Anthropology and tribal welfare, *Adibasi* 2(1), p 6-8.

——, 1958, Reply to the letter to the editor regarding his "The tribal population in West Bengal", by B.K. Roy Burman, *Man in India* 38(3) June-September, p 215-216.

——, 1958, The tribal population in West Bengal, *Man in India* 38(1) January-March, p 60-64, tables.

——, 1960, Micro-revolution : A plea for coordination between physical and cultural anthropology, *Journal of Social Research* 3(1) March, p 1-6, illustrations, references.

Sarkar, Sabita Ranjan, 1969, Some aspects of material culture of the tribals of West Bengal, *Bulletin of Cultural Research Institute* 8(3-4), p 85-86.

Sathe, Madhusudan Dattatraya, 1988, Katkari labour in charcoal making, *Economic and Political Weekly* 23(34) July 30, p 1565-1567.

Satish Kumar, 1985, Development in tribal areas : An overview, *Link* (Supplement) 27(26) February 3, p 13-18, tables.

Satpathy, Gopinath, 1964, Gadabas, *Adibasi*, January, p 151-156.

Satya Raju, R., 1986, Role of government in Scheduled Tribes development, *Kurukshetra* 34(4) January, p 21-24.

Satyanarayana, B.S., 1982, Educational problems of Scheduled Caste college students in Karnataka, *Journal of Higher Education* 7(3) Spring, p 253-260, bibliography, footnotes, tables.

Satyanarayana, T.V., 1986, Cheaper foodgrains for tribals, *Indian and Foreign Review* 23(16) June 16, p 8-9.

——, 1986, Subsidised foodgrains for tribals, *Yojana* 30(7) April 16, p 19-20.

Satyarthi, Devendra, 1944, In Aboriginal India, *Rural India* 7(6) July, p 247-252.

Saxena, Devendra, 1965, Demography and social anthropology, *Indian Journal of Social Research* 6(3) December, p 246-250, references.

Saxena, N.C., 1985, Caste and Zamindari abolition in U.P., *Mainstream* 23(42) June 4, p 15-19, tables.

Sayanna, V.V., 1950, The social class structure and its influence on rural economy with special reference to the prestige classes in rural society, *Rural India* 13(5) June, p 198-209.

Sebastian, M.K. and **Bhandari, M.M.**, 1984, Cultivation of wild plants for the uplift of tribals in the forest areas of Rajasthan, *Tribune* 16(3-4) September, p 30-35, bibliography.

——, 1987, Magico-religious beliefs about plants among the Bhils of Udaipur district, Rajasthan, *Folklore* 28(10) October, p 244-247.

Seerval, H.M., 1985, Reservation in education and public service, *Monthly Commentary on Indian Economic Conditions* 27(1) August, p 79-86.

Sen, Biswajit, 1965, The Monpas of Tawang, *Vanyajati* 13(1) January, p 23-26.

Sen, D.K., 1967, Racial studies in India : Recent trends, *Journal of Indian Anthropological Society* 2(1) March, p 1-18.

Sen, Gopi Nath, 1983, Life and culture of the Santals, *Modern Review* 147(7-8) July-August, p 214-222.

——, 1983, Some socio-religious aspects of the tribal people of West Bengal, *Modern Review* 147(3-4) March-April, p 81-86.

——, 1984, Patriotic lyrics of the Santals, *Modern Review* 148(3-4) March-April, p 100-111.

Sen, Jyoti, 1966, Problem in tribal transformation, *Man in India* 46(4) October-December, p 319-330.

Sen, Sachin, 1964, Impact of modern forces on castes and tribes, *Journal of Social Research* 7(1-2) March-September, p 113-118.

Sen, Suchibrata, 1984, The Santals of Jungle Mahals : An agrarian history, 1793-1861, *Indian Archaeology* 33(2) July-December, p 86-88.

——, 1985, The Santals of Jungle Mahals, *Times of India* February 24, p 1, col 1-4.

Sengupta, A.K., 1967, Hinduisation and tribalisation : Two case studies, *Folklore* 8(12) December, p 433-438, references.

Sen Gupta, Gouranga Gopal, 1959, The Kacharis of Assam, *Indian Folklore* 2(3) July-September, p 226-227.

Sen Gupta, N.K., 1988, A note on the survey and investigation on some physical conditions and nutritional patterns in relation to the tribal people in Singhbhum, *Man in India* 68(4) December, p 473-476.

Sen Gupta, Nirmal, 1988, Reappraising tribal movements : Legitimisation and spread, *Economic and Political Weekly* 23(19) May 7, p 943-945; 23(20) May 14, p 1003-1005; 23(21) May, 21 p 1054-1055.

Sen Gupta, P.N., 1953, Population studies and living conditions of the tribes in the Padam and Minyong areas of Abor hills (Assam), *Bulletin of Department of Anthropology* 2(1) January, p 91-112, tables.

——, 1956, Studies on the nutritive values of tribal alcoholic beverages, *Bulletin of Department of Anthropology* 5(1) January, p 67-80.

—— and **Biswas, S.K.**, 1956, Studies on the diet and nutritional status of the Malapantaram, Muthuvan and Ullatan tribes of Travancore, *Bulletin of Department of Anthropology* 5(2), p 9-19, tables.

Sen Gupta, S. and **Dutta, M.N.**, 1985, A note on ridge count of finger patterns of the Wanchos of Arunachal Pradesh, *Resarun* 11(2) Autumn-Winter, p 23-26, bibliography, tables.

——, 1985, Palmar main line index and transversality in Wanchos of Arunachal Pradesh, *Resarun* 11(2) Autumn-Winter, p 39-41, bibliography, tables.

Sen Gupta, S. C., 1966-67, Tribal education : Present position and future progress, *Indian Education* 6(1-2) December-January, p 37-62, tables.

Sen Gupta, Sabuj and **Pathak, S.**, 1988, A study of sexual maturation in the tribal (Koles) girls of Koteswar, Marwa region of Madhya Pradesh, *Man in India* 68(4) December, p 470-472, bibliography, tables.

Sen Gupta, Sarthak, 1982, Study of sexual maturation in Ahoms girls, *Indian Journal of Physical Anthropology and Human Genetics* 8(1) April, p 63-66, bibliography, tables.

——, 1984, Finger prints of the Bangnis of Arunachal Pradesh, *Resarun* 10(1) Spring-Summer, p 25-30, bibliography, tables.

Sengupta, Shekar, 1966, The role of James Long in sociology and folklore study in India, *Folklore* 7(8) December, p 462-471, references.

Seshadri, H.V., 1987, Ralegana Sindi : A name for social metamorphosis, *Organiser* 38(40) February 15, p 10.

Shah, A.M., 1982, Division and hierancley : An overview of caste in Gujarat, *Contribution to India Sociology*, New Series, 16(1) January-June, p 1-33.

——, 1990, Reservations : Double talk on castes, *Hindustan Times*, September 7.

Shah, Ghanshyam, 1985, Caste, class and reservation, *Economic and Political Weekly* 20(3) January 19, p 132-136, footnote.

——, 1985, Economic differentiation and tribal identity: A case study of Chaudhries, *Perspectives in Education* 1(2) April, p 129-131.

——, 1987, Middle class politics : Case of anti-reservation agitation in Gujarat, *Economic and Political Weekly*, Annual Number 22, (19-21) May, p AN155-AN72.

Shah, P.G., 1952, Cultural synthesis in India, *Journal of Anthropological Society of Bombay* (NS) 6(2) September, p 62-65.

——, 1954, The Second Tribal Welfare Conference, 11th, 12th and 13th November, 1953, *Journal of Anthropological Society of Bombay* (NS), 8(1) March, p 76-79.

——, 1956, The use of multi-purpose employment co-operative societies for the Scheduled Tribes of India, *Vanyajati* 4(1) January, p 29-31.

——, 1958, Caste and social education : Sublimation of caste impulse, *Indian Journal of Adult Education* 19(3) October, p 1-4.

Shah, U.M., 1984, Cooperatives and tribals, *Tribe* 16(3-4) September-December, p 7-19.

——, 1986, Cooperatives and tribals, *Khadi Gramodyog* 31(7) April, p 314-322.

——, 1986, Tribals and cooperattives, *Kurukshetra* 34(4) January, p 4-8.

Shah, Vimal, 1966, Tribal education in Gujarat, *Vanyajati* 14(3) July, p 109-112.

Shahabuddin, Syed, 1987, New approach to tribal India, *Janata* 42(16) October 4, p 7-8.

Shaik, Abdul Azeez Saheb and **Shaik, Gousia Begum**, 1990, Struggle against starvation : A study of the Yanadi food getting techniques, *Man in India* 70(2) June, p 169-184.

Shaileshwar Prasad, 1960, Where tribes and castes meet : Some preliminary observations, *Journal of Social Research* 3(2) September, p 132-144, references, tables.

Shakir, Moin, 1974, Scheduled Caste : Beyond the system, *Economic and Political Weekly* 9(16) April 20, p 629-631.

Shamsuddin, 1966, Gholeng school: Adivasis heaven, *Educational India* 33(4) October, p 123-126, illustration.

——, 1988, Glimpses of Bastar, *Social Welfare* 34(11) February, p 2-3.

——, 1989, The tribal world of Bastar, *Social Welfare* 35(10) January, p 17-20.

Shankara Narayan Rao, N.P., 1985, Identity of the Yeravas of Kodagu, *Quarterly Journal of the Mythic Society* 76(3-4) July-December, p 211-228.

Shanker, Prem, 1968, Education and Rorschach affective factors of the Harijans, *Indian Psychological Review* 4(2) July, p 95-100, references.

Shankraiah, A. and **Ghanshyam Das O.**, 1985, PDS in a tribals village, *Kurukshetra* 34(3) December, p 30-32.

Sharma, A.C., 1949, Illiteracy of Aborigines in India, *Educational Review* 55(4) April, p 67-69.

——, 1950, Report of the Aborigines education Section, *Educational India* 16(10) April, p 286-287.

——, 1951, Eradication of illiteracy among Aborigines, *Educational India* 17(7) January, p 216-218.

——, 1951, Eradication of illiteracy among tribal women and girls, *Education Quarterly* 21(1) April, p 44-46.

Sharma, Arvind, 1986, Manu on determinants of castes, *Man in India* 68(3) September, p 255-258.

Sharma, B.D., 1979, Tribal development : The concept and the frame, *Journal of Indian Education* 7(2) July, p 70.

——, 1985, Administration for tribal development, *Journal of Social and Economic Studies* (New Series) 2(4) October-December, p 361-379.

——, 1985, Tribal welfare legislation and enforcement, *Cochin University Law Review* 9(1-2) March-June, p 19-47.

Sharma, Bansi Ram, 1984, Dr. Siddheswar Varma's notes on tribal languages of Kinnaur in Himachal Pradesh, *Vishveshvaranand Indological Journal* 22(1-2) June-December, p 138-148.

Sharma, D.D. 1988, Language loyalty and maintenance: (A case of Chinals of Lahaul. *Panjab University Research Bulletin (Arts)* 19(2) October, p 111-119, footnote.

Sharma, Govind P., 1984, Trends in the study of Scheduled Castes, *Indian Anthropologist* 14(2) December, p 119-131, bibliography.

Sharma, H.R., et al, 1987, Pattern of income, consumption and employment, *Economic Affairs* 32(2) June, p 81-88, appendix, tables.

Sharma, J.C., 1970, Convergence and divergence of dermatoglyphic traits in human populations based on a study of the four tribal groups of Bastar, *Eastern Anthropologist* 23(1) January-April, p 17-35.

——, et al, 1985, A study of some of the genetic traits in the Kond tribe of Orissa, *Journal of Indian Anthropological Society* 20(1) March, p 50-58, bibliography, tables.

Sharma, K.K.N., 1989, A note on the distribution of matrimonial distance of the Khairwar tribal population of Surguja district, Madhya Pradesh, *Man in India* 69(3) September, p 267-271, bibliography, tables.

Sharma, K.L., 1950, Changing class stratification in rural Rajasthan, *Man in India* 50(3) July-September, p 257-268, references.

——, 1984, Caste and class in India : Some conceptual problems, *Sociological Bulletin* 33(1-2) March-September, p 1-28, bibliography.

——, 1990, A backward step, *Indian Express*, September 19.

Sharma, K.N., 1969, Developmental planning for M.P. tribes, *Bulletin of Tribal Research and Development Institute* (Bhopal) 7(1-2) June-December, p 19-25; *Journal of Social Research* 12(1) March, p 93-99.

Sharma, K.R., 1977, Specific problems of tribal students in non-tribal schools, *Education Quarterly* 28(4) January, p 30-32.

——, 1983, Scheduled Tribes and equality of educational opportunity, *Indian Education* 12(10) January, p 10-13.

——, 1983, A study of educational backwardness of tribal students, *Education Quarterly* 35(2) april, p 33-38.

——, 1984, A study of language development scholastic achievement and tribal students, *Research Bulletin* 14 (1-2) March-June, p 3-21, tables.

——, 1984, Tribal students and role of schools, *Primary Teacher* 9(4) October, p 11-13.

key-in-start here JOSHI

Sharma, Khem Raj, 1890, Cultural effects on education of the tribals, *Vanyajati* 37(1) January, p 14-16.

Sharma, O.P., 1989, Literacy trends : Selected tribes *vis-a-vis* mother-tongue, *Economic Times*, January 20, p 5. col. 3-6.

Sharma, R.S., 1984, Sudras in ancient India, *Journal of the Institute of Economic Research* 19(2) July, p 32-33.

——, 1985, Developing educational technology for deprived sections of the Indian society, *Bulletin of Non-formal Education* 3(3) December, p 1-17.

Sharma, Ranbir and **Kamal, Amir Chand**, 1986, Growth of political consciousness : A study of Pangwals tribes of Himachal Pradesh, *Punjab Journal of Politics* 10(1) January-June, p 67-81, tables.

Sharma, S.K., 1987, Hopes for Harijans, *Haryana Review* 21(10) October, p 17-18.

Sharma, S.L. and **Srivastava, R.N.**, 1967, Institutional resistance to induced Islamisation in a converted community : An empirical study in sociology of religion, *Sociological Bulletin* 16(1) March, p 69-80, references.

Sharma, Suryanarayan, 1985, Accent on tribal area development, *Commerce* 151(2873) August 17, p 325-326.

Sharma, T.R., 1962, A tribal community in an industrial context : A case study in Jamshedpur city, *Journal of Social Research* 5(1) March, p 114-123, references, tables.

Sharma, V.S., 1958, The Scheduled Tribes of Himachal Pradesh and their problems, *Vanyajati* 6(3) July, p 117-122.

Shashi, S.S., 1969, A sociological study of the Gaddi tribes in Himachal Pradesh, *Tribe*, June 4, p 32.

——, 1970, Folk dances and dances of the Gaddis, *Folklore*, March 11, p 91.

——, 1970, Nomads of the Himalayas, *Times Weekly* 1(6) September 20, p 1, col. 3; p 3, col. 1-5.

——, 1970, A sociological study of the Gaddi tribe in Himachal Pradesh, *Indian Behavioural Science Abstract* 1(3) July, p 259.

——, 1971, The Baigas of Madhya Pradesh, *Children's World*, October 10, p 18.

——, 1971, The Gaddis of the Himalayas, *Children's World*, August 29, p 11.

——, 1971, The Nagas of North-East India, *Children's World*, September 19, p 18-20.

——, 1971, Song and dance of the Gaddies, *Caravan*, p 14.

——, 1973, Gaddi women of Himachal, *Hindustan Times*, (Sunday Magazine), March 25, p 8, col. 1-4.

——, 1973, Gujar women, *Hindustan Times* (Sunday Magazine), May 27, p 4. col. 1-3.

——, 1973, Women of Kinnaur, *Hindustan Times* (Sunday Magazine), September 2, p 8, col. 1-6.

——, 1975, The Naga warfare, *Contemporary Social Sciences*, 8, April-June, p 9.

——, 1982, Origin of Gypsies, *Link*, February 28, p 17.

——, 1983, Romas still cherish old memories, *Statesman*, March 21, p 8.

——, 1986, Roma : The Indian Gypsies, *Indian and Foreign Review* 24(1) October 31, p 14-15.

——, 1986, Tribal women of India, *Kurukshetra* 34(4) January, p 215-16.

——, 1988, Gujjars : The Nomads of the Himalayas, *Kurukshetra* 36(4) January, p 13-14.

——, 1988, Kurbas : Shepherds of Karnataka, *Mainstream* 26(14) January 16, p 27-28.

——, 1988, Santhals in Naxalite movement, *Mainstream*, November 12, p 60.

Shastri, Lal Bahadur, 1965, Serve tribals in a dedicated spirit (Speech delivered at the 7th All Indian Tribal Conerence held at Gunter (A.P.), 1964). *Vanyajati* 13(1) January, p 1-2.

Shastri, Raghuvira Mitthulal, 1931, A comprehensive study into the origin and status of the Kayasthas, *Man in India* 11(2) April-June, p 116-159, footnotes.

Shaw, Biswanath, 1958-59, Vocational education in the Ashram School, *Adibasi* 3(3-4) August-January, p 31-34.

Shekharappa, Veera, 1984, Labour in an unorganised sector : Rural Scheduled Castes women, *Vision* 4(2) October-December p 4-14, bibliography, tables.

Sher, Sher Singh, 1959, The Panchayat system of the Sansis is of Punjab, *Sociological Bulletin* 8(1) March, p 97-102.

——, 1960, Ex-criminal tribes of Northern India need reclassification on more authentic and scientific grounds, *Journal of Social Research* 3(2) September, p 35-42, tables.

——, 1962, A demographic study of Sansis, *Vanyajati* 10(4) October, p 145-160, references, tables.

——, 1963, Demography of Sikligars, *Vanyajati* 11(2) April, p 79-81, tables.

Shesh, S., 1965, Phonology of Abuj Mariya, *Bulletin of Tribal Research and Development Institute* (Bhopal) 5(1-2) June-December, p 35-49, tables.

Sheth, D.L., 1979, Politics in caste conflict, *Seminar* 23(3) January.

——, 1985, The great reservation debate, *Indian Express* (Magazine) May 12, p 1+; *Sarvodaya* 33(1-2) July-August, p 9-19.

——, 1986, The problem of reservations : Economic backwardness or sócial injustice ? *Indian Journal of Adult Education* 47(5) May, p 9-15; 47(6) June, p 4-7, + ; 47(7) July, p 14-21.

——, 1987, Reservation policy revisited, *Economic and Political Weekly* 22(46) November 14, p 1957-1962, footnote.

Shourie, Arun, 1990, Three sets of facts on Mandal : Rank 413? So sorry, Rank 14246 ? But of course, *Indian Express*, September 2.

Showeb, M., 1984, Changing socio-cultural orientation of Harijans, *Interdiscipline* 16(1) April, p 93-117, bibliography, tables.

Shrikant, L.M., 1953, Tribal social welfare, *Indian Journal of Social Work* 14(3) December, p 292-295.

——, 1954, Forest co-operative societies in Bombay, *Vanyajati* 2(3) July, p 94-99.

——, 1954, Tribal welfare, *Indian Journal of Social Work* 14(4) March, p 360-366.

——, 1955, Progress of tribal welfare work in 1954, *Vanyajati* 3(3) July, p 124-127.

——, 1956, Some suggestions for constructive welfare workers in scheduled areas, *Vanyajati* 4(2) April, p 58-59, references.

——, 1956, Tribal welfare in Western India, *Vanyajati* 4(4) October, p 100-102.

——, 1957, Social service among the tribals, *Vanyajati* 5(2) April p 54-57.

——, 1959, Evaluation of tribal welfare work in Nellore district (Andhra Pradesh), *Vanyajati* 7(4) October, p 124-126, illustration.

——, 1960, Evaluation of work of non-official associations in Bombay, Madras and Kerala, *Vanyajati* 8(1) January, p 3-5.

_____, 1961, Scheduled Tribes of Andaman and Nicobar Islands, Their conditions and needs, *Vanyajati* 9(3) July, p 90-98.

_____, 1961, Tribal welfare under Panchayat Raj, *Vanyajati* 9(4) October, p 136-144.

_____, 1962, Tribal welfare with special reference to the tribal development blocks, *Indian Journal of Social Work* 22(4) March, p 379-385; *Vanyajati* 10(1) January, p 4-12.

_____, 1963, Welfare work in NEFA area, *Vanyajati* 11(4) October, [illegible]45-146 +.

_____, 1964, Tribal problems and publicity, *Vanyajati* 12(4) October, p 159-160.

_____, 1966, Education Commission and backward classes, *Vanyajati* 14(3) July, p 95-98.

_____, 1966, Measures proposed for the spread of education amongst the Scheduled Tribes, *Vanyajati* 14(3) July, p 133-138, tables.

_____, 1967, Cooperative movement among tribals : Andhra Pradesh Scheduled Tribes Cooperative Finance Development Corporation, *Vanyajati* 15(2) April, p 53-55 +, maps, tables.

_____, 1967, Co-operative movement among tribals III : The Madhya Pradesh State Tribal Co-operative Development Corporation Limited, Bhopal, *Vanyajati* 15(3) July, p 101-108, tables.

_____, 1967, Cooperative movement among the tribes, *Vanyajati* 15(1) January p 1-4; 15(3) October, p 101-08.

_____, 1968, Socio-economic aspects of prohibition, *Vanyajati* 16(2) April, p 37-40 ; 69-70.

_____, 1968, Tribal Development Blocks Community development blocks, *Vanyajati* 16(4) October, p 119-122 +.

_____, 1969, Tribal development blocks, *Vanyajati* 17(2) April, p 35-36+.

_____, 1970, Seminar on tribal forest labour cooperatives, *Vanyajati* 18(2) April, p 49-50.

Shrivastava, Aruna, 1986, Tribals habitats under the impact of urbanisation and industrialisation, *Man and Life* 12(1-2) January-June p 69-76, bibliography.

Shrivastava, L.R.N., 1966, The problem of integration of the tribal people, *Indian Journal of Social Work* 27(1) April, p 51-57.

_____, 1968, Plans and programmes of social education for the tribal people, *Bulletin of Cultural Research Institute* 7(1-2), p 39-50.

Shrivastava, O.M., 1978, Continuing education and tribal development : The role of colleges near tribal areas, *Indian Journal of Adult Education* 39(4) April, p 15-26.

Shukla, Rajiv, 1990, Mandal Commission: Where does the Jan..ta Dal stand?, *Sunday*, September 9-15.

Shukla, Ravi Shankar, 1955, Tribal welfare work in Bastar district (M.P.), *Vanyajati* 3(2) April, p 78-80.

Shyam Chaudhuri, N.K., 1952, The enumeration and treatment of tribes in the Indian Census : A study in retrospect, *Man in India* 32(3) July-September, p 160-166, tables.

Shyam Lal, 1970, Educational development among Bhangis in Jodhpur, *Tribe* 7(1) January, p 26-31, tables.

_____, 1973, Sanskritisation and social change among Bhangis in Jodhpur city, *Indian Journal of Social Work* 34(1).

_____, 1984, Planting a mission among the Bhils of South Rajasthan, *Man and Life* 10(1-2), January-June, p 77-96, bibliography, tables.

——, 1986, Socio-religious movements among the tribals of Banswara district, Rajasthan, *Man and Life* 12(3-4) July-December, p 159-172, bibliography.

Shyam Manohar, 1964, Education in tribal areas with employment bias, *Indian Education* 3(10) September, p 18-24.

——, 1968, A new deal for tribal development block, *Indian Education* 7(9) August, p 39-45.

Shyama Nand Singh, 1986, Reservation controversy in Andhra Pradesh, *Mainstream* 27(44) July 29, p 15-20 bibliography, tables.

——, 1988, Roots of caste war in Bihar, *Mainstream* 26(14) January 16, p 28-29.

——, 1989, Politics of Job reservation, *Mainstream* 27 (44) July 29, p 15-20, bibliography, tables.

Sidhu, L.S., et al, 1985, Sexual dimorphism, physique and body composition of adult Bhotia : A high attitude population, *Indian Anthropologist* 15(2) December, p 115-126, bibliography.

Sidhu, S. and **Sidhu, L.S.**, 1987, The impact of age at menarche and age at marriage on fertility among Scheduled Caste women of Punjab, *Guru Nanak Journal of Sociology* 8(2) October, p 41-46, bibliography, tables.

Sil, Ajit Kumar, 1990, Adaptation of the migrant Oraon in their present habitat in Sundarbans, *Geographical Review of India* 52(1) March, p 89-90.

Sills, David L., 1961, Social research and anthropology in India, *Journal of Anthropological Society, Bombay* (NS) 11(2), p 36-47, footnotes.

Singh, Ashok K., 1989, Socio-cultural characteristics of Dushads, *Vanyajati* 37(4) October, p 56-61.

Singh, B.K., 1989, A study of nutritional status of tribal farmers in Ranchi district of Chotanagpur in Bihar, *Economic Affairs* 34(1) January-March, p 58-63, tables.

Singh, C.S.K., 1985, Bhils participation in politics in Rajasthan in the 1920s, *Social Scientist* 13(4) April, p 31-43, footnotes.

Singh, K.M.P., 1984, Tips on training needs and middle management for tribal areas, *Survey* 24(1-2), p 19-25, bibliography.

Singh, K.S., 1982, A note on the types of earlobe among the Tangkhul Nagas of Manipur, *Indian Journal of Physical Anthropology and Human Genetics* 8(1) April, p 73-76, bibliography, tables.

——, 1990 Environment, technology and management in tribal areas, *Man in India* 70(2) June, p 123-130.

Singh, R.G., 1986, Atrocities on tribals, *Khadi Gramodyog* 32(7) April, p 358-361, tables.

Singh R.R., 1968, A new approach to tribal welfare, *Vanyajati* 16(3) July, p 100-109.

Singh, R.Y., 1972, Bhils of Malwa Region: Their habitat, economy and society, *National Geographical Journal of India* 15(3-4) p 223-239.

Singh, V.P., 1990, Speech of the Prime-Minister (at) National Conference on Problems of Scheduled Tribes, Vigyan Bhawan, New Delhi, 31st March, *Vanyajati* 38(2) April, p 3-6

Singh, Y.P., 1986, Housing programme for Scheduled Castes in U.P., *Kurukshetra* 34(8) May, p 4-7.

Sinha A.C., 1967, Leadership in a tribal society, *Man in India* 47(3) July-September, p 222-227, references.

Sinha, A.K., 1986, Chotanagpur tribals of Baratang Island : A brief note, *Journal of Social Research*, 29, September, p 73-79.

Sinha, Arun, 1986, Caste and faction in Bihar politics, *Times of India*, July 9, p 7-8.

Sinha, B,C., 1985, Origin and evolution of caste system, *Vedic Path* 47(4) March, p 31-34, bibliography.

Sinha, H.K., 1960, Tribal education in Bihar : A preliminary statistical analysis, *Journal of Social Research* 3(1) March, p 85-92, references, tables.

Sinha, H.S.P. and **Ranjan, R.**, 1981, An analysis of tribal loanees in repayment of loans, *Indian Journal of Extension Education* 17(3-4) September-December, p 54-65, references, tables.

Sinha, R.K., 1983, Self-image and emerging identify of the Bhilala, *Vanyajati* 31(3) July, p 9-16.

——, 1984, Alienation among Schedule Castes in an urban setting, *Indian Journal of Social Research* 25(2) August, p 151-161.

——, 1984, Birth rites and rituals among the Bhilala, *Vanyajati* 32(3) July, p 5-8.

Sinha, Rakesh Ranjan, 1967, Traditional political institutions and tribal development, *Vanyajati* 15(3) July, p 135-138.

Sinha, S.C. et al, 1969, The concept of Diku among the tribes of Chotanagpur, *Man in India* 49(2) April-June, p 121-138, references.

Sinha, S.P., 1989, Nehru's testament for tribal development X-rayed, *Vanyajati* 37(4) October, p 39-49.

Sinha, Surajit, 1957, Tribal cultures of peninsular India as a dimension of little tradition in the study of Indian civilisation : A preliminary statement, *Man in India* 37(2) April-June, p 93-118, references.

——, 1959, Bhumij-Kshatriya social movement in South Manbhum, *Bulletin of Department of Anthropology* 8(2) July, p 9-32, references.

——, 1965, Tribe-caste and tribe peasant continuum in Central India, *Man in India* 45(1) January-March, p 57-83, references, tables.

——, 1968, Tribal solidarity and messianic movements, *Contributions to Indian Sociology* (NS) December 2, p 112-118, references.

——and **Bhattacharya, Ranjit**, 1969, Bhadralok and Chhotalok in a rural area of West Bengal, *Sociological Bulletin* 18(1) March, p 50-66, references.

Sinha, Surendra Prasad, 1961, Kherwar movement in Hazaribagh district (1870-1880), *Vanyajati* 9(3) July, p 98-104.

——, 1961, The nature of religion of Birsa (1895-1900), *Journal of Social Research* 4(1-2) March-September, p 316-322, references.

Sinha V., et al, 1976, Parental deprivation in relation to intelligence of denotified tribes, *Asian Journal of Psychology and Education* 1(2) July, p 38-39.

Sirajuddin, S.M., 1984, Reproduction and consanguinity among Chenchus of Andhra Pradesh, *Man in India* 64(2) June, p 181-192, bibliography.

Sircar, D.C., 1955, The Dravidian problem, *Man in India* 35(1) January-March, p 31-38.

Sirsalkar, P.R., 1984, Evaluation of Ashram Schools managed by the voluntary agencies in Maharashtra State, *Tribal Research Bulletin* 7(1) September, p 7-8.

——, 1985, Primitive tribes : Challenge for development, *Tribal Research Bulletin* 7(2) March, p 7-8.

Sivadasan Pillai, K., 1988, Equality of educational opportunity and the Scheduled Castes, *Progressive Education Herald* 3(1) October, p 40-42.

Sivakumar, S.S. and **Sivakumar, Chitra**, 1979, Class and jati at Asthapuram and Kanthapuram : Some comment towards a structure of interest, *Economic and Political Weekly*, 14, Annual Number, February, p 265-286.

Sivananda, P., 1979, Caste, class and economic opportunity in Kerala: An empirical analysis, *Economic and Political Weekly* 14, Annual Number, February, p 475-480.

Sivaswamy, K.G., 1984, Serf labour among the Aboriginals, *Indian Journal of Social Work* 8(4) March, p 310-319.

Social Service Quarterly (Periodical), 1920, Temple entry satyagraha, *Social Service Quarterly* 15(2) October, p 57-58, editorial.

——, 1923, Depressed Classes Mission Society, *Social Service Quarterly* 9(1) July, p 47-48, editorial.

——, 1925, Bhils in South Gujarat, *Social Service Quarterly* 11(1) July, p 28-29, editorial.

——, 1926, Untouchables in Nadiad, *Social Service Quarterly* 11(4) April, p 154-155.

——, 1927, Depressed classes Institute, *Social Service Quarterly* 1293) January, p 144-145.

——, 1928-31, Bhil Seva Mandal, *Social Service Quarterly* 13(4) April, 1928, p 176-177; 15(1) July, 1929, p 31-32; 17(2) October, 1931, p 82, editorial

——, 1930, Socio-economic reconstruction among hill tribes in the South, *Social Service Quarterly* 16(4) April, p 153-154, editorial.

——, 1934, Mr. Bakhals Depressed Classes (Protection of rights) Bill, *Social Service Quarterly* 20(2) October, p 75-77, editorial.

——, 1934, Disabilities of depressed classes, *Social Service Quarterly* 20(1) July, p 25-26, editorial.

——, 1934, Harijan uplift, *Social Service Quarterly* 19(4) April, p 159-160, editorial.

——, 1935, An appeal to all friends of Harijans, *Social Service Quarterly* 20(3) January, p 114-115, editorial.

——, 1936, Harijan Sevak Sangh, Bombay, *Social Service Quarterly* 22(1) July, p 24, editorial.

——, 1937, Temple Entry Proclamation, *Social Service Quarterly* 22(3) January, p 116-119.

——, 1938, Harijans in Index, *Social Service Quarterly* 19(4) April, p 160-161, editorial.

——, 1938, Harijans in Savantvati, *Social Service Quarterly* 24(3) January, p 129-130, editorial.

——, 1938, Harijan Temple Worship Act, *Social Service Quarterly* 24(1) July, p 28-30, July-December, p 27-38, editorial.

——, 1940, Indian Aborigines Friends Society, *Social Service Quarterly* 26(2) October, p 79-81.

——, 1952, The abolition of caste distinctions, *Social Service Quarterly* 37(1) July, p 10-12, editorial.

Solanki, M.S., 1985, Only half of reserved jobs are filled, *Link* 27(36) April, p 7-8.

Som, Sujit, 1983, Incidence of mild digital hair among the Santal of Orissa, *Vanyajati* 31(3) July, p 23-27.

Som, T.K., 1988, Transformation of Riang economy in the context of rubber plantation industry : A micro study in Tripura, *Man in India* 68(2-3) June-September, p 145-166, bibliography, tables.

Somasekhar, A., 1987, Tribal development in Andhra Pradesh : Certain issues, *Man and Life* 13(1-2) January-June, p 67-76, bibliography.

Somasundaram, A.M., 1947, Segregation or assimilation?, *Man in India* 27(1) March, p 66-73.

——, 1949, A note on the Gadabas of Koraput district, *Man in India* 29(1) January-March, p 36-45.

——, 1950, Glimpses into primitive culture of India, *Man in India* 30(4) October-December, p 28-45.

Sonalkar, Wandana and **Shakir, Moin**, 1987, Caste, politics and development in Maharashtra, *Mainstream* 25(30) April 11, p 25-31, bibliography.

Sood, Renu, 1980-1981, Role of achievement, anxiety alleviation and value discrepancy in academic achievement of Scheduled Caste students, *Journal of Higher Education* 6(1-3), p 117-22 references, tables.

Soren, Bhabatosh, 1969, A few words concerning literary drive in the tribal communities, *Bulletin of Cultural Research Institute* 8(1-2), p 5-7.

Soren, Sonaram, 1955-1956, Social and cultural problems of the Adibasis in Orissa, *Adibasi*, 1, p 1-4.

Sowaid, M., et al, 1986, A study of parent child interaction and achievement motivation among tribal high school students, *Journal of Institute of Educational Research* 10(3) September, p 24-27, references.

Srinivas, M.N., 1952, Social anthropology and sociology, *Sociological Bulletin* 1(1) March, p 28-37.

——, 1979, Future of Indian caste, *Economic and Political Weekly* 14, Annual Number, February, p 237-242.

——, 1984, Some reflections on the nature of case hierarchy, *Contributions to Indian Sociology* (New Series) 18(2) July-September, p 161-167.

——, 1985, The Poleyas in the Kodava society, *Journal of Historical Studies* 19, p 75-79, bibliography.

Sripal, K.B. and **Knight, A. John**, 1986, Socio-economic profile of tribals of Tamil Nadu, *Kurukshetra* 34(4) January, p 35-37.

Srisalkar, P.R., 1985, Primitive tribes: Challenge for development, *Tribal Research Bulletin* 7(2) March, p 7-8.

Srivastava, B.N., 1966, Education Commission and tribal education, *N I E Journal* 1(2) November, p 78-82.

Srivastava, Harish C., 1990, A socio-economic and demographic profile of the Kamar tribe of Madhya Pradesh, *Man in India* 70(2) June, p 101-122.

Srivastava, Jai Prakash, 1954, Aggressiveness in Scheduled Caste children, *Education* 33(4) April, p 16-19 ; 33(5) May, p 10-13.

Srivastava, L.R.N., 1966, Hair style, head dress and their social significance among some of the tribes of North East Frontier of India, *Bulletin of Cultural Research Institute* 5(1-2), p 110-125, footnotes, references.

Srivastava, L.R.N., 1966, The problem of integration of the tribal people, *Indian Journal of Social Work* 27(1) April, p51-57.

——, 1969, The problem of modernisation of the tribes of North East India, *Bulletin of Cultural Research Institute* 8(1-2), p 21-25.

Srivastava, Manju and **Srivastava, Saraswati**, 1983-84, The Mandal Commission report : A critique, *Journal of State Politics and Administration* 6(2) July-December ; 7(1) January-June, p 75-86, bibliography, footnotes.

Srivastava, Om Prakash, 1960, Tharus in Balrampur Tahsil, *Vanyajati* 8(1) January, p 28-30.

Srivastava, P.K., 1963, The Gonds of Sagar district (M.P.) : Culture contact and consequences, *Vanyajati* 11(1) January, p 12-14.

Srivastava, R.M. and **Kharde, R.L.**, 1983, Traditional beliefs of tribal Mundas associated with cattle husbandry, *Indian Journal of Extension Education* 19(3-4) September-December, p 77-82, references, tables.

——, 1984, Tribal economy : An analytical view, *Tribal Research Bulletin* 7(1) September, p 12-15.

Srivastava, R.N., 1988, Moving wheels of machine : The impact of mining industrialisation at the Bastar tribal region of Central India, *Man and Life* 14(3-4) July-December, p 119-137.

Srivastava, R.P., 1953, Rang-Bang in the changing Bhotia life, *Eastern Anthropologist* 6(3-4) March-August, p 190-203, footnotes.

Srivastava, Rajni, 1982, Sociological problems in tribal education : A case study, *Indian Educational Review* 17(3) July, p 110-113.

——, 1983, Some psychological problems of tribals of Mirzapur : A case study, *Indian Educational Review* 18(2) April, p 106-110, tables.

Srivastava, Ratish, 1984, Tribals of Madhya Pradesh and Forest Bill of 1980, *Man in India* 64(3) September, p 320-327.

Srivastava, S.K., 1960, Current trends in Social Anthropological research in India, *Journal of Social Sciences* 2(2) July, p 107-115, references.

Srivastava, S.L., 1967, The Jat : A caste stereotype, *Folklore* 8(10) October, p 370-375.

Srivastava, Shab Lal, 1950, Stratification and etiquette in village communities, *Man in India* 50(3) July-September, p 269-279.

Srivastava, Shakuntala, 1961, A note on the question of dress for the tribals (with an apology to Dr. Verrier Elwin), *Sociological Bulletin* 10(2) September, p 42-45.

Subba, Tanka Bahadur, 1984, Caste and agrarian structure : A study in hill Darjeeling and Sikkim, *Man in India* 64(1) March, p 59-68, bibliography.

——, 1985, Caste relations in Nepal and India, *Social Change* 15(4) December, p 23-26, bibliography.

——, 1988, Tribal handicrafts of Sikkim : A profile, *Man in India* 68(4) December, p 431-441, bibliography.

Subhashini, A.V., 1987, Tharavads : Kerala's Nair homes, *Indian Management* 7(8) July, p 52-63.

Subramanian, K.S., 1987, Behind rural violence, *Mainstream* 25(45) July 25, p 19-25.

——, 1987, Violence against Schedule Castes in India: Overview, problems prospects, *Man and Development* 9(1) March, p 26-42.

Subrahmanyam S., 1986, Problems of school dropouts: A study with a special references to Scheduled Castes and Scheduled Tribes in Andhra Pradesh, *Education Quarterly* 38(3) Autumn, p 28-32.

Sudama, G.R. and **Thiagarajan, A.P.**, 1981, Enrolment of the Scheduled Castes in general colleges : A case study of Tamil Nadu, *Experiments in Education* 9(4) June, 63-69, tables.

——, 1982, Academic difficulties of college youth : A case study of the Scheduled Castes, *Indian Education* 12(5-6) August-September, p 23-29.

Sudhakar Babu, M., et al, 1984, Variation in taste perception to P T C in two tribal populations of Andhra Pradesh, *Indian Anthropologist* 14(1) June, p 63-68, bibliography.

Suguna, A.V., et al, 1988, The role of descent groups among the Mannedoras, *Man in India* 68(4) December, p 454-458, tables.

Sujatha, K., 1987, Inequality in educational development of tribes : A case study of Andhra Pradesh, *Journal of Educational Planning and Administration* 1(2) April, p 108-125, bibliography, footnotes, tables.

Sukumaran, Tatapuram, 1984, The Ezhavas in Kerala, *Malayalam Literature Survey* 8(3-4) July-December, p 11-117, bibliography, footnote.

Sundaram, S., 1984, Harijans perception of themselves, *Interdiscipline* 16(1) April, p 65-72, bibliography.

Sundaresh, Aruna, 1986, Constitution, law and reservations, *New Frontiers in Education* 16(2) April-June, p 33-40.

Sundaresan, V. and **Subha Reddy, B.V.**, 1982, Equality for tribals : The role of education, *Experiments in Education* 9(12) February, p 213-215.

Sunil, K.P., 1989, Children of a lesser God, *Illustrated Weekly of India* 110(26) June 25, p 36-39.

——, 1989, Crucible of conflict, *Illustrated Weekly of India* 110(41) October 8, p 22-25.

Surana, M.B., 1985, Socio-economic survey of tribals in the proposed M.A.D.A. pocket in Buldbana district, *Tribal Research Bulletin* 7(2) March, p 9-13.

——, 1986, Supply of milch animals to Adivasis in Dbule district, *Tribal Research Bulletin* 9(1) September, p 11-15.

——, 1987, Research designs for evaluation of Tribal development programme, *Tribal Research Bulletin* 9(2) March, p 5-8, bibliography.

Suresh Singh, 1966, Development schemes as a factor of change in tribal areas, *Journal of Social Research* 9(2) September, p 52-64.

Suri, Dona, 1985, Reservations : Are they still valid ? *Tribune*, April 14, p 1, col. 1-8.

Suryavanshi, Bhagwan Singh, 1959, Life in the dormitories of the tribals: The Oraons, *Indian Folklore* 2(1) January-May, p 45-47.

——, 1959, Romances in the tribals : A living page from the life of the tribals, *Indian Folklore* 2(3) July-September, p 223-225.

Swain, Laxmidhar, 1985, Santal tribes : Infant feeding practices, *Social Welfare* 32(3) June, p 22-23.

Swaminathan, M.S., 1982, Educational development of the Scheduled Castes, *Journal of Indian Education* 8(1) May, p 40-45, tables.

Swaminathan, Srilata, 1987, Endless night in Dabi Pada, *Indian Express* (Magazine) January 25, p 4, col. 1-8.

Swaminathan, T., 1985, The magical script, *Link* (Supplement) 27(26) February 3, p 55-63.

Synghal, S., 1984, Integrated tribal development projects, *Kurukshetra* 32(12) September, p 6-8 +.

Talesara, Rajendra, 1984, Agricultural development among tribals : Issues and aspects, *Prashanika* 13(1) January-March, p 27-33.

Tandon, J.S., 1959, The Bhatra of Bastar, *Bulletin of Department of Anthropology* 8(2) July, p 33-54.

Tarlok Singh, 1966, Education in tribal areas, *Folklore* 7(10) October, p 397-401.

Tavleen Singh, 1988, Murder and mayhem in Jehanabad, *Indian Express*, September 4, p 1, col. 1-8.

Thakkar, A.V., 1918, Disabilities of municipal sweepers in Bombay, *Social Service Quarterly* 3(3) January, p 120-124.

——, 1935, The Harijan problem, *Social Service Quarterly* 21(1) July, p 6-8.

——, 1941, Census of Assam tribals, *Man in India* 21(4) October-December, p 243-247.

——, 1942, Among Santals and Pahadias, *Rural India* 5(1) January, p 6-8.

——, 1945, Education among tribal people, *Social Service Quarterly* 32(1) July, p 1-4.

——, 1949, Some pressing problems of primitive tribes, *Eastern Anthropologist* 3(1) September p 1-2.

——, et al, 1939, Gul Maharaj : The Bhil Saint, *Rural India* 1(5) March, p 258-259.

Thakur, D.S., et al, 1989, Socio-economic conditions of scavengers in Himachal Pradesh, *Social Change* 19(3) September, p 42-55.

Thakur, Devendra, 1984, Township and its impact on tribal urbanisation, *Monthly Commentary on Indian Economic Conditions* 26(3) October, p 7-10.

——, 1985, Bihar tribals share benefits of green revolution, *Link* 28(19) December 15, p 26-27; *Monthly Commentary on Indian Economic Conditions* 27(4) November, p 7-9.

Thakur, Laxmi and **Nathawat, S.S.**, 1987, Cognitive performance of Scheduled Caste children, *Indian Educational Review* 93(7) July, p 113-116, bibliography, tables.

Tharyan, P., 1990, Attack caste, not Mandal, *Hindustan Times*, September 8, p 11, col. 2-5.

Thiagarajan, A.P., 1981, A study of the Scheduled Caste students in some Secondary schools of Tamil Nadu, *Indian Education* 11(5) August, p 22-26, tables.

——, 1987, Educational progress of Scheduled Castes, *Experiments in Education* 15(5) May, p 94-96.

Thirupati Rao, U., 1987, Job reservation policy in India, *Indian Educational Review* 93(2) February, p 29-31.

Thomas, C., 1964, Tribal welfare in Maharashtra State, *Social Action*, 14(4) April, p 179-184.

Thusu, Kidar Nath, 1959, The Dhurwa of Marenga, Bastar district, *Bulletin of Department of Anthropology* 8(2) July, p 67-73, references.

——, 1962, The Riang agricultural practices, *Bulletin of Anthropologi[illegible] Survey of India* 11(3-4), p 157-174, appendix, references.

——, 1963, The Dhurwa tribe of Bastar, *Vanyajati* 11(1) January, p 16-21.

——, 1965, The Panchayat system of the Dhurwas of Bastar (M.P.), *Man in India* 45(2) April-June, p 134-151, footnotes.

Times of India (Newspaper), 1985, Disgrace abounding, *Times of India*, August 5, p 8, col 1-2, editorial.

——, 1987, A new approach, *Times of India*, September 14, p 6, col 1-2, editorial.

——, 1988, An effective reposite, *Times of India*, February 9, p 6, col 1-2, editorial.

——, 1989, Tribals short charged: *Times of India*, May 11, p 4, col 1-2, editorial.

Tribune (Newspaper), 1988, The neglect of the tribal genus, *Tribune*, July 24, p 1, col 1-8, editorial.

Tripathi, C.B., 1987, Development of Scheduled Caste women, *Journal of Social Economic Studies* 4(4) October-December.

——, 1988, Approaches to tribal development and experience : General policies, administrative approach and personnel policies and their implementation : An all India review, *Man in India* 68(4) December, p 335-355.

Tripathi, G.P., 1985, Scheduled Tribes and tribal legislation in Madhya Pradesh, *Cochin University Law Review* 9(1-2) March-June, p 105-116.

Tripathi, Premananda, 1985, Administration for tribal development : An analytical review. *Indian Journal of Public Administration* 31(3) July-September, p 870-878.

Tripathi, R.S., 1989, Agricultural economy of the Kols in Manikpur Block, Uttar Pradesh, *Vanyajati* 37(3) July, p 3-8.

——— and **Vishwakarma, J.P.**, 1990, Castes in rural areas of Bundelkhand (U.P.) : A study of major characteristics and process of change, *Geographical Review of India* 52(1) March, p 84-88.

Tripathy, Sangam, 1989, A silent revolution of forest dwellers and tribals, *Janata* 44(7) April, p 15-16.

Trivedi, D.N., 1990, Multiplier versus unitary development : Nation building and citizenship : An Indian case, *Man in India* 70(1) March, p 16-25.

Trivedi, H.V., 1986, The T S P area in Rajasthan and its socio-psychological development barriers spectrum, *Rajasthan Economic Journal*, 10(1) January, p 53-63, bibliography, tables.

Trivedi, Harshad R., 1989, Nehru and tribals, *Indian Journal of Public Administration* 35(2) April-June, p 286-291.

Trivedy, Shikha, 1989, A matter of faith, *Illustrated Weekly of India* 110(25) June 18, p 42-45.

Tucker, Richard, 1980-81, The early setting of the non-Brahmin movement in Maharashtra, *Indian History Review* 7(1-2) July-January, p 134-159, footnote.

Uday Bhaskar Reddi, I. and **Chattopadhyay, R.N.**, 1986, Industrialising tribal areas, boon or bann, *Yojana* 30(5) March 16, p 18-20.

Uma Singh, et al, 1969, A genetic investigation of the Gujars: Blood groups and A.B.H. secretion, *Anthropologist* 16(1-2) March-September, p 57-61, references, tables.

Umeshrao, 1939, The weavers of India, *Rural India* 1(7) May, p 419.

Upadhyaya, Ram Narain, 1959, The Nimadi folksongs, *Indian Folklore* 2(4) October-December, p 298-299.

Uplankar, A.T., 1989, Protective discrimination and the equality of opportunity, *Social Change* 19(3) September, p 3-15.

Upreti, H.C., 1967, The position of women among Khasas of Kumaon, *Journal of Social Research* 10(1) March, p 37-45, references.

Ursekar, H.S., 1970, Constitutional concern for Harijans and Adivasis, *Social Service Quarterly* 55(4) April, p 97-105.

Vaid, Minnie 1985, Gujarat is going the way of Assam, *Illustrated Weekly of India* 106(8) June 30, p 36-37.

Vaish, Prerana, 1984, Role of mineral in the tribal development of TSP region of Rajasthan, *Tribe* 16(3-4) September-December, p 20-29.

Vaniker, P.G., 1954, Missionary approach to the tribal welfare, *Indian Journal of Social Work* 14(4) March, p 376-382.

Vankatasha Murthy, G.B., 1987, The soligas of B.R. hills : A demographic study, *Journal of Family Welfare* 34(1) September, p 54-58, bibliography, tables.

Vanyajati (Periodical), 1953, Backward Classes Commission, *Vanyajati* 1(2) April, p 25-26, editorial.

———, 1964, In memoriam : Nehru and the tribes, *Vanyajati* 12(3) July, p 109-110, editorial.

———, 1984, Scheduled Tribes and 1981 Census figures, *Vanyajati* 32(3) April, p 1-4, editorial.

Varma, R.P., 1984, Educating the disadvantaged : A few suggestions, *National Journal of Education* 6(2) May, p 1-6, references.

Varma, S.C., 1959, Problem of drinking in the primitive tribes, *Eastern Anthropologist* 12(4) June-August, p 252-256.

_____, 1961, Tribal problems, *Bulletin of Tribal Research Institute* (Chhindwara) 1(2) December, p 16-18.

_____, 1984, The Bhil kills, *Man in India* 64(4) December, p 440-444.

Vazeruddin, Mohammad, 1985, Scientific analysis of caste system, *Tribune*, May 12, p 1-8.

Velayudhan, R., 1940, A study of social conditions among the Pulayas (Harijans) of Kolady in Travancore State, *Indian Journal of Social Work* 1(3) December, p 393-403, tables.

Venkataih, N., 1980, Non-formal education for adult tribes, *Experiments in Education* 8(3) May, p 54-56.

Venkataraman, S.R., 1950, Education of the Aborigines, *Indian Educational Review* 56(7) July, p 129-132, ; 56(8) August, p 150-152.

_____, 1951, The Scheduled Tribes, *Social Service Quarterly* 36(4) April, p 114-117, tables.

_____, 1954, The Todas, *Vanyajati* 2(3) July, p 82-85.

_____, 1959, Some problems of tribal welfare work, *Social Service Quarterly* 44(3) January, p 77-82.

_____, 1959, The Tribal Welfare Conference at Bordi, *Vanyajati* 7(1) January, p 29-35.

_____, 1962, Education of Aborigines, *Social Service Quarterly* 43(4) April, p 119-126.

_____, 1963, The life of the Aboriginal child, *Social Service Quarterly* 48(4) April, p 105-109.

_____, 1964, Education as a basic factor in tribal welfare, *Social Service Quarterly* 49(3) January, p 88-92.

_____, 1967, Social welfare and exercise of human rights regarding tribes, *Social Service Quarterly* 53(2) October, p 54-58.

_____, 1969, Tribal development block, Yercaud : An impression, *Social Service Quarterly* 54(3) January, p 77-79.

_____, 1984, Tribes of Palani and Kodal hills, *Vanyajati* 32(3) July, p 13-15.

_____, 1984, Villies of Chingleput district, *Vanyajati* 32(2) April, p 5-11.

Venkataramana, M., et al, 1989, Housing pattern in Scheduled Castes of Andhra Pradesh : A micro-empirical study, *Vanyajati* 37(4) October, p 62-75.

Venkatashan, D., 1988, Innovations and their impact on the Onge of Little Andaman, *Man in India* 68(4) December, p 413-423, bibliography.

Verghese, Alexander V., 1984, Education, earning and occupation of weaker castes, *Journal of Higher Education* 9(3) Spring, p 373-381, references.

Verghese, B.G., 1990, Quake remedies, *Indian Express*, September 12.

Verma, B.P. and **Sharma, Keshav**, 1989, A comparative study of locus of control and self concept of higher, Backward and Scheduled Caste students, *Progress of Education* 63(9) April, p 205-208.

Verma, B.R., 1985, Rationale of reservations, *National Herald* (Sunday Herald), August 11, p 1 +.

Verma, O.P., 1979, Determinants of status in ancient India, *Journal of Bihar Puravid Parishad*, 3, p 87-90.

Verma, Ram Swaroop, 1985, Socio-psychological make-up of Tharu and Boksa adolescents, *Bhartiya Shiksha Shodh Patrika* 4(2) July-December, p 27-33.

Verma, Sneh Veena, 1961, Working of the multi-purpose tribal blocks in M.P., *Vanyajati* 9(2) April, p 48-55.

Vidyarthi, Lalit P., 1955, Education in tribal Bihar, *Man in India* 35(1) January-March, p 39-45.

——, 1957, Anthropology, authority and tribal welfare, *Eastern Anthropologist* 11(1) September-November, p 14-24, references.

——, 1959, Anthropology and administration in India, *Journal of Social Research* 2(1-2) March-September, p 59-71, references.

——, 1963, Approach to tribal integration in India, *Vanyajati* 11(2) April, p 47-50.

——, 1964, The changing face of tribal Bihar : Some preliminary observation on the concept of detribalisation, *Journal of Social Research* 7(1-2) March-September, p 53-61, references

——, 1966, Nehru's approach to tribal culture, *Vanyajati* 14(4) October, p 170-175, references.

——, 1966, Social anthropological researches in India : Some preliminary observations, *Journal of Social Research* 9(1).

——, 1968, Cultural change in the tribes of modern India, *Journal of Social Research* 11(1) March, p 1-36, references, tables.

——, 1972, Needed urgent research for Fifth Five Year Plan for tribal Bihar, *Research Journal of Ranchi University* December 8.

——, 1976, Tribal development in Independent India and its future, *Man in India* 56(1) p 172-183.

Viegas, Philip, 1987, Land control and tribal struggle for survival, *Social Action* 37(4) October-December, p 325-344, footnotes.

Vimal Chandra, 1965, Key to tribal development, *Vanyajati* 13(4) October, p 143-145.

Vinoba Bhave, 1958, Tribal welfare workers and their role in gramdan work, *Vanyajati* 6(4) October, p 143-145 +.

Vishwa Mohan, 1964, Remnants of shifting cultivation, *Eastern Anthropologist* 17(1) January-April, p 31-38, references.

Viswam, S., 1985, The reservation conundrum, *Mainstream* 23(35) April 27, p 3-5 +.

Volchock, B. Ya, 1964, The interaction of castes and tribal communities in Central India, *Journal of Social Research* 7(1-2) March-September, p 104-122, references.

Von Furer-Haimendorf, Christoph, 1945, Aboriginal rebellions in the Deccan, *Man in India* 25(4) December, p 208-217.

——, 1946, Agriculture and land tenure among the Apa Tanis, *Man in India* 26(1) March, p 20-49, footnotes, illustrations.

——, 1949, Anthropology and administration in the tribal areas of the North-East Frontier, *Eastern Anthropologist* 3(1) September, p 8-14.

——, 1949, Problems and prospects of Indian anthropology, *Man in India* 29(3-4) July-December, p 147-168.

——, 1971, Tribes and Hindu society, *Contributions to Indian Sociology*, (New Series), 5, December, p 24-33.

—— and **Von Furer-Haimendorf, Elizabeth**, 1946, Notes on tribal justice among the Apa Tanis, *Man in India* 26(3-4) September-December, p 181-195.

Vyas, Ambalal, 1957-58, Why this emphasis on vocational bias in education in Ashrams ? *Adibasi* 2(1), p 45-49.

——, 1963, 15 Years progress of tribal education in Orissa, *Vanyajati* 11(2) April, p 51-54.

——, 1970, How backward the tribal areas of Orissa State are?, *Vanyajati* 18(3) July, p 131-133, tables.

Vyas, N.N., 1968, Economic aspect of tribal life, *Rural India* 31(6) July-August, p 216-218, tables.

——, 1984, Some spatial aspects of tribal culture and development, *Tribe* 16(3-4) September-December, p 1-6.

—— and **Chaudhary, N.D.**, 1983, The socio-economic implications of Guinea worm : A disease in tribal setting, *Tribe* 15 (1-2) March-June, p 15-26.

Wadia, A.R., 1953, Tribal Welfare Conference, Lohardaga, Bihar, November, 11-13, 1953, *Indian Journal of Social Work* 14(3) December, p 296-300.

——, 1958, Casteism and untouchability : An analysis, *Indian Journal of Adult Education* 19(3) October, p 28-33.

——, 1966, A note on the tribals and the Government, *Journal of Anthropological Society of Bombay* 12(1), p 12-14.

Wandrekar, D.N., 1949, Educational progress of the Adivasis in the Konkan track of Bombay Province, *Eastern Anthropologist* 3(1) September, p 3-7.

——, 1966, Tackling the problem of the poverty of the Adivasis, *Vanyajati* 14(3) July, p 99-108.

——, 1966, The progress of the movement of the forest labourer's cooperatives, *Vanyajati* 14(4) October, p 165-170.

——, 1967, Forest labour cooperatives or corporations, *Vanyajati* 15(4) October, p 184-187.

——, 1968, Co-operatives and the forest workers, *Vanyajati* 16(1) January, p 5-10, illustrations.

Wilkinson, T.S., 1961, Isolation, assimilation and integration in their historical perspective, *Religion and Society* 8(3) September, p 13-25.

——, 1962, Isolation, assimilation and integration in their historical perspectives, *Bulletin of Tribal Research and Development Institute* (Chhindwara) 2(1) June, p 19-28.

——, 1962, Reorientation of tribal education, *Social Action* 12(4) April, p 202-207.

Yadav, Bhupender, 1985, Growing up in wilderness, *Link* (Supplement), 27(26) February 3, p 19-23.

—— and **Navsharan G. Singh**, 1985, Tribals : Myth and reality, *Link* (Supplement) 27(26) February 3, p 48-54, tables.

Yadav, S.K., 1982, A study of the Scheduled Castes awareness about the schemes for their educational progress, *Indian Educational Review* 17(1) January, p 85-93.

——, 1983, Research review on implementation of educational schemes of Scheduled Castes, *Indian Educational Review* 18(3) July, p 12-22, references.

——, 1988, Educational wastage amongst Scheduled Castes : A research review, *Indian Educational Review* 23(1) January, p 90-98, bibliography.

Yagnik, Achyut and **Desai, Harshad**, 1985, The wages of populism, *Illustrated Weekly of India* 106(8) June 30, p 38-39.

Zaidi, Sunita, 1989, The Mughal State and tribes in seventeenth century Sind, *Indian Economic and Social History Review* 26(3) July-September, p 343-362.

Zide, Norman H. and **Munda, Ram Dayal**, 1969, Revolutionary Birsa and the songs related to him, *Journal of Social Research* 12(2) September, p 37-60, references.

Zutshi, G.L., 1957, Functions of the Pattapara among the Kannikars, *Vanyajati* 6(2) April, p 84-86.

——, 1959, Preliminaries regarding applied research among backward classes, *Vanyajati* 7(3) July, p 84-93.

——, 1961, Place of forests in tribal economy, *Vanyajati* 9(1) January, p 32-36.68

FIVE

AUTHOR APPROACH

Added Entries

Abdul Azeez Saheb Shaik
See Shaik, Abdul Azeez Saheb

Abdul Aziz
See Aziz, Abdul

Abdul Gaffoor, Khaja
See Gaffoor, Khaja Abdul

Abdul Kalam
See Kalam, Mohammad Abdul

Abrahi Ayrookuzheil, A.M.
See Ayrookuzheil, A.M. Abrahi

Adhikary, M.M., *jt author*
See Samanta, R.K. and Adhikary, M.M., 1988

Advani, L.K.
See Anon, 1990

Agarwal
See also Aggarwal, Agrawal

Aggarwal, Pratap
See Anon, 1986, (Book review)

Ahmad
See also Ahmad

Ahmad, S. Hasim, *jt author*
See Negi, Raghunath Singh and Ahmad, S. Hasim, 1982.

Ahmed
See also Ahmad

Ahmed Khan, G.
See Khan, G. Ahmed

Ahsan Quamar
See Quamar, Ahsan

Aijazuddin Ahmad
See Ahmad, Aijazuddin

Aikara, Jacob
See Anon, 1981, (Book review)

Aiyer
See Anon, 1990

Akbar Ahmad
See Ahmad, Akbar

Alam, Javeed
See Anon, 1985, (Book review)

Alam, M. Jabbar
See Jabbar Alam, M.

Amir Hasan
See Hasan, Amir

Anantha Krishna Iyer, L.K.
See also Anon, 1984, (Book review)

Anderson, Robert S.
See Anon, 1982, (Book review)

Archer, W.G.
See also Anon, 1986, (Book review)

Archer, W.G., *jt author*
See Culshaw, W.J. and Archer, W.J., 1955.

Ashok K. Singh
See Singh, Ashok K.

Babu
Under full surname, e.q., Sudhakar Babu, M.

Badri, Rama
See Rama Badri

Bag, Dulal Chandra
See Anon, 1987, (Book review)

Baghel, A.S., *jt author*
See Paul, S.P. and Baghel, A. S., 1987.

Bambawala, U. *jt author*
See Ramanamma, A. and Bambawala, U., 1985

Bandyopadhyay
See Lakshmi, G.R. and Bandyopadhyay, 1980

Banerjee, Swapan Kumar, *jt author*
See Das, Amal Kumar and Banerjee, Swapan Kumar, 1963

Banerjee—Guha, Swapna *jt author*

Warora, S.G. Geogaonkar
See Deogaonkar, Warora, S.G.

Yadappanavar, Arvind, *jt author*
See Lakshmaiah, T. and Yadappanavar, Arnivd, 1988

Yadav, Bhupender, *jt author*
See Pramod Kumar and Yadav, Bhupender, 1985

Yengneshwar, V., *jt author*
See Divakar, P. and Yengneshwar, V., 1986

Zia ul Haq
See Anon, 1986

APPENDIX

COMMISSIONS/COMMITTEES

CENTRAL AND STATES
(Including Pre-Independence Relevant References)

CENTRAL

Advisory Committee on the Revision of the Lists of Scheduled Castes and Scheduled Tribes, 1965.

Backward Classes Commission, 1953-1955.
Chairman: Shri Kakasaheb Kalelkar

Backward Classes Commission, 1979-1980.
Chairman: Shri B.P. Mandal

Commission on the Hill Areas of Assam, 1965-66.

Committee on Customary Rights to Scavenging,1965.

Committee on Untouchability Economic and Educational Development of the Scheduled Castes and Connected Documents, 1965.

Education Committee for the Andaman and Nicobar Islands, 1955.

Environmental Hygiene Committee, 1948

Excluded and Partially Excluded Areas (Other than Assam) Sub-Committee, 1947.

High Power Panel on Minorities, Scheduled Castes and Scheduled Tribes and Other Weaker Sections
Chairman: Dr. Gopal Singh

National Commission on Labour, Committee to Study Working and Service Conditions of Sweepers and Scavengers, 1967.

National Commission on Labour, Study Group for Tribal Labour (Agricultural and Industrial), 1968.

National Committee on Development of Backward Areas.
Chairman : B. Sivaraman

North-East Frontier (Assam) Tribal and Excluded Areas Sub-Committee, 1947.

Scavenging Conditions Enquiry Committee, 1957.

Scheduled Areas and Scheduled Tribes Commission, 1960.

Study group on the Welfare of Weaker Sections of the Village Committee, 1960.

Study Team on Social Welfare and Welfare of Backward Classes, 1958-1959.
Chairman/Leader : Smt. Renuka Ray

Study Team on Tribal Development Programmes, 1966 : Report on All India

Study team on Tribal Development Programmes, 1966 : Report on Andaman and Nicobar Islands.

Study Team on Tribal Development Programmes, 1966 : Report on Andhra Pradesh

Study Team on Tribal Development Programmes 1966 : Report on Assam.

Study Team on Tribal Development Programmes, 1966 : Report on Bihar

Study Team on Tribal Development Programmes, 1966 : Report on Dadra and Nagar Haveli.
Study Team on Tribal Development Programmes, 1966 : Report on Himachal Pradesh
Study Team on Tribal Development Programmes, 1966 : Report on Kerala
Study Team on Tribal Development Programmes, 1966 : Report on Madhya Pradesh
Study Team on Tribal Development Programmes, 1966 : Report on Madras
Study Toam on Tribal Development Programmes, 1966 ; Report on Manipur
Study Team on Tribal Development Programmes, 1966 : Report on Mysore
Study Team on Tribal Development Programmes, 1966 : Report on Nagaland
Study Team on Tribal Development Programmes, 1966 : Report on North East Frontier Agency
Study Team on Tribal Development Programmes, 1966 : Report on Orissa
Study Team on Tribal Development Programmes, 1966 : Report on Rajasthan
Study Team on Tribal Development Programmes, 1966 : Report on Tripura
Study Team on Tribal Development Programmes, 1966 : Report on West Bengal.

STATES

Andhra Pradesh

Backward Classes Commission, 1968-1970.
Chairman: Shri Mandhai Pershad
Committee of the Fifth Legislature Assembly to Recommend Further Measurers for the Welfare of Backward Classes, 1977.
Chairman: Shri Agisam Veerappa

Bihar

Backward Classes Commission, 1971-1976.
Chairman: Shri Mungeri Lal

Bombay

Scavengers' Living Conditions Enquire Committee, State of Bombay, 1954.

Gujarat

Backward Classes Commission, 1972-1976.
Chairman: Shri A.R. Bakshi

Jammu and kashmir

Backward Classes Committee, February-November 1969.
Chairman: Shri J.N. Wazir
Backward Classes Committee, 1976-1977.
Chairman: Justice (Dr.) Adarsh S. Anand
(Gajendragadkar) Commission, 1967-1978.
Chairman; Gajendragadkar

Karnataka

Backward Classes Committee, 1960-1961.

Chairman: Dr. R.Naganna Gowda

Backward Classes Commission,1971-1975.

Chairman: Shri L.G. Havanur

Kerala

Evaluation Committee, 1961-1963.

Chairman: V.K. Vishwanathan

Backward Classes Commission, 1964-1965.

Chairman: Shri G.Kumara Pillai

Backward Classes Reservation Commission, 1967-1970.

Chairman: Shri M.P. Damodaran

Maharashtra

Committee to Report on Reservation of Backward Classes in the Services, 1961-1964.

Chairman: Shri B.D. Deshmukh

Mysore

Committee to Recommend Steps for Adequate Representation for Non-Brahmins in the Services of the State, 1918.

Chairman: Shri L.C. Miller

Punjab

Committee on Backward Classes, 1951.

Evaluation Committee, 1965-1966.

Chairman: Shri Brish Bhan

Vidhan Sabha Committee on Welfare of SC & ST and Backward Classes, 1975-1976.

Tamil Nadu

Backward Classes Commission, 1969-1970.

Chairman: Shri A.N. Sattanathan

Uttar Pradesh

Most Backward Classes Commission, 1975-1977

Chairman: Shri Chhedi Lal Sathi

West Bengal

Committee (on Backward Classes) to Find out Whether It was Necessary to Invoke the Powers Vested in the State Government under article 15(4), 16(4) and 29(2) Read with Article 15(4) of the Constitution, August 1-30, 1980.

PRE-INDEPENDENCE RELEVANT REFERENCES

1871

Criminal Tribes Act, 1871.

1885

Madras Government, Grant-in-Aid Code to Regulate Financial Aid to Educational Institutions Providing Special Facilities for Students of Depressed Classes, 1885

1911

Criminal Tribes Act, 1911.

1919

Montague—Chelmsford Reforms of 1919

1935

Government of India Act, 1935.

CICIL LIST

CONCEPTS IN COMMUNICATION, INFORMATICS & LIBRARIANSHIP (CICIL)

General Editor: S.P. AGRAWAL

CICIL-1 Development of Library Services in India: Social Science Information
S.P. Agrawal Rs. 150

CICIL-2 Development of Documentation in India: Social Science Information
S.P. Agrawal Rs. 250

CICIL-3 UNESCO and Social Sciences: Retrospect and Prospect
S.P. Agrawal and **J.C. Aggarwal** Rs. 250

CICIL-4 INDIANA : A Bibliography of Bibliographical Sources
M.K. Jain Rs. 200

CICIL-5 Dimensions of Library and Information Science: Kaula Festschrift
V. Venkatappaiah (Eds.) Rs. 600

CICIL-6 Book Numbers: Some Indian Methods
M.P. Satija and **S.P. Agrawal** Rs. 100

CICIL-7 National Policy for University Libraries in India: Problems and Perspectives
N.B. Inamdar and **L.S. Ramaiah** (Ed.) Rs. 250

CICIL-8 Media Utilisation for the Development of Women and Children
B.S. Thakur and **Binod C. Agrawal** Rs. 150

CICIL-9 Terrorism: An Annotated Bibliography
Susheela Bhan (Ed.) Rs. 275

CICIL-10 Transnational Library Relations: The Indo-American Experience
M.B. Konnur Rs. 175

CICIL-11 Geography of Marketing and Commercial Activities in India (Documentation on Research Information)
R.S. Dixit Rs. 130

CICIL-12 Information India 1988: Global View
S.P. Agrawal and **J.C. Aggarwal** Rs. 200

CICIL-13 Women's Education in India: Historical Review, Present Status and Perspective Plan
S.P. Agrawal and **J.C. Aggarwal** Rs. 360

CICIL-14 Cultural Communication in India: Role and Impact of Phonograms
J.M. Ojha (in press)

CICIL-15 Second Historical Survey of Educational Development in India: Select Documents 1985-1989
S.P. Agrawal and **J.C. Aggarwal** Rs. 490

CICIL-16 Documentation Encyclopaedia of UNESCO and Education
J.C. Aggarwal and **S.P. Agrawal** Rs. 800 (set of 2 parts)

CICIL-17 Attitude Towards Information: A Study of Post-Graduate Teachers and Researchers in Social Sciences
N.G. Satish (in press)

CICIL-18 Librarianship and Bureaucratic Organisation: A Study in the Sociology of Library Profession in India
P.K. Jayaswal Rs. 175

CICIL-19 Literature Search
K.A. Isaac Rs. 150

CICIL-20 Child Education in India: Index to Scholarly Writings in Indian Educational Journals and Newspapers since independence
S.P. Agrawal and **Naresh Kanta** Rs. 100

CICIL-21 Lok Sabha and Vidhan Sabha Elections in India 1989 & 1990: Process and Results with Comparative Study of Manifestos
S.P. Agrawal and **J.C. Aggarwal** Rs. 250

CICIL-22 Islamic Studies in India: A Survey of Human, Institutional and Documentary Sources
Mohamed Taher Rs. 180

CICIL-23 Panchayati Raj: An Annotated Bibliography
N.B. Inamdar, N.G. Satish and **Anil Takalkar** 290

CICIL-24 Information India 1989-90: Global View
S.P. Agrawal and **J.C. Aggarwal** Rs. 500

CICIL-25 First Handbook of Psychological and Social Instruments
Udai Pareek and **T. Venkateswara Rao** (in press)

CICIL-26 Educational and Social Uplift of Backward Classes: A What Cost and How? Mandal Commission and After
S.P. Agrawal and **J.C. Aggarwal** Rs. 275

CICIL-27 Mass Media and New Horizons: Impact of TV & Video an Urban Milieu **H.R. Trivedi** Rs. 180

CICIL-28 Indian Writings on Education : An Indicator to India Educational Journals Grouped by Subject Deseriptor 1979 to 1986 (in two parts) **S.P. Agarwal** Rs. 90 (per set)

CICIL-29 Nation in Crisis
S.P. Agrawal and **J.C. Aggarwal** Rs. 200

CICIL-30 Information India 1990-91: Global View
S.P. Agrawal and **J.C. Aggarwal** Rs. 500

CICIL-31 Development of University Libraries in India Afte Independence
O.P. Gupta Rs. 270

CICIL-32 Handbook on Child : With Historical Background
Pramila Pandit Barooah Rs. 320

CICIL-33 Weaker Section in Indian Society : Undiscovered Past Uncertain Present and Unpredictable Future Index Writings in Indian Scholarly Journals and 10 Natior Newspapers Classified under 1500 Descript 1886-1990
S.P. Agrawal and **Rajeev Kumar Sharma** Rs. 600

CICIL-34 Communication Informatics and Librarianship in India : Introductory Guide to Publications Based on a Survey Libraries in Capital of City India
S.P. Agrawal and **Pushpa Rani Sharma** Rs. 720